Jerry Elliott
Crawfordsville, IN
September - 2013

CLASS OF 1862 — WABASH COLLEGE

SERVICE IN THE WAR FOR THE UNION

JOHN C. BLACK
SERGT. MAJOR 11TH IND. ZOUAVES APR. 1861   COLONEL 37TH ILL. INF.
TWICE SEVERELY WOUNDED   BVT. BRIG. GENERAL U.S.V.

ZERAH F. BLAKELY
MINISTER OF THE GOSPEL

FRED A. CLARK
PRIVATE 11TH IND. ZOUAVES APR. 1861 · 1ST LIEUTENANT 29TH IND. INF. CAPTAIN AND A.D.C.

JOHN E. CLELAND
1ST SERGEANT 70TH IND. INF. AUG. 1862   CAPTAIN 44TH U.S.C. TROOPS

JOHN JACKSON
CAPTAIN 4TH IND. CAV. AUG. 1862 · COMMENDED FOR VALOR IN GENERAL ORDERS
CAPTURED AT VARNELL STA. GA. MAY 9 1864 AND DIED IN CONFEDERATE PRISON
COLUMBIA S.C. NOV. 20 1864

EDWARD B. KINGSBURY
PRIVATE 11TH IND. ZOUAVES APR. 1861 · CAPTAIN 125TH ILL. INF. MORTALLY WOUNDED
AT CHATTAHOOCHEE BRIDGE GA. JULY 5 1864 AND DIED AUG. 13 1864 DANVILLE ILL.

MONROE M. MILFORD
PRIVATE 11TH IND. ZOUAVES APR. 1861 · DIED APR. 16 1884 ATTICA IND.

LYCURGUS RAILSBACK
CHAPLAIN 44TH U.S.C. TROOPS JULY 1864 · DIED AUG. 5 1897 SHREVEPORT LA.

WILLIAM H. H. SCOTT JR.
PRIVATE 12TH ILL. INF. APR. 1861   DIED NOV. 29 1861
AT FRANKFORT KY. OF DISEASE CONTRACTED IN SERVICE

JOSEPH R. WEBSTER
PRIVATE 11TH IND. ZOUAVES APR. 1861 · MAJOR 88TH IND. INF.
LIEUT. COLONEL 44TH U.S.C. TROOPS

**LET THOSE WHO COME AFTER US
UPHOLD LAWFUL AUTHORITY THAT
THE REPUBLIC MAY LIVE FOREVER**

JUNE 17 1913

500 STRONG

Wabash College Students in the Civil War

Edited by Dr. James J. Barnes and

Patience P. Barnes

Nancy Niblack Baxter, Contributing Editor for the Publisher

Hawthorne Publishing

© 2013 Dr. James J. Barnes and Patience P. Barnes

All rights reserved. Some historical photos were available using GFDL conventions through massive multi-author collaboration sites.

ISBN 978-09831994-8-9

Images, unless othewise noted or covered under the GFDL convention, are from the Robert G. Ramsay, Jr. Archival Center at Wabash College.

Archival material for Henry Campbell and other original material has been provided by Beth Swift, archivist at the Ramsay Archival Center.

Hawthorne Publishing
15601 Oak Road
Carmel, IN 46033
317-867-5183
www.hawthornepub.com

DEDICATION

To the Wabash College men who served during the Civil War and helped spread the fame of her most honored name.

Dear Alma Mater, at thy shrine of cherished memory
The hosts of Wabash meet to pledge undying loyalty.
Within these sacred portals thy fires shall brightly flame
And herald our devotion to thy most honored name.

Carroll Ragan, Class of 1901
Son of Civil War veteran Gillum Ragan, Class of 1862

and to the Wabash history students 120 years later who researched these men's lives.

ACKNOWLEDGMENTS

The references at the end of each biographical sketch will indicate the extent to which we are indebted to a wide variety of local history societies, county and state libraries, cemetery offices, and county clerk bureaus. We are also most grateful for the continuing help from Wabash College archivists Donald Thompson, Johanna Herring and Beth Swift. Reference librarian Jeffrey Beck has also performed yeoman service for us.

Charles Hill, Genealogy Collection Librarian at the Indiana State Library routinely provided Wabash students with a lucid introduction to pursuing family histories, and Stephen E. Towne of what is now the Indiana State Archives patiently demonstrated how to locate veterans' records. Steve is now assistant archivist at IUPUI. Patricia Galloway and Janice Clauser have worked tirelessly over the years on this and many of our other publications.

Nancy and Arthur Baxter, as soon as they learned about this project, enthusiastically supported it and have shared their professional expertise as editor and publisher.

The following is a list of Wabash students who took my history seminar on research methods and delved into the lives of early Wabash undergraduates who served in the Civil War.   JJB

Arnold, Michael L.
Babcock, Michael J.
Baber, Andrew R.
Baylor, Paul E.
Bettuo, Bart M.
Bisbecos, Peter A.
Blackman, Shane E.
Bogan, Jared T.
Broadwater, Ned L.
Brown, David A.
Bunton, Herbert L.
Burdick, Brian L.
Butler, Michael G.
Cain, Bradley S.
Chadwick, Jeffrey A.
Cheviron, J. Stephen
Childress, Clinton S.
Clark, Eric J.
Clary, Jesse B.
Cole, John D.
Cook, Aaron M.
Coy, Douglas A.

Craig, D. Scott
Craine, Patrick K.
Crockett, William J.
Crossey, Michael D.
Cunningham, Jeffrey A.
Dawson, Scott A.
Deener, Jamey L.
Demske, Mark J.
Dennis, Aaron M.
DeWald, Brian C.
Dorrel, Andrew J.
Doty, Christopher D.
Eaton, Brent E.
Eichhorn, Kevin J.
Elderkin, T. Andrew
Elston, Gordon S.
Engledow, Eric J.
Eversole, Michael E.
Fahl, Christopher A.
Ferguson, William D.
Fox, Daniel A.
Fronek, Justin T.

Fruits, Kevin L.
Fulton, Michael J.
Gant, Charles M.
Gerold, Sean A.
Glover, Dominic W.
Grasch, Kenneth L.
Grove, Ryan S.
Guiden, Timothy A.
Gumz, Mark J.
Hammer, William J.
Hanson, Matthew G.
Harris, Timothy R.
Hartman, Brian J.
Hecker, William F.
Hill, Jonathan M.
House, S. Kelley
Huber, Michael D.
Huggler, Lyndall J.
Hunt, Wesley C.
Imm, Eugene
Jackson, Sean R.
Jansen, Paul A.

Jernagan, Craig E.
Johnson, Lewis J.
Kalinowski, Isaiah R.
Kallister, William K.
Kelleher, Matthew H.
Kelley, George D.
Kerr, Andrew T.
Kielbasa, Mark S.
Krakowka, Ben H.
Kristensen, Michael R.
Largura, Burton V.
Lee, Eric J.
Legg, Eric R.
Lewinski, Michael J.
Lewis, Douglas W.
Lindseth, Eric L.
Long, Jerry L.
Maldonado, Frank
Marshall, David J.
McKinley, Michael S.
McLaughlin, Harry R.
McWilliams, Fred M.
Miller, Alan R.
Miller, Eric B.
Miller, Miles B.
Miller, Patrick R.
Mills, Joshua T.
Moore, Kurtis F.
Murtaugh, Thomas P.
Nink, William J.
Nogen, Michael B.
Ogle, Mark R.
Ostrowski, Todd
Parkison, Paul T.
Perez, Daniel W.
Pfennig, Joseph M.
Pope, Kurt A.
Pope, Nathaniel N.
Price, Matthew M.
Primetica, Branko
Prince, Kenneth M.
Reidenbach, Gary R.
Reynolds, David T.
Riegel, Christopher I.
Robinson, Paul E.
Roetter, Frederick A.
Ross, Curtis A.
Ross, Daniel J.
Rutherford, Mark W.
Sausser, Mark C.
Schmelzer, Frederick E.
Shepherd, Thomas E.
Smith, Kelly R.
Springer, Douglas L.
Stafford, John M.
Stalker, Kevin R.
Stark, Jared L.
Stevenson, Mark R.
Sullivan, Michael P.
Swetnam, Douglas S.
Tan, Zhen-Ming
Thibault, Michael A.
Tragesser, Micah G.
Troglia, Gerald R.
Umbarger, Christopher A.
Underwood, Christopher L.
Upchurch, John G.
Urbaska, James S.
Valaika, George C.
Vega, Robert D.
Vieck, Alan M.
Waltz, D. Brent
Ward, Matthew J.
Weir, David B.
Weir, Donald E.
West, Donald J.
Whistler, Richard E.
White, Marion Z.
Williams, Craig M.
Williams, James R.
Woosley, Nicholas S.
Worrell, Mark J.

INTRODUCTION

This book comes out of my curiosity as a teacher at Wabash and a professor of history. My search into the stories of Wabash College students who served in the Civil War in America started with the bronze plaque on the east wall of Center Hall that honors the 307 Wabash students who served between 1861 and 1865, from generals to non-commissioned soldiers, listed alphabetically. I wondered where each of these men came from; what battles they fought in; which teachers might have taught them at the college; and how they survived the rigors they encountered, or in some cases, from which they perished. It occurred to me that the answers to these questions might also intrigue my senior history majors. Together we might be able to learn some interesting details about their collegial predecessors and at the same time discover the satisfactions of doing original research. Moreover, the results would add greatly to the known history of the college.

At first it was disconcerting to discover how little information there was in our college archives at that time. There were at that time few handwritten letters, diaries, scrapbooks, or memoirs. The only data we could find came from the official college catalogues that listed every student who enrolled in a particular academic year, as well as his hometown or county. With only these bare facts, and nothing more, we might have had to abandon the project. But we persisted.

Originally, each history major was assigned twenty-four men and asked to locate their service records at what was then the Archives Division of the Indiana State Library. Eventually, by using pension applications and personal inquiries, we ascertained that about 80 percent served as volunteers, while others were in the state militia (the Indiana Legion), the regular United States army or navy, or volunteer regiments of neighboring states.

We soon found that the definition of military service needed to include physicians and surgeons, clergy, provisioners of the camps, desk officers, and others who took part in the war.

Since we were able to find the hometown or state of almost everyone, we could use the federal censuses to identify a student's family, age, and place of birth. The Indiana State Library also contains marriage and death records for many counties as well as cities and towns.

As we learned about our Wabash veterans, we expanded our search, using correspondence and telephone calls to distant libraries and archives, since former students tended to move several times after leaving the college, locating in Texas or California or Washington state. It was cause for celebration to find an obituary in a local paper or a living family member.

From the outset it was apparent that most of the veterans were much younger than we had anticipated. Although the college offered a Classical Course leading to a bachelor of arts degree, most students were enrolled in the

Preparatory Department (high school) and were likely to be ten to sixteen years old. The fact that there was a prep school in addition to a college accounts for the astounding total of 529 soldiers from a small Presbyterian college in the Midwest, which had only been in existence thirty years when the major battles of 1862 got underway. The search for specifics beyond the bare facts was often elusive, but we all persisted, hoping for interesting life stories. Often we got these, and I believe they are at the heart of the interest of the collection.

By the end of the fall semester of 1981, the students in the seminar were ready to present their research in the form of brief biographical sketches of each of their twenty-four veterans. These were then combined and became part of the college archives, greatly adding to what the college knew about them. Later history majors continued researching students who were not memorialized on the plaque, and to our surprise, found more than two hundred other veterans, bringing the total of those who served in the war to more than five hundred.

The students were able to hunt down almost every veteran, but there were some who defied our collective efforts, so I decided to pursue the especially elusive ones. The quest led me into communication with people nationwide for more than twenty-five years.

Some years passed, and then a publication opportunity presented itself when a Wabash graduate, Art Baxter, who owned a publishing company specializing in Indiana history, thought our material was a good match with their publishing interests.

My wife Patience, herself a scholar of and writer about history, has edited all of the biographical sketches for publication. She has traced many loose ends and followed many leads to their logical conclusions, filtered by her own knowledge of Wabash families.

So now the collection is ready for reading, ready to stimulate the continuing curiosity of Wabash graduates, history buffs, and Civil War enthusiasts.

For a summary of the findings about the soldiers in this collection, see the Afterword of this book.

James J. Barnes
Wabash College
Crawfordsville, Indiana

Accounts of Wabash Soldiers' Origins, Wartime Careers, and Lives

ABDILL, EDWARD C. (1840–1901)

Most troops from Indiana went to the western theater of the war, many to the Mississippi valley, where a desperate struggle was underway to seize the river, restore trade, and cut the Confederacy in half. Edward Abdill joined the Eleventh Indiana Regiment. After some training, his regiment sailed for St. Louis and then to Paducah, Kentucky, where it remained for the next few months, but early in 1862, it saw action both at Fort Henry and at Fort Donelson.

In April Abdill took part in the Battle of Shiloh, and soon thereafter fought at Corinth, Mississippi. By June he was stationed at Memphis, and for the next year he was involved in skirmishes or battles in Arkansas and Missouri. In July 1863 he participated in the siege of Vicksburg and was promoted to second lieutenant. He then transferred to the First Indiana Cavalry and served with this unit until December 1863, when he became a first lieutenant and adjutant of the 120th Indiana Regiment.

Edward Abdill was born at Perrysville on 14 May 1840. His father, Irad, was born about 1813 in Ohio and settled in Vermillion County sometime in the late 1830s. He was a tinsmith and later a hardware dealer. His wife, Rebecca Ann Watson, was two years his senior and born in Kentucky. Their other children were George, Louis, William, and Heinram.

In the autumn of 1856, Abdill entered the Normal School of Wabash College, remaining only one academic year. He then returned home and joined his father in the hardware business. On 31 August 1861 he enrolled at Perrysville in Company B of the Eleventh Indiana Regiment. Later that day he was formally mustered in at Indianapolis and committed to three years of service.

During April 1864, in the latter part of his war experience, his 120th Regiment went to Nashville and then to eastern Tennessee as part of the First Brigade of the First Division of the Twenty-Third Army Corps. On 2 May the division joined the campaign against Atlanta, which included both the Battle of Resaca (15 May) and Kennesaw Mountain (27 June). Atlanta fell on 1 September, but Abdill missed witnessing the victory since he had secured a medical discharge on 14 August and had returned home.

While on leave during the war, he traveled to Vermilion County, Illinois, to marry Anna Bell Peters on 13 August 1863. They eventually had four children: Charles, Bertha, Catherine, and Henry (Harry).

From 1865 to 1868 Abdill ran a hardware store in Fairmount, Illinois, and later joined with one of his older brothers to establish Abdill Brothers, a hardware business in Danville, Illinois. This occupied him for the rest of his life. He died at home on 20 February 1901 and is buried in Spring Hill Cemetery. Anna died in Danville on 20 June 1922.

References: Military files located at the Indiana State Archives and at the National Archives in Washington, DC. The staff at the Danville Public Library supplied copies of the *Danville Daily News*, 21 Feb. 1901, and *Past and Present of Vermilion County, Illinois* (1903), pp. 983–85.

ADAMS, ALBERT WILLARD (1840–1862)

Albert Adams was born on 9 April 1840 in Logan, Hocking County, Ohio. Sometime in the 1850s his family moved to Carbondale, Illinois, and in the fall of 1859, enrolled their son as a freshman at Wabash College. He returned as a sophomore, but when war broke out in April 1861, he interrupted his studies and went home to enlist in a local Illinois regiment.

On 28 May 1861 he enrolled as a private in Company K of the Eighteenth Illinois Volunteers. Promotion came quickly, and by July he was the regimental sergeant major. Not long thereafter he was again promoted, this time to adjutant of the regiment.

By the beginning of 1862 the regiment was encamped at Cairo, Illinois, where Adams wrote to his parents:

> The future, as concerns this world, matters but little to me. I have been in the service long enough to have learned that the present only is all-important; and that all brilliant anticipations for the future are utterly futile. ... I know not but that tomorrow will leave me lying dead on some battlefield; and again, for all I know, or can do, we may remain where we are for years. All ahead is dark as midnight—the only bright spot around me is directly overhead, and that light is too dim. I am too young to be where I am, but I never sought the position, and cannot honorably leave it.

In another letter home he reflected again upon his chances for survival:

> I know the storm will pass eventually, but, ere the sun shines again in peace and happiness upon our landscape, many a noble oak must receive a lightening stroke; must bend and break beneath the raging tornado. It may be my lot to fall with the rest; if so, I can only say "whatever is, does right."

Soon after these letters were written, Adams died in camp at Cairo. Tributes were forthcoming from the college magazine: "His standard shows that he always recited well, although many of his lessons were studied while engaged in sawing wood to pay for his board." President Charles White affirmed that "Adams is pure gold."

Adams had hoped eventually to become a minister and had probably received some financial aid while at Wabash. Mindful of this, he requested his father to repay such a debt from any back pay owed him from the army, should he die while in service.

References: I. Osborne and T. Gronert, *Wabash College: The First Hundred Years* (1932), pp. 126–27; *Wabash Magazine*, III (Dec. 1861), p. 93; *Wabash Magazine*, III (April 1862), pp. 203–06; and the service record in the Illinois State Archives, Springfield.

AKEY, ALFRED (1838–1923)

Alfred Akey was born on 1 April 1838 near Mount Eaton, Ohio, one of ten children. His parents were Robert and Phian Zimmerman. By the time he entered Wabash in the fall of 1858, his home was Lima, Ohio. He was enrolled in the Preparatory Department for two years, during which time his family moved to Nottawa Township, St. Joseph County, Michigan.

In the autumn of 1860, young Akey enrolled in Jefferson College (now Washington and Jefferson College) in Washington, Pennsylvania, as a member of the freshman class. He might have continued as a sophomore, but the Civil War intervened. On 15 May 1861 he was mustered into the Tenth Reserve Regiment, later known as the Thirty-Ninth Pennsylvania Volunteers, and was described as 5 feet 6 ½ inches tall, with dark complexion, grey eyes, and dark hair. He spent that summer in Virginia at Camp Pierpont. Due to an injury to his foot in early October, he secured a medical discharge on 1 December 1861. He did not return to Jefferson College, but stayed with his family. He was treated for about a year by his local doctor, but thereafter he was unfit for manual labor.

In 1882 Akey's former Wabash College classmate and fellow Civil War veteran, Joseph R. Webster, prepared an affidavit on his comrade's behalf to convince the United States pension bureau that Akey was not impaired physically before the war, and thus was harmed by the war and eligible for a pension: "since when at college in Crawfordsville, Indiana, he was strong and vigorous and distinguished above the average for leaping and running and similar athletic sports."

Eventually Akey read law with William Saddler and was admitted to the St. Joseph County bar on 9 August 1864. He married Genie J. Allison, a native of New York, on 23 May 1867. She was ten years his junior, and their only child, William, was born the following year.

For the remainder of his life, Akey practiced law in St. Joseph County. Eventually the injury he suffered in the war proved fatal. He died on 11 April 1923, and his widow passed away in 1931. They are both buried in Prairie River Cemetery.

References: 1860 U.S. census; Nottawa Township Public Library; *Centreville Observer*, 12 April 1923, p. 1, and 21 May 1931; and *Portrait and Biographical Album of St. Joseph County, Michigan* (1889).

ALEXANDER, JAMES CYRUS (1833–1865)

James Alexander was born in the first brick house built in Paris, Illinois. The young man was eighteen when he entered Hanover College in southern Indiana. During the academic year 1852–53, he interrupted his studies at Hanover to attend Wabash College as a freshman, probably because his elder brother John went to Wabash.

On 24 August 1859 Alexander married nineteen-year-old Emma Bodine Graydon of Indianapolis. They soon moved to Clinton, Missouri, where their first child, Milton, was born on 9 August 1860. Emma gave birth to a second child, Willie, at her former home in Indianapolis on 9 May 1862, but the baby soon died. Their third child, James, was born in his father's hometown of Paris on 22 February 1863, but the senior James Cyrus lived only two years after his son's birth. He died of dysentery on 29 March 1865, leaving his young wife and children to manage on an inheritance of $1,000.

A search of state and federal archives yielded no positive record of Alexander's military record, yet there are two independent sources testifying to his having been in the Union Army. One is the memorial tablet affixed to Center Hall at Wabash College, where his name appears along that of his older brother, and second is the 1889 history of Edgar County that records James Alexander as having served.

References: 1850 U.S. census for Edgar County; Charles A. Hand and A. Joyce Brown of Paris, Ill.; *Portrait and Biographical Album of Vermilion and Edgar Counties, Illinois* (1889); and written reminiscences of Lucy Lamon, sister of James Alexander, 1923, in the possession of the Paris Public Library.

ALEXANDER, JAMES W. (1833–1865)

James W. Alexander was one of nine children born to John and Rhoda Thornhill Alexander. His parents were both born about 1801 in Virginia and married sometime in the mid- to late 1820s. James was born in Brown County, Ohio, and his siblings included Sarah, Bernard, Robert, John, William, Hugh, Nancy, and Mariah. About 1841 the family moved from Ohio and settled in the town of Warren in Indiana. John took up a variety of trades, including farming, brickmaking, and surveying.

At about the age of thirteen or fourteen, young James entered the Normal School of Wabash College, but remained only one year, 1856–57, returning home to join his father making bricks until the Civil War broke out.

On 21 September 1861 both James and his brother John enrolled at Anderson, in Company C of the Thirty-Fourth Regiment. In March or April 1862, their parents learned of John's death at New Haven, Kentucky. James continued in the Thirty-Fourth Regiment after his term of service was up in December 1863. He almost made it through the war but died on 5 March 1865 from an illness he contracted while stationed at Brazos Island, Texas.

References: Military service records at the Indiana State Library, and *Biographical Memoirs; Huntington County, Indiana* (1901), p. 526, at the Huntington Public Library.

ALEXANDER, JOHN WASHINGTON SHIELDS (1822–1863)

The life of John Alexander strikingly exemplified the ideal of the citizen soldier. Twice he interrupted his career to answer his nation's call to arms: the first during the war with Mexico and the second following the outbreak of the Civil War. He did not survive the latter.

In January 1863 he sustained a serious wound to his foot at the Battle of Stones River near Murfreesboro, and his younger sister Lucy later recalled the anxiety felt by the whole community of Paris, Illinois: "Soon after this battle my younger brother brought my wounded brother home—our house was crowded with anxious friends to get news from these people right from the battlefield—the high cavalry boot from the wounded foot was filled to the top with letters from the soldiers to their families."

Many months passed before Alexander returned to command his regiment, the Twenty-First Illinois, supported by a crutch. However, he still led his troops into battle on horseback at Chickamauga. On the second day of fighting, 20 September 1863, he was shot and fell from his horse and died. His body was returned to his hometown for burial.

Alexander was born in Giles County, Tennessee, on 10 December 1822. He was the elder brother of James Cyrus Alexander, and his father Milton served in the Black Hawk War of the early 1830s.

In the autumn of 1841 Alexander enrolled at Wabash College as a freshman and pursued a classical course of study leading to a bachelor of arts degree in the summer of 1845. Soon after, the conflict with Mexico broke out, and in 1846 he was commissioned a first lieutenant in the Fourth Illinois Infantry. He fought in the Battles of Vera Cruz and Cerro Gordo.

After his discharge from the army, he married Elizabeth Howard on 17 July 1848. She had grown up in Rockville, the daughter of General and Mrs. Tilghman Howard. They had two children: Howard (1849–1853) and Elizabeth Adelia (1852–1888).

Alexander's wife died on 22 September 1855, and two years later he married Lucinda Canady of Charleston, Illinois. She died giving birth to a stillborn infant in October 1858. By this time, Alexander's mercantile business had stabilized, and for the next few years he enjoyed a comparative degree of prosperity.

When the Civil War broke out, the former Wabash student lost little time offering his experience to the newly formed Twenty-first Illinois Regiment. He began his duties as a lieutenant colonel in May 1861, but when the colonel of the regiment, Ulysses S. Grant, was raised to brigadier general, Alexander took Grant's place as colonel. It was at the head of this regiment that he met his death in the war.

References: Charles A. Hand and A. Joyce Brown of Paris, Ill.; "Obituaries of Some Alumni," Wabash College Archives; and military service records at the Illinois State Archives, Springfield. See also the sources cited for James Cyrus Alexander.

ALEXANDER, SCYLURUS W. (1832–1911)

Some soldiers bypassed infantry regiments in their home territories to enroll in what might have been considered more adventuresome or interesting units. On 15 August 1862 Scylurus Alexander enrolled in the Twenty-Third Light Artillery attached to the Forty-Seventh Indiana Regiment. According to the records, he was a sergeant, standing five feet eleven inches tall, with fair complexion, grey eyes, and brown hair. He was promoted to second lieutenant on 24 October 1862 and to first lieutenant on 14 April 1865. In November 1864 he was involved in a battle near Columbia, Tennessee, which caused him to be deaf in the right ear, and he was mustered out with his battery at Indianapolis on 2 July 1865.

Scylurus Alexander was born at Eaton, Preble County, Ohio, on 19 January 1832. His mother, whose name is not known, apparently left property to each of her three children: $1,000 for Scylurus, $400 for his sister Kezia, and $400 for another sister Josephine. His father, John Alexander, was born in Kentucky about 1800, and by 1860 was living in the town of Huntington, Indiana, where he was a debt collector.

Alexander completed two years (1855–57) in the Preparatory Department of Wabash College, studying to be a doctor. However, by 1862 he was a tailor, a profession he continued for the rest of his life.

Alexander was married four times. His first wife was Mary Jane Straup of Huntington, whom he wed on 24 April 1859. She must have died, as he married Edith Wisner in the late 1860s. When Edith died at Woodland, St. Joseph County, in 1871, he wed Mrs. Sarah Mathews, and they moved from St. Joseph County to Iowa in 1877. Three years later this marriage ended in divorce. He remained in Iowa until about 1885 and then moved to St. Louis, where he married his fourth wife, Frances Mary Hulford, on 23 January 1889. They moved to Dardanelle, Arkansas, and had a son, John, and a daughter, Verena.

By 1907 Alexander was living in a soldiers' home at Leavenworth, Kansas, where he died on 4 August 1911.

References: Military pension file at the National Archives, Washington, DC; and the Huntington County Public Library.

ALLEN, ARCHIBALD CAMERON (1815–1883)

Chaplains served a useful and compassionate role in the northern and Confederate armies, where almost all individual soldiers were active in one denomination or another and sources of comfort were few and far between. Archibald Allen, who was to become a most-admired chaplain in the Federal army, was born on 4 March 1815 near Shelbyville, Kentucky. In 1831 his family moved to Waveland, Indiana, near Crawfordsville, where he continued his education privately. In the mid-1830s he entered Miami University in Oxford, Ohio. For reasons that are not clear, he decided to return to Montgomery County and enrolled in Wabash College in the autumn of 1836 as a junior. Two years later he received a bachelor's degree, the first ever awarded by Wabash College.

Following his experience at Wabash, Allen went to seminary at Princeton and was licensed to preach in 1842 by the presbytery of Kaskaskia, Illinois. By then he had married and brought his wife, Elizabeth Affleck of Pittsburgh, west with him. She was Scottish by birth. Over the years the couple had six children, five daughters and one son.

Allen's clerical duties took him to a wide variety of parishes. During the 1840s he served churches in Hillsboro, Illinois; Tuscumbia, Alabama; and Grand Gulf, Mississippi. In 1851 he assumed the duties of pastor at the First Presbyterian Church of Terre Haute and stayed there six years before serving briefly at Hopewell.

Shortly before the Civil War broke out, the minister came to Indianapolis and volunteered as a chaplain to the Seventieth Indiana Regiment in August 1862. For the next three years he was intimately involved with the life of the regiment. Several of his fellow officers were Wabash College alumni. One of these, John Cleland, later recalled how effective Allen was as a chaplain: "Venerable, dignified, unselfish, he was a real chaplain—brave and true on the field, faithful in the camp, tender in the hospital, where wounds and disease and homesickness ruled the hour."

Another testimony came from the regiment's colonel (and future president of the United States), Benjamin Harrison. In a dispatch dated 20 May 1864 and written in the field near Cassville, Georgia, Harrison noted: "Rev. A. C. Allen, chaplain, deserves mention for his untiring labors night and day to relieve the wants and suffering of our wounded."

Allen lived in Indianapolis for nearly twenty years, but according to his obituary, "After the war [his] health began to fail—the beginning of the secret, mysterious trouble in his brain that finally resulted in his death. . . . He often said that, while speaking, his mind became a blank and sometimes the conviction came to him that he would expire in the pulpit." Nonetheless, "He could not be idle, and he gave himself freely, with but little remuneration, to mission work in the vicinity of Indianapolis." Archibald Allen died at his home on 28 August 1883.

References: *Wabash Magazine*, XII (Jan. 1872), p. 75; Wabash College Archives, "Obituary of Some Alumni," p. 94; S. Merrill, *The Seventieth Indiana Volunteer Infantry* (1900), pp. 111–12; *Indianapolis News,* 29 Aug. 1883; Presbyterian Church, Indiana Synod Minutes (1882–1884), pp. 91–93.

ALLEN, JOHN BEARD (1845–1903)

John Beard Allen was born in Crawfordsville on 18 May 1845. His father, Joseph S., was a physician in town. His middle name came from his mother, Hannah Cora Beard.

At the age of sixteen Allen entered the Wabash College Preparatory Department. After three years (1860–63), and following his freshman year, he was forced to leave because of poor health. By June 1864 he had recovered sufficiently that he was able to enlist in Company F of the 135th Regiment, and for one hundred days he served in Tennessee and Alabama. He was then released in time to enter his sophomore year at Wabash (1864–65).

In the spring of 1865, Allen accompanied his family when they moved to Rochester, Minnesota. He was hoping to study law. After apprenticing with a local judge, Charles C. Wilson, Allen undertook formal legal studies at the University of Michigan at Ann Arbor, culminating in graduation and admission to the Minnesota bar in 1869. At about this time he married Celia Bateman of Rochester.

In March 1870 the former soldier ventured west to the territory of Washington. Settling in Olympia, he earned a solid reputation as a lawyer, and in 1875 he was appointed United States attorney for the territory. He retained this position for the next ten years, although he changed his residence in 1881 to Walla Walla.

In the federal elections of 1888, he was elected to represent Washington Territory in the United States Congress, serving from 4 March to 11 November 1889, when Washington became a state. Allen then was elected one of Washington's new senators, serving from 20 November 1889 to 3 March 1893.

Following his congressional career, Allen resumed practicing law in Seattle, where he died on 28 January 1903. His widow, two daughters, and two sons survived him.

References: *National Cyclopedia of American Biography*; *Who Was Who in America*; *Wabash Magazine*, VI (June 1866), p. 5; *Wabash Magazine*, VII (June 1867), pp. 10, 16; *Indianapolis Journal*, 11 Dec. 1889; *Biographical Directory of the American Congress*; and material at the Olmsted County (MN) Historical Society.

ALLEN, JOSEPH SHEPHERD (1814–1874)

In early days it was not unusual for both a father and a son to attend Wabash College a generation apart. Only a few Wabash fathers and sons also served in the war, however. Yet this was true for Joseph Shepherd Allen and his son John Beard Allen.

Joseph, subject of this biography, was born in Indiana on 19 November 1814 and was living in Crawfordsville some twenty years later when he joined the

Wabash College Preparatory Department in the autumn of 1834. He returned the following year, listing Lafayette as his residence. He married Hannah Beard of Crawfordsville on 14 March 1839, and they had at least seven children.

Allen studied medicine, and at the time of the 1850 census he owned real estate worth $3,500. The family was still living in Crawfordsville when the Civil War erupted, and Dr. Allen secured a commission from Governor Morton and became chief surgeon of the Tenth Indiana Regiment in September 1861.

In February 1862 Allen was placed under arrest for angering his fellow officers, then released without charges filed against him. Outraged that he was not reinstated fully, the surgeon complained to Governor Morton, but delays ensued, and he was relieved of all his duties in the active regiment by his regimental commander. Meanwhile, the regiment moved south in March, leaving Allen in charge of one hundred wounded men at Somerset, Kentucky, without adequate supplies and assistance.

It was not until June 1862 that he was exonerated and permitted to rejoin the Tenth Regiment stationed in Corinth, Mississippi, but once again, he felt compelled to petition Governor Morton to recall the regiment because there was so much illness in its ranks. Unsuccessful in his plea, he resigned his commission in October 1862 and returned to Crawfordsville.

In March 1865 Allen and his family moved to Rochester, Minnesota, where his medical practice flourished, but his wife's health declined, and she died of tuberculosis on 26 December 1868, leaving him with four children: John, Cora, Katie, and Joseph Jr.

In February 1872 he suffered a stroke that paralyzed his right side, forcing him to give up his practice and move his family west to Olympia, Washington, where his son John had settled.

He died on 11 June 1874 and is buried in the Tumwater Masonic Cemetery.

References: H. W. Beckwith, *History of Montgomery County* (1881), p. 34; *History of Montgomery County, Indiana* (Bowen and Co., 1913), p. 93; G. T. Williams, *Pioneer Physicians and Surgeons of Montgomery County, Indiana* (1943), pp. 21–22; N. H. Guthrey, "Joseph S. Allen," *Minnesota Medicine*, XXXII–XXXIV (1949–1951), pp. 59–60. See also: letters from J. S. Allen to Governor Morton in the Indiana State Archives; *Rochester Post*, 1 July 1855, 30 June 1866, 24 Sept. 1870, 10 Feb. 1872, 20 April 1872, and 8 June 1872. Allen's death was reported in the *Washington Standard*, 13 June 1874.

ALLEN, PERRY W. (1839–1930)

Some men's service was short, particularly in the early months of the war when the war's potential duration was not clearly understood as yet. Selected regiments were mustered in for three months or less in Indiana. Such was the case with the unit Perry Allen joined. He was born at Frankfort on 19 January 1839, the son of Robert M. and Phoebe White Allen, and attended Wabash for only one academic year, 1856–57. By 1860 he was working as a clerk in a Williamsport grocery store.

On 25 April 1861 Allen enlisted in Company B of the Tenth Indiana Regiment for a term of three months. He was described as being five feet nine inches tall, with auburn hair, grey eyes, and a light complexion. By 10 June his regiment had reached Parkersburg in western Virginia, where their major engagement in one of the first land battles of the war, at Rich Mountain, occurred from 10 to 13 July 1861, after which he was mustered out at Indianapolis on 6 August.

He returned to Williamsport and on 14 January 1864 married Sarah E. Jones, who was born in Attica and was about five years older than he was. At the time he owned his own grocery store in Williamsport, but by 1866 he was in business in Delphi. The following year he joined his younger brother Frank in a store in Omaha, Nebraska, where his first child Harry was born in 1868. In 1870 a second child, Robert, was born at Neosho Falls, Kansas.

In 1872 the family moved back to Williamsport, where Allen became the proprietor of the City Meat Market and General Produce, and where their two daughters, Mable (1873) and Josephine (1876) were born.

In the 1880s or 1890s the family was in Big Timber, Montana, where Sarah died on 23 December 1910. In August 1926 Allen entered a soldiers' home at Retsil, Washington, and died there on 20 December 1930. He is buried in Seattle.

References: Military pension file at the National Archives in Washington, DC, supplemented by Walter Salts of Warren County, who directed our attention to various local sources, including issues of the *Warren Republican*, 2 Feb. 1865, 12 July 1866, and 25 April 1872.

ANDERSON, JAMES H. (1838–1886)

James Anderson was born in Vermillion County in 1838 and entered the Preparatory Department of Wabash College in the fall of 1857, staying for three years before returning to the family farm.

At the outbreak of the Civil War, he lost little time in enlisting as a private in the Eighteenth Indiana Regiment on 16 August 1861, destined for action in Missouri. On a march from Otterville to Springfield in November, he contracted bronchitis and was given sick leave. He rejoined his regiment in March 1862, but found that he could not sustain the rigors of military service and secured a medical discharge in May at St. Louis.

He resumed his life as a farmer, and in 1865 he married a widow, Frances (Fanny) Ammerman Foucannon, who was several years his senior and had lost her first husband three years before in the war. They had five children: West (1870), Frederick (1872), Marietta (1873), William (1876), and Carrie (1881).

In the 1870s the family apparently moved from Vermillion County, Indiana to the town of Newell, Vermilion County, Illinois, where Allen described himself as an "itinerant minister." He died on 14 March 1886, but Fanny survived him for many years, eventually moving in with her daughter, Marietta, who lived in Terre Haute. She was modestly sustained by her husband's veteran's pension of $30 per month.

References: Military service and pension files, National Archives, Washington, DC.

ANDREW, ABRAM PIATT, III (1843–1935)

Abram Andrew III was born on 2 January 1843 in Michigan City. When he was four years old, the family returned to the town of LaPorte, where his father, Abram Jr., picking up the spirit of the times, began to speculate in land that increased in value so much that he became a wealthy man. Andrew attended the local schools and then enrolled in Wabash College in the autumn of 1860, entering for the last of the preparatory years. During 1861–62 he completed his freshman year, but on 12 August 1862 he enrolled for three years in the Twenty-First Indiana Light Artillery and was commissioned as an officer. He was with the Army of the Cumberland in Kentucky and Tennessee and was promoted from second lieutenant to first lieutenant, and finally to captain, before being mustered out on 26 June 1865 in Indianapolis.

Soon afterwards he joined his brother-in-law and journeyed south to rent a plantation in Louisiana, intending to grow cotton, employing ex-slaves as field hands. All went well until the "army worm" devastated the crop and he was forced to give up farming and return to LaPorte, where in 1869 he founded a bank named in honor of his father. For the next sixty-one years he ran this establishment, in that period of time setting a record for continuous proprietorship. Only poor health forced him into retirement in 1930.

On 16 April 1872, he married Helen Merrill, who was born in Ohio, but had settled in LaPorte. They had two children, Helen and Abram. His son attended Wabash College briefly, but completed his bachelor of arts degree at Princeton University in 1893, secured a PhD at Harvard, and taught economics there from 1901 to 1909, eventually being elected to the United States House of Representatives.

Abram Andrew III also tried his hand at politics, first as county chairman for the Republican Party in the early 1870s and then as unsuccessful candidate for mayor of LaPorte in 1873.

On 27 October 1935, Allen died at his home. Known as "Captain Andrew," he had by then become an institution in his town.

References: Indiana State Archives; J. P. Dunn, *Indiana and Indianans*, III (1919), pp. 1374–76; and *LaPorte Herald-Argus*, 28 Oct. 1935.

ANDREW, EDWIN ANDERSON (1840–1884)

At the time when it was typical for students to remain at Wabash College for only a year or two, Edwin Andrew spent 1865–67 in the Preparatory Department, followed by four years in the college's classical course of study, graduating in June 1871 at the age of thirty-one. Prior to this he spent four years in the Twelfth Regiment of the Indiana Volunteer Infantry.

His first tour of duty began in May 1861 and concluded the following spring. At this time he was described as a twenty-one-year-old man, five feet ten inches tall, with dark hair, fair complexion, and grey eyes. His occupation was that of a farmer, but when he re-enlisted in the same regiment in August 1862, he described himself as a carpenter. He served until June 1865 and rose to the rank of captain, claiming that he hiked about ten thousand miles during those three years.

With this background, it was natural that he led the Cadet Corps at Wabash College in the years immediately after the war. He was also the first student to be initiated into the newly formed Gamma chapter of the Phi Kappa Psi fraternity in December 1870.

Soon after graduation in 1871, he married Elizabeth Wheeler, and they had a son, William. He also became a licensed minister in the Methodist Episcopal Church of Indiana and held a series of brief pastorates in Kentland, 1872–73; Remington, 1874–75; Chesterton, 1875–76; and Colfax, 1878–80. Between 1876 and 1878 he served at a church in Evanston, Illinois.

In 1881, partly for reasons of ill health, Andrew changed vocations and accepted a professorship of mathematics and natural philosophy at Willamette College in Salem, Oregon, but after a year he returned to Evanston, where he retired. He died on 14 August 1884.

References: Methodist Episcopal Church, *Northwestern Indiana Conference*, XXXIII (1884), p. 58; National Archives in Washington, DC; *Wabash Magazine*, XI (June 1871), p. 149; *Wabash Magazine*, XII (March 1872), p. 148; and information from Phi Kappa Psi via M. Stuart Douglas, Wabash class of 1985; 1850 U.S. census for Van Buren Township, Kosciusko County and 1880 U.S. census for Colfax, Clinton County; Phi Psi information from M. Stuart Douglas, class of 1985.

ANDREW, JOHN H. (1829–1862)

Uncertainty surrounds the war career of John H. Andrew and much else of his life. When Andrew attended the Preparatory Department of Wabash College between 1846 and 1848, his middle initial did not appear. However, during the Civil War, the college catalogues indicate that he was in the army and referred to him as J. H. Andrew.

While Andrew was at Wabash, the town of Lafayette was listed as his residence, and it seems likely that he was the son of Jesse and Sarah Andrew, born in Tippecanoe County on 16 July 1829. In the 1850 census he described himself as a saddler, like his father.

Several men with the name John Andrews married women either in Montgomery or Tippecanoe Counties in the 1850s, but it is impossible to be certain which one might be the student in the Wabash Alumni Directory for 1932, which suggests he died in 1862.

References: Tippecanoe County Historical Association.

ANDREW, JOHN WAUGH (1831–1862)

John Waugh Andrew was born on 7 January 1831, probably in Lebanon, Ohio, where his parents were married on 26 March 1830. His mother, Martha Waugh, died on 23 September 1831, and his father, Daniel Andrew, died on 13 March 1839, when John was just eight years old. His uncle, Abram Piatt Andrew Sr., provided funds for him to study in the Preparatory Department of Miami University at Oxford, Ohio, from 1842 to 1844 and arranged for him to go to Wabash in the autumn of 1846.

After two years of college Andrew gravitated to LaPorte, where his uncle had been one of the town founders in 1832, and by 1859 Andrew and a partner had established a thriving drugstore.

Another link to Wabash College came when his cousin, Abram Piatt Andrew III, attended between 1860 and 1862.

On 22 July 1861 Andrew received his commission as a lieutenant in Company E of the Twentieth Indiana Regiment. He went to Maryland the following month, assigned to guard railroad lines, then his regiment embarked on a steamer bound initially for Hatteras Inlet, North Carolina, one of the early battles of the war. On 9 November 1861 he again boarded a steamer with his regiment, bound this time for Fortress Monroe, Virginia. In May 1862 they took part in the capture of Norfolk. Along with many other Union forces, they became involved in the peninsular campaign, where they sustained a serious defeat at the Battle of the Orchards (25 June 1862), with 144 killed and wounded. Andrew met his death on 30 June at the Battle of Frayser's Farm and White Oak Swamp.

Before the war, Andrew had purchased cemetery lots in the Pine Lake Cemetery of LaPorte, where he memorialized his parents, Daniel and Martha. A tablet also memorializes their son.

References: Miami University Archives, Oxford, Ohio; Tippecanoe County Historical Association; Fern Eddy Schultz of LaPorte County; *LaPorte Herald*, 12, 19, and 22 July 1862.

AUSTIN, ABNER VANHOOK (1828–1896)

Abner Austin was born in Crawfordsville on 29 November 1828, one of the ten children of Nancy and John B. Austin. His father distinguished himself as Montgomery County auditor for sixteen years.

Austin entered the Preparatory Department of Wabash in the fall of 1844 and matriculated as a freshman for the Classical Course in the fall of 1846. Unlike many of his contemporaries, he completed that higher course of studies and received an AB degree in June 1850. For a brief time he studied medicine, but changed to law, which became his life's profession.

On 8 September 1853 he married Catherine V. Huffman of Crawfordsville, and two years later they had their first son, Harry M. About this time they moved to Rushville, Illinois, where their second child, Fred H., was born.

When the Civil War broke out, they were living in Crawfordsville, and Austin was an early volunteer in the Tenth Indiana Regiment. Upon the expiration of his three months' commitment in August 1861, he re-enlisted for three years in the Eighteenth Indiana. He enrolled in the 130th Indiana for a third tour of duty in February 1865.

He was mustered out in August 1865 at Stevensville Station, Virginia, and returned to his family, which had moved to Darlington by the latter 1860s. Sometime in the 1870s they moved again to Thorntown, where he died on 8 May 1896. He is buried in the Jamestown Cemetery.

References: Boone County cemetery records; Montgomery County marriage records and U.S. census for 1860; *Daily Argus News*, 8 May 1896; *Portrait and Biographical Record of Montgomery, Parke and Fountain Counties, Indiana* (1893), p. 702.

The curriculum in the 1840s

Four-year Classical Course
Latin
Greek: Xenophon, Homer, Demosthenes
Latin: Horace, Cicero, Tacitus: essays and orations and declamations.

Scientific Course: from the catalogue
Algebra, Trigonometry, Geometry, Natural Philosophy, Physics
Senior Year: Chemistry, Mineralogy and Geology.

Rhetorical Course
English Language and Literature
Forensics, Philosophy, Ethics and Logic
All students had one term of Theology, and Constitution of the U.S.
*In early years preparatory students outnumbered college students 2 to 1.
An Agricultural Course was offered for a year or two.

Preparatory Department
Had been incorporated with the college earlier and students of all ages were often together.
In 1847 Caleb Mills separated the Preps from the college. Some younger men were in the fraternities.
Also in the late 1840s Mills implemented a teachers' course, Normal.

Normal School
A three-year course, department, but if you completed 2 years you could get a teacher's certificate.
Hovey, Mills and Campbell were the teachers for "such branches as are deemed important to be mastered by every one who designs to honor the profession of a teacher." General courses in English, math, science and natural and intellectual philosophy, logic, surveying and navigation. Latin and German were recommended but not required.
All the courses had religious training, liberal Presbyterianism.
Discipline could be administered if you swore, drank, attended "Thespian" performances, committed a prank like stealing the chapel bell or were "ungentlemanly" or attended an unauthorized secret society.

References: James I. Osborne and Theodore Gregory Gronert *Wabash College: The First Hundred Years*

BABB, JOHN PINCKNEY (1836–1918)

Many Civil War soldiers, particularly from the Midwest, complained that their soldierly duties seemed to always consist of guarding railroads. These duties often entailed protecting northern army supply lines late in the war. While it is true that this was a relatively safe place to be during the Civil War, it was also incredibly boring. John Babb was one of the soldiers guarding railroads for the 137th Indiana Regiment.

Babb was born in Pennsylvania on 28 May 1836. His father, after whom he was named, was in the construction business. The senior Babb died sometime in 1840–41, and John's mother, Mary Schriner Babb, reared her seven children in Wilkes-Barre, Pennsylvania, until she died in 1844 or 1845. Among John's siblings were two brothers, Clement and Edwin, and a sister, Mary.

About 1849 Babb joined his older brother Clement, a Presbyterian minister, in Indianapolis, and in the autumn of 1849 he enrolled in the Preparatory Department of Wabash, where he remained for two years, witnessing his brother Clement become a trustee of college, a post he held from 1850 until 1858.

From 1851 to 1861 John Babb held a succession of jobs in Pennsylvania and Ohio, one of which was as a reporter for the *Cincinnati Gazette*. After marrying Nettie Hatfield Williams, he became a farmer in North Vernon and became the father of three sons, Clifford, Clement, and Walter.

In May 1864 Babb felt compelled to join the army and signed on with Company B of the 137th Indiana Regiment for a term of one hundred days. The regiment's assignment was to guard the railroad lines that Sherman's army depended on for supplies. At Tullahoma, Tennessee, Babb assumed the duties of a clerk in the commissary office and extended his service for another month before mustering out as a sergeant at Indianapolis on 21 September 1864.

An interesting part of Indiana Civil War history can be observed by noting how many ex-soldiers left Indiana for other states, especially in the west. In 1874 the Babb family migrated to Santa Clara County, California, where Babb purchased sixty acres of choice land outside of San Jose, at the foot of Mount Hamilton. He developed twenty-five acres into Hill Crest Orchard, which produced apricots, peaches, plums, cherries, almonds, and apples and cultivated a vineyard with a variety of grapes. The remainder of the ranch was devoted to growing hay and raising cattle.

One of the reasons that Babb went to California was that his older brother Clement had settled there. However, Clement died in 1906, while John lived until 1 March 1918. He was buried in Oak Hill Cemetery in San Jose.

References: Jennings County Public Library and San Jose (CA) Public Library. See also: *North Vernon Sun*, 1 March 1969; *North Vernon Plain Dealer*, 15 Nov. 1923; H. S. Foote (ed.), *Pen Pictures from the Garden of the World: or Santa Clara County California* (1888), pp. 252–53; J. M. Guinn, *History of the State of California* (1904), p. 1180.

BACON, CYRUS J. JR. (1837–1868)

Thirteen thousand doctors served in the Civil War. It was not difficult to be commissioned surgeon or assistant surgeon because medical training was rudimentary, based on apprenticeships or attendance at what were often proprietary medical schools. Cyrus Bacon served in the Union army as an assistant surgeon. His story is both typical of, and slightly more interesting than, those of the many other Indiana medical officers.

Cyrus Bacon Jr. was the third of five children born to Cyrus Sr. and Melinda Guernsey. He was born in Michigan and attended Wabash for only one year, 1853–54. At this time his family was living in Cass County, Michigan, and he became apprenticed to a physician in Edwardsburg, Dr. I. G. Bugbee. After completing his medical education in Washington, DC, Bacon began his practice in Mishawaka in 1858.

With the coming of the Civil War and the consequent demand for qualified doctors, Bacon enrolled at Monroe, Michigan, in Company B of the Seventh Michigan Regiment on 22 August 1861 as assistant surgeon. He committed to three years of service and secured an honorable discharge in May 1862 in order to become a surgeon in the regular United States Army.

In 1865 Bacon was stationed in Texas. In 1867 he was transferred to Baton Rouge, Louisiana, where he served another year.

At the end of the summer of 1868, the surgeon started for home, presumably on a riverboat, because his health had seriously deteriorated, but when he reached St. Louis, he was unable to continue his journey, and he died on 3 September. His remains were conveyed to Niles, Michigan, where he is buried in the Silverbrook Cemetery. As far as is known, he never married.

References: 1860 U.S. census for Edwardsburg, Michigan. See also: H. S. Rogers, *History of Cass County, Michigan*, pp. 143–45; *History of Cass County, Michigan* (1880), pp. 282–83; and the records of the Silverbrook Cemetery.

BACON, DAVID (1827–1899)

David Bacon was the oldest of the five children of Cyrus Sr. and Melinda Guernsey, mentioned above. He was born in New York State on 9 September 1827, but in 1834 his family moved to Michigan, where his brother Cyrus Jr. was born. A third brother, James, also attended Wabash but apparently did not serve in the Civil War.

David Bacon reached the Preparatory Department of Wabash in the autumn of 1850 from his home in Niles, Michigan. He remained at Wabash two years and then returned to Niles to study law.

In September 1857 he married Lydia A. Griffin, age twenty. She too had originally come from New York State. Their first son, Irving, was born in 1859 but died two years later. Paul was born in 1860, Earnest in 1864, and Marion in 1866, and these children grew to maturity.

On 27 August 1861 Bacon entered military service as captain of Company K of the Sixth Michigan Regiment. At the end of April 1862, New Orleans fell to the northern troops, and the Michigan Sixth was soon stationed nearby. On 5 August 1862, at the Battle of Baton Rouge, Bacon was badly wounded. A bullet passed through both of his shoulders. He was medically discharged on 3 September and made his way home to recover his health.

In the latter 1860s and early 1870s, Bacon practiced law in partnership with John King in Niles. By the early 1890s he seemed to be by himself as an attorney, at 214 Main Street.

By then he was no stranger to family tragedy. His wife, Lydia, had died in October 1888, and their daughter, Marion, had drowned in 1890. He lived until 25 July 1899 and is buried in Niles's Silverbrook Cemetery.

References: Much valuable help was provided by the Niles Community Library. Some information comes from various Niles or Berrien County directories. Bacon's medical discharge and his subsequent disability is covered in his pension file at the National Archives in Washington, DC.

BAKER, ROBERT FULTON (1831–1890)

Fulton Baker, as he liked to call himself, was born in Jefferson on 6 July 1831, the oldest of twelve children born to Abner and Catherine Hood Baker, whose marriage in August 1830 was reckoned to be the first wedding by settlers in the county.

Baker spent the years 1848–50 in the Preparatory Department of Wabash College and continued for his freshman and sophomore years (1850–52). Records of Clinton County show his marriage to Sarah A. Hopple on 5 April 1853.

After leaving Wabash, he went to seminary for a year intending to become a Presbyterian minister, but soon began studying homeopathic medicine and practiced in Cincinnati for about five years. In the late 1850s he moved to Moline, Illinois, where remained for about ten years.

In Moline he tried to enlist in the Illinois Volunteers, but he was turned down because of his unorthodox homeopathic training. Undeterred, he went to New York City and took a course at Bellevue Hospital medical school, which qualified him for military service in the 132nd Illinois, On 1 June 1864 he signed in for one hundred days, which he served in the Chicago area, and was mustered out on 17 October 1864.

After the war, Baker married a widow, Jane Eliza Dimock Battisace, in Elizabeth, New Jersey, in 1868 and relocated his medical practice from Moline to Davenport, Iowa. Jane's daughter from a previous marriage, Jannette (Jennie), took the surname Baker, and in September 1869 Jane gave birth to a son, Robert

DeWitt Baker.

For over twenty years, Fulton Baker practiced medicine in Davenport. However, his devotion to duty proved fatal: He contracted influenza while treating a patient and died of pneumonia on 28 January 1890. He was buried at Oakdale Cemetery.

References: Helpful information provided by Mrs. Enid Burghard of Oregon City, Oregon. See also: Iowa Historical Society of Iowa City; *Portrait and Biographical Record of Boone and Clinton Counties, Indiana* (1895); *History of Clinton County, Indiana* (1886); *Davenport Democrat*, 29 Jan. 1890.

BALDWIN, JOSEPH ELIHU (1826–1914)

For those who know Wabash, the name of Baldwin is invariably associated with the college's first president, Elihu, so it is not surprising that his son, Joseph, was a student here from 1838 to 1846. Little is known of Joseph's time at Wabash except that he belonged to the Western Literary Society and won a prize for speaking during his sophomore year.

Baldwin was one of eight children born to Elihu and his wife, Julia, who met in a stagecoach on Long Island (New York) and married years later. In 1835, when the younger Baldwin was nine years old, the family left New York City, where his father was minister of a prosperous church, and ventured to Crawfordsville in the frontier outposts of Indiana so Elihu Baldwin could become the first president of Wabash College.

Premature death, a sad mark of the times, plagued the Baldwin family, and Elihu passed away in 1840, when Joseph was only fourteen and his mother, forty. She continued to live in Crawfordsville and raise her children there, but died in 1849 while Joseph was teaching in Lafayette and Indianapolis.

At some point in the early to mid-1850s, Baldwin returned to New York to study law at a Buffalo firm, and he was admitted to the bar in 1858. In early 1860 he traveled to St. Louis and established a law practice there.

As the Civil War spread from the East to the border states of the West, the citizens of St. Louis were determined to have their own militia, and so on 12 August 1862 Baldwin enrolled in Company C of the First Regiment of the Missouri National Guard for three years. He later recalled that he witnessed Joseph O. Shelby's Confederate cavalry raid at Potosi, Missouri, in 1863.

Baldwin's military service ended on 24 September 1864, and he decided to settle in Potosi, where he ran for election to the state senate and served from 1864 to 1866. He took special interest in the founding of a school of mines at Rolla and in the construction of a great bridge over the Mississippi at St. Louis, probably the first road and railroad bridge across the Mississippi built by James Eads after the Civil War.

In the summer of 1872 he moved to Topeka, Kansas, and established a successful law practice. When he died on 4 October 1914, he was said to be the oldest lawyer in Topeka. Baldwin was buried in Mount Hope Cemetery.

References: Johanna Herring, formerly the archivist at Wabash College, provided substantial help reconstructing the lives of the Baldwin family. See also: *Wabash Magazine*, VI (Dec. 1914), p. 52; J. I. Osborne and T. G. Gronert, *Wabash College: The First Hundred Years* (1932).

BALL, LAFAYETTE (1836–1921)

Three Ball brothers attended Wabash and also served in the Civil War: Lafayette, Zephaniah, and Zopher. All six children of Solomon and Lucetta Ball were born in Montgomery County, where the family owned sixty-five acres of land. Lafayette Ball was born in Crawfordsville on 13 November 1836.

In the fall of 1859, at the age of twenty-two, Ball embarked upon a formal education at Wabash, attending one year. In 1862 he enlisted in Company L of the Ninetieth Indiana Regiment. He was described at the time as a farmer, five feet nine inches tall, with light complexion, light hair, and blue eyes.

At first, Ball's military service was relatively uneventful, alternating between Kentucky and Tennessee, with no major engagements. Then, at the beginning of July 1863, the regiment's Fifth Cavalry pursued Morgan's Confederate cavalry in southern Indiana and Ohio and inflicted a crushing defeat at Buffington Island, Ohio; seven hundred were killed and wounded, leaving a remnant of three hundred who retreated into Pennsylvania.

Ball's military career came to an abrupt end on 11 October 1863, when he was wounded in the hip at Rheatown, in eastern Tennessee. For five months he was out of action, and in March 1864 he received an honorable and medical discharge. The injury left his right leg somewhat shorter and his foot splayed out.

Back in Crawfordsville, Ball enrolled at Wabash in the autumn of 1864. The following summer, on 4 July 1865, he was married to Barbara Van Hook, a native of Crawfordsville, by the president of the college, Joseph Tuttle. Their first son, Harry V., was born in 1866, followed by Frank S. in 1868, Martha E. in 1870, Luke S. in 1871, and Margaret in 1874.

They apparently farmed in Iowa and Indiana before moving to Kansas, where Ball died of pneumonia on 12 March 1921. His wife died on 10 December 1928.

References: Military pension file at the National Archives in Washington, DC, and valuable information provided by Joseph L. Druse of East Lansing, Michigan.

BALL, WILLIAM STAUGHTON (1836–1917)

William Ball was born on 12 March 1836 in the town of Albion, Orleans County, New York. His father Thomas was a minister and presumably moved every few years.

The younger Ball entered the Preparatory Department of Wabash in the fall of 1853 and returned the following year, 1854–55. On 1 August 1862 he enrolled in Company C of the Fourth New York Heavy Artillery at Rochester, New York, and rose from private to second lieutenant before being discharged at Washington, DC, on 26 June 1865. He was described as being five feet four inches tall, with light complexion, blue eyes, and brown hair.

On 12 June 1867 Ball married Mary Catherine Eddy of Lewiston, Niagara County, New York. For a brief time they lived in Charleston, South Carolina, and then in November 1868 settled in Greensboro, North Carolina, where Ball established a law practice and became a United States commissioner of land disposal as well as editor of a newspaper, the *New North State*.

Ball was a staunch Republican, but by the early 1890s, North Carolina was coming under the influence of Democrats and white supremacists, so he moved first to New Jersey and then to Brooklyn, New York, where he continued to practice law until his death on 29 April 1917.

References: Military pension files; Greensboro Public Library: *Greensboro Patriot*, 9 Feb. 1871; E. S. Arnett (ed.), *Greensboro North Carolina* (1955), pp. 248–49; and William D. Bennett of Raleigh, North Carolina.

BALL, ZEPHANIAH M. (1841–1927)

A son of Solomon and Lucetta Ball and brother of Zopher and Lafayette, Zephaniah Ball was born in February 1841 and lived in Crawfordsville during most of his childhood.

Like his brothers who also attended Wabash College and served in the Civil War, he entered the college's Normal School in 1860 but left in April 1861 to join the Indiana Eleventh Regiment, Company G, nicknamed the Indiana Zouaves. His regiment saw little action, and he was mustered out on 4 August 1861.

Ball returned to Wabash the following fall and completed two years of Preparatory Department studies. During this time he was a member of the Calliopean Society.

On 20 August 1863 he was commissioned a first lieutenant in the Montgomery Guards of the Indiana Legion and at the same time became a college freshman. On campus he organized a small company for manual at-arms drill in support of the Union cause.

In the spring of 1864 Ball left Wabash for Vicksburg, where he was commissioned a lieutenant in the U.S. Forty-Ninth Colored Infantry. He was discharged on 15 April 1866 and returned to Indiana to marry Louisa Smock. They had two children, Howard and Allen.

The census of 1870 listed Zephaniah Ball as a druggist residing in Brown Township, Montgomery County, but by 1895 he lived in Crawfordsville at 311 South Washington Street.

He joined the Grand Army of the Republic at Steadman Post No. 245 on 20 October 1883 and transferred his membership to the McPherson Post No. 7 in Crawfordsville on 6 July 1889. GAR records indicate that he died in February 1927 at the National Soldiers Home in Virginia.

References: F. M. Mills, *Early Days in a College Town* (1924), p. 212; GAR, *Descriptive Book*, McPherson Post No. 7; Crawfordsville city directories; GAR *Roster*, McPherson Post No. 7, p. 144; correspondence with Joseph L. Druse of West Lansing, Michigan; *History of Montgomery County, Indiana* (Bowen and Co., 1913), p. 104.

BALL, ZOPHER (1834–1895)

Zopher Ball was one of three sons of Solomon and Lucetta Ball to attend Wabash College. He was born on the family farm one mile west of Crawfordsville in October 1834.

During 1860–62 he sampled both the Normal and the Scientific courses of study at Wabash, after which he began his formal medical training under the supervision of a Dr. Sloan. This was followed by several years at Rush Medical College in Chicago, from which he graduated in 1865.

During his years at Wabash Ball volunteered for three months with the Eleventh Indiana Regiment, serving from April to August 1861. Two summers later he also responded to the emergency call for defense against Morgan's raid, devoting nine days in July 1863 to Company C of the 108th Regiment.

Following the war he settled in Waveland, west of Crawfordsville, where he married Sarah E. McNutt on 3 January 1867 and practiced medicine for the next thirty years. They eventually had one daughter and three sons. Sarah died on 16 March 1895, with her husband Zopher succumbing a week later on 23 March. He was honored both in life and in death by the GAR and by the Masons.

References: *Journal of the Indiana State Medical Association*, XXXVI (Nov. 1943), p. 609; 1860 and 1870 U.S. censuses for Montgomery County; Montgomery County marriage and death records; *Crawfordsville Journal*, 29 March 1895. Also: Thomas V. Ball of Ringgold, Pennsylvania.

BARLOW, GEORGE WILSON (1838–1907)

George Barlow was born on 3 January 1838 in Lagro, the son of Wilson B. and Hannah Barlow. He came to Wabash in 1858 and spent the next two years in the Preparatory Department, skipping the academic year 1860–61 but returning the following autumn as a junior. He graduated in June of 1863.

Back in Lagro he undertook a variety of jobs, including schoolteacher, tanner, and surveyor. However, the pressure to serve in the war was strong, and he joined the Indiana Fourteenth Light Artillery in November 1864. When the war ended in the spring of 1865, he was relieved of his one-year obligation and was again confronted with the need to choose a career.

The following autumn Barlow entered Lane Theological Seminary in Cincinnati, Ohio. Three years later he graduated, married Amanda Sandford, and was ordained by the Presbytery of Fort Wayne. His first parish was in Mason, Michigan, where he remained for a decade—a surprisingly long time. One can only surmise that this was an effective minister of the gospel, appreciated by his congregation. Another lengthy tenure was at Calvary Chapel in Detroit from 1879 to 1892. He served shorter terms at the Presbyterian Church of Lapeer, Michigan (1892–95), Cairo, Illinois (1895–1903), and the Cadillac Avenue Church of Detroit (1903–07).

The Barlows had three children. Two daughters died in infancy; only their son, Perry Arthur, born 16 May 1870, reached maturity.

Barlow possessed a facility for ancient languages dating from his years at Wabash College. His reputation was such that the Wabash Board of Trustees asked him to return from Lane Seminary in the spring of 1866 to replace the recently deceased Professor Atlas Hadley. He reluctantly declined, but received an honorary doctor of divinity degree from his alma mater in 1891.

He died in Detroit on 7 January 1907, shortly after his sixty-ninth birthday.

References: 1905 Wabash College alumni questionnaire; *Wabash Record*, XXXI (Feb. 1907), p. 180; *The Michigan Presbyterian*, XIV (Feb. 1907); Lane Theological Seminary, *General Catalogue, 1829–1899*, p. 73.

BARLOW, JAMES MILTON (1845–1922)

James Barlow was born in Washington Township, Hendricks County, on 13 September 1845, one of eight children born to Harvey R. and Sarah E. Smith Barlow.

He was only fifteen years old when the Civil War broke out, so he bided his time until he was eighteen and then enrolled in Company H of the 132nd Regiment in nearby Danville on 30 April 1864. He signed up for one hundred days and was mustered out the following September.

Brief as his service was, it proved both exciting and traumatic. In July he managed to become detached from his regiment and joined the march on Atlanta, stringing along with soldiers from other units. During this time he contracted malaria and spent ten days in the hospital. Coming home allowed him to partially recover his health, but he never again felt able to do any heavy manual labor.

Before coming to Wabash in the autumn of 1867, he may have been an apprentice for a lithographer in Cincinnati. Registering in the Preparatory Department, he indicated that his home was in Danville, Hendricks County, Indiana.

Barlow acquired seven hundred acres of farmland near Plainfield, and he married Sarah E. Hornaday on 17 May 1871. They had eight children. Barlow combined being a farmer with teaching, a common practice because the growing and harvesting seasons coincided with summer vacations. He reckoned that he taught or administered at twenty-two different schools during his career.

In 1897 he was elected to the House of Representatives of the Indiana General Assembly, and from 1901 to 1903 he served in the Indiana State Senate. He also served as a justice of the peace for twenty years.

Barlow died in Plainfield on 29 August 1922, while his wife, Sarah, lived until 1937.

References: J. V. Hadley, *History of Hendricks County, Indiana* (1885), pp. 562–63; *Portrait and Biographical Record of Boone, Clinton and Hendricks Counties, Indiana* (1895), pp. 1033–35; and *Biographical Directory of the Indiana General Assembly* (1880), I, p. 14.

BARNES, JOHN A. (1837–1900)

In the period before the war broke out in Indiana, when political tensions were high and ardent patriotism strong, particularly among young men, "marching units" became popular around towns in Indiana and other states, North and South. Calling themselves names like "The Wide-Awakes" or "Putnam Guard," these units practiced what they imagined were military drill tactics while carrying squirrel rifles or other local arms. Wabash men are shown marching on campus in the lithograph which is the cover of this book. These drilling units, along with regular militia, were the antecedents of the Civil War Indiana Legion, men who stayed in Indiana to protect the state instead of going to the battlefield. John Barnes was a member of the Carroll County "Rough and Ready Guard."

Barnes was born in Ohio about 1837, one of four brothers. The eldest, Samuel, briefly attended Wabash from 1852 to 1853, but did not serve in the Civil War.

John Barnes attended the Preparatory Department of Wabash from 1852 to 1854, citing his hometown as Pittsburg, Carroll County. He was still living in Pittsburg in 1860, listed as a student.

A few months after the outbreak of war, Barnes helped to organize the Carroll County "Rough and Ready Guard" of the legion. He received a commission as its captain on 25 July 1861. He seems not to have enrolled in a regular regiment of Indiana volunteers.

In July 1892 he was appointed from the state of Illinois as United States consul to the city of Chemnitz in the German state of Saxony. He retained this post until May 1893, and in October 1897 he became American consul in the German city of Cologne. He was performing these duties when he died on 27 March 1900.

References: *Carroll County Citizen*, 7 April 1900; *Hoosier Democrat*, 7 April 1900; J. H. Stewart, *Recollections of the Early Settlement of Carroll County* (1872), pp. 370–71.

BARNETT, JAMES F. (1837–1915)

James Barnett was born on 2 February 1837 at Camden, Ohio, the only son of James and Jane Creason Barnett. He had ten sisters, most of whom were born in Montgomery County, Indiana. The family lived on a farm near Ladoga which was valued at $1,500 in 1850 and $4,000 in 1860. Barnett undoubtedly worked on the family farm until he enrolled at Wabash College in the fall of 1856. He spent two years in the Preparatory Department, and then presumably returned to farming.

On 22 April 1861 Barnett enlisted in Company G of the Eleventh Indiana Regiment for a term of three months. He was described as being five feet ten inches tall, with fair complexion, grey eyes, and light hair.

When Confederate cavalry commander John Hunt Morgan threatened southern Indiana in July 1863, Barnett served briefly as a captain in an unknown unit, but after about a week he was released along with the many other volunteers.

Following the war he returned to farming in Montgomery County until 1868, when he acquired a farm near Wellsville, Kansas, where he remained the rest of his life. Barnett never married. He died on 24 February 1915.

References: U.S. census records and his military pension file at the National Archives, Washington, DC.

BASSETT, EDWARD ELNATHAN (1831?–1898)

Edward Bassett was one of seven children born to Horace and Amanda Fairchild Bassett at Aurora. His siblings were Harriet, Julia, Harvey, and Horace and two unknowns.

His father, Horace, was born in 1782 in Mansfield, Connecticut, but settled in Dearborn County as early as 1820. Between 1822 and 1830 he represented his district almost every year in the Indiana General Assembly, and in 1834 he was appointed clerk for Judge Jesse L. Holman of the United States District Court.

The sons of both Bassett and Holman attended the recently founded Wabash College.

Edward Bassett entered the Preparatory Department in 1844, and in 1847 he became a freshman in the classical course of study. He graduated with a bachelor of arts degree in 1851 and the following year studied law in Indianapolis.

He began practicing law in Terre Haute with a firm headed by Judge S. B. Goskins and later became a partner of Colonel John P. Baird. Bassett married Mary B. Gilman on 20 June 1860 and on his first wedding anniversary joined Bracken's Cavalry, part of the Twenty-Eighth Regiment of Indiana Volunteers. Because of his age, he was immediately commissioned a second lieutenant of Company K. His brief service took place mostly in western Virginia, where he was honorably discharged on 28 April 1862, presumably for medical reasons, since later in life he suffered from rheumatism, spinal injury, and kidney problems.

In 1863 the Bassetts moved to Clinton, Iowa, where the veteran practiced law and became an assistant adjutant general, dealing with claims against the state arising from the war.

In the early 1870s Bassett spent two years in Springfield, Illinois, editing the *State Journal*, and subsequently relocated to Chicago, where he practiced law until about 1878, when he returned to Indianapolis as a partner of Charles Test and John Coburn.

His wife died some time during the 1880s, after which Bassett lived in the Enterprise Hotel, where he died on 28 March 1898, survived by his son, Van. G. Bassett.

References: *The Soldier of Indiana in the War for the Union* (1866), I, p. 77; *The Wabash* (May 1898), p. 263; *Indianapolis Journal*, 29 March 1898; *Indianapolis Sentinel*, 29 March 1898. There is also a pension file for Bassett at the National Archives in Washington, DC. Edward's father, Horace Bassett, is included in the *Biographical Directory of the Indiana General Assembly* (1980), I, pp. 16–17.

BASSETT, GEORGE WASHINGTON (1827–1896)

George Bassett was the older son of Elnathan and Livea Buck Bassett, born in 1827 in what was then known as Canada West and later referred to as Hamilton in the Province of Ontario. A younger brother, James, also attended Wabash College and served in the war.

After attending the Preparatory Department for one year, in 1855–1856, he was named principal of the Belleville Academy in southern Illinois, but the following year he returned to Crawfordsville for a year of tutoring at his alma mater before deciding to study law in Cincinnati. With his law degree in hand, George Bassett returned to Iowa and tried to establish himself in Des Moines, but in 1859 he went to Fort Dodge to become partner with Judge W.N. Meservey.

Following the Union's humiliating defeat at Bull Run, Iowa Senator James

Harlan arranged with his relative, Colonel Joseph Harlan, to have the Iowa Volunteers who made up Company A merge with the 11th Pennsylvania Cavalry stationed at Washington D.C. in 1861. George Bassett received a commission of second lieutenant in this unit and went with the regiment to Annapolis, Maryland, and then by steamer to Fortress Monroe. He served for 15 months, and was promoted to first lieutenant in August 1862. He was twice wounded, the second and more serious time at Franklin, Virginia, justifying a medical discharge on 25 January 1863.

Returning to Fort Dodge, Bassett ran for the state senate and served for two years. In 1865 he was appointed agent for a newly-opened land office in Fort Dodge with the responsibility of administering a federal land grant for an agricultural college at Ames, Iowa, and during the next 20 years he either leased or sold about 200,000 acres for the new institution. After a varied career in railroad management, he died in 6 February 1896.

References *Fort Dodge Evening Messenger,* 7 Feb. 1896; E.D. Ross, *A History of Iowa State College* (Ames, 1942), p. 76; *Annals of Iowa,* II (April 1896), 40; *ibid.* VI (Jan. 1905), 571, 577; C. Cole, *The Courts and the Legal Profession of Iowa,* I (1907), 223.

BASSETT, HARVEY BERTRAND (1835–1862)

Harvey Bassett was born in 1835 in Aurora, one of seven children born to Horace and Amanda Bassett.

He followed his elder brother Edward to Wabash College, becoming a member of the freshman class in the fall of 1850 and sharing Room 41 of South Hall dormitory with Edward.

Harvey Bassett remained through his sophomore year of 1851–52 and then joined his father's office as an assistant to the clerk of the circuit and district courts, a job he had on 12 April 1861, when the war broke out. That July he joined Company H of the Twentieth Regiment for three years.

The Twentieth Indiana had been organized at Lafayette and was sent to Hatteras Inlet, North Carolina. At Newport News it witnessed the engagement between the *Merrimac, Cumberland,* and *Congress* and prevented the enemy from taking possession of the *Congress*. It was one of the most distinguished of Indiana's rare eastern regiments, enduring withering fire the second day at Gettysburg and losing 152 killed and wounded. Bassett, however, did not see that battle, as he died before his fellow soldiers were deployed at the Wheatfield.

Earlier, in a letter written in camp about seventeen miles from Baltimore, Maryland, Harvey Bassett was especially eloquent about what he witnessed:

> The daily routine of camp is finished; the pale moonlight sleeps on grassy banks or struggles faintly through the dense foliage overhead

on our snow-white tents; the sentinels are pacing the lonely watches in silence; the smouldering fires are fast dying out; the shrill cry of the katydid mingles with the voices of the men, as, gathered in groups around in tents, or on the grass, they make the clear night resonant with their Methodist song singing, now their only solace after the long tedious drills, and previous to the last roll-call at nine o'clock and the tap for all lights out. Today I heard a quail and a meadow-lark in a stubble field near us.

You cannot imagine how such things affect one under peculiar circumstances. The whistle of Bob White, the first heard since I left home, made me homesick, tired of my situation, and long to be again at home in the West... About ten o'clock at night the flames burst through the deck of the "Congress" and, igniting her rigging, spread a luminous glare over the heavens and across the harbor. Her tall masts resembled columns of fire. Her shrouds, ropes and sails looked like silver threads. Before midnight her guns became heated and discharged their loads all around, but did no damage beyond sinking a small sloop. Shortly after her magazine blew up, throwing cinders far heavenward amidst clouds of sparks and flakes of rope; then the mass sank beneath the waves, carrying down the burned and charred bodies of many a gallant tar...

In June 1862 Bassett was badly wounded at the Battle of Chickahominy and was taken prisoner by the Confederates, who brought him to Richmond, Virginia, where he died on 3 July 1862.

References: D. Stevenson, *Indiana's Roll of Honor* (1864), I, p. 653; 1850 U.S. census for Indianapolis; Merrill & Co., *The Soldier of Indiana in the War of the Union* (1866), pp. 484–85.

BASSETT, HENRY S. (1841–1913)

Henry Bassett's background was similar to that of two other Bassetts, George and James, who appear in this narrative. All three were born in Canada and lived for a time in Iowa. Perhaps they were cousins, but nothing definitely links them together.

Henry Bassett was born in Ingersoll, Canada, on 21 April 1841. His parents were Gilbert and Mary, who also had two daughters. In 1844 the family moved from Canada to Scott County, Iowa; ten years later they moved to Forestville, Minnesota. Bassett traveled the distance to Crawfordsville in the autumn of 1858 to spend the next three years in the Preparatory Department of Wabash.

On 22 August 1862 he secured a commission as a second lieutenant in Company K of the Sixth Minnesota Regiment, which was activated the following October. He was promoted to the rank of first lieutenant on 5 January 1863, remaining active for three years. He mustered out on 19 August 1865 at Fort Snelling in Minnesota.

In January 1866 Bassett enrolled at the University of Wisconsin, from which he received a degree in civil and military engineering in June 1871. Returning to Forestville, he studied law and was admitted to the Minnesota bar in 1874. He was elected judge of the probate court in Forestville, a post he retained until 1882, when he went into private legal practice. On 13 July, presumably of that year, Bassett married a widow, Georgiana A. Smith, who had one son, Edward R. Smith, from a previous marriage. The Civil War veteran died at home on 27 August 1913.

References: Minnesota Historical Society and an obituary in the *Proceedings of the Minnesota State Bar Association*, 14th annual session (1914), p. 266.

BASSETT, JAMES (1834–1906)

During the first half of the nineteenth century, it was rare for any Wabash student to complete the four-year Classical Course and graduate with a bachelor of arts degree. Yet all three Bassett brothers did just that: Daniel A., graduating in 1854; George W. in 1855; and James in 1856. Both James and George also served in the Civil War.

James Bassett was born on 30 January 1834 near what is now Hamilton, Ontario, Canada. His parents, Elnathan and Olivia Buck Bassett, moved to Maquoketa, Iowa, in the 1840s, and James made his way to Crawfordsville in the autumn of 1849. He graduated in 1856 and studied to become a minister.

When the Civil War broke out, Bassett joined the Fifty-Sixth Regiment of Illinois Volunteers on 12 November 1861 and served as a regimental chaplain in Chicago, mustering out on 5 February 1862.

While he was a minister in the town of Neenah, Wisconsin, Bassett married Abigail W. Jones on 3 May 1864. They remained there until 1869, when they relocated to Chicago. In 1871 the family, now with three daughters, accepted an arduous and hazardous overseas assignment from the Presbyterian Board of Foreign Missions to go to Tehran, Persia, the first missionaries sent there from the United States.

Besides preaching the gospel, Bassett established a school in Tehran and taught in the Persian language, translating various Christian materials so that they could be read by educated Persians. In 1879 the serious illness of one of their children necessitated a return to the United States. En route they stopped in London, where Bassett supervised the printing of his translations into Persian.

After a short time in America, the family returned to Tehran, but in 1884 Bassett reluctantly concluded that he must seek employment elsewhere, since he could not afford to live abroad and educate his children satisfactorily. From his years abroad emerged two published books: *Persia, the Land of the Imams: A Nar-*

rative of Travel and Residence (New York, 1886) and *Persia; Eastern Mission: A Narrative of the Founding and Fortune of the Eastern Mission* (Philadelphia, 1890).

By the mid-1890s Bassett was semi-retired, living with his family at Wading River, near Jamaica, Long Island, New York. The family resided there for the next decade, when, for presumed reasons of health, Bassett journeyed west to California. He died in Los Angeles on 10 March 1906, survived by his wife, four daughters, and one son.

References: *Wabash Record*, vols. XXVIII and XXX (July 1904 and July 1906), pp. 26, 107; *Los Angeles Times*, 12 March 1906; Illinois State Archives, Springfield; Lane Theological Seminary, *General Catalogue* (1899), p. 62.

BATES, HERVEY, JR. (1834–1929)

Hervey Bates Jr. was the son of the first sheriff of Marion County, a wealthy banker who commissioned the building of the Bates Hotel at the corner of Washington and Illinois Streets in Indianapolis. Abraham Lincoln is supposed to have stayed at this hotel and spoken at or near it enroute to his inauguration on 11 February 1861.

Hervey Jr. was born in Indianapolis in August 1834 and had two older sisters. He attended Wabash's Preparatory Department for only one year, 1852–53. After leaving Wabash, Bates became involved in the wholesale grocery business, and according to the 1860 census, he had a sizeable fortune: $22,000 of real property and $13,000 of personal.

Like the others we have already mentioned in this narrative, Bates responded to the threat of Morgan's raid into southern Indiana by enlisting in Company E of the 107th Regiment. However, once it was clear that the Confederates were no longer a menace, he served only a short time longer, from 9 to 18 July 1863, and the next month became adjutant of the City of Indianapolis Guards, a branch of the Indiana Legion. In the following spring, on 18 May 1864, Bates enrolled in the 132nd Regiment for one hundred days and served until 6 September as an adjutant and a major. His duties consisted mainly of the seemingly never-ending and uninteresting duty of guarding railway lines in Kentucky and Tennessee.

Bates's marriage to Charlotte Cathcart likely took place in 1855 or 1856. They had two children, Hervey III (1857) and the future Mrs. John Perrin.

Bates presumably managed the Bates Hotel for a number of years and then sold it. In 1901 the structure was torn down to make way for the new Claypool Hotel.

Bates's wife, Charlotte, died in 1907 and is buried in Crown Hill Cemetery, Indianapolis. Bates continued living in Indianapolis for many years but about 1918 joined his daughter and son-in-law in Pasadena, California, where he died on 25 January 1929. He does not appear in the index to Crown Hill Cemetery, but the American Legion graves register indicates that he was buried there.

References: *Indianapolis Journal*, 7, 8, and 10 July 1876; *Indianapolis Star*, 26 Jan. 1929; J. P. Dunn, *Indiana and Indianans*, IV (1919), p. 1698; and assorted Indianapolis city directories.

BEACH, JOHN HENRY (1843–1864)

John Beach was born in Rockaway, New Jersey, the eldest son of Joseph H. and Elvira, who had two other children, Sarah and Edmond.

One wonders why the Beach family sent John across the country to Crawfordsville to attend Wabash. Perhaps it was because John aspired to a career in the Presbyterian ministry, for which an undergraduate degree was desirable. He embarked on the Classical Course in the autumn of 1862.

During his sophomore year Beach was one of six editors of the college magazine and was chosen as a featured speaker in December 1863 at the college oration ceremonies. All too prophetically, his speech was titled "The Nobility of Sacrifice" and was quoted in the *Wabash Magazine*: "If we cannot be heroes of the twilight, it is still noble to speak and to live for the truth in the midday of our own age."

In the spring of 1864, the editors of the college magazine, along with students in Beta Theta Pi fraternity, of which Beach was a member, decided to embark on military service *en masse*. On 25 April they all enrolled in Company H of the 135th Regiment of Indiana Volunteers and reported for duty in Indianapolis on 23 May. Their assignment was to guard the railroad lines through Alabama that carried needed supplies for General Sherman's Atlanta campaign.

Unfortunately Beach died of some mysterious disease at Bridgeport, Alabama, on 30 June 1864. Like his fraternity brothers, he probably signed up for the army as a summertime occupation, a commitment of only one hundred days that would have allowed him to return to college in the fall.

References: Alumni records of Beta Theta Pi fraternity in the Wabash College Archives; and the *Wabash Magazine*, V (May 1864), p. 215, and VI (Dec. 1865), pp. 72–74.

BEARD, THOMAS J. (1822–1901)

The Beard family was associated with Wabash College from its earliest days. In September 1834, as the college prepared to open for the second year, a call went out for a new steward, a job that involved running a boardinghouse for new students. Thomas's parents, John and Marie Beard, assumed this responsibility when their son turned twelve years old, so he grew up familiar with the college.

Thomas Beard was born on 19 February 1822 in Wayne County. Sometime in 1822–23 the family moved to Montgomery County. In 1836 young Beard entered Wabash College and continued his studies until June of 1840. Before eventually becoming a farmer, he worked at a general store and for the state's engineering service, and he helped run the first railroad between Crawfordsville and Lafayette.

In 1844 Beard married Lovia Fields, who died in 1848 leaving no offspring. In 1855 he married Susan Tiffany. They had two children, George (1857) and Mary (1860).

Beard's military service proved disastrous to his health. He enrolled in Company K of the Eighty-Sixth Regiment in Crawfordsville on 22 August 1862 and was mustered in at Indianapolis on 4 September. He was forty years old with hazel eyes, five feet seven inches tall, with light complexion and hair. Within ten days the regiment reached Covington, Kentucky, where Beard was laid low with chronic diarrhea, a condition that persisted for two months, forcing him to remain behind when the regiment moved on. In December he entered the hospital at Nashville, Tennessee, suffering from a disease of the lungs, and he was officially discharged on 14 January 1863. The following July he joined the 108th Regiment in response to Morgan's raid, but this service lasted only ten days. His infirmities recurred periodically, and by the time he applied for a pension in 1886 he was described as "completely disabled."

After the war Beard was a member of the Capital police force in Washington, DC, and later became a printer at Indianapolis and worked on the *State Journal*. By the mid-1890s he and his wife had moved to Stillwater in the Oklahoma Territory, presumably because of his worsening health. Thomas died there on 19 May 1901. His widow Sue lived until 1912.

References: H. W. Beckwith, *History of Montgomery County* (1881), p. 166; *Crawfordsville Journal-Dispatch*, 23 July 1887; minutes of the Wabash College prudential committee of the board of trustees, 2 Sept. 1834; J. Bowerman, "Beard Played Major Role in School Reform," *Montgomery Magazine* (Oct. 1978), p. 6 for additional information and military pension file at the National Archives in Washington, DC.

BEARSS, OMER D. (1844–1920)

Omer Bearss was born in Peru, Indiana, on 5 February 1844, the son of Daniel R. and Emma Cole Bearss. His father owned substantial property in Peru and was a prosperous merchant who served several stints in the Indiana General Assembly.

In the autumn of 1861 young Bearss came to Crawfordsville for one year of college-level education in the Wabash Normal School. He then enlisted, like many others, in Company F of the 109th Regiment on 10 July 1863, in response to the Confederate threat of Morgan's raid. Once this subsided, Bearss was mustered out seventeen days later.

On 7 June 1865 in Miami County, Bearss wed Mary (Mollie) Celeste Hann. They had two children who grew to adulthood, Edwin and Georgina.

Bearss lived out his long life in and about Peru, looking after his family's extensive landed interests. He died on 10 March 1920, and his wife, on 26 June 1921. They are buried in the Bearss family cemetery.

References: *Peru Journal*, 11 March 1920; *Peru Journal*, 27 June 1921; J. H. Stevens, *History of Miami County* (1896); B. Fuller, *History of Miami County, Indiana* (1887); *Biographical Directory of the Indiana General Assembly*, I (1980), p. 19.

BENEFIEL, JAMES HARVEY (1817–1887)

James Benefiel was born in 1817 somewhere in Montgomery County, the son of George Washington and Marjory Van Cleeve Benefiel. He entered the College's Preparatory Department in 1836 and, except for the years 1838–39, remained until the spring of 1843.

On 4 January 1842 Benefiel married Jane McConnell, who was born on 30 January 1820 in Hamilton County, Ohio, but had lived in Montgomery County since 1826. Her younger brother, John Newton, also attended Wabash College. The couple's first child, Amelia, was born in 1843; their second child, William, was born about 1849.

The Benefiel grocery store flourished in Crawfordsville, and by 1860 the family owned real estate, including the shop, with a worth of $5,000, with cash on hand of $1,500.

When the Civil War broke out, Benefiel was forty-three years old and doubtless too old to enlist, but as a gesture of support for the newly recruited local young men, he handed out Bibles as they boarded the train that took them to their first training camp. However, shortly before the end of the war and in light of the need for soldiers, he enrolled on 28 March 1865 in Company B of the 154th Indiana Volunteers. When he mustered out on 14 August 1865, he held the rank of corporal.

He may have returned to his grocery business in Crawfordsville. Early on the morning of 10 April 1887 he died at his home, survived by his wife, his son, and his daughter, Amelia (who by this time had married W. M. Scott). His widow died on 6 February 1901.

References: 1860 U.S. census for Union Township, Montgomery County; H. W. Beckwith, *History of Montgomery County* (1881), pp. 32 and 97; Evelyn Benefiel Stout, *The Benefiel Family of Indiana and their Descendants* (1983); [Crawfordsville] *Daily Argus News*, 11 April 1887; *Crawfordsville Daily News Review*, 6 Feb. 1901.

BEVAN, EDWARD B. (1839–1862)

Edward Bevan was born in South Wales. His father, Philip Bevan, was a missionary on the frontier of Indiana, seeking to establish new churches for the

American Missionary Society along the Ohio River. Edward was the sole survivor among Philip's five sons, four of whom perished from scarlet fever in 1860.

In the autumn of 1857 Bevan entered the Preparatory Department of Wabash College, indicating that his home was Jeffersonville, Indiana. He spent four years at Wabash, completing his sophomore year before leaving Crawfordsville in the summer of 1861 to join the army. But for the war, he had hoped to graduate and become a Presbyterian minister like his father.

In the late summer and early autumn of 1861, Colonel Thomas J. Wood was raising volunteers from Indiana to augment the Army of the Ohio, and Bevan became one of the mounted orderlies assigned to his personal staff. Initially, Wood's Second Cavalry, part of the Sixth Division, rallied at Camp Nevin, fifteen miles south of Louisville. In early December the training camp moved to Bardstown, Kentucky, and after the fall of Fort Henry and Fort Donelson in February 1862, they went to Nashville, Tennessee, to prepare for the Battle of Shiloh that occurred in early April.

Bevan never took part in this famous encounter, however, because he contracted typhoid fever and died on 6 April 1862.

In a letter to the college, his father wrote, "It is indeed a sore affliction to us. But had he lived longer he could not, perhaps, have died better, nor in a better cause."

References: *Wabash Magazine* III (Dec. 1861 and June 1862), pp. 93, 379–80. See also: *History of the Ohio Falls Cities and Counties* (1882), p. 530; G. T. Scribner, *Indiana's Role of Honor* (1866), p. 619; *The Soldier of Indiana in the War of the Union* (1866), II, p. 233. Quotations are from L. C. Rudolph, *Indiana Letters* (1979), III, pp. 1033–34, 1062; and from the *Wabash Magazine* cited above.

BILL, ARMINIUS WESLEY (1845–1929)

Wesley Bill was born on 5 June 1845 in Glastonbury, Connecticut, the eldest of the three children of Rowena Cleveland and Frank Wesley Bill. His sisters were Mary Irene, born in 1848, and Lorinda, born in 1850. Their father was a Methodist minister, and in 1854, at the age of thirty-four, he undertook a missionary voyage to Peru, but died along the way. His widow carried on as best she could for several years, but then she too died. Son Wesley was adopted by an uncle, and in 1859 they headed West and settled in Sheffield, Illinois, where Bill had a job as a clerk when the Civil War broke out.

In September 1861 Bill enrolled in what was informally called the Western Sharp-Shooters and was ordered to report to the Benton Barracks near St. Louis. The regiment was under the command of Major General John C. Frémont, and by December it had been incorporated into a new and larger Fourteenth Missouri Volunteer Infantry. The regiment saw action at Columbia and Mount Zion and then sailed up the Mississippi and Ohio Rivers, where it was involved in the

Battles of Fort Henry and Fort Donelson and then in the Battle of Shiloh in April 1862. Soon thereafter the regiment was renumbered the Sixty-Sixth Illinois and was involved in skirmishes and raids in Mississippi and Alabama.

In November 1863 eighteen-year-old Bill was granted an honorable discharge, but he lost no time reenlisting in the same regiment and subsequently took an active role at the Battle of Atlanta and later in operations in South and North Carolina.

In the latter stages of the war, Bill worked in a hospital behind the lines, having been co-opted as a steward and later promoted to an assistant surgeon with the rank of lieutenant. Mustered out in Kentucky on 7 July 1865, he returned to Sheffield and studied medicine with a doctor before entering the College of Physicians and Surgeons in New York City in 1866. In the spring of 1867 Bill came back to Indiana to work with a doctor in Plymouth, and it was from here that he applied to Wabash College.

Bill spent 1867–70 at Wabash in the Preparatory Department but began to drift away from an interest in medicine to studying religion, and he was accepted into the Chicago Theological Seminary in the autumn of 1870. In September 1873 he was ordained and began serving as pastor at the Bethany Congregational Church of Chicago.

In August 1874 he was called to the First Presbyterian Church in Menominee, Michigan, where he met another native from Connecticut, a teacher named Harriet Woodford. They were married in 1875 and eventually had a son and a daughter.

In addition to his normal parish duties, Bill was active in helping other communities organize and begin new Presbyterian churches in towns like Ford River, Wisconsin (1877); Stephenson, Michigan (1879); and Florence, Wisconsin (1880). A nervous breakdown forced him into early retirement in the late 1880s.

In 1892 he seemed well enough to undertake another ministry, this time in Bainesville, Texas. After some other pastoral experiences, he returned to Menominee, where he involved himself in guest preaching, public lectures, and participation in the local GAR post.

Bill died on 10 January 1929, outliving his son Clarence, who had died the previous year. His widow died in Seattle on 21 May 1935 while visiting her daughter, Mrs. Francis Harrigan. Both husband and wife are buried in Menominee.

References: Archives of the First Presbyterian Church of Menominee and the Presbyterian Historical Association of Philadelphia. Special thanks are also due to Vicki Evans Hardin for clarifying the early history of the Bill family. Further assistance was rendered by the Newberry Library of Chicago, the Chicago Theological Seminary, and the Spies Public Library of Menominee. Information about Bill's military service came from the Illinois State Archives, Springfield.

BINFORD, JAMES WILLIAM (1845–1896)

James Binford was born in Crawfordsville on 2 November 1845, the youngest of three brothers. His siblings were Edward J. and Ambrose Whitlock Binford, both of whom attended Wabash but did not serve in the Civil War. James was three years old when his father, William (1801–1848) died, leaving his wife, Elizabeth Ann Jones Binford (1813–1897), a wealthy widow.

From 1859 to 1862 James Binford was in the Preparatory Department of Wabash College, but as soon as school was out, he joined the Eighteenth Light Artillery under Colonel Eli Lilly. He was not yet eighteen years old, but committed for three years with the eager Hoosiers constituting the unit, who were to "fight manfully for our just and holy cause." Colonel Lilly's battery was sent to Kentucky to repel the threatened Confederate advance but saw no action there. In February 1863 word came from Kentucky to Crawfordsville that Binford was seriously ill, and a family friend, Dr. Herndon, tried to secure his discharge, but without success. Binford eventually recovered and served as a company clerk for his full term of service, being mustered out on 30 July 1865.

On 30 September 1868 he married a local Crawfordsville woman, Mary Alice Vance, who was a few months older than he, having been born on 7 September 1845.

In 1869 Binford went into partnership with Eli Lilly. The colonel had recently become bankrupt and needed the cash that his former comrade could call upon. Together they created the Red Front drugstore on the east side of the town square in Paris, Illinois. In 1876 Lilly decided to return to Indianapolis and produce medicine on his own, and he persuaded Binford to distribute these compounds throughout southern Indiana and Kentucky. Lilly eventually established a pharmaceutical empire, while Binford continued his quiet profession of druggist in Paris.

James and Mary Alice Binford had two daughters, Augusta (1870–1948) and Mrs. Mary Binford Graham (1878–1962).

Binford died of consumption in Paris on 22 May 1896, but his body was returned to Crawfordsville for burial in Oak Hill Cemetery. Mary Alice died in Los Angeles on 21 May 1928, and her body was returned for burial near her husband. A street in Crawfordsville carries the family name.

References: J. W. Rowell, *Yankee Artilleryman*, (1975), pp. 62, 266–67; R. C. Clark, *Three Score Years and Ten: A Narrative of the First Seventy Years of Eli Lilly and Company, 1876–1946* (1946), p. 15; *Crawfordsville Star*, 10 Jan. 1889; *Crawfordsville Weekly Journal*, 29 May 1896; and information from Charles Hand of Paris, Illinois.

BLACK, JOHN CHARLES JR. (1839–1915)

The older son of John C. and Josephine Culbertson Black, John Black Jr. was one of the most distinguished soldiers to enlist in the Union army from Wabash College. He was a native of Lexington, Mississippi, born on 27 January 1839. His brother, William P., also attended Wabash.

Not long after John Black's birth, the family moved to Woodford County, Kentucky, where William, Mary, and Josephine were born. The family soon relocated to western Pennsylvania, where John Sr., a Presbyterian minister, died in 1844. In 1847 Josephine and her children settled in Danville, Illinois, where son John grew up and attended the local schools. He came to Crawfordsville for the fall term at Wabash in 1857, completing his freshman and sophomore years as a student in the Classical Course before the war interrupted his college education. Along with brother Will, Black enrolled for three months on 18 April 1861 in the Eleventh Indiana Regiment, which was being recruited in Crawfordsville. After this brief exposure, both re-enlisted in the army from their hometown of Danville, Illinois.

Black had risen to the rank of sergeant in the Eleventh Indiana and in his second wartime experience was advanced significantly to become major of field and staff for the Thirty-Seventh Illinois. In the coming three years, he saw action in no less than thirteen battles or skirmishes in Missouri, Arkansas, Alabama, and Mississippi, and his promotions included lieutenant colonel on 11 July 1862, full colonel on 31 December 1862, and brevet brigadier general in the spring of 1865. In 1893 he was awarded a Congressional Medal of Honor for his Civil War bravery: leading his regiment against a fortified Confederate position when other attacks had failed at the Battle of Prairie Grove, Arkansas.

Black remained in the army well after the South surrendered, but resigned on 15 August 1865, returning home to Danville, where he married Adaline L. Griggs and was admitted to the Illinois bar in 1867. After a few years of legal practice, he moved to Champaign and later to Chicago. In 1872 he put himself forward unsuccessfully as a candidate for lieutenant governor of Illinois.

Black was appointed U.S. Commissioner of Pensions and spent the years 1885–87 in Washington, DC. In 1892 he was chosen to represent Illinois in the House of Representatives, and in 1895 he was appointed U.S. attorney for the Northern District of Illinois. In 1899 he was called by President Teddy Roosevelt to be a member of the Civil Service Commission and became its president, serving until 1913.

Black was a frequent visitor to Wabash and speaker to Wabash students, coming to the campus in 1900, 1902, and 1915. In 1915, shortly before his death, he spoke eloquently about the meaning of the Civil War to Wabash. When Europe was already immersed in a world war, he spoke then about America's becoming militarily prepared. He died in Chicago on 17 August 1915 and was interred in the Spring Hill Cemetery in Danville, survived by his son, John.

References: *Biographical Directory of the American Congress* (Washington, 1961), pp. 558–59; *Who Was Who*, I, part 2, p. 190; *Wabash College Record*, XIV (Oct. 1915), pp. 134–36; *Dictionary of American Biography* (1929), II, p. 313; *Civil War Centennial Commission of Illinois, Civil War Medal of Honor Winners from Illinois* (1962), p. 5; M. Dearing, *Veterans in Politics: The Story of the G.A.R.* (1952).

John Charles Black, Jr.

William Perkins Black

BLACK, WILLIAM PERKINS (1842–1916)

William Black followed in his older brother's footsteps much of his life. He came to Wabash in the fall of 1860 to join John Charles, who had already been at the college the previous three years. He served in the same two regiments as John did during the Civil War, and he also became an attorney. Yet William carved out a distinguished military and legal career in his own right, heightening the contemporary impression that these were two remarkable brothers.

Born on 11 November 1842 in Woodford County, Kentucky, William Black grew up in Danville, Illinois, entering Wabash's freshman class at the age of eighteen, but he did not quite complete the school year because the war started and students rushed to enlist in the Eleventh Volunteers. Black enlisted on 18 April 1861. During his initial ninety days' service, the regiment went from Indianapolis to Virginia and back, and he was mustered out on 4 August.

Both brothers helped organize a new regiment in Danville, Illinois, and on 13 August 1861 William enrolled in the Thirty-Seventh Illinois Volunteers for three years and was appointed captain of Company K. One month later the regiment reported for active duty in Chicago and was dispatched to Missouri and Arkansas.

By March 1862 the Thirty-Seventh Regiment, along with others, comprised a formidable Federal force of about eleven thousand troops under General Samuel R. Curtis. They camped on Sugar Creek, north of Fayetteville, Arkansas, in anticipation of a major fight with fourteen thousand Confederate soldiers under General Earl Van Dorn. Skirmishes began on the night of 6 March. The Confederates shammed sleep while stealthily trying to encircle the Union forces, but this tactic failed. The Battle of Pea Ridge (7–8 March 1862) raged throughout the day and into the next, but gradually the Confederates were pushed back and eventually retreated. This battle was reckoned to have been the largest to date west of the Mississippi and proved decisive in forcing the South to withdraw most of its soldiers from Missouri. Black conducted himself with such courage that he was later awarded the Congressional Medal of Honor, as his brother had been.

Black was mustered out in Chicago on 12 September 1864 and returned to Danville, where he devoted one year to being provost marshal for the Seventh Congressional District of Illinois. He then took up residence in Chicago and read law in the firm of Arrington and Dent.

In the meantime, in 1869 Black married Hortensia M. McGreal of Galveston, Texas, and eventually they adopted one son, William P. E. Perkins.

Although a Republican for many years, Black decided to back the unsuccessful presidential candidacy of Horace Greeley in 1872. From then on Black was an active Democrat, urging others to vote for William Jennings Bryan on various occasions.

What came to alter Black's life and career dramatically in 1886 were the so-called Haymarket riots. On 3 May 1886 in Haymarket Square, Chicago, strikers from the McCormick Harvester Works were demonstrating for shorter hours and better conditions when police fired upon the crowd, killing six. The next night some two thousand workers and others returned to the square to protest the police brutality. Not surprisingly, the police were out in force, and while the crowd listened to one of their leaders, someone threw a bomb at the police, killing seven. Some eighty bystanders were also injured.

In the ensuing days the authorities rounded up all known radicals, including anarchists, and finally decided to charge eight of them with the bombing. Even if it could not be proved that any of these defendants had been directly involved, they had contributed to an atmosphere of revolution and violence.

A local committee of liberal and concerned citizens tried to raise money for a legal defense of the accused radicals, but no attorney in town would take the case, if for no other reason because the committee could not afford to pay them very much. Finally the committee approached Black and tried to persuade him to undertake the defense, even though his background was in corporate, not criminal, law.

Black was inclined initially to turn them down, but when he too found that no other lawyer would take the case, he gave even more serious consideration to the request. He consulted a friend of his, who was a judge, to see what he would advise. As he told his friend, "I think I can foresee that he who undertakes the defense of these anarchists will be looked upon with at least great disfavor." Black threw himself wholeheartedly into what he knew would probably be a losing cause.

Of the seven defendants who finally came up for trial on 21 July, all were initially found guilty and sentenced to death. Subsequently, two were given life terms, one committed suicide, and four were hanged. Black had been intimately involved in all stages of the proceedings, including the futile effort to have the United States Supreme Court hear the case on appeal.

Black was not mistaken about the repercussions of taking the case. Almost immediately his law partner of many years, Thomas Dent, insisted upon dissolving their firm. In coming years Black saw his income reduced by about two-thirds, as one client after another forsook him. Eventually he set himself up in a new firm, that of Black and FitzGerald, and later in partnership with his brother as Black and Black.

There had never been any firm evidence supporting the involvement of the defendants in the bomb explosion, and Black had done all he could to try and save what may very well have been innocent men.

Black died at the home of his son in Chicago on 3 January 1916.

References: Many of the materials consulted for William Black are the same as those cited for his brother, John. See also H. Kogan "William Perkins Black: Haymarket Lawyer." *Chicago History* V(summer 1976), 85-94. There is a sketch of Black's life in J.W. Leonard, *The Book of Chicagoans* (1905). p. 6.

BLACKWELL, JOHN QUINCY ADAMS (1834–1914)

John Blackwell was born in Orleans on 10 November 1834, one of six children of Ezekiel Blackwell (1786–1871) and Elizabeth Dickey Blackwell (1790–1841). After the death of his wife, Blackwell's father married Lovey Kittridge of Bedford in 1842.

In the autumn of 1852 Blackwell entered Wabash's Preparatory Department, naming Bedford as his hometown. In 1854 he began his freshman year in the Classical Course, graduating in 1858, after which he studied at the Jefferson Medical College in Philadelphia.

On 29 December 1859 he married Catherine Wolfe of Crawfordsville. The couple began their married lives in Pleasant Hill. Between 1861 and 1878 they had seven children, two of whom died in infancy. Those who survived were Henry, Frank, Theodore, Antoinette, and Bessy.

In July 1862 Blackwell became a first lieutenant in Company D of the Twelfth Indiana Regiment. He wrote to his wife from Camp Morton, outside Indianapolis, reflecting the boredom and lack of action in prison detail in the war: "I have no congenial spirits here to mingle with and I often long for the old college acquaintances and friends with whom I used to live so pleasantly."

On 12 September 1863 he was promoted to surgeon and attached to the 115th Indiana Regiment. After fewer than two years of his three-year commitment, he was allowed to leave the army on 25 February 1864.

After the war he returned to Bedford to practice medicine. In the early 1870s he and his family moved to Foristell, Missouri, and by 1878 he was the local mail agent for the Missouri-Pacific Railroad. By 1900 they were residing in Wellsville, Missouri, where he died on 28 January 1914.

References: 1905 Wabash College alumni questionnaire; quotation from letters in the Indiana Historical Society, Indianapolis; alumni directory of the Phi Delta Theta fraternity (1888); and information from the state historical society at Columbia, Missouri.

BLAIR, JOHN W. JR. (1838–1870)

John W. Blair Jr. was born in Jefferson in 1838, one of five children of John W. Sr. and Eliza Blair. His siblings were Robert, Aneliza E., Anson H., and Harriet (Hattie). In 1852 the family moved to Crawfordsville, and in the fall of 1853 John Jr. became a member of the Wabash College Preparatory Department for one year, returning in 1855 after a year's absence.

Blair worked in his father's successful grocery and meat-packing business until the Civil War began, and on 11 August 1862, at the age of twenty-four, he enrolled in Company K of the Eighty-Sixth Indiana Volunteers for three years. At the time he was described as six feet tall, with blue eyes, light hair, and a fair complexion. Illness forced him to request an honorable discharge in February 1863.

Returning home, Blair continued working in the family store and married. However, perhaps from the lingering effects of his military service, Blair died in 1870. His wife Sarah and her baby, Rosa, died in childbirth on 7 March 1871. All three are buried in Oak Hill Cemetery in Crawfordsville.

References: T. Gronert, *Sugar Creek Saga* (1958), p. 97; Montgomery County cemetery records; last will and testament of John W. Blair Sr.; *Crawfordsville Saturday Mercury*, 10 March 1871; H. W. Beckwith, *History of Montgomery County* (1881), pp. 131, 133–34, 185, 264; *History of Montgomery County, Indiana* (Bowen and Co., 1913), p. 144; and J. A. Barnes, *The Eighty-Sixth Regiment of Indiana Volunteer Infantry* (1895), p. 593.

BLINN, JOHN J. P. (1841–1863)

John Blinn was born to Horace and Dorothea Blinn in Terre Haute on 8 April 1841. He had an elder sister, Charlotte, and three younger siblings: Horace, Julia, and Sarah.

Blinn entered the Preparatory Department in 1857, and the next year became a freshman and then a sophomore. According to the diary of a fellow student, fifteen-year-old Benjamin F. Paddock, John's father died that year.

While still a sophomore, Blinn was mustered into service at Terre Haute on 7 June 1861. He secured a commission as adjutant to Major William Harrow of the Fourteenth Indiana Regiment. His regiment spent sixteen months in Virginia losing hundreds at the Battle of Antietam, where Blinn was wounded in the face and subsequently discharged that October. He took part in fourteen engagements. The Fourteenth Indiana was a much-lauded regiment in the Gibraltar Brigade, which turned the Confederate guns on Cemetery Hill at a crucial moment of the battle and Blinn was proud of his affiliation with this illustrious unit and of serving as adjutant.

To the surprise of everyone at Wabash, Blinn was back for the beginning of term in January 1863 and would have continued his studies uninterrupted, but his former commander, William Harrow, was now a general and asked him to become brigade assistant adjutant general, so at the end of March he reentered the army with the rank of captain.

On 3 July 1863, in the heat of battle at Gettysburg, he sustained a shell wound in his thigh. The next day he wrote to his mother: "Your soldier boy is wounded. But we whipped the enemy and the old flag is again victorious, glorious. My wound is a very serious one and I fear amputation may be necessary. I may die but mother: God give you strength and grace to bear the affliction. My country called and I came to die upon her altar. God bless and keep you. I can write no more."

Upon receiving his letter, Dorothea rushed to his bedside, arriving in time to share his last few delirious days. He died on 13 July 1863, and his body was returned for burial in Woodlawn Cemetery, Terre Haute.

References: *Wabash Magazine*, III (Dec. 1861), p. 93; *Wabash Magazine*, IV (March 1863), p. 158; *Wabash Magazine*, IV (May 1863), p. 240; *Wabash Magazine*, V (Dec. 1863), p. 78; unpublished Blinn letter at the Vigo County Public Library; *The Soldier of Indiana in the War for the Union*, II (1869), p. 122; N. Baxter, *Gallant Fourteenth* (1980), pp. 39, 59, 152, 187; *History of Vigo County, Indiana* (1891); *Terre Haute Daily Express*, 21 July 1863. Martha L. Brogan, "Family Values," *Common-Place* 5, no. 3 (April 2005).

BLOOD, NATHAN W. (1836–1898)

Nathan Blood was born in Washington Township, Miami County, son of Royal and Polly Stiles Blood. His siblings included Albert, James, Lucius, Mary, Frances, Sarah, and Silas. At the time that the 1860 census was taken, Polly had died, and Royal had remarried a sixty-year-old New Hampshire woman named Mary.

In the autumn of 1853, Blood entered the Preparatory Department of Wabash College, where he remained for two years.

On 2 July 1861 Blood enrolled in Lafayette in Company A of the Twentieth Indiana Volunteers for three years. Two years later, on 7 November 1863, he was wounded at Kelly's Ford near Culpepper, Virginia, and was inactive until February of the following year, when he was sufficiently restored to re-enlist beyond his initial commitment of three years. On 12 July 1865 he was mustered out of service at Jeffersonville, Indiana.

He married Sarah A. Beaumont in Connecticut on 15 September 1873. By 1887 he and his family were farming near Le Sueur, Minnesota, where he applied for a military pension. Later the couple moved to Helena, Montana, where Blood died on 5 August 1898. Sarah lived until 1918. They apparently had no children.

References: Miami County Historical Society and his pension file at the National Archives in Washington, DC.

BOLEY, JOSEPH (1837–1864)

Andersonville Prison in Georgia claimed over fifty thousand prisoners in its filthy and disease-ridden premises. Joseph Boley was one of them. The son of Henry and Matilda DeWeese Boley, he was a farm boy who came to Wabash from near Byrneville.

Boley was enrolled in the Normal School of Wabash College for the school year 1859–60 and then returned to work on the family farm. On 16 August 1862 he registered in New Albany for three years' military service and became a private in Company C of the Eighty-First Regiment. His first major battlefield action came on 31 December, when Confederate troops under General Bragg attacked the Federals under General Rosecrans, driving them back to the Murfreesboro-Nashville Road, where they made their stand.

The Federal troops, including the Eighty-First Regiment, occupied Murfreesboro until June 1863, when they moved to Winchester, Tennessee, for two months. On the move again, they crossed the Cumberland Mountains to Stevenson, Alabama, and on 9 September forced the Confederates to evacuate Chattanooga, Tennessee. Boley was taken captive during the Battle of Chickamauga (20 September 1863) and was incarcerated in Andersonville, where he died on 19 July 1864. He had a brother, Henry, who also served in the Eighty-First Regiment of Indiana Volunteers but survived Chickamauga. Framed detailed maps of the Battle of Chickamauga decorate the hallway of the ground floor in Baxter Hall at Wabash College.

References: W. H. Terrell, *Report of the Adjutant General of the State of Indiana* (1869), III, pp. 43–44; muster roll card in the Archives Division of the Indiana State Library; and information from the Corydon Public Library.

BOOTH, DAVID C. (1841–1864)

David Booth was born in about 1841, probably in the town of Allensville, where his father, Levi, was a Presbyterian minister.

The family moved several times before 1858, when young David made his way to Crawfordsville from Seymour to spend the years 1858–60 in the Preparatory Department of Wabash College. The census of 1860 listed his father as a forty-seven-year-old clergyman from New York State with real property in Seymour amounting to $1,500; his mother, Sarah, age forty-three, was listed as a native of Maine. His siblings were Mariah, sixteen; Ellen, fourteen; and Levi, thirteen.

On 28 August 1861 Booth enrolled as a private in Company K of the Thirty-Ninth Regiment, which was attached to the Eighth Indiana Cavalry. He committed for three years but died at home in Seymour on 6 May 1864, presumably after serving for two years before falling ill and being sent home for his final days.

References: Indiana State Library Archives and the Seymour Public Library.

BOOTS, JAMES F. (1836–1913)

James Boots was born in Crawfordsville in 1836, the eldest of seven children. His father, Oli, came originally from Ohio, and his mother, Martha, from Virginia.

During the academic years 1857–59, Boots attended the Normal School of Wabash College. He then worked as a laborer for two years before signing up for three months' military service in the Tenth Indiana Regiment in the spring of 1861. Once he completed this tour of duty in August, he went back to Crawfordsville until April 1862, when he reenlisted in the Twentieth Indiana Light Artillery with the rank of sergeant. He was mustered out as a corporal in June 1865, relatively unscathed.

During the following decades in Crawfordsville, Boots pursued a variety of careers: county surveyor, farmer, mill operator, and owner of a sash and door company. By the 1880s he had also acquired land in Colorado and was speculating in gold mines, one of them the Bridal Veil Mining Company.

He joined the local GAR McPherson Post No. 7 in 1880 and remained active in this veterans' organization until shortly before his death at home on 30 November 1913. He was survived by his widow, Ethelinda, two brothers, two sisters, and one half-brother.

References: Records of GAR McPherson Post No. 7 in the Crawfordsville Public Library; *Crawfordsville Daily Dispatch*, 12 July 1887; *Crawfordsville Journal*, 30 Nov. 1913; *History of Montgomery County, Indiana* (Bowen and Co., 1913), pp. 660–61.

BOUDINOT, CHARLES T. (1842–1918)

Charles Boudinot was born in Terre Haute on 13 May 1842, son of John and Celia Boudinot, both of whom died before 1860. He was one of their five children. The others were Mary, Henry H., Edward J., and Elliott.

Before attending Wabash College, Boudinot enrolled in Company C of the Eleventh Regiment from Terre Haute on 18 April 1861, committed to three months' service. Mustered out in Indianapolis on 4 August, he began his freshman year in the spring or early summer of 1862, joining his brother, Henry, who was completing his junior year.

Instead of returning to school in the autumn of 1862, Boudinot decided to re-enlist in the army, this time for three years, and on 14 August 1862 he enrolled in Company G of the Eighty-Fifth Indiana Regiment. Later that fall he was promoted to sergeant major. He presumably fought at the Battle of Thompson's Station or Spring Hill in early March 1863, when so many of his fellow Hoosiers were taken prisoner. That debacle was led by Wabash alumnus John Coburn, described in another section of this book. Boudinot escaped capture and prison camp, but he became severely ill the following year and was given a medical furlough followed by a medical discharge in May 1865.

Returning to Terre Haute he met and courted Flora E. Smith, born 27 May 1844, who hailed from near Cleveland, Ohio. They were married on 12 June 1866 and subsequently had three children, one of whom died in infancy. The two who survived to adulthood were Blanche E., born 1871, and Roy E., born 1872.

For a few years after their marriage, the couple remained in Terre Haute.

In September 1868 they moved to Rockville, where their children were born and Boudinot was involved in the milling business.

In April 1888 the family moved to Omaha, Nebraska, where Boudinot was employed as a clerk for the Omaha Milling and Elevator Company. He was with the company until 1908, when he became bookkeeper for Updike Milling Company.

During the 1890s and thereafter, Boudinot was rarely free from pain, which dated back to his service in the army. Exacerbating his condition was an accident at work in 1893, when his leg was caught in a stairway, badly wrenching it and rendering him unable to do manual labor. Eventually he qualified for a veteran's pension, but the infection in his leg worsened, and in February 1905 the leg had to be amputated.

In August 1911 Charles and Flora took up residence in Frankfort, Kentucky, and it was there that the veteran died on 17 February 1918. Flora lived until the age of ninety-three, dying on 12 July 1937. They are both buried in the Frankfort Cemetery.

References: Boudinot's pension file at the National Archives in Washington, DC; Vigo County Public Library; Kentucky Historical Society of Frankfort.

BOWMAN, BENJAMIN D. (1851–1936)

Benjamin Bowman may deserve recognition as the youngest Wabash student to have served in the Civil War.

He was born in either Adams or Brown County, Ohio, in 1851, son of Mary McIlwee Bowman (1815–1893), widow of Benjamin Bowman (1802–1850), who married her husband's brother, Aaron Bowman (1817–1889) in 1850 after Benjamin Sr. died. From her first marriage, her children were William, Patrick, Thomas, and Hannah. Benjamin, John, and Eliza were offspring of her second marriage.

This would have made Benjamin Bowman a mere youth, age thirteen, when he joined the army. Perhaps the recruiting sergeant suspected he was well underage, but since his term of service would only be for one hundred days, and since he claimed to be seventeen, and since the army needed soldiers in the worst way in 1864, he was not turned down. The regiment was slated to do mostly guard duty anyway and not likely to be involved in combat.

Bowman joined Company C of the 156th Ohio Regiment on 2 May 1864 at Dennison, Ohio. During his one hundred days of service, he was stationed first in Cincinnati, then in Paris, Kentucky. He was honorably discharged at Camp Dennison on 1 September.

Upon his release from military service, he entered the Preparatory Department of Wabash College and remained there for three years, repeating the freshman year in 1865–66 and 1866–67, after which he returned home to Winchester in Adams County, Ohio.

According to the 1870 census, Bowman lived with his parents and was a teacher. He married Biancy Hawk (1853–1927) on 29 December 1870, and they had one child, John.

Bowman outlived his wife by about nine years, dying on or about 16 December 1936. Because of his youth when serving in the war, he became one of the last veterans from his unit to die. He and his wife are buried in Point Cemetery, Green Township, Adams County.

References: Adams County Genealogical Society of West Union, Ohio. See: *Adams County News*, 17 Dec. 1936; Ohio Historical Society of Columbus. See: H. S. Axline (comp.), *Official Roster of the Soldiers of the State of Ohio in the War of the Rebellion*, IX (1889), pp. 229, 234.

BOWMAN, GEORGE W. (1818–1894)

The 1840s can still be considered part of the founding period at Wabash College. One of the most earnest students and a founder of Wabash's chapter of Beta Theta Pi was also a Civil War soldier. But before he went to war, he had an interesting and significant career connected to both Wabash and academia.

George Bowman was born on a farm near Martinsburg, Berkeley County, Virginia (now West Virginia), on 28 February 1818, the fourth of seven children born to George and Elizabeth Bowman. His parents died when he was a child, so the young man was brought up by a guardian until the age of twenty, when he headed west to join his older brother, Charles A. Bowman, in the town of Delphi.

George Bowman attended Wabash from 1845 to 1848 and was a charter member of the Tau chapter of Beta Theta Pi fraternity. Sometime in the spring of 1848, during his junior year, Bowman became ill and had to leave the college. He had hoped to return in the fall of 1848 to finish his senior year, but the prospect of marrying Ruth Angel proved too tempting. To support her, he took up teaching in the local Carroll County schools. By 1850 they had moved to Monticello in nearby White County, but Ruth died in September, perhaps giving birth to a daughter named after her mother, Ruth Angel.

In the autumn of 1852, Bowman fulfilled his dream of returning to Wabash, graduating in June 1853. While at Wabash he boarded with the college's first and most prominent teacher, Caleb Mills, and some years later Bowman named one of his sons after his mentor.

Bowman was such a natural and dedicated teacher that a story was told, perhaps apocryphal, that in his youth he had taught a slave to read, and the latter's mistress was so pleased that she gave Bowman a dollar, with which he bought himself an algebra book.

In 1858 he married again, this time to Mary Dill Piper of Piper's Run, Pennsylvania. She eventually gave birth to seven children: Phoebe, Anna, Rebecca, George, Caleb Mills, Mary Margaret, and Carrie.

Despite being a forty-four-year-old married man, Bowman enrolled in the Twelfth Regiment of Indiana Volunteers on 20 June 1862 and was promoted rapidly from lieutenant to captain of Company D. Because of the threatening movements of Confederate troops under General Kirby Smith, the Twelfth Indiana was rushed to Kentucky to take part in the Battle of Richmond (29–30 August 1862). The regiment sustained heavy losses, but Bowman survived and marched through Kentucky, Tennessee, and Alabama, arriving in time to participate in the siege of Vicksburg in July 1863.

On 25 November 1863 he was badly wounded at the Battle of Missionary Ridge, Tennessee, and carried off the field for dead. However, he not only managed to revive but also to make his precarious way back home to Monticello.

Bowman's medical discharge from the army took place in March 1864, and he returned to being a teacher and later a superintendent of schools in White and Carroll Counties.

At the time of his death, a local newspaper paid tribute to him: "No citizen of White County, living or dead, has had a larger part in molding the character of the present generation. His influence, though quiet and unpretentious, was of the kind that took hold upon the lives of those who came in contact with him, and it was always on the side of right." Caleb Mills would have been proud.

Bowman taught up to four weeks before his death on 29 November 1894. He was survived by his wife and four of their children.

References: *Wabash Magazine* XIX (1894–1896), p. 187; J. H. Stewart, *Recollections of the Early Settlement of Carroll County, Indiana* (1872), p. 327; T. B. Helm, *History of Carroll County, Indiana* (1882), p. 203; *Monticello Herald*, 6 Dec. 1894; and the Delphi Public Library.

BOWMAR, JOSEPH MARSHALL (1839–1889)

Wabash student Joseph Bowmar was in the Confederate army. He was one of the few from the college who served for the South. Bowmar came from Kentucky.

He was born on 12 November 1839 at Versailles, Woodford County, Kentucky, and his father was Hermann (1805–1863), a lawyer and clerk of the county court from 1835 to 1862. His mother was Mrs. Emeline Tunis Tarrant (d. 1848). They had, in addition to Joseph, two other sons, Daniel and Robert.

Joseph Bowmar was fifteen when he entered the Preparatory Department in the autumn of 1853, but he left the following spring to work for his father as deputy clerk of the county court. He kept this job until 1859, when he began the first of two years with the state auditor's office in Frankfort.

In September 1862 Bowmar helped to raise a company of cavalry in Woodford County and was elected its first lieutenant. The Fifth Kentucky Cavalry soon came under the command of General John Morgan. In the coming months the former Wabash student was promoted to the rank of captain and made a regimental adjutant.

On 4 July 1863 Morgan brought his raiders to Tubb's Bend of the Green River, in expectation of crossing into Kentucky. However, he was thwarted by the Twenty-Fifth Michigan Volunteers, withdrew briefly, and ordered a surprise crossing of the Ohio River into Indiana. By this time Bowmar had been badly wounded at Green River and taken captive. Under the most disconcerting circumstances some weeks later, he and General Morgan both found themselves in the Ohio Penitentiary at Columbus. Morgan later escaped, but Bowmar spent a total of twenty-one months in Yankee prisons, mostly at Fort Delaware.

In March 1865 he was released and was chosen a member of the personal guard protecting President Jefferson Davis, but the day before his capture, with Union troops closing in, Davis released his guard.

After the war Bowmar worked for the banking firm of Ridgley and Son in Springfield, Illinois, and in 1868 accepted a position with Merchants National Bank of Chicago, where he remained almost fifteen years. In 1876 he married Charlotte Turner, and they had four daughters: Charlotte, Frances, Elizabeth, and Katharine.

Bowmar's health was never robust, and by the early 1880s he suffered from lung disease. Seeking a warmer and drier climate, he took a job as assistant cashier of the First National Bank of Decatur, Texas. The move brought him a reprieve, but in May 1889 his lung condition dramatically worsened, and he and his family returned to Versailles, Kentucky, where he died on 4 June. He is buried in the town cemetery.

References: Woodford County Historical Society. See: *Kentucky: A History of the State* (5th ed., (1887); W. C. Railey, *History of Woodford County* (1968), p. 86; E. F. Van Der Doort (comp.), "Bowmar Families and Allied Families," a collection of miscellaneous papers at the Woodford County Historical Society; *Woodford Sun*, 6 April 1889.

BOYLAND, WILLIAM H. (1844–1909)

William Boyland was born in Crawfordsville on 25 September 1844. His father was a carpenter who had settled in Crawfordsville in the early 1840s, shortly after his marriage.

Boyland's mother may have died in childbirth or shortly thereafter, since William did not have any siblings.

Boyland spent only one year, 1855–56, in the Normal School of Wabash College, but curiously, when he enrolled in Company H of the Eleventh Regiment at Indianapolis on 26 March 1862, he described himself as a student. He became a private, committed for three years' service.

On 16 May 1863 he was wounded in the fierce Battle of Champion's Hill,

Mississippi, part of the Vicksburg campaign, from a gunshot to the head, and could not return to active service until September. He fell ill again in April 1864 and returned home briefly for medical treatment. He was mustered out at Baltimore in March 1865.

After the war Boyland spent time in Crawfordsville and Lafayette, but later admitted, when applying for a pension, that he was "scarcely ever at one place long enough to become acquainted with anyone." However, on 8 April 1868 he married Ellen J. Mann in Crawfordsville. The young couple lived for several years with her parents at Clarks Hill, where Boyland established himself as a stonemason.

Sometime in 1870 or 1871 the Boylands moved to Frankfort. William Boyland continued to carve monuments in marble but was increasingly plagued by chronic bronchitis, and his doctor affirmed that he was unfit for manual labor.

Ellen died at Frankfort on 5 July 1881, and two years later, on 23 January 1883, William married Mary C. Wharton of Newark, Licking County, Ohio. They remained in Frankfort until 1897 and then moved to Celina, Ohio, where they settled in St. Marys, on the western edge of Auglaize County, Ohio. William Boyland died there on 4 July 1909 and is buried in Bunnell Cemetery, Frankfort.

References: Boyland's military pension file at the National Archives in Washington, DC. See also: H. W. Beckwith, *History of Montgomery County* (1881), p. 56. The Frankfort-Clinton County Library was most helpful. See for example: *History of Clinton County, Indiana* (1886), p. 527; *Frankfort Crescent*, 13 July 1881; and *Frankfort News*, 6 July 1909.

BRADEN, ROBERT FLOYD (1833–1877)

In an early letter to his family from Booneville, Missouri, Robert Braden of the Twenty-Sixth Indiana Regiment wrote, "We have had fine times for the past week; traveling in a nice steamboat is a very nice way of playing Soldier and I think I could serve my country cheerfully, if it required no greater exertion than I have had to make." Soon, however, his situation changed. During the winter of 1861–62, his regiment began preparations for a head-on fight with the Confederates.

Braden had originally secured a commission as second lieutenant in the state militia in 1853, and so when the Civil War began, he became a first lieutenant in Company G of the Twenty-Sixth Indiana Volunteers on 9 August 1861. At the time, he was described as five feet eight inches tall, with grey eyes, dark hair, and a light complexion.

On 6 February 1862 he was promoted to captain of Company B, which obliged him to serve for three more years, ending up at Pea Ridge, Missouri. That autumn his unit shifted the field of operations to Arkansas, where Braden participated in the heavy fighting at Prairie Grove, the same encounter of 7 December in which fellow Wabash student, John C. Black, so distinguished himself.

Braden was at Vicksburg in July 1863 and took part in the surrender, and he was eventually mustered out on 2 June 1865.

Braden was born at Jefferson on 21 September 1833 and attended Wabash from 1851 to 1852 in the Preparatory Department. His older brother Hector was enrolled at the college from 1850 to 1851, and Robert followed. Their father was said to have freed his slaves and paid for their passage back to Liberia before he and his family departed from Virginia in 1830 and made their way to Indiana.

Braden returned home from service in the war and by 1868 was working in Frankfort at the Clinton County Bank. In the early 1870s he moved to Lafayette and became assistant cashier of the First National Bank. Shortly before his death Braden was promoted to cashier. He never married, and he died in Lafayette on 12 October 1877.

References: Ronald and Susan Beach of Muncie, Indiana. See also: *Biographical Record and Portrait Album of Tippecanoe County, Indiana* (1888), p. 469. Of special interest is Mrs. W. R. Braden, "Selected Letters of Robert F. Braden, 1861–1863," *Indiana History Bulletin*, XLI (Aug. 1964), pp. 110–22.

BRANYAN, JAMES C. (1838–1912)

James Branyan was born in Madison County, Ohio, on 24 October 1838, the son of John and Nancy Black Branyan, who had both been born in Ireland. He had two brothers: W. A. and John Branyan. In 1845 the family moved to Huntington Township, Huntington County, where the father continued to farm.

At the age of nineteen the young Branyan enrolled in the Marion Academy of Grant County, remaining for two years. In 1860 he entered the freshman class at Wabash, pursued the Classical Course of studies, and graduated with a bachelor of arts degree in June 1864. He was not on hand to receive his diploma, however, because on 27 May he had enlisted in Company I of the 138th Indiana Regiment. His service consisted of guarding rail and river transport in Kentucky, and he emerged from the military, honorably discharged as a sergeant, on 30 September 1864.

Returning to Huntington County, he began to study law, and on 3 October 1865 he married Emma Woodrow, a local woman. They eventually had five children: Anna (who died at age one), Vivian, Everett, John, and Wilbur.

In 1866 Branyan served briefly as county surveyor and ran unsuccessfully as a Democrat for the United States House of Representatives, but law was his true calling. He was admitted to the bar, but within a year wanderlust took over, and he and his wife moved first to Decatur County in 1867, followed by a move to Kansas for a year. He later served in the Indiana House of Representatives and as a judge in the Fifty-sixth Indiana circuit court.

James Branyan died at home on 28 April 1912. His wife died in 1913.

References: *Huntington Herald*, 29 April 1912, p. 8; *History of Huntington County, Indiana* (1886), pp. 452–53; Leander Monks, *Courts and Lawyers of Indiana*, pp. 319, 762; and *The Bench and Bar of Indiana*, p. 561. We are also most indebted to help from the Huntington Public Library. See also: *Biographical Directory of the Indiana General Assembly* (1980), I, p. 36.

BROWN, EDMUND RANDOLPH (1845–1930)

Edmund Brown was born 9 August 1845 in Indian Creek Township, Pulaski County, the third child of Ira and Sophia Blew Brown, who were among the earliest settlers of this area of Indiana. Their other children were Michael, James W., and Stephen I., all of whom went to Wabash.

At the age of seventeen, Edmund enrolled in Company C of the Twenty-Seventh Indiana Volunteer Infantry Regiment, signing the rolls at Indianapolis on 12 September 1861. He was promoted to corporal, but declined further promotion to sergeant. The Twenty-Seventh was one of the most active regiments from Indiana and had the second-highest mortality rate of all Indiana regiments. The fought at Antietam (where Brown was wounded), Chancellorsville, and Gettysburg and also took part in the Atlanta campaign.

Brown was discharged on 1 October 1864 and immediately enrolled at Wabash in the first-year English course. The following year he was a freshman, and the year after that, a junior, graduating in 1868 with a bachelor of science degree. While at Wabash, Brown joined the Phi Gamma Delta fraternity.

Although he had aspired to be a writer, Brown entered Lane Theological Seminary of Cincinnati, graduating in 1871. He served as a Presbyterian pastor in Mechanicsville, Iowa, for three years, but left the ministry because of poor health caused by his war injuries.

After spending a year recovering his health at home in Indiana, Brown began a career in business. He worked successively in Pulaski, Star City, and Winamac, and he married Emma Jane March of Pulaski on 1 March 1879. They had two children: Arthur Halleck (Wabash, 1905) and Genevieve.

Brown remained in Monticello for a substantial period, but then switched to a banking career, moving to Akron. In 1917 he purchased a large interest in the Citizens National Bank of Winamac and became its president, remaining in that position until the bank consolidated with the First Trust and Savings Bank in 1920–21, at which time he retired.

Brown was a prolific writer throughout his life. Although he never became an editor (his early ambition), he wrote several newspaper articles and had a weekly column in the *Winamac Republican*. He also served as his regiment's historian, compiling and writing the regimental history. Active in the Grand Army of the Republic, he was Commander of the Department of Indiana in 1906.

Brown died on 15 March 1930 and is buried in the Winamac Cemetery. He was survived by his wife and their two children.

References: Edmund Brown, *The Twenty-seventh Indiana Volunteer Infantry in the War of the Rebellion* (1899); *Indianapolis Star*, 16 March 1930; *Pulaski County Democrat*, 20 March 1930; D. E. Thompson, *Indiana Authors, 1917–1966* (1974); *Winamac Republican*, 20 March 1930. Additional information was kindly provided by Wilbur D. Jones of Alexandria, Virgina.

BROWN, JAMES WHITCOMB (1846–1895)

As was mentioned in the biography of Edmund Brown, James Brown was one of four Brown brothers to attend Wabash and also enlist in the Civil War.

James was born in Pulaski County in 1846, the fourth child of Ira and Sophia Blew Brown. On 4 October 1861 he enrolled in Company H of the Forty-Sixth Regiment of Indiana Volunteers and was commissioned a second lieutenant. On 29 March 1862 he became a first lieutenant; he then was made captain on 22 April 1863. Having signed up for three years, he was granted an honorable discharge on 28 December 1864.

Brown entered the Preparatory Department of Wabash in the autumn of 1865, naming Crawfordsville as his hometown. The following year he left the college, but a year later traveled south to Greencastle to attend Asbury University for the academic year 1867–68. At some point he attended Indiana University, and it is unclear whether he graduated.

On 19 October 1870 Brown married Mattie H. Hiatt of Crawfordsville.

During 1871–72 he studied law at the University of Chicago, and he began practicing in the recently settled community of DeWitt, Nebraska, where he also functioned as a railroad land agent. In the early 1880s he moved to Oketo, Kansas, and for a few years he boarded with a friend, John Dolen. However, his health deteriorated substantially, and in the fall of 1894, he entered a home for infirm soldiers in Leavenworth. He returned to Oketo a few days before his death from cancer of the throat on 12 June 1895. He is buried in Oketo.

References: T. H. Bringhurst, *History of the Forty-sixth Regiment of Indiana Volunteer Infantry* (1888); *Wabash Record Bulletin*, 28 November 1925, p. 14; *History of the State of Nebraska* (2 vols., 1882); *Marshall County* (Kansas) *News*, 21 June 1895.

BROWN, MICHAEL (1841–1915)

Michael Brown was the third of these same four brothers to attend Wabash and also serve in the Civil War. He was born at the family homestead in Indian Creek Township, Pulaski County, on 20 April 1841. Clearly his family placed a premium on formal education, since Michael spent a year at an academy in Logansport before entering Franklin College in the 1850s. In the fall of 1860, he joined the Preparatory Department of Wabash. The following year Brown became a member of the freshman class, but on 22 October 1862 he enrolled in Company B of the Forty-First Regiment of Indiana Volunteers. Not long afterwards he transferred to Company C, where he remained for the next three years.

His regiment was attached to the Army of the Cumberland, and he first saw action at Middleton, Tennessee, on 24 June 1863. Skirmishes or battles followed: Shelbyville (27 June 1863), Mossy Creek (26 December 1863), and Fair Gardens (27 January 1864). Together with many other Indiana regiments, the Forty-First fought in the Battle of Chickamauga.

Brown was taken prisoner near Dalton, Georgia, on 9 May 1864 and confined in the notorious prison camp at Andersonville until mid-October, when he rejoined his unit at Florence, South Carolina. On 22 July 1865 he was mustered out at Nashville.

Returning to Pulaski County, Brown married his sweetheart, Mary Alice, and taught school for a year before entering the University of Michigan law school in October 1866. When he graduated in the spring of 1868, Brown established his own practice in Big Rapids, Michigan, where he remained for forty years. Brown made a name for himself in legal circles. Not only did he plead cases before the United States Supreme Court, but he also served as vice president of the Michigan Bar Association and a member of its legal examining board. For more than twenty years he was the attorney for the Grand Rapids and Indiana Railroad.

He was elected mayor of Big Rapids in 1873 and three years later was appointed to fill a vacancy on the Michigan's Fourteenth Circuit Court. Poor health forced his retirement as a judge in 1881.

In 1903 Brown visited Billings, Montana, and five years he later moved there and found a new law partner, Fred Hathhorn. He died at home in Billings, on 20 December 1915, survived by his wife, son, and three daughters. He is buried in the Billings Cemetery.

References: Obituary for Michael Brown in the *Billings Gazette*, 21 Dec. 1915. See also: *Wabash Record Bulletin*, XXIII (28 Nov. 1925), p. 14.

BROWN, STEPHEN IRA (1848–1925)

Stephen Brown was born on 17 June 1848 in Pulaski County, the fourth son of Ira and Sophia Brown and the fourth to attend Wabash. He also followed his three older brothers by entering the Union army.

At only sixteen years old he enrolled on 19 October 1864 at Indianapolis in Company H of the Forty-Sixth Indiana Regiment, which was commanded by his older brother James. Undoubtedly his family connection enabled him to enter military service even though he was under the age of eighteen. At this time he was described as having blue eyes, light hair, a fair complexion, and a height of five feet eight inches. Since he had committed for only one year, he was mustered out on 4 September 1865.

After the war Brown attended Valparaiso University from 1865 to 1866. He then returned to Pulaski County and taught school the next year. In 1867 he enrolled at Asbury University for a year, and then returned home again. Finally, in the autumn of 1869 he entered Wabash College's Preparatory Department and stayed for two years.

On 28 January 1873 Brown married Emma M. Messerly at Winamac, and he began reading medicine under Dr. D. F. Moss of Pulaski. He later attended the Indiana Medical College in Indianapolis, from which he received a degree in medicine and surgery in 1875. He began practicing at Merrillville, then moved to Medaryville in 1882 and later to Francesville, finally settling in Knox in 1901.

Brown served as the doctor for the Nickel Plate Railroad for more than twenty-five years and was a member of the pension board for Starke County. He was an ardent Methodist and was active for more than fifty years in Masonic circles. He was also a respected member of the Grand Army of the Republic, serving six terms as medical director for Indiana and one term as the surgeon general of the national GAR.

Brown died in Knox on 5 October 1925, survived by his wife and five daughters. One daughter and one son preceded him in death.

References: *Starke County Democrat*, 7 Oct. 1925; *Wabash Record Bulletin*, XXIII (28 Dec. 1925), p. 16; *Journal of the Indiana State Medical Association*, Nov. 1925, p. 433.

BROWN, WILLIAM H. (1837–1910)

William H. Brown's father was born in New York State about 1801, while his mother, Rhodisa, was born in Virginia about 1806. Nothing is known about their early lives, but the family was living in Ohio from the late 1820s to the late 1840s. They then came to Indiana and settled on a farm in Pierson Township, Vigo County, and are shown living there in 1850. William Sr. was a reasonably successful farmer, with land worth over $4,000.

William H. was born in Zanesville, Ohio, on 29 September 1837. Among his siblings were John, David, Hugh, Rebecca, Mathias, and Caroline. It was from the Indiana farm that the young man made his way to Wabash College to attend the Normal School for the year 1854–55. For some reason he never returned, perhaps because he was needed on the farm. By the time the 1860 census was taken, Brown was also teaching school. He had a modest holding of land worth $200 and personal property of $100.

On 18 September 1861 he went to the town of Hartford, Indiana, and enrolled in Company D of the Forty-Third Indiana Regiment. This new private in the Union army was described as being five feet eight inches tall, with dark hair, dark complexion, and grey eyes. We know little of his military service except that he rose to the rank of first lieutenant and was mustered out of the army at Indianapolis on 30 December 1864.

About 1865 he married sixteen-year-old Lena from Ohio. In the coming years she bore him four children: Eva, Cora, Linneus, and John. She may have died by 1877, since William married Louisa F. Mundy in Vigo County on 18 November 1877. Louisa seems not to have had any children of her own and to have died some time prior to 1898.

During the 1870s Brown left his farm in Pierson Township and acquired one in Harrison Township, still quite near to Terre Haute. He remained there until 1887, when he headed west to Colorado. By then his health was greatly impaired, and he was unable to farm for himself. He spent about four years at Booneville and another four at Tribune, Kansas, before returning to Colorado, living at Cotopaxi until about 1899. Then he moved to Poncha Springs, where he died on 14 June 1910.

References: David N. Lewis of the Vigo County Public Library was most helpful in identifying the right family among the many Browns who lived in the county. There is a very useful military pension file on William Brown at the National Archives, Washington, DC.

BRYANT, CHARLES T. (1838–1924)

Charles Bryant was born on 29 April 1838 in South Bend, one of five children of Alfred and Adrianna Bryant. His younger brother, Henry, also attended Wabash and took part in the Civil War. His other siblings were Mary, Alice, and Edwin, who also attended Wabash, but did not join the army.

Bryant's father was a graduate of Princeton Theological Seminary and began his Presbyterian ministry in South Bend, where his three boys were born. In 1843 the family moved to Michigan, and five years later they settled in Niles, where son Charles was living when he entered Wabash in the autumn of 1852. For two years he was enrolled in the Preparatory Department and then returned to Niles to become a farmer, specializing in growing fruit trees. At this time he was described as being five feet six inches tall, with dark eyes, dark hair, and dark complexion.

On 11 November 1861 Bryant enrolled in Company E of the Seventy-First Ohio Infantry Regiment for a term of three years, and in January 1864, almost a year before his term of duty expired, he re-enlisted in the same company and regiment while they were stationed at Gallatin, Tennessee. Bryant was promoted on 7 April to sergeant major of the regiment. On 15 December 1864, at the Battle of Nashville, he was gravely wounded, and he eventually received a medical discharge on 25 June 1865.

Back in Niles, Bryant resumed growing fruit, and in 1868 he purchased eleven acres of prime land at South Haven in Van Buren County. Visiting his orchards one could see 20 apple trees, 190 peach, 250 pear, and many plum. He also grew cherries, quince, currants, gooseberries, raspberries, and blackberries. This outstanding farmer in the prime orchard area of Michigan was elected secretary of the recently founded Pomological Society for the scientific growing of fruit in 1871.

On 9 April 1872 he married Sarah A. Cox at Bangor, Michigan. She bore five children, one of whom died in infancy. Those growing to maturity were Alfred, Philip, Carroll, and Benjamin, but Philip died as a young man in 1901.

Sarah died on 30 September 1907, and Charles moved in with his son Alfred, but eventually went to Chicago to be near his two other sons, Carroll and Benjamin. He died there on 9 May 1924.

References: Pension file at the National Archives, Washington DC. See also the obituary of Charles Bryant's father, Alfred: *Lansing Republican*, 4 June 1881; O. W. Rowland, *History of Van Buren County* (1912), I, pp. 322–23; *South Haven Daily Tribune*, 1 Oct. 1907; and *The South Haven Directory*, 1898–1900, p. 230.

BRYANT, HENRY M. (1841–1919)

Henry Bryant was born on 13 September 1841 in South Bend, the second son of Alfred and Adrianna Bryant. In 1854–55 he followed his older brother Charles to Wabash, where he was enrolled in the Normal School, but after one academic year he returned to Niles, Michigan, to work as a nurseryman at the family farm.

On 1 September 1861 he joined Company F of the Twelfth Michigan Volunteers as a sergeant, and he first saw action at Shiloh in April 1862. On the march to Corinth in Mississippi, he came down with typhoid fever and was sent to a barracks hospital in St. Louis, where he was astonished to encounter his father, the Reverend Alfred Bryant. The father had been summoned by a false rumor of his son Henry's death. Permission was given to the older Bryant to take Henry home for further nursing. Henry Bryant received a medical discharge in June because he was deemed unfit for "manual labor."

On the advice of a local Michigan doctor, Bryant joined a wagon train heading west in the spring of 1864. He stopped off first in Salt Lake City and then followed some new friends to Helena, Montana, where he remained until 1869. At that point he traveled to Walla Walla, Washington, and settled in for a while, from 1870 to 1875. His next relocation was to Seattle (1875–79) and Ellensburg, Washington, where he married Lilly B. Peterson in 1882. Lilly died a few years later, on 11 February 1885.

For many years the United States War Department denied Bryant a pension on the grounds that he was sick even before he entered military service. Late in life he secured a pension of $27.00 per month, which was increased to $33.00.

He moved to Orting, Washington, in 1900, explaining to the pension board that he could no longer work even as a clerk, and relocated to several more towns in Washington before being admitted in 1917 to a veterans' home in Retsil. There he enjoyed occasional visits from his nephew, A. Bryant, a furniture dealer in nearby Bremerton.

He died on 7 July 1919 and is buried next to his wife in the Ellensburg Cemetery.

References: Military pension file from the National Archives in Washington, DC; *Bremerton News*, 9 July 1919.

BRYANT, JAMES RAY McCORKLE JR. (1838–1907)

James Bryant was born in Williamsport on 9 September 1838, the son of James R. M. and Dorcas Gardner Ellis Bryant. His siblings included John, Thomas, Joseph, and Theodore.

He entered Wabash in the Normal School in 1858. On 30 May 1859, at the end of his first year, his mother died in Crawfordsville. Bryant returned to the college for one more year.

Before marrying Helen Riley of Crawfordsville on 9 September 1862, he served thirty days in the military with Company G of the Seventy-Sixth Indiana Volunteers, where his duty consisted mainly of guarding steamboats along the Ohio River.

The 1870 census for Montgomery County describes Bryant as a well-established railroad freight agent and Helen as a twenty-seven-year-old mother of three children: Ellen, Maggie, and Augustus H.

The family seems to have moved sometime in the latter 1870s to Old Orchard, St. Louis County, Missouri, where James continued working as a railroad cashier until he retired. He died at home on 5 April 1907 and is buried in Oak Hill Cemetery, St. Louis County, Missouri.

References: 1870, 1880, and 1900 U.S. census information. See also: *Crawfordsville Daily Journal*, 8 April 1907, p. 8; and *St. Louis Post*, 5 April 1907, p. 20.

BRYANT, ROBERT ELLIS (1827–1906)

If like other armies, the northern army traveled on its stomach, then the commissary was worthy of plenty of notice, if only because it was so necessary. That did not mean the commissary was always appreciated. Soldiers easily tired of "fatback" and wormy crackers, the fare that all too often appeared as the evening menu choice.

In October 1861 Robert Bryant of Wabash was appointed a captain in the United States Army's Commissary of Subsistence. He was activated on 3 February 1862 under the command of General Lew Wallace in Paducah, Kentucky, and on 26 March wrote to his father from Crump's Landing on the Tennessee River, "Being in the grocery trade, I am not permitted to take any part in the fight, my orders being to take care of the stores."

After the Battle of Shiloh, Bryant was directed to establish his supply center at Corinth, Mississippi, and despite orders to stay clear of the fighting, he was close enough to it to be taken captive by a Confederate regiment. His brother John had supposedly joined the army of the Confederate States and was in the regiment that took Robert prisoner, yet neither recognized the other.

When General Ulysses S. Grant laid siege to Vicksburg in 1863, he requested Robert Bryant, by then released, to establish his commissary in St. Louis. Bryant eventually allocated supplies not only for the immediate region along the Mississippi but also in Arkansas and Kentucky and points east.

On 13 March 1865 Bryant received a double promotion in recognition of his "meritorious service," rising from captain to brevet major and then to brevet lieutenant colonel. On 18 August he was mustered out of service.

Bryant was one of ten children of James Ray McCorkle Bryant and Dorcas Gardner Ellis. He was born in Washington, DC, on 5 June 1827.

In 1835 the family made their way to Indiana by wagon and steamboat and settled in Montgomery County, where the young man enrolled at Wabash College in the Scientific, Teachers and Preparatory Department for two years.

The Civil War was not Bryant's first experience with war. With the outbreak of the war with Mexico in 1846, he lost no time enrolling on 15 June in Company K of the First Regiment of Indiana Volunteers, whose captain was the local Crawfordsville politician and future United States senator Henry S. Lane. His regiment spent the better part of the year in Mexico. In July 1847 he and others from his regiment sailed from Mexico to New Orleans, but the vessel capsized off the shore of Padre Island, and they found themselves marooned for ten days before they could reach the mainland. They tried to establish a camp along the Rio Grande amidst insufferable heat and bad drinking water, and many took ill and died. Bryant was lucky to escape these hazards and was able to make his way to New Orleans, where he became clerk to Major Van Ness.

Returning to Crawfordsville, Bryant found the town buzzing with anticipation of bringing the electric telegraph to Montgomery County. Local inhabitants had raised the money for this new technology, and Bryant was sent to Dayton, Ohio, to learn how it worked. He then set up an office in Crawfordsville and proposed marriage to Ellen (or Helen) Sweetser in February 1848.

The young couple moved to Lafayette, where Robert oversaw a telegraph office. After two years they moved back to Crawfordsville, where eventually Bryant got a job as a passenger agent for the Monon Railroad.

After the Civil War he was involved in a variety of jobs, including selling insurance and real estate. In 1871 he was elected to the Crawfordsville City Council. Then, in 1874, he founded the Crawfordsville Casket Company at 309 West Pike Street, in partnership with William Robertson.

Ellen died in 1872, and two years later Bryant married Susan H. Rice. They had two children, Frank and Edith, and also adopted a daughter, Clara. Robert Bryant sustained a stroke in 1900, and although he recovered some of his faculties, he retired from the casket company in 1902. He died on 21 December 1906 and is buried in Oak Hill Cemetery. His daughter, Edith, married a Wabash alumnus, Chase Harding, but she died early, in 1919. Her mother, Susan, followed on 1 May 1923.

References: *Crawfordsville Journal*, 28 Dec. 1906; *Crawfordsville Weekly News Review*, 28 Dec. 1906; *Wabash Record* (Jan. 1907), p. 51; *Crawfordsville Star*, 6 Feb. 1872; Miriam L. Luke and Frances Ferguson, "Some Descendants of Thomas Bryant of Chester County, Pennsylvania" (1977); *Crawfordsville Journal Review*, 1 May 1923; *Biographical Directory of the Indiana General Assembly*, I (1980), pp. 43–44; Robert E. Bryant, "A brief Sketch: the Autobiography of Col. Robert Bryant," *Crawfordsville Journal*, 24 Dec. 1906, published posthumously.

BUEHRIG, HENRY ERNST JR. (1842–1888)

Henry Buehrig Jr. was the son of a German-born hotelkeeper, Henry Ernst Buehrig, and his wife Rebecca, an Englishwoman. He was born in 1842 in Louisiana and had two siblings: Rebecca and William.

Beuhrig attended the Preparatory Department of Wabash College for only one year, 1854–55, giving his home as Indianapolis, where his father owned a successful boardinghouse. After he left Wabash, he presumably returned home to help out with his family's small hotel.

On 23 October 1863 Beuhrig enrolled in the Indiana Fourth Light Artillery at Indianapolis. His muster card noted that he was five feet ten inches tall, with light eyes, hair, and complexion. The following November he saw action at the Battle of Lookout Mountain (24 November 1863) south of Chattanooga.

On 21 September 1864 he was transferred to the Seventh Indiana Battery, which merged with the Army of the Cumberland at Nashville, and remained at Fort Rosecrans in Murfreesboro until the end of the war. He was discharged at Indianapolis on 20 July 1865.

After his father's death in September 1872, Beuhrig maintained his father's saloon at 37 East South Street in Indianapolis. Beuhrig died in Indianapolis on 1 June 1888 and is buried in Crown Hill Cemetery, along with his father. His mother died on 12 December 1898.

References: The Buehrig family name often appeared as Buchrig, as it did in Henry Jr.'s military service record at the Archives Division of the Indiana State Library. However, the name is spelled Buehrig in the U.S. censuses of 1850 and 1860, plus Indianapolis city directories. See also the index to Crown Hill Cemetery at the Indiana State Library.

BUFFINGTON, H. JULIAN (1847–1932)

Julian Buffington was the only child of Taylor and Ann Buffington. He was born in Fayette, Kentucky, on 4 July 1847. His parents came to Crawfordsville in 1850, and by 1860 the family was prospering, with both father and son working as a carpenters.

On 26 April 1864 sixteen-year-old Julian enrolled in Company D of the 135th Regiment of Indiana Volunteers. He was described as having a fair complexion, light hair, hazel eyes, and standing five feet seven inches tall. His regimental obligation was for one hundred days, which was spent as so many other Indiana soldiers did in Kentucky and Tennessee guarding railway lines.

Released from the army on 29 September 1864, he came home and entered the English Course of study at Wabash College. However, within six months he committed to another tour of duty. On 17 March 1865 he enrolled in Company K of the 154th Regiment, from which he was discharged on 4 August 1865 at Stevenson Station, Virginia.

Back in Crawfordsville, Buffington assisted his father as a carpenter, day laborer, and plasterer. The family lived at 109 W. Chestnut Street, adjacent to the college, and it is quite likely that Buffington assisted his father once he had secured the contract from the college to construct the north wing of Center Hall in 1868–69.

On 16 October 1873 Buffington married Georgian Devitte, who died sometime during the next ten years. On 11 June 1885 he was wedded to Fannie T. Brown, whom he outlived. She died on 21 October 1926 and is buried in Oak Hill Cemetery, and he followed on 15 March 1932.

References: Indiana State Library Archives; minutes of the Wabash College Trustees' Prudential Committee in the Ramsay Archives of the Lilly Library; and marriage and cemetery records in the Crawfordsville Public Library.

BUTTNER, ANDREW LEWIS (1845–1913)

Andrew Lewis, or Lewis Andrew, Buttner was born in Allen County on 26 February 1845, son of Andrew and Catherine Antrup Buttner.

In 1860 he was living with two of his siblings, an older sister, Catherine, and a younger brother, Frederick.

On 12 October 1864 he enrolled at Fort Wayne in Company G of the 142nd Regiment for a term of one year. At the time he was described as slightly over five feet eight inches tall, with red hair, sandy complexion, and blue eyes. He entered as a private, but on 10 May 1865 he was promoted to corporal. On 14 July 1865 he was mustered out of service at Nashville, Tennessee.

In 1866 he came to Wabash from Fort Wayne and was distinctive in that he remained at college for five years and graduated with a bachelor of arts degree in

Classical Studies in 1871. He was portrayed in the college magazine as a redheaded soldier who was impulsive and combative: "As a writer he is fresh but odd."

Following graduation from Wabash, Buttner spent a year in Indianapolis studying law and getting married. In about 1873 he changed course and went to Yale Divinity School, from where he graduated in 1876 and secured a pastorate in Elkhart, Indiana, presumably as a Congregationalist.

From about 1878 to 1882 Buttner was in Fort Wayne, teaching school and functioning as a supply minister to local churches. He then moved to Gallatin, Tennessee, and combined working for a lumber company with his ministry, eventually buying his own lumber business in Long Creek, Tennessee. While in Gallatin he married for the second time to Mattie Blanche Whiteside. They had one son.

During the 1890s and early 1900s Buttner owned a lumberyard in Drake, Allen County, Kentucky, and continued preaching whenever possible. His wife, Mattie, died there in 1905, and on 20 July 1909 he embarked upon a third marriage, to Nola M. Morris.

About 1910 Buttner had to give up preaching because his voice had become impaired. He and Nola moved to Loxley, Baldwin County, Alabama, where he died of tuberculosis on 14 November 1913.

References: *Wabash Magazine*, IX (Dec. 1868), p. 56; *Wabash Magazine*, XI (June 1871), p. 149; *Wabash Magazine*, XII (March 1872), p. 148; Yale University, *Obituary Record, 1911–1915*, p. 703; plus alumni sections of the annual catalogues of Wabash College.

CAMPBELL, HENRY (1846–1915)

Henry Campbell is one of the most familiar names in the history of Wabash College because he kept a meticulous diary of his years of military service in the Civil War, and that diary found a home at the college.

Campbell was born in Crawfordsville on 2 June 1846, the first son of John Paxton and Mary Collette Campbell, who later gave birth to Stephen and Mary. His father was a successful dry goods merchant with impressive real and personal property, and he also had a long association with Wabash, serving on its board of trustees from 1857 to 1875.

The younger Campbell entered the Preparatory Department of Wabash in the autumn of 1861 and completed one year before trying to join the army. Although he was just sixteen years old in the summer of 1862, he tried to pass himself off as eighteen, the minimum age for enrollment, but it was hard to fool Colonel Eli Lilly of the Eighteenth Indiana Light Artillery, who knew the Campbell family well. However, just when it looked as though Henry would be rejected, Colonel Lilly let him stay with the battery, not in the capacity of a regular soldier, but as the regiment's bugler, a tale told in Campbell's diary entry for 5 August

1862. For the next two years the boy fulfilled his responsibilities so well that he was given an honorable discharge on 24 November 1864 so that he could re-enlist as a second lieutenant in the 101st United States Regiment of colored infantry.

At war's end Campbell returned to Crawfordsville and re-entered Wabash in the fall of 1866 in its English Course, studying there for only one year. He remained in town, living with his parents and working at a hardware store. On 13 October 1870 Campbell married Allie Houston, and after his father died, he joined his brother Stephen in establishing the dry goods firm of Campbell Brothers.

Sometime in the 1890s Allie died, and Henry became a vice president of the First National Bank, a short walk from his home at 201 South Grant Avenue. He was married a second time to a woman whose name was either Ettie or Rita.

He had a daughter, the future Mrs. Jesse Greene, from either his first or second marriage.

Campbell walked to work on Saturday, 17 July 1915, but died the following Thursday, 22 July, and was buried in Oak Hill Cemetery. Wabash has been proud and gratified to have his fine Civil War diary.

References: *Wabash Magazine*, XI (Dec. 1870), p. 54; *Wabash Record* (Oct. 1915), p. 134; *Crawfordsville Daily Journal*, 22 July 1915; Crawfordsville city directories and indexes to marriages and cemeteries.

CANBY, EDWARD RICHARD SPRIGG (1817–1873)

Some Wabash students entered the service through the regular U.S. Army. The career of Richard Canby brought him into the war from West Point and command in the prewar military. He was one of the most distinguished officers the college produced, commanding in significant fields of military operation.

Canby was born at Platt's Landing, Boone County, Kentucky, on 9 November 1817. He was one of six children, and his brother, Charles, also attended Wabash, although Charles does not seem to have served in the Civil War. His parents were Israel T. and Elizabeth Piatt Canby. Canby was the highest-ranking Civil War veteran to have attended Wabash College.

After one year at Wabash in 1834–35, he secured a place at the United States Military Academy at West Point, where he pursued his studies and training from 1835 to 1839, graduating thirtieth out of thirty-one in his class. On 1 August 1839 he married Louisa Hawkins of Crawfordsville. Their daughter, born in 1842, lived only a short time.

As a second lieutenant Canby spent 1840–46 in Florida dealing with the Seminole tribe, whom the government accused of harboring runaway slaves. Afterwards he was assigned a similar role in Arkansas, moving Native Americans west of the Mississippi River while the federal government designated state boundaries. When the war with Mexico broke out, he was a first lieutenant, and after leading major engagements, he was promoted to captain in 1848.

For the next few years Canby continued to enforce U.S. Indian policy in New Mexico, rising in rank from major to lieutenant colonel. In May 1861, shortly after the outbreak of the Civil War, Canby was promoted to a full colonel and made head of the newly organized United States Army's Nineteenth Regiment stationed at Fort Defiance, New Mexico. His main task was to prevent Confederate troops from moving out of Texas westward toward California.

In the spring of 1862, he became a brigadier general and was ordered to Washington, DC, where he did staff work for the next two years. In July 1863 draft riots broke out in New York City when the Union army enforced the draft to swell its diminished ranks after Gettysburg. Angry mobs demonstrated against being forced into the army and took out their rage against blacks in the city. Canby was sent to command as part of the force to restore order. As Horace Greeley was said to have commented about Candy, "He is a man full of fire and energy, and evidently will not be trifled with, with impunity."

Canby's final and highest rank, major general, came in May 1864 when he took charge of the Military Division of West Mississippi. On 12 April 1865 his forces captured Mobile, Alabama, and accepted the surrender of the last Confederate army in the field. He was mustered out in September 1866.

After the war Canby remained in the army, reverting to the lower full-time rank of brigadier general. From 1865 to 1870 he administered Reconstruction in the southern states. On 8 August 1870 he was appointed commander of the Pacific Coast Department of the Columbia in Portland, Oregon. On 11 April 1873, while attempting to make peace between the Modoc Indian chiefs and state authorities in California, he was suddenly stabbed to death. His body was returned for burial in Crown Hill Cemetery, Indianapolis.

References: E. J. Warner, *Generals in Blue* (1964); United States Military Academy at West Point; the Johnson County Public Library; M. L. Heyman, *Prudent Soldier: A Biography of Major General E. R .S. Canby* (1959).

Edward R. S. Canby: Service in the far west and many other fields

Interest in the Civil War almost always is focused on the major battles in the East, on the series of big-name battles in the Mississippi Valley, like Vicksburg, and on the bloody Southern encounters in Tennessee and Georgia. Extremely interesting battles were fought early in the war in the West as the Confederacy attempted to extend its territory and slave-holding rights and seize valuable resources and access to the riches of Colorado and the seaports of California.

New Mexico territory became a battleground as Federal forces who had been stationed at the U.S. government's forts in the thinly populated regions throughout the Southwest and around scattered small towns confronted Texan Confederate westerners. Texas for its part had seceded; organized Confederate forces of rangers, farmer/ranchers and veterans of the Texas wars organized themselves into mounted regiments to capture the main supply depot at Ft. Union and from there take the Colorado gold fields and ultimately seize California with its riches and seaports to expand a Confederate empire. It was early in the war and hopes were sky-high.

When appointed Commander of the Department of New Mexico in 1861, Colonel Edward R. Canby faced a number of challenges. In early 1861, the U.S. government had ordered most of the regular troops stationed in the territories of New Mexico/Arizona back east. This forced Canby to consolidate the remaining companies of regulars in three different forts in New Mexico. This outpost position was specifically designed to challenge any invasions from Texas and to protect the major supply depot for the southwest at Fort Union in northeast

New Mexico. To replace the departing Regulars, Canby had to rely on raising New Mexico Volunteers and militia. In late 1861, his forces suffered a serious setback when the initial invasion forces from Texas captured over seven hundred Regulars after the abandonment of Fort Filmore, forcing Canby to further group his remaining troops at Fort Craig, a hundred miles south of Albuquerque. He developed a defensive strategy when the large force of Texans threatened under General Henry Hopkins Sibley, formerly a Federal officer, who had convinced Jefferson Davis to let him seize New Mexico and other western territories for the Confederacy.

After irritating delays, Sibley's frontier army started marching up the Rio Grande and came to confront Canby and the Federal forces at Fort Craig. In a wild melee which has been called one of the most ferociously fought of the war, Sibley's units forced Canby's better organized Federals back.

Though defeated in the actions at this Battle of Valverde, Canby's forces were able to retreat to the confines of Fort Craig. The exhausted Texans did not have adequate forces or siege guns to seize the Fort. The result is that the Texans marched north and ultimately met defeat before a combined force of U.S. Regulars and Colorado Volunteers who marched down in response to pleas from the governor of New Mexico and challenged the Texans at Glorieta Pass. Canby then executed a successful maneuver that "encouraged" the Texans to leave the territory while avoiding further large battles and significant casualties. He escaped the burden of attempting to capture and then being required to deal with (house and feed) the Texan army. The Texan Confederates abandoned their last post at Mesilla in July 1862 and returned to Texas. The dream of a Southern empire was over.

In judging Colonel Canby's military performance in New Mexico, one can say he was unsuccessful in "winning" the battles in which he participated; however, he executed a successful strategy of preserving military resources and stores and of eventually forcing the Texans to leave. They never came back.

For his strategic success in pushing the Texans out of New Mexico, Canby was promoted to brigadier general of volunteers effective March 31, 1862. After reorganizing the Department of New Mexico in the wake of the Texans' withdrawal, he then turned over command to his successor, Brigadier James Carlton on September 18, 1862. Upon being ordered to the East, General Canby reported to Washington. There he served as assistant adjutant general of the army for almost a year, and then commanded Federal troops in New York

City during the draft riots that followed the Battle of Gettysburg. In 1864, he assumed command of the military district of West Mississippi where he was severely wounded by Confederate guerrillas. Late in the war, as a major general of volunteers, he commanded the army in the Department of the Gulf, attacking the fortifications at Mobile, Alabama. He also accepted the surrender of Richard Taylor as commander of the Confederate forces of Alabama and Louisiana at the conclusion of the war.

Following the war, Canby was promoted to the rank of brigadier general in the regular army. He and his wife subsequently moved to the Pacific Northwest to command the Department of the Columbia. As a result of a disturbance involving the Modoc tribe which broke out in 1872, General Canby accompanied a peace commission in an attempt to settle the disagreements with the Modocs. During those peace talks, two of the Indians shot and killed General Canby with the guns they had hidden. Thus ended the life and career of one who had been called the "prudent soldier," the only general officer killed during the Indian Wars. (The story of the Texas and New Mexico campaigns is interestingly told in Donald S. Frazier's book *Blood & Treasure*.)

--James P. Houghton

Jim Houghton is president of the Glorieta NM Battlefield Coalition and serves in both Federal and Confederate reenactive units.

CARICO (CARRICO), JOHN R. (1830–1863)

John Carico enrolled in the Normal School of Wabash College in 1854–55 and gave his hometown as Terre Haute, Vigo County, Indiana. He may be the same John Carico who was born in Parke County on 7 August 1830.

In 1860 he joined Company E of the Forty-Third Regiment, and when he was mustered in on 8 November 1861 for three years, he was five feet five inches tall, with light hair, fair complexion, and blue eyes. He gave his occupation as a wagon maker in Carlisle.

By June 1862 Carico was noted as absent from his regiment on account of illness and was presumed to be recuperating in hospital at Carlisle. However, in April 1863 the army decided that he must have deserted. Carico does not appear in later censuses, which suggests that he died in or out of the hospital in southern Indiana.

References: National Archives in Washington, DC.

CARLIN, ROBERT LINSEY (1832–1914)

Robert Carlin was born on 28 June 1832 in Noblesville, one of twelve children of Joseph G. and Margaret Carlin.

He was enrolled in the Preparatory Department of Wabash College for only one academic year, 1849–50, and then worked in Noblesville as a cabinetmaker. On 27 March he married Fanny Gaskill, who later had a daughter, Carrie, but Fanny died in childbirth. The young father found that he could not cope alone with a newborn baby, so Carrie was brought up by others in Fanny's hometown of Shelbyville.

On 8 July 1852 Carlin married Rhoda Ann Cottingham, and they had four children: William F. (1856?), Martha (1856?), John G. (1858?), and Frank (1861?). He supplemented his furniture business as the conductor of a military band as well as of a Presbyterian choir in Noblesville. In July 1863, when Morgan led his raid into southern Indiana, Carlin volunteered for military service in Company E of the 109th Regiment. One week later, his brief career as a soldier ended abruptly with the mustering out of the regiment.

In 1875 the Carlin family moved from Noblesville to Indianapolis. Robert and his sons established a music store, where they sold pianos and other instruments.

In 1889 Rhoda Carlin sought a divorce in the face of her husband's liaison. He later married Laura Clampitt on 7 July 1889. Robert Carlin then retired on his savings and lived another twenty years, dying at home in Indianapolis on 31 August 1914. He was survived by Laura and two sons, William and John. His body was conveyed from Indianapolis to Noblesville, where he was buried in Crownland Cemetery along with other members of his family.

References: Mr. and Mrs. Earl Owens of Salem, Oregon, and obituaries in the *Hamilton County Ledger*, 31 Aug. and 2 Sept. 1914.

CARNAHAN, JAMES RICHARD (1841–1905)

James Carnahan, a native of Dayton, Indiana, born in 1841, seems to have been so determined to go to Wabash to get an education that he proposed to save everything he earned for several years, without spending a cent, in order to pay tuition. So as not to be tempted to spend any of his tuition money, he carefully deposited his modest earnings in a bank that unfortunately went bankrupt during the panic of 1857. Undaunted, he started saving all over again, and by the autumn of 1859 he had the six dollars necessary to gain admission to Wabash. This determination was also reflected in his pursuit of a bachelor's degree.

On 18 April 1861 Carnahan enrolled at Crawfordsville in Company I of the Eleventh Regiment and committed to three months' volunteer service, facilitated by prewar training in the Montgomery County Guards under Lew Wallace.

On 15 August 1862 he enlisted at Lafayette for three years in Company K of the Eighty-Sixth Regiment, entering as a first sergeant by virtue of his previous military experience, and by December he had become a second lieutenant. On his muster card he was described as five feet nine inches tall, with dark eyes and complexion and black hair. Promotion to the rank of the captain of Company I of the Eighty-Sixth came on 4 September 1863, just a few weeks before the Battles of Chickamauga and Missionary Ridge. He described that battle in this way:

> The whole side of the mountain is now covered with our forces, struggling and clambering toward the top. The little band that has fought its way in advance of the others now grows impatient, and fears lest some others may rush forward and snatch the first awards of victory from them. The command "fix bayonets" is given, and again the order to "charge," and these two regiments with a shout disappear amidst the smoke; and, with loud huzzas plants a new flag, now in threads, on the rebel fort, and rallying round it, fights for its maintenance until our army reaches them.

Carnahan participated in thirty-three military engagements as well as acting for a time as a staff officer for Brigadier General Thomas Wood, commander of the Fourth U.S. Army Corps, before being mustered out at Nashville, Tennessee, on 6 June 1865.

Finishing his senior year at Wabash, 1865–66, he joined the Indianapolis law firm of Ray, Gordon, and March and studied for the bar examination, which he passed in 1866. This led to his being appointed prosecuting attorney in the Tippecanoe County criminal court, a job he held from 1867 to 1873.

In the fall of 1867 Carnahan married Sue Patterson of Indianapolis, and in the coming years they had three daughters: Lorene, Lida, and Nellie. Then in 1874 he was elected judge of the same criminal circuit court in Tippecanoe County. Following Carnahan's six years in the Lafayette criminal court, Indiana governor Porter appointed him adjutant general for the state, which carried a rank of brigadier general in the Indiana Guard. This new position occasioned a move to Indianapolis to a fashionable address in Woodruff Place, where he lived for many years, becoming active in the Knights of Pythias. Facts of his death cannot be substantiated.

References: *Wabash Magazine*, VIII (Dec. 1867), p. 79; *Wabash Magazine*, IX (June 1869), p. 157; *Wabash Record* (July 1904), p. 19; T. Gronert, *Sugar Creek Saga* (1958), pp. 166–67; unpublished materials in the Indiana Historical Society, James R Carnahan collection, M311; J. P. Dunn, *Memorial Record of Distinguished Men of Indianapolis and Indiana* (1912), pp. 393–96; *Indianapolis News*, 3 Aug. 1905; J. F. Tuttle, "Father Carnahan of Dayton," (1879).

CARR, CHAUNCEY R. (1835–1919)

Chauncey Carr was born in about 1835, one of four sons of Moses C. and Mary Carr. His father was a merchant in Terre Haute. His brothers were John, Moses, and Theodore. Shortly before Carr entered Wabash in the fall of 1860, both of his parents died.

Carr spent two years in the Preparatory Department (1860–62) and then volunteered on 21 July 1862 for thirty days of military service in Company I of the Seventy-Sixth Indiana Regiment. He spent eight days with a company of the Indiana Legion until the Morgan threat subsided. After his short stint with the Seventy-Sixth, he returned to Wabash for another year (1862–63) as a freshman.

In 1868 Carr embarked upon a medical career, first becoming an apprentice to Dr. William Hill in Bloomington, McLean County, Illinois. He then was admitted to New York City's Bellevue Hospital Medical College and received his diploma in 1871. During 1871–72 he spent nine months back with Dr. Hill in Bloomington, Illinois, followed by six months in Rockford, Illinois. In 1873 went to New York to work in the Eye and Ear Infirmary.

On 28 May 1874 Carr married Ella B. Hayes, a native of Bloomington. They moved into the house in which Ella had grown up and eventually produced a family of five: Edna (1875), Chauncey R. Jr. (1877?), Helen (1886), Damon (1888), and Elizabeth (1890). All but Chauncey Jr. grew to maturity.

After a long and successful medical practice, Carr died in Bloomington on 17 April 1919. He is buried in Evergreen Cemetery next to Ella, who lived until 1944.

References: Vigo County Public Library and the McLean County (Illinois) Historical Society; *Wabash Magazine*, VII (July 1866), p. 10; H. C. Bradsby, *History of Vigo County, Indiana* (1891), p. 480; S. B. Gookins, *History of Vigo County, Indiana* (1880), p. 480; *McLean County Medical Society*, (1905), p. 24; and C. L. Kessler, *Home Town in the Corn Belt* (1950), pp. 102–03.

CARR, WALTER BRUCE (1841–1913)

Though Indiana sent a major portion of enthusiastic young men to the war in regular units, particularly in the early days of the war, being in the northern army was not without controversy in the state. Confederate sympathizers agitated, and some formed units of the Knights of the Golden Circle or other so-called "Copperhead" organizations that pressed for a quick end to the war. Being in the local defenders' Indiana Legion was not without its difficulties; members of the Legion were often called "shirkers" for not enrolling in a regular unit, instead leaving the fighting to others.

A less vocal but just as earnest group were the Friends, the Quakers, strong in eastern Indiana but present in several Indiana communities. Some Quakers went to the war; others objected and did not go or served as medical assistants. Occasionally there were Quaker impersonators, and it appears at least one Wabash College student was cast in this role by his parents to avoid having their son go to war. Walter Bruce (or Bruce Walter) Carr was born in the town of Liberty on 8 July 1841. His parents were Thomas and Elizabeth Carr. He had two sisters, Phoebe and Evelyn, and an older brother, Henry M., who was born in about 1829.

In 1855 the family moved to Crawfordsville, where his father was a minister of the Christian Church and a blacksmith. Later the younger Carr entered the Normal School of Wabash College, and as soon as the Civil War began, he felt led to enlist as his older brother had done. However, his parents hoped to discourage this and sent him to a Quaker school. Soon, however, after he had entered the school, he eluded his instructors' watchful eyes and going to Terre Haute enlisted and secured recruitment papers. A few days later he re-appeared at the school and in a short time had enlisted sixteen of the boys of the school and started to the front as Captain of Company K, 58th Indiana Infantry.

So the story went. However that may be, it is clear that he secured a commission as captain of Company K on 15 November 1861. What is less clear is the matter of his discharge on 1 May 1862. He may have undergone a court martial, but if so, he was exonerated, because on 23 July 1863 he was commissioned a first lieutenant in the Union Guards of Montgomery County, a unit of the Indiana Legion. On April 1864 he became a major in the Montgomery County Guards. Local lore has it that during the war, the local Copperheads decided to have a meeting at the Mount Tabor schoolhouse, and Carr decided to crash the meeting. A local newspaper reported, "A member of the order stood up to announce that there was an enemy in the camp. A committee was appointed to put Carr out, but it was dissuaded from performing the task by his big army revolver."

On 21 May 1864 Carr became the captain of Company I of the 135th Regiment of Indiana Volunteers for one hundred days. He was switched to Company D and guarded railway lines in Kentucky and Tennessee until mustered out at Indianapolis on 29 September.

Returning to Crawfordsville, he became a full-time farmer, cultivating 205 acres three miles south of town. He married a local woman, Emma Jeanetta Baker, on 7 November 1886, and they had one son, Thomas, who died in infancy.

Plagued by chronic illness, Walter died at home, 109 Vance Street, Crawfordsville, on 18 April 1913. He is buried in Oak Hill Cemetery and was survived by his wife.

References: *History of Montgomery County* (Bowen & Co., 1913), pp. 843–44; *Revised Montgomery County Atlas* (1898); *Crawfordsville Journal*, 25 April 1913; unidentified newspaper clipping of 17 June 1902 at the Crawfordsville Public Library; and military pension file at the National Archives, Washington, DC.

CARTER, JOHN M. (1839–1918)

John Carter was born in Richmond on 5 August 1839. His father died shortly afterwards, leaving John, his older brother, Robert, and his younger brother, Thomas, without a father.

John's mother, Millie Carter, remarried twice, the second time in 1855 to Enoch Sales. Sales proved to be a harsh taskmaster who refused to let John go to school. Thus, at the age of seventeen, John could neither read nor write and decided to run away. He was taken in by Joseph Ratliff of Richmond and allowed to attend the Whitewater Academy in Centerville, Indiana (1858–59).

From 1859 to 1861 young Carter was in the Preparatory Department of Wabash College and, like many students in the spring of 1861, responded to the call for recruits and joined Company I of the Eleventh Regiment for a term of three months in April 1861.

On 15 October 1861 he enrolled at Anderson in Company G of the Forty-Seventh Regiment and became a corporal. At the time he was described as five feet ten inches tall, with blue eyes, light hair, and light complexion. He served well beyond his commitment of three years and was mustered out at Baton Rouge, Louisiana, on 23 October 1865.

Toward the end of the war, Carter was a steward in a hospital for black troops in Shreveport, Louisiana, a job that undoubtedly led to his pursuing medicine, first in Middletown, near Anderson, and then Cincinnati, graduating in 1868.

On 5 November 1868 he married Marcy C. Savage at Centerville and almost immediately moved to Jackson Centre, Ohio. Their only child, Ida, was born there on 6 July 1873, but lived only until 1 September.

Carter practiced medicine for many years and ultimately secured a military pension in the 1880s for his many service-related afflictions. Toward the end of his life, he went to Hot Springs, Arkansas, in search of a healthier environment, and he died there on 8 July 1918. He is buried in Crown Hill Cemetery in Centerville next to his wife.

References: *Directory of Soldiers' Register of Wayne County Indiana* (1865), p. 271; the Morrisson–Reeves Library of Richmond, Indiana; and his military pension file at the National Archives, Washington, DC.

CATICK, JOHN C. (1834–1904)

John Catick was born in Warren County, Ohio, in October 1834. In 1850 he enrolled in the Preparatory Department of Wabash College for one year. His father, Henry, was a saloonkeeper and grocer in Crawfordsville, and his sister was known on campus as "beautiful Lizzie."

After his brief time at Wabash, it must be presumed that he worked for his father in the grocery store, but his name does not appear in the Indiana census for 1860. However, on Christmas Day 1863 he joined Company K of the Eleventh Cavalry, 126th Indiana Regiment, at Crawfordsville. He was described as being five feet seven inches tall, with blue eyes and light hair and complexion, and indicated his occupation as a dentist.

On 22 March 1864 Catick was promoted to corporal, followed on 1 November 1864 by the rank of quartermaster sergeant. He was formally discharged at Fort Riley, Kansas, on 4 September 1865.

On 16 March 1868 Catick married Rachael Johnson of Topeka and became a farmer. He and Rachael had four children, two of whom died in childhood: Benjamin (1889–1893) and John Martin (1872–1874). Two girls, Louisa, born in 1870, and Blanche, in 1884, seem to have grown to adulthood.

Catick died in Topeka on 20 April 1904 and Rachael on 17 April 1917. They are both buried in Topeka.

References: F. M. Mills, *Early Days in a College Town*, (1924) pp. 70, 157; H. W. Beckwith, *History of Montgomery County* (1881), p. 89; Mrs. Katy Matthews of Topeka, Kansas; *Topeka Daily Capital*, 1 April 1917; 1900 U.S. census for Topeka; and military pension file at the National Archives, Washington, DC.

CAVEN, JOHN F. (1838–1866)

John Caven was born on 14 February 1838 in Illinois, one of four children of Martha B. Caven and her first husband. He had three sisters: Martha, Evaline, and Harriet. Circa 1850–51 his mother married a successful Crawfordsville grocer, Henry Williams, and by 1860 she and Henry had a son and a daughter.

When Caven entered Wabash in the fall of 1857, he was slightly older than most of the students in the Preparatory Department. He proceeded to study as a freshman and sophomore in the Classical Course.

In the spring of 1861, soon after the outbreak of war, there was a mass exodus from the college into the ranks of the Eleventh Indiana Regiment, made especially easy because recruitment took place in Crawfordsville. Being older than most of his classmates, Caven secured a commission as a second lieutenant of Company H on 23 April 1861 for three months. Once he was released at Indianapolis on 4 August 1861, he turned around and enlisted again, this time as a first lieutenant of Company G of the Eleventh Regiment. On 20 November 1861 he was promoted to captain in Company G. Soon afterwards he was wounded in the thigh and went home to Crawfordsville for several months to recuperate. However, restless to rejoin his company, Caven returned by March, sooner than some thought that he should have. Several of Caven's fellow officers petitioned Governor Oliver P. Morton of Indiana to appoint him major of the Eleventh Regiment as a replacement for the recently retired Crawfordsville soldier Isaac Elston, but their pleas went unheeded. Caven served three years, participating in the Battles of Fort Donelson, Shiloh, Champion's Hill, Vicksburg, Port Gibson, and Little Rock before mustering out on 23 November 1864.

He died in Louisville, Kentucky, on 8 February 1866 of some sort of paralysis, and his body was brought back to Crawfordsville for interment in Oak Hill Cemetery.

References: *History of Montgomery County* (Bowen & Co., 1913), p. 781; *Wabash Magazine*, II (March 1861), p. 179; *Wabash Magazine*, IV (Dec. 1863), p. 74; *Wabash Magazine*, VII (Feb. 1866), p. 76; *Crawfordsville Weekly Review*, 10 Feb. 1866; and file of letters for the Eleventh Regiment at the Indiana State Library Archives.

CHAMBERS, WILLIAM B. (1842–1917)

William Chambers was born in Rockridge County, Virginia, in October 1842, one of seven children of William and Susan Chambers. The others were John, Susan, Martha, Joseph, Sarah, and Jane. The family settled in Montgomery County, Indiana, in the early 1850s, where the father and son farmed.

The younger Chambers spent only 1855–56 in the Normal School of Wabash College, after which he rejoined his family. On 8 October 1862 at Indianapolis he enrolled in Company L of the Fifth Indiana Cavalry, attached to the Eightieth Regiment. Chambers was described as being five feet eight inches tall, with a light complexion, hazel eyes, and sandy hair. Later he transferred to Company D of the Sixth Cavalry, part of the Seventy-first Indiana Regiment. Chambers was honorably discharged as a corporal at Murfreesboro on 15 September 1865.

After the war Chambers acquired his own land near Mace in Montgomery County. On 10 September 1870 he married Amanda Lope, and their children included Henry, Adrian, Arinda, Wilbert, and Lola.

Amanda died on 3 January 1917. Chambers continued living on his acres until 1918, but illness forced him to live his last days with his son-in-law, Homer Linn. He died on 14 June of that year and is buried along with his wife in the Knights of Pythias Cemetery in Mace, Indiana.

References: *History of Montgomery County* (Bowen & Co., 1913), p. 104; *Crawfordsville Weekly Journal*, 21 June 1918.

CHAPIN, GEORGE TARVIN (1838–1864)

George Chapin was one of four brothers to attend Wabash College, two of whom took part in the Civil War. The other two were Jonathan Edwards and Lucius Philander. A fifth brother, Elisha Cowgill, also served in the war but did not attend Wabash. George was the youngest, born in Greencastle in 1838. His parents were Lucius Rousseau and Sarah Cowgill Chapin, and they also had seven daughters: Susan Lucretia, Martha Ann, Harriet Eliza, Mary Agnew, Sarah Rousseau, Ruth Ellen, and an unknown other daughter.

Chapin entered the Preparatory Department of Wabash in the autumn of 1856 but left at the end of the first year, returning in the fall of 1858 to complete two more years of formal education before joining his father on the family farm. His father died on 1 February 1861.

At the outbreak of war, as we have shown, one of the first Indiana regiments to be organized was the Tenth, and Chapin promptly enrolled at Greencastle on 20 April. Four days later he reported for duty at Indianapolis, and by June he was moving from one town to another in Virginia, including Clarksburg, Parkersburg, and Marietta.

By 6 August 1861 Chapin's regiment was back in Indianapolis, ready to be mustered out after their three-month commitment, but Chapin re-enlisted for three more years, this time in Company I of the Twenty-Seventh Regiment. His previous military experience gave him an advantage, and he was given the rank of sergeant. In January 1863 he was promoted to second lieutenant, then to first lieutenant in March.

The Twenty-Seventh narrowly survived the rout of Federal troops at the Battle of Ball's Bluff in Virginia on 21 October 1861, but it was not so lucky a year later at the Battle of Antietam in Maryland, where Chapin was wounded. In a letter home to his brother Henry about the battle, he wrote, "It is the bloodiest one of the war, it raged from morning light till dark." He estimated that his regiment, which had entered the fight with about 400 soldiers, emerged with 18 killed and 192 wounded. His company lost 3, while 16 were injured.

Chapin's regiment remained in Virginia during the spring and early summer of 1863, but it was hastily rushed to southern Pennsylvania to take part in the battle of Gettysburg. On 5 July 1863 he described the carnage to his brother John: "We have just passed through the most terrible battle ever fought on the continent." He guessed that his regiment had sustained a loss of one hundred killed and wounded.

In a letter to his brother John, Chapin wrote that he might apply for a transfer to a black regiment, realizing that although it did give advancement opportunities, some would accuse him of being an abolitionist. Chapin seems actually to have been in agreement with most of the views of the abolitionists. He said that slavery was a "curse of our country, the cause of all our troubles, misery—the cause of the war, and I hope the war will have the good effect to wipe it from the face of this country forever."

Whether or not he applied for a transfer is unknown, but in any case, time ran out for him at the Battle of Resaca, Georgia. He had a premonition of his imminent death, which he confided to a friend, and was hit in the head by a musket ball. He died on 15 May 1864 and was buried in the national cemetery at Chattanooga.

References: Chapin family letters in the Wabash College Archives and in the manuscript section of the Indiana Historical Society. Quotations are taken from the latter collection. See also: *Greencastle Banner*, 8 July 1886; and E. R. Brown, *The Twenty-Seventh Indiana Volunteer Infantry* (1899), p. 474, which contains a photograph of George Chapin.

CHAPIN, HENRY EWING (1835–1878?)

Of the four Chapin brothers who went to Wabash, least is known about Henry. He was born in Greencastle in 1835 into the very large farming family described in the account of his brother, George.

In the autumn of 1853, he joined his older brother John at Wabash, and the two roomed together. After Henry had been at college for a few months, John wrote to another brother, Elisha, that Henry was "decidedly another person since he has been here … I have not known him so cheerful for years … his mind is constantly employed with something useful … when he is through his studies he reads or writes. He has now a great ambition to be a writer." Henry also demonstrated another talent while he was at Wabash for two years: He began to play the violin and take voice lessons, and again John proudly announced that the teachers at Wabash "think he is a prodigy in music."

When the other Chapin boys went away during the war, his mother and sisters depended on son Henry to run the farm. The effort proved a struggle for him and adversely affected his health. In addition, money was scarce, so he reluctantly decided to sell one of the family's horses and cut timber and hauled it to the sawmill to make ends meet.

There is no record of Chapin undertaking military service, yet the Wabash College magazine included his name among those in the army in the spring of 1864. It is always possible that he enlisted in a neighboring state, but more likely his muster-in card was lost, denying later inquirers evidence of his brief soldiering.

He continued to farm in Putnam County during the 1860s and most of the 1870s and seems not to have married, but shared the homestead with his mother, Sarah, and a few of his sisters. He is listed on a register of voters compiled in 1877 but does not appear in the 1880 census, and oddly is not alluded to in the later family correspondence.

References: Henry is alluded to in the Chapin family correspondence at the Wabash College Archives, but there are no letters to or from him. For other references to the family, see the sources cited at the end of the sketches for his brothers, George, John, and Lucius.

CHAPIN, JONATHAN EDWARDS (1829–1911)

Getting higher education in "high frontier" Indiana was not easy. Young men were often needed on the farm or in small-town family businesses, and money was scarce. Wabash College was not accessible by train until 1851, and coach routes went only through major towns. Jonathan Chapin in his later years recounted the challenges he faced in 1850 as he sought admission to the college. From his home in Putnamville, since he could not get a train or carriage to Crawfordsville, he packed his things in carpetbags, slung them over his shoulder, and walked forty-five miles. Arriving before the beginning of the term, he took odd jobs in town until he had earned six silver dollars to present to the college treasurer for admission to Wabash. Of the four Chapin brothers who attended Wabash, John seems to have been the most studious. From 1850 to 1852 he was in the Preparatory Department, and then he progressed from a freshman to a senior between 1852 and 1856.

Chapin was born in Maysville, Kentucky, on 3 December 1829, the oldest of twelve children born to Sarah Cowgill and Lucius Rousseau Chapin. (See the account of his brother, George, for a fuller treatment of the family.) The year following his graduation, 1856–57, he stayed in Crawfordsville as a teacher, either at the college or at a local primary school.

In the autumn of 1857, Chapin was admitted to Lane Theological Seminary in Cincinnati, and for the next four years he took course work there while preaching and teaching in nearby localities. Even before his ordination in 1861, he acted as a Presbyterian minister in Worthington and Allensville in Ohio.

In 1862 he began eight years at a church in Plymouth, Indiana, interrupted in 1864 by a leave of absence in order to represent the Christian Commission and its work with the troops. The Christian Commission, created in response to the suffering of troops after First Bull Run, visited camps to distribute supplies, including medical needs, religious consolation, and reading material.

Initially serving in East Tennessee, Chapin wrote that it was "the farthest boundary between the Union and Rebel lines," but soon he followed various Indiana regiments to Huntsville, Alabama, where he was only ten miles from the Confederates. As he explained in a letter to one of his sisters, his pastoral duties were a mixture of the sacred and the secular: providing soldiers with writing paper and selling them postage stamps, and distributing Bibles, religious tracts and magazines. There was even a lending library with five hundred volumes. As a chaplain, he visited the sick and wounded in addition to conducting formal religious services.

Toward the end of his mission to the troops, Chapin searched for the grave of his brother George, which took him to the battlefield at Resaca, Georgia. He wrote his brother Lucius, who was also in the army: "I stopped at Resaca, got a good headboard for George's grave. I cut his name on it with chisel and knife."

Chapin returned to Putnamville in August 1864 and resumed his duties as pastor. On 9 August 1867 he married Mary Anderson. In May 1870 they moved to Neenah, Wisconsin, where Mary died two years later. On 28 October 1873 he married Harriet (Hattie) Lucretia Ely in Hector, New York. Their only daughter, Ellen Ely (Nellie), was born in 1879.

Chapin was the Presbyterian minister in Neenah for thirty-three years and remained an emeritus pastor for the remaining eight years of his life. He died on 4 February 1911.

References: The letters of John E. Chapin are in the Wabash College Archives and the Indiana Historical Society. See also: the *Wabash* Magazine, XXXV (April 1911), p. 127; memorial program of the Presbytery of Winnebago, Wisconsin, 12–14 Sept.1911; *Neenah Daily Times*, 4 Feb. 1911; Lane Theological Seminary, *General Catalogue, 1829–1899* (Cincinnati, 1899), p. 63, and *Ouiatenon*, VI (1895), pp. 38–40.

CHAPIN, LUCIUS PHILANDER (1832–1915)

Lucius, nicknamed Lew, was born at Maysville, Mason County, Kentucky, on 4 March 1832, the second of the four brothers to attend Wabash and who are described in this series of biographies. A fifth brother, Elisha, volunteered but died in the war.

Lucius Chapin enrolled in the Preparatory Department of Wabash College in the autumn of 1851. He remained for only one school year, then studied law and was admitted to the bar.

On 2 August 1859 he married Ruby Alice Osborn in Terre Haute, Indiana. They eventually had three children: Alice, Lucius, and Hanna.

On 11 August 1862 Chapin journeyed to Terre Haute in order to enroll in the Fourth cavalry of the Seventy-Seventh Indiana Regiment. On 22 November the recruits assembled in Indianapolis to begin their formal training. Soon they were at Camp Platter near Henderson, Kentucky, and for the next six months they were stationed either near Henderson or Caseyville, Kentucky.

Mid-April 1863 found the regiment in Tennessee, either at Nashville or Murfreesboro. Details are lacking, but somehow Chapin was badly wounded in late June 1863, and from 29 June until 23 November 1863, he was recuperating in Hospital No. 3 at Nashville. Serious as his condition was in the early weeks, his letters to his family and especially to his wife were usually cheerful and positive. Meanwhile his fellow soldiers had experienced several major and serious battles, such as Chickamauga in September.

Chapin reported back to duty in late November 1863 and along with others wintered in east Tennessee. He took part in the Battle of Fair Gardens on 27 January 1864. By May of that year the Seventy-Seventh Regiment was with General Sherman's forces in Georgia as part of the campaign against Atlanta. That crucial city fell in early September, and then Chapin found himself back in Tennessee in October and in Kentucky near Louisville in November. By late February 1865 the Seventy-Seventh was in Alabama and eventually made its way back to

Tennessee. They were duly mustered out at Edgefield on 29 June 1865.

During much of the 1870s and 1880s, Chapin was a lawyer in Greencastle in partnership with Judge Claypool. He was also elected mayor of that city for two terms, 1876–80. Toward the end of the 1880s, he seems to have given up his law practice for the ownership of a grocery store. Still later, from 1898 to 1902, he was Greencastle's postmaster.

Alice Chapin died on 6 November 1907, and Lucius followed on 7 March 1915. They are both buried in Forest Hill Cemetery, Greencastle.

References: There is a sizeable collection of letters to and from Lucius Chapin in the Wabash College Archives. See also: J. W. Weik, *History of Putnam County, Indiana* (1910), pp. 59, 112, 175; *Biographical and Historical Record of Putnam County* (1887), p. 301; Putnam County Sesquicentennial Committee, *A Journey Through Putnam County History* (1966), p. 42; *Greencastle Herald Democrat*, 12 March 1915.

CHESNUT (CHESTNUT), JAMES D. (1834–1886)

James Chesnut was born in Chillicothe, Ohio, in 1834, the son of Robert Thomas Chesnut and Harriet Carpenter. Both of his parents were from Ohio. Their other children included Augustus, Ellen, Lucy, Laura, and Elizabeth.

In the spring of 1833, the Chesnut family moved from Ohio to Lafayette, Indiana, and it was from here that James made his way to Wabash College in the autumn of 1848. He remained for three years but never received a degree. While at college he clerked at a dry goods store in Lafayette.

In 1852 he joined the California gold rush and in one year made $7,000. He was ready to come home when he was inveigled into taking part in the odd scheme of freebooter William Walker's Independence Brigade, which traveled into western Mexico, where Walker declared himself president of southern California.

In the late 1850s Chesnut went to the newly created state of Kansas and helped design the town of Wyandotte. In 1860 he was in Central City, Colorado, operating his own sawmill.

With the outbreak of the Civil War in 1861, Chesnut enlisted Native Americans and blacks for the Union Army and became a colonel in Company A of the Twelfth Kansas Infantry, which served along the Kansas-Missouri frontier, guarding rail lines and confronting Confederate guerrillas.

Chesnut was mustered out in June 1865 and went to Montana, where he discovered coal in the Rocky Canyon Trail Creek area and became a wealthy entrepreneur. In 1867 he settled in Bozeman and established Chesnut's Corner Saloon, a "high class establishment," as it was described locally, where local businessmen congregated to read newspapers and talk politics.

In the early 1880s he left Bozeman to reside in a town named after himself, but misspelled: Chestnut. Here he operated a hotel, for railway travelers.

James died on 21 January 1886, a subject of several tales of romance among locals, but never married.

References: Tippecanoe County Historical Association; Bozeman Public Library. See also: R. P. DeHart, *Past and Present of Tippecanoe County, Indiana*, pp. 331–32; M. Leeson, *History of Montana* (1885), pp. 606, 1110; and Phyllis Smith, *Bozeman and the Gallatin Valley* (1997), p. 81.

CLARK, ALBERT BARNES (1842–1883)

Albert Clark was born in LaPorte on 24 August 1842, one of three sons of Amzi and Candice Roberts Bailey Clark. All of the brothers attended Wabash College. Edward Payson and Frederick Augustus also served in the Civil War. They also had a sister, Catherine.

Albert Clark came to Wabash in the fall of 1858 and spent two years (1858–60) in the Preparatory Department, followed by two years (1860–62) as a freshman and a sophomore. He was an effective student orator, winning first prize for declamation at the end of his freshman year. As a sophomore, he was chosen to speak about the Netherlands. He also joined Beta Theta Pi fraternity. At the end of his sophomore year, he transferred to Yale and joined the Skull and Bones society, graduating Phi Beta Kappa in June 1864.

In November 1864 he became a paymaster for the navy, attached to the Gulf Squadron under Admiral Farragut. His health was always poor, and he left the service in 1865.

Clark then returned to New Haven, Connecticut, and sold insurance while at the same time learning stenographic shorthand, which he used as a court reporter in Chicago from 1867 to 1870. He also acted as private secretary to banker J. N. Scammon and worked for Robert Todd Lincoln, the son of President and Mrs. Mary Todd Lincoln.

In 1870 he joined the United States Geographic Survey, headed by Clarence King, Yale class of 1862. Returning to Indiana in 1871, Clark married Mary Teegarden of LaPorte on 21 November 1872. The couple eventually had four children: Elsie, Marjorie, Kate, and Donald. In 1873 the family moved to Washington, DC, where Clark became private secretary to Senator Matthew H. Carpenter of Wisconsin, who was president *pro tem* of the U.S. Senate from March 1873 to December 1874.

In 1875 the family moved to rural Richland, California, and bought twenty-two acres of prime land on which they planted fruit trees. They sold oranges commercially and are credited with the idea of wrapping each orange in paper before shipping.

Clark founded and presided over the Santa Anna Valley Irrigation Company but contracted lung disease in 1882, followed by typhoid fever. He died on 24 April 1883.

References: Beta Theta Pi alumni directories; *Wabash Magazine*, III (June 1862), p. 380; *Wabash Magazine*, V (May 1864), p. 178; E. D. Daniels, *A Twentieth Century History and Biographical Record of LaPorte County, Indiana* (1904), pp. 415–16; Rose Clark's reminiscences in *LaPorte, Indiana: The First Hundred Years* (1932), Vol. IV, pp. 1739–46; *California of the South: A History* (1933), Vol. IV, pp. 667–69; and the *Yale Obituary Record, 1880–1890*.

CLARK, FREDERICK AUGUSTUS (1840–1920)

The West often beckoned irresistibly to Civil War veterans, as it did to other Americans in the generation after the end of hostilities and the return of the South to the Union. Fred Clark fought actively in the western campaigns, but drawn by foreign climates and opportunities, he sought his fortunes farther west.

Fred Clark was born in LaPorte, Indiana, on 25 June 1840, two years before his brother, Albert, whose story is also told in this narrative. Clark would almost certainly have graduated from Wabash had not the Civil War intervened. He entered the Preparatory Department in 1856 and continued in the Classical Course from 1858 to 1861. He was completing his junior year when news came of the firing on Fort Sumter, and so he enrolled in the Eleventh Indiana Regiment on 18 April 1861.

Clark's initial military commitment in Company I of the Eleventh Indiana was only for three months, but he re-enlisted in Company C of the Twenty-Ninth Regiment as a first lieutenant on 27 August. His second assignments included Nashville in November 1863 and Chattanooga in February 1864, but his health deteriorated seriously, forcing him to apply for a medical discharge. His certificate of disability, dated 30 March 1864, declared his malady to be "tubercular disease of the left lung, which has given him occasional difficulty for the last two years and for the last three months has unfitted him for any military duty, he being confined to his room." He was officially discharged on 10 April 1864.

After being mustered out, he spent part of 1865 in Chicago, and then traveled to Connecticut to visit his younger brother in New Haven. In 1867 he joined his older brother, Albert, on the expedition to chart the fortieth parallel, led by geologist Clarence King. Clark stayed in Nevada for a while and then moved on to Wyoming in 1868.

From 1869 to 1878 Clark worked for the government in Washington Territory, which would later become Washington State, and afterwards spent a brief time (1878–79) in Arkansas. He finally settled about as far as one can go in the continent, in San Francisco, where he married Sarah Louise Dutcher. In December 1887, after a divorce, Clark married a widow, Mrs. Mary Adeline Clements, who had a daughter, Pearl Adeline Clements, whom Frederick legally adopted.

Ever restless, Clark eventually returned back East. In 1904 he was employed by the United States Military Academy at West Point, where his supervisor wrote of him, "Although Mr. Clark is an older man than was desired for the place, he is fully able at present to fulfill all the requirements for the office."

In June 1913, at the age of seventy-three, Clark returned to Wabash College to receive a bachelor of arts degree. With his new degree he moved to New York City, where he died on 13 December 1920. His stepdaughter arranged for him to be buried in the Presidio National Cemetery in San Francisco, an appropriate spot for a man who had lived coast to coast.

References: See sources for Frederick Clark's brother, Albert; and also: *Indianapolis News*, 18 June 1913; *Wabash Magazine*, III (Dec. 1861), p. 93; information from the archives of the U.S. Military Academy, West Point; and military pension file from the National Archives, Washington, DC.

CLARK, RICHARD M. (1843–1865)

Richard Clark was born either in 1843 or 1844 in Salem. His parents, Richard Sr. and Martha Neal Clark, were from Kentucky. His siblings were Sarah, James, Martha, and Henry.

He responded to the call for volunteers by enrolling at Salem in Company E of the Fifty-Third Regiment on New Year's Day 1862. He was five feet nine inches tall, with blue eyes, light hair, and fair complexion, and he committed himself to three years' service. He was not actually mobilized for duty until 19 February 1862 at New Albany, and in less than nine months he was disabled by an injury. He spent at least twenty days in a hospital at Memphis and was formally discharged at Bolivar, Tennessee, on 18 October 1862.

Prior to serving in the military, Clark described himself as a mechanic and a painter, and he continued such work until lured by a college education at Wabash in the autumn of 1863. He spent one year in the Normal School at the college, but did not return in the fall of 1864, perhaps because of ill health. He died on 3 September 1865. He is buried in Crown Hill Cemetery, Salem.

References: Washington County Historical Society; 1850 and 1860 U.S. censuses; and his military service file at the National Archives, Washington, DC.

CLAYPOOL, HORATIO RANDOLPH (1828–1912)

One of the lamentable parts of service in the northern army was the tangled politics that often dominated life within units and beyond. Horatio Claypool's army experience illustrates this complicated situation. Since the North had a volunteer army until the draft was instituted in 1862, men were often serving with others from their town or area, and local quarrels or personalities affected officer designations. In early days, regiments and companies voted on their own leaders; as the war advanced, officer designation became more formalized. In Indiana,

Governor Oliver P. Morton retained final power. Since "advancement" was a primary goal on the part of a good many soldiers in the ranks and would spell future recognition in local communities, the race to the top sometimes became combative and ugly. Reputations could be ruined by "reports from the field." Claypool is an example of the toll unit politics took on a soldier. It is not clear to this day whether rumors and charges against him had any validity.

Claypool was born somewhere in Indiana on 24 February 1828. From 1849 to 1851 he was at Wabash College in its Preparatory Department. He then read law, perhaps back in his hometown of Attica, and was admitted to the Indiana bar in 1852. For the next two years he was a county prosecutor for the Twenty-Seventh District Court. Thereafter he apparently went into private practice.

During 1858–59 he published a magazine called *The People's Friend*. On 4 January 1859, in the town of Covington, he married Agnes L. Craine. Later that same year Claypool was elected to the Indiana House of Representatives.

Details are vague, but it seems as though Claypool entered some kind of state militia in May 1861 and was appointed a captain. In November 1861 he wrote to Governor Morton, lamenting the lack of field officers from Fountain County even though it had furnished some seven hundred recruits to date. Morton presumably took the hint and on 21 February 1862 commissioned Claypool a captain of Company B of the Sixty-Third regiment. He was not mustered in until 1 May, but soon found himself transported to the state of Maryland. One night in early June, while on guard duty in the rain, he became so chilled as to bring on painful rheumatism thereafter. This would plague him in years to come.

Nothing is more curious about his military service than its ending on 7 March 1863. He was branded as disloyal, and reports of this reached Morton. No clear explanation has survived to account for the grounds of his dismissal. The charge was equally puzzling to many of his men in the Sixty-Third regiment. Some forty-five non-commissioned officers and privates wrote a letter to Governor Morton on 14 March protesting his removal. They explained how they had "heard with deep regret that our worthy and esteemed Captain H. R. Claypool has been dismissed ... without any investigation or trial; that simply, on the representations of a few evil and designing persons who desire preferment...." The letter writers further explained that many of them would not have been "in the service had it not been with the understanding that H. R. Claypool was to be our Captain. He has been with us over fourteen months and some of us have known him a long time previous to our enlistment...." They testified to his efficiency and most especially to his loyalty, and they asked "for the good of [the] company and the service to have him restored...." If that was not possible, they petitioned the governor not to promote their current first lieutenant, "for he has not done one thing for the company."

The efforts of his men were unavailing, and Claypool found himself out of the service with a cloud hanging over him. He returned to Covington to live out his long life as a lawyer and occasional teacher. He and Agnes had four children: William (1859), Vernon (1862), Sally (1864), and Mary (1870).

In 1873 he served another year in the Indiana House of Representatives. From about 1886 on, Claypool was so troubled by rheumatism as to regard himself as three-quarters disabled for any physical labor. His doctor began giving him morphine for the pain, and by 1890 Claypool was injecting himself with the drug. It would seem quite likely that he became addicted to it, but that did not prevent him from living for several more decades. He died at Covington on 19 September 1912. Agnes decided to move to South Bend, Indiana, and later to Evansville, where she died on 29 May 1918.

References: Letters concerning Claypool's military service are in a folder for the Sixty-Third Regiment at the Archives Division of the Indiana State Library. His military pension file is at the National Archives, Washington, DC. See also: *Portrait and Biographical Record of Montgomery, Parke and Fountain Counties, Indiana* (1893), p. 324; *Biographical Directory of the Indiana General Assembly*, I (1980), p. 56.

CLELAND, JOHN EDWARD (1840–1919)

John Cleland was born in Greenwood on 30 December 1840, the son of Philip Sidney and Hannah Maria Titcomb Cleland, who also had three daughters: Tarne, Narcissa, and Maria.

In the autumn of 1856, Cleland joined the Preparatory Department of Wabash College, where he spent two years. He then began his freshman year in the Classical Course. As an undergraduate he was especially well known for his writing and involvement in student publications, and unlike many students at that time, he persevered and graduated in June 1862.

Even before finishing college, Cleland signed onto the state militia unit at New Albany, which was part of the Indiana Legion. Soon after graduating, on 1 August 1862, he committed to three years of military service, enrolling in Company I of the Seventieth Regiment. On 3 April 1864 he transferred as a captain to become adjutant general of the Forty-Fourth U.S. Colored Regiment stationed in Alabama. He was honorably discharged on 12 January 1865.

After the war Cleland went to Indianapolis to study law but after two years became involved in real estate. On 29 June 1869 he married Elizabeth J. Coughlin of Fitchburg, Massachusetts. They eventually had three children: Harriet, Frank, and Ethel.

In 1871 Cleland followed his literary interests and opened a bookselling and stationery business in Indianapolis that occupied him until the end of the century.

In 1899 he turned his hand to accounting in order to pave the way for another career as business director of the Indianapolis school system from 1900 to 1917. During these years he was also appointed secretary of the State Board of Education and also the president of the Indianapolis Literary Club.

The Cleland family lived a long time in Indianapolis. Elizabeth died in

1919, and John died on 27 December 1920, just three days short of his eightieth birthday. He was buried in Crown Hill Cemetery, survived by his three children.

References: 1905 alumni questionnaire in the Wabash College Archives. See also: *Wabash Magazine*, V (Feb. 1864), p. 153; *Wabash Record* (Jan. 1904), p. 15; and *Indianapolis News*, 28 Dec. 1920.

COBB, JAMES ALFRED (1845–1927)

James Cobb often went by his middle name, Alfred, while official records lists him variously as James A., and A. G. Cobb. Let us call him Alfred. He was born on 10 August 1845 in Aurora, Dearborn County, son of John and Maria Coffyn Cobb. He had at least two brothers, D. W. and Thomas J., as well as an adopted sister, Mary Walsh.

Cobb was at Wabash for only one year, 1863–64, in the Preparatory Department. Before the end of term, on 9 May 1864, he enrolled in Company I of the 134th Regiment. His tour of duty lasted one hundred days, and he spent most of his time guarding the rail lines between Nashville, Chattanooga, and Memphis, Tennessee. In June, while camped at Decatur, Alabama, he came down with severe diarrhea and piles, symptoms that afflicted him periodically for the rest of his life. He was mustered out on 3 September 1864.

After the war Cobb returned to Aurora, and later he moved to Illinois. Along the way he met Martha Ella Trumbower of Cincinnati; they were married on 2 November 1869. They eventually had three children: Jesse (1870), Grace (1872), and John (1880). The latter two predeceased their parents.

During the 1870s and 1880s the Cobb family returned to Alfred's hometown of Aurora, where Cobb manufactured chairs. In 1893 they went to Salt Lake City, Utah and then to Los Angeles.

While a passenger in an automobile in Pasadena on 1 May 1927, he was involved in an accident that fractured his skull and ended his life. He was buried in Forest Lawn Cemetery, as was his widow.

References: Pension records on file with the Department of Veterans Affairs in Indianapolis.

COBURN, JOHN (1825–1908)

John Coburn is regarded by members of Beta Theta Pi as the founder of the Wabash chapter of that fraternity. By Civil War buffs nationwide, however, he is known as a Civil War brigade commander who earned a reputation both notorious and commendatory. For three years, 1862–65, the regiment of this brigade stayed together, an unusual situation in the war. The brigade under Coburn's leadership served well in Kentucky until these units, the Eighty-Fifth Indiana, the Thirty-Third Indiana, the Nineteenth Michigan, and the Twenty-Second Wisconsin experienced disgrace when their commanding officer surrendered at Thompson's Station, Tennessee, on 5 March 1863. Coburn later explained his actions:

In early March 1863, he reported, he led his regiment, along with several thousand other Federal troops, into an ambush by an estimated fifteen thousand Confederates at Thompson's Station (or Spring Hill), Tennessee. Entirely cut off, they attempted a bayonet charge. In Coburn's own words: "I was convinced that a massacre would ensue, to little purpose; that a few might escape, but that many would fall in a vain struggle for life with unequal weapons. I ordered a surrender. I believe it was justified by the circumstances." Taken prisoner, they marched or were conveyed by boxcars from one prison camp to another until they reached Richmond and its renowned Libby Prison. According to Coburn, "Neither food, medical attendance, air or water were furnished, as the barest, sheerest, humanity would dictate. The iron-hearted monsters who had charge of the prison had no regard for suffering or for human life. We were closely confined the whole time; no visitors allowed; our correspondence withheld or destroyed for the most part." Coburn was exchanged on 5 May 1964 and ended his three-year commitment in September 1864.

Coburn was criticized for surrendering his troops but his options were anihillation or surrender. Present-day Civil War historians Larry Ligget and Frank Welcher have presented a more favorable view of Coburn's career and the battle at Thompson's Station than observers at the time. They effectively show that Gordon Granger, commander of the fort at Franklin, was less than ten miles away and should have sent support. Coburn's mostly green troops were facing the corps of two of the Confederacy's hardest fighting generals, Earl Van Dorn and Nathan Bedford Forrest. Coburn's brigade was outnumbered five to one. Few brigade commanders could have handled the situation as well as Coburn did. Later in the war the brigade acquitted themselves admirably at Resaca and Averasboro and Peach Tree Creek in the Atlanta campaign. They were the first troops to enter Atlanta. After the war Coburn advocated for the publication of *The War of the Rebellion: Official Records of the Union and Confederate Armies*. He and his brigade had moved towards erasing the stain unfairly placed on them.

Coburn was born on 27 October 1825 in Indianapolis, one of four sons of Henry Peter and Sarah Malott Coburn. His brothers were Edwin, Augustus, and Henry, and his sister was Caroline. He was educated at Marion County Seminary before attending Wabash from 1844 to 1846. His founding of Beta Theta Pi fraternity was the inauguration of the first Greek letter fraternity on the campus.

After two years at Wabash, he returned to Indianapolis. For the next three years he studied law and was admitted to the bar in 1849.

Coburn lost little time getting into politics and was elected in 1850 for a one-year term in the Indiana House of Representatives. On 9 March 1851 Coburn married Caroline Test in Indianapolis. They had a daughter, Sarah, who only lived from 20 November to 1 December 1852. They had no other children.

John Coburn. Courtesy Craig Dunn Collection

March 5, 1863: The Battle of Thompson's Station, morning. Courtesy Larry Ligget

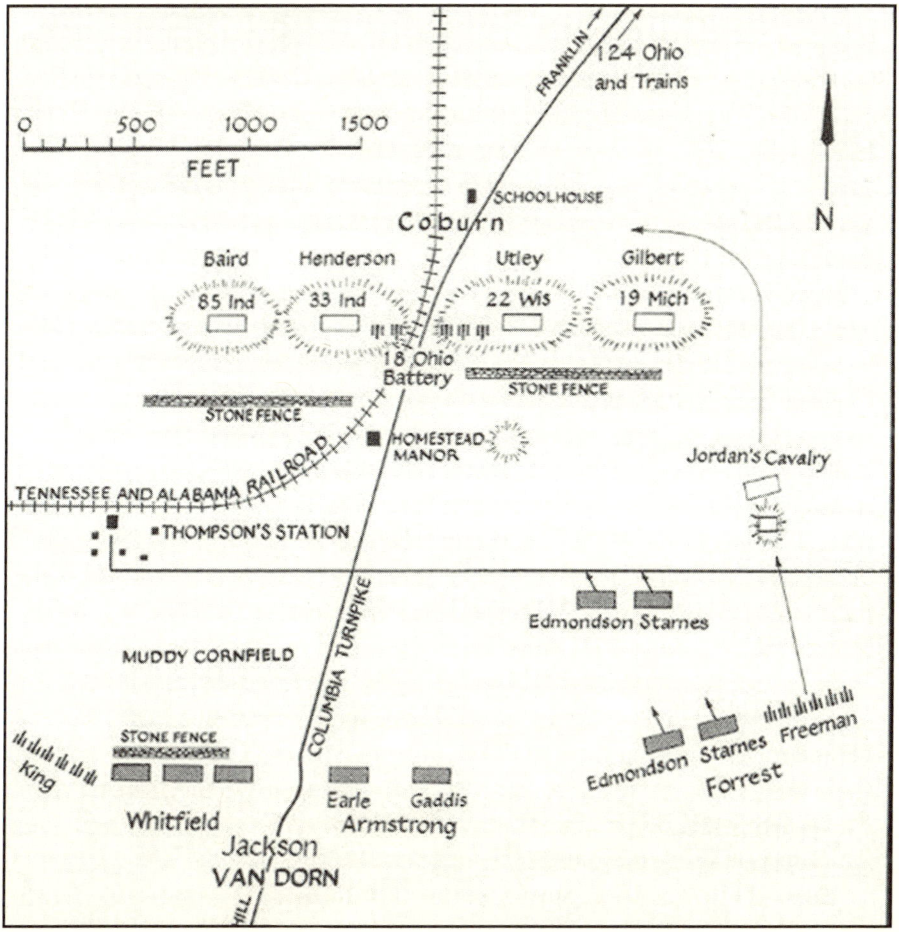

Coburn's next foray into politics came in 1859, when he was elected to the court of common pleas for Marion County, a post he retained until the outbreak of the Civil War. Being a fraternity brother of Governor Morton no doubt facilitated his appointment as colonel of the Thirty-third Indiana Regiment.

Following the war Coburn threw himself into legal and political affairs again. In October 1865 he was elected judge of Indiana's Fifth Circuit. Tempted by the opening of a congressional seat, he ran as a Republican in 1866 and enjoyed four successive terms in the House of Representatives, from 4 March 1867 to 3 March 1875. However, his bid for a fifth term met with defeat. The citizens of Indianapolis had good reason to be grateful for his many years of congressional service. As one wrote in *Early Reminiscences of Indianapolis*, "It is to his exertions and influence the people of this city are mostly indebted for the present free delivery system, by which they receive their mail matter at their doors."

Coburn was active in the life of Wabash College. From 1886 to 1896 he was second vice president of the Indiana Historical Society and then assumed the office of first vice president for life. He died on 28 January 1908, and his wife, Caroline, followed on 7 March 1909. They are both buried in Crown Hill Cemetery in Indianapolis.

References: *Biographical Directory of the American Congress* (1961), pp. 712–13; and *Biographical Directory of the Indiana General Assembly* (1980), I, p. 69. *Indianapolis News*, 29 Jan. 1908; L. J. Monks, *Courts and Lawyers of Indiana* (1916), III, p. 1141; J. H. B. Howland, *Early Reminiscences of Indianapolis* (1870), pp. 203–05; and 1905 Wabash College alumni questionnaire. The quotations by Coburn of his surrender and imprisonment in 1863 are to be found in E. Root et al., *The War of the Rebellion* (1901), series I, Vol. XXIII, part I, pp. 85–93. Dr. Erik Lindseth, Wabash Class of 1983, supplied background information on the Tau chapter of Beta Theta Pi. See also: Larry Ligget and Frank J. Welcher, *Coburn's Brigade* (Guild Press of Indiana, 2000). Larry Ligget generously reviewed and assisted in the writing of the above biography of Coburn.

COLLETT, EDWARD TIFFIN (1820–1878)

Wars have always taken a tremendous toll on the soldiers who fought them, and the Civil War was no exception. Suicides among soldiers occurred on both sides of the conflict both during and after the war. As many as one thousand men in the northern army killed themselves on active duty, with more suicides attributed to the Confederacy during the war. Discouragement over the failure of the Lost Cause, debilitating physical conditions towards the end of the conflict, and worries over those at home contributed to southern men's desperation. At the Battle of Franklin near the end of the war, six Confederate generals were killed, some of them observed by their troops seemingly hurling themselves toward the front of the action.

Edward Collett killed himself after the war, and it is not clear whether the psychological or physical effects of the war were among the causes of his suicide. Most of the war-related suicides occurred when men returned home and lived in pain from wounds or illness, could not adjust to new demands on the home front, or suffered from stress and "replay" of battlefield trauma. By the early 1900s physicians were recognizing certain symptoms like heart palpitations, shortness of breath, and mental distress and connecting them, for the first time in history, to re-experiencing the horrors of the war.

The first son of Josephus (1787–1872) and Elizabeth Tiffin Collett, Edward Collett was born in Terre Haute. There were two other children fathered by Josephus, who married three or four times.

The young Collett grew up on a farm in Vermillion County. In the autumn of 1836, he made his way from Eugene to Crawfordsville and enrolled in the college's Preparatory Department, where he remained for one academic year. He then apprenticed with a local doctor in Eugene and went to the University of Louisville Medical College in Kentucky. By 1857 he was practicing back in his hometown, but in 1860 he was in Lawrence County, Missouri.

On 18 August 1862 he joined the newly organized Indiana Seventy-First Regiment at Indianapolis as an assistant surgeon. Collett's regiment incorporated the Sixth Indiana Cavalry and almost immediately left for Kentucky. Two weeks later the regiment took part in the Battle of Richmond, where 215 were killed or wounded and 347 taken prisoner. Only 225 escaped to make their way back to Terre Haute. They returned to Kentucky and met with another disaster in December 1862, when 400 were taken prisoner by a much larger Confederate force. Again the regiment withdrew to Indiana, where it remained at Indianapolis until August 1863. Meanwhile Collett tended the sick in Cincinnati, but in February 1863 he resigned from the army and returned to Kansas. He was left five hundred acres of land by his father, but no money. He committed suicide without heirs.

References Rowena Horr of Topeka, Kansas, and John Collett of Indianapolis. See also: H. D. O'Donnell, *Eugene Township (Vermillion County Indiana): The First One Hundred Years, 1824–1924* (1953).

COLTRIN, NATHANIEL POTTER (1820–1877)

Nathaniel Coltrin does not appear on the Center Hall tablet commemorating Wabash College students who served in the Civil War. Born in Steubenville, Ohio, on 17 February 1820, he was the eldest of at least twelve children born to John and Ruth Potter Coltrin. Two of his younger brothers, Samuel and Isaac, also went to Wabash and served in the war.

In 1840 Coltrin entered the Preparatory Department, and in the autumn of 1841, he became a member of the freshman class, which graduated in July 1845 with bachelor of arts degrees.

In the autumn of 1846, Coltrin enrolled in Cincinnati's Lane Theological Seminary and after only one year was preaching at Auburn, Indiana. He was ordained in the Presbyterian Church in 1850 and for seven years served as a pastor in Illinois, including service in the towns of Jacksonville, Chandlerville, and Plymouth. From 1857 to 1877 he was a Congregational minister in Griggsville, Litchfield, Wythe Township, Sandoval, Clement, and Centralia.

In June 1864 Coltrin became chaplain of the Thirty-Third Illinois Volunteers and traveled to New Orleans to remain with the troops until well after the war. He was mustered out on 29 November 1865 at Vicksburg, Mississippi.

He apparently never married and died on 23 December 1877. He is buried in Elmwood Cemetery, Centralia, Illinois.

References: Illinois State Archives; *History of Pike County, Illinois* (1880), pp. 515, 519–21; *History of Hancock County, Illinois* (1880), pp. 581, 625–26.

COLTRIN, SAMUEL EDMUND (1830–1905)

As we have seen in the case of the older brother, Nathaniel, Samuel Coltrin was born on 24 May 1830 on the family farm in Lost Creek Township, Vigo County, one of twelve children born to John and Ruth Coltrin.

Following the death of his father in 1848, Coltrin worked on the farm until the autumn of 1851, when he entered the Preparatory Department of Wabash College and spent one year.

By the time of the 1860 census, Coltrin was well established, with real property valued at $1,500 and personal property of $500. He married Elizabeth D. Chamberlain on 28 March.

On 30 August 1862 Coltrin joined Company M of the Fourth Indiana Cavalry at Indianapolis for three years. He was released from service in June 1865 at Edgefield, Tennessee, the state in which he had spent much of his time in the army.

He devoted the rest of his life to farming, supplemented at times with teaching. His eldest son, Edwin, born about 1862, also became a teacher. His other children were Mary (1863?), Charles (1867?), Emma (1871?), and Nina (1873?). A sixth child, Lucy, lived only from 1864 to 1875.

Samuel's wife, Elizabeth, died in 1899, and he followed her on 5 June 1905. They are buried in the Coltrin Cemetery near Terre Haute.

References: H. T. Bradsby, *History of Vigo County, Indiana* (1891), p. 618; and military pension file at the National Archives, Washington, DC. See also the sources for Nathaniel.

CONDIT, AARON DAYTON (1843–1910)

Aaron Condit was one of the three children of Charlotte T. Coon and Daniel Dayton Condit, the other two being John and Blackford. Aaron was born on 17 March 1843 in Terre Haute, where he attended the local schools.

In September 1862 he enrolled in the second year of the Preparatory Department at Wabash, returning the following year as a freshman, but in May 1864 he enrolled in Company C of the 133rd Indiana Regiment for a term of one hundred days. The regiment initially pursued a guerrilla band commanded by General Nathan Bedford Forrest, but failing in this quest, it marched to Alabama and was involved in guard duty and occasional skirmishing.

Condit was released from the army in early September 1864, just in time to enter Dartmouth College, where he was one of twenty-eight in his class and graduated in 1868. On 29 September 1869 he married Elizabeth Amelia Lord, a native of Vermont. Between 1872 and 1873 he worked as a druggist in Mankato, Minnesota, and then moved to St. Paul to establish his own drugstore.

In 1876 a son, Dayton Lord Condit, was born, the only one of Aaron and Elizabeth's five children to survive past infancy. In the 1880s Condit changed careers and became an agent for real estate, insurance, and loans.

Although he had served only one hundred days in the Civil War, he contracted chronic diarrhea in the service, a sickness that plagued him throughout his life and contributed to his demise in St. Paul on 28 February 1910.

References: Dartmouth College Archives. See the Dartmouth College Report of 1913 and Dartmouth *Alumni Magazine* (March 1911), p. 186.

CONNER, JOHN COGGSWELL (1842–1873)

Occasionally, a Wabash student's father also attended the college and served in the Civil War with his son. William W. Conner was at Wabash in 1834–35 and went on to become Hamilton County clerk. John Conner was the eldest of his six children with Amanda Coggswell and was born in Noblesville, Hamilton County, on 27 October 1842.

John Conner attended the college's Normal School from 1858 to 1860 and then went to the United States Naval Academy in Annapolis, Maryland, from 1861 to 1862. He didn't graduate from the academy, but he received a commission as a second lieutenant of Company F of the Sixty-Third Indiana Regiment and soon was promoted to first lieutenant. He received a medical and honorable discharge on 20 June 1864 and returned to Noblesville to begin studying law.

In 1866 Conner ran for election to the Indiana General Assembly. Failing this, he reentered the army, securing a commission in July 1866 as a captain in the Forty-First United States Regiment of colored troops stationed in Texas, where he remained for three years, resigning in November 1869.

Once Texas was readmitted to the Union in 1870, Conner ran for the United States Congress. He entered the House of Representatives in March 1870 and was elected for another term from 4 March 1871 to 3 March 1873.

At some point Conner married Alice Finch. They had two daughters, Julia and Helen. Conner died in Washington, DC, on 10 December 1873, and Alice died on 25 March 1878, when she was only thirty-one years old. Both are buried in Noblesville, Indiana.

References: J. P. Dunn, *Memorial Record of Distinguished Men of Indianapolis and Indiana* (1912), pp. 387–89; *Biographical Directory of the American Congress*; J. H. Burgess, *Hamilton County in the Civil War* (1972), pp. 216–17; information from the Noblesville Public Library and from the United States Naval Academy.

CONNER, WILLIAM WINSHIP (1820–1890)

William Conner was born in Connersville on 27 May 1820, one of two sons (the other was Henry J. Conner) of John and Lavina Winship Conner. From 1834 to 1835 he was enrolled in the Preparatory Department of Wabash, and he then attended Hanover College.

Conner married Amanda Coggswell on 11 November 1841, and they went on to have six children, the eldest of whom was John. William entered Indiana politics in 1843, being elected to the house at the early age of twenty-three, and served in the senate from 1845 to 1848. He served as Hamilton County clerk from 1859 to 1862.

He joined the Sixty-Fifth Indiana Regiment as a first lieutenant and when Morgan's raid threatened southern Indiana in 1863, he served as a captain in the 109th "Minutemen" Regiment of Indiana Volunteers for the brief period of 10–17 July 1863. Once the threat abated, he returned to his farm near Noblesville.

He was the editor of the *Noblesville Ledger* and served as state adjutant general in 1873. He also was a Whig/Republican, Freemason, and Odd Fellow.

Amanda died in 1871, but William lived until 16 April 1890.

References: David G. Vanderstel, Conner Prairie; *Biographical Directory of the Indiana General Assembly* (1980), I, p. 76; see also the sources for William Conner's son, John.

COOPER, LOUIS (1837–1917)

The first name of this Wabash student was spelled Lewis, but his gravestone shows a different spelling: Louis. He was born in Franklin Township, Montgomery County, in January 1837. His father was Jonathan and his mother Lizabeth. His siblings were Lizabeth, born in 1833; Curttia (?), 1840; John, 1843; George,

1848; and James, 1850.

Louis Cooper attended the Normal School of Wabash for only the one year, 1860–61, returning to the family farm near Darlington to help his widowed mother and siblings. At about this time he was married to Elizabeth, and they had two children, Mary and John.

Cooper joined Company I of the Eleventh Indiana Regiment on 27 February 1865 and was mustered out at Baltimore on 26 July.

He worked the farm as late as 1900. Elizabeth died sometime during the next ten years, and he married sixty-nine-year-old Phoebe Armstrong Hampton in 1913. Louis died on 9 February 1917 and is buried in the St. James Lutheran Cemetery of Franklin Township.

References: Obituary in the *Crawfordsville Daily Journal*, 9 Feb. 1917, p. 1.

CORY, AUGUSTUS M. (1843–1924)

Augustus Cory and his older brother Daniel both came to Wabash from nearby Thorntown in the autumn of 1860. They were the sons of David and Margaret Cory. Augustus was born on 31 January 1843. He also had two sisters, Mary and Malvina.

With the completion of his second year at Wabash in June 1862, Cory enrolled in Company D of the Seventy-Second Regiment in Boone County. By November the regiment was in Tennessee, where it remained for much of the following year and saw action on 19–20 September 1863 at Chickamauga, Georgia. In early 1864 the regiment joined others under General Sherman as they carried out raids in Mississippi. On 22 February Cory was wounded while trying to cover the retreat of General William Sooy Smith against the onslaught of the Confederates under Nathan Bedford Forrest at Okolona, Mississippi. Later that spring he rejoined his regiment as it supported Sherman in the campaign against Atlanta. His three years in the army came to an end at Nashville, where he was honorably discharged as a sergeant on 26 July 1865.

Returning to Thorntown, Cory secured employment with the Shipp dry goods company and married the boss's daughter, Mary Alabama Shipp, on 12 October 1868.

In 1882 the couple moved to Minnesota, and five years later they took up residence in Minneapolis, where Cory became a salesman for the Wyman-Partridge Company.

Cory died at home in Minneapolis on 2 September 1924 and was buried in Lakewood Cemetery, survived only by his wife Mary.

References: Thorntown Public Library and an obituary in the *Minneapolis Tribune*, 2 Sept. 1924.

CORY, DANIEL WEBSTER (1841–1921)

Daniel Webster Cory often reversed his names, leading to some confusion. He was the elder of two brothers to attend Wabash College and to serve in the Civil War. We have just documented the story of brother Augustus. Their parents were David and Margaret, who lived in Thorntown.

Cory was born in Boone County on 18 January 1841. He entered the Normal School of Wabash in the fall of 1860 and remained only one school year. On 23 July 1861 he heeded the call for recruits and enrolled as a private in Company G of the Eleventh Regiment for three years. The regiment gathered at Indianapolis and by the end of August was encamped at Paducah, Kentucky. In early April 1862 they saw action at Fort Henry, Fort Donelson, and Shiloh. At Crump's Landing in Virginia, Cory was badly wounded. After a lapse of sixty days he rejoined his regiment stationed at Memphis, but he was granted an early discharge at New Iberia, Louisiana, on 14 December 1863. Undeterred by the lingering results of his injury, Cory re-enlisted in the Eleventh and on 19 September 1864, while under fire at Opequon Creek, Virginia, he fell victim to a shell burst that permanently affected his hearing. He served until the war's end and was discharged at Baltimore on 26 July 1865.

Cory returned to Thorntown to become a farmer and married a local woman, Nancy M. Fall, on 25 February 1866. Their first child, Nora, died in infancy in 1867. Their other children were Thorley, born 1868; Mattie, 1870; Eva, 1872; Charles, 1874; and Josie, 1878.

From 1879 to 1882 the family was in Vermilion County, Illinois, then moved to Michigan for two years before settling first in Franklin County, Nebraska, and finally in Merna, Nebraska, where Daniel Cory died on 12 December 1921.

References: Cory pension file at the National Archives, Washington, DC.

COWAN, EDWARD HOWARD (1846-1942)

Edward Cowan was born in Frankfort, Indiana, on 21 December 1846, the son of Harriet Janney Cowan and John Maxwell Cowan, Wabash class of 1842. Edward had two brothers, James and John, both of whom went to Wabash, and a sister, Laura.

At the age of 15, young Edward enrolled at Wabash College, and spent the school year 1862-1863 in the Preparatory Department. The following year he was admitted to the freshman class, and returned in 1864-1865 to repeat his freshman year, probably because his family moved to Crawfordsville when his father became a judge of the Indiana 8th circuit court.

He stayed on at Wabash for two more years, and then left to study medicine at Stockwell with Dr. Moses Baker, the first physician-surgeon in Indiana to successfully perform a Caesarian section where both mother and child lived. Eventually Edward graduated from the Miami Medical College of Cincinnati and spent a brief residency in New York City before returning to Crawfordsville.

His military service was relatively brief, sandwiched between his two freshman years during the summer of 1864. After outfitting himself with military clothing and gear to the amount of $21.38, he accompanied his regiment, the 135th, through the states of Tennessee and Alabama.

In 1877 he married Lucy Ayers of Louisville, Kentucky. They eventually had two children: Elizabeth and John. Lucy died in 1924, and shortly thereafter Edward retired from active practice.

Over the years Edward did a good deal of travelling, both within the United States and abroad. After his wife's death, he began spending winters with his daughter, Mrs. Lewis R. Ferguson of Dallas, Texas, and then returning to 408 South Grant Avenue in the spring. During his annual visit in 1942 he took ill and was unable to journey back to Crawfordsville and died on 2 August 1942. He was interred in Oak Hill Cemetery after a memorial service in the Wabash College Chapel.

At the time of his death he was the last of the Civil War veterans residing in Montgomery County, and the last survivor among the Wabash College alumni.

References: *Montgomery County Magazine* (June 1977); Crawfordsville Chamber of Commerce, Citizens Historical Association (1934); *Indianapolis Star*, 3 August 1942.

COWGILL, CARY E. (1843–1914)

Cary (or Carey) Cowgill was born in Winchester on 5 August 1843, one of six children of Calvin and Mary Flannigan Cowgill. The others were Caroline, Emily, Kate, and Thomas and one other. Three years later the family moved to the town of Wabash, Indiana, which would remain their home for the rest of the century.

Cowgill's father was a successful lawyer and legislator, having served in the Indiana General Assembly from 1851 to 1852 and also as a member of the United States House of Representatives from 1879 to 1881. Cary followed in his footsteps, not only becoming a lawyer but also serving a term in the Indiana legislature in 1873–74.

Cowgill went to a college preparatory school in his hometown from 1858 to 1862 and then enrolled at Union College in New York State. However, illness forced him to return home, and he entered Wabash College as a sophomore on 1 November 1862. For unknown reasons Cowgill left college in February 1864 and returned home to become a temporary clerk in the office of the provost marshal, headed by his father.

At the call for troops to support General Sherman's march on Atlanta, Cowgill volunteered, and on 18 May 1864 he enlisted as a second lieutenant in Company G of the 138th Regiment for a term of one hundred days. The regiment's assignment was to guard rail lines in Tennessee that were vital to resupplying Sherman's forces. He mustered out on 30 September 1864.

Cowgill returned to Wabash and began studying law in his father's office. He was admitted to the bar in 1866 and for a time served as a deputy district attorney. He practiced law in Wabash for forty-eight years and included among his important clients the Cincinnati, Wabash and Michigan Railroad and the Cleveland, Cincinnati, Chicago and St. Louis Railroad. The Cowgill-DeHart House still stands as a landmark at 86 Walnut Street.

On 10 September 1877 Cowgill married Nancy E. Stuart, and they had two children: Stuart Calvin (1880–1951) and a stillborn infant in 1885. Nancy died in 1934. Cowgill lived until 4 May 1914 and was buried at Falls Memorial Gardens in Wabash.

References: Wabash County Historical Society Newsletter (summer 1980), pp. 1–3, and *Biographical Directory of the Indiana General Assembly* (1980), I, p. 81.

COX, WILLIAM H. (1840–1887)

Service in artillery in the Civil War was exciting but dangerous. Cannons were heavy and unwieldy and often had to be hauled over hills and rocky terrain. Misfire explosions were common. William Cox went from classrooms at Wabash, where he studied from 1857 to 1859, to the light artillery, with a brief stay as a clerk in Lafayette. From then on his service career was full and contradictory.

On 20 November 1861 Cox secured a commission as second lieutenant in Company C of the Tenth Light Artillery but was not called until 25 January 1862. During the next two years he was involved in battles or campaigns in Mississippi, Alabama, Tennessee, Kentucky, and Georgia, including Nashville, Shiloh, and Corinth.

Cox returned to Lafayette briefly to recruit new volunteers and then was assigned to the Fourteenth Army Corps of the Department of the Cumberland in Nashville. In December 1862, acting as an inspector, he procured forty-eight bushels of corn and sought reimbursement from the army. This outraged one of his commanding officers, who complained "that he had foraged without an order in direct opposition to orders from these headquarters." Cox was placed under arrest pending an inquiry, and by 25 January 1863 he was released and exonerated.

In September 1863 Cox and his Tenth Battery were in the thick of things, and he described his precarious situation to his superiors from a ridge at Lookout Mountain, Tennessee. He regarded his location as "the key to Chattanooga." However, the Confederates were bombarding his position, and he doubted if he and his comrades could hold out much longer, unless added fortifications were built and more troops and guns brought forward. Several weeks later, in early October, he was still clinging to Lookout Mountain and describing for his commanders the exchanges of artillery taking place.

In November 1863 Cox received a medical discharge and returned to his family at 40 North Fifth Street in Lafayette, where he had been born in 1840. The date of his marriage to Henrietta M. (Cox) is uncertain.

In the mid-1870s Cox went to Denver, Colorado, where he died on 17 March 1887. There is some ambiguity surrounding his death. According to a local newspaper, he was working as a contractor for the Union Pacific Railroad when he was murdered at Naomi, Colorado. He may have been badly wounded there and survived long enough to sign a will that left everything to his wife.

References: Tippecanoe County Historical Association, Ms. Dorothy Van Cleef in particular. Quotations regarding Cox's military experiences are in *The War of the Rebellion*, Series I, Vol. XX, part 1, pp. 477–78; series I, Vol. XXX, part 3, pp. 829–30; and series I, Vol. XXX, part 4, p. 103. See also: R. P. Dehart, *Past and Present of Tippecanoe County, Indiana*, I (1909), p. 221; *Biographical Record and Portrait Album of Tippecanoe County, Indiana* (1888), p. 308; [Lafayette] *Leader*, 27 April 1877 and 17 June 1877; the National Archives, Washington, DC; and the *Summit County Journal*, 19 March 1887.

CRAIG, SAMUEL M. (1838–1870)

Samuel Craig was born on 8 June 1838 in Franklin Township, Montgomery County. His parents were Jemima and David, and his siblings included William, David, Charles, and Cynthia.

When Craig entered the Normal School at Wabash College in the fall of 1857, his family had moved to Crawfordsville from a farm nearby. He studied at the college for one academic year and then returned to farming.

On 18 September 1861 he enlisted in Company B of the Tenth Indiana Volunteers for a term of three years. He was badly wounded at Mill Springs, Kentucky, on 19 January 1862 and spent a long time in hospital before being given a medical discharge on 5 July 1862. He died in Montgomery County on 26 August 1870 and is buried in the Masonic Cemetery at Crawfordsville.

References: *History of Montgomery County, Indiana* (Bowen and Co., 1913), I, p. 107; and the Military Archives Division of the Indiana State Library.

CRAIG, WILLIAM (1829–1886)

William Craig was born in 1829 and entered the Normal School of Wabash College in the fall of 1847, when he was living in Newport under the guardianship of someone listed as O. Craig. During the course of his two years at Wabash (1847–49), he secured an appointment to the United States Military Academy at West Point, thanks to Indiana congressman R. W. Thompson.

Craig married sometime in 1852 and graduated from the academy in 1853. The next year he was posted to Kentucky as a brevet second lieutenant. The following year he went to the New Mexico Territory, where he spent the next ten years and became successively a second lieutenant and first lieutenant in the United States Eighth Infantry. He seems to have spent the time before the Civil War out west. A Las Vegas newspaper characterized Craig as "one of the bravest young officers ever stationed on the frontier. As an Indian fighter prior to 1860 he had few equals, and was beloved by such men as Kit Carson, St. Brain, Simpson and Kent for his rare courage and the trials and hardships they together endured in combating the Navajos and Apaches along the Rio Grande Valley."

A few weeks after the outbreak of the Civil War, Craig was promoted to captain and assumed new duties as an assistant quartermaster in western Virginia, a tour of duty that lasted until August 1862, when he returned to New Mexico in a similar capacity.

Craig resigned from the army in April 1864 and devoted the next few years to farming near Fort Garland, Colorado, until gold-mining fever seized him. For the rest of his life he combined large-scale ranching with mineral exploration.

He died in Santa Fe on 27 May 1886, known by the honorific title of Colonel Craig, and was survived by his widow.

References: W. H. Powell, *List of Officers of the Army of the United States, 1789–1900* (1900); *Annual Register of the Association of Graduates Office, United States Military Academy* (1886); G. W. Cullum (comp.), *Biographical Register of the Officers and Graduates of the United States Military Academy* (1891). The above quotation comes from a Las Vegas newspaper cited in *Annual Reunion of the Association of Graduates Office, United States Military Academy* (1886), II, pp. 130–31.

CRANE, JACOB H. (1835–1910)

Jacob Crane was born in Fountain County on 21 October 1835, the son of Elizabeth Sharp and Henry Crane. His siblings were Lockey, Jonathan, George, Joseph, and Mary

Crane attended Wabash, studying in the Normal School for one year, 1855–56, and then returned home to work on his father's farm and teach at a local school.

He was in New York State when the Civil War broke out, and he enlisted in Company H of the Second Regiment of New York Cavalry on 3 August 1861. At the time he was described as having gray eyes, dark hair, and a dark complexion and standing five feet six inches tall. Being older than many of the other recruits, he was made a sergeant, and soon found himself in Washington, DC. Early in 1862, while marching from Winchester to White House Landing, Virginia, he was stricken with severe rheumatism, a condition that bothered him the rest of his life. He was mustered out in December 1863 but almost immediately re-enlisted at Stevensburg, Virginia, and served until 23 June 1865.

Back in the Midwest, Crane settled briefly in Vermilion County, Illinois, and then resumed farming in Indiana in Fountain County. In 1882 he joined his younger brother, Joseph, in a move to Tennessee, where he farmed for the next eight years. In 1890 he took up residence in Bryson City, Swain County, North Carolina, and died there on 24 July 1910. He is buried in the Bryson City Cemetery, survived only by his younger brother, George, of Veedersburg, Fountain County, Indiana.

References: *History of Fountain County, Indiana* (1983), pp. 297, 307, 469; T. Clifton, *Past and Present of Fountain and Warren Counties, Indiana* (1913), p. 546; and military service and pension files at the National Archives, Washington DC.

CRANE, SAMUEL C. (1825–1905)

Details of the life of Samuel Crane are sketchy. His parents were James Coggswell and Mary Hubbard Crane, and both were from New York City, where Samuel was probably born in May 1825. He entered the Preparatory Department of Wabash in 1837 at the age of twelve, and after five years he embarked on the Classical Course that led in June 1846 to a bachelor of arts degree. In 1848 he was a teacher, and ten years later he edited a newspaper in Pennsylvania, the *Bradford Weekly Miner*, a stint that lasted a little over a year.

In December 1863 Crane enlisted in Company G of the 124th Indiana Regiment, which was sent to Tennessee to engage the Confederates in major action and subsequently to Georgia, where it skirmished at Lost Mountain and Kennesaw Mountain. During July and August 1864 Crane participated in the siege of Atlanta, and the following spring he fought in North Carolina. He was wounded four times and given a medical discharge on 8 May 1865.

In 1878 he was a special correspondent for the *Masonic Advocate*, published in Indianapolis. At some point he married Mary E. Belden Beckley of Meriden, Connecticut, a widow with three children. They lived in Guilford, Connecticut, where Samuel died on 16 October 1905. Mary died on 11 July 1910, and they are both buried in the Alderbrook Cemetery in Guilford.

References: *Wabash Record*, XXX (Nov. 1930), p. 64; *Wabash Record*, (Jan. 1906), p. 62; V. Hatch (ed.), *Illustrated History of Bradford, McKean County, Pennsylvania* (1901), pp. 20–22; [Guilford] *Shoreline Times*, 19 Oct. 1905 and 14 July 1910. Also the Carnegie Public Library of Bradford and the Guilford Public Library.

CRAWFORD, CHARLES MARSHALL (1845–1917)

Charles Crawford was born in Crawfordsville, Indiana, on 22 September 1845, the son of Henry and Lydia Marshall Crawford. He had an older brother, Henry E., whose mother, Mary Cochran, was his father's first wife, and a sister,

Clara. His father is credited with opening the first general store in town in 1827.

At the age of fourteen, young Charles came to Wabash and enrolled in the Preparatory Department. In the autumn of 1862, he became a freshman and returned the next year as a sophomore. In December 1863 he was one of the featured speakers at a special college convocation, speaking on "The Conquest of Granada."

In the spring of 1864, the call came for troops to support Sherman's march on Atlanta, and Crawford responded by enrolling in Company D of the 135th Indiana Regiment. He was formally recruited by Captain Walter Bruce Carr, who had attended Wabash just before Crawford arrived. The regiment spent most of its one hundred days guarding the railroad lines through Tennessee in order that Sherman be adequately supplied for the Atlanta campaign. On 29 September 1864 Crawford was mustered out at Indianapolis.

Like many others, service in the army put an end to Crawford's further formal education at Wabash. He attended a commercial college in Poughkeepsie, New York, before returning to Crawfordsville.

During the 1870s he was president of the Crawfordsville Casket Company, and in 1878 he married Anna Clara Milligan. They had two children, Alexander M. and Lydia M.

In 1884 he became president of the Indiana Wire and Fence Company, and eventually he was appointed first vice president of the Elston Bank. In 1900 he authorized the construction of a new hotel and called it the Crawford Hotel, characterized as "one of the best, neatest and coziest hostelries in the state" in a standard history of Montgomery County. It still functioned in the 1960s.

When Wabash College compiled its first alumni directory in the 1890s, it characterized Crawford's occupation as "capitalist," which nicely summed up his successful business career, spent mostly in his hometown of Crawfordsville.

Late in his life Crawford entered a sanitarium in Battle Creek, Michigan, where he had a stroke and died on 30 August 1917. His widow lived in Crawfordsville until she died in 1939. Both are buried in Oak Hill Cemetery.

References: *Wabash Magazine*, V (Feb. 1864), p. 59; *Wabash Magazine*, VII (June 1866), p. 14; *Crawfordsville Journal*, 7 Sept. 1917; *History of Montgomery County, Indiana* (Bowen and Co., 1913), I, pp. 656–58.

CRAWFORD, HENRY E. (1840–1923)

Henry Crawford was the only surviving child of Henry and Mary Cochrane Crawford. Mary died at the age of twenty-five, probably of complications from Henry's birth on 28 January 1840. Henry's father was an extraordinarily wealthy farmer in Montgomery County, with land valued at $50,000 in 1860 and $100,000 in 1870. With his second wife, Lydia Marshall, he had another son, Charles Marshall, who also went to Wabash and served in the Civil War.

Crawford spent 1853–56 in the Preparatory Department of Wabash College, followed by a return to the family farm until August 1862, when he enrolled for three years as a private in Company C of the Seventieth Indiana Regiment, commanded by the future president of the United States, Colonel Benjamin Harrison. The regiment went first to Louisville by train and remained there several months protecting rail lines, but in November it was sent to Tennessee, where it became part of the extensive Atlanta campaign. By the fall of 1864, it formed part of Sherman's march through Georgia, culminating at Savannah, and then was diverted into South Carolina. When Lee surrendered, they were in North Carolina, and Crawford was mustered out at Washington, DC, on 8 June 1865.

On 24 February 1886 Crawford married Katherine McDonald. They had two children, one of whom died in infancy; the other was named Kitty May.

Although Crawford owned extensive farms throughout the county, he also maintained a residence in Crawfordsville, where he died on 24 August 1923. He is buried in Oak Hill Cemetery together with his widow, who died in 1933.

References: *Crawfordsville Journal*, 24 Aug. 1923; Crawford family file at the Ramsay Archives, Wabash College.

CRAWFORD, JAMES BRATTIN (1833–1882)

There seem to have been many Crawfords in Crawfordsville; some suppose its founders gave their name to the village carved out of a wilderness. Instead, it was named after a political official named Crawford.

Our James Crawford was born on 18 September 1833, the second white male child born in the frontier village of Crawfordsville. He was one of the six children of John and Sarah Daniels Crawford, the others being Albert, Alice, Laura, Thiston, and John.

Crawford studied in the Preparatory Department of Wabash College for four years, 1847–51, but then withdrew. He married Martha E. Andrews of Montgomery County on 23 September 1857. She may have died in childbirth, because he married Mary J. Crain (or Crane) on 12 April 1859. During the Civil War Crawford spent two years in the quartermaster's office in Indianapolis. During Morgan's raid, he joined the 108th Infantry Regiment (Minutemen) briefly.

Between 1865 and 1868 he assisted his father, the newly appointed postmaster for Crawfordsville under the Andrew Johnson administration, and then undertook a series of assistant clerkships under several clerks of the circuit court.

In the mid-1870s Crawford took a job with the state auditor's office in Indianapolis. Returning to Crawfordsville, he worked for the wholesale grocery firm of T. N. Lucas. Crawford died from consumption on 23 March 1882.

References: *Crawfordsville Evening Journal*, 24 March 1882; *Crawfordsville Weekly Review*, 25 March 1882.

Archibald Allen

Zeph Ball

John Beach

Ben Bowman

Edmund Brown

Henry Campbell

Albert Clark

J. E. Cleland

A Soldiers' Album

CRAWFORD, JOHN A. (1841–1917)

John Crawford was the son of Elizabeth Cline and John Crawford and one of seven children. He was born on the family farm a few miles west of Rob Roy.

When he enrolled at Wabash in the autumn of 1861, he was working as a farm laborer, but heeded the call for military service on 14 June of that year and was mustered into Company G of the Fifteenth Indiana Regiment for a term of three years, mustering out on 25 June 1864.

On 8 April 1869 he married Margaret Marquess; they had five daughters and one son.

Crawford returned to farming grain and cultivating a fruit orchard. He died on 27 August 1917 from injuries suffered while pruning his fruit trees. Margaret lived a few more years and died in 1926. They are both buried in Beulah Cemetery, Shawnee Township.

References: Betty Clawson of the Fountain County Historical Society. See also: *Attica Ledger Tribune*, 31 Aug. 1917.

CROUSE, JEROME H. (1843–1908)

It is difficult not to compare the careers of the many ten-day soldiers who joined the fray to repel Morgan the Raider with those who spent three or four years in the midst of bullets and bloody assaults. It must be supposed that all did their part, but the three-year soldiers themselves were very aware of the difference.

Jerome Crouse seemed to seek action and had a wartime career filled with excitement, danger, and pain. He had been born at Dayton, Indiana, on 30 December 1843 and attended the Preparatory Department at Wabash from 1860 to 1862. He enrolled in the Tenth Light Artillery at Lafayette on 3 January 1862 for three years.

According to the diary of his fellow Wabash student, Henry Campbell, Crouse distinguished himself, especially at the Battle of Chickamauga in Tennessee in September 1863, and had a lucky break that could have been a serious injury: "Sergt. Crouse received a shot through the rear of his saddle, passing through his blanket, overcoat & portable writing desk, and lodged in his coat tail." Other battles in which Crouse participated were Pittsburg Landing, Corinth (3–4 October 1862), Murfreesboro (13 July 1862), Stones River (31 December 1862–2 January 1863) Lookout Mountain (24 November 1863), Mission[ary] Ridge (24–25 November 1863), and Atlanta.

At one point the remnant of his battery was put aboard a gunboat, and Crouse served temporarily in the navy. He had many harrowing escapes, including being run over by a caisson and having his arm almost torn off while trying to stop a team of sixteen stampeding mules. Although small of stature and prone to poor health, he served his time in the army until he was discharged at Nashville in January 1865.

Returning to Dayton, he studied medicine with his father before attending Rush Medical College in Chicago, graduating in 1867. After an additional year at the Jefferson Medical College of Philadelphia, he served as a physician in Dayton and its environs.

On 6 October 1868 he married Sophia Catherine Bartmess, but she died the following March. In 1894 he married a widow, Lena Nicely, who had one son, David. Crouse died on 16 June 1908 and is buried in the Dayton Cemetery.

References: *Wabash Magazine*, III (Feb. 1862), p. 190; *Wabash Magazine*, VII (June 1866), p. 8; *Biographical History of Tippecanoe, White, Jasper, Newton, Benton, Warren, and Pulaski Counties, Indiana* (1899); and *Lafayette Daily Courier*, 16 June 1908.

CROSIER, EDWARD STOKOE (1832–1891)

Being a surgeon was not the only way Wabash students, former and prospective, performed some sort of medical service in the War Between the States, as it was sometimes called in the years after it was fought. Their service might range from being a hospital steward or hospital visitor to an ambulance driver. Still, being a surgeon gave men the top respect from all who served, and it was a grueling and physically difficult job in those early days of medicine.

Edward Crosier was indeed a surgeon, perhaps head surgeon, of General Hospital No. 6, one of the largest and most significant hospitals in the North, in New Albany. Previous to that he had been a captain in the Mauckport Rifles, a contingent of the Indiana Legion, from October 1861 to February 1862.

Crosier was born on 5 March 1832, the oldest of seven children born to Adam and Sarah Douglas Crosier of Laconia, Boone Township, Harrison County. Their other children were Elizabeth, Douglas, Mary, Isabell, Robert, and Minerva.

Prior to entering Wabash he was a farmer, as was his father. He was enrolled in the Preparatory Department for only one year, 1852–53. However, by the spring of 1856, he had secured admission to the medical department of the University of Michigan at Ann Arbor. His training there sheds light on the medical training of the day.

During his first year at Michigan, Crosier wrote several postcards to his parents telling them about the exams he was required to take in order to be admitted: "In Latin I will have no difficulty, but the rub will be in Greek." In November he described his daily routine: "We go to college early in the morning and have lectures until 12 o'clock and then one lecture after dinner and then are in the dissecting room until dark. The rest of the time I have to study like everything."

Crosier secured his MD in 1861, and because he was a mature student, he was placed in a position of responsibility right away at the hospital in New Albany, where he stayed during the war.

In 1867 he acted briefly as the editor of the *New Albany Commercial*. The proprietor, James P. Luse, was appointed surveyor of customs for Louisville and persuaded Crosier to leave New Albany and become his assistant in Kentucky. Crosier initially married Sarah A. Neely in Harrison County on 19 March 1868, but married a second time in Floyd County on 8 December 1869. He and Caroline Vincent had two children: Irene born about 1874 and Ethel about 1878.

He was professor of chemistry and microscopy at Louisville Medical College from 1870 to 1871. Crosier married again in the late 1880s and had a daughter, Gertrude, with his third wife, Lena. Together they ran a pharmacy below their residence.

He died at home on 9 June 1891 and is buried in the Crosier Cemetery in Boone Township, Harrison County.

References: B. N. Griffing, *An Atlas of Harrison County, Indiana* (1882), p. 45; F. A. Bulleit, *Illustrated Atlas and History of Harrison County, Indiana* (1906), p. 76; New Albany-Floyd County Public Library; *New Albany Daily Ledger*, 10 June 1891; and the Alumni Records Office, University of Michigan, the source of the postcards cited.

CRUFT, CHARLES (1826–1883)

Charles Cruft was born on 12 January 1826 in Terre Haute. His parents were John F. and Elizabeth Armstrong Cruft, two of the first settlers in the Terre Haute region.

The eldest of eight children, Cruft graduated from Wabash College in 1842 at the remarkable age of seventeen. Returning to his hometown, he taught school, worked as a bank clerk, and studied law under W. D. Griswold. In 1848 he was admitted to the bar and quickly rose to prominence. From 1855 to 1858 he was president of the St. Louis, Alton, and Terre Haute Railroad, and he formed a law partnership with John P. Baird that developed into the most highly respected and lucrative law firm in Terre Haute. He published the *Terre Haute Express* newspaper in 1860.

At the outbreak of the Civil War, Cruft was a civilian in Washington, DC, and witnessed the first Battle of Bull Run, probably from the roads where "spectators" had come to see what they believed would be something like a performance of military theater, but which turned into a frightening rout for the Federals. In the weeks following, as the Union Army seemed to falter, Cruft returned to Indiana and raised the Thirty-First Indiana Regiment on 2 September 1861, becoming its colonel. He joined Ulysses S. Grant at Fort Donelson and then at Shiloh, where Cruft was severely wounded but still remained on his horse to lead the troops until the end of the day. His bravery undoubtedly played a part in his promotion to brigadier general on 16 July 1862. He subsequently commanded brigades in the Army of the Ohio and the Army of the Cumberland and participated in the Battles of Murfreesboro; Richmond, Kentucky; Chancellorsville (2–3 May 1863); Chattanooga, (November 1863); Chickamauga; the Atlanta Campaign; Franklin (30 November 1864); and Nashville (15–16 December 1864). He was breveted major general on 5 March 1865 and was mustered out of service the following August.

Charles Cruft returned to his law practice with Baird and for several years was a member of the Republican state central committee, once as a presidential elector. A prominent Mason, he rose to the highest Masonic post in Indiana, the Grand Commander of the Knights Templar. He always retained the commitment to learning he had shown at Wabash College and was a cofounder of Rose Polytechnic Institute, laying its cornerstone on 11 September 1874.

On 23 March 1883 General Cruft succumbed to heart disease in his home at Terre Haute. Having never married, he was survived by two brothers and a sister. He is buried in Woodlawn Cemetery.

References: *Indianapolis News*, 23 March 1883; *Terre Haute Express*, 24 March 1883; C. C. Oakey, *Greater Terre Haute and Vigo County*, vol. I (1908); Henry C. Bradsby, *History of Vigo County, Indiana* (1891); H. W. Beckwith, *History of Vigo and Parke Counties* (1880); L. F. Cronim, *An Account of Vigo County* (1922); D. N Lewis of the Vigo County Public Library. See also: E. J. Warner, *Generals in Blue* (1964), pp. 104–05.

Brigadier General Charles Cruft

CULLEN, JOHN C. (1837–1917)

John Cullen was another wartime surgeon. He was one of two Cullen brothers who attended Wabash and also served in the Civil War. The other was William Allen Cullen. Their siblings were Alice, Emma, and Elizabeth. John was born at Patriot on 17 December 1837, son of William and Louisiana Early Cullen.

About 1850 the family moved from Patriot to Rising Sun, where John lived before coming to Wabash in the autumn of 1854. He stayed at the college through the spring term of 1857 and then returned to Rising Sun to study medicine with Dr. W. H. Sullivan before spending 1858 as an intern in the medical department of the University of Michigan at Ann Arbor.

In 1858 he began his practice in Indiana, in Florence, and married twenty-one-year-old Belle Morgan of Rising Sun in June 1860. In February 1863 he was offered a commission to serve as an assistant surgeon in the Twelfth Indiana Regiment, and in April 1864 he was promoted to a full surgeon with the rank of major in the Sixteenth Indiana Regiment stationed at Alexandria, Louisiana. He was mustered out on 30 June 1865 at New Orleans. While in the army Cullen fought during many encounters, including Champion's Hill and Port Gibson, Mississippi, in May 1863; the siege of Vicksburg in July of that year; the campaign along the Red River in Texas in March 1864; the battle of Pleasant Ridge [Hill] (9 April 1864); and the fighting around New Orleans.

Once released from the army, Cullen enrolled at the Ohio Medical College of Cincinnati. In early 1866 he moved to Anderson to be a partner with Dr. Thomas Jones until 1875, when he began to practice alone. By the 1880s he was so sufficiently unwell that he stopped traveling around the countryside seeing patients and only treated them in his office.

Cullen's wife, Belle, died sometime in the 1880s or 1890s, and he married a widow, Mrs. Harriet Pittsford, who had a daughter, the future Mrs. George Hewitt.

John Cullen died on 18 January 1917 at his home of fifty years in Anderson, survived by his stepdaughter and two of his sisters. He was buried in the East Maplewood Cemetery of Anderson.

References: *Journal of the Indiana State Medical Association*, X (Feb. 1917), p. 72; *A Portrait and Biographical Record of Madison and Hamilton Counties, Indiana* (1893), pp. 746–47; and sources cited for his brother, William Cullen. See also his obituary in the *Anderson Herald Bulletin*, 19 Jan. 1917.

CULLEN, WILLIAM ALLEN (1836–1912)

William Cullen was the elder brother of John and was born in Patriot, Indiana, on 6 August 1836. He spent 1853–56 at Wabash, moving up from the Preparatory Department to the freshman class.

Determined to become a lawyer, Cullen studied for a year at Asbury before securing admission to the bar. In 1857 he began practicing law in Rushville. He traveled to Rising Sun to marry 14 October twenty-year-old Frances S. Davis. The following year she gave birth to their only child, Hannah.

Cullen's legal career flourished, and as a Democrat he became editor of the *Rushville Jacksonian*, but with the coming of war in 1861 he converted to the Republican Party and became a staunch foe of the local anti-war elements. Governor Oliver P. Morton relied on him for recommendations for military or political preferment.

During Morgan's jaunt through Indiana, Cullen very briefly joined the 111th Regiment, but on 1 March 1864 he undertook a more substantial commitment and accepted a commission as a lieutenant colonel of the 123rd Indiana Regiment. Unfortunately, he became ill and sought a medical discharge.

In Rushville after the war, he combined his two interests, law and the Republican Party, and in 1888 was elected an Indiana delegate to the Republican national convention. However, it was as a judge that he distinguished himself: serving until 1871 at the Twenty-Second Court of Common Pleas, two years at the Fourth Circuit Court, and from 1873 to 1876 at the Eighth Circuit Court.

Cullen was elected a state senator for the years 1865–69 and was a member of the Indiana House of Representatives from 1869 to 1871.

Throughout his life Cullen combined legal work with farming. He served on the board of directors of the Rushville National Bank and the State Bank of Indiana at Indianapolis. He died at Rushville on 3 May 1912, survived by daughter, Hannah, and by his brother John.

References: *Rushville Republican*, 6 May 1912; *Biographical Directory of the Indiana General Assembly*, I (1980), pp. 87–88; *History of Rush County, Indiana* (1921), p. 691; and special assistance by Stephen Towne of the Indiana State Archives.

CUNNINGHAM, GEORGE B. (1841–1862)

George Cunningham was born in Terre Haute in about 1841, the son of Eliza and Nathaniel Cunningham. His siblings were Charles, George, Welton, Mary, Nathaniel, and Sarah. He attended Wabash from 1858 to 1860. In early 1859 the family moved to Indianapolis, where Nathaniel served as Indiana's state treasurer from February 1859 to February 1861.

George was mustered into the Twentieth Indiana Volunteers at Lafayette on 22 July 1861 and was in Company G for a term of three years. The regiment, which later distinguished itself so admirably the second day of Gettysburg, was a part of the Union Army of the Potomac and remained with it during 1862, but Cunningham died at Richmond, Virginia, on 29 June 1862.

References: Indiana State Library Archives and the 1850 and 1860 U.S. census.

CURRY (CURREY), JAMES BARNES (1824–1886)

James Curry was born in Crawfordsville on 10 March 1824, the son of Jane Barnes and Thomas M. Curry. His siblings were Sarah, Elizabeth Jane, Amanda, Helen, Mary Josephine, and Caroline. James's father, a doctor, served two terms in the Indiana House of Representatives while owning farmland in both Montgomery and Carroll Counties.

Young Curry attended Wabash from 1836 to 1838. When his father died in 1848, Curry maintained the family farm and became the guardian of his four younger siblings.

On 5 October 1855 Curry married Mary Ellen Philbrick of Kokomo and moved to Plymouth County, Iowa, where their first son, Thomas, was born. Their other children included Mary, Emma, May, Harry, Dick, Bonnie, and a son, Autumn.

Curry was caught up in Civil War fever like so many others. At the relatively old age of thirty-six, he enlisted in the Sixty-Fifth Missouri Volunteers at Chillicothe on 6 September 1862. On 1 December of that year, he was relieved of duty and allowed to return home. On 13 January 1864 at St. Louis he joined Company A of the Missouri First Volunteer Artillery, which he seems to have left. Later that year, as the Federal troops tried to push Confederate forces under General Sterling Price out of Missouri, fresh recruits were called for, and Curry answered the call on 18 October 1864. A week later he saw action as a member of the Fourth Provisional Militia Cavalry. Other skirmishes were to follow, and he was not discharged until 11 March 1865.

Curry lived out the rest of his life at Oregon, dying on 19 February 1886. He is buried in Maple Grove Cemetery. It is not known what became of his wife, Mary Ellen.

References: *Biographical Directory of the Indiana General Assembly*, I (1980), p. 89; and help from the Oregon Public Library and the Missouri State Archives.

CURTIS, WILLIAM B. (1837–1900)

William Curtis was born on 17 January 1837 at Braden, Vermont. In August 1850 his family moved to Chicago, where his father served as the pastor of the First Presbyterian Church. From 1851 to 1853 he was enrolled at Wabash and, according to one of his classmates, underwent a trial "on the charge of a surreptitious translation of the college clock to the seminary grounds," presumably to the local female academy in Crawfordsville, presaging future Monon Bell transportings by Wabash students. He was strong and athletic from college days on.

When Curtis joined Company A of the Nineteenth Illinois Volunteer Infantry Regiment, he gave his occupation as gymnast. He entered service as a sergeant and was promoted to second lieutenant on 6 August 1861. The regiment patrolled the Mississippi between Cairo and St. Louis and subsequently participated in capturing Forts Henry and Donelson. When the Confederates abandoned Bowling Green, Kentucky, in February 1862, the Nineteenth Illinois undertook its occupation.

In August 1862 Curtis resigned from the Nineteenth in order to assume a new appointment as captain and assistant adjutant general in the Union Army Fourteenth Corps, Third Brigade, Fourth Division, under the command of Brigadier General John Basil Turchin, formerly a distinguished officer in the Russian army (his real name was Ivan Vasilovitch Turchinoff).

After the war, Curtis went to Washington and worked with the government spying agency, undertaking several trips to Europe before returning to Chicago and joining his brother, Henry M., in a wholesale fish and oyster business. The great Chicago fire in 1871 destroyed the business, and Curtis moved to New York City, which provided the opportunity for him to exploit his extraordinary athletic prowess. In 1876, 1878, and 1880 he won first place in contests featuring the hammer throw, and gained the unofficial title of "Father of American Rowing" as well as "Father of American Amateurism."

Curtis was the founder of the New York Athletic Association and for twenty years edited a sporting magazine. He seems never to have married. He died on 30 June 1900 while climbing Mount Washington in New Hampshire and was eulogized in the *Chicago Times Herald*: "In aquatic sports, running, throwing the hammer, and lifting weights, Mr. Curtis surpassed all his contemporaries."

He was survived by two brothers, Edward H. and Henry M. Called "Father Bill" by his contemporaries, he did as much as anyone to promote amateur athletics in America.

References: Illinois military service records, the 1850 U.S. census, and various Chicago city directories. See also: R. Hickok, *Who was Who in American Sports* (1971), pp. 67–68; and the *Chicago Times Herald*, 4 July 1900. Special thanks to John J. Kearns of New York City, who is preparing a biography of William Curtis.

CUSTER, JOSEPH L. (1841–1907)

Joseph Custer was one of those Wabash students whose name was never entered upon the Civil War memorial tablet affixed to the east wall of Center Hall. However, the commencement program for June 1865 included his name among those who had served.

He was born in Fayette County, Pennsylvania, on 11 February 1841, one of three children born to Hannah Downard Custer and George W. Custer. In 1847 his parents relocated to Highland County, Ohio, but his father died in 1851. His mother then married Samuel Malcolm, and the family moved to Grant County, Indiana, where Custer did a variety of jobs in and about the town of Marion.

On 15 May 1861 Custer enrolled in Company I of the Twelfth Regiment of Indiana Volunteers, but in July he fell seriously ill and was given a medical discharge. That autumn he was a member of the freshman class at Wabash, but his one year of formal higher education was interrupted by the death of his stepfather.

Custer spent part of the year 1863 in Indianapolis as an enlistee in the office of the provost marshal, and again he secured an honorable discharge, to return to his legal studies in Marion. In March 1864 he was admitted to the Indiana bar, and he twice served as district attorney for the Fourteenth Judicial District.

In June 1865 he married Angela T. Leas, and they eventually had three sons: George, Burr, and Robert. He ran as a Republican for the Indiana Senate in 1868 but was narrowly defeated. Not until the early 1890s did he again run for office, and this time he was successfully elected judge of the Forty-Eighth Judicial Circuit, serving from 1892 to 1899.

Over the years he established several enterprises, including the Custer Electric Manufacturing Company and the Custer Lumber Company. Custer died at his home in Marion on 23 September 1907.

References: Grant County marriage records and 1860 U.S. census; *Marion Chronicle*, 23 Sept. 1907; *The Biographical Memoirs of Grant County*, (Bowen and Co., 1901), pp. 232–34.

DAGGY, CHARLES WHITE (1844–1929)

Charles Daggy was born in Putnam County on 20 January 1844, the youngest son of Jacob and Hannah Cyple Daggy, who had eight other children: Addison, William, Sarah, Elizabeth, Eliza, James, and Franklin.

Daggy entered the Twentieth Light Artillery on 8 April 1863, describing himself as a farmer who had blue eyes and light hair. He earned the rank of first sergeant during the war and was mustered out on 28 June 1865.

Following in the footsteps of his brothers Addison and William, Daggy entered Wabash College as a second-year English student in the fall of 1865. He successfully completed his freshman and sophomore years before returning to Greencastle to resume farming.

On 1 May 1873 Daggy married Sarah Ellen Lee. They had three children: Roscoe, Florence, and Maynard. Daggy combined being a farmer with acting as a partner in the Black and Daggy shoe store in Greencastle. He died on 12 January 1929 and was buried in Forest Hill Cemetery.

References: Elizabeth Daggy of Greencastle provided help sorting the complicated Daggy family relationships.

DAGGY, FRANKLIN P. (1842–1910)

Frank Daggy was one of a number of brothers and cousins from Greencastle who attended Wabash College, some of whom also served in the Civil War. Frank was one of eight children born to Hannah and Jacob Daggy, mentioned above. His father was a substantial farmer, and his sons worked alongside him on the farm.

Frank spent 1860–61 in the Normal School of Wabash College, but at the outbreak of war enrolled in Company A of the Seventy-Eighth Indiana Regiment on 28 July 1862 at Greencastle, committing himself to sixty days' service. When Morgan's cavalry threatened southern Indiana, Daggy returned as a volunteer in Company C of the 105th Regiment.

He married Laura Hutchenson at Greencastle on 11 February 1883, but she died quite soon after their wedding. He subsequently joined his older brother, James, in York, Nebraska, where he went into business as a merchant and later into real estate and insurance. He also married again, and he and his wife Callie had one child, Robert.

Badly in debt and fearful of the spreading paralysis in his body, Daggy hanged himself on 9 May 1910 and was buried in York's Greenwood Cemetery.

References: York (Nebraska) Public Library. See also: *York Teller*, 11 May 1910; *Blue Valley Journal*, 12 May 1910; *York Republican*, 11 May 1910.

DAGGY, SILAS (1838/9–1862)

Silas Daggy was born in Monroe Township, Putnam County, in 1838 or 1839, one of at least eleven children born to Cecelia and Michael Daggy. He spent 1857–58 in the Normal School of Wabash College and then joined his older brother, Samuel, in Tuscola, Illinois. Samuel was a doctor and ran a drugstore, where Silas worked as a clerk.

In August 1862 a call went out for volunteers from Douglas County, Illinois, and Silas Daggy responded, becoming a private in Company B of the Seventy-ninth Illinois Regiment. Soon he was promoted to quartermaster sergeant. On 12 September the regiment departed for Louisville, Kentucky, and merged with other regiments to become part of the Second Division of the Army of Kentucky, which headed for Nashville, Tennessee, on 7 November. However, Daggy was not among them because he had contracted typhoid fever. He died in a hospital in Lebanon, Kentucky, on 9 November.

References: Information provided by Elizabeth Daggy of Greencastle. See also: *Wabash Magazine*, IV (Dec. 1862), pp. 77, 80; Tuscola Public Library and Abraham Lincoln Presidential Library at Springfield; *County of Douglas, Illinois* (1884), p. 115.

DAGGY, THEODORE FRELINGHUYSEN (1848–1874)

Theodore Daggy was born in 1848 in Putnam County, the son of Cecelia and Michael Daggy. He had two brothers, Silas and Samuel, discussed earlier, and one sister. In rapid succession, his father, mother, and brother died in 1860, 1861, and 1862, necessitating his move to Tuscola, Douglas County, Illinois, to live with his married sister.

At the age of seventeen he went to Danville, Illinois, and enrolled in Company B of the 154th Illinois Infantry on 14 February 1865. He committed to serving for one year and was mustered out at Murfreesboro, Tennessee, on 22 May 1865.

Returning to Tuscola, he made plans to attend college and in September entered the Preparatory Department at Wabash. After two years he embarked on the Classical Course as a freshman and graduated in June 1871. In the undergraduate magazine he was characterized as ". . . quite bashful, and easily embarrassed, yet he is passionately fond of society," and he was acknowledged to be a proficient writer and speaker.

Back in Tuscola, Daggy studied law under Thomas Rundy and eventually became his partner. He never married. In the summer of 1874 he contracted typhoid fever and died on 9 August. Daggy was a member of the local Presbyterian church, and his funeral was led by the pastor, Edwin Black, also a Wabash alumnus, class of 1850. Daggy was buried in Tuscola.

References: Primarily a handwritten ledger in the Wabash College Archives titled *Obituaries of Some Alumni*. Information was also provided by Elizabeth Daggy of Greencastle, Indiana.

DAGGY, WALLACE L. (1844–1904)

Wallace Daggy was born on 15 May 1844, one of two children of Lucretia Black (1825–1849) and Benami Daggy. His parents migrated from Virginia to Indiana in 1823 and eventually settled in Putnam County. His mother died in 1849, and in 1850 Benami married Lucy Stoner. In 1856 the family moved to Starke County, Indiana, where Benami farmed.

In 1859 Wallace Daggy returned to Putnam County and worked as a clerk for a Mr. Hawkins. On 2 October 1861 he joined Company H of the Forty-Third Indiana Volunteers at Greencastle. The regiment was drawn mostly from the county and was sent first to Calhoun, Kentucky, where it remained till February 1862, and then to Missouri, where it was involved in attacks upon New Madrid and Island No. 10 (2 March–8 April 1862). In May and June the Forty-Third saw action in Tennessee and took pride in being one of the first regiments to enter Memphis. The following year the regiment operated in Mississippi and Arkansas, where it especially distinguished itself at the Battle of Helena July 1863.

In January 1864 those who had served in the regiment since it was organized were given the choice to be discharged or to re-enlist. Daggy was one of four hundred who chose to stay and was soon promoted from corporal to sergeant. After especially heavy losses on 30 April 1864 at Camden, Arkansas, the regiment was granted a brief furlough at Indianapolis, but in July again skirmished in Kentucky. Most of the remainder of the regiment's service was back in Indianapolis, guarding Confederate prisoners at Camp Morton. Daggy was promoted to second lieutenant in October 1864 and captain in January 1865.

On 14 June 1865 Daggy returned home and enrolled in the English course of study at Wabash for one year, then moved to where his father and stepmother were living in Starke County. In 1867 he started a grocery store in LaPorte County at Westville, and about this time married Caroline Bladen. They had seven children.

He moved to Spencer, where he established a hardware business in 1868 and became involved in community affairs, eventually serving as chairman of the town council. Wallace Daggy died in Spencer on 26 November 1904 and was buried in Westville Cemetery, LaPorte County.

References: C. Blanchard, *Counties of Clay and Owen, Indiana* (1884), p. 833; *Biographical and Historical Record of Putnam County, Indiana*, pp. 278–80.

DALE, FRANK C. (1848–1885)

Frank Dale was born in White County on 18 March 1848, the son of Lucinda Spencer (1819–1850) and Levi S. Dale (1812–1857). His siblings were George Spencer Dale (1843–1849) and Maria A. Dale (1845–1849).

On 17 August 1863, at the age of fifteen, he was mustered into Company K of the Indiana 116th Regiment, having told the recruiting officers that he was eighteen. He served initially for six months in Kentucky and Tennessee and was mustered out on 2 March 1864. Two months later, on 24 May 1864, he caught up with Company E of the Indiana 125th Regiment in Nashville, Tennessee, and served for one hundred more days, again telling officials that he was eighteen years old. He spent most of his time in Tennessee and northern Alabama guarding crucial railroad lines before mustering out on 29 September 1864.

In the autumn of 1865, Dale enrolled at Wabash College from his home in Monticello. He began as a second-year student in the English Course and continued in the Preparatory Department during 1866–67.

Dale married Lucy Keefer of Wooster, Ohio, on 11 January 1870. She died two years later on 29 February 1872.

In 1874 Dale began to practice medicine in Logansport, Indiana, but in 1876 moved to California, where he married Francenia Haines on 27 August 1880. He died on 30 April 1885.

References: White County Historical Society. See also: W. H. Hamelle, *A Standard History of White County, Indiana* (1915), pp. 630–31; *Counties of White and Pulaski, Indiana* (1883), p. 20; J. Z. Powell, *History of Cass County, Indiana* (1913), pp. 405, 414.

DAVIS, CHARLES W.

In the fall of 1844 Charles Davis entered the Preparatory Department of Wabash College, indicating that he was from Thorntown. He returned in 1845–46 as a freshman to pursue the Classical Course of study and continued through his sophomore year, 1846–47. According to the college archives, Davis served in the Civil War as a surgeon, but because his name is not in the military files at the Indiana State Library, he must have served from another state.

According to the census of 1850, Davis may have been living with his brother, William P. Davis, a thirty-seven-year-old physician. He may have married Miram (Myram) Olive in Boone County on 6 November 1850. William P. Davis later moved to Des Moines, Iowa, and quite possibly Charles joined him there.

References: Karen Zach of the Crawfordsville Public Library provided the information about cemetery inscriptions for Boone County. Dian Moore, archivist at the Crawfordsville Public Library, also furnished potential evidence.

DEAN, GEORGE W. (1841–1897)

George Dean was born in Harrison County, but by the time he entered Wabash in the fall of 1860, his family was living in New Albany. He spent two years in the Preparatory Department at Wabash College before joining Company H (and later Company B) of the Ninety-Third Indiana Regiment on 20 August 1862 in Orange County. He enlisted for a term of three years and was described as being five feet five inches tall, with fair complexion, hazel eyes, and black hair. He stated his occupation as farmer at the time of his enlistment.

Throughout his military service, Dean was plagued by health problems. On 1 March 1865, while on Dolphin Island, Mobile Bay, Alabama, he contracted typhoid fever, and in April he was transferred to a hospital outside of Philadelphia, where he was diagnosed as insane in June. He was given a medical discharge on 30 August 1865 after being promoted to the rank of sergeant.

After the war Dean resumed farming in Harrison County, the place of his birth, and married Elizabeth Ellen Loughmiller on 5 November 1868. They had four children: Clara, Kate, Tilly, and Philip. Dean ran a variety store from his home in Byrneville.

Still, his mental problems persisted. He was committed to the Southern Indiana Hospital for the Insane in Evansville and died there on 1 September 1897.

References: Betty Menges of the New Albany-Floyd County Public Library. See also: *Wabash Magazine*, VII (June 1866), p. 8; *History of the Ohio Falls Cities and its Counties* (1882), p. 129; E. S. Payne, *Bible and Cemetery Records* (1967), I, p. 173, concerning Floyd County; A. M. Frederick, *The Wolfe Cemetery, 1821–1981* (1982), p. 52; *New Albany Weekly Ledger*, 4 June 1919; and military pension file at the National Archives, Washington, DC.

DEGROFF, LEONARD R. (c. 1838–1874/1875)

Leonard Degroff was born in New York State about 1838, the son of Harriet (b. 1801?) and Amos (1799?–1891) DeGroff. His siblings included Mary, Melissa, Griffin, and Sarah. During the 1840s the family settled in Michigan City, LaPorte County.

Degroff came to Wabash in the fall of 1853 as a student in the Preparatory Department for one academic year. On 15 September 1861 he secured a commission as a first lieutenant in the Fourth Indiana Light Artillery. On 10 May 1862 he was granted a medical discharge.

After his military service he married Josephine E. Dresden and had one daughter.

Degroff died at Valparaiso on 15 October 1874 or 1875 and was buried in the Greenwood Cemetery in Michigan City.

References: Military files at the Indiana State Library and the National Archives in Washington, DC. Also Fern Schultz of LaPorte, Indiana.

DEMING, ARTHUR (1843–1885)

Arthur Deming was born in Terre Haute, Vigo County, on 4 November 1843, son of Sarah C. Patterson and Demas Deming (1787–1865). His siblings were Demas Jr., Henry, and Sophia.

In the autumn of 1860, the young Deming entered the Preparatory Department of Wabash College, but like so many other Wabash students, enrolled in Company I of the Eleventh Indiana Regiment on 18 April 1861 for a term of three months. He was out of the service on 4 August and prepared for a second year (1861–62) at Wabash, after which he went abroad for a year to study in Geneva. This was followed by another year of travel throughout the Continent.

In the mid-1860s he became a partner in the firm Tuell, Ripley, & Deming in Terre Haute, but left for Lawrence, Kansas, in 1867. He wrote to his sister in January 1868, "I am plodding away here, in the hope of getting away independent. Dame Fortune has jilted me several times, but hope, lingers still behind."

By late 1871 Deming was back in Terre Haute, and in 1874–75 he worked for the First National Bank. The spring of 1877 found him thriving in Rome, Italy. As he wrote to his mother, "I have been reading history in a condensed school book form, and have enjoyed myself exceedingly well hunting up places and things referred to."

In a letter dated 11 July 1877, written from the coal mining and industrial Welsh port of Swansea, he lamented, "The only thing one sees are clay hills, mountains of cinders from the factories, a filthy river and bay, a smoke clouded sky and a poor brutal lot of people."

Once back in the United States in 1878, he bought some choice acres near Effingham, Illinois, and was a successful farmer until his death on 12 July 1885.

References: David N. Lewis of the Vigo County Public Library. See also: *Wabash Magazine*, VII (June 1866), p. 8; *Greater Terre Haute and Vigo County* (1908), p. 146; *Terre Haute Express*, 14 July 1885.

DEMING, BENJAMIN OWEN (1829–1864)

Benjamin Deming was one of four brothers who attended Wabash College. The others were Charles R., James, and Augustus E., and these young men had two younger sisters, Gertrude (Emily?) and Anna. Their parents were Hester Carpenter and Elizur P. Deming.

Elizur had grown up in Great Barrington, Massachusetts, and studied medicine at Williams College. Within about a month of graduation, he went to Wilkes-Barre, Pennsylvania, to marry Hester on 7 July 1818. The newlyweds then made their way to Milford, Ohio, where Dr. Deming set up in practice. A few years later the Demings moved westward.

Benjamin Deming was born on 22 July 1829 in Chillicothe, Ohio. In 1834 the family moved to Lafayette, Indiana, where Elizur was elected as a Whig in 1841 to the Indiana General Assembly House of Representatives. Two years later he ran unsuccessfully for governor.

The younger Deming entered the Preparatory Department at Wabash in 1842–43 and became a freshman in the Classical Course the following year. He stayed the full four years and received a bachelor of arts degree in June 1847, then returned to Lafayette.

In 1863 the Seventh Cavalry of the 119th Regiment of Indiana Volunteers was organized at Lafayette, and Deming enrolled as a second lieutenant on 20 July. He was mustered in at Indianapolis on 7 October. Deming died ten days after being wounded on 20 June 1864 in a skirmish at White's Station, Tennessee.

References: Tippecanoe County Historical Association. See also: *Biographical History of Tippecanoe, White, Jasper, Newton, Benton, Warren, and Pulaski Counties* (1899), p. 12, and his military service record at the Indiana State Library Archives.

DEMING, CHARLES R. (1831–1869)

Charles Deming was born on 9 October 1831 in Chillicothe, Ohio, one of the group of four young brothers who attended Wabash: Benjamin, Charles, James, and Augustus. A few years after Charles Deming's birth, the family had to leave their Ohio community because of local hostility to father Elizur's abolitionist activities. They settled in Lafayette, where Elizur pursued his career as a physician. In the autumn of 1847 Charles Deming embarked on the first of three years in the Preparatory Department of Wabash College.

By the time the Civil War began, he was practicing law in Lafayette, and on 26 March 1862 he enrolled in the Sixteenth Battery of Light Artillery attached to the Sixteenth Indiana Volunteers, securing a commission as a first lieutenant. Deming's first battle experience was at Slaughter Mountain, Virginia, on 9 August when Union General John Pope's troops faced Stonewall Jackson. A few weeks later he fought at the Battle of South Mountain under a fellow Hoosier, Major General Ambrose Burnside.

In May 1863 Deming was promoted to captain, and the regiment became known as Deming's Battery for its strong performance during a number of battles in Virginia (Rappahannock), Maryland (Antietam), and Washington, DC. At the end of his three-year commitment, Deming was mustered out on 21 April 1865, but in June he re-enlisted with a United States regiment of veteran volunteers, although his health was not good. He received a medical discharge in November 1865.

He married Alice C. Milburn on 11 December 1865 in Grace Church, Baltimore, Maryland, and they had two children: a daughter, Edith Gertrude (1866), and a son, Elizur (1868).

Returning to Indiana, Deming tried his hand at farming, but found the exertion too much and considered becoming a physician. He died of lung disease on 4 December 1869.

References: Military pension file at the National Archives in Washington, DC; *Biographical Record and Portrait Album of Tippecanoe County, Indiana* (1888), p. 238; *Past and Present of Tippecanoe County, Indiana* (1909), I, p. 221.

DEWOLF, JOSEPH E. (1842–1917)

Joseph Dewolf was born in New York State on 24 February 1842, the son of Mary and C. E. DeWolfe. His father was the successful owner of a hardware store in Michigan City, where his son worked before coming to Wabash in the fall of 1858.

The younger Dewolf returned to the Preparatory Department each year until he completed the 1860–61 academic year, then enrolled in the Fourth Indiana Light Artillery on 27 September 1861 for three years. In January 1863 he acted as a clerk and orderly for his regimental commander, and following the Battle of

Stones River near Murfreesboro, Tennessee, received a commendation for having been so cool and effective during the battle, including carrying vital messages to and from the front.

Dewolf was mustered out on 6 October 1864 and returned to his father's mercantile firm for a few years before establishing a hardware business of his own in 1867. On 2 September 1868 he married Gertrude Ward, who was born in 1842 in New York State. They had three children: Charles, Clara, and Jesse.

Dewolf retired from active business in 1904 but lived in Michigan City until his death on 20 December 1917. He is buried in Greenwood Cemetery.

References: *Wabash Magazine*, III (Dec. 1861), p. 93; *History of LaPorte County, Indiana* (1880), p. 761; [Michigan City] *Evening News*, 22 Dec. 1917.

DICKEY, WILLIAM MATHER (1835–1923)

William Dickey was born on 25 February 1835, the son of Margaret Osborn Steele and John M. Dickey, the pastor of the Presbyterian church in New Washington. He had a sister who was a child of his father's first wife, Nancy W. McClesky. Nancy died in 1816.

Young Dickey attended Wabash from 1851 to 1858, first in the Preparatory Department and then in the Classical Course, graduating with a bachelor of arts degree. In the years following graduation, he presumably studied medicine, preparatory to beginning his life's career as a physician.

On 28 August 1862 he enrolled in Company G of the Ninety-Third Indiana Regiment at New Albany. Entering for a term of three years, he was described as nearly six feet tall, with dark complexion and hair and blue eyes. He rose to the rank of corporal before falling into the hands of the Confederates at Brices Crossroads, Guntown, Mississippi (10 June 1864). He was incarcerated in the infamous Andersonville.

Dickey was exchanged for a Confederate prisoner on 19 September 1864 and was brought to Atlanta. By late October he had rejoined his regiment, enabling him to serve his full time in the army and be discharged at Memphis on 30 August 1865.

After the war Dickey returned to New Washington and practiced medicine for the next few years before the urge to travel lured him to Missouri (1869–72), Montana (1872–76), and Oregon (1876–1923).

On 2 November 1886 he married Mary Bugle in Lone Rock, Gillam County, Oregon. She had been married twice before, the first marriage ending in divorce and the second in her husband's death. In 1891 they moved to Cottage Grove, Lane County, where they lived for twenty years. When Mary's health deteriorated, they relocated to Myrtle Creek, Douglas County, where she died on 30 August 1920. Afterwards, Dickey lived intermittently at the Soldiers Home at Roseburg, Oregon, where he died on 8 March 1923.

References: Dorothy Tombleson of Condon, Oregon, provided material from the *Condon Globe Times*, 24 Sept. 1920. Lee H. Schick of Hood River, Oregon, supplied references in the *Biographical and Military Histories of Patients at Roseburg Soldiers Home*. See also: pension file at the National Archives in Washington, DC.

DODDS, OZRO J. (1840–1882)

Students at Wabash and other colleges reacted in different ways in 1861 when they heard the electrifying news that the Federal fort, Sumter, near Charleston, had been fired on. Many of these young college men, prime candidates for military service, rushed to their own hometowns to seek whatever fortune brought with their own friends. Some enlisted right in the college community. Some joined a unit together.

Ozro Dodds, who had been a Wabash student but in 1861 was finishing his BA at Miami University in Oxford, Ohio, put together his own company.

Here is his story: Before Dodds's senior year was formally ended, war broke out. When word of the bombardment in South Carolina reached the Ohio campus, a large gathering of students and staff met in the chapel. At this point Dodds announced his intention to form a company of volunteer soldiers. He explained that he was familiar with close order drill, having learned it in Crawfordsville from Lew Wallace. More than 150 students flocked to join the Oxford Rifles, but many were underage or otherwise unable to serve. However, about thirty, with Ozro leading them, boarded a train to join the Twentieth Ohio Volunteer Regiment. Ironically, southern students travelled on the same train en route to joining the Confederate forces.

Ohio was a logical choice for the new unit: Dodds was born in Cincinnati, Ohio, on 23 March 1840, the son of Eliza McMaster and William Dodds, who had five children, three of whom reached maturity. He had attended Hughes High School in Cincinnati, entering Wabash College as a sophomore in the fall of 1858. He completed two years (1859–60) before transferring to Miami University.

Dodds served as captain of Company B for three months and was then appointed captain of Company F of the Eighty-First Ohio Volunteer Infantry. During the spring and summer of 1863, he functioned as a quartermaster under General G. M. Dodge and then became lieutenant colonel and commander of the First Alabama Union Cavalry on 18 October 1863. The First Alabama was one of a few units in Alabama formed of Union supporters. It included a wide variety of men from Alabama and Tennessee and recruits from other states. The First acted as scouts and raiders and provided screens for infantry on the march.

On 2 May 1864 Dodds resigned his commission and returned to Cincinnati, where he enrolled in the law school of the University of Cincinnati, graduating in 1866. Once he began practicing law, he married Mattie D. DeSilver of Brooklyn, New York, on 23 February 1869, but she died prematurely on 12 August 1870.

Dodds entered politics and served in the Ohio House of Representatives in 1870 and 1871, and when a vacancy occurred in the United States Congress for Cincinnati, he filled it from 8 October 1872 to 3 March 1873.

On 24 December 1874 he embarked on a second marriage with a Miss Lamison of Lima, Ohio. Dodds served as a trustee of Miami University from 1875 until he died on 18 April 1882. He was buried in the Spring Grove Cemetery. There were no children from either marriage. A fitting epitaph, and a tribute that would have pleased him, was the dedication in 1961 of Dodds Hall at Miami University in Oxford.

References: *Wabash Magazine*, III (Dec. 1861), p. 93; *Wabash Magazine*, IV (Dec. 1862), p. 74; *Wabash Magazine*, V (Dec. 1863), p. 77. James Blount of Hamilton, Ohio, and Robert T. Howard of Oxford, Ohio, provided several valuable items: *Official Roster of the Soldiers of the State of Ohio in the War of the Rebellion, 1861–1866*, I (1893); W. S. Hoole, *Alabama Tories: The First Alabama Cavalry* (1960); *Cincinnati Inquirer*, 19 April 1882; *Beta Theta Pi* (April 1882); *Cincinnati Commercial*, 19 April 1882; also the Walter Havighurst Special Collections Library of the King Library, Miami University.

DOOLEY, ALVAH H. (1838–1903)

Alvah Dooley was born in 1838 in Boone County, the son of Jane E. Hunter and Newton Dooley, who had five other children besides Alvah: Pamela, John, William, Joseph, and Nancy.

While attending the Preparatory Department of Wabash College for one year, he indicated his home was Northfield, Union Township, Boone County. On 22 April 1861 he joined many of his fellow students and enrolled for three months in Company I of the Eleventh Indiana Regiment.

According to the 1880 census, Dooley lived in the twelfth ward of Indianapolis and worked as a newspaper editor. His wife, Mary, came from Illinois and was thirty-six years old. By 1886–87, Dooley was in Kansas City, Missouri, employed by the News Depot, and the city directory for 1892–93 confirmed that he was still there and now serving as editor for the *Kansas City Star*. His last known address in 1892 was in Excelsior, Kansas, about twenty miles from Kansas City, where he died in 1903.

References: H. W. Beckwith, *History of Montgomery County* (1881), p. 48; and the Kansas City Public Library.

DORMAN, JAMES HARVEY (1831–1905)

James Dorman was born on 7 November 1831, the eldest of eleven children born to Lucy Chowning Kemper and Peter Eldy Dorman.

When young Dorman entered Wabash in the fall of 1852, he indicated that his home was Warsaw, Gallatin County, Kentucky. He stayed only one year in Crawfordsville, returned home for a year, and spent 1854–55 at Indiana Asbury University (now DePauw University). From 1859 to 1861 he read law with Hiram Kelso of Owenton, Owen County, Kentucky, and also taught school before being admitted to the Kentucky bar and starting to practice law.

On 6 October 1862 Dorman joined others in Owen County and enlisted in Company C of the Fourth Kentucky Cavalry, Confederate Army, under General Humphrey Marshall. He reckoned later that he had taken part in forty-two engagements and come through totally unscathed. Two of the notable conflicts in which he fought were the Battle of Blue Springs, Tennessee, in October 1863 under Cerro Gordo Williams and the siege of Knoxville in November 1863 under James Longstreet.

In the autumn of 1862, he met Elizabeth (Lizzie) Gaines, a native of Sullivan County, Tennessee, and toward the end of the war Dorman got permission to take a leave, go to Sullivan County, and marry Lizzie on 16 March 1865. He was there with his bride when Robert E. Lee surrendered.

For about a year both Lizzie and James taught school in Verona, Boone County, Kentucky. Then they returned to Owenton, and Dorman hung out his lawyer's shingle. For ten months virtually no clients entered his law office, but gradually he built a successful practice. He was one of the founders of the First Baptist Church and was elected to the Kentucky State Senate, serving from 1869 to 1874. Elected judge of the Owen County Court in 1874, he held this position for four years.

James and Lizzie Dorman had four children: William, Virginia, James, and Fanny. While visiting his daughter, Virginia, in August 1905 at Oak Grove, Tennessee, Dorman took ill and died. He was buried in the Odd Fellows Cemetery in Owenton, as was Lizzie in 1922.

References: Owen County Public Library: [Owenton] *News Herald*, 10 Aug. 1905 and 17 Aug. 1905; W. H. Perrin, et al., *Kentucky: A History of the State* (1887), pp. 786–88; M. S. Houchens, *History of Owen County, Kentucky* (1976), p. 93; L. and R. H. Collins, *History of Kentucky* (1966), p. 670. See also: DePauw University, *Alumni Record* (1920), p. 410; and the Kentucky Department of Libraries and Archives, Frankfort, for information about Lizzie Dorman's efforts to secure a pension.

DOSTER, JAMES TAYLOR (1832–1863)

James Doster was born on 22 May 1832 in Winchester, Virginia, the eldest of seven children of Rachel Doyle (1807–1931) and Alfred Doster (1809–?). His siblings were John William, Jane, Simon, Edmond, Susan Frances, and Frank. The Doster family came to Jefferson, Indiana, sometime between 1844 and 1850.

James Doster was in the Normal School at Wabash for the school year 1854–55. On 13 March 1856 he married Sarah Jane Eyre (1833–?) and they had two children, Edward and Mary Alice. In 1860 Doster was a teacher and was elected county surveyor for two years.

During the summer of 1862, the Eighty-Sixth Indiana Regiment of Volunteers was organized at Lafayette, and Doster enrolled in Company I as a second lieutenant on 14 August. Coincidentally, the captain of this company was a Wabash alumnus, James R. Carnahan. The regiment was mustered in on 4 September at Indianapolis and went immediately to Cincinnati, taking up a defensive position at Covington, Kentucky, and then embarked on a steamboat for Louisville. Ten days later it joined with the Fourteenth Brigade of the Fifth Division of the Army of the Ohio and vainly pursued Confederate General Bragg and his troops.

As his regiment approached Knoxville, Tennessee, on 10 December 1863, Doster was mortally wounded. He is buried in the Shiloh Cemetery of Perry Township, near the town of Colfax, Indiana.

References: Frankfort Community Public Library. See also: J. Claybaugh, *History of Clinton County, Indiana* (1913), pp. 137, 170; *History of Clinton County, Indiana* (1886), pp. 360, 383; Indiana State Archives; and J. A. Barnes, *The Eighty-Sixth Regiment* (1895).

DOUGLASS, FRANK MINOR (1843–1930)

Frank Douglass was born in Peru on 6 May 1843, the son of Catherine Strother and Samuel A. Douglass.

When Douglass entered the Preparatory Department of Wabash College in the fall of 1861, he indicated that his home was Dayton in Tippecanoe County. He stayed only a few months, and on 7 January 1862 he enrolled at Lafayette in the Tenth Battery of Indiana Light Artillery for three years. At the time he was described as a farmer, five feet eight inches tall, with light hair and blue eyes.

In May 1862 Douglass was thrown from a horse and injured his back, resulting in his being conveyed by steamboat along the Tennessee River to Evansville and then to a hospital in Louisville, where he was laid up for ten months.

After his release he rejoined his battery in March 1863, determined to serve out his full three years. He did and was then discharged at Chattanooga on 24 January 1865.

Not long after war's end, Douglass returned to Louisville, this time as a medical student. He secured his degree at the Louisville Medical Institute and embarked on a career as a physician. On 16 November 1876, in Martinsville, Indiana, he was joined in marriage to Elvira Anntonie Farrow. They settled in Kansas, first in Emporia, then in Kansas City, and later in Mount Leonard.

In 1892 the family moved to Clinton, Missouri, where Douglass practiced until he died at home on North Main Street on 9 March 1930, survived by his wife and three of his six children.

References: Military pension file from the regional office, Dept. of Veterans Affairs, Indianapolis; the Henry County (Missouri) Public Library and the county scrapbook for March 1930; and *The Hoosier Genealogist*, XXXVIII (March 1998), p. 49.

DUNLAP, DANIEL A. (1840–1865)

Daniel Dunlap was born in 1840 in Perrysville, the younger son of Nancy Ann and John Dunlap. He had a sister, Mary, and his older brother, James R., also attended Wabash. As a teenager, Daniel worked as a clerk in his father's clothing store, the first shop of its kind to be established in Perrysville. In the autumn of 1859, he entered the Preparatory Department of Wabash College, remaining for one academic year.

On 31 August 1861 he was mustered into Company B of the Eleventh Indiana Regiment of Volunteers that was sent to Kentucky and later Tennessee. It participated in the Battle of Corinth (Mississippi) in October 1862. The regiment then went to Arkansas. There Dunlap secured a medical discharge on 2 January 1863 and returned to Perrysville. His family did their best to restore his health, but he died in 1865.

References See those for Daniel's brother, James R. Dunlap.

DUNLAP, JAMES R. (1838–1909)

James Dunlap was born in Perrysville on 18 September 1838, the son of Nancy Ann and John Dunlap. He had a younger brother, Daniel, who also attended Wabash, and a sister, Mary. Before coming to Wabash in 1856 to enroll in the Normal School, James clerked in his father's shop. He spent one school year at Wabash and then made his way to Urbana, Illinois, where the 1860 census listed him as a merchant.

On 6 August 1862 he enrolled at Urbana in Company G of the Seventy-Sixth Illinois Regiment as a second lieutenant. He was described as five feet eight inches tall, with black hair, dark eyes, and a dark complexion. Committed to three years of service, he was promoted to first lieutenant on 5 January 1863, and later that year was transferred to the United States Signal Corps, attached at first to the staff of General James B. McPherson and then to General Francis P. Blair. On 22 July 1865 he was mustered out of the army at Galveston, Texas.

After the war he returned to the family farm in Vermillion County and married Mary Russell Bell. They eventually had ten children. In 1880 Dunlap was elected a county commissioner, a post he held for many years.

Dunlap died of Bright's disease on 1 November 1909 and was buried in Hicks Cemetery of Highland Township, Vermillion County.

References: Newport-Vermillion County Public Library. See also: [Newport] *Hoosier State*, 10 Nov. 1909; and military service record at the Illinois State Archives, Springfield.

DUNN, BENJAMIN IRVINE (1822–1890)

Benjamin Dunn and his younger brother, James, had good reason to come to Wabash College: Their uncle, Williamson Dunn, donated the land overlooking Sugar Creek that became the first site of the new institution in 1833. Williamson Dunn had encouraged Benjamin's brother, Nathaniel, to leave Kentucky and settle in the growing frontier town of Crawfordsville, and Benjamin followed.

Benjamin Dunn was born on 21 July 1822 in Madison County, Kentucky, one of ten children of Sophia W. Irvine and Nathaniel Dunn. He enrolled in the Preparatory Department in 1835 and graduated with a bachelor of arts degree in July 1845. For a time he taught school in Kentucky, but his health was precarious in those years, and he returned to Crawfordsville and studied medicine with Dr. James G. McMechan. After several years he went to Chicago for more formal training at Rush Medical College, coming back to Crawfordsville in 1850.

By 1852 he was restless and decided to venture westward to Macomb, Illinois. By 1854, like so many doctors of the time, he added a drugstore to his medical office. His partner in this new enterprise was J. D. Yeiser, whose sister-in-law, Lucy J. Craig of Kentucky, happened to be visiting at the time. She and Dunn lost little time deciding that they were meant for each other, and they were married on 17 May 1854. Over the coming years the couple were to have ten children.

When the Civil War erupted, Dunn was nearly forty years old and understandably did not rush into volunteer service. However, by the summer of 1864, he decided to lend his medical talents to the cause. In June he was commissioned an assistant surgeon in Company C of the 137th Illinois Regiment and soon found himself attending the wounded in Memphis. On 21 August his regiment was overrun by a surprise raid of Confederate cavalry under the command of Nathan Bedford Forrest. Dr. Dunn was taken prisoner and to his consternation soon found himself caring for the sick and injured in a Rebel hospital. That did not last long, and he was then permitted to rejoin the rest of his regiment, shortly to be mustered out thereafter on 24 September 1864. He returned to Macomb, to his family and his medical practice, but his own health was never quite the same. Dunn suffered much in years to come, but continued his healing labors as best he could for the next quarter century. He died at home of heart failure on the evening of 23 October 1890. He was survived by his wife and seven of their children.

References: S. J. Clarke, *McDonough County History* (1878), pp. 236, 634; *History of McDonough County, Illinois* (1885), pp. 414–15; *Crawfordsville Weekly Journal*, 10 Jan. 1891; and H. W. Beckwith, *History of Montgomery County* (1881), pp. 170–71.

DUNN, JAMES ERWIN (1817–1894)

James E. Dunn was born on 7 May 1817 in Madison County, Kentucky. In 1825 his parents moved to Crawfordsville, and at the age of seventeen, Dunn entered the Preparatory Department of Wabash College. The following year, he was joined there by his younger brother, Benjamin. In all, James remained in school for three years, 1834–37.

He then began to clerk at various stores in town for the next half dozen years or so. Toward the end of the 1840s, he took a job with the railroads, helping to survey the line from Lafayette through Crawfordsville to Indianapolis. With regular employment assured, Dunn felt financially able to marry Matilda Burbridge on 20 November 1849. She was a long-time resident of Crawfordsville, having come there with her parents, Judge and Mrs. William Burbridge, in 1823 from Kentucky. James and Matilda Dunn went on to have six children: Emma E., William A., Samuel, Fannie M., Walter G., and George G.

When work on the railroad was completed, the couple tried their hand at farming on land a mile and a half south of town. This lasted for the years 1855–58, and then Dunn resumed clerking for hardware and other stores, both in Crawfordsville and in Thorntown. It was not until 1877 that he took a chance on farming again, with eighty-three acres north of Crawfordsville. This time it proved a success, and he remained there the rest of his life.

Several sources have stated that Dunn briefly served in an Indiana regiment during Morgan's raid. Repeated attempts to verify this military experience proved fruitless until some stretch of the imagination turned up the right person with the wrong name. On 11 July 1863 a James E. Drum enrolled in the 108th Regiment as it gathered in Crawfordsville; it is likely to have been Dunn. By 17 July all the fuss was over, Morgan had galloped over to Ohio, and the members of Dunn's regiment were disbanded.

About a year or so before his death, Dunn met with a serious horse and buggy accident. It left him partly crippled, and what with his rheumatism as well, he was reduced to getting around on foot by means of crutches. Some part of his wound never quite healed, and eventually blood poisoning set in, leading ultimately to his death at home on 25 January 1894. He was survived by his wife and several of their grown children.

References: H. W. Beckwith, *History of Montgomery County* (1881), pp. 170–71; *Crawfordsville Star*, 26 Jan. 1894; *Crawfordsville Daily Journal*, 26 Jan. 1894; *Weekly Argus News*, 3 Feb. 1894.

EDWARDS, GILBERT H. (1841–1861)

Gilbert Edwards was born in the town of Pinckneyville, Illinois, in 1841. He entered the Preparatory Department at Wabash College in the fall of 1860 when he was living in the household of his sister, Bridget, and her husband, William Lorry. His occupation at the time was recorded as "law student."

In May 1861 he returned to Anna, Union County, Illinois, and enrolled in Company A of the Eighteenth Illinois Infantry for a term of three years, with the rank of corporal. His regiment was one of the first organized in Illinois, and it was ordered to Cairo, a crucial point at the junction of the Ohio and Mississippi Rivers. There the Eighteenth Illinois carried out reconnaissance missions into Missouri and Confederate states to the south.

On 30 August 1861 Edwards fell victim to an epidemic of malaria and died. He had the sad distinction of being the first Wabash College student to die in the Civil War and was buried in Pinckneyville.

References: *Wabash Magazine*, III (Feb. 1862), p. 101; military service record from the Illinois State Archives; the *Wabash Alumni Directory*, the annual college catalogues, and *The Wabash*, June, 1866, p. 5.

ELLIOTT, JAMES WALTER (c. 1833–1895)

James Elliott, a product of Wabash's Preparatory Department, had his own signal moment in Civil War history. He was one of about six hundred survivors of the infamous explosion of the steamship *Sultana*, which was carrying Andersonville prisoners and others finally home up the Mississippi in 1865.

Elliott was born in Jefferson County in about 1833, the eldest of seven children of Elizabeth Craig and Anthony Elliott. His siblings were Elizabeth, John, Simeon, Mary, Allen, and Daniel.

He spent two years (1852–54) in the Preparatory Department of Wabash before advancing to his freshman year, continuing until graduation in June 1858. His lively interest in preaching led to his becoming a minister and also a schoolteacher.

On 18 April 1861 at Lafayette, he enrolled in Company E of the Tenth Indiana Regiment, which was sent to Virginia. Mustered out at Indianapolis on 6 August, Elliott immediately re-enlisted as a sergeant of Company G, Tenth Indiana Regiment, for a term of three years. He was promoted to first lieutenant, and in March 1864, he became a captain in the Forty-Fourth United States Colored Troops. He was captured on 7 September 1864 and sent to Andersonville prison camp. Upon his release he met another Wabash man, Benjamin Marshall Mills, member of the class of 1868 and the son of the college's first professor, Caleb Mills, in Vicksburg, Mississippi. In a letter to his mother dated 19 April 1865, Mills wrote, "He [Elliott] is the only officer of the Black Troops that I know of among the prisoners. He has seen a hard time but is ready to help with it until the war is over."

On 27 April 1865 Elliott was aboard the ship being used as a conveyor of released prisoners, the SS *Sultana*, when the boiler exploded and more than half of the 2,021 passengers were killed. Somehow Elliott escaped and escorted survivors to Indianapolis.

He died in Alabama in 1895.

References: *Wabash College Record*, July 1903, p. 26; J. E. Cleland, "The College and the Civil War," *Wabash College Record-Bulletin*, July 1918, p. 8. Stephen E. Towne of the Indiana State Library Archives helped disentangle the record.

ELSTON, ISAAC COMPTON, JR. (1836–1925)

Isaac Elston Jr. was born in Crawfordsville, Indiana, on 5 February 1836, the sixth of nine children of Maria Aiken and Isaac Elston Sr. At the tender age of ten, he embarked on his formal education in the Preparatory Department of Wabash College, where he studied from 1846 to 1849.

In 1853 his father founded the bank in Crawfordsville that bore his name for more than a hundred years. That same year Isaac Jr. joined a group of gold miners on their way to California. He contracted malaria and returned home. He attended the University of Michigan at Ann Arbor for a year and then joined a Crawfordsville firm of grain merchants, Lee, Gilkey and Company. In 1860 he entered the family bank.

On 18 April 1861 Elston enrolled for three months as captain of Company I of the Eleventh Indiana Volunteers, but soon after being released on 4 August re-enlisted and was promoted to major. He went with the Eleventh to the actions at Fort Donelson, Fort Henry, and Shiloh.

Elston resigned from the Eleventh Regiment on 8 April 1862 in order to join the staff of his brother-in-law, General Lew Wallace. This was officially confirmed on 9 July, when Elston became a lieutenant colonel and aide-de-camp of the general.

On 7 August 1862 he married Sarah Mills of Marietta, Ohio, but soon returned to Wallace's staff. However, duties in fortifying Cincinnati and taking charge of Camp Chase in Columbus, Ohio, followed by providing support to a commission inquiring into the conduct of Major General Don Carlos Buell, didn't really suit him. He resigned on 8 June 1863.

During part of 1864, Isaac and Sarah lived in Memphis, Tennessee, where he helped to found the First National Bank. In 1866 he went into the brokerage business in Cincinnati, followed by a brief stint with a lumber company in Buchanan, Michigan.

With the death of his father in 1867, Elston came back to Crawfordsville and not only assumed the presidency of the family bank but also expanded his business interests to include the Logansport, Crawfordsville and Southeastern Railroad; the Poston Paving Brick Company, the YountWoolen Mills; the Union Trust Company of Indianapolis, the Crawfordsville Wire Bound Box Company; the Indianapolis, Bloomington and Western Railroad; and the Sand Creek Coal Company.

Isaac and Sarah Elston had six children: Marie, Katharine, Mary, Nancy, Isaac III, and Joan. The Elstons first lived in the house later given to Wabash College to be used by its presidents. Then Isaac built another, more modern family home at 400 E. Wabash. Sarah died in 1920 and Isaac on 2 July 1925. They are both buried in Oak Hill Cemetery in Crawfordsville.

References: Crawfordsville Public Library; *Crawfordsville Journal*, 2 July 1925; D. E. Thompson, "Elston had a Spirit of Adventure in his Early Years," *Montgomery Magazine* (April 1989), p. 5; *History of Montgomery County, Indiana* (1913), p. 694; and Stephen E. Towne of the Indiana State Library Archives.

ELTZROTH, WILLIAM C. (c. 1835–1887)

William Eltzroth was born in Winchester, Randolph County, about 1835, the son of John Eltzroth, a native of Ohio. The young Eltzroth attended the Normal School of Wabash College for one school year, 1854–55. He then returned home to marry Mary Jane Clayton, a resident of Miami County, on 9 September 1855. By 1860 they were living in Waltz Township, Wabash County, and had three children: Eliza, Martha, and Isabella. In 1874 they had a son, Rollie. On 28 August 1861 at Indianapolis, Eltzroth enrolled for three years in Company A of the Eighth Indiana Cavalry, Thirty-Ninth Indiana Regiment. He was described as being a shoemaker, five feet nine inches tall, with light hair and complexion and blue eyes. In 1862 his regiment was sent to Kentucky, but Eltzroth contracted chronic diarrhea that plagued him for the next two years. He spent time in and out of hospitals in New Albany or Madison, Indiana, until discharged at Indianapolis on 9 September 1864.

Following the war he and his family returned to Mary Jane's home county of Miami County and lived in the town of Amboy. In November 1876 they moved to Fulton County, where they lived the rest of their lives.

References: Census records; the Indiana State Library Archives; and the military pension files at the National Archives in Washington, DC.

EMERSON, JOHN B. (c. 1845–1910)

John Emerson's name appears on the memorial tablet affixed to the east wall of Center Hall, yet he is not mentioned in the college's catalogues or records.

129

A search of the censuses of 1850 and 1860 suggest he most likely was born in about 1845 in New Hampshire and attended Wabash's Preparatory Department from 1860 to 1861.

Emerson's father was Roswell B. Emerson (1812?–1892), and his mother was Mary (1823?–1876), both natives of New Hampshire. In addition to John, they had three other children: Lucy, Mary, and George. The family was living in Indianapolis, Marion County, Indiana, in 1860.

On 20 September 1861 Emerson enrolled in Indianapolis in Company B of the Second Cavalry attached to the Forty-First Indiana Regiment, although he was probably only fifteen years old. Instead of serving three years, he was mustered out on 1 January 1863.

When Confederate General John Hunt Morgan and his cavalry threatened southern Indiana, Emerson enrolled in the 107th Indiana Regiment at Indianapolis on 2 July 1863, serving until the threat evaporated. In May 1864 he joined the 132nd Regiment for another tour of duty that lasted one hundred days.

After the war Emerson returned to helping his father, who was a carpenter. He also found part-time employment in Indianapolis manufacturing building materials. On 18 October 1874 Emerson married Amarilla McCaw in Indianapolis, and they had two daughters, Ettie (1877) and Mary (1880). Amarilla died on 19 October 1886, and Emerson lived with his two unmarried daughters.

From 1900 to 1910 Emerson was superintendent at a lumber, lime, and coal company. He died on 19 February 1910 and is buried alongside his parents and wife at Crown Hill Cemetery.

References Dr. Carl Cowen at the Indiana State Library; census records; and Indianapolis city directories.

EMERSON, THOMAS H. (c. 1846–1921)

Thomas Emerson was born in New Hampshire in about 1846 and was among the surviving children of Frances and Thomas P. Emerson. His siblings who survived to maturity were Frank, Harry, and Mary.

In 1847 the Emerson family moved from New Hampshire to Lafayette, Indiana, where the father started a jewelry store.

In the autumn of 1863 Emerson entered the Preparatory Department of Wabash College. He nearly completed the school year, but enrolled on 10 May 1864 in Company D of the 135th Indiana Regiment for one hundred days. The regiment went to Kentucky and Tennessee to guard railroad lines, and in early September 1864 Emerson was discharged. He returned to Lafayette, where he lived for the rest of his long life. He died of cancer on 19 June 1921.

References: Dorothy Van Cleef, volunteer at the Tippecanoe County Historical Association. See also: *Lafayette Journal and Courier*, 20 June 1921.

> ### Colored regiments: the road to advancement
>
> In the early months of the Civil War, free African Americans were not allowed to join the Union army, but some were taken in by the United States Navy. During the course of 1862 black regiments were formed in occupied Louisiana, South Carolina and Kansas. In 1863 Massachusetts formed two black regiments, the 54th and 55th, the former of which became a legend for its heroism and sacrifice. Lincoln's Emancipation Proclamation, freeing slaves residing in the Confederate states, also had a provision for recruiting African Americans into the United States army. Most of these initially were used for labor service and garrison duty. Gradually so-called colored regiments were organized in various Northern states, until by war's end there were 166 such regiments comprising some 300,000 African Americans. Invariably their officers were white. About 60 of these colored regiments saw action on the field of battle, resulting in the death of 143 white officers and 2,751 African American soldiers.
>
> Wabash men, like others who did not find "advancement" easily in the Northern army, particularly near the end of the war, sought command in these colored regiments.

ENGLE, JOHN B. (1844–1883)

John Engle was born in Crawfordsville on 15 August 1844, the only son of Elizabeth D. Beard of Crawfordsville and Philip E. Engle of Harper's Ferry.

From 1860 until 1862, Engle studied in the Preparatory Department of Wabash College. Soon after school let out in the latter year, he enrolled at Crawfordsville in Company K of the Eighty-Sixth Indiana Regiment. He entered as a corporal, obligated to three years of service. On 19 September 1863 he was taken captive at the Battle of Chickamauga and endured many months in prison, first at Belle Island, Richmond, Virginia, and afterwards fourteen months at Andersonville. He survived, returned to his regiment, and was mustered out at Nashville, Tennessee, on 6 June 1865.

Returning to Crawfordsville, Engle again enrolled in Wabash College, but he joined the regular United States Army in February 1866 as a second lieutenant in the Seventeenth Regiment, with military duty on the western frontier. He rose steadily through the ranks, becoming a first lieutenant in 1867 and captain of Company A of the Fifteenth U.S. Infantry in 1875. For unknown reasons, he resigned from the army on 18 September 1878.

Back in Crawfordsville, he joined the GAR in 1879, listing his occupation as student. On 13 October 1881 he married Ida Ellis, and he died on 26 December 1883. He is buried in Oak Hill Cemetery.

References: Diane Hammill of the Crawfordsville Public Library. See also: *Crawfordsville Weekly Journal*, 5 Jan. 1884; *Wabash Magazine*, V (Dec. 1863), p. 76; *Wabash Magazine*, IX (June 1869), p. 78.

ENSMINGER, SAMUEL L. (1844–1921)

Samuel Ensminger was born on his family's farm three miles south of Crawfordsville on 2 October 1844. His parents were Jane Fulton Canine and Joseph Ensminger. Their other children were Ellen, Isabel, Sophronia, and Chalmers.

Financial records of Wabash College state that in April 1852 Joseph Ensminger and Son contracted to do the brick work on the Normal School. Two years later, in the fall of 1854, Samuel became a student at the college, remaining a year.

At the outbreak of war in April 1861, sixteen-year-old Ensminger tried to enlist at Lafayette, but his father caught wind of it and brought him home. However, the next year, on 21 March, the young man enrolled for three years in Company H of the Eleventh Indiana Volunteers. In the fall of 1863, he was promoted to corporal, in the spring of 1864 to sergeant, and in March 1865, to first lieutenant of Company A of the Eleventh Indiana Regiment. After taking part in the ravaging of the Shenandoah Valley (scorched earth tactics) under General Philip Sheridan, he was badly wounded at the Battle of Cedar Creek, Virginia (19 October 1864), and was discharged at Baltimore on 26 July 1865.

Following the end of the war, the young veteran entered the Preparatory Department of Wabash College in the autumn of 1865. He started as a freshman in 1867. He stayed through his junior year, but spent 1870–71 as an apprentice with a local doctor. Ensminger then went to Cincinnati and enrolled in the Miami Medical College. He graduated in two years and went into practice with a former Wabash student and Civil War vet, Dr. Edward H. Cowan. They were physicians together from 1875 to 1890. Ensminger became known as an exceptional surgeon as well as physician.

In 1876 he married Louise Webb Austin (1854–1929), and they had one son, Leonard Ensminger (1878–1963), who became a physician as well. Their well known office was at 118 East Main Street in Crawfordsville.

In 1918 Ensminger was the victim of a stroke, but lived for three more years, dying on 25 September 1921. Louise died eight years later, and they are both buried in Oak Hill Cemetery.

References: GAR and McPherson Post No. 7 records at the Crawfordsville Public Library. See also: *War Papers Indiana Commanders* (1898), p. 486; G. T. Williams, *Pioneer Physicians and Surgeons of Montgomery County* (1943–1944); *Crawfordsville Journal*,

26 Sept. 1921; *Wabash Magazine*, XI (March 1871), 127; *Wabash Magazine* (June 1871), p. 146; Minutes of the Prudential Committee of the Wabash trustees; *Wabash Record Bulletin* (25 Oct. 1921), p. 17.

ESSEX, JULIUS (1843–?)

Julius Essex was born near Hope on 19 January 1843, the son of Rebecca Frey and Benjamin "Thomas" Essex. He had an older sister, Miranda, born in 1836.

The young man worked on the family farm before enrolling in the Normal School of Wabash College in 1857–58. He moved to Columbus, where he joined Company I of the Thirty-Third Indiana Volunteers. He was alleged to have deserted the army by 19 January 1863. By the time of the 1870 census, Essex was living in Columbus and had the job of deputy recorder. He had a twenty-two-year-old wife, Catharine, a native of Ireland, but no children.

It is unclear when and under what circumstances he died.

References: Tri-City Library of Jamestown, Indiana. See also: Bartholomew County Genealogical Society, *Bartholomew County Indiana* (1999), p. 154; *Biographical Record of Bartholomew County, Indiana* (1904), pp. 350–52, 500–01; *Hope Area Families* (1984), p. 262; *Biographical Directory of the Indiana General Assembly*, I (1980), p. 120; and the *Columbus Republican*, 28 Dec. 1876.

ESSICK, MICHAEL LUTHER (1834–1913)

Michael Essick was born in Guernsey County, Ohio, on 20 February 1834. His older brother, William J. Essick, graduated from Wabash College and went on to have a distinguished career in the Presbyterian ministry. The parents of these boys were Grizelda Todd and Samuel Essick, who moved to Gilead in Miami County, Indiana, in 1839.

Michael Essick grew up helping his father on their farm and in their tannery. Their home was on the Underground Railroad, and the boy sometimes helped guide fugitive slaves to or from his house. He spent four years at Wabash, two in the Preparatory Department (1852–54) and two as a freshman and sophomore (1854–56). In 1857 Essick moved to Manhattan, Kansas, where he bought a team of oxen and hauled stone for a new schoolhouse. Coincidentally, he married the schoolteacher, Ellen L. Rowley, on 31 October 1858. They eventually had five children, but three died in infancy.

For the next few years Essick practiced law, supplementing this with surveying. He was also elected to the state senate.

On 28 August 1862 he enrolled in Company G of the Eleventh Kansas Volunteer Cavalry and was honorably discharged on 20 September 1863. He had fought at the Battles of Prairie Grove (7 December 1862), Cave's Hill, Maysville (26 October 1862), and Van Buren (December 1862). He transferred to the Sixth

Kansas Cavalry as a first lieutenant, and between April and August of 1864 he served in Arkansas,

In 1865 Essick and his family settled in Rochester, Indiana, and for several years he was proprietor and editor of a Republican newspaper, the *Chronicle*. In 1867 he was elected for a two-year term as prosecutor of a circuit that covered eight counties, after which he returned to his private law practice.

Michael Essick died in Rochester on 19 September 1913.

References: Fulton County Public Library. See also: S. Willard, *Fulton County Folks* (1974), pp. 63–64; *Rochester Weekly Republican*, 20 Sept. 1913; and the Kansas State Historical Society.

EVANS, MARION PUTNAM (1827–1862)

Marion Evans was born in Owen County on 28 February 1827. He and his family moved to Tipton, Indiana, in 1841. According to the 1850 census, he was not living with his family, but with Newton Jackson, so there is no record of his parents' or his siblings' names. During the 1850s he was active in the Austin Masonic lodge and with building a new schoolhouse.

On 3 August 1852 he married eighteen-year-old Sarah Jane Smith. They had five children, only two of whom, Horace and Fremont, survived to adulthood.

Before the war Evans was a successful farmer and merchant, and in 1857 he was elected to the House of Representatives of the Indiana General Assembly for Howard and Tipton Counties.

On 29 November 1861 Evans responded to efforts being made to recruit young men from Tipton and neighboring counties into the Forty-seventh regiment. He joined 134 other volunteers and received a commission as first lieutenant and adjutant in Company K. Although he was committed to serve for three years, he had to resign on 4 September 1862 because of severe illness brought on by chronic diarrhea. He went directly home to Tipton and was nursed by his wife, but to no avail. He died eight days later and was buried in the Old Fairview Cemetery. In July 1866 Sarah Jane married Isaac H. Montgomery.

References: Donna Ekstrom, the Tipton County historian. See also: G. Kemp, *Tipton County: Her Land and People* (1976), p. 291; *Biographical Directory of the Indiana General Assembly*, I (1980), p. 121; and the *Tipton Daily Tribune*, 7 Nov. 1930.

FAIRCHILD, ADDISON M. (1843–1889)

Addison Fairchild was one of four Fairchild brothers to attend Wabash College. The others were John Bigelow, Hiram Orlando, and Asa Albert Fairchild. Addison Fairchild was born in Newtown, Fountain County, on 29 June 1843. His parents were Laura Porter Bigelow and John B. Fairchild. John was a Presbyterian minister, which meant the family moved every few years. While the family lived in the town of Wabash between 1857 and 1863, Addison Fairchild spent 1861–62 as a freshman at Wabash College.

On 4 January 1864 he enrolled in Company A of the Seventy-Fifth Indiana. His regiment merged with the Fourteenth Army Corps, one of three armies led by General William Tecumseh Sherman, that invaded Georgia and fought in the Battles of Missionary Ridge, Resaca, Kennesaw Mountain, Atlanta, and Savannah.

In May 1865 Fairchild was promoted to corporal and was transferred to Company K of the Forty-Second Indiana Regiment. He was discharged on 21 July 1865. It was later recorded that "his greatest thrill was being part of the Grand Review in Washington, D.C., before President Lincoln at the close of the war." This magnificent parade celebrated the virtual close of hostilities on 23 and 24 May 1865 and revived the spirits of the capital, which was still in mourning for the assassination of Lincoln. Over eighty thousand men of the Army of the Potomac headed the parade.

Somewhat at loose ends after the war, Fairchild returned to Marinette, Wisconsin, where his family was living, and took a job as a bookkeeper at the local sawmill, the Ludington Company. In 1868 he opened a pharmacy, and in 1870 his brother, Charles, joined him in the business.

In 1869 Fairchild married Maria Elizabeth Wright. They had four children.

He was chief of the Marinette Fire Department for sixteen years and treasurer of the school district for nine years. An enthusiastic Republican, he served as clerk of the circuit court and as town clerk. He was immersed in Masonic activities and was vice-president of the Marinette Mineral Land Company.

His wife died in 1887, and in 1888 he married Phyllis B. Brown, who became the first telephone operator in town when the exchange was put in the family drugstore.

Fairchild died on 2 September 1889, and his wife Phyllis on 28 October 1899. Both are buried in Woodlawn Cemetery in Marinette.

References: Stephenson Public Library of Marinette, Wisconsin. See also: T. B. Helms, *History of Wabash County, Indiana* (1884), p. 180; *Menominee River Memories* (1976); and *The West Shores of Green Bay Wisconsin* (1896), pp. 680–81.

FARNER, JOHN F. (c. 1844–1864)

John Farner was born about 1844, presumably in Connersville, where he was living when he enrolled at Wabash College for the academic year 1859–60. He attended Wabash for three years, the initial two in the Preparatory Department and the last (1861–62) as a freshman.

When he returned home to Connersville, he joined Company K of the Sixty-Ninth Indiana Regiment of Volunteers on 2 August 1862, committing to three years of military service. During the next year and a half, he rose to the rank of sergeant. Then, on 13 March 1864, while he and his comrades marched across a pontoon bridge spanning a bayou near Saluria, Texas, the structure collapsed. He and others were pitched into the water, and John drowned.

References: Indiana State Library Archives; *Wabash Record-Bulletin*, 26 March 1923, p. 31. See also a copy of a manuscript speech that Theodore Ristine delivered in March 1865, in the possession of the Wabash College Archives.

FERGUSON, SAMUEL B. (c. 1840–1885)

Samuel Ferguson was born in Perrysville in 1840, one of at least five children of Herbert and Elizabeth Ferguson. He came to Wabash in the fall of 1855 and spent two years in the Preparatory Department, then entered the Classical Course, which he pursued for another two years.

On 31 August 1861 he enrolled in Company B of the Eleventh Indiana Regiment of Volunteers for three years. By early 1862 he was clerk for General Charles Ferguson Smith, accompanying him at the battles of Fort Henry and Fort Donelson. In mid-March General Smith was replaced by General Ulysses S. Grant, and Ferguson continued as clerk for him. Shortly before the siege of Vicksburg, Ferguson was promoted to assistant adjutant general with the rank of captain, and he remained in service until well after the war ended, being released on 29 January 1866.

Returning to Perrysville, he rejoined his parents and became involved in the buying and selling of cattle. About 1875 he moved to Danville, Illinois, and died there on 6 July 1885. He is buried in the Hicks Cemetery of Highland Township, Vermillion County.

References: Newport-Vermillion County Library; the 1870 U.S. census; and the *Danville Daily Commercial*, 6 July 1885.

FINCH, HENEAGE BYRON (1835–1867)

Drunkenness was a persistent and devastating plague for the armies, both North and South. Liquor was readily available from camp rations and sutlers and almost anywhere else, and "strong drink" was seemingly desired by soldiers to pass the time and stimulate comradeship, relieving boring camp life. In reality, addiction, which was not clearly understood at the time, caused many a blunder in crucial leadership situations and ruined many an officer's career. Tens of thousands of man-hours were lost to drunkenness.

Whiskey spelled disaster for Heneage Finch. This privileged young man was born in 1835, the eldest of seven children of Nancy Allen and Fabius Maximus

Finch. His brother, John Allen Finch, also attended Wabash and served in the Civil War. Heneage Finch grew up in and around the city of Franklin, Indiana. His father had been an early settler in the Connersville and Noblesville areas and was a respected judge. The family was related by marriage to Indiana pioneers John and William Conner and friends with Governor Oliver P. Morton, Senator Henry S. Lane, and a large number of influential Indiana families.

Wabash College catalogs state that Finch spent two years in the Preparatory Department from 1854 to 1856, and in 1857–58 he was a sophomore in the Scientific Course.

With the outbreak of the war, he enlisted for three months in the Seventh Indiana Regiment as quartermaster sergeant of field and staff under Colonel T. J. Wood. Finch spent most of his service in what is now West Virginia, engaging in a number of skirmishes but no major battles. Mustered out on 2 August 1861, he re-enlisted for three years in the Thirty-Third Indiana Volunteers, commanded by Wabash College graduate Colonel John Coburn.

Perhaps it was the Wabash connection that induced Coburn to overlook Finch's dereliction of duty as a first lieutenant and quartermaster: Finch did not file a report or keep adequate books for two years. As Lieutenant Colonel James M. Henderson wrote to Judge Finch, "His first introduction into the regiment was not in any way agreeable to the officers, yet sir, we had too much respect for Governor Morton to then ask for his transfer." Henderson continued, "I, as well as other officers of the regiment, have spoken to Lieutenant Finch on the subject of dissipation, have advised and counselled him, as we would a brother, upon the inevitable ruin he was bringing upon himself. He has been threatened by Brigade and Divisional commanders with dismissal from the service, and yet, he has paid very little attention to anyone, counselling himself with a favorite expression of his, 'We did not mean it.'"

Finch was prevailed upon to resign from the army in November 1863. He returned home, and a few years later, on 17 July 1866, he married Mary M. Morrison. The couple had a daughter.

On 7 October 1867 the *Indianapolis Journal* announced that, "after a long and painful illness," Finch had died. He was buried in Greenlawn Cemetery, Franklin.

References: Unpublished letters in the Indiana Historical Society; C. W. Taylor, *The Bench and Bar of Indiana* (1895), pp. 276–79; *Indianapolis Journal*, 7 Oct. 1867.

FINCH, JOHN ALLEN (1842–1899)

John Finch was born in Franklin on 15 November 1842, younger son of Nancy Allen and Fabius Maximus Finch. John and his brother, Heneage, whose story is told above, were two of seven children.

John Finch entered the Preparatory Department of Wabash College in the autumn of 1858, advanced to the freshman class the next year, and graduated in June 1863. He was an active member of the Beta Theta Pi fraternity. The Finch Fellowhip is named for John and his father, Maximus.

During the summer of 1862, between his junior and senior years, he served as clerk in the quartermaster's department, but this experience greatly weakened his health, and he did not return to campus until January of 1863. Six months later he took his degree and enrolled in the 114th Indiana Regiment in response to the Morgan episode, serving from 9 to 21 July.

For the next few years, Finch studied law. He was admitted to the bar in 1866. He joined his father in the firm of Finch and Finch, but ill health still troubled him, and he sought relief in travel throughout the United States and Europe. His wanderings provided the opportunity to write letters and articles that were published in the *Indianapolis Mirror*, the *Indianapolis Sentinel*, and the *New York Tribune*.

In the course of publishing with the *Tribune*, he became acquainted with its editor, Horace Greeley, whom Finch supported against Ulysses S. Grant at the Republican Convention of 1872.

In 1879 Finch was appointed to an Indiana commission with instructions to recommend revisions in the law governing insurance. Gradually he became an expert and went to all states and territories of the nation as a consultant, preparing materials for *Annual Digest of Life and Accident Insurance Cases*, begun in 1887, and *The Insurance Agent, His Risks, Duties and Liabilities*.

In a contemporary biographical work titled *Men of Progress*, Finch was characterized as "a man of wide reading, close observation, keen sympathies and a cultured taste. He is at home with almost any subject."

Finch never married. He died unexpectedly on 30 May 1899, while on a visit to St. Paul, Minnesota.

References: *Wabash Magazine*, IV (July 1863), pp. 257–59; *Wabash Magazine*, XI (March 1871), p. 138; *Wabash Magazine*, XII (Jan. 1872), p. 76. Good biographical sketches appear in W. Cumback and J. B. Maynard, *Men of Progress* (1899), pp. 266–67 and C. W. Taylor, *The Bench and Bar of Indiana* (1895), pp. 276–79.

FISK, DANIEL WILLARD (c. 1838–?)

Daniel Fisk was born about 1838–39 in Pierpont, Ohio, one of six sons of Jerusha and James L. Fisk.

The family settled in Lafayette in about 1846, and Daniel attended Wabash College for the school year 1855–56. He then returned to Lafayette, where he became an apprentice in the law firm of Chase and Wilstach and was admitted to the bar in 1859. In 1860 the family moved to St. Paul, Minnesota.

His service record could not be found.

In the summer of 1866 all six of the Fisk brothers took part in an expedition from Minnesota to Montana, and three of them (Robert, Daniel, and Andrew) established a newspaper, the *Helena Herald*, which proved very successful and was not sold until 1902.

On 12 October 1878 Daniel Fisk married Julia Walker, who was born in Pennsylvania on 30 May 1855. She died in Helena on 27 December 1898. With the sale of the *Helena Herald* in 1902, Fisk became treasurer of Helena. He presumably died before the 1910 census was taken.

References: See those cited for his older brother, Robert, below. See also an obituary for Julia Fisk in the *Helena Daily Independent*, 29 Dec. 1898.

FISK, ROBERT EMMETT (1837–1908)

Robert Finch was born on 9 August 1837 in Pierpont, Ohio, the third of six brothers. His other siblings were John, James, Daniel, Van, and Andrew. Their father was James L. Fisk, and the mother of the older boys was Jerusha. Andrew's mother was Teresa Loveland Fisk, and she may have given birth to one or more of the others.

The parents settled in Lafayette as early as 1846. Robert and Daniel both enrolled in the Preparatory Department at Wabash in 1855–56. Robert then joined his older brother James in working on the *Lafayette Daily Courier*, and a year or two later he worked at the city clerk's office.

By 1860 the Fisks had left Indiana. Many of them went to St. Paul, Minnesota, while Robert made his way to New York City, where he briefly worked at a printing firm before raising a company of volunteers from Brooklyn, becoming its lieutenant within the larger New York Sixty-Sixth Regiment. His regiment went immediately to Virginia, where on 7 May 1864, he sustained a bad concussion when an artillery shell burst near him during the Battle of the Wilderness, the first battle of Lieutenant General Ulysses S. Grant's Virginia Overland Campaign against General Robert E. Lee.

In New York City, recovering from his injury, Fisk became restless and recruited another company, Company G of the 132nd New York Infantry, and became its captain. By the autumn of that year, he was stationed at New Berne, North Carolina. While there, a quilt from Connecticut found its way to him from Vernon in that state, where women made quilts for the Union troops at the front. When Fisk wrote to thank the ladies, he was put in touch with the younger sister of one of the seamstresses, Elizabeth Clarke Chester. She and Fisk struck up a correspondence for the rest of the war, and when he was released from the army in June 1865, he traveled to Vernon to meet Lizzie. Within a few weeks they were engaged to marry, but the young veteran felt that he must first make his fortune.

In 1862 gold had been discovered in Montana, and Fisk and several of his brothers decided to try their luck. During the winter of 1865–66 Fisk worked for the *Hawk Eye* of Burlington, Iowa. The expedition to the gold fields of Montana took place during the summer of 1866, with the Fisk brothers reaching Helena in September. By November three of them, Robert, Daniel, and Andrew, started a Republican-backed paper, the *Helena Herald*.

Robert Fisk returned to Vernon, Connecticut, and married Lizzie on 21 March 1867. They honeymooned in New York City, where Fisk purchased printing presses and paper stock for the Helena newspaper. These supplies had to accompany them by train and riverboat to Montana. For the next thirty years, Fisk was chief editor of the *Helena Herald*, while Lizzie raised seven children: Grace, Robert, Loveland, James, Florence, and sons R. C. and Asa. Lizzie wrote letters depicting the joys and sorrows of living in a mining frontier town that span twenty-five years, a collection housed at Wabash.

After a mild stroke, Fisk retired and sold the newspaper in 1902. He and Lizzie then moved to Berkeley, California, where he died on 27 December 1908. Lizzie lived until 21 April 1927.

References: Dorothy Van Cleef of Lafayette, Indiana, and Dolores Harris of Helena, Montana. See also the obituaries and other articles relating to the Fisk brothers in the *Helena Daily Independent*, 28 Dec. 1908 and 29 Dec. 1908; Rex C. Myers (ed.), *Lizzie: The Letters of Elizabeth Chester Fisk, 1864–1893* (1989).

FLESHER, HENRY BROWN (1835–1911)

Henry Flesher was born in Augusta County, Virginia, on 1 January 1835. His parents were Elizabeth B. (1800–1872) and John (1803–1886). They had five children, with three dying in infancy, leaving only Henry and his sister, Mary A.

The family left Virginia in about 1837 and settled for two years in Preble County, Ohio, before continuing westward to Indiana to settle on a farm north of West Lebanon. Young Flesher worked on the farm until the autumn of 1855, when he enrolled in the Preparatory Department of Wabash College. There he earned a reputation as a singer in the "Hoosier Quartet." He remained for two academic years and then returned to Warren County as a teacher. He first taught at the Bell School in Pike Township and then at the Perrysville High School.

On 15 August 1862 he joined the Eighty-Sixth Indiana Regiment for three years, and he soon was promoted to hospital steward. His regiment saw action at major battles such as Stones River and Chickamauga. On 19–20 September 1863 Flesher was tending the wounded on the field while his fellow soldiers were in retreat and was consequently taken captive and confined in Libby Prison at Richmond, Virginia. Luckily, after three months, he was part of a prisoner exchange and was granted a furlough to go home. He lost little time in persuading Anna M. Kirkpatrick to marry him at Perrysville on 18 February 1864.

Flesher was released from the army at Nashville on 12 June 1865 and returned to Warren County. Soon he and Anna bought a farm near West Lebanon, where they made a specialty of growing grain and livestock, supplemented later by the cultivation of fruit. They had three children: Elizabeth, Mary, and Harry. Anna died on 2 October 1902, while Henry lived for another decade. He died at home on his farm on 7 December 1911 and is buried in the West Lebanon Cemetery.

References: Mr. and Mrs. Walter Salts of West Lebanon. See also: *Attica Ledger Tribune*, 14 Dec. 1911; *Warren Review*, 21 Dec. 1911; and *Biographical History of Tippecanoe, White, Jasper, Newton, Benton, Warren and Pulaski Counties, Indiana* (1899), pp. 961–62.

FOOTE, HORACE S. (1842–1928)

Born in Painesville-on-the-Lake, Ohio, in 1842, Horace Foote grew up in Peru, Indiana. His parents were Emily Forbes and Carter Foote, and he was one of nine children.

Foote showed an aptitude for reading and writing at an early age, and at ten years old he helped a local printer set type for a political journal during the 1852 presidential campaign. At the age of fourteen he entered the Preparatory Department of Wabash College and remained four years, completing his freshman year in the spring of 1861.

In August 1861 Foote was one of ninety-eight men from Peru to enroll in Company A of the Eighth Cavalry, attached to the Thirty-Ninth Regiment of Indiana Volunteers. During 1861–62 the Eighth Cavalry served mostly in Kentucky as part of the Army of the Ohio and then became attached to the Army of the Cumberland in 1863–64, seeing action in Tennessee, Georgia, and Alabama. Foote was promoted to first lieutenant on 1 April 1864 and to captain on 11 May 1864, and at the end of the year he was honorably discharged. Returning home, he found his father dying from consumption. In 1865 Horace Foote married Sarena Higgins. They had three children, but only one survived to adulthood.

During the late 1860s the Footes settled in San Jose, California, where he founded, with D. M. Adams, the first morning newspaper, the *Daily Independent*. This marked the beginning of a distinguised writing career. As a journalist he was affiliated with San Jose *Herald*, *Mercury*, and *Times*, and in 1884 he began a magazine of horticulture and viticulture called the *Santa Clara Valley*. He also became the unofficial county historian for the last forty years of his life.

From about 1895 to 1920, Foote served as clerk of the San Jose board of supervisors. In 1920 he formally retired but continued his various real estate interests. He died on 6 November 1928, survived only by his daughter, Mrs. George Whitney of Campbell.

References: R. Bakehorn, *Civil War Veterans of Miami County* (1979 photocopy), p. 24; A. L. Bodurtha, *History of Miami County, Indiana* (1905), p. 520; *History of Miami County, Indiana* (1887), p. 308; *San Jose Mercury Herald*, 7 Nov. 1928 and 8 Nov. 1928; E. T. Sawyer, *The History of Santa Clara County, California* (1922), p. 115; F. Rall, *The History of San Jose and Surroundings* (1872), p. 314.

FORD, JAMES MITCHELL (1841–1927)

James Ford was born in the Indiana town of Wabash on 31 May 1841, one of seven children born to William J. and Mary McGee Ford. He entered the freshman class of Wabash College in the autumn of 1861, but stayed only one term and finished the school year in Indianapolis.

Ford may have joined an Indiana regiment early in the war but became ill and returned home. However, on 1 March 1864 he enrolled in Company H of the 130th Regiment as a first sergeant for three years. In September that year he was promoted to second lieutenant, and in April 1865 he was promoted to first lieutenant, completing his military obligation at St. Louis, Missouri, on 8 June 1865. While in the army, he was part of the Federal force under General Sherman, heading to Atlanta. Before mustering out he was transferred to Jefferson County, Missouri, where he joined the department of ordnance.

After the war Ford went to the University of Michigan at Ann Arbor, pursued a degree in medicine and pharmacy, and graduated in 1869. The same year he married Beulah Kirk, and they eventually had a son, Ernest. He spent another year doing postgraduate work and then returned home to Wabash to become a partner in the medical practice of Dr. Andrew J. Smith.

After a career as a druggist and land speculator, about 1885 Ford moved to Denison, Texas, to become president of the First National Bank. A few years later he relocated to Phoenix, Arizona, where he was elected to the territorial senate in 1891 and focused his energies and investments on copper mining.

In 1907 the family settled in Alhambra, California. Ford died at home on 13 November 1927 and is buried in the Inglewood Park Mausoleum.

References: Wabash Carnegie Public Library. See also: *Biographical Memoirs of Wabash County, Indiana* (1901), pp. 626–27; University of Michigan, *Catalogue of Graduates, 1837–1921* (1923), p. 401; University of Michigan Office of Alumni Records; and the *Alhambra Post Advocate*, 14 Nov. 1927. Information about Kansas City was provided by Mary Burt.

FRENCH, JOHN LOUIS (1832–1912)

John Louis French was born on 23 May 1832 near Vevay, the son of Mary Ann Weaver and William French, whose father had been a veteran of the American Revolution.

By the time French entered the Preparatory Department of Wabash College in the autumn of 1853, his family had settled in Jacksonville, Indiana. He attended Wabash for six years, culminating in his graduation in the summer of 1859.

He spent the next three years at Lane Theological Seminary in Cincinnati and on 24 September 1862 was ordained by the Madison Presbytery. From 1862 to 1869 he served as pastor of the Presbyterian church in Batavia, Ohio, and toward the close of the Civil War in 1865, he also functioned as chaplain for the Forty-First Regiment of the Ohio National Guard.

Because his throat had been damaged by diphtheria, French could not effectively preach, so he gave up plans to become a full-time minister and became chief clerk in the contract department of the U.S. Post Office in Washington, DC, a position he retained until 1881.

On 17 October 1871 he married Agnes Laura Cherwell of New York State. They had two sons, Harry G., born on 23 December 1872, and Leon L., who was born on 11 January 1874 and subsequently attended Wabash.

Following the death of his wife, John French joined his son Leon in Searchlight, Nevada, where he died on 28 March 1912, just short of his eightieth birthday.

References: 1905 alumni questionnaire in the Ramsay Archives, Wabash College; *Lane Theological Seminary General Catalogue: 1829–1899*; and the *Wabash College Record* (July 1912), p. 20.

FRENCH, JOHN S. (1829–1914)

John S. French was born in Mercer County, Kentucky, on 13 July 1829, one of five children of Mary Smock and Simon French.

In 1822 the family settled in Marion County, Indiana, where French's father established himself as a chairmaker until 1844, when he moved his business to Montgomery County. Proximity to Wabash College facilitated son John's attendance at the Preparatory Department from 1846 to 1850 and then as a freshman between 1850 and 1851.

For the next six years French taught school locally, but at about the age of twenty-seven, he embarked on a career in medicine, becoming an apprentice for two years with Dr. J. W. Straughan of Parkersburg. He subsequently paid tuition and studied at Rush Medical College in Chicago. By 1860 he was established as a physician in Waveland, where his wife, Jemima Mann, gave birth to two children, Rebecca and David. Two years later they moved to Alamo, where a third child, Thomas, was born.

At the beginning of December 1863, French enrolled as an assistant surgeon in Company B of the 120th Indiana Volunteers. In April 1864 he became regimental surgeon attached to the field and staff headquarters in Georgia. In January 1866, well after the war ended, he was mustered out and returned home.

However, in his absence, his wife had died, so French married for a second time in May 1866. He and Mary Stubbins settled in Coal Creek near Crawfordsville, and Mary raised John's three children while bearing two of her own, Sophia and Frederick Charles.

After Mary died, John French moved back to Crawfordsville in 1880 and became active in the local Presbyterian Church, the GAR post, the Odd Fellows, and the Republican Party. Toward the end of his life, he moved to Pittsboro, Hendricks County, where he died on 19 September 1914.

References: G. T. Williams, *Pioneer Physicians and Surgeons of Montgomery County, Indiana* (1943); *Journal of the Indiana State Medical Association*, III (10 Oct. 1914), p. 484; and the *Descriptive Book of McPherson Post No. 7*.

FRY, SPEED SMITH (1817–1892)

Speed Fry was one of the oldest Wabash College students to serve in the Civil War. Before that, he had seen action in the Mexican War, as well.

He was born in Boyle County, Kentucky, on 9 September 1817. After attending Center College in Danville, Kentucky, Fry transferred to Wabash in the fall of 1837 and became a sophomore. He graduated in 1840 and returned to Danville to study law with his uncle. Admitted to the Kentucky bar in 1843, he practiced for three years until the conflict with Mexico erupted. He then spent portions of 1846–47 as a captain in the Second Kentucky Volunteer Regiment. Returning to Danville, he resumed his law practice, and in 1857 he became a judge in Boyle County.

When war broke out in 1861, Fry was immediately appointed a colonel of the local Union militia, but soon he was drawn into a regular regiment as colonel of the Fourth Kentucky Infantry.

On 21 March 1862 Fry was appointed Brigadier General of Volunteers, a position he held until 24 August 1865. After the war he ran unsuccessfully as a Republican for Congress and was supervisor for internal revenue collection as well as superintendent of the Soldiers Home in Louisville, Kentucky. He died on 1 August 1892 and was buried in the Bellevue Cemetery, Danville.

References: Kentucky Historical Society; E. J. Warner, *Generals in Blue* (1964), pp. 163–64.

FRY, THOMAS WALKER JR. (1839–1868)

Thomas Walker Fry Jr. and his father, Thomas Walker Sr., both served in the Civil War. The junior Thomas Fry and his brother, William R., both were born in Crawfordsville and attended Wabash College. Their father was a pioneer surgeon in Montgomery County, a member of the vestry of the newly founded St. John's Episcopal Church, and an early trustee of the college. He married Maria W. Rochester in November 1837, and they had five children: Thomas Jr., William, Lewis, Julia, and Letticia.

Thomas Jr. joined the Preparatory Department at Wabash as an eleven-year-old in the fall of 1850 and graduated in June 1859. After one year of law school in Lexington, Kentucky, he returned to Crawfordsville, hoping to be admitted to the Indiana bar, but answered the call of duty on 21 April 1861 and became a first lieutenant in Company H of the Eleventh Indiana Regiment under the command of Lew Wallace. After completeing his three-month commitment, he re-enlisted for three more years in the same regiment. He transferred to Company E and by December became a second lieutenant, followed shortly by promotions to first lieutenant and captain and designation as assistant quartermaster, the post he retained until mustering out of the army on 31 May 1866.

When Fry returned from the war, he discontinued his pursuit of a law career and started a business venture, endorsed heartily by the local newspaper: "Our friend, Capt. Tom W. Fry, we are pleased to learn has opened out in trade at the town of Pleasant Hill, this county. It is his intention to keep on hands at all times a a sufficient stock of dry-goods, groceries and drugs, to meet the immediate demand of that people, and at prices as low as like articles can be purchased at retail. . ."

Within two years he died, circumstances unknown, at the age of twenty-nine.

References: G. T. Williams, *Pioneer Physicians and Surgeons of Montgomery County, Indiana* (1943); *Crawfordsville Weekly Journal*, 5 July 1866; student newspaper, the *Geyser*, 5 March 1873; *Crawfordsville Star*, 23 June 1874; and *Wabash College Record*, I (July 1903), p. 26.

FRY, WILLIAM R. (1843–aft. 1880)

William Fry was born in Crawfordsville, one of the five children of Maria W. Rochester and Dr. Thomas Walker Fry Sr., as we have seen in the sketch of his older brother, Thomas Walker Fry Jr. Their sisters were Julia and Letticia, and their other brother was Lewis.

Fry was enrolled in the Preparatory Department at Wabash from 1856 to 1858 and the Normal School from 1860 to 1863.

He enlisted in the military, with records only showing that he was in the Army of the Cumberland in 1864. He married Fanny Hough of Crawfordsville on 15 November 1866. Initially they lived with her father, George Hough, who was in the insurance business, and Fry joined him. By the mid-1870s the couple were in Rockville, where Fry was part owner of a drugstore.

In 1880 the Frys appear in Crawfordsville census with two children: George, age twelve, and Jane, age four. Fanny died two years later and is buried in Oak Hill Cemetery. Fry moved away from Montgomery County by 1890, and the date and place of his death is unknown.

References: See the sketch of William's older brother, Thomas W. Jr. Also: H. W.

Beckwith, *History of Montgomery County* (1881), p. 269; *Crawfordsville Weekly Journal*, 1 Dec. 1864; *Crawfordsville Saturday Mercury*, 2 Oct. 1875; and the Rockville Public Library.

FULLENWIDER, JAMES CAMERON (1838–1863)

James Fullenwider was born in 1838 in Waveland, one of eleven children raised by Lavinia Erwin Allen and Eleazer (1802–1870) Fullenwider. James grew up knowing all about Wabash College because his uncle and physician, Samuel Fullenwider, was one of the founders of the college, and his older brother, Samuel, matriculated at the college between 1847 and 1849.

Fullenwider attended Waveland Academy and in the autumn of 1858 enrolled at Wabash as a sophomore. He pledged the Beta Theta Pi fraternity. Unlike most of his peers, he pursued the Classical Course of study and graduated in June 1861. He had planned to go to Lane Theological Seminary in Cincinnati, but instead he made his way in September to Indianapolis and volunteered service to Company E of the Thirty-Third Indiana Regiment, whose colonel was John Coburn, a fellow Beta and Wabash graduate, class of 1846. He soon became a quartermaster sergeant, but on 4 March 1863 his regiment was involved the battle at Thompson's Station (or Spring Hill) in Tennessee, where the unit was lured into a trap and found itself surrounded by vastly superior numbers of Confederates. Coburn spared the lives of as many of his troops as possible by surrendering and being imprisoned. Fullenwider was active in command at the time, also. Unfortunately, he was so seriously wounded that he died the next day.

His body was brought back to Waveland for burial in the Presbyterian Township Cemetery.

References: *Wabash Magazine*, IV (July 1863), p. 331. See also: H. W. Beckwith, *History of Montgomery County* (1881), p. 110; the American Legion Register of Graves, Indiana State Library Archives. For Fullenwider family background, see Henrietta Bromwell, *The Bromwell Genealogy* (1910), p. 212; and Harry Fullenwider of Crawfordsville.

FULWIDER, JAMES M. (ca. 1837–1894)

James Fulwider was born in Virginia in about 1837, one of eleven children of Sarah Houff and Joseph Henry Fulwider. The family was in Montgomery County, Indiana, in 1850, and by the time of the next census (1860), James was living on his own in Crawfordsville.

He married Mary Melinda York of Edgar County, Illinois, on 6 September 1861. On 19 October 1864 Fulwider enrolled in Company B of the Seventy-Second Indiana Regiment of Volunteers, giving his occupation as a farmer. In July 1865 he transferred to Company B of the Forty-Fourth Indiana Regiment.

He was mustered out at Nashville, Tennessee, on 14 September 1865.

That autumn Fulwider entered Wabash College and remained for two academic years before resuming farming somewhere in Illinois. In 1869 he was divorced, and on 31 March 1872 he married Armilda Frazier in Guthrie, Iowa. They settled in Tuscola, Illinois. In March 1875 Armilda contracted malaria. She died one month later on 8 April from a miscarriage.

The following year the widower married Sarah Smith, the woman who had nursed Armilda during her protracted illness. She was about twenty-three and bore many children: Sarah (1879), Evangeline (1880), Arthy (1882), James (1884), Joseph (1886), Jacob (1888), and John (1891).

James Fulwider suffered from several health problems and was granted a monthly pension of six dollars by the government. He died on 5 February 1894, leaving his widow landless and penniless, according to her application for a widow's pension.

References: Indiana State Library Archives; *Family Histories: Montgomery County, Indiana* (1989), p. 169; military pension file in the National Archives, Washington, DC.

GALEY, MILTON H. (1837–1894)

Milton Galey was born in Crawfordsville on 14 September 1837, one of six children of Lucy Whilhite and William W. Galey. His siblings were William L., Frances R., Beal V., Virgil, and Louise. Beal Galey also attended Wabash briefly. For many years their father was a tailor, but with the death of his wife in 1854, he took up farming.

Milton Galey entered the Preparatory Department of Wabash College in 1853, but, stirred by the attack on Fort Sumter in April 1861, like so many others from Crawfordsville, he enrolled in Company C of the Eleventh Indiana Regiment for three months. During this time he went to Cumberland, Maryland, and Harper's Ferry, mustering out at Indianapolis on 4 August.

He and Beal studied dentistry with Dr. J. F. Canine, and in 1867 they opened their own dental practice in Crawfordsville. On 29 December 1870 Galey married thirty-year-old Frances McClintock. They had one son, Scott. The Galeys were active in the Methodist church, and Milton also was involved with the Knights of Pythias. Along with Beal, Milton was part of a Crawfordsville quintet that sang throughout the state.

Frances Galey died on 6 November 1891 and Milton on 2 March 1894. They are buried in Oak Hill Cemetery.

References: H. W. Beckwith, *History of Montgomery County* (1881), pp. 165–66; *History of Montgomery County, Indiana* (Bowen and Co., 1913), p. 1215; *Crawfordsville Daily Journal*, 3 March 1894; and *Crawfordsville Star*, 13 Nov. 1891.

GALEY, SAMUEL T. (1837–1907)

Samuel Galey was born in September 1837 at the family homestead six miles southeast of Crawfordsville. His parents were Caroline Beatty and James Galey. Samuel's older brother, William M., attended Wabash briefly in 1848–49.

Prior to his admission to Wabash in 1861, Galey was teaching school and living with his mother and brother. His father died some time prior to 1850. Galey volunteered for emergency military service for the Morgan raid in 1863. Once the raider turned east and the crisis for Indiana subsided, Galey's service in the 108th Indiana Regiment ended, having lasted only from 11 to 18 July 1863.

That September he married a local woman, Emma Robinson, and they eventually had two sons, Clarence and Howard. Galey was a carpenter. He died on 24 September 1907 and is interred at the Masonic Cemetery in Crawfordsville.

References: *Crawfordsville Daily Journal*, 25 Sept. 1907, p. 1; and FamilySearch.org. There is also a Galey family genealogy compiled by Warren Galey in the Crawfordsville District Public Library.

GERRISH, JAMES L. (1836–1930)

James Gerrish was born on 15 November 1836 at Boscawen, New Hampshire, one of six children of Eliza Dodge and Abiel Gerrish. His siblings were Maria, Martha, Mary, Jane, and Anna.

Soon after the family moved to a farm in West Creek Township, Lake County, in 1856, Gerrish came to Crawfordsville for a year of study in the Preparatory Department of Wabash College.

In August 1862 he enrolled for three years in Company A of the Ninety-Ninth Indiana Infantry Regiment. Records describe him as five feet nine inches tall, with light complexion, dark hair, and grey eyes. One day in early November 1862, two runaway horses trampled him in their fright, leaving him badly injured. Although he continued to serve until honorably discharged near Washington, DC, on 5 June 1865, he spent much of his service time in the hospital.

On 15 February 1866 Gerrish married Lena D. Dyer fron Wheaton, Illinois. They eventually had four children. Two of these, Carrie and Agnes, died young, while Henry and Catherine (Kittie) grew to adulthood. Gerrish settled first in Lowell and farmed there until 1871, when he moved to Lockport, Illinois, only to return to Lowell in 1874 to resume farming. In the 1880s he expanded into cattle breeding, and in 1891 he relocated to Hammond and began a meat-packing business. He also became a meat inspector for the United States government.

Gerrish's health deteriorated to the point that he found it difficult to keep working, so he and Lena moved to Fort Worth, Texas, in February 1903 to seek a more congenial climate. Gerrish died on 8 March 1930 at the couple's home.

Lena died a few months later, on 1 July. They are both buried at Greenwood Cemetery, Fort Worth.

References: Lake County Public Library of Merrillville and the Hammond Public Library. See also: D. R. Lucas, *New History of the 99th Indiana Infantry* (1900), p. 31; W. F. Howat, *Standard History of Lake County, Indiana* (1915), I, p. 137; W. A. Goodspeed and C. Blanchard, *Counties of Porter and Lake, Indiana* (1882), p. 755; *History of Lake County, Indiana* (1931), II, p. 180; and his military pension file at the National Archives, Washington, DC.

GASKILL (GASKELL), JOHN W. (ca. 1834–1863)

John Gaskill was born in about 1834 somewhere in Indiana, the eldest child of Abigail Rippey and John Wesley Gaskill. His siblings were Nancy, Newton, Jasper, and Elizabeth. When he entered the Normal School at Wabash in the fall of 1857, the young man declared Frankfort to be his hometown. He stayed the course until June 1860.

On 13 August 1862 he mustered in to Company K of the Seventy-Second Indiana Volunteers as a corporal, and within a few months he was promoted to second lieutenant. He died at Murfreesboro on 20 February 1863.

Reference: Frankfort Public Library.

GEIGER, HENRY H. (1840–1912)

Henry Geiger was born near Rockville on 9 April 1840, the youngest of three boys. His oldest brother, William, also went to Wabash and served in the Civil War. The middle brother was James. Geiger spent three years at Wabash (1858–1861) in the Preparatory and Normal School. He then presumably worked on his father's farm before enrolling as a corporal in Company A of the Eighty-fifth Indiana Infantry at Annapolis, Indiana. On 2 September the regiment was fully organized at Terre Haute and set off for Kentucky. Between September 1862 and February 1863, it moved throughout the state, from Covington and Falmouth to Lexington, Danville, and Louisville. Next, it was on to Nashville and Franklin in Tennessee. At the Battle of Thompson's Station many were forced to surrender and march to Libby Prison at Richmond, Virginia. They were released and allowed to return to Indianapolis, but by June the regiment was back in Tennessee at Murfreesboro. Because of illness, Geiger was honorably discharged on 17 August.

In 1865 Geiger left Indiana and settled in Missouri, first in Jackson County and then in the spring of 1866, at Maryville, Nodaway County. By 1870 he had his own sawmill, and the following year he married Martha S. Davis. Their first child, Edgar, was born in 1872 but soon died. Then came Elizabeth in 1875, Henry M. in 1881, and John, who died in infancy, in 1886. The family lived in Maryville for at least twenty years, during which time Geiger was elected for two years as Nodaway County treasurer and appointed twice as postmaster (1873 and 1878). He also bought and sold livestock.

About 1887 the Geigers moved to Denver, where Martha died shortly thereafter. In 1892 Henry married Sarah Burgess, and they headed farther west to Seattle. Henry Geiger died at home on 5 April 1912.

References: Maryville (Missouri) Public Library. See also: *Past and Present of Nodaway County*, I (1910), pp. 341–42; *History of Nodaway County, Missouri* (1882), pp. 284–85, 760–63; M. L. Cooper, *The Civil War and Nodaway County, Missouri* (1989), p. 108; *Maryville Tribune Weekly*, 12 May 1912; and *Seattle Daily Times*, 6 April 1912.

GEIGER, WILLIAM M. (1834–1908)

William Geiger was the older of two brothers to attend Wabash and serve in the Civil War; the other was Henry, just described. William Geiger was born on 21 December 1834 in Charleston, Indiana. Later the family moved to Rockville, and it was from there that William came to Crawfordsville in the autumn of 1852 to enter the Preparatory Department of Wabash College. He spent two years in this department and a further two years (1854–56) as a freshman and a sophomore. Afterwards, he presumably returned to Parke County and worked on the family farm.

On 5 April 1859 at Bethany, Geiger married Rebecca James Mann. They would have four sons: Charles, William, David, and Joseph. When Geiger reported for duty as a first lieutenant of Company I of the Thirty-First Indiana Regiment, he was recorded as being six feet tall, with light hair, fair complexion, and blue eyes. During his three years' enlistment, he also was a regimental musician.

After training at Camp Vigo near Terre Haute, the regiment proceeded to Camp Calhoun on the Green River in Kentucky, which proved to be a very unhealthy location. In the coming months ten soldiers died of disease and exposure. Geiger contracted chronic diarrhea and was allowed to resign on 7 January 1862.

After the war the Geiger family settled on a farm in Parke County. He owned seventy-eight acres and was known as an artist and a farmer. He also speculated in land in both Parke and Montgomery Counties, and by 1879 he lived in the town of Waveland.

In 1904 Geiger styled himself a photographer in Denver, living initially at 2829 Perry Street and later at 3252 West 30th Avenue, where he died on 23 February 1908. His wife, Rebecca, lived until 17 March 1918. They are buried in Fairmount Cemetery in Denver.

References: Rockville Public Library; and his military pension file at the National

Archives in Washington, DC. See also: *Parke County Centennial Memorial* (1916), pp. 22–23.

GEORGE, WILLIAM A. (ca. 1826–1895)

William Alexander George was born in Ohio, the only child of Rhoda A. McDonald and Ellis Barrett George. He attended Wabash in 1840–41, indicating his home was in Danville, Illinois.

At the time of the 1860 census, George was farming land valued at about $8,000 in Fall Creek Township, Madison County. His wife, Mary A., was in her early thirties, a native of North Carolina, and a mother of four: Lucretia, Cynthia, William, and John.

George was among those who rushed to join the army when the Morgan scare alarmed southern Indiana. He joined Company I of the 110th Indiana Regiment on 10 July, but the regiment was quickly dissolved after that time, and he was dismissed on 13 July.

His family was on the farm in Fall Creek Township in 1880, and their twenty-one-year-old son, John, lived with them. George died on 19 July 1895 and is buried in Bunker Cemetery of Madison County.

References: Census records and the Anderson Public Library.

GERHART, JOHN R. (ca. 1845–1884)

John Gerhart was born in Lebanon, Pennsylvania, in about 1845. In 1863 he lived in Thorntown, Indiana, and worked as a harness maker. After serving ten days with Company A of the 102nd Indiana Regiment when Morgan threatened, John and his brother, Isaac N. Gerhart, returned to Thorntown.

On 21 March 1864 Gerhart enrolled in Company G of the Eleventh Indiana Volunteers. Reporting for duty on 8 May, he boarded a ship to Fortress Monroe, near Washington, DC, and between August and December marched and counter-marched throughout Virginia and participated in battles at Cedar Creek, Opequan (10 September 1864), Fisher's Hill (21–22 September 1864), Woodstock (9 October 1864), and Harrisonburg. In January 1865 his regiment was stationed at Baltimore until they were mustered out on 26 July 1865.

Gerhart served under a former Wabash student, Captain John Caven, who probably urged him to enter Wabash, which he did in the autumn of 1865. He studied for two years and then married a local Crawfordsville girl, Sarah Eva McMechan, on 22 July 1867.

The Gerharts remained in Crawfordsville until sometime in the early 1870s, when they moved to South Bend. Gerhart worked as a trimmer of carriages and then as a clerk with the post office, sorting mail aboard trains journeying between

Chicago and Cleveland. His work was well regarded, and he was promoted twice during the next ten years.

In 1883, for unknown reasons, he stole several sacks of mail, and when questioned by railroad detectives, he admitted his guilt. After nine months at the "northern prison," presumably Michigan City, he was pardoned by Governor Albert Porter. However, his wife divorced him and with her two children moved back to Crawfordsville to live with her father.

Gerhart moved to South Bend and took up lodgings with Dr. A. G. Miller on Michigan Street. On the evening of New Year's Day 1884, he took strychnine, and in spite of everything that Dr. Miller tried to do to save him, Gerhart died.

References: *Crawfordsville Weekly Journal*, 5 Jan. 1884; and *South Bend Tribune*, 2 Jan. 1884.

GIFFORD, THOMAS (ca. 1841–1930)

Thomas Gifford was born about 1841 in the town of Charleston, son of Rachael Terrell and A. G. Gifford. He had two sisters: Sarah (1842) and Mary (1844).

On 5 August 1862 young Gifford enrolled at Charleston in Company D of the Seventy-Seventh Indiana Regiment, committed to serving for three years. He saw action at the Battle of Chickamauga in September 1863 and in May 1864 joined General Sherman's campaign against Atlanta. That October he was at Columbia, Tennessee, and during February and March of 1865 was in Alabama. He was duly mustered out at Edgefield near Nashville, Tennessee, on 29 June 1865.

Gifford was back in Indiana that autumn in time to enter Wabash as a freshman, but he attended only a year and left to marry Amanda McGee of Charleston on 30 October 1866. They eventually had two children, Anna and Harry.

Sometime in the late 1870s, the Gifford family moved to New Albany. For fifty years, Gifford worked as a member of the staff at the Hutchinson Memorial Presbyterian Church. He died at home of a stroke on 9 July 1930 and was survived by his children. His wife pre-deceased him.

References: *New Albany Tribune*, 9 July 1930; and indexes to marriages for Clark County, Indiana.

GILKEY, JOSEPH A. (1829–1893)

Joseph Gilkey was born in Indiana in 1829 and became a student in the Preparatory Department of Wabash College in 1853–54, citing his residence as Alamo. He stayed for one year.

In about 1857 he married Milicent, and together they had at least six children: William (who died as an infant), Mary, Ella, Annie, Herbert, and Robert. In the 1860 census Gilkey indicated that he was a teacher.

At age thirty-five Gilkey enrolled in Company F of the 135th Indiana Regiment for one hundred days. At the time he was described as five feet six inches tall, with light complexion, brown hair, and blue eyes. He served from 29 April to 29 September 1864, mainly guarding rail lines in Tennessee and Alabama.

Rejoining his wife and children, he farmed near Alamo until the early 1870s, when he relocated several times throughout Indiana, including Bloomingdale, Alliance, and Winamac. During these years he was a teacher and hotelkeeper. By the mid-1880s, he was living in the town of Andrews.

In 1888 Gilkey sustained a stroke that paralyzed his left side. This may have occasioned his entry into the soldiers' home in Marion. On 8 September 1890 he married Adeline Fletcher in Fountain County, but he died of a second stroke on 12 April 1893.

References: *History of Montgomery County, Indiana* (Bowen and Co., 1913), p. 161; *Crawfordsville Journal: Souvenir Edition* (1894), p. 11; and military pension file at the National Archives, Washington, DC.

GILLAM, WILLIAM HIRAM (1843–1906)

William Gillam was born in Delphi in 1843, the only son of Maria Grantham and Solomon Gillam. He had one sister, Mary Ann, and two stepsisters, Susan and Maria.

On 13 October 1861 Gillam enrolled at Logansport in Company E of the Forty-Sixth Indiana Infantry Regiment. He was promoted to sergeant in May 1862 and to second lieutenant in 1863, eventually becoming captain in a regiment of African American troops.

In the autumn of 1868, he entered the freshman class at Wabash, one of the older veterans then coming in after the war. He pursued the Classical Course and graduated with a bachelor of arts degree. The college magazine of June 1872 featured verbal portraits of the graduating class, and Gillam was said to be of robust frame, slightly above medium height, with black eyes and hair. The magazine noted, "His mind is of the solid type. To do himself justice he requires considerable time to study his subject. But, this condition granted, he is probably the most forcible writer in the class. Earnestness, rising sometimes to eloquence, characterizes his speaking. He is a great reader, and is never so well satisfied as when surrounded by books, magazines and newspapers. His disposition is sober, with a tinge of melancholy."

Following Wabash, Gillam traveled to St. Louis to study law and by 1874 was living in Belleville, Illinois, entering legal practice and teaching at a school for African American children. According to a college publication of 1903, he was still practicing law in Belleville. Three years later he was dead.

References: Belleville Public Library and Carroll County Historical Society Museum. See also: *Wabash Magazine*, XII (June 1872), p. 159; and T. H. Bringhurst and F. Swigart, *History of the Forty-Sixth Regiment* (1888), p. 183.

GILLUM, HOWARD SOLOMON (1845–1870)

Howard Gillum was born at Harveysburg in July 1845, one of five sons of Emiline Sowers and Osborn Gillum. His brothers were John, Ira, William, and Charles, two of whom also served in the Civil War.

On 1 July 1863 Gillum enrolled for six months' service in Company C of the 116th Indiana Regiment. His regiment left Indiana in August and went first to Dearborn, Michigan, then to Nicholasville, Kentucky. By early October he was in battles in Tennessee at Cumberland Gap, Blue Springs, and Bull's Gap, and Walker's Ford, moving in January 1864 to Tazewell and Maynardsville, all rugged and remote areas where the men suffered severe hardship. They were relieved to spend their last month of service back in Indiana, and they mustered out at Lafayette, Indiana, on 2 March 1864.

Returning home, Gillum worked on the family farm for the next few years. In the fall of 1867, he entered the Preparatory Department of Wabash College. He returned the next year (1868–69) and the embarked on his freshman year in the autumn of 1869. That December he walked home anticipating a well-earned vacation, but he came down with a chill and became seriously ill. He died on 7 January 1870 and is buried in the Harveysburg Cemetery in Kingman.

References: H. W. Beckwith, *History of Fountain County* (1881), p. 406; *Wabash Magazine*, X (March 1870), p. 173.

GLASSCOCK, OLIVER B. (1843–1864)

Many of the war careers of the men from Wabash are regrettably sad and cut off too soon by disease. Oliver Glasscock was one of these, dead of "fever" before he could return home. These fevers, which men and physicians alike labeled "camp fever," were sometimes passing sicknesses but often were serious or fatal. Malaria, typhoid, smallpox, tuberculosis (consumption), and measles were diseases, sometimes epidemics, of both the northern and southern armies. Men could often recover from fevers if they could get away from camp and be nursed by loving hands in a clean, quiet place. Still, these afflictions claimed far too many victims in the camps of the times.

Oliver Glasscock was born in Ohio in 1843, one of three children of Sarah Baughman and Samuel H. Glasscock. His siblings were Eliza and John. At the age of eighteen he entered the Preparatory Department of Wabash College, indicating that his home was Delphi. He remained one year, 1861–62.

Glasscock enrolled in Company D of the Twelfth Indiana Volunteer Infantry Regiment on 20 July 1862. In December he was promoted from private to sergeant. He contracted an unstipulated fever and died near Scottsboro, Alabama, on 17 May 1864.

References: Carroll County Historical Society Museum. See also: *Wabash Magazine*, VII (June 1866), p. 8.

GOODHUE, SAMUEL NEWELL (1836–1931)

Samuel Goodhue was born on 23 July 1836 at Paris, in Jennings County. His parents were Esther Shillidaey and Walter Bennet Goodhue, a physician. His siblings included Florella, Alvin, James, Richey, Emma, and Tilman.

His parents had moved to Paris in about 1835, and Samuel left the family homestead from there to enter the Preparatory Deparment of Wabash in the fall of 1849. He remained for two years. By 1855 Goodhue was in Floyd County, Iowa, and in 1857 he moved to Clarksville, Iowa, where he worked as a teacher and bank cashier. On 2 June 1860 he married Margaret McRoberts, an Irish woman living in Marion, Iowa. They had one child, Walter F., born in Clarksville in 1861.

On 11 August 1862 Goodhue joined Company G of the Thirty-Second Iowa Infantry. When he enlisted, records show he described himself as a schoolteacher, five feet seven inches tall, with fair complexion, blue eyes, and light hair. He was stationed at Cape Girardeau, Missouri, as a hospital steward when he contracted a pulmonary disease as well as arthritis, which resulted in a medical discharge for him in December 1863.

In February 1864 Goodhue returned to Cape Girardeau and joined the quartermaster's department as a clerk. In January 1865 he switched to the commissary department and in June joined a similar department in Denver, Colorado, until October 1865, when he was mustered out.

Returning to Marion, Goodhue established a grain and produce business and combined mercantile activity with holding local government offices such as deputy recorder. In 1872 he and Margaret adopted a daughter, Ida, and in 1878 he founded a real estate agency, Goodhue and Woods.

Margaret died in 1904, and Goodhue moved to Cedar Rapids and married a New York native, Julia Fisher. They resided there until 1915, when they moved to Los Angeles. In 1930 a doctor wrote to the government pension office saying that Goodhue was weak and infirmed and required constant care. He died the following year on 17 October.

References: Jennings County Public Library; Mrs. Frances Hickman of Greencastle, Indiana; Cedar Rapids (Iowa) Public Library; Linn County (Iowa) Heritage Society; Iowa State Historical Society Library of Des Moines; and Iowa State Historical Society of

Iowa City. See also: M. Oxley, *History of Marion Iowa*, II (1880), p. 16; *History of Linn County, Iowa* (1878), pp. 621–22; and his military pension file.

GOOKINS, JAMES FARRINGTON (1840–1904)

James Gookins was the son of Mary Osborn and Samuel Barnes Gookins, born in Terre Haute, Indiana, on 30 December 1840. His father was a distinguished lawyer and justice of the Indiana Supreme Court.

Gookins entered the Preparatory Department of Wabash in the autumn of 1859 and advanced as a freshman into the Classical Course the following fall. He went on to complete his sophomore year, 1861–62, but illness prevented him from returning as a junior.

Before his health declined, Gookins served from April to August 1861 in Colonel Lew Wallace's Company I of the Eleventh Indiana Infantry, mostly in southern Indiana or what is now West Virginia. In the autumn of 1862, he went to Cincinnati to study art and volunteered his services to Wallace, now a major general seeking to prevent Confederate troops from making inroads into Ohio. Gookins's talent as an artist was increasingly recognized, and *Harper's Weekly* began to feature his battlefront sketches, such as the one that appeared in the 31 May 1862 issue portraying the Battle of Pea Ridge in Arkansas.

In 1866–67, inspired by the grandeur of the Rocky Mountains, he went to Colorado and painted scenery that later became a hallmark of his work and provided further opportunities to appear in *Harper's Weekly*.

In 1869 he moved to Chicago and helped found the Academy of Design.

On 14 June 1870 Gookins married Cora Donnelly in Terre Haute and then sailed for Europe, where he studied at the Royal Academy in Munich under artists like Raab Wagner and Carl von Piloty. Before returning to the United States in 1874, he also worked in Paris, London, and Vienna.

Gookins helped found the Indiana School of Art, which opened in Indianapolis on 15 October 1877. The school closed in 1879, and Gookins then spent most of his time concentrating on architectural and municipal concerns. He lobbied the Indiana legislature to appropriate funds for a new statehouse, and in 1887 he served as secretary of the Soldiers and Sailors War Memorial commission. At the same time he devoted much energy to planning a new waterfront for Chicago, in anticipation of the world's fair of 1893. He also encouraged Marshall Field to contribute to Chicago's beautification, resulting in the Field Museum of Natural History.

From 1894 on, Gookins promoted the financing and construction of a subway system for downtown Chicago, and it was in this connection that he went to New York City in the spring of 1904. On 23 May he died while staying at the Navarre Hotel. His body was returned to Terre Haute, where he is buried in Woodlawn Cemetery alongside his wife.

References: *Indianapolis Star*, 20 July 1940; *Wabash Record* (July 1904), pp. 17–18; *Wabash Magazine*, V (May 1864), pp. 175, 179; *Wabash Magazine*, VII (April 1867), p. 45; *Art and Artists of Indiana*, p. 116; Sheldon Swope Art Gallery, "A Retrospective Exhibition of Paintings and Lithographs by James Farrington Gookins" (1966); *Terre Haute Tribune-Star*, 9 July 1978; the Vigo County Historical Society: unidentified newspaper article, "Terre Hautens Cherish Art of J. F. Gookins, Pioneer Painter."

GORDON, EDWIN JOHN (1839–1863)

Edwin Gordon was born in Salem, Washington County, Indiana, on 30 January 1839, one of ten children of Eliza Roberts Dennis and John William Gordon, a successful merchant in New Albany. Edwin's siblings were John Jr., Josephine, Eliza, Newton, Theresa, Ella, Emma, Emerson, and Lillian.

In 1856 he enrolled at Wabash and stayed two years before returning to New Albany. On 4 October 1859 he married Isabella (Bella) A. Gorner. They had one daughter, Eva, who was born in 1860, the same year in which Gordon established his own merchandise shop.

Three years later Gordon responded to the Confederate raid into southern Indiana, according to the local newspaper: "When Morgan invaded Indiana, and her patriotic sons were called upon to drive the enemy from our borders, Mr. Gordon, as a member of the Purdue Rifles, at Lafayette, where he was living, responded to the call, and with his company followed in the pursuit to Buffington Island, and participated in the engagement which resulted in the capture of most of the invaders. It was during this campaign that his fatal illness was brought upon him, and he is another added to the long list of martyrs in his country's cause."

Edwin died on 7 August 1863 and was buried in New Albany's Fairview Cemetery.

References: New Albany Public Library; *New Albany Daily Ledger*, 8 Aug. 1863, p. 2; and Familysearch.org.

GORDON, JOHN H. (1836–1911)

John Gordon was born most likely in the town of Salem in Indiana in November 1836, the fourth of thirteen children born to Eliza A. and John Gordon. His younger brother, Newton, also went to Wabash and served in the Civil War.

Young Gordon entered Wabash in the autumn of 1855 and spent two years in the Scientific Department. Midway through his course, his family moved from Salem to New Albany and helped Gordon start a mercantile business. On 1 July 1858 he married Helen King of New Albany, and they eventually had six children: Charlotte, Horace, Roland, George, Marcellus, and Stella.

Gordon's military service lasted from 8 to 15 July 1863 and was in response to Morgan's raid on southern Indiana. He was a member of the local

Floyd County Regiment Number 7 of the Indiana Legion.

Remaining in New Albany, Gordon gave up the merchandising business and became a bookkeeper. His wife pre-deceased him, and he went to live with his daughter, Charlotte, Mrs. Samuel Miller, in Castlewood, Kentucky, a suburb of Louisville. He died there on 26 November 1911. His body was returned to New Albany for burial.

References: Betty C. Menges of the New Albany-Floyd County Public Library; *New Albany Weekly Tribune,* 1 Dec. 1911.

GORDON, NEWTON (?–1921)

As we have seen in the case of his older brother, John, Newton Gordon was one of thirteen children born to Eliza A. and John Gordon while they were living in Salem, Indiana.

When Newton Gordon registered as a freshman at Wabash in the fall of 1861, he lived in New Albany. The following summer he enrolled in Company E of the Eighty-First Indiana Regiment and was described as five feet four inches tall, with blue eyes, dark hair, and a dark complexion.

When the regiment was fully organized on 29 August, it went to Nashville, Tennessee, by way of Louisville, in pursuit of General Bragg's Confederate forces. On 20 December 1862 Gordon was honorably discharged, presumably due to illness. Like his brother, he responded to Morgan's raid into southern Indiana, joining Company F of the 108th Indiana Regiment from 10 to 18 July 1863.

Before the war he was a clerk, but afterwards he worked for a railroad.

His wife, Ella G., bore two children, Fred and Mary. For many years they lived in New Albany, where Gordon died on 11 January 1921.

References: Besides the references shown for Newton's brother, John, see the *New Albany Daily Ledger*, 12 Jan. 1921.

GORDON, OLIVER WALKER (1836–1927)

Oliver Gordon was born on 29 March 1836 in Wayne County, Indiana, to Deborah Mendenhall and William M. Gordon. His siblings were Luther, Leroy, Eliza Jane, Esther, Arrenetta, Lydia, and Lucy. The family moved to Iowa in 1844 but returned to settle in Thorntown in the early 1850s.

Gordon entered the Preparatory Department of Wabash College in the fall of 1853 and remained only one academic year.

When the Civil War broke out, Gordon was in Iowa studying law, but he became an assistant surgeon to Dr. Hughes in a hospital at Keokuk. Later he worked with Surgeon Woods in U.S. Army hospitals and attended to the medical care of a regiment of colored troops.

After the war he studied medicine and went into practice in Iowa, first at Bloomfield, then in Mount Pleasant, and still later in Chicago, where he edited a medical journal. For a time he joined his brother, Leroy, in Minneapolis, and finally settled in Council Bluffs, Iowa, in 1883.

His first wife was Mary Wright of Des Moines, and they had two children, William and Annie. His second wife was Mary C. Williams Walker of Council Bluffs, and their children were Deborah and Luther, plus four others from her previous marriage to Thomas Walker.

Gordon practiced medicine for many years in Council Bluffs, and after Mary died, he moved in with one of his stepdaughters, Mrs. D. D. Carter. He died on 15 March 1927 and is buried in Walnut Hill Cemetery.

References: Council Bluffs (Iowa) Free Public Library; *Biographical History of Pottawattamie County, Iowa* (1891), p. 429; *Biographical Directory of the Indiana General Assembly*, I (1980), p. 148; *Council Bluffs Non Pareil,* 17 March 1927; and Mrs. Rose Mele of Des Moines.

GRAY, HARVEY (?–?)

Harvey Gray was a student at Wabash for two years, 1857–59. He lived at home in Crawfordsville with his father. He enrolled for his junior year, but was not listed in the 1860 college catalogue, leading to the possibility that he moved during that year.

According to the memorial tablet, he served the war, but he is not listed in an Indiana regiment, suggesting that he may have served out of state.

GRAY, HENRY HARRISON (1842–1885)

Henry Gray was born at Marion, Iowa, on 22 November 1842, the youngest of eight children of Priscilla Moore (1800–1852) and Thomas Gray (1789–1843). His siblings were Mary, Catherine, Hannah, Richard, John, Elizabeth, and Thomas.

Gray came to Wabash College in the autumn of 1856 and studied for one year in the Preparatory Department. He then enrolled in the Iowa Conference Seminary at Mount Vernon (which became Cornell College in 1858) and continued there as a freshman and sophomore.

On 24 September 1861 he enlisted in Company K of the Ninth Iowa Volunteers at Marion, in the same company as his older brother, John. After the Battle of Pea Ridge in Arkansas, Gray rose quickly from private to corporal to quartermaster sergeant, and after re-enlisting on 23 January 1864 became a lieutenant, mustering out at Louisville, Kentucky, on 18 July 1865.

He then made his way to Ann Arbor, Michigan, in order to study law, receiving a diploma from the University of Michigan in 1867.

By 1869 he had opened a legal practice in Waverly, Bremer County, Iowa, and the following year he married Marie L. Mathews, a native of Canada. Their children were Alice, Harry (Henry), Ann, and Eddy. In addition to practicing law, Gray was mayor of Waverly for one term. For unknown reasons, he took his own life on 29 September 1885. He is buried in Harlington Cemetery.

References: Genealogical Society of Cedar Rapids, Iowa, and the Iowa Graves Registration Service.

GREENWOOD, FRANCIS A. (1837–1864)

Frank Greenwood was born in 1837, most likely on a farm in Rob Roy. His mother may have died in childbirth, because his father soon married Frances Timberlake, who provided Frank a stepsister, Minerva, in 1838.

In the autumn of 1852, Greenwood entered the Preparatory Department of Wabash, and in 1855–56 he became a freshman in the Classical Course, coming back as a sophomore.

Greenwood was living in Hillsboro in 1860, working as a clerk. Two years later, on 5 March 1862, he married Amelia E. McCormick. The following August he signed up for three years in the Indiana Eighteenth Light Artillery. Rising quickly from private to corporal, he saw action throughout the state of Tennessee in 1863: in June, Hoover's Gap (24 June); in September, Chickamauga; in October, Farmington (7 October); and in November, Missionary Ridge. From May to November 1864, he took part in the march through Georgia, and on the banks of the Chattahoochee River near Atlanta, he received a devastating wound to his knee that resulted in his death on 17 October.

References:: H. W. Beckwith, *History of Fountain County* (1881), pp. 193–94; Archives Division of the Indiana State Library.

GREGORY, JAMES B. (1832/3–1887

James Gregory was the eldest of four children born to Martha and Robert C. Gregory. His siblings were William, Mollie, and Julia. He was probably born in Crawfordsville in 1832 or 1833. When he was six or seven years old, his father, a salesman, combined studying law with spending the academic year 1839–40 as a student at Wabash.

In 1843 the family moved to Lafayette, from where young James entered the Preparatory Department of Wabash in the fall of 1846. He left the college for the next two years but returned in 1849.

Sometime during 1854–55 Gregory married Martha McCutcheon from Ohio. They had two children, a daughter, Minnie, and a son, McCutcheon. At this time Gregory was a prosperous farmer in Wea Township, Tippecanoe County.

On 14 August 1862 he joined Company I of the Eighty-sixth Indiana Regiment at Stockwell and committed to three years' service. He was promoted rapidly and became captain of Company C on 25 April 1863 at Murfreesboro, Tennessee. He saw action at numerous battles in 1863 and 1864: Chickamauga, Missionary Ridge, Stones River, Chattanooga, and Lookout Mountain, but contracted a serious illness at Knoxville that led to a medical discharge on 25 March 1864.

Sometime in the early to mid-1880s, Gregory went to El Paso, Texas, perhaps because of failing health. While visiting Hot Springs, Arkansas, he died on 25 June 1887. He is buried in Springvale Cemetery in Lafayette.

References: Dorothy Van Cleef of Lafayette; J. A. Barnes, *The Eighty-Sixth Regiment of Indiana Volunteer Infantry* (1895), p. 573; *Lafayette Daily Courier*, 26 Jan. 1885; El Paso (Texas) Public Library.

GREGORY, RALPH SHAW (1842–1917)

Ralph Shaw Gregory was born on 28 February 1842 on a farm near Granville, Niles Township, Delaware County. He was the youngest of Mary Braddock and Samuel Gregory's six children.

In about 1860 he was sent to a private academy in Muncie run by Messrs. Ferris and Bell. Then, in the autumn of 1861, he entered the Preparatory Department of Wabash College. He remained for one year before enrolling for three years in Company B of the Eighty-Fourth Indiana Regiment on 8 August 1862.

His regiment was initially assigned to defend Covington, Kentucky, and Cincinnati against possible attacks by Confederate General Kirby Smith, then went to West Virginia and Tennessee, where it distinguished itself at Chickamauga. Ralph was promoted to first sergeant on 10 November 1863, but he fell from a horse and received a medical discharge at Shellmound, Tennessee, on 4 December 1863.

In the autumn of 1864, Gregory returned to Wabash and embarked as a freshman in the Classical Course. He returned for his sophomore and junior years. However, in the fall of 1866, his namesake, Ralph Shaw, endowed a scholarship at Asbury University, and Gregory won the stipend. He was also granted senior status, so he was able to graduate with a bachelor of science degree in June 1867.

In 1868 he superintended schools at Huntington and Wabash while reading law on the side. His legal mentor was Carleton E. Shipley of Muncie, and once he was admitted to the bar in 1869, he joined Shipley as a partner. Shipley died the following year, and Gregory became a partner of Alfred Kilgore, but Kilgore died in 1871. A third partnership with James M. Templer lasted ten years, and then

Gregory practiced on his own until associating with A. C. Silverburg.

On 5 July 1880 Gregory married Anna C. Madden of Piqua, Ohio. Their son Walter was born in 1882 and their daughter Florence in 1884.

Although a staunch Republican for many years, he broke with his party in 1896 over the issue of bimetalism and became a delegate to the Democratic Party convention in Chicago that chose William Jennings Bryan as its Free Silver candidate.

Gregory served as Delaware County attorney between 1912 and 1916 and city judge of Muncie from 1916 until 1917. He died on 13 January 1917, survived by his wife and children.

References: W. Comback and J. D. Maynard (eds.), *Men of Progress of Indiana* (1899), pp. 90–92; *Muncie Star*, 14 Jan. 1917; T. B. Helms, *History of Delaware County, Indiana* (1881) pp. 214–15; *Representative Men of Indiana* (1880), I, p. 33; G. W. H. Kemper, *A Twentieth Century History of Delaware County, Indiana* (1908), pp. 673–74.

GREGORY, ROBERT CROCKET (1811–1885)

Although unusual, on occasion a father and a son each attended Wabash and also served in the Civil War. Robert and James Gregory provide one example. Robert was born in Kentucky on 15 February 1811, one of ten children born to Elizabeth Lee and James Gregory. A brother, Benjamin Franklin, also attended Wabash in its first year of existence (1833–34).

Gregory moved with his family from Kentucky to Indiana and at age sixteen persuaded his parents to let him take a job as clerk in a Fort Wayne dry goods store operated by the emerging entrepreneur and statesman Samuel Hanna, four of whose ten sons went to Wabash.

In 1829 Gregory took a sales job in Fountain County and married Elizabeth C. Brier on 4 October 1830. Eventually they had four children: James, William, Mary (Mollie), and Julia.

In June 1832 the family moved to Crawfordsville, where Gregory combined doing business with studying law under Hosea Humphreys, who later became professor of classics at Wabash. He was also a captain in the Indiana Militia during the Black Hawk War, a conflict stemming from a land dispute between the United States and Native Americans.

Once admitted to the Indiana bar in 1838, Gregory entered the Preparatory Department of Wabash at the relatively advanced age of twenty-eight, already having served as a trustee since 1833. During the next few years he practiced law in Crawfordsville, and in 1841 he was elected a state senator.

Relocating to Lafayette, he ran as a Whig for the United States House of Representatives in 1852 but was defeated by another Wabash man and Democrat, Daniel Mace. On 10 July 1863 he joined Company A of the 108th Indiana Regiment as a first lieutenant in response to Morgan's raid and was mustered out seven days later.

In October 1864 he was elected to the Indiana Supreme Court and served from January 1865 to January 1871. He died at home on 25 January 1885.

References: C. W. Taylor, *The Bench and Bar of Indiana* (1895); *Biographical Directory of the Indiana General Assembly*, I (1980), p. 153; H. W. Beckwith, *History of Montgomery County* (1881), pp. 115, 518; *Biographical Record and Portrait Album of Tippecanoe County, Indiana* (1888), pp. 228, 236, 241, 694; *Lafayette Daily Courier*, 26 Jan. 1885.

GRIFFITH, THOMAS JEFFERSON (1837–1924)

Thomas Griffith was born in Clinton County near Frankfort on 2 April 1837, the only son of Mary and Thornton Griffith. He had two sisters, Joanna and Nancy.

The Griffith family had long associations with Montgomery County, beginning in the 1830s when they lived in Crawfordsville and acquired a farm near Darlington. For the academic year 1853–54, Mary Griffith took temporary lodgings in Crawfordsville so that Thomas could stay with her while he was enrolled in the Preparatory Department of Wabash College.

For the next ten years, Griffith had a variety of jobs, including teaching school at Ridge Farm in Ripley Township, Montgomery County. He helped on the family farm in Darlington and by 1863 was a salesman in William Bowers's dry goods store in Crawfordsville. Later he managed a branch store for Bowers in Rockville, Parke County.

From 8 May to 29 September 1864, he guarded railroad lines in Tennessee and Alabama as a recruit in Company D of the 135th Indiana Regiment, whose captain was a fellow Wabash student, William Bruce Carr. This duty put him in touch with a regimental surgeon, Dr. J. S. McClelland, with whom he studied medicine before going to the University of Michigan in Ann Arbor during the winter of 1865–66 and to Miami Medical College of Cincinnati the following year.

Griffith began practicing at Darlington in 1867, and on 4 October 1871 he married Martha E. Hutchings in Madison, Indiana, who had the rare distinction of being a medical doctor herself. For nearly two decades both of them practiced medicine at Darlington. In 1888 they moved to Crawfordsville and continued as doctors for the rest of their lives. Thomas Griffith died on 6 January 1924, and Martha on 28 December 1925. They are both buried in the Odd Fellows Cemetery at Darlington.

References: H. W. Beckwith, *History of Montgomery County* (1881), pp. 549–50; *Crawfordsville Journal Review*, 7 Jan. 1924; *History of Montgomery County* (Bowen and Co., 1913), p. 338; P. Cline, "Griffiths had Successful Medical Practice," *Montgomery County*

Magazine (May 1995), p. 7; Diane Hammill of the Crawfordsville Public Library; and a pamphlet published by the Montgomery County Historical Society, *Martha Hutchings Griffith: Montgomery County Pioneer Physician* (2001).

GRISARD, FREDERICK L. JR. (1840–?)

Frederick L. Grisard Jr. was born in Vevay, Switzerland County, Indiana, on 26 February 1840, the elder of two brothers, both of whom went to Wabash and served in the Civil War. His parents were Zeller C. Simon and Frederick Louis Grisard Sr., who had six other children: James, Lucilla, Perret, Rudolph, Louise, and Zeller.

From 1858 to 1860 Grisard was enrolled in Wabash College's Normal School. He then went to Cincinnati for a year of commercial study at Bartlett's College before returning to Vevay and working in the family store, Grisard and Sons.

In September 1862 Grisard was appointed captain of one of the companies of the Tenth Regiment of the Indiana Legion, and later served for a few days when Morgan threatened southern Indiana in July 1863. On 25 November 1862 he married Mary Ann McMakin, and they eventually had four children: Addie, Mamie, Lou, and Emma.

In 1878 Grisard bought out his father's interest in the hardware store and ran it himself for the next ten years. He was also elected to the Vevay city council for 1877–81 and served as town clerk. A city directory for 1887 lists him in business at the same location, but after this he simply disappears. He was not buried in Vevay may have moved elsewhere before 1900.

References: *Representative Men of Indiana* (1880), I, pp. 30–31; *History of Dearborn, Ohio and Switzerland Counties, Indiana* (1885), p. 1220; and the Switzerland County Public Library, Vevay.

GRISARD, JAMES S. (1842–1910)

As we have seen in the case of his older brother, Frederick, James was one of seven children born to Zeller C. Simon and Frederick Louis Grisard Sr. His birth took place on 28 June 1842 in Vevay, Switzerland County.

In the autumn of 1860, the youth registered in the Normal School of Wabash, staying only until April 1861, when he, along with many other students, enrolled in Company I of the Eleventh Indiana Regiment (Zouaves) commanded by Lew Wallace. Three months later he was mustered out at Indianapolis and returned to Vevay to work in the Grisard and Sons store. He also served in the Indiana Legion.

In about 1867 Grisard married Florence Lucy Roberts and moved to Cincinnati, where their two sons, Willie and John Simon, were born. Grisard worked for some years as a salesman for the Meader Furniture Company. In 1880 he returned to Indiana and settled in Evansville, where the family included John, Laura, Anna, Russell, and Hattie.

In 1910 Grisard was living on his own in a boardinghouse in Vevay, where he died in September. He was buried in the local cemetery.

References: See the references for James's brother, Frederick; also the Hamilton County branch of the Ohio Genealogical Society; the Cincinnati Historical Society.

GROENENDYKE, CHARLES (1844–1932)

The Groenendyke family had the distinction of sending five sons to Wabash: Charles, John, Henry, Edward, and Frank. Equally remarkable was that four of them served in the Civil War.

Charles Groenendyke was born on 28 October 1844 in Eugene. His parents were Sarah Coleman (1813–1869) and James Groenendyke (1798–1856), and besides his four brothers, he had four sisters: Ann, Lucy, Eliza, and Nancy.

Groenendyke spent the 1863–64 academic year in the Preparatory Department at Wabash, and on 13 May 1864 he enrolled at Crawfordsville for one hundred days of service in Company H of the 135th Indiana Regiment. Most of those days were spent guarding railroad lines in Tennessee and Alabama. He was discharged at Indianapolis on 29 September, just in time to return to Wabash as a freshman in the Classical Course of study. Four years later, in June 1869, he received his bachelor of arts degree. At college Groenendyke compiled an impressive record. In his sophomore year he won first prize in oratory, and during his sophomore and junior years he edited the *Wabash Magazine* in addition to serving as the president of his class.

After the death of his father in 1856 and his mother in 1869, Groenendyke had been dependent upon his older brother, Edward, for lodging and support. Soon he could independently earn his living in the Hoosier state. From 1869 to 1870 he was principal of the high school in Eugene, and during 1870–72 he served as principal of the high school in Homer. All this time Groenendyke studied law on the side, and in 1873 he moved to Lafayette, where he practiced law for the next eight years before leaving for Fargo, North Dakota.

He practiced in Fargo for a few years before returning to Lafayette, but in 1889 he relocated again, this time to Lockett, Colorado, to try his hand at farming. This lasted three years, but was cut short by an offer to become superintendant of schools in Salida and later at San Luis. Eventually he settled in Del Norte, near two of his siblings, and became town clerk and recorder.

Entering a soldiers' and sailors' home in Monte Vista, he died on 2 February 1932 and is buried in the local cemetery there.

References: The public libraries of Newport and Clinton, Vermillion County. See also: H. L. O'Donnell, *Eugene Township: First One Hundred Years* (1963), p. 276; *Wabash Magazine*, IX (June 1869), pp. 86, 94; H. Groenendyke, *The History and Genealogy of the Groenendyke Family* (1950); and libraries in Fargo, North Dakota, and Del Norte, Colorado.

GROENENDYKE, EDWARD (1842–1930)

Edward Groenendyke was born on 16 September 1842 at Eugene. As we have seen in the case of his brother, Charles, Edward was one of the nine children born to Sarah Coleman and James Groenendyke. Four of these brothers served in the Civil War.

Young Edward entered the Preparatory Department of Wabash in the fall of 1857 and spent 1859–61 in the more difficult Classical Course.

On 23 July 1861 Groenendyke enrolled for three years in Company I of the Eleventh Indiana Regiment (Wallace's Zouaves) alongside his brother, Henry. When he reported for duty on 31 August, he had been promoted to corporal.

A year later, in September 1862, Groenendyke was transferred to the Ninety-Seventh Indiana Regiment as a second lieutenant of Company K. A further promotion came in January 1863 to the rank of first lieutenant and adjutant of field and staff. However, toward the end of that year, he had to take sick leave from the front. He paid a visit to Wabash College. Soon thereafter he was given a medical discharge on 11 January 1864.

Groenendyke returned to Eugene after the war and became a woolen manufacturer, moving to Lafayette in 1873, where he went into the insurance business. By 1906 he was residing at the Maryland Hotel, 168 Raymond Street, in Pasadena, California. There in the Golden State he raised his nephew, Edward Henry Groenendyke, after the boy's father, John, died. Edward Groenendyke died on 31 October 1930. He is buried in Mountain View Cemetery.

References: See references for Edward's brother, Charles; *Wabash Magazine*, III (Dec. 1861), p. 93; *Wabash Magazine*, V (Dec. 1863), p. 75; *Pasadena Star News*, 1 Nov. 1930; and the Pasadena Historical Society and the Pasadena Public Library.

GROENENDYKE, HENRY (1841–1863)

Henry Groenendyke is another Wabash student among the five brothers born at Eugene on 28 January 1841. Groenendyke spent only one school year, 1857–58, at Wabash and then presumably returned home.

On 22 April 1861 he was mustered into Lew Wallace's Company I of the Eleventh Indiana Regiment as a corporal. Once his initial commitment of three months expired, he re-enlisted on 31 August in the same company that his younger brother, Edward, had joined in July. Groenendyke was promoted to second lieutenant on 4 October 1862, and in 1863 he became an officer in the United

States Signal Corps. However, during the siege of Vicksburg he contracted acute dysentery and died on 16 September 1863. His body was returned to Indiana for interment in the Groenendyke Cemetery at Newport.

References: See references for his brother, Charles; also Wabash *Magazine*, V (Dec. 1863), p. 79.

GROENENDYKE, JOHN (1833–1886)

John Groenendyke, born at Eugene on 24 December 1833, was the eldest of nine children of Sarah Coleman and James Groenendyke, who sent five of their sons to Wabash, all but one of whom served in the Civil War.

Groenendyke entered the Preparatory Department in 1851 and returned every year until his father died in 1856. He returned to Eugene and took charge of the family's general store until 1860 and declared himself a farmer.

Along with his brother Henry, Groenendyke enrolled in Lew Wallace's Eleventh Indiana Regiment for three months in April 1861. On 23 October 1861 he married Eleanor M. Shaw. They eventually had four children: Flora (1862), Sarah (1864), Henry Edward (1877), and Elizabeth (1879).

In 1873 Groenendyke served in the House of Representatives of the Indiana General Assembly. Soon thereafter he moved to Lafayette, along with members of his extended family, and from 1879 to 1882 worked for the United States Internal Revenue Service. Beginning in 1881 he worked for the United States government in Terre Haute, where he was an excise officer in a distillery pasting official seals on bottles. Groenendyke died on 20 September 1886 and was buried in Highland Lawn Cemetery at Terre Haute.

References: See references for John's brother, Charles; also the *Biographical Directory of the Indiana General Assembly* (1980), I, p. 155.

GROVER, JOHN B. (1822–1895)

John Grover was born in Madison on 7 April 1822, the eldest child of Elizabeth Brisben and Nicholas D. Grover. He came to Wabash College from Logansport in the fall of 1839 and stayed for three years, returning to Logansport to run a drugstore.

In June 1846 Grover joined Company G of the First Regiment Indiana (First Indiana Volunteers) and went to Mexico to fight in the Mexican-American War that grew out of the United States' annexation of Texas in 1845.

In 1852 Grover married Julia Sharpe in Cass County, and they eventually had three children: Jennie, Cassius, and Julia. The family moved to Columbus, Ohio, in about 1862, and enlisted in the 197th Regiment of Ohio Volunteers.

After the war Grover returned to Columbus and served as a bookkeeper for the Baltimore and Ohio Railroad as well as the Pan Handle Railroad. He retained these positions until 1872, when the family moved back to Logansport. There he continued working for the Pan Handle.

Grover died at Logansport on 1 January 1895 and is buried in Mount Hope Cemetery.

References: Cass County Historical Society; Thomas B. Helm, *History of Cass County, Indiana* (1882), pp. 116, 331–32, 510; *Biographical Directory of the Indiana General Assembly* (1980).

GUTHRIE, JAMES F. (1844–1910)

James Guthrie was born in Ohio on 22 September 1844. In the fall of 1855, he made his way from Three Rivers, Iowa, to Wabash College and spent one school year in the Normal School.

On 1 June 1861 at Keokuk, Iowa, he enrolled in Company E of the Third Iowa Infantry Regiment. He was unusually tall for his time; standing at six feet one, he stood head and shoulders above most of his comrades.

Guthrie was struck by a musket ball on his left side at Blue Mills Landing, Missouri, on 17 September 1861. He carried it in his body the rest of his life. As a result of repeated hospital stays at Liberty and Kansas City, Missouri, then in Wyandotte, Kansas, he was able to rejoin his regiment, but on 12 July 1863 at Jackson, Mississippi, he injured his arm badly.

Due for release from military service sometime in the latter half of 1863, he nevertheless chose to re-enlist as a veteran volunteer on 4 January 1864 at Hebron, Mississippi, in Company A of a combined Second and Third Iowa Regiment and mustered out at Davenport, Iowa, on 12 July 1865.

On 28 April 1864 Guthrie married Mary Ann Bridgeman of Des Moines. Their children were Sarah Ellen (1864), Alice (1868), Meira (1870), and Hollas (1875). After the war they lived in Kansas, where Guthrie took up farming, but by 1880 they had moved to Lincoln, California, About 1890 they settled in Tacoma, Washington, where Mary Ann died on 30 May 1894.

Guthrie married for a second time on 15 March 1904 at Santa Cruz, California, and he and Fannie Miller went to live in Stockton, California, where he died on 30 April 1910. He is buried in the Stockton Rural Cemetery.

References: Jasper County (Iowa) Genealogical Society; Iowa State Historical Society of Des Moines; and the Newton (Iowa) Public Library; and a military pension file at the National Archives, Washington, DC.

HADLEY, CYRUS R. (1839–1917)

Cyrus Hadley was born in Danville on 27 July 1839, one of eight children of Mary Hadley and Simon Hadley. An older brother, Atlas, became a professor at Wabash, and a younger brother, Joshua, not only attended Wabash but also served in the Civil War.

Hadley was in the Normal School at Wabash for one school year, 1859–60.

On 13 July 1863 he enrolled in Company B of the 117th Regiment at Danville for six months and was formally discharged at Indianapolis on 23 February 1864. He was described as being five feet eight inches tall, with grey eyes, dark hair, and dark complexion.

Hadley married Nancy Carter of Danville on 25 June 1865, and they had two children: Loftus (1867) and Maggie (1869). He was a farmer, and the family moved frequently. From 1870 to 1874 they lived in Tuscola, Illinois, but Hadley was listed as a landlord in Danville in the 1880 census. Between 1898 and 1902 they lived in Cherry Vale, Kansas, and then moved to Garden City, Cass County, Missouri, returning to Indiana in 1911 and settling on a farm in Lebanon.

Nancy Hadley died on 11 May 1914 and Cyrus on 28 November 1917. They are both buried in Oak Hill Cemetery, Lebanon.

References: *History of Hendricks County, Indiana* (1885); *Lebanon Reporter*, 12 May 1914 and 28 Nov. 1917; military pension file, National Archives, Washington, DC, and the Lebanon Public Library.

HADLEY, JOSHUA CLINTON (1842–1907)

Joshua Hadley was another son of Simon and Mary Hadley. Born in Danville on 25 February 1842, he was one of eight children. Joshua spent three years at Wabash College, 1859–62, the last in the freshman class, and joined the Beta Theta Pi fraternity.

On 22 July 1862 Hadley enrolled at Danville for three years in Company K of the Seventieth Indiana Volunteer Infantry and rose steadily in rank, culminating as a captain on 23 April 1865. He mustered out near Washington, DC, on 8 June 1865 after seeing action at the Battle of Atlanta and witnessing Sherman's march through Georgia to the sea.

After the war he returned to Danville and then went to Cincinnati, where he worked as a billing clerk for the Marietta and Cincinnati Railroad Company.

In 1869 Hadley married a Cincinnati woman, Margaret B. Chester. Eventually they had three children: Jay, George, and Mary. In 1870 they came to Indiana, moving to Logansport, where Hadley became paymaster for the newly formed Vandalia Railroad. He helped superintend the construction of the line between Logansport and Terre Haute. In 1881 the family went to Chariton, Illinois, where Hadley was the trainmaster of the Chicago, Burlington and Quincy

Railroad for one year before returning to Logansport to become a partner with George Ash in the Logansport Furniture Company.

He served seven years on the Logansport city council, and in 1888 he ran unsuccessfully as a Republican candidate for the Indiana Senate.

Hadley died on 13 January 1907 and is buried in Mount Hope Cemetery, Logansport. His wife and children survived him.

References: Logansport-Cass County Public Library. See also the references cited in the entry for his brother, Cyrus. *Logansport Daily Reporter*, 14 Jan. 1907; *Biographical and Genealogical History of Cass, Miami, Howard and Tippecanoe Counties, Indiana* (1898), pp. 629–31.

HAINES, WILLIAM WIRT (1837–1921)

William Haines was born in Rising Sun on 9 May 1837, one of the eleven children of Elizabeth and Matthias Haines. In the autumn of 1853, he entered the Preparatory Department of Wabash College, where he remained for three academic years, 1853–56.

On 14 August 1861 he enrolled at Indianapolis as a sergeant in the Second Battery, Light Artillery. A year later he was promoted to second lieutenant and in November 1862 to first lieutenant. During 1863–64 he was an ordnance officer at Fort Smith, Arkansas, keeping track of stores and equipment and rendering quarterly reports as to what inventory was on hand. He was mustered out at Indianapolis in September 1864 and later claimed to have participated in twenty-six battles and skirmishes.

On 14 October 1866 at Rising Sun, Haines married Jane (Jennie) S. Frank, who came from across the Ohio River in Henry County, Kentucky. They had eight children, two of whom died in infancy, and one, John, who died in adulthood. Their other five children were Matthias, Verlinda, Hattie, William W., and Matilda (Tillie). Haines acquired a farm near Millwood, Missouri, where he grew crops and bred livestock. From 1874 to 1878 he served as a justice of the peace.

In 1889 the family purchased another farm in Lincoln County, near Olney, where they remained for the rest of their lives. Jane died on 2 June 1900, while her husband lived until 14 April 1921. They are both buried in the Olney Cemetery. In his last will and testament, Haines provided well for his five children, including an extra $8,000 for his blind daughter, Matilda.

References: William Haines's grandson, William W. Haines of Olney, and Mrs. Jane Haines Kientzy of Silex, Missouri, provided local newspaper obituaries, background information on the Haines family, copies of William's will, and some of his military service records. See also: *History of Dearborn and Ohio Counties, Indiana* (1885), p. 214.

HALL, HARVEY P.R.C. (1825–1864?)

Bodies of unknown numbers of soldiers could never be returned home after death. Battlefield deaths, as at Antietam (estimated at 3,650), were often overwhelming, and bodies were stacked up several feet high for burial crews to take care of in mass graves. Embalming was often out of the question, though families frequently traveled to battlefield sites to try to bring the remains home. Many times burial places could never be traced. Harvey Hall was typical of those whose final resting place was never found.

Hall was born in Ohio in 1825, one of ten children of Jane Buell and Dr. Daniel C. Hall. The family moved in 1829 to Pike Township, Warren County, Indiana, where Harvey lived when he spent from 1843 to 1846 at Wabash College, starting in the Preparatory Department.

At the time of the 1850 census, Hall was married, a farmer with a twenty-year-old wife, Minerva, and a one-and-a-half-year-old daughter, Martha.

On the eve of the Civil War, the family lived in Nodaway County, Missouri, where he enlisted at St. Joseph on 16 August 1861 in the Thirteenth Missouri Volunteer Infantry. He was five feet ten inches tall, with light complexion, light grey eyes, and brown hair. On 20 September he was wounded at the First Battle of Lexington, Missouri, also called the Battle of the Hemp Bales. When Hall rejoined his regiment in October, it had become the Twenty-Fifth Missouri Regiment, and he was assigned to Company K (Cavalry). He sustained gunshot wounds in his scapula and spine on 6 April 1862 at the Battle of Shiloh that led to his medical discharge at Corinth, Mississippi, on 21 July 1862.

In 1863–64 he was in a military unit, perhaps a local militia, and died somewhere in Arkansas. His brother James later wrote that "he [Harvey] had been sent with a small body of picked men on a foraging expedition for the troops, when they were attacked by a superior force of Confederates." He was never seen again, so where he died and was buried is unknown. Missouri was a particularly chaotic and unpredictable arena in the fighting.

References: Walter Salts of Warren County, Indiana; Maryville (Missouri) Public Library; and the Missouri State Archives in Jefferson City. See also: *Biographical History of Tippecanoe ... Warren and Pulaski Counties, Indiana* (1899), p. 91; and *History of Warren, Benton, Jasper and Newton Counties, Indiana* (1883), pp. 181–82; and his military service file at the National Archives, Washington, DC.

HALL, SAMUEL J. (1835–1915)

Samuel Hall was born at Newport in Vermillion County on 13 April 1835, one of twelve children born to Nancy Jordan (1806–1878) and William B. (1798–1863) Hall. His siblings were Harriet (born 1822), Lucy Ann (1826), Elizabeth (1828), Mary S. (1830), Charles (1833), Emily (1838), Amanda (1840), John D.

(1842), Ellen (1844), Melvin L. (1846), and James W. (1850).

Hall spent two years (1852–54) in the Preparatory Department of Wabash College, after which he returned home to help on the family farm.

In October 1861 he helped organize Company I of the Forty-Third Indiana Regiment and was appointed the company's captain. He committed for three years' service and soon traveled from Terre Haute to Kentucky and then to Tennessee, where he took part in the siege and capture of Fort Pillow in early 1862. By June of that year he had been reassigned to the Department of Missouri and the Mississippi River, and during the next two years he saw action in Arkansas at Helena (4 July 1863), Little Rock (10 September 1863), Elkin's Ford (or Ferry) (3–4 April 1864), and Jenkins Ferry (30 April). In January 1865 he was honorably discharged.

In 1867 Hall married Elizabeth Ann Head (1844–1929) of nearby Eugene. In the coming years he expanded his farm holdings until they amounted to 540 acres and also started a meat-packing business.

One of Hall's younger brothers, Melvin L., attended Wabash briefly during the school year 1865–66. His sister Elizabeth also married a Wabash College man, Luther T. Woodward.

Hall died in Newport on 6 July 1915 and is buried in the Eugene Township Cemetery.

References: H. O'Donnell, *Newport and Vermillion Township: The First One Hundred Years* (1969); *Biographical and Historical Record of Vermillion County, Indiana* (1888); W. McClean, *The Forty-Third Regiment of Indiana Volunteers* (1903).

HAMILTON, DAVID HENRY (1830–1895)

David Hamilton was born in Clinton County on 27 May 1830, one of five children of Elizabeth Strahan and James S. Hamilton. His siblings were Orville (1819), Susan (1826), John (1838), and Ezekiel (1843).

From 1847 to 1849 Hamilton was enrolled in the Preparatory Department at Wabash College. In 1850 he began the study of law and for a year served as a prosecuting attorney for the Boone County Court of Common Pleas.

On 8 May 1852 he married Mary Jane Hillis, a resident of Boone County, who died prematurely on 13 June 1854. On 25 December 1855 he married Elizabeth Benefield Van Nuys. They were unfortunate when it came to their offspring, all of whom died as children, one of the striking and deplorable facets of life in the nineteenth century that strikes modern readers as particularly tragic. No fewer than six children died between 1862 and 1866.

In 1857, besides practicing law, Hamilton secured a teaching contract in Lebanon to teach sixty-five days between November and the end of February. This provided him with a salary of $108, less a charge for fuel in the schoolhouse.

On 3 June 1862 Hamilton received a commission as a captain of Company G in the Fifty-Fifth Indiana Regiment for a term of three months, during which he was assigned to guard prisoners at Camp Morton, Indianapolis. Then in mid-August the regiment was sent to Kentucky, where it engaged in the Battle of Richmond on 30 August. Many Hoosiers were taken captive but were paroled during September and October and allowed to return to Indianapolis to be mustered out.

Returning to Lebanon, Hamilton resumed his law practice. Sometime during the 1870s he moved to Iowa, where he died on 2 January 1895 and is buried in Taylor Township, Appanoose County.

References Lebanon Public Library; Ralph W. Stark, "Early Schools in Lebanon," *Boone Magazine* (June 1980) pp. 10–11; L. M. Crist, *History of Boone County, Indiana* (1914) pp. 215, 319, and 451. For an obituary of David's older brother Orville, see *Lebanon Patriot*, 4 Oct. 1878.

HARBERT, WILLIAM SOESBY (1842–1919)

Little attention seems to be paid in these or any other Civil War records to the spouses of the Wabash students and alumni who went to the war. The women are usually mentioned as "he married" or "he left behind" Belle or Eleanor or whatever woman it was who remained home. In reality their lives were often difficult: they took care of several small children, managed the farm alone or with whatever help they could get, and endured. They are unsung heroes in the war. Occasionally an interesting story of a spouse highlights a woman in her own right during the mid-nineteenth century.

William Harbert, whose career was outstanding in and out of the war, chose a mate with a spirit as independent as his, a woman who managed to shake Wabash up at a time when women had no effect on the college. She was 150 years before her time.

Harbert was born in Terre Haute on 17 September 1842, the oldest of four children born to Amanda Watson and Solomon Harbert. His younger siblings were Lucinda, Mary, and Edward. Before entering the Preparatory Department of Wabash College in the fall of 1859, he spent several years at Franklin College. He left Wabash in the spring of 1861 and took a year (1861–62) at the University of Michigan at Ann Arbor.

On 14 August 1862 he enrolled in Company C of the Eighty-Fifth Indiana Regiment at Terre Haute and was promoted to second lieutenant on 4 September. In 1863 he temporarily transferred to the Thirty-Third Indiana Regiment under Colonel John Coburn, a former Wabash College student. As commissariat Harbert's job was to keep track of stores behind the front. However, that March the Thirty-Third was involved in the previously described disastrous battle about nine miles from Franklin, Tennessee. Not only were Coburn and Harbert taken prisoners at Thompson's Station, but former Wabash students Levin T. Miller,

Henry C. Johnson, James C. Fullenwider were also marched to Libby Prison. A Wabash man was killed. The prisoners were confined at Libby in Richmond, but were fortunate to be exchanged.

Harbert subsequently returned as a first lieutenant in his original Eighty-fifth Indiana Regiment, which saw action in Georgia in 1864 at the Battle of New Hope Church (25–28 May), Lost Mountain (27 June), and Kolb's Farm (22 June). They then joined Sherman in his March to the Sea and arrived in Savannah by December 1864. At some point Harbert was promoted to brevet captain of Company C and also served as an aide-de-camp to Major General W. T. Ward of the Third Division of the Twentieth Army Corps, eventually ending at Fort Lincoln near Washington, DC, where he was mustered out on 12 June 1865.

The following autumn he entered the University of Michigan law school and was admitted to the bar in 1867. In 1869 he was living in Des Moines, Iowa, a partner in the law firm of Harbert and Clark and also serving as a United States assistant district attorney.

On 18 October 1870 he returned to Crawfordsville to marry the local author and vice president of the Indiana Suffrage Association, Elizabeth Morrison Boynton (1845–1925). Boynton had applied unsuccessfully to be admitted to Wabash. Instead of admission, she was granted permission to attend lectures at this all-male institution. Their three children were as follows: Arthur Boynton (1871–1900), Corinne Boynton (1873–1958), and Boynton Elizabeth "Bess" (1875–1949).

In 1874 the Harberts moved to Chicago, where William Harbert entered the law firm that then became Harbert and Daly. When Daly died several decades later, Harbert included his son Arthur in Harbert, Curran and Harbert. When Arthur died in 1900, William practiced on his own for the next five years and served also as a judge. The family lived at 1412 Judson Avenue in Evanston during these years, and Lizzie continued to be active in the cause of women's suffrage. She was a friend of Susan B. Anthony and other leaders in the woman's rights movement. For eight years she wrote a column titled "Woman's Kingdom" for the *Chicago Inter-Ocean* newspaper. She also published three books and contributed numerous articles to a variety of journals.

In 1906 William and Lizzie moved to Pasadena, California, where their two daughters, Corinne and Bess, lived. William died on 24 March 1919, before the Nineteenth Amendment to the Constitution was passed on 18 August 1920, but Lizzie survived until 19 January 1925 to witness the fruits of her life's passion and surely to exercise the great privilege of voting.

References: *Wabash Magazine*, V (July 1863), p. 327; *Wabash Magazine*, XI (Dec. 1870), p. 54; *The Book of Chicagoans* (1905), p. 261; Vigo County Public Library; Evanston (Illinois) Public Library; and Pasadena (California) Public Library. The Crawfordsville Public Library has a large file on Elizabeth Boynton Harbert, compiled by Jean Thompson.

HARLAND, WILLARD H. (ca. 1829–1896)

Willard Harland was born in Indiana, possibly Crawfordsville, in about 1829, the son of Sarah Messick and Ambrose Harland. From 1840 to 1843 he was enrolled in the Preparatory Department of Wabash College, and he continued as a freshman from 1843 to 1844. A contemporary, Frank Mills, later described Willard as "fat, hearty, and good natured."

He married Sarah Leffingwell, a native of Vermont, on 14 May 1849 in Marion, Iowa. They eventually had at least six children, but several died in infancy. Those who survived were Pliny C. and Linneus (twins), Horace L., and Willard H. Jr.

In 1850 Harland was a clerk, according to the census, while in 1860 he was described as a lawyer.

On 25 June 1861 he enlisted in Company A of the Sixth Iowa Infantry as a second lieutenant, but became a first lieutenant on 1 November, adjutant a week later, and captain on 1 January 1862. His company was made up entirely of Linn County volunteers and suffered heavy casualties at the Battles of Shiloh and Missionary Ridge in Tennessee; Big Shanty (9 June 1864) and Kennesaw Mountain in Georgia; and in Jackson, Mississippi.

What Harland did after the war is a mystery. He does not appear in either the 1870 or 1880 censuses for Linn County, although Sarah died at Marion on 19 March 1891.

Harland died in the town of Willis, Texas, on 16 March 1896 without leaving a will. His property consisted mainly of mules and wagons with an estimated value of $515.

References: State Historical Society of Iowa; Iowa Dept. of Veterans Affairs; Genealogical Society of Linn County; and the Willis (Texas) Public Library. See also: abstracts of the *Marion Sentinel* at the Linn Genealogical Society; and F. M. Mills, *Early Days in a College Town* (1924), p. 155.

HARRISON, REUBEN E. (1839–1914)

Reuben Harrison was born in 1839 when the family lived in Byrneville. He was the son of Cecelia Byrn and Benjamin Harrison. He entered the Normal School of Wabash in the fall of 1860 and stayed for his freshman year, 1861–62.

On 20 August 1862 he was mustered in to Company G of the Sixty-Seventh Indiana Regiment.

On 21 March 1867 Harrison married Harriet Bright of Indianapolis. However, when the 1870 census was taken, Florence B. Bell is shown as his wife. They had two children, both of whom died young: Roy Harrison and Ruby Florence Harrison (1874–75). In 1886 they had another child, Robert, who was living with them in 1910.

In 1870 and again in 1880 the census indicates that Harrison was a successful lawyer in Indianapolis, possessing real property worth $14,000 and personal effects valued at $5,000.

By 1910 the couple were partners in a general store. The precise date of Harrison's death is uncertain, but he was interred in Crown Hill Cemetery, Indianapolis, on 21 January 1914.

References: Crown Hill Cemetery, Indianapolis.

HARRISON, TEMPLE COLE (1835–1876)

Perhaps few students were so highly regarded while at Wabash as Temple Harrison. A classmate later wrote of him, "It is perhaps not too much to say that no man has ever been graduated at Wabash College who attracted more attention or was more beloved. . . . There was something about him—his awkwardness—his kindliness—his poverty—his perseverance—his geniality—that irresistibly attracted."

This young man so admired by his peers was born on 15 March 1835, the oldest of seven children of Cecelia Byrn (1811–1864) and Benjamin Harrison (1805–1852). One of his brothers, Reuben, covered earlier, also attended Wabash. His other siblings were Esek, Mary, Sarah, Theodore, and Tilghman.

The family lived on a farm near Byrneville in Morgan Township, Harrison County.

Harrison entered the Preparatory Department of Wabash College in the autumn of 1858, indicating that his home was Byrneville. The allusion in the opening quotation to his poverty was genuine, as it is said that he arrived on campus with only one dollar in his pocket and worked his way through college for five years. Between 1859 and 1863 he pursued the Classical Course, culminating in a bachelor of arts degree.

Less than a month after graduation, Morgan's raid attracted many recruits. Harrison joined the fray and was discharged at Indianapolis on 17 July 1863.

He then went to Indianapolis and began the study of law. He made a specialty of helping veterans prosecute claims so that they could redeem their land warrants. On 12 December 1867 he returned to Crawfordsville to marry Frances (Fanny) Jennison. They had one child, Helen.

In 1871 he served on the Indianapolis City Council and began to speculate in real estate. At first he did very well, but the panic of 1873 wiped him out financially and psychologically. His untimely death on 4 May 1876 was described in his obituary: "The remains of Temple C. Harrison were found yesterday afternoon lying near an old outhouse of Simon Sipp. Whisky had done its work, and the wreck of a most promising life was consummated. . . . It is possible that the immediate cause of Mr. Harrison's death was an overdose of hydrate of chloral which he had been taking to quiet his nerves." It was generally accepted, however, that he had not tried to commit suicide.

References: *Wabash Magazine*, VIII (Dec. 1867), p. 79; *Wabash Magazine*, XI (March 1871), p. 138; *Obituaries of Some Alumni*, Ramsay Archives, Wabash College; and *Indianapolis Daily Sentinel*, 5 May 1876.

HARRISON, THOMAS JEFFERSON (1824–1871)

Thomas Harrison was born in Shelby County, Kentucky, on 8 June 1824, the son of Sarah and Joshua Harrison. When he was six years old, the family moved to a farm near Crawfordsville, where they were still living in the autumn of 1846 when son Tom entered the Preparatory Department of Wabash College. He remained for two years and then went to Kokomo to study law with Judge Nathaniel R. Lindsay.

In 1851 Harrison was admitted to the Indiana bar and continued practicing with Judge Lindsay, whose daughter he married when she turned sixteen in 1853. They subsequently had four children: Sarah, Jane, Thomas, and Lulu.

In 1859 Harrison was elected as a Republican to the lower house of the Indiana General Assembly, where he served until 1860. At that time he returned to Kokomo to practice law until the outbreak of the Civil War.

On 21 April 1861 he initially signed up for three months as captain of Company D of the Sixth Regiment of Indiana Volunteers, but after being mustered out in August 1861, he returned to Kokomo and helped to organize the Thirty-Ninth Indiana Regiment, becoming its colonel at the age of thirty-seven. The regiment was deployed first to Kentucky and then farther south, and Harrison saw action at Fort Donelson, Shiloh, and Stones River, where 380 out of 480 either died or were wounded or missing. In 1863 the regiment was reorganized as the Eighth Cavalry and fought at Chickamauga, and later in the war it carried out raids in Alabama and Georgia.

On 31 January 1865 Harrison was brevetted a brigadier general, and on 15 June he was released from military service.

After the war his family settled on a farm near Nashville, Pulaski County, Tennessee, where he supplemented cotton farming with ownership of a lumberyard, a mill, and a limestone.

In 1870 he was appointed U.S. marshal for the middle district of Tennessee, but on 28 September 1871 he had a sudden heart attack and died. His body was returned to Kokomo, where his wife resided for many years.

References J. P. Dunn, *Representative Citizens of Indiana* (1912), p. 657; *Biographical Directory of the Indiana General Assembly* (1980), I, p. 170; *Kokomo Daily Dispatch*, 25 Aug. 1897; *Kokomo Tribune*, 3 Oct. 1871; *Kokomo Democrat*, 5 Oct. 1871. William McKibben of Kokomo furnished a wide variety of items relating to the Harrison family.

HARTMAN, DAVID W. (1839–1898)

David Hartman was the eldest son of Elizabeth Lee (1810–1847) and William Hartman (1804–1891), born in Crawfordsville on 31 January 1839. His siblings were John A., Samuel L., Martha A., and William.

Young David attended Wabash for one year (1853–54) in the Preparatory Department. According to the 1860 census, he was a painter.

All the boys in the family except William served in the army. John was a lieutenant at Pittsburg Landing, and Samuel raised an artillery company from Crawfordsville. David's military career began on 20 April 1861. His unit, Company G, Tenth Indiana Regiment, was under the direction of a former Wabash College student, Colonel Joseph J. Reynolds, and later under Colonel Mahlon D. Manson. The regiment headed for Parkersburg, in western Virginia, by way of Cincinnati and Marietta, Ohio, and by 10 July, they reached the foot of Rich Mountain, where they charged the Confederates' works and routed the enemy. Their work being completed, they returned to Indianapolis, where they were mustered out on 2 August 1861.

On 4 September 1861 Hartman married Julia Wade, with whom he had three children, two of whom grew to adulthood: Ferris and Aletha. Following Julia's death, David married Mrs. A. F. Wise and they had a son, Robert.

In 1870 Hartman was a printer and a charter member of the GAR, McPherson Post No. 7, when it was reorganized in 1879. He was a trustee of the Union Township schools from 1891 to 1895. In recognition of his service, the teachers of Union Township presented him with a gold-tipped cane on 21 March 1895 and resolved, "We the teachers of Union Township in institute assembled, do, through our President, tender you this cane as a support for your declining years and as a slight token of our appreciation of you as a friend and our regard for you as an employer and public officer, with a hope that your future years may be many, blest with health, prosperity, and best of all, contentment." He died at home on 29 January 1898 and is buried at Oak Hill Cemetery in the family plot.

References: Wabash College archives; American Legion archives; H. W. Beckwith, *History of Montgomery County* (1881); *History of Montgomery County* (Bowen and Co., 1913); *Crawfordsville Journal*, 22 March 1895; 1860 and 1870 U.S. census for Montgomery County; and Montgomery County Cemetery Records, Oak Hill Cemetery.

HASKELL, WILLIAM A. (1837–1901)

William Haskell was born in Jefferson County, Indiana, on 8 March 1837, one of twelve children born to Rosy Brown and Amos Haskell. As a farmer, Amos was just scraping by, if one may go by the census of 1860. William's siblings were Honorwell, Hallowell, Arminta, Thomas, Eunice, Catherine, Sarah, Freeman, Oliver, Richard, and Martha.

In the 1850s the family resided in Crawfordsville, facilitating son William's entry in the fall of 1854 into the Preparatory Department of Wabash College, where he spent two years. He then entered the freshman and sophomore class for 1856–58.

The family returned to Jefferson County and farmed in Milton Township. There, on 11 September 1861, Haskell enrolled in Company F of the Sixth Indiana Regiment for three years. At the time he was five feet seven inches tall, with light complexion, dark hair, and blue eyes. He was plagued with illness during most of his military service. Exposure to the cold brought on lung disease that landed him in the hospital near Nashville, and in March and April of 1862, and a year later he was similarly hospitalized at Huntsville, Alabama. Between hospitalizations he returned to his regiment and was able to complete his full three years, mustering out at Indianapolis on 22 September 1864.

Settling in Brooksburg, he resumed farming. On 6 July 1865 at Madison, he married Nancy Jane Burress. They had two children, James (1871) and Christie (1872).

In spite of his weak lungs, Haskell lived until 27 March 1909, when he died of pneumonia. Nancy died a year later, on the anniversary of her husband's death. They are buried in Mount Zion Cemetery, Vevay, Switzerland County.

References: 1850 and 1860 U.S. censuses as well as William's military pension file at the National Archives, Washington, DC.

HAWKINS, JOHN PARKER (1830–1914)

John Parker Hawkins was another Wabash student who attended West Point and became a career soldier, spending all of his active life serving his country. His record is impressive for both dedication through many postings and length of service.

He was born on 29 September 1830 in Indianapolis, the son of Elizabeth Waller and John Hawkins. He had three sisters: Louisa, Miriam, and Margaret. Both of his parents had distinguished English ancestors: his father's family included Admiral Sir John Hawkins, who commanded the English fleet at the battle that defeated the Spanish Armada in 1588, and his mother's line included the English poet Edmund Waller.

In the 1820s the family moved to Covington so that the senior Hawkins could take up farming. The depression of 1837 hit them hard, and they abandoned farming in favor of a mercantile business in Crawfordsville. That too failed after a few years, and John Sr. again tried to farm, acquiring a spread of one thousand acres. However, he and his wife died soon thereafter.

Bereft of both parents, John Hawkins was nevertheless determined to acquire an education and a career, and in 1846 he entered the Preparatory Department of Wabash College. In 1847 he was accepted at West Point and enrolled there on 1 July 1848, graduating in 1852, fortieth in a class of forty-three. While there he became acquainted with Phillip Sheridan, who was to serve with distinction and in 1883 was appointed general-in-chief of the U.S. Army.

Upon his graduation from West Point, Hawkins served on the frontier and was appointed second lieutenant of the Sixth Infantry on 1 July 1852. He was transferred to the Second Infantry on 23 June 1854 and then promoted to first lieutenant on 12 October 1857. One year later, in October 1858, he was made regimental quartermaster, a position he still held when war broke out. While still a lieutenant, Hawkins was involved in First Bull Run, and he subsequently served in the western army under Frémont's command.

On 3 August 1861 Hawkins was promoted to captain and helped organize Grant's commissary department. At the Battle of Shiloh he was an aide-de-camp to General Grant, who appointed him brigadier general of volunteers with the job of organizing and leading black troops. In February 1865, after a brief illness,

The Siege of Mobile, Alabama. Hawkins and his men were in the thick of battle. Hawthorne Publishing Historic Photo Collection, original from Harper's Weekly, *May 27, 1865.*

Hawkins and his men were ordered to New Orleans, where an advance on Mobile, Alabama, was being planned. He was subsequently brevetted major general for "gallant and meritorious service during the siege of Mobile." He spent the remainder of the war in New Orleans, in charge of a military district composed of parts of Texas and Louisiana. He received an honorable muster out of the volunteer service on 1 February 1866 and returned to the commissary department of the regular army.

On 10 October 1867 Hawkins married Jane B. Craig, daughter of Colonel Henry Knox Craig.

On 3 September 1889 he was promoted to lieutenant colonel, to colonel on March 12, and to brigadier general on 22 December 1892. He retired on his sixty-fourth birthday, 29 September 1894, as required by law, and lived in Indianapolis for twenty more years until his death on 7 February 1914. Hawkins is buried in Crown Hill Cemetery, Indianapolis, along with his parents.

References: F. B. Heitman, *Historical Register and Dictionary of the United States Army* (1903), p. 513; E. J. Warner, *Generals in Blue* (1964), pp. 218–19; *Who Was Who in America 1896–1942* (1943), I, p. 536; Indiana Scrapbook Collection, Vol. III, at the Indiana State Library; *Indianapolis Sun and Star*, 9 Feb. 1914; Hawkins, *Reminiscences* (1913), pp. 24–30, 75–76.

HAWLEY, HENRY M. (1834–1914)

Henry Hawley was born on 2 November 1834 in Bloomington, Indiana, where his father, Ransom E. Hawley Sr. (1802–1889), was a Presbyterian pastor. His mother, Sarah Hall, was a native of Connecticut. Henry had two sisters, Lucy and Emeline, and a younger brother, Ransom Jr., whose career is described later in this book.

By 1844 the family had moved to Putnamville. Hawley entered the Preparatory Department of Wabash College in 1850 and stayed for two years. According to the census of 1860, he described himself as a laborer married to Eliza, a native of Ohio. They had a daughter, Mary. Hawley was from all accounts in the war, but his record is hard to substantiate.

After the war Hawley was a freight agent in Terre Haute for the Evansville and Crawfordsville Railroad while also farming. He died at home on 14 July 1914 and is buried in Woodlawn Cemetery.

References: David N. Lewis of the Vigo County Public Library; *Terre Haute Tribune*, 15 July 1914; and D. Clark, *Historically Speaking* (1981), pp. 275–76.

HAWLEY, RANSOM EDWARDS JR. (1844–1927)

Ransom Hawley Jr. was born in Putnamville, Indiana, on 8 July 1844, the second surviving son of Sarah Hall and Ransom Hawley, whose first child, Josiah, had died at birth. Ransom's elder brother, Henry, whose life has just been described, also went to Wabash and served in the war; their sisters were Lucy and Emeline. Ransom entered the Preparatory Department of Wabash in the fall of 1860. On 22 April 1861 he wrote to his parents:

> The war excitement has by no means abated, yet the second volunteer company from this town left this morning. It is the third from this county. On Saturday the ladies of the city met at McCellands Hall to make tents, shirts, etc. for the soldiers. There were 40 students at

prayer this A.M., about 20 attend recitations, about 40 have gone, and about 20 will go this week. And now I want to go, and is it strange when the flag of our country has been torn down and a traitor's flag planted instead? When nearly every student has gone to the war, or is going there, or going home, but when 4 or 5 go to recitation, and such tremendous excitement is going on constantly, is it strange that a boy whose Grandfathers both did their country's service, is it strange that he. . . would not want to go too?

In spite of this strongly stated reasoning, Hawley's parents refused permission for him to enlist, reminding him that he had not yet turned seventeen and that they had contributed their older son, Henry, to the Union cause.

Following Hawley's second year in the Preparatory Department (1861–62), his parents allowed him to enroll in Company A of the Seventy-Eighth Indiana Regiment toward the end of July. He committed to sixty days of service, and within a month he was in Uniontown, Missouri, where the regiment was attacked by Confederate troops on 1 September. Hawley was one of twenty wounded. Taken prisoner, he was released just in time to return to Indiana for his freshman year at Wabash. At the college he won renown for reading the multi-volume history of Greece by George Grote.

In early July 1863 Hawley signed on for the emergency force opposing Morgan and was soon released. Still anxious to serve, Hawley enrolled in the 115th Regiment from his hometown of Putnamville for six months beginning 14 August and ending 24 February 1864. Since he could not return to college in the middle of the year, he signed up for another one hundred days, this time with Company F of the 133rd Regiment, which he joined on 6 May 1864.

Wabash did not immediately readmit him the following autumn, so he entered Indiana University at Bloomington, but transferred back to Wabash and completed the academic year 1864–65. The next year he returned to Indiana University as a senior and graduated in June 1866. He became a Presbyterian minister, serving in several areas.

On 16 May 1872 Hawley married Minerva Andrews in North Vernon. Their first child, Ralph Andrews Hawley, was born in 1873 but died eight months later. Their only other child, Marietta Louise, was born in 1875 and survived both her parents. Minerva died at Terre Haute in 1904, and Hawley married sixty-year-old Minnie Marples of Georgetown, Illinois. For several decades they made their home in Terre Haute, where Hawley occasionally assisted at a nearby Methodist church. He died on 20 January 1927 and is buried in Woodlawn Cemetery.

References: David N. Lewis of the Vigo County Library; *Wabash Magazine*, IV (Dec. 1862), p. 78; *Wabash Magazine*, VII (June 1866), p. 10; Lane Theological Seminary, *General Catalogue, 1829–1899*, p.76; *Cambridge City Tribune*, 10 Nov. 1910; *Terre Haute Gazette*, 28 Nov. 1889; S. Otto, *History of Edinburgh, Indiana* (1886), p. 177; *Terre Haute Tribune*, 21 Jan. 1927.

HAYES, GEORGE WARREN (1838–1910)

George Hayes was born in Terre Haute on 7 April 1838, the only child of Eliza Warren and Benjamin Hayes. In the autumn of 1854 he entered the Preparatory Department of Wabash College. After two years of study, he advanced to the freshman year, where he was one of the rare students who remained for four years in the Classical Course. He graduated in June 1860 and enrolled at Lane Theological Seminary in Cincinnati, but after one year decided not to become a Presbyterian minister. During the next four years (1861–65) he taught at schools in Terre Haute and Montezuma (Parke County), Indiana, and Waverly, Illinois.

On 21 July 1862, at Evansville, Hayes was admitted as a corporal in Company I of the Seventy-Sixth Indiana Volunteers for thirty days of military service, after which he married Mercy E. Safford, a graduate of Oberlin College, on 25 November 1862. A son, George Washington Hayes, was born in 1865. Mercy died of tuberculosis two years later at Aurora, Illinois. George remarried and had a daughter, but their names are unknown.

Hayes gradually phased out of teaching and became a special agent in northern Illinois for the Aetna Insurance Company between 1864 and 1874. He then moved to Milwaukee, where he worked as a special agent in Illinois, Wisconsin, Iowa, and Minnesota for the Franklin Fire Insurance Company of Philadelphia. In 1879 he headed the Milwaukee office of the Western Assurance Company of Toronto, and in 1893 he added the British-American Assurance Company of Toronto to his responsibilities.

After retiring, Hayes moved to Seattle, Washington, to live with his daughter. He died there on 13 November 1910. In 1982 his grandson, George W. Hayes III, arranged to have his grandfather's ashes conveyed from Seattle to Oberlin, Ohio, for reburial in the Safford family plot.

References: *Wabash Magazine*, IV (Dec. 1862), p. 80; A. J. Aikens, *Men of Progress: Wisconsin* (1889), pp. 609–10; *Elyria Chronicle Telegram*, 4 May 1982; *General Catalogue of Lane Theological Seminary, 1829–1899*, p. 69; *Alumni Directory of Phi Delta Theta Fraternity* (1888); *The Chronicle: The Weekly Review of Insurance* (Nov. 1910). Also the Milwaukee Public Library and George W. Hayes III of Port Richey, Florida.

HEATON, FRANCIS MILLER (1834–1908)

Francis, known as Frank, was born in Crawfordsville in July 1834, one of three sons of Sarah and James Heaton, the Montgomery County recorder. His brothers were James and Edgar, and his sisters were Elizabeth, Cornelia, and Laurie.

He attended the Preparatory Department for one academic year, 1852–53. According to the 1860 census, Heaton was a bookseller with a wife, Harriet, and a one-year-old son, Charles. They eventually had three more children: Edith, Anna, and Mary. The family moved during the 1860s to Washington, DC, where Heaton worked for the government land office. Harriet presumably died, and in October 1870 Heaton married Mable. They had one son, Arthur. Heaton remained with the land office for twenty-eight years and then became a lawyer specializing in real estate and land claims.

Heaton's military service record is problematic. There is no doubt he was in the war, since his obituaries allude to this, and he was a member of the military order of the Loyal Legion in Washington. However, finding where and when he served has been challenging. One possibility is a *Franklin* Heaton who served in the Thirty-Fifth Regiment of Indiana Volunteers; this Heaton mustered into Company G on 8 February 1865 and was released on 30 September 1865.

On 30 October 1908 Heaton was struck and killed by an automobile while crossing the street in Chevy Chase, Maryland, where he was living with his daughters Edith and Mary.

References: Martin Luther King Library, Washington, DC; *Washington Post*, 31 Oct. 1908, pp. 3, 5, 7; and *Washington Evening Star*, 31 Oct. 1908, p. 2.

HERNDON, HENRY (1842–1865)

Henry Herndon was born in Crawfordsville in 1842, the only son of Elizabeth N. Lindsay and Dr. Milton Herndon, both of whom were from Kentucky but came to Indiana in 1834. Their other children were Rebecca, Louisa, and Emma. Two sons, William and John, died young.

Henry spent one year, 1854–55, in the Normal School of Wabash College, and when the 1860 census was taken, he was working as a clerk in an office in Crawfordsville.

On 11 July 1863 Herndon responded to the call for troops to oppose Morgan's raiders in Company C of the 108th Regiment. He was released on 17 July. However, on 12 May 1864 he signed up for one hundred days' service in Company D of the 135th Regiment along with other recruits from Tippecanoe, Montgomery, Boone, and Clinton Counties. He reported for duty at Indianapolis on 23 May but soon thereafter was discharged because of illness. For nearly a year he clung to life, but he died on 11 March 1865 and was buried in the Odd Fellows Cemetery at Crawfordsville.

References: H. W. Beckwith, *History of Montgomery County* (1881), pp. 88, 94; *Crawfordsville Weekly Journal*, 6 June 1872 (obituary for Milton Herndon); and Indiana State Library Archives.

HERRON, WILLIAM PARKE (1843–1927)

William Herron was born in Crawfordsville on 17 June 1843, the son of James D. (1798–1874) and Rebecca Young (1802–1888) Herron. James grew up in South Carolina and Rebecca in Pennsylvania. James reached Montgomery County and took up farming as early as 1825, and he presumably married Rebecca about 1830. In addition to William, their large family included daughters Rebecca, Mary Jane, Margaret, Janette, and Eliza and son Howard.

William entered Wabash College's Preparatory Department in the fall of 1858. He persevered for four years and then took up arms in the cause of the Union.

On 14 July 1862 at Crawfordsville, Herron enrolled in Company B of the Seventy-Second Indiana Volunteers. He had signed up for three years, and by 24 October 1862 he was promoted to the rank of second lieutenant. On 24 February 1863 further advancement came in the form of a captaincy. This latter coincided with his transfer to Wilder's brigade of mounted infantry. Herron was badly wounded at Chickamauga and again, though less seriously, at Farmington, Tennessee (7 October 1863). For six months he filled in as major, and toward the end of the war he was provost marshal of Macon, Georgia. Herron's division was responsible for capturing Confederate President Jefferson Davis near Irwinville, Georgia, on 10 May 1865.

Returning to Crawfordsville after the war, Herron decided to set out for the Northwest Territories and remained there for three years. Back in Crawfordsville in 1870, he worked as a bookkeeper and was elected county treasurer from 1873 to 1875.

On 20 January 1875 Herron married Ada Patton of Lafayette. They had six children: daughters Jesse and Florence and sons Charles, William, Frederick, and Austin. All four of their sons attended Wabash College.

Herron assumed the presidencies of the first gas company in Crawfordsville, the Wire and Nail Company (of which he was also treasurer), and the First National Bank. He was a longtime member of the board of trustees of the State School for the Deaf.

Herron died at home, 407 W. Wabash Avenue, on 19 June 1927, and is buried in Oak Hill Cemetery.

References: H. W. Beckwith, *History of Montgomery County* (1881), pp. 37–38, 115; *History of Montgomery County, Indiana* (Bowen and Co., 1913), pp. 1201–04; *Wabash Magazine*, XII (June 1872), p. 213; *Crawfordsville Journal*, 20 June 1927.

HIATT, JOHN MILTON (1840–1869)

John Hiatt was born about 1840 in Randolph County, where his parents Mary and Harmon Hiatt had settled after moving from North Carolina. He was the oldest of their four children. He had two sisters, Louise and Martha, and a younger brother, Joel, who also attended Wabash and fought in the war. Joel's wartime and life career is described later.

John came to Wabash from Noblesville in 1854 and was a student in the Preparatory Department for three years. His family then moved to Crawfordsville, and he completed his freshman through junior years but transferred to Miami University in Oxford, Ohio, for his senior year, graduating in June 1861. The young man appears to have studied medicine in Peoria, Illinois, for the next couple of years before attending Rush Medical College in Chicago.

In May 1864 Hiatt tried to become a surgeon, writing Oliver P. Morton:

> I am a very poor man and unable to remain in the city to solicit the favor and recommendation of colonels and other officers for an appointment. My recommendations from Dr. Todd, Dr. Babbs and other medical men of Indianapolis and elsewhere were filed with Mr. Slater, your secretary, last week. If I can be of service to God and my native state, I want an appointment in the public service—three months—three years—anywhere.

Morton got him into the Officers' Hospital at Louisville. He died from unknown causes in Crawfordsville on 20 March 1869.

References: Indiana State Library Archives and the archivist of Miami University.

HIATT, JOEL WILLIS (1850–1926)

Joel Hiatt was born in Noblesville on 10 June 1850, one of two sons of Mary and Harmon Hiatt. He had two sisters, Louise and Martha, and an older brother, John M., who also attended Wabash and served in the war and whose career was chronicled earlier.

Hiatt may have set a record for the number of years he was in and out of Wabash. At the age of eleven, in the fall of 1861, he entered the Preparatory Department, remaining until the spring of 1864, when he enrolled in Company B of the Tenth Indiana Regiment on 23 March 1864 at Lafayette, although he had not yet turned fourteen. He stood five feet six inches and had hazel eyes, dark hair, and a light complexion. On 30 March he reported for duty, posing as a nineteen-year-old clerk, but it did not take long for someone uncover his deception, and he was discharged.

Back at home he awaited the beginning of the fall term of 1864 at Wabash and joined the Prep class again, remaining for his freshman through junior years. The college magazine said of him, "He is gathering laurels of honor as a student and a gentleman." However, he then dropped out of college for several years to take up carpentry. In 1871 he returned to Wabash, repeated his junior year, and graduated in June 1873.

After graduation Hiatt briefly attended Harvard Divinity School, but left to become principal of the high school in Mount Vernon, Indiana. During 1876–78 he was superintendent of schools at New Harmony and married Mary Frances Fitton.

From 1885 to 1895 he was documents clerk for the House of Representatives in Washington, DC, but then returned to New Harmony to go into trade.

His wife died on 5 April 1919, and Hiatt died at home in New Harmony on 25 March 1926.

References: 1905 alumni questionnaire in the Ramsay Archives, Wabash College; *Wabash Magazine*, XLlIII (June 1868), p. 2; *Wabash Magazine*, IX (June 1869), p. 92; *Wabash Record* (July 1903), p. 30; E. H. Ziegner Jr., *Phi Gamma Delta at Wabash* (1941), pp. 16, 38; and the New Harmony Workingmen's Institute Library.

HICKS, NAPOLEON B. (1838–1894)

Napoleon Hicks was born on the eighty-acre family farm one mile west of Perrysville on 10 October 1838. His father, George W. Hicks, was born in Rehoboth, Bristol County, Massachusetts, on 10 April 1795. He first reached Indiana in 1820 and purchased eighty acres of land in Vermillion County. He then returned east and eventually married Mary Curtis on 7 September 1826 in Allen's Hill, Ontario County, New York. She had been born in Canandaigua, New York. They had eleven children.

In addition to farming, George Hicks built up a prosperous pork-packing business, sending boatloads of meat down various rivers to New Orleans. Napoleon's mother died on 7 February 1868 near Perrysville; his father died on 1 October 1878.

When Napoleon Hicks entered Wabash in the fall of 1857, he indicated his home was Perrysville. He stayed the one year and then presumably went back to the family farm. He seems to have moved soon thereafter to a farm in Vermilion County, Illinois. It was from Illinois that he joined the army on 15 August 1861. He became a private in Company K of the Thirty-Seventh Illinois Regiment. While at the battle of Prairie Grove, Arkansas, in December 1862, he came down with some kind of lung disease. This pretty well incapacitated him, and he secured a medical discharge on 22 May 1863.

Hicks was described as being five feet eight inches tall, with fair hair and blue eyes. By the time of the 1870 census, he was living in Chetopa, Kansas. His occupation was that of a miller. By 1880 he was living in Frio, Texas, and his occupation was that of a stock raiser. A few years later he indicated he was growing sheep on his Texas land. The last we hear of him is in the early 1890s, where he was living in San Antonio. Upon his death on 17 February 1894, his body was conveyed to Perrysville, and he was buried in the Hicks family cemetery. The brick house that his father erected, vintage 1840, continues to stand and is inhabited by descendants of the Hicks family.

References: Much good help was provided by the Vermillion County Historical Society of Newport. One of the descendants, Carl D. Hicks, was anxious to provide whatever information he could. Finally, we are indebted to Norman Peters of Washington for locating a pension file for Napoleon at the National Archives.

HILL, DANIEL FRANKLIN (1839–1895)

Recruits could aspire to some special non-commissioned jobs, usually given to a soldier for demonstrated meritorious or responsible behavior in uniform. Daniel Hill of Pittsboro was designated as a "color ensign," which meant he carried the flag. Both U.S. and regimental flags were considered almost sacred symbols during the war, being borne ahead of or in the midst of the troops. They were rallying points during battles. The flag bearer was a particular target for those firing, and if one ensign bearer was shot, another soldier would pick up the flag and bear it on.

Daniel Hill was born on 26 January 1839 in Pittsboro, the son of Rebecca Homaday and Samuel Hill. In the autumn of 1859, Hill entered the Preparatory Department of Wabash College. He was in the freshman class when the war interrupted his academic life on 31 August 1861 and he decided to enlist in Company I of the Eleventh Indiana Regiment for a term of three years. As a sergeant and color ensign, Hill saw action in battles at Fort Henry and Fort Donelson, Shiloh, and Corinth, where he contracted typhoid fever. At first it was doubtful whether he would survive, but gradually he regained enough strength to be granted a ninety-day furlough, but this respite failed, resulting in a medical discharge.

In May 1864 Hill re-enlisted for one hundred days as adjutant of the 132nd Indiana Infantry and spent most of this time in Tennessee and Alabama guarding railway lines.

In February 1865 Hill committed to a third tour of duty as a captain of Company G in the 148th Indiana Regiment. Suffering from leg problems, he was released from the army the following September.

On 28 November 1867 he married Sarah J. McVeigh of Hendricks County. Their one and only child, Harry Edwin, entered Wabash College in the Class of 1890.

After the war, Hill spent ten years as railroad stationmaster in Pittsboro while studying law. He was admitted to the bar in 1872, later serving as prosecuting attorney. He died on 10 June 1895.

References: *Wabash Magazine*, III (Dec. 1861), p. 93; *Wabash Magazine*, V (May 1864), p. 175; *1888 Alumni Directory of Phi Delta Theta Fraternity*; *Portrait and Biographical Directory of Boone, Clinton and Hendricks Counties, Indiana* (1895), pp. 952–53.

HOBBS, MARMADUKE MENDENHALL COFFIN (1829–1907)

Marmaduke Coffin Hobbs was born on the family farm near Salem on 20 March 1829. His parents were Lydia and Elisha Coffin Hobbs, Quakers born and married in North Carolina. Coffin is a prominent name in Indiana's Quaker history.

Hobbs' early schooling took place at the Washington County Seminary. From 1849 to 1851 he was a freshman and sophomore at Indiana University, then transferred to Wabash College for his junior and senior years. While in Crawfordsville he boarded with Caleb Mills, the first faculty member of Wabash. Hobbs was a founding member of the Phi Delta Theta fraternity at Wabash, and while at Wabash he became a Presbyterian. Following graduation in June 1853, he returned home and served for three years as superintendent of the Salem Academy.

On 5 September 1854 Hobbs married Ellen Cutshaw. Early in 1856 he converted to Methodism and divided his time during the next two years between serving as an itinerant minister and studying at Asbury (DePauw) University, with the goal of becoming a minister.

From 1859 to 1860 he served at a church in Evansville, followed by several years at one in Vincennes. Once the Civil War started, he secured a commission as the chaplain of the Eightieth Indiana Regiment. From September 1862 until November 1864, he accompanied his regiment, but at Kenesaw Mountain, Georgia, he was felled by sunstroke and had to resign.

For the next ten years Hobbs "lived a quiet and retiring life," but by 1874 he resumed the duties of a preacher and spent the next two years in Petersburg. There followed churches in Mount Vernon (1876–78) and Princeton, until the mid-1880s. His last active post was Presiding Elder of the Vincennes district.

Hobbs married three times, and lost each wife to untimely death. His children were Clara, Schuyler, Oscar, and Emma.

About 1890 he retired to enjoy a tranquil existence on his farm west of Salem. In June 1902 he returned to Wabash and offered the invocation at the dedication of the Center Hall tablet that commemorates those Wabash College students who served in the Civil War.

He died of a heart attack on 5 January 1907.

References: Alumni directories of the Phi Delta Theta Fraternity; *Wabash Record* (March 1903), p. 4; *Wabash Record* (July 1907), p. 89; Minutes of the 76th Session of the Indiana Annual Conference of the Methodist Episcopal Church (1907), p. 429; 1905 Wabash College alumni questionnaire; W. W. Stevens, *Centennial History of Washington County, Indiana* (1916), pp. 665–66.

HOLMAN, JESSE LYNCH (1830–1883)

The career of Jesse Lynch Jr. was somewhat overshadowed by that of his father, Jesse Lynch Sr., who studied law with Henry Clay, was elected to the Indiana territorial assembly and to the Indiana Supreme Court, was judge of the federal district court, and in 1839 helped found Franklin College and served as its president for three years.

Jesse Jr. was born 2 April 1830 near Lawrenceburg, in a house that today is called Veraestau and is designated an historical monument open to the public. His siblings were Richard, Emerine, Eliza, William, Lucy, and Mary Ann.

He pursued the Classical Course for four years at Wabash and graduated in 1849. Afterwards he studied law in Aurora, Dearborn County, and was a practicing attorney in 1850. On 15 August 1854 Holman married Jane (Jennie) Smith in Cincinnati. Their children were Richard (1858), Frank (1860), Mary (1862), and Abigail (1868).

On 16 August 1861 Holman was appointed captain of Company A of the Eighteenth Indiana Infantry. Organized at Indianapolis on that day, the regiment left for Missouri the following morning to link up with the forces of General John C. Frémont that successfully besieged Springfield. They later fought a major battle at Pea Ridge and marched toward Helena, Arkansas, reaching there in July. Holman was promoted to major on 21 June 1862 but had to resign this commission because of poor health. By October he had rejoined his regiment and was promoted to lieutenant colonel. During the winter of 1862–63, complaints reached his commanding officers that Holman was persistently drunk, and he was arrested pending an investigation that resulted in his being allowed to resign from the army on 29 March 1863.

He returned to Dearborn County and farmed until 1870, when he joined several other families and moved to Humboldt, Kansas, where they lived for only one year.

During the next decade Holman became an expert in scientific farming. He died on 12 July 1883 and is buried in Riverview Cemetery, Aurora.

References: *Wabash College Record* (July 1903), p. 24; *Wabash Magazine*, XI (March 1871), p. 138; *Aurora Spectator*, 16 July 1883; *Lawrenceburg Journal-Press*, 15 July 1883; the Aurora Public Library; also Pamela Greenwood of Tulsa, Oklahoma, a descendant of the family.

HOLMES, GEORGE W. (1841–1910)

George W. Holmes was born in Crawfordsville on 22 February 1841, the third son of Eliza Ann Ristine and Magnus Holmes. He had two older brothers, Henry and John, and a younger sister, Ella. His parents were married in 1826 in Crawfordsville and remained there until they moved to Marion, Iowa, where

Eliza's brother Henry lived. Magnus died in 1846.

In the autumn of 1855, young Holmes enrolled in the Wabash College Preparatory Department. He left in the spring of 1858 without advancing as a freshman and rejoined his family in Marion.

On 1 July 1861 Holmes enrolled in Company A of the Iowa Sixth Regiment as a fourth sergeant. Promotions came steadily that year: third sergeant (November); second sergeant (December); in 1862: first sergeant (March); second lieutenant (April); and in 1863 (July) captain of Company K.

In 1866 Holmes joined his uncle, Henry Ristine, in the latter's medical practice in Marion and the following year became a partner in the local drugstore, Nutt and Holmes.

In 1871 Holmes graduated from Bellevue Hospital in New York City and rejoined his uncle, who moved his practice in 1873 to Cedar Rapids, Iowa. There Holmes married Eliza Wisner on 17 June 1874.

Two months later, the Presbyterian Board of Foreign Missions sponsored Holmes as a medical missionary to Persia (present-day Iran), where he spent three years in Urumieh, northern Iran. His first child, Mary, was born there on 11 December 1877. Holmes was asked by the crown prince of Persia to become his personal physician. In 1881 the family moved to Tabriz, and on 6 April 1885 a son, Harold, was born.

In 1889 Eliza Holmes became seriously ill, and the family returned to Cedar Rapids, where she died on 28 June 1890. Holmes traveled to New York City to take some postgraduate medical courses and met Lucy Sturges Hale, a physician in her own right. They were married on 13 September 1892 and went as medical missionaries to Hamadan in Iran the following year.

In 1896 the crown prince became Mozaffar-Din Shah and asked Holmes to attend him personally again. However, Holmes and his wife felt that their calling was to remain with the Board of Foreign Missions in Iran until 1899.

The family spent 1900–01 in Wellesley, Massachusetts, and in 1906 they settled in Boonton, New Jersey, where Holmes died on 11 May 1910. He requested that his remains be buried next to those of his father, Magnus, in Oak Hill Cemetery, Crawfordsville.

References: 1850 U.S. census for Linn County, Iowa; *Boonton Weekly Bulletin*, 12 May 1910; G. T. Williams, *Pioneer Physicians and Surgeons of Montgomery County*; scrapbook of Theodore H. Ristine in the Wabash College Archives; *History of Lynn County, Iowa Part II* (1878); the Iowa State Historical Society; and Jamshid Javid of Tappan, New Jersey.

HOLTON, ROBERT C. (1842–1913)

Robert Holton was born in Falmouth, Kentucky, in 1842, the son of Nicholas Holton. Robert's older brother was George, and his two sisters were Jennie and Mary. The family moved from Kentucky to Crawfordsville in 1851. Both boys attended Wabash and lived with their father. Robert Holton spent 1854–56 at the college.

In 1858 the family moved to Missouri, and for the next few years Holton worked as a compositor on various newspapers in the state. On 2 June 1862 he enlisted in Company D of the Twenty-Fifth Missouri Volunteers and steadily rose through the ranks. In early 1864 he transferred to Company B of the First Missouri Engineers, and by the time he mustered out on 22 July 1865, he was a colonel.

Following the war, he joined his parents in Danville, Illinois, and worked at local newspapers. On 10 March 1866 Holton married Mary Virginia Lemon.

By 1874 Holton had become foreman of the printing department of the *Danville Commercial News*, and two years later he bought a share in the paper. In the mid-1880s he was secretary, and he became the city editor in the early 1890s.

His wife died on 6 February 190, and with a lifelong drinking problem, he was admitted to the National Military Home in Danville. However, the problem persisted, and his older brother's suicide three years earlier perhaps contributed to his taking his own life on 20 February. He was buried in Springhill Cemetery at Danville.

References: Danville Public Library; H. W. Beckwith, *History of Vermilion County* (1879), p. 376; *Danville Commercial News*, 21 Feb. 1913, p. 1; and *Danville Press Democrat*, 21 Feb. 1913; pension file, National Archives, Washington, D.C.

HORNADAY, ENOS C. (1839–1919)

Enos Hornaday was born in Liberty Township, Hendricks County, on 20 October 1839 to Eliza and Simon Hornaday. He was one of five children. His siblings were Balam, Edwin, Edom, and Elizabeth.

When he entered Wabash in the fall of 1860, he declared his hometown to be Pittsboro and expressed an interest in a medical career. However, the war not only interrupted his one year in the Preparatory Department, but also dashed his plans to become a physician. He was one of the many students who joined Company I of the Eleventh Indiana Volunteer Infantry in Crawfordsville on 18 April 1861, and after an obligatory three months, he was mustered out at Indianapolis on 4 August.

The following August Hornaday re-enlisted in the same regiment at Indianapolis as a sergeant and was promoted in late 1863 to second lieutenant. He may have established a record among Wabash students for the number of states in which he served: Kentucky, Tennessee, Mississippi, Arkansas, Missouri, Louisiana, Florida, Pennsylvania, and Virginia. He was involved in battles at Fort Donelson, Shiloh, Port Gibson, Vicksburg, and Jackson, and he was badly wounded in the leg at Champion's Hill and in the chest at Jackson, Mississippi.

In the summer of 1864, his regiment went by boat from New Orleans to Virginia, where it joined General Philip Sheridan in the Shenandoah Valley campaign. He fell ill and was granted a medical discharge on 27 August.

Returning to Hendricks County, Hornaday married Viola C. Dillon in February 1879. Their children were sons Herbert Porter and Edgar and daughters Erie, Ruth, and Maud.

In 1880 Hornaday was elected county treasurer, a post he held for two years before moving to Danville, where he acquired a farm of seventy-three acres and was elected township trustee. He died in 1919 and is buried in the Old Greenlawn Cemetery of Brownsburg, Hendricks County.

References: Pittsboro Public Library; *Wabash Magazine*, III (Dec. 1861), p. 93; *Wabash Magazine*, IV (Dec. 1863), p. 74; *Portrait and Biographical Record of Boone, Clinton and Hendricks Counties, Indiana* (1895), pp. 1051–52.

HUBARD, WILLIAM C. (1828–1912)

William Hubard was born on 26 December 1828 in the frontier county of Vermillion, Indiana, one of two sons of Noah Hubard. He had a brother, Scott. As Mormons, the family faced religious intolerance and moved frequently as a result. When young William entered the Preparatory Department of Wabash College in the fall of 1841, his home was in Vermillion County. He stayed only one school year at Wabash and then took up blacksmithing.

Hubard's whereabouts for the next two decades are uncertain. His parents went out to Salt Lake City, but there is no evidence that he joined them. On 3 July 1863 at Indianapolis, Hubard joined Company K of the Seventh Cavalry, attached to the 119th Regiment. On 28 August he was promoted to first lieutenant and on 11 September to captain. The regiment moved to Union City, Tennessee, and in 1864 participated in a battle at Egypt Station, Mississippi, in February 1864 and then spent the year guarding railroad lines between Memphis and Charleston.

Although he had enlisted for three years, Hubard resigned his commission on 11 April 1865 at Nashville and came to Montgomery County in 1866 to marry his sweetheart Elizabeth. In the 1870 census Hubard is listed as a blacksmith with real property of $500 and personal property of $200; Elizabeth is twenty-five years old, and her daughter, Martha, two, and Adeline (Ida), eight months. Ten years later they were living in Scott Township in Montgomery County, and their family had grown by three: Minnie, James, and Floyd. In 1900 they moved to Darlington, Franklin Township, where Hubard continued blacksmithing until he died on 7 June 1912. He is buried in the Odd Fellows Cemetery along with his wife.

References: *Eugene Township: The First 100 Years; Darlington, Yesterday and Today* (1976), pp. 47, 71, 76; also various cemetery and census records.

HUMPHREY, FRANK WARREN (1839–1863)

Frank Humphrey was born in Crawfordsville on 17 April 1839, the son of Caroline Starr and Hosea Dayton Humphrey. His father was a member of the board of trustees of Wabash College and in 1841 was named professor of Latin, a teaching post he held until he died in 1845.

In the fall of 1857, Frank Humphrey came to Wabash from Waverly, Illinois, and studied one year in the Normal School.

In August 1862 he enrolled for three years in Company G of the 101st Illinois Regiment. The following June his regiment carried out a raid at Holly Springs, Mississippi (20 December 1862), with disastrous consequences. Many were taken prisoner, but Humphrey and a few others boarded a Union ram, the *Switzerland*, and tried to run the Confederate blockade at Vicksburg to seek safety. However, the Confederate batteries laid down a withering fire, and Humphrey was badly wounded. He died aboard the hospital ship, the *Woodford*, on 7 June 1863.

References: *Wabash Magazine*, V (Dec. 1863), p. 77; J. I. Osborne and T. G. Gronert, *Wabash College: The First Hundred Years* (1932).

HUNT, JABEZ (1841–1922)

Jabez Hunt was born in September 1841 in Milford Township, Wayne County, one of six children of Joanna Meredith and Jesse Hunt. He attended the Normal School and then Preparatory Departments between 1860 and 1862, and then returned home to Richmond.

In May 1864 he signed up for one hundred days of military service in Company A of the 149th Ohio Volunteer Infantry. In July the regiment rushed to Monocacy in Maryland to reinforce General Lew Wallace, whose forces were trying to stem a surprise Rebel attack that potentially threatened Washington. After slowing down the Confederates, the Union troops fell back on the Capital and defended it. The regiment was involved up and down the Shenandoah Valley from 22 July to 22 August. Hunt was mustered out in Ohio on 30 August 1864.

The 1870 census found Hunt living in Wayne Township, Wayne County, along with Mary, age twenty-six, born in Ohio. There were no children in the household. However, records are confusing, and one interpretation is that Jabez and Mary Elizabeth Samms were not formally married in Wayne County until 16 February 1875. She seems to have died in about 1881.

Hunt married Martha B. French in Wayne County on 4 October 1882. From this marriage there were at least six children, three of whom died in infancy. Those who survived included Rex (1889), Paul (1895), and Geniva (1899).

Jabez Hunt died in Centerville on 3 July 1922 and was buried in Crown Hill Cemetery there.

References: Census records. See also: *History of Wayne County, Indiana* (1884), I, p. 709; and *Directory and Soldiers Register of Wayne County, Indiana* (1865), p. 320.

HURLBUT, WALTER C. (1838–1920?)

Walter Hurlbut was born in Quincy, Illinois, in 1838, the son of Susan Jones and Ralph Hurlbut. His siblings were Charles (1831), Elizabeth (1834), and Edward (1840).

He attended Wabash for one academic year, 1852–53, and on 1 October 1859 he married Mary Livinia Brockway of Quincy, Illinois. Mary died in March 1862.

On 14 April 1862 Hurlbut enlisted in the Fifty-Sixth Illinois Regiment of Volunteers. In early 1863 he was promoted to lieutenant and soon thereafter was named assistant quartermaster for the Seventh Division, Seventeenth Army Corps, Department of the Tennessee. In June 1863 he was transferred to the front at Vicksburg, and he resigned in July 1864 as a captain.

According to the 1900 census, Hurlbut was living in a soldiers' home in Marion. The date of his death is problematic. Some sources put it on 15 January 1910, while others suggest that the year was 1920. He is buried in the Silent Cemetery, Marion, Indiana.

References: Betty Menges of the New Albany-Floyd County Public Library; also the libraries of Quincy, Illinois, and Marion, Indiana. His military service file, but not a pension record, is at the National Archives, Washington DC.

HUSTON (HOUSTON), WILLIAM R. (1829–1880)

William Huston was born in Ohio on 22 November 1829. He entered Wabash's Preparatory Department in the autumn of 1843, and two years later he became a freshman, leaving the college in 1847. Throughout these years he indicated that New Winchester, Indiana, was his home. When the 1850 census was taken, he was living as a laborer with the Charles Malone family in Lagro Township, Wabash County.

He married Elizabeth S. McGuiness of Mount Etna on 13 February 1851. They had twelve children between 1852 and 1873. When the Civil War broke out, they were living in Antioch, Indiana, where Huston enrolled in Company E of the Forty-Seventh Indiana Regiment for a term of three years.

On 1 November 1861 the regiment was fully mustered and during December made its way to Missouri. Huston was stricken with bronchitis and was hospitalized twice before sustaining a gunshot wound in May 1863 that again landed him in the hospital.

In spite of his illnesses, he re-enlisted in December 1863 for three years as a veteran volunteer and was promoted to corporal, but in May 1864 he came down with measles. He survived this debilitating disease and was mustered out at Baton Rouge, Louisiana, on 23 October 1865.

It is likely that he and his large family resumed farming in Huntington County, where his wife presumably had family. According to the 1880 census, all seemed to be going well, but a few months later Huston suddenly died on 3 November, a few weeks short of his fifty-first birthday. He is buried in the Mount Etna Cemetery alongside Elizabeth, who lived until 1916.

References: Widow's pension file at the National Archives, Washington, DC. See also: (Huntington) *Indiana Herald*, 10 Nov. 1880, p. 5.

INGERSOLL, JOSEPH (c. 1836–1862)

There were two men with the same name who not only lived in Montgomery County but also served in the Civil War. One was accused of murder and escaped from the local jail. The other was a student at Wabash.

Joseph Ingersoll of Wabash was born in about 1836 in Ohio, a son of Hannah Elizabeth and Stephen Ingersoll. Hannah died in Crawfordsville in 1849, and in 1855 Stephen married Susan Smyth, who helped raise Stephen's children from his first marriage.

From about 1846 to 1856, the senior Ingersoll was a partner with George Haugh in running what was formerly the Ristine Tavern in Crawfordsville. Both Ingersoll boys attended Wabash: Dunham from 1846 to 1853 and Joseph in 1850–51 and again in 1853–54.

On 3 September 1861 Joseph joined the Eleventh Ohio Light Artillery. Initially he was a private, but by February 1862 he was promoted to wagoner at Hamburg, Tennessee.

On 19 September 1862 at Iuka, Mississippi, Federal troops under Generals Grant and Rosecrans confronted Confederates led by Sterling Price. By day's end, several hundred were dead on each side, Ingersoll among them. He was buried at Corinth, Mississippi.

References: *Wabash Magazine*, V (May 1864), p. 239; service records at the Ohio Historical Society and the National Archives, Washington, DC. Karen Zach of the Crawfordsville Public Library aided in distinguishing between two Joseph Ingersolls.

JACKSON, JOHN (1834–1864)

John Jackson was born in Ohio on 21 March 1834, one of six children of Matilda Gunter and David Jackson. His siblings were James (born and died in 1828), Mary Margaret (1830), Mary Ann (1832), James C. (1836), and William

(1839). His mother died in 1845 and his father in 1847, leaving John and his brothers and sisters under the guardianship of William Dunkle.

Citing Delphi as his home, Jackson entered the Preparatory Department of Wabash College in the fall of 1856, enrolling as a freshman in the Classical Course in 1858 and graduating in June 1862.

On 8 August 1862 at Crawfordsville, he joined Company I of the Fourth Indiana Cavalry, Seventy-Seventh Regiment, as a second lieutenant. He was six feet one with a fair complexion, and he listed his occupation as carpenter. In April 1863 he became a first lieutenant and in March 1864 a captain. During the winter of 1863, his regiment was in east Tennessee, but by May 1864 it had joined forces with Sherman's troops marching on Atlanta, and Jackson was taken prisoner by the Confederates near Dalton, Georgia.

He was confined at Columbia, South Carolina, where he died on 20 November 1864.

References: Indiana State Library Archives and the Carroll County Museum.

JENNISON, ALBERT CUNNING (1842–1908)

Albert Jennison was born in Crawfordsville on 17 August 1842, one of five children of Margaret McMasters and Ozro P. Jennison, a civil engineer for whom the street along the south edge of the Wabash campus is named. Albert's younger brother, Henry, also attended Wabash, while his father was an early trustee of the college.

Young Albert entered Wabash in the fall of 1858 and progressed through his junior year until the war caused an end to his college experience. In August 1862 he enlisted in the Fourth Cavalry of the Seventy-Seventh Indiana Volunteers, committing to three years of service. However, the following March he caught pneumonia, and he came home to convalesce.

By the autumn of 1864, he was able to resume his senior year of college and graduate with the class of 1865. The following year he taught school, but the lure of his father's occupation led him to become an engineer for five years in the late 1860s and early 1870s until he decided to study and practice law. From 1878 to 1890 he specialized in real estate law, abstracting titles and financing loans, but his health, never very good since the war, forced him to restrict his business activities.

On 18 October 1883 Jennison married Mary E. Cumberland. Their first son, Albert C., was born in 1885, and their second, John B., in 1889, but died in 1894. Mary passed away a few years later, and on 9 October 1900 Albert married Anna M. Pickarts.

During the last year of his life, Jennison was a virtual invalid. While visiting his mother-in-law in Madison, Wisconsin, he was stricken and died on 4 June 1908, just prior to attending his son's graduation from Wabash.

References: *1905 Alumni Questionnaire*, Wabash College Archives; 1860 and 1870 U.S. censuses for Montgomery County, *Crawfordsville*.

JENNISON, HENRY S. (1846–1895)

Like his older brother Albert, Henry Jennison was the son of Margaret McMasters and Ozro P. Jennison. Born in Crawfordsville in 1846, Henry entered the Normal School of Wabash College in the autumn of 1861 and stayed for two years. During Morgan's raid Jennison joined Company C of the 108th Indiana Regiment, serving only from 11 July to 17 July.

On 27 March 1864 he committed to a much longer tour of duty: three years in Company I of the Eleventh Regiment. He was five feet eight inches tall, with blue eyes and a fair complexion. By 8 May his regiment reached New Orleans, remaining there until July and then proceeding eastward and northward via Fortress Monroe, Washington, DC, and Harper's Ferry, Virginia. On 12 August 1864 he was involved in his first major skirmish at Cedar Creek, Virginia, then a battle at Winchester followed by an even heavier engagement on 19 September at Opequan Creek, Virginia, where he was badly wounded, losing a thumb. After convalescing at home, he rejoined his regiment and was mustered out at Indianapolis on 26 July 1865.

According to the 1870 census for Crawfordsville, Jennison was listed as a circus performer. In 1891 he indicated that his work was gardening. He never married and died at home, 411 Perry Street (later renamed Jennison Street), on 11 March 1895. He is buried in Oak Hill Cemetery.

References: *Crawfordsville Weekly Journal*, 15 March 1895; and the Crawfordsville Public Library.

JENNISON, JAMES STEELE (1825–1894)

James Jennison was born in Vermont on 18 August 1825, the youngest of the eight children of Ruth Porter Steele and Samuel Jennison.

He spent one year in the Preparatory Department at Wabash College, 1839–40, and probably lived with his brother, Ozro P. Jennison, the father of Albert and Henry, whom we've just shown went to Wabash. James's older brother, George H., also attended Wabash but did not serve in the Civil War.

During the 1840s Jennison moved to Cincinnati, Ohio, where he married Frances Barker on 19 March 1849. He then traveled to Marion, Iowa, where he went into a printing partnership with his brother George. They acquired the *Prairie Star* newspaper and changed its name to the *Linn County Register*. In a few years George yielded the sole proprietorship to James, who also began another paper in Mount Vernon, Iowa.

The financial crash of 1857 forced Jennison into bankruptcy, and the fam-

Frank C. Dale

Ozro Dodds

John Finch

Charles Groenendyke

Temple Harrison

John Hawkins

A Soldiers' Album

John Jackson

ily moved back to Cincinnati. Jennison resumed being a printer, and by 1860 he and his wife had three children: Esther (age ten), Guy (six), and Erwin (three). On 21 August 1862 Jennison enrolled in Company F of the Seventy-Ninth Ohio Infantry as a private. He was honorably discharged at Louisville on 30 June 1865.

In 1890 he applied for an increase in his military pension from the National Military Home of Dayton, Ohio. He died on 19 November 1894.

References: J. A. Vinton, *The Giles Memorial* (1864), pp. 265, 276; Linn County (Iowa) Genealogical Society. See also his military pension file at the National Archives, Washington, DC.

JEWETT, EDWARD DUNCAN (ca. 1839–1919)

Edward Jewett was one of three children born to Mary Moore and Merrick A. Jewett of Terre Haute. His father was the founder and preacher of the First Congregational Church, the only Congregationalist parish in Indiana at the time. Edward's older brother, David, also attended Wabash but did not serve in the Civil War. Their younger sister was named Mary.

Jewett spent two years in the Normal School of Wabash College, 1855–57, and then joined his brother in farming. On 4 May 1864 at Terre Haute, Jewett enrolled in Company D of the 133rd Indiana Regiment, committed to serve one hundred days. His regiment went to Tennessee and Alabama to guard railroad lines, and on 8 June at Bridgeport, Alabama, he was badly injured while trying to repair a wagon. Though he was mustered out the following September, the back injury along with rheumatism plagued him the rest of his life.

In 1866 Jewett married Jennie Boone in Cincinnati, and for the next few years they lived in Terre Haute. Then in 1869 they moved to Kansas, first to Topeka, and then to Emporia. Jewett was a traveling salesman. In 1872 the family joined Jewett's father in Paris, Texas; the father died on 2 April 1874. Edward and Jennie Jewett had five children: Edith (1869), Joseph (1871), Merriah (1875), Margaret (1877), and Asa (1879).

In 1885 Edward Jewett returned to Terre Haute and was employed as a merchant. A few years later he went back to Paris, Texas. Jewett died on 21 June 1919 at Adamson, Oklahoma.

References: L. C. Rudolph (ed.), *Indiana Letters*; city directories of Terre Haute; *Terre Haute Express*, 4 April 1874; *Terre Haute Evening Gazette*, 13 April 1882; *Terre Haute Express*, 12 September 1882; and a military pension file at the National Archives, Washington, DC. Also David N. Lewis of the Vigo County Public Library.

JOHNSON, GEORGE W. (1830–1889)

George Johnson was born in Brown County, Ohio, in 1830, one of six children of Anna Morrow and James L. Johnson. His siblings were Hiram, Henry C., Hannah, Mary and another unidentified sibling.

By the time Johnson entered the Preparatory Department of Wabash College in the autumn of 1850, his father, who was a large landowner and a successful merchant in Williamsport, had died (1847). Perhaps because of that, Johnson stayed only one academic year at the college and then returned to work at the family farm.

On 30 April 1864 he joined Company K of the 135th Indiana Regiment as a private for one hundred days, although he was not mustered in until 24 May. He soon found himself near Stevenson, Alabama, but when he contracted pneumonia he was confined in hospital for three weeks. Returning to his regiment, he again fell ill and was mustered out as a sergeant at Indianapolis in September 1864.

Following the war Johnson resumed farming in Warren County, although his health was never robust. He spent the year 1888 in a soldiers' home in Dayton, Ohio, returning to Williamsport the next year. He died on 30 August 1889.

References: Military pension file at the National Archives, Washington, DC; *Counties of Warren, Benton, Jasper and Newton, Indiana* (1883), p. 162; and Mr. and Mrs. Walter Salts of West Lebanon, Indiana, who were able to distinguish between the several George Johnsons of Warren County.

JOHNSON, HENRY CLAY (1834–1815)

Henry Johnson was born on 6 December 1834 in Brown County, Ohio, the youngest brother of George W. Johnson, whose parents, Anna Morrow and James L. Johnson, had six children (see entry for George). The family moved to Warren County in 1835, where his father died in 1847 and his mother in 1856.

Young Johnson spent one year (1851–52) in the Preparatory Department of Wabash College. On 30 December 1858 he married Elizabeth Tebbs. During the coming years, they had six children: Lewis H., Lillian, Anna, Harry, George W., and Kate, who died at an early age.

Shortly before the outbreak of the Civil War, Johnson and his family moved to Indianapolis, where he assumed the duties of clerk of the Indiana Supreme Court. Once the war began, they moved back to Williamsport, where Johnson helped to organize Company K of the Thirty-Third Regiment of Indiana Volunteers.

On 2 September 1861 Johnson became a second lieutenant, and after seeing action at the Battle of Camp Wildcat (Laurel County, Kentucky, 19–21 October), he was promoted to first lieutenant and joined the staff of the regimental commander, Colonel John Coburn, a former Wabash College student. Both were taken prisoner following the Battle of Thompson's Station on 4–5 March 1863, and Johnson, like other former Wabash students, both soldiers and officers, spent seven weeks in the Confederate Libby Prison before being released in a prisoner exchange.

Johnson eventually rejoined his regiment and took part in the Battle of Atlanta and General Sherman's March to the Sea. Before war's end he was promoted to captain (27 March 1865), and he was mustered out at Louisville on 21 July 1865.

Following the war he returned to Williamsport, and for the next thirty years he served in the office of the Warren County clerk, at first as deputy clerk. He was elected county clerk in 1878 and 1882. In 1879 he also became clerk to the circuit court.

Johnson presumably retired about the turn of the century and moved to Grand Rapids, Michigan. In 1914 he and his wife joined their son, Harry, at Harry's home in Edwardsville, Illinois, where Johnson died on 30 November 1915. He is buried in the Old Hillside Cemetery, Williamsport.

References: Mr. and Mrs. Walter Salts and Mrs. Opal Johnson of Warren County, Indiana. See also: *Counties of Warren, Benton, Jasper and Newton, Indiana* (1883), p. 162; *Wabash Magazine*, IV (July 1863), p. 327; *Williamsport Pioneer*, 3 Dec. 1915; *Williamsport Review-Republican*, 9 Dec. 1915; *Edwardsville Intelligencer*, 1, 3 and 4 Dec. 1915.)

JOHNSON, MAHLON V. (1838–1930)

Mahlon Johnson was born in Crawfordsville on 28 December 1838, one of six children of Ann and Chillion Johnson. His father was a well-known tinsmith and stove maker in town. His brothers and sisters were Angeline, Elizabeth, Susan, Mary, Edgar, and Walter, who did not serve in the war.

The teenaged Johnson spent 1853–54 in the Preparatory Department of Wabash College and then probably joined his father in business. On 21 September 1861 at Indianapolis, he enrolled in the Indiana Seventh Light Artillery for a term of three years. As a first sergeant, he carried a considerable amount of responsibility for a twenty-two-year-old.

Johnson married Catherine Patterson in Crawfordsville on 11 December 1861. Their three children were Arthur, the future Mrs. Ernest Pease, and Frederick.

After three months of training, Johnson's battery moved to Louisville in December and by February 1862 was in Nashville, Tennessee. They moved too late to reach the Battle of Shiloh but in time to take part in the battle at Corinth in October. Other major battles that Johnson participated in were Stones River, Chickamauga, and Missionary Ridge. In January 1864 he re-enlisted as a veteran for another year, and he was mustered out at Indianapolis on 7 December 1864.

In 1873 Johnson was in Denver, Colorado, working in the construction business, including contracts with new railroads such as the Colorado Central. For a few years he lived in Golden and then moved back to Denver, attracted by the coal business. Between 1883 and 1893 he was superintendant of the Fox Coal Mining Company's properties in Boulder and also developed mines in Frederick and Trinidad, Colorado.

About 1894 he and his family returned to Denver, where he died at the age of ninety-one on 18 January 1930, one of the older veterans of the war.

References: F. M. Mills, *Early Days in a College Town* (1924), p. 37; H. W. Beckwith, *History of Montgomery County* (1881), pp. 120, 129, 134, 210, 261, 303; *History of Montgomery County* (Bowen and Co., 1913), pp. 346, 460, 474–75, 506; and the Denver Public Library staff for researching Mahlon's Colorado career, e.g. *Denver Post*, 25 January 1930.

JOHNSTON, WITTER H. (1837–1911)

Witter Johnston was born in 1837 at Sidney Plains, New York, one of five children of Adelia Hall (1808–1882) and Milton Johnston (1800–1890), a farmer. His siblings were Lauren, Susan, Dorcas, and Milton.

Johnston spent two years in the Preparatory Department of Wabash College, 1851–53, and then returned to Sidney Plains, presumably to help with the family farm. On 14 August 1862 he enrolled in Company I of the 144th New York Volunteer Infantry, and when he was mustered in on 6 September, he was appointed a second lieutenant. Soon thereafter he was promoted to first lieutenant and helped to guard Washington, DC. In April and May 1863 he participated in the siege of Suffolk, Virginia, and from August to November he witnessed the northern bombardment of Fort Sumter, South Carolina. During all of 1864 and the early months of 1865 his regiment remained in South Carolina.

On 27 November 1864 Johnston became a captain of Company F, a regiment of 225 men that engaged in a major fight at James Island, South Carolina, on 10 February 1865. One man was killed and twenty-five were wounded, among them Witter. His left ankle was shattered by a bullet, and a few weeks later his leg was amputated four inches below the knee. He was formally granted a medical discharge on 15 May 1865.

Seemingly undeterred by this setback, he moved to Binghamton, New York, in order to study law, and he was admitted to the bar in about 1869. Two Wabash contemporaries, Dr. George Bassett and Dr. Harley G. Ristine, urged Johnston to come west and settle at Fort Dodge, Iowa, so in 1869 the young veteran agreed and soon established a law practice there. In July 1877 he married Malvina (Mallie) McBride, and in 1881 their son, Witter L., was born. Mallie died on 30 January 1886, and Johnston married Mallie's younger sister, Margaretta, on 2 August 1887. They may have had a son, Walter, born in 1888, who predeceased them; a daughter, Malvina, was born in the early 1890s.

When Johnston was appointed deputy clerk of the United States District Court, he gave up his law practice. In 1903 he helped found the Fort Dodge Public Library and served as president of its board of directors until his death.

He died on 6 June 1911. He had lost his son, Witter, the year before, and his wife Margaretta had died in 1900. However, he was survived by his daughter, Mallie, a student at Mount Holyoke College in Massachusetts.

References: Fort Dodge Public Library: *The Witter Johnston Foundation*. See also: *Fort Dodge Messenger*, 6, 7 and 9 June 1911; F. Pfisterer (comp.), *New York in the War of the Rebellion* (1912), pp. 3667–71; J. H. McKee, *Back "In War Time": History of the 144th Regiment, New York Volunteer Infantry* (1903), pp. 34–35, 214–15, 306; and military pension file, National Archives, Washington, DC.

JONES, GEORGE WHEELER (1839–1895)

George Wheeler Jones was born in Bath, New York, on 4 February 1839, one of six children of Charlotte and John Wheeler. His siblings were James, Mary, Lydia, Frank, and Lotte.

In January 1846 the family made the arduous journey from New York to Covington, Indiana, where John practiced medicine. In the fall of 1853, George ventured forth to Crawfordsville and the Preparatory Department of Wabash College. He was there just one school year, but then returned a few years later for two more in the prep program: 1857–59. He might well have come back in the fall of 1859, but poor health precluded this. Instead, he began to study medicine at home with his father.

During 1860–61 Jones took a year of formal medical education at the Northwestern Medical College in Chicago. He then settled down to practice in Terre Haute, but by then the war was raging, and he offered his services. Details are lacking, but he spent some time in 1861–62 as a volunteer medical officer with the Twenty-Sixth Illinois infantry. In September 1862 he formally joined the Sixty-Third Indiana Regiment as an assistant surgeon.

Jones was probably one of many in the regiment who were stationed at Indianapolis until December 1863. Then, in the early months of 1864, they made their way through Kentucky to Tennessee. In May 1864 they joined up with Sherman's forces in order to be part of the Atlanta campaign. From here on out, the fighting was continual, culminating in their reaching the outskirts of Atlanta on 17 July. Much more fighting lay ahead in and about this major target. By November 1864 the regiment was back in Tennessee, and by February 1865 was in North Carolina. Jones was finally mustered out at Indianapolis on 20 May 1865.

On 16 August 1865 at Indianapolis he married Evelyn K. Enos. Eventually they would have a daughter and a son, names unknown. Soon after the wedding, George and Evelyn settled in Danville, Illinois, where the doctor built his practice for the next thirty years. He also served as the surgeon for the Chicago, Danville and Vincennes Railroad.

In the spring of 1894, he placed himself under the care of the College Hill Sanitarium of Cincinnati, so that they could treat his condition of "nervous prostration." He returned to Danville about Thanksgiving but soon felt the need for more rest, so he went to the island of Bermuda. He died at the Princess Hotel, Hamilton, on 6 January 1895, and is buried in Spring Hill Cemetery, Danville. Evelyn died on 3 May 1909, probably in the town of Putnamville, Indiana.

References: Danville Public Library; National Archives in Washington, DC; *Wabash Magazine*, IV (July 1863), p. 247; *Danville Evening Commercial*, 8 and 21 Jan. 1895; H. W. Beckwith, *History of Vermilion County* (1879), p. 443; Lotte E. Jones, *History of Vermilion County, Illinois* (1911), pp. 784–87.

After the war how did the pension system work?

In 1862 the United States government made provision for military pensions. Modest amounts would be paid to the families of those killed, while disabled soldiers would receive a pension. The amount was increased in 1864, and over the following decades pensions were augmented and children of veterans under the age of 21 were also covered with payments. In 1890 the law was changed to include any veteran who could no longer perform manual labor and who could trace this infirmity to service-related problems.

As a result of a new pension law of 1904 any veteran over the age of 62 could henceforth receive a pension, and the amounts went up in 1907 and 1912. Many former Wabash students who served in the Civil War eventually secured a pension, while some applied repeatedly over the years but to no avail. They could not prove satisfactorily that their infirmities were linked to their war service.

Pension fraud was a major problem as the years went along; the government had reason to demand proof of war-time injury. Claimants had physicians and former tentmates try to claim for a friend a huge variety of infirmities ranging from irritable colon to "nervous prostration." Possibly all of these things were exacerbated by the war but how could one be sure? At least writing to get friends to certify infirmities kept the old soldiers in touch.

JONES, HARVEY A. (ca. 1838–1863)

Harvey Jones was born in Tippecanoe County in about 1838. His mother's name was Mary; she was widowed before 1850, but by then Harvey had seven siblings: Albert, James, Deborah, Lewis, Levi, Calvin, and Asa. He spent two years, 1854–56, in the Normal School at Wabash and subsequently became a schoolteacher.

It would appear that Jones enrolled in Company B of the Forty-Third Indiana Regiment on 19 September 1861 at Terre Haute. At some point in 1863 he was detached from his regiment to assist a corporal sutler in the sutler's quest for supplies, but he died of "bilious fever" on 17 August 1863.

References: Indiana State Library Archives; and the U.S. censuses of 1850 and 1860.

JONES, JAMES H. (1837–1920)

James Jones was born on 5 October 1837 in Tippecanoe County, the son of Matilda and Thomas S. Jones. His father died in the mid-1840s, and his mother married Peter Brown in about 1846.

Jones spent the 1853–54 academic year in the Preparatory Department at Wabash and then returned home to help his stepfather on his farm. Jones's military service is confusing. According to the records at the Indiana State Library, a twenty-year-old James Jones enrolled in Company C of the Fortieth Indiana Regiment in the late autumn of 1861 and was discharged in June 1862. However, the obituary of this former student at Wabash says that he helped raise Company D, not C, and that he was badly wounded at the Battle of Missionary Ridge near Chattanooga in November of 1863.

After the war Jones went back to Tippecanoe County and farmed on his own. On 7 March 1872 he married his stepsister, Margaret Brown. They had no children but adopted a foster daughter. He served as county recorder from 1872 to 1874.

Jones gave up farming in about 1890 and went into business as Jones and Brown with one or more of his stepbrothers, a partnership that lasted for thirty years. He died at home on 5 July 1920 and is buried in Grandview Cemetery.

References: *Biographical Record and Portrait Album of Tippecanoe County, Indiana* (1888), p. 225; *Lafayette Journal Courier*, 6 July 1920; and census and marriage records.

JONES, WILLIAM MARLOW (ca. 1831–1910)

William M. Jones was born in Crawfordsville about 1831, the son of Resin (Rezin) V. Jones and his first wife. He had two siblings or stepsiblings: Virgil R. and Carrie. In the autumn of 1849, he entered the Preparatory Department of Wabash College and returned for his freshman year in 1851–52. After this he joined his father in the hotel business in Lafayette.

By 1864 young Jones and his father had moved to Indianapolis, where they ran a "first class" hotel. In March of that year, William sought the support of prominent Hoosiers to recommend him to a captaincy in the army's Department of Commissary of Subsistence. Luminaries such as United States congressman Godlove Orth and Indiana governor Oliver P. Morton wrote on his behalf, and he received his commission in April 1864.

Early in his service he was charged with conveying cattle from Nashville to Chattanooga. In June 1865 he contracted a seemingly temporary paralysis that unfortunately persisted off and on throughout his life. However, by the following December he was active at Mobile and Montgomery, Alabama. On 4 February 1866 he was promoted to a brevet major and four days later was honorably discharged.

After the war he spent some twenty-five years in Alabama, where his wife, Lavenia Jenners Duval, gave birth in 1884 to their only child, Georgiana. Eventually the family returned to Lafayette, Indiana. William died in hospital there on 22 March 1910 and is buried in Greenbush Cemetery, where Lavenia is also interred.

References: Tippecanoe County Historical Association; Lafayette city directories for 1858–63; *Lafayette Weekly Courier*, 25 March 1910; and military pension file, National Archives, Washington, DC.

JORDAN, JAMES H. (1842–1912)

James Jordan was born at Woodstock, Virginia, on 21 December 1842, the son of Elizabeth Burke and Charles B. (1802–1874) Jordan.

The young man joined Company B of the Forty-Fifth Indiana Volunteer Regiment, Third Cavalry, on 22 August 1861 and served for three years in spite of being badly wounded at the Battle of Culpeper Court House, Virginia, on 8 November 1863. He had been wounded also at Gettysburg the previous July. After being released from formal military obligations in 1864, he entered the Indiana Legion to guard the border between Indiana and Kentucky.

During the school year 1864–65, Jordan enrolled as a student in the English course of study at Wabash and then transferred to Indiana University at Bloomington, where he graduated in June 1868. Back in Corydon, he studied law in combination with coursework at Indiana University and received a law degree in

1871. Later in 1871 he moved to Clinton, Missouri, and practiced law briefly before returning to Martinsville, Morgan County, his home for the rest of his life.

In 1873 Jordan was appointed city attorney. He was twice elected to the Indiana Supreme Court, in 1894 and 1900, and eventually became its chief justice. From 1891 to 1895 he also served on the Indiana University board of trustees.

On 13 January 1886 he married Emma R. Johnson in Sandusky, Ohio. The couple seems not to have had any children. Jordan died at Martinsville on 5 April 1912, and Emma died four years later. They are buried in Greenlawn Cemetery.

References: C. W. Taylor, *The Bench and Bar of Indiana* (1895), p. 192; *Men of Progress of Indiana* (1899), p. 181; B. D. Myers, *Officers of Indiana University, 1820-1950*, p. 405; *Biographical Record of Prominent and Representative Men of Indianapolis and Vicinity* (1908), pp. 1222–23; L. J. Monks, *Courts and Lawyers of Indiana*, III (1916), p. 1219; and Arville L. Funk of Corydon, Indiana.

KENDALL, HOWARD C. (1848–1913)

Howard Kendall was born at Monticello on 28 August 1848, one of the six children of Mary Eliza and Charles W. Kendall. His siblings were Walter, Maria, Sallie, Charles, and May.

On 10 May 1864 at Lafayette, Kendall, described as five feet eight inches tall with light complexion, blue eyes, and auburn hair, enrolled in Company E of the 135th Indiana Regiment for one hundred days, which he spent mostly in Kentucky and Alabama guarding railroad lines. He was mustered out at Indianapolis on 29 September 1864.

Returning to Monticello, he clerked in a store until the fall of 1865, when he began studying English at Wabash College in the Preparatory Department. The following year, 1866–67, he was promoted into the freshman class, but he left to take employment in various railroad companies, including the Panhandle, the Rock Island, and the St. Paul and Pacific.

In 1874 Kendall moved to Duluth, Minnesota, and worked for the Northern Pacific Railway and the St. Paul and Duluth Railroad. Then in 1885 he became involved in the operation of livery stables, including the H. C. Omnibus and Hack Line. On 23 May 1894 he married Mary Balmer of Calumet, Michigan. Howard Kendall died in Duluth on 28 November 1913.

References: White County Genealogical Society; Northeast Minnesota Historical Society of Duluth; *History of White and Pulaski Counties, Indiana* (1883), p. 225; military pension file at the National Archives, Washington, DC.

KENT, EDWARD P. (ca. 1838–1890)

Venereal disease was a plague in both armies, but reliable statistics are available for the northern army only. Surgeons reported after the war in the documents of the *Medical and Surgical History of the War of the Rebellion 1861–1865* that 73,000 soldiers were treated for syphilis and 109,000 for gonorrhea. Edward Kent was one of those treated for the latter, although it would obviously be unfair to remember him only for that statistic. Camp followers were a constant accompaniment of marching armies, and many officers' reports complain of the toll illicit sexual activity was taking on the troops. Treatment was often with compounds containing mercury.

Kent was born on 12 June 1838 at Greenwood, the younger son of Fannie Capron and Eliphalet Kent, a Presbyterian clergyman. The family moved about a fair amount, but eventually settled in Shelbyville. However, during the years that Edward attended the Preparatory Department of Wabash, 1853–55, they resided in Crawfordsville, so Edward lived at home.

After attending college, Kent returned to Shelbyville and on 16 June 1859 married Mary A. (Annie) Montgomery. They eventually had four children: Walter, Fannie, Edward, and Lydia.

On 26 February 1864 at Walker, Indiana, Kent enrolled for three years in Company I of the Thirteenth Cavalry attached to the 131st Regiment. He was promoted to the rank of sergeant during the summer of 1864, but in the spring of 1865, he contracted severe rheumatism while stationed at Macon, Mississippi, and it was at this time that he was hospitalized suffering from gonorrhea. He was mustered out well after the war had ended, on 18 November 1865 at Vicksburg.

At first he returned to Shelbyville until the mid-1870s. However, by 1875 he and Mary were living at Telluride in Colorado. They stayed there for a decade before coming back to Shelbyville, where Edward died on 24 June 1890.

References: Military pension file, National Archives, Washington, DC. See also the sources for Edward's brother, George.

KENT, GEORGE E. (1836–1920)

George Kent was born in Greenwood on 4 September 1836, son of Fannie Capron and Eliphalet Kent, a Presbyterian minister. His mother died in 1848, leaving him with his father, a sister, Frances, and a brother, Edward, covered above. His father married a second time to a widow, Fanny Henderson, who had two children: Joseph H. and Lydia D. Joseph graduated from Wabash College.

Kent's father had moved his family to Crawfordsville in the early 1850s to facilitate the education of his sons at the college. In the autumn of 1853, Kent entered the Preparatory Department of Wabash College. He stayed for three years and then took charge of his father's farm in Montgomery County. After a few years he rejoined his family in Shelbyville.

On 2 May 1864 he enrolled in Company E of the 132nd Indiana Regiment, committing to one hundred days of service. Once the regiment gathered in Indianapolis on 18 May, it went by train to Tennessee, where its main duty was to guard railroad lines, as it also did in Alabama. Kent was mustered out in early September.

After the war Kent returned to Shelbyville, and on 28 March 1866 he married Hattie Hill. They had one son, Frank. Kent went into the grain business with his brother-in-law, F. W. Hill; their elevator burned down twice. In 1873 he became a partner in the Shelby Water Mill. He remained in the milling business until he retired in 1906 and was also active in civic affairs.

Kent's first wife died in February 1873, and he married Nettie C. Harter, with whom he had two daughters, Anna and Laura. Nettie died in 1894, but George lived until 20 February 1920. He is buried in the Shelbyville City Cemetery.

References: *Shelbyville Democrat*, 20 February 1920; *History of Shelby County, Indiana*.

KETCHAM, JOHN LEWIS (1844–1915)

John Ketcham was the older of two brothers who attended Wabash and served in the Civil War. John Jr. was born in Indianapolis on 3 January 1844. His siblings were Frank, Edwin, Henry, William, Elizabeth, and Susan.

Ketcham entered the Preparatory Department of Wabash College in the autumn of 1860 and stayed for two years. In mid-July 1862 he enrolled for three years in Company K of the Seventieth Indiana Regiment. The following autumn his regiment was in Kentucky, and from late November to June 1863 it was stationed at Gallatin, Tennessee, guarding the mail line to Nashville. On 10 April 1864 Ketcham was promoted to the rank of sergeant, just before Sherman's Atlanta campaign, including battles in May at Resaca and Cassville, Georgia (19 May 1864). These were followed by battles at Kennesaw Mountain in June and at Peachtree Creek (20 July 1864). After the fall of Atlanta in September, Ketcham's regiment was one of many involved in Sherman's march through Georgia, culminating in the fall of Savannah in December. On 27 March 1865 he became the regimental quartermaster, and he was discharged at Washington on 8 June 1865.

In the autumn of 1865, Ketcham entered the freshman class at Williams College in Massachusetts. In the spring of his senior year he had to drop out of school because of the accidental death of his father, but he received his diploma nonetheless as a member of the class of 1869.

For the next ten years he worked for the Indiana Banking Company of Indianapolis. On 27 April 1870 he married Lilla McDonald, and they eventually had eight children: Eleanor, Priscilla, Elizabeth, David, Ralph, Arthur, William, and John L.

After his years at the bank, Ketcham became a partner in the architectural iron works of Haugh, Ketcham and Co. Later still he was secretary and treasurer of the Brown-Ketcham iron works. Toward the end of his working life he was also a director of the Indianapolis Gas Company. He died at home on 29 December 1915.

References: A descendant of the Ketcham family, Mrs. Martha J. Stafford; Williams College, *Sketch of the Class of Sixty-Nine*, p. 17; *Wabash Magazine*, VII (June 1866), p. 7; alumni directory of the Phi Delta Theta fraternity (1888); *Indianapolis Star*, 30 December 1915.

KETCHAM, WILLIAM ALEXANDER (1846–1921)

William Ketcham was born on 2 January 1846 in Indianapolis, one of the sons of Jane Merrill and John Lewis Ketcham, who served in the Civil War. His siblings were John, cited before, Frank, Edwin, Henry, Elizabeth, and Susan.

In 1859 Ketcham had the opportunity to study in Germany for two years. He came to Wabash in the autumn of 1861. He stayed through his sophomore and junior years and pledged the Phi Delta Theta fraternity. He was also chosen president of his junior class.

When he turned eighteen in January 1864, he enrolled for three years in Company C of the Thirteenth Regiment of Indiana Volunteers. Promotions came rapidly: second lieutenant in December 1864, first lieutenant soon thereafter, and captain of Company I in May of 1865. Five months after the war ended, he was mustered out on 25 September 1865. Years later he wrote his recollections of those days, especially the months of May and June 1864 when the Thirteenth Regiment was part of the Army of the Potomac.

Ketcham was determined to complete his formal education and sought admission to Dartmouth College, receiving his bachelor of arts degree in the spring of 1867. He then decided to follow in his father's footsteps and pursue a career in law. Returning to Indianapolis, he received tutelage from both his father and Judge David McDonald, securing admission to the bar in 1868 and joining his father's law practice.

His contact with Judge McDonald proved to have an additional advantage. On 25 June 1873 he married the judge's daughter, Flora, and they subsequently had six daughters and one son: Flora (1876), Agnes (1878), Jane (1880), Lilla (1882), Henry (1884), Lucia (1888), and Dorothy (1892).

In 1894 Ketcham became Indiana Attorney General, filling this role from 1895 to 1899. In 1902 he received much notoriety by winning a case against the Vandalia Railroad. In later years he and his family resided on north Capitol Avenue, and it was there that he died on 27 December 1921.

References: Martha J. Stafford, a descendant of the Ketchams; copies of William's reminiscences dated 26 January 1910 are in the Indiana State Library and the Indiana Historical Society. See also: *Wabash Record,* December 1902, p. 24; January 1903, p. 18; July 1903, p. 20; and January 1922, p. 16; 1888 Phi Delta Theta alumni directory.

This photograph is of downtown Crawfordsville in the 1860s—at the intersection of Washington and Main Streets looking west. The building in the middle of the picture is the Hanna Building, the spot where Wabash held classes following the fire of 1838.

KIBBY, THOMAS ALEXANDER (1845–1924)

The seventh of the eight children of Jane Vannest and Thomas Kibby, Thomas Kibby was born in Clinton on 22 April 1845.

On 9 October 1861 he enrolled in Company A of the Forty-Third Indiana Regiment, committing to three years of service. He was only sixteen years old, which ordinarily would have disqualified him for army duty, but an exception was made because he was a "musician," presumably a bugler. His regiment saw action at New Madrid and Island No. 10 in Missouri; Yazoo Pass in Mississippi (February 1863); Helena, Arkansas, and Little Rock and the Camden Expedition (April 1864). Kibby was mustered out at Indianapolis on 19 October 1864.

In the fall of 1871 Kibby came to Crawfordsville and joined the Preparatory Department at Wabash College for one year. During the 1870s and 1880s he pursued a variety of occupations, including farmer, teacher, and county assessor. In 1878 he became co-owner of a Clinton newspaper, the *Western Indianian*, but sold his interest two years later.

On 12 March 1882 Kibby married Josie Lyday. They had three children: John, Jane (Jennie), and Auverne. They lived with Thomas's father on the ninety-acre farm one mile north of Clinton. Thomas Kibby died on 19 October 1924.

References: *Biographical and Historical Record of Vermillion County, Indiana* (1888); and a descendant of the Kibby family, John Russell of Indianapolis.

KING, EDWARD CLINTON (1825–1904)

Edward King, the oldest of the seven children of Sarah and John King, was born in Terre Haute on 22 April 1825. His siblings were Richard, John, Robert, Sarah, Mary, and Lucy. Brother Robert also went to Wabash and served in the war.

King attended the Preparatory Department at Wabash for one year, 1843–44. Two years later he struck out on his own to Wisconsin, remaining there for a decade, marrying Mary Ann Stone in 1851, and trying his hand at various jobs, including real estate. With the death of his father in 1857, he returned to Terre Haute and joined the family firm of King Brothers, dealers in coal.

In early May 1864 the 133rd Regiment was actively recruiting soldiers in Wisconsin, and so although he was thirty-nine years old, King enrolled in Company D for one hundred days. He was put to work guarding railroad lines in Tennessee and Alabama and was mustered out in September.

After the war the Kings returned to Wisconsin, reaching there about 1870 and settling in Darlington, where Mary Ann died in 1877. In 1879 King found a partner and established the banking firm of Judge, King and Co. In 1885 they put up a new building and changed the company's name to the Citizens National Bank. King served as its vice president until he died on 11 August 1904.

References: *Darlington Republican Journal*, 18 August 1904; *History of Lafayette County, Wisconsin* (1881), p. 720; Vigo County Public Library; Darlington (Wisconsin) Public Library.

KING, GEORGE EDWARD (1839–1927)

George King was born at Lafayette, Indiana, on 30 October 1839, one of four children of Delilah DeVault and George King. His siblings were Nancy, Charles, and Jennie. The family lived in Middleport Township, Iroquois County, Illinois, in 1855 while young George attended Wabash in the Normal School. After two years he returned to work in his father's general store, King and Wagner.

On 12 August 1862 King, described as five feet eleven inches tall with grey eyes and light hair and complexion, enlisted in Company F of the 113th Illinois Infantry. He reported for duty as a sergeant at Chicago on 21 October and was promoted to the rank of captain on 2 March 1863 while at Camp Butler, Illinois. On 10 June 1864 he was taken captive at Guntown, Mississippi, and imprisoned at Columbia, South Carolina. King escaped on 16 November and rejoined his regiment until 20 June 1865, when he mustered out at Memphis.

After the war he resumed his career as an attorney in Iroquois County and was elected to the state legislature. He also served as a local master in chancery.

On 5 October 1870 King married Mary Elizabeth Arnold Tillinghast at Watseka, Illinois. Eventually they had three children: Mable, Herman, and Alice. At some time the family moved to Chicago, where King was in the real estate business for a dozen years.

He later located in Michigan, first in Traverse City, then in Coloma, where he died on 26 October 1927. He is buried in Oak Hill Cemetery at Watseka, Illinois.

References: Iroquois County (Illinois) Genealogical Society; Coloma (Michigan) Public Library; *Watseka Republican*, 2 November 1927; *Iroquois Times*, 13 November 1874; *Watseka Republican*, 13 June 1934; *Coloma Courier*, 4 November 1927.

KING, ROBERT A. (1833–1880)

Robert King was born in Terre Haute on 26 July 1833, the son of Sarah and John King, and quite naturally followed his older brother Edward to Wabash College. He was one of seven children, and in addition to Edward, his known siblings were Richard, John, Sarah, Mary, and Lucy.

Like his older brother, King spent one year in the Preparatory Department, 1851–52, and presumably returned to Terre Haute to work for his father. In 1858 he was appointed a deputy sheriff.

King was one of the first to enlist at Terre Haute in late April 1861, joining the Eleventh Indiana Regiment for three months. When released in August, he immediately registered as a second lieutenant in Company F for three years, but four months later, on 7 January 1862, he was "dismissed" for unknown reasons. He marred Harriet Lackey on 5 December 1873 and died in Terre Haute on 11 March 1880. He was buried in Woodlawn Cemetery.

References: David N. Lewis of the Vigo County Public Library; *Terre Haute Daily Express*, 12 March 1880.

KINGSBURY, EDWARD BEECHER (1836–1864)

Those who fought in the middle of the war years in the battleground areas of the western theater, deep in the South, were obviously more likely to be wounded or maimed than those who were stationed at the railroads in the war. All must be credited with service, no matter where it was, but in '63 and '64 the South was fiercely trying to score breakthrough victories and had enough man- and firepower to execute real damage on northern soldiers' bodies.

Edward Kingsbury was an idealistic soldier who did not shy away from serious conflict, and the price he paid was typical of many in those fierce conflicts in Tennessee and Georgia, which were eventually part of the definition of the western theater. Kingsbury escaped injury fighting at Lookout Mountain and Missionary Ridge in Tennessee in November 1863 and Kennesaw Mountain in Georgia in June 1864. However, on 5 July he was badly wounded near Marietta. Forty years later, a fellow Wabash student, John Cleland, recalled, "I saw him in a hospital at Chattanooga—what was left of him. He had left an arm on the red field, but he was cheerful, happy, glad of his life, and planning what a man might do with one good arm. He was taken home that his wounds might heal in peace, but death would not have it so, and soon the news came to us, far down in Georgia, 'Captain Kingsbury is dead.'"

Edward Beecher Kingsbury was born in Danville, Illinois, on 20 October 1836, one of eight children of Fannie Goodwin and Enoch Kingsbury, a Presbyterian minister. He and his youngest brother, Samuel, attended Wabash, and both of them served in the Civil War. An older brother, James, graduated from Wabash in 1855.

Kingsbury entered the freshman class in the fall of 1858 and graduated from the Classical Course in June 1862. He was one of the speakers at commencement, choosing as his topic, "Submission to law, the condition of Liberty."

Kingsbury managed to fit in his initial army experience during the late spring and early summer of 1861 without interrupting his college studies. He enrolled in Lew Wallace's Eleventh Indiana Regiment in April and was out by August 1861. Then, on 16 July 1862, following his graduation, he signed on for further military service, joining Company C of the 125th Illinois Regiment for three years. He was five feet ten inches tall, with dark eyes, dark hair, and dark complexion. Promotions came rapidly: by September he was a sergeant major; in December, a first lieutenant in Company I, while the regiment was at Nashville; and captain at Rossville, Georgia, on 23 March 1864.

After Kingsbury's death in Danville on 18 August 1864, his father Enoch proclaimed, "I have cause for profound gratitude to God that my son died a patriot and not a traitor to his country."

References: Danville Public Library; *Wabash Magazine*, III (June 1862), p. 379; *Wabash Magazine*. XXVII (March 1903), p. 26; K. Stapp, *Footprints in the Sand* (1975), p. 21; letter from Edward's mother to Wabash College, 1 December 1877, Ramsay Archives.

KINGSBURY, SAMUEL D. (1846-1911)

Samuel Kingsbury was born on 5 July 1846. He was the youngest of three Kingsbury brothers to attend Wabash, the others being James G. and Civil War soldier Edward B. The boys grew up in Danville, Vermilion County, Illinois. Their parents were Fanny G. and Enoch Kingsbury, a Presbyterian clergyman. In addition to their three sons, they had two daughters, Martha and Mary.

Samuel fit his military service around his school schedule at Wabash, entering the Preparatory Department in the fall of 1863, and joining Company H of the 135th Indiana Regiment in Crawfordsville on 3 May 1864. He served in Tennessee and Alabama guarding railroad lines until 29 September 1864 when he mustered out at Indianapolis in time to start his second year at the college

After his two years at Wabash he returned to Danville, indicating that he was a copyist. In 1870 he moved to Indianapolis and married Lucy E. Brown on 16 July 1873. Their four children were: Samuel (1875); Fanny (1876); Harry (1879) and Lucy (1883). Between 1883-1890 the family lived in Urbana, Illinois, and then moved first to Tacoma, and then to Seattle, Washington.
Shortly before his death, Samuel moved into the Washington Veterans Home in Port Orchard, where he died on 23 June 1911. He was buried in Seattle.

Sources: Danville Public Library; military pension file, National Archives, Washington DC.

KING, WILLIAM SMITH (1840–1911)

William King (who often went by his middle name, Smith) was born in Danville on 26 August 1840. His father, William A. King, was born in Kentucky about 1814 and reached Hendricks County, Indiana, sometime in the early 1830s. His wife, Eliza J., was born in Ohio about 1819; the couple's only daughter was Martha.

The elder King was a druggist in 1850, when the census was taken, with real property worth a comfortable $2,000. Ten years later he had become a merchant, and his net worth was much enhanced, with real property of $4,000 and personal property (merchandise, presumably) of $9,000.

Young William attended the Preparatory Department of Wabash College for two years, 1859–61. Instead of returning in the fall, he joined the Eleventh Indiana Regiment in the spring of 1861 and served for some fifteen months before resigning for reasons of disability. In January 1863 he was appointed first lieutenant to the Shuler Guards of Hendricks County, one of many units of the state militia. Then, on 24 June 1863, he enrolled at Danville in Company B of the 117th Regiment of Indiana volunteers. This time he was a captain committed to six months' service, which ended at Indianapolis on 23 February 1864. It was during this stint that he and his comrades had especially harsh winter conditions to contend with as they made their way through the Cumberland Gap. Shoes were in short supply, and they were on quarter rations in the bitter cold.

Within a few months, King was back in service again. In May 1864 he was made captain of Company H of the 132nd Regiment and spent most of his duty in Tennessee and Alabama, guarding railroad lines. Out of the service in September 1864, he gave himself a bit over six months of civilian comfort before joining the 156th Regiment on 1 April 1865 as captain of Company A, on guard duty in the Shenandoah Valley, mustered out at Winchester, on 4 August 1865.

On 11 April 1867, in Marion County, Indiana, King married the twenty-seven-year-old Laura Hoyt. Their children were Russell, Lucien, Frost, Hoyt, Abby, and Kathryn.

King pursued a variety of careers following the war's end. From 1876 to 1880, he was Center Township trustee for Marion County, more or less co-terminus with Indianapolis. At some point in his life he was a travelling agent for a metropolitan newspaper, the *Indianapolis Journal*, and on another occasion he worked for the Internal Revenue Service.

He died from a stroke at a cousin's home on 12 December 1911, and his body was brought back to Indianapolis for burial in Crown Hill Cemetery. An obituary mentions that he was survived by his six children, but there is no mention of his wife, which suggests she may have predeceased him.

References: *Wabash Magazine*, III (February 1862), p. 190; G. S. Cottman (comp.), *Indiana Scrapbook of Colleges*, Indiana Division of the Indiana State Library.

KIRKPATRICK, GEORGE W. JR. (1835–1921)

George Kirkpatrick was born on 21 May 1835 in Sheffield Township, Tippecanoe County, Indiana, one of ten children born to Katherine Porter and George W. Kirkpatrick. In 1848 the family moved to Wea Township, and it was from a farm here that George came to Wabash College in the autumn of 1856 to study for one year in the Normal School. He then embarked on his medical studies, living in Crane Station, Sheffield Township.

In January 1864 Kirkpatrick received a commission as an assistant surgeon in the Seventy-Second Indiana Volunteers, the regiment in which his older brother, Samuel, was lieutenant colonel. By April he caught up with his unit at Mooresville, Alabama, and joined the regiment that was advancing on Atlanta. Once this key city fell, the regiment returned to Alabama and participated in the fall of Selma and Montgomery in April 1865. Kirkpatrick was mustered out of service on 28 June 1865 at Nashville.

After the war he returned to Crane Station and resumed his medical practice. On 7 September 1866 he married a local Tippecanoe County woman, Lovena E. DeHart, and they would go on to have two daughters and two sons, James N. and Milo D.

George Kirkpatrick had a long and successful career as a physician, not retiring until about 1906. He and Lovena then moved to Lafayette, where she died on 28 June 1912. He died 21 September 1921 and is buried in Wildcat Cemetery.

References: *Biographical Record and Portrait Album of Tippecanoe County, Indiana* (1888), p. 561; *Lafayette Journal and Courier*, 22 September 1921; and *Lafayette Daily Courier*, 28 June 1912.

KNAPP, CHARLES H. (1845–1898)

Charles Knapp was born in Terre Haute on 7 September 1845, the son of Susan Beach and Charles C. Knapp (1813–1888), a successful contractor, builder, and mason. Charles C. Knapp was a native of Sussex County, New Jersey. His first wife died presumably about 1840, and soon thereafter he moved to Terre Haute, Vigo County, Indiana. He met there and married a widow, Susan Beach, ten years his senior. From her earlier marriage, Susan had two children: Mary and Silas. From her marriage with Charles Knapp, she had two others: Sarah and our student, Charles H.

Young Charles came to Wabash College for two years as a freshman, from 1862 to 1864. He joined Company I of the Eleventh Indiana Regiment for three years and was described at that time as being eighteen years old, with black eyes and dark hair and complexion. He stood five feet seven inches tall. At some point Knapp was promoted to corporal and was praised in the *Wabash Magazine*: "Knapp entered the 11th Indiana, and after participating in the closing victories of the war, returned home covered all over with military glory."

After the war Knapp spent a few years as a businessman in his hometown of Terre Haute before venturing west to Chillicothe, Missouri, followed by a stint as a travelling salesman based in McPherson, Kansas.

On 8 October 1873 Knapp married Anna Rezzer in Newton, Massachusetts. They had four children: Harry, Cora, Susan, and Mary. By April 1881 they were in Phoenix, Arizona Territory, where they settled permanently. Knapp became deputy clerk and eventually clerk for the federal district court.

Anna died on 10 January 1889 and three years later Knapp married Mary Davidson from Alexander, Louisiana. Knapp died on 27 November 1898.

References: Arizona Historical Society of Tucson and the Arizona Historical Foundation of Phoenix; *Wabash Magazine*, VI (June 1866), p. 10; *Terre Haute Evening Gazette*, 24 December 1888; *Terre Haute Express*, 24 December 1888; *Arizona Republic*, 28 November 1898; *Phoenix Daily Herald*, 28 November 1898.

KNIGHT, JONATHAN LEE (1837–1915)

Jonathan Knight, who often went by his middle name, Lee, was born in Carroll County on 6 July 1837, the son of Sarah Woodington and William Knight (1804?–1849).

He briefly attended Wabash as a freshman in 1857–58.

On 10 April 1860 he married a local Delphi woman, Margaret Ann Leonard, and they eventually had ten children.

Until he enlisted in Company A of the Seventy-Second Indiana Regiment on 24 July 1862, Knight worked as an engraver of marble. By mid-August he and his fellow volunteers set out for Kentucky, where for two months they found themselves involved in steady skirmishes. They then moved on to Tennessee, where they were discharged on 27 December.

Initially the Knights moved to Iowa, where their second daughter was born, but in August 1867 they took up residence at Topeka. Knight became a photographer and went on to create an illustrious career using this new technology. His photographs of state legislators and other eminent Kansans were widely admired, and when Archduke Alexis of Russia visited Topeka, Knight was his official photographer. He supplemented his formal career with stints of public service, including the office of city clerk, county clerk (1876–1882), and county commissioner (1889–1895). His civic duties inspired him to invent one of the early models of the adding machine, which brought him considerable income.

In January 1906 Knight's wife died, and soon thereafter, he entered a soldiers home in Kansas City for five years to be near one of his daughters. Unaccountably he then moved to Fond du Lac, Wisconsin, and continued to participate in local government and service organizations. He died there on 27 June 1915. His body was returned to Topeka for interment next to his wife. Six daughters survived him.

References: *Topeka Capital*, 11 January 1906, 28 June 1915, and 1 July 1915; and Rowena Horr of Topeka.

KREPPS, ANDREW JACKSON (1828–1910)

Andrew Krepps was born in Washington County, Pennsylvania, on 28 May 1828, the son of Emeline and Solomon G. Krepps. Sometime in the 1840s his family moved to Vernon, Jennings County, Indiana, and it was from there that he made his way to Crawfordsville in the autumn of 1849 to enroll at Wabash College.

After one academic year, young Krepps left the college and took up carpentry. Five years later, on 1 November 1855, he married Mary Elizabeth Hurley of DeWitt County, Illinois, and they eventually had eight children: Charles, Elizabeth, Elvin, Mary, Elmer, Stella, Josie, and Olive.

On 15 August 1862 Krepps enlisted in Company I of the 107th Illinois Infantry. Activated in October of that year, the regiment made its way to Louisville to guard railroad lines, moving to Tennessee in February 1863. In November and December the regiment participated in the Knoxville campaign. From May to September 1864, Krepps took part in the siege of Atlanta and then joined the pursuit of Confederate General Hood. Toward the end of 1864, his regiment operated in northern Alabama and in Nashville. During March and April of 1865, it took part in skirmishes in the Carolinas.

Mustered out late in 1865, Krepps returned to his family in DeWitt County and acquired eight acres of farmland five miles north of Farmer City, Illinois. He worked his land there until about 1892, when he moved into the city. Wife Mary died in 1896, but Krepps lived until 15 March 1910. They are both interred in Maple Grove Cemetery.

References: Public Library, Farmer City, Illinois.

LAROSE, NOAH S. (1817–1886)

Noah LaRose was born in Ohio in 1817, one of eight children born to Anna Maria Shearer and Philip S. LaRose. His siblings included John and Joshua, but others' names are unknown.

The young Wabash student came to Crawfordsville from a sizeable farm in Cass County in the fall of 1839. He spent the next two years in the Preparatory Department of Wabash College and then returned to work on the family farm. He served as county surveyor from 1846 to 1849 and then moved into the town of Logansport and was Cass County clerk from 1856 until 1864.

In July 1863 LaRose enlisted in Company G of the 110th Indiana Regiment as the regimental clerk for the Morgan episode, but served only from 9 to 15 July. In the 1870s LaRose had real estate holdings worth $9,000 and personal property of $2,000. He was re-elected Cass County clerk from 1872 until 1876 while continuing to farm. LaRose died in 1886 and is buried in Bethel Cemetery, Clay Township, Cass County.

References: Cass County Public Library; J. O. Powell, *History of Cass County, Indiana* (1913), pp. 829, 1204–05.

LAWSON, MICHAEL MEDSKER (1844–1924)

To look through this collection of Civil War biographies is to be struck, dismayed, by the number of illness-related disabilities the war caused. Still, in spite of coming home with the lingering results of typhoid fever, amputation infections, tuberculosis, or malaria, men attempted to pick up the threads of their lives and move on. Sometimes the faith they had found or cultivated at the college inspired them to lead quite contributive lives. Michael Lawson was one of these who "soldiered on" successfully in spite of his rather severe war disability.

He was born in Hillsboro, Ohio, on 21 February 1844, the only child of Elizabeth and Isaac R. Medsker. His father's first two wives died, and he grew up with nine half brothers and half sisters. In 1853 the family moved to Danville, Indiana, where the eighteen-year-old enrolled in the Seventieth Indiana Volunteers on 30 July 1862 for three years. He stayed with his regiment throughout the war, including Sherman's March to the Sea, and was mustered out in June 1865.

Military service greatly impaired Lawson's health, so it was not until the fall of 1866 that he entered the Preparatory Department of Wabash College. Two years later he became a freshman and remained with his class until graduating in

June 1872. He later noted that had supported himself throughout college with a variety of odd jobs, supplemented by the "usual aid for ministerial students." Having this career in mind, he spent the next three years as a theological student at Lane Seminary in Cincinnati, Ohio.

He married Katherine Darrah of West Ely, Missouri, in 1875, and toward the end of 1876 their first child, Darrah Campbell, was born. However, death claimed the baby, and a few months later Lawson assumed his first full-time post as minister of the Presbyterian church in Kingston, Ohio. Over the years, he served churches in St. Marys, Ohio; Ossian, Indiana; Lema, Indiana; and Indianapolis. He returned to Crawfordsville in 1904 to be the minister of the local Presbyterian church at a time when his son, Isaac, was an undergraduate at the college.

Lawson made his last move to a new church in Nashville, Arkansas. Wabash asked him to preach in the college chapel in May 1919. He died on 27 March 1924 at the home of his daughter and son-in-law in Fordyce, Arkansas.

References: Ms. Dorothy E. Templin of Danville, Indiana; 1905 Wabash College alumni questionnaire; *Wabash College Record*, October 1904, July 1912, July 1919, and September 1924; Lane Theological Seminary, *General Catalogue*, 1829–1899, p. 88.

LEFEVRE, SAMUEL J. (1841–1917)

Samuel LeFevre was born in Miami, Ohio, on 16 April 1841, the only son of Martha Jewett (1817–1865) and William C. M. LeFevre (1814–1869), a physician. He attended Wabash for one academic year, 1854–55, and then moved with his family to Gibson County, Illinois, where his father acquired 320 acres of farmland that he worked for the next six years.

On 14 August 1862 LeFevre enrolled in Company K of the Seventh Illinois Regiment at Paxton. He participated in the siege of Vicksburg in 1863. In the course of capturing Fort Blakely near Mobile, Alabama, on 9 April 1865, he was wounded in the left foot. He was mustered out of service three months later.

After the war he returned to the family farm and married Laura Carver of Norton, Massachusetts, on 23 December 1866. They became the parents of two daughters, Anna and Mary Etta. In 1872 LeFevre opened a coal and lumber business, supplementing his farming income, and in 1891 he founded Gibson County's first electric power plant. He died on 27 September 1917, and Laura died on 8 September 1922. They are both buried in Drummer Township Cemetery.

References: Troy (Ohio) Historical Society; Paxton (Illinois) Carnegie Library; Susan H. Truax of Pittsboro, Indiana; *Paxton Record*, 4 October 1917 and 14 September 1922, *Portrait and Biographical Record of Ford County, Illinois* (1892), pp. 410, 481, 490, 493.

Why so many Presbyterians?

Why so many Presbyterian enrollees, converts, ministerial prospects, professors and administrators?

From early times, there were links between the Presbyterian community of Crawfordsville and the founding and development of Wabash College. The local church went back to 1824, and one of its founders, Williamson Dunn, eventually donated land for the college. The first pastor, James Thomson, arrived in 1827, and five years later he would be one of the founders of Wabash College. By the early 1830s the local Presbyterian church had increased to about 120 members. In April 1832 the church went on record "deeming the education of young men for the ministry of great importance to the interests of religion."

In that same year, Edmund O. Hovey of Vermont took up his calling as a home missionary and made his way to Crawfordsville. He would be intimately bound up with the college thereafter.

On 21 November 1832 nine "founding fathers" formally established Wabash College. The Presbyterian link was clear, with five of the founders ministers. Once the college was underway, students were expected to attend some church in Crawfordsville on Sunday morning and then chapel at the college later in the day. In 1838 the local church split over issues such as slavery, and Thomson led about one hundred of his flock into a new Center Church. It was this one that had the closest ties with the college students and faculty. As a Wabash student and Civil War vet later recalled, "The pulpit of Center Church in those stirring days was a center of the Union cause in this place and was frequently used for public meetings." Of the thirty-one members of Center Church who served in the Civil War, all but six had been, at one time or another, students of Wabash College.

Finally, the first six presidents of the college were all Presbyterian ministers, even though the college was not officially church-related. Between 1863 and 1866 President Joseph Tuttle also performed the duties of Center Church's ministry, until they secured a new pastor. The last ministerial president was George Lewis Mackintosh, who guided the college from 1907 to 1929.

LEMA, ALBERT S. (184–1862)

Albert Lema was born in Dansville, New York, in 1842, son of Julia and P. L. Lema. He had one sister, Julia, born in 1844. How and why a young man from so far distant and with so many good colleges in his own area made his way to Wabash College is somewhat puzzling, but he enrolled in the Normal School in the fall of 1855, remaining for one academic year.

On 12 November 1861 he enrolled at Dansville in Company I of the Thirteenth New York Volunteer Infantry. He was promoted to second lieutenant in the spring of 1862. In June of 1862 at the Battle of Gaines Mill in Virginia, he was badly wounded in his shoulder and leg. His leg had to be amputated, and a week later, on 4 July, he died at Watt's Farm, near Richmond, and was buried somewhere nearby.

References: Dansville (New York) Public Library; *Dansville Advertiser*, 7 August 1862; his military service file, National Archives, Washington, DC.

LEMMON, LEONIDAS W. (1844–1911)

Leonidas Lemmon (sometimes spelled Lemon) was born in Union County on 26 January 1844. He moved to Montgomery County in 1856, but his parents' names are unknown.

On 11 July 1863 at Crawfordsville, Lemmon joined Company C as a private, and when the Morgan furor passed, he was mustered out at Indianapolis on 17 July. On 21 February 1865 at Thorntown, he enrolled in Company H of the Eleventh Indiana Regiment, describing himself as five feet ten inches tall, with hazel eyes, black hair, and fair complexion. He gave his occupation as a painter. His time in the military was interrupted by a bout of mumps, which landed him in the hospital at Fort Marshall near Baltimore from 12 April to 23 May 1865.

He was mustered out on 26 July 1865 and returned to Crawfordsville in time to enter Wabash College that fall. For two years he studied in the English course, and he was characterized in the college magazine as the "Crawfordsville Angelo." Does this mean that he was painting murals and portraits instead of walls? We cannot tell at this distance. He married Mary Flora Miller of Montgomery County on 8 February 1868 and lived in the neighboring town of Ladoga until 1874. They had one son, Byron.

Mary died on 7 April 1883, after they had moved to Santa Barbara. On 1 May 1898 Lemmon married a divorcee, Ida West, aboard the *Genova*, a ship anchored in the channel of Santa Barbara. Sometime afterwards he entered a soldiers home in Los Angeles County and died on 3 April 1911.

References: H. W. Beckwith, *History of Montgomery County* (1881), p. 81; *History of Montgomery County* (Bowen & Co., 1913), p. 117; *The People's Guide* (1874); *Craw-*

fordsville Review, 16 July 1863; *Wabash Magazine*, VIII (March 1868), p. 74; and military pension file, National Archives, Washington, DC.

LEONARD, CHARLES HENRY (1841–1902)

Charles Henry Leonard was born in Mount Vernon, Indiana, on 3 June 1841, son of Lucretia Knowles (1817–1852) and Charles Frederick Leonard. His siblings were Mary, Anna, Isaac, and William.

Leonard entered Wabash in the autumn of 1861 and remained for only one academic year. He then presumably joined his father in the mercantile business until he enrolled in Company G of the 136th Indiana Volunteers on 21 May 1864 for one hundred days that were spent mostly in Tennessee guarding railroad lines.

On 30 June 1881 Leonard married Florence M. Gorman, a schoolteacher, in Owensville. Their only child, Manning, was born in about 1884. Leonard died on 9 October 1902 and was buried in the Owensville Cemetery, survived by Florence, who lived until 1933 and was interred next to her husband.

References: Alexandrian Public Library of Mount Vernon, Indiana; John C. Leffel, *History of Posey County, Indiana* (1913), pp. 371–73; Manning Leonard, *The Leonard Genealogy* (1896); Owensville Public Library; Princeton Public Library.

LEWIS, EDWIN RUFUS (1839–1907)

Some veterans returned from war to teach at Wabash, and their "practical life experiences" may or may not have played into their success as teachers.

Edwin Lewis was a promising student and became a well recognized—if controversial—professor at Wabash. He was born at Madison on 2 April 1839, the only son of Sophronia West and James E. Lewis, a plow-maker by trade. His two sisters were Harriet and Frances.

He entered the Preparatory Department of Wabash in the fall of 1855 and showed academic ability, advancing through the freshman, sophomore, and junior years in three years. He repeated his junior year at Amherst College in Massachusetts and graduated in the spring of 1861. An accomplished violinist, he helped form the first orchestra at Amherst.

Returning to Indiana, Lewis joined General Lew Wallaces's Eleventh Indiana Volunteers as a first lieutenant and aide-de-camp to the general. Following the Battle of Shiloh in April 1862, after which Wallace was effectively sidelined for many months, young Lewis resigned and presumably went back to Massachusetts.

In September 1862 he enrolled in the Twenty-First Massachusetts Regiment and quickly rose through the ranks from private to sergeant major to first lieutenant and finally captain. He saw action at the battles at Antietam, Spotsylvania Court House, and Petersburg, and he was wounded at Fredericksburg and Knoxville. He was mustered out on 30 August 1864 and married Harriet Goodwell in Amherst. They had one son, Edwin S., who graduated from Wabash College in 1888.

Lewis entered Harvard Medical School in 1864 and graduated in 1867. The following year found him back in Amherst practicing medicine until 1869, when he enrolled in Union Theological Seminary in New York and became an ordained Presbyterian minister in November 1870.

From 1871 to 1884 Lewis taught chemistry at the Protestant College in Beirut, Syria. His wife died there in 1878. In 1882, as a guest teacher at Wabash, he gave a commencement address supporting the theories of Charles Darwin and was summarily dismissed by the college's trustees.

Lewis returned to Crawfordsville, seemingly forgiven for advancing non-Biblical theories, and accepted the post of professor of chemistry at Wabash. In 1885 he married a widow from Philadelphia, Ellen Poole Milford, who died in 1889. In 1892 he met and married his third wife, Rose Baldwin, in Indianapolis, where he practiced medicine and was involved in numerous civic organizations. In 1896 they moved to Washington, DC, where Lewis worked for the pension office as a medical expert for ten years before returning to Indianapolis in 1906. He died on 31 January 1907, leaving a legacy of books about chemistry, geology, and music. One of these, consisting of hymns and tunes, was written in Arabic. He gave his collection of fossil fish to the British Museum, which designated it the Lewis Collection.

References: Archives of the Harvard Medical School and of Amherst College. At Amherst there is a letter from Lewis to Professor William Montague, detailing Lewis's complicated military service.

LINGEMAN, SAMUEL (1839–1864)

Samuel Lingeman and his twin sister, Catherine, were born in 1839 in Ohio. Their parents, Anna Elizabeth and Johann Lingerman, emigrated from Germany to the United States in 1832. Originally, the family name was spelled with an "r," which was later dropped. Samuel had an older brother, John. The family settled in New Winchester, and it was from Hendricks County that young Samuel made his way to Wabash College in the fall of 1858. He spent three years in the Normal School before enlisting in the service for the North.

While at Wabash Lingeman wrote to his older brother saying that he was unable to pay his last term's tuition, and if funds were not forthcoming, he would have to withdraw from the college. Presumably John obliged, since Samuel remained in school.

Like many other students in April 1861, Lingeman left the college before the end of term in order to enroll in Company I of the Eleventh Indiana Regiment for three months. Then, on 7 October he joined Company C of the Fifty-First Regiment as a first lieutenant, described as six feet tall, with blue eyes, light hair, and a fair complexion.

In November 1862 he wrote to his older brother from Silver Springs, Tennessee, lamenting his deteriorating health and hoping to get to Nashville, where the medical facilities would be better. Meanwhile he asked his brother to send him Confederate money, real or counterfeit, since the locals would accept only Confederate bills: "All money is good with us, that is anything in the shape of a banknote with pictures and a little writing in cursive."

A year later, to his relief, he was promoted to captain and became a member of a general court martial, which meant that he might be separated from his regiment and left behind in Nashville. Again, he wrote to John:

> I have thought that my proper place now was with the men with whom I enlisted and that they and the people at home looked to me to take care of them but I again remember that I am a stranger to them—a foreigner by parentage and only an American by birth and education, and am by most of my acquaintances considered *only a Dutchman*—and consequently any exercise of authority is looked upon by them as arbitrary and uncalled for under these considerations. I have come to the conclusion to accept an easier to me and better situation so long as I can get them and thereby fitting myself for better positions in afterlife, for I do think that the common soldiers or officers life to be a poor place for improvement at least in the present state of affairs, indeed officers and soldiers of the line are but *slaves* to their commanders. *We are all slaves to one another.* I have no doubt that I will be censored for not taking charge of my company but I don't care for what people at home might say so long as I can have the confidence of my companions in the army. I am not well. I am able to "go around" and look very well, but the cold I caught on my way here has settled on my lungs and the surgeon says that if I do not take good care of myself that I will never recover. So much for this war.

In February or March 1864 he returned home to New Winchester, where he died of pneumonia on 20 March 1864, never able to marry Lydia Barlow, to whom he was engaged before the war. He was initially buried at New Winchester but later was moved to the Lingeman family cemetery at Brownsburg to lie near his parents.

References: Dr. Byron S. Lingeman of Wellesley Hills, Massachusetts; Mrs. and Mrs. Harold B. Lockwood of Anderson, Indiana; Frances Fisher of Pittsboro, Indiana. The letters quoted above are in the possession of Dr. Lingeman.

LIVINGS, FRANCIS (1837–1918)

Francis Livings was born on 14 December 1837 in Allensville, the son of Lucy Norton and Everson Livings. His father was a farmer who also worked on a riverboat on the Ohio River. He had a younger brother, Theodore, who went to Wabash and served in the war, and a sister, Louisa.

From 1858 to 1861 Livings attended the Preparatory Department of Wabash College, and within a couple of months of completing his third year, he enrolled at Madison in Company A of the Third Cavalry attached to the Forty-Fifth Regiment. He was, records say, five feet three inches tall and had grey eyes, blonde hair, and pale complexion. From October 1861 to January 1862, he was sick in a hospital. The following May he was given the responsibility of tending cattle, and in October he was taken prisoner by the Confederates. Trying to escape on horseback, he failed to jump a wide ditch and injured his groin. Soon thereafter he came down with typhoid fever and was hospitalized in Richmond on 20 November 1863. Paroled at City Point, Virginia, on 16 April 1864, he almost immediately entered a Union hospital at Baltimore. Upon his release in June, he rejoined his regiment and was mustered out with his comrades on 7 September 1864.

Back in Allensville he married Martha L. Harris on 10 November. They eventually had ten children: Carrie, Julia, Olive, Laura, Chester, Flora, Alice, Fanny, Harry, and a boy that died prematurely. They lived briefly in Bartholomew County but returned to Switzerland County, where Livings became an insurance salesman because his delicate health precluded his doing manual labor.

In October 1912 he moved to Hamilton, Ohio, where he died on 7 August 1918.

References: Switzerland County Public Library; *Livings History of Dearborn, Ohio and Switzerland Counties, Indiana* (1885), p. 1107; military pension file, National Archives, Washington, DC.

LIVINGS, THEODORE (1839–1917)

Theodore Livings was born on 15 September 1839 at Allensville, the younger son of Lucy Norton and Everson Livings. Like his older brother, Francis, he came to Wabash and served in the war.

Before coming to Wabash young Theodore taught school locally in Switzerland County. He entered the Preparatory Department in the autumn of 1860. Lacking the means to pay for tuition, he worked as a janitor at the college and a sexton at the Methodist church. He was also a member of the Phi Gamma Delta fraternity. Livings completed his freshman year in the Classical Course, but while he was home for the summer, he raised Company D of the Ninety-Third Regiment Indiana Voluntary Infantry on 1 August 1862 and received a commission as second lieutenant. Later that month Livings became an adjutant of field and staff, and in June 1864 he was appointed aide-de-camp to Colonel William L. McMillen at Ripley, Tennessee. He received a commendation in July 1864 for acting with great coolness and bravery during the Battle of Tupelo, Mississippi (14–15 July 1864).

Once he was discharged from the army on 10 August 1865, Livings returned to Wabash for his sophomore year, but instead of continuing on at the college, he went to Indianapolis to study law and go into practice.

On 7 April 1870 he married Mary Ann Jackman, and they had two children: Lucy Norton (1871) and Frederick Theodore (1873). In the late 1880s the family moved to Washington, DC, where Livings worked as a clerk in the United States Pension Office. Livings died in the District of Colombia on 17 March 1917.

References: District of Columbia Public Library; Switzerland County Public Library; *Wabash Magazine*, VIII (June 1868), p. 16; *Wabash College Record* (July 1903), p. 20; *War of the Rebellion*, series I, vol. 39, part 1, pp. 115, 260.

LOCKWOOD, WILLIAM WIRT (1835–1906)

William Lockwood was born on 24 December 1835 on a farm near New Paris, Preble County, Ohio, the younger son of Belinda Jackson and George W. Lockwood. His father died in 1837 and his mother in 1840, leaving the boys to be brought up by an uncle, Daniel D. Lockwood.

In the spring of 1845, they moved to Peru, where Lockwood attended the local schools and occupied himself with various jobs. In the summer of 1860, he came to Crawfordsville, enrolled in Wabash College, secured a room in the college's dormitory, and took to his studies. However, before the academic year was over, he withdrew for financial reasons and proceeded to take a job as a teacher in Williamsport.

In August 1862 Lockwood enrolled in Company E of the Eighty-Sixth Indiana Volunteers. Marching through Kentucky and Tennessee exhausted him, and for a while he had to leave the regiment, but by the end of the year, he was able to take part in the Battle of Murfreesboro. However, poor health continued to debilitate him and resulted in his spending the last two years of the war as a clerk in the Quartermaster's Department in Indianapolis, from which he was discharged on 17 June 1865.

Lockwood stayed in Indianapolis after the war and became a clerk at the post office for two years, then returned to Peru to pursue his long-standing ambition of teaching. On 23 December 1869 he married Mary E. Waite, moving then to Illinois, where he became principal of the schools in the town of Forrest and Mary obtained a job as a teacher. Later Lockwood became superintendent of schools in Odell, Illinois, while his wife concentrated on rearing their six sons and four daughters.

In the spring of 1878, the family moved back to Peru, where Lockwood purchased a one-third share in the *Peru Republican*, the local newspaper. He was always an ardent Republican and an active member of the Methodist church, where he sang in the parish choir. He also was a Mason and member of the GAR post and the Knights of Pythias fraternity. Six of his children went to DePauw University.

When he was not quite seventy, Lockwood was involved in a serious accident. On the night before Thanksgiving, a horse-drawn cab ran him down, and his foot had to be amputated. While undergoing surgery he is said to have had enough presence of mind to ask, "Is the paper up?"

He died on 16 February 1906 and is buried in Mount Hope Cemetery, Peru.

References: *Biographical and Genealogical History of Cass, Miami, Howard and Tipton Counties, Indiana* (1898), I, pp. 83–85; *Denver Indiana Tribune*, 22 February 1906; *Amboy Independent*, 23 February 1906; *Peru Republican*, 23 February 1906.

LOGAN, WILLIAM McCLURE (1821–1862)

One of Wabash's earliest students, William Logan, was born in Montgomery County, Ohio, on 10 April 1821, the son of Ann and Alexander Logan. He had two siblings, Mary Ann and John M. His parents moved to Fountain County, Indiana, in 1822 and joined the Presbyterian church in Richland Township. From there Logan enrolled in the Preparatory Department of Wabash in 1835, spending until 1840 at the college.

On 2 September 1847, in Fountain County, he married America Oglesby Sanford, who had a two-year-old son, Horace. During the 1850s they moved to Allen County, Kansas.

On 16 January 1862 Logan enlisted at the town of Iola in Company H of the Ninth Kansas Cavalry. Later that year he contracted typhoid fever, and he died in the military hospital at Fort Scott on 13 September 1862.

References: H. W. Beckwith, *History of Fountain County* (1881), p. 347; Lawrence McKinney and Miriam Luke of Fountain County; military service file, National Archives, Washington, DC.

LOVEJOY, JAMES COLLINS (1819–1905)

James Lovejoy was born in Orange County, Vermont, on 24 June 1819, the son of Jemima Kingsbury and John Lovejoy. The year after he was born, the family moved to Connersville, where his father pursued farming. James Lovejoy's younger brother, Halsey R., also came to Wabash College. Their other siblings were John, Emily, Caroline, Eugene, Solon, and Virgil.

Lovejoy entered the Preparatory Department in the fall of 1835, only the third year of the college's existence. He did not come back the following year, but returned between 1837 and 1839. At the death of his father, he probably worked on the family farm in Tippecanoe County. He also taught school and began to study medicine, eventually supplementing his informal education with study at Rush Medical College of Chicago.

On 4 July 1847 Lovejoy married Emeline Bunnell of Independence and started a family that would include twelve children. Until 1854 he practiced medicine in Warren and White Counties and then moved to Des Moines, Iowa, where he continuing doctoring but also went into partnership with his brother, Halsey, in a lumberyard and a dry goods store.

In 1859 the Lovejoys settled in Old Rippey, Greene County, Iowa, where Lovejoy became captain of the home guards during the war. He helped organize a company of new recruits and received a commission to be their doctor, but the local inhabitants prevailed upon him to stay home to care for the wounded soldiers who returned home and to assist families whose husbands, fathers, and sons were away in service. He was never idle. In addition to his medical work, he was Greene County supervisor, coroner. and school superintendent.

Lovejoy died on 6 September 1905 and is buried in the Old Rippey Cemetery. Emeline died on 29 December 1907.

References: E. B. Spillman, *Past and Present of Greene County, Iowa* (1907), pp. 188–91; [Old Rippey] *Jefferson Bee*, 12 September 1905; State Historical Society of Iowa, Iowa City; Rippey (Iowa) Public Library.

LOWRY, ALFRED (1842–1922)

Alfred Lowry was born in Bainbridge on 11 December 1842, the son of Maria Jane Hanna and Samuel Gardner Lowry. His siblings were Almira, Julia, Lucinda, Ann, Jane, Philip, and Leander. Two stepbrothers, Samuel Doak and William Henry, also attended Wabash and served in the Civil War.

Although the family moved to Minnesota in 1857, young Alfred returned to Indiana in the autumn of 1862 to enter the Preparatory Department of the college, following in the footsteps of his four older brothers. He remained there for two years, interrupted briefly by Morgan's Raid into southern Indiana. On 11 July 1863 he joined Company C of the 108th Regiment and was mustered out six days later. Somehow, during that short time, he was wounded, rendering him unfit for further military service.

Lowry returned to Minnesota and took up farming on land about halfway between the towns of Austin and Albert Lea. In November 1870 he married a teacher from Freeborn County, Henrietta J. Hicks, and they eventually had three daughters: Edith, Olive, and Anna.

In the 1890s the family moved into Austin, where many of their relatives lived and where he was a builder and contractor until 1912, when they went to St. Charles, Illinois, to live with their married daughter, Edith. Lowry died there shortly after his eightieth birthday, on 18 December 1922, survived by his wife and daughters.

References: For further Lowry family background, see the sketches for Samuel and William Lowry. Austin (Minnesota) Public Library; *Austin Daily Herald*, 5 January 1923.

LOWRY, SAMUEL DOAK (1826–1875)

Samuel Lowry (often called by his middle name, Doak) was born in Sand Creek, Indiana, in 1826, one of four brothers who attended Wabash in the 1830s and 1840s. His parents were Almira Thomas and Samuel Gardner Lowry, a Presbyterian minister. All four boys joined the college in the January term of 1835, when Doak was scarcely nine years old. He was not enrolled in the college every year because the family relocated frequently. However, when the Lowrys returned to Crawfordsville in 1846, Lowry came back and graduated in June 1849.

On 30 September 1852 Lowry married Emily Moberly at nearby Fayetteville, and in 1854 they had a daughter, Alice C. Lowry. Lowry then began teaching mathematics and natural science at the Cane Hill Collegiate Institute, a new school that the Presbyterian church had opened in Boonsboro, Arkansas, and the first chartered college in the state. He was appointed acting president for four years, 1856–60.

Two pieces of evidence testify that Lowry served in the Confederate Army, although neither specifies his company or regiment. In 1872 he returned to Wabash College for the first time since he had left in 1849, and after his visit the college magazine mentioned that he had fought with the Confederacy. A second allusion to his belonging to a southern regiment is in a letter from Fontaine Richard Earle, a former president of Cane Hill College, who mentions that his letter would be conveyed by Mr. Lowry.

Lowry and his brother, William, constituted one of the many instances when a family was split by members serving on opposite sides of the conflict.

In the fall of 1869 Trinity University opened in Tehuacana, Texas, and Lowry was a member of its faculty, still teaching math and science. In the University catalogue for 1871–72, he is listed as principal of the Female Department, while his daughter, Allie (Alice) is noted as a student. He died at Tehuacana in 1875.

References: *Wabash Magazine*, XII (January 1872), p. 76; The Twenty-Fourth Annual Announcement and Catalogue of Trinity University (1892), pp. 5–7; *History of the Cumberland Presbyterian Church* (1899), pp. 576–77; D. E. Everett, *Trinity University: A Record of 100 Years* (1969), pp. 8–10; "History of Cane Hill College," *Publications of the Arkansas Historical Association*, III, pp. 184–200; E. E. Richardson, *Early Settlers of Cane Hill* (1955), pp. 55–58; "The Earle-Buchanan Letters,'" *Arkansas Historical Quarterly*,

XXXIII (1974), pp. 126–31; Baylor University; Washington County Historical Society of Fayetteville (Arkansas); Fayetteville (Arkansas) Public Library; University of Arkansas; Archives and Special Collections of Trinity University, San Antonia; Arkansas History Commission, Little Rock.

LOWRY, WILLIAM HENRY (1828–1911)

Four Lowry brothers born to Almira Thomas and Samuel Gardner Lowry attended Wabash in the 1830s and 1840s, as has been shown. William, the youngest, was born at Sand Creek in March 1828. One of his older brothers, Samuel Doak Lowry, fought for the Confederacy. The other two older brothers were James T. and Theophilus. Eleven days after William was born, his mother died. His father, a Presbyterian minister, married Maria Jane Hanna in February 1829. She became the mother of Almira, Julia, Lucinda, Ann, Jane, Philisa, Alfred, and Leander.

In 1834 the family settled in Crawfordsville, where Lowry's father was asked to be a member of the board of trustees of Wabash College. At the opening of the term in January 1835, the four Lowry boys were enrolled. William remained in the Preparatory Department until June of 1838, when the family moved, first to Rockville and then to Bainbridge. Putnam County was enough closer to the college that William Lowry returned in the fall of 1846 for two more years.

On 28 June 1849 Lowry married Mary Ann Thornton. They had three children: Julia, Annabel, and Charles. In the early 1860s Lowry entered the army. His wife died while he was in the service, and after the war, on 24 September 1865, he married Eliza Watkins, a schoolteacher he met in Freeborn County, Minnesota, where his parents were living with his children. His father performed the ceremony. William and Eliza eventually had seven children: Frederick, Frank, Eva, Mary, Doak, Arthur, and Raymond.

They moved from Minnesota to Iowa, to Nebraska, then back to Minnesota, Lowry plying his trade of blacksmithing. In 1898 they joined many of his siblings and stepsiblings in Austin, Minnesota. With the death of Eliza on 4 March 1909, Lowry left Austin to live with his daughter, Mrs. Clark (Julia) Seeley, in Westbrook, where he died on 17 January 1911. Both he and his wife are buried in Fairview Cemetery, Oakland, in Freeborn County.

References: State Historical Society of Iowa, Iowa City; Mower County (Minnesota) Genealogical Society; Austin (Minnesota) Public Library; Minnesota Historical Society, St. Paul; Freeborn County (Minnesota) Historical Society; *Crawfordsville Weekly Journal*, 12 April 1884; *Mower County Transcript*, 29 September 1886; *Austin Register*, 30 September 1886.

LUSK, SALMON P. JR. (1843–1863)

Salmon P. Lusk Jr. was born 1843 in Parke County, on land given to his father as a veteran of the War of 1812. Today it is part of Turkey Run State Park, and the gristmill the father built on Sugar Creek stood until 1847, when it was swept away by a flood. His mother was Mary Beard Lusk, and her other children were William, John, Lydia, and Susan.

Before coming to Wabash in the fall of 1861, young Salmon not only helped his father at the mill, grinding grain, sawing wood, and shipping pork to New Orleans, consignments that filled twenty flatboats a year, but he also joined the Union Greys, a regiment of the state militia or Indiana Legion. Following his year in the Preparatory Department of the college, he enrolled in the regular army, and on 5 August 1862 was admitted into Company A of the Eighty-Fifth Indiana Regiment for three years as a corporal, advancing to sergeant during the next six months.

At the Battle of Thompson's Station, Tennessee, on 4 March 1863, when Coburn surrendered the troops rather than having them killed, Lusk was one of the one hundred Union troops killed that day. His remains were returned to Parke County and buried in Bethany Cemetery, where he was joined six years later by his father.

References: *Wabash Magazine*, IV (July 1863), p. 332; *Parke County Centennial Memorial* (1916); H. W. Beckwith, *History of Vigo and Parke Counties, Indiana* (1880), p. 448.

LYNN, WILLIAM H. (1840?–1883)

William Lynn was born in Crawfordsville in about 1840, the son of Lucinda McConnell and James W. Lynn. He had two younger sisters, Margaret and Mary.

Lynn entered the Preparatory Department of Wabash in the autumn of 1853 and remained until 1856. He then joined his father in a grocery business on Green Street before securing a commission as a first lieutenant of Company K of the Eighty-Sixth Indiana Regiment on 23 August 1862. He saw action at the Battle of Perryville before moving on to Tennessee, but because of poor health he had to resign at Nashville on 30 November 1862 in spite of a three-year commitment.

Returning to Crawfordsville he resumed his involvement in the grocery store business and became quite successful. On 2 January 1878 he married Marie Lizzie Heath, but they apparently had no children.

Lynn died on 16 December 1883, survived by his widow, and was buried in Oak Hill Cemetery alongside his mother and father.

References: H. W. Beckwith, *History of Montgomery County* (1881), pp. 39, 231,

376; *History of Montgomery County* (Bowen & Co., 1913), p. 99; and *Saturday Evening Journal* of Crawfordsville, 22 December 1883; Oak Hill Cemetery, Crawfordsville.

LYNN, WILLIAM H. H. (1838–?)

William H. H. Lynn (his name is subject to confusion with William H. Lynn, the previous entry) was born in Indiana in 1838, one of eleven children of Mary Webb and James Lynn. His siblings were Elizabeth, Rebecca, Minerva, Martha, Melinda, Jackson, James, Levi, John, and Sophronia.

Lynn spent two years, 1860–62, at Wabash College as a sophomore and a junior. Prior to this he was a laborer on his father's farm. Between his first and second year, he fit three months of military service into his schedule, enrolling at Lafayette on 17 April 1861 in Company A of the Tenth Indiana Regiment.

On 6 May 1864 he enlisted as a sergeant for one hundred days in Company I of the 138th Regiment and subsequently disappeared. He may have departed from Indiana without leaving any trace of where he had relocated.

References: F. Bash, *History of Huntington County, Indiana* (1914), I, 199; *Wabash Magazine*, IV (July 1863), p. 254; Huntington Public Library.

LYON, THOMAS VALENTINE (1841–1902)

Thomas Lyon was born in Owen County on 19 January 1841, one of thirteen children of Mary Payne and Valentine Lyon. His mother died in 1853, and his father then married Zerelda Myers, who gave birth to seven children.

On 16 September 1861 Lyon joined the federal volunteers as a musician in Company E of the Thirty-Third Indiana Regiment at Indianapolis, and his military service seemed to have lasted until early 1862, when a combination of ailments made him unfit to continue in the army. On 27 April he was formally discharged at Lexington, Kentucky.

Lyon seems to have taken up teaching until good health returned, and then on 2 January 1864 at Indianapolis, he joined the Twentieth Light Artillery, initially as a bugler. He also helped to recruit new soldiers. That summer the battery went to Bridgeport, Alabama, but he again experienced various problems and ended up in the hospital, eventually becoming a hospital steward before mustering out at Indianapolis on 23 June 1865.

In 1866 or 1867 he married Minerva Virginia. By 1868 they were living in Manhattan, Kansas, where their first child, Harry Clay, was born. Their other children were all born in Riley County, Kansas: May Belle in Manhattan in 1870; Thomas (1872) and Minnie Eva (1875) in Fairview Farm; Frank, purportedly in Lamoille Post Office in 1882; and Fred (1886) in Grant Township.

The Lyons moved in about 1895 to Fayetteville, Arkansas, where Thomas died on 22 October 1902. He was survived by his wife, who relocated to Idaho Falls and died on 17 June 1924.

References: A descendant of Thomas, Jack Lyon of Greencastle, Indiana; military pension file, National Archives, Washington, DC; *Fayetteville Democrat*, 30 October 1902; Greencastle Public Library; Ozarks Regional Library of Fayetteville, Arkansas.

Artillery was not for sissies...
From the diary of Henry Campbell "Three Years in the Saddle"

On the 12th day of July 1862 young Henry Campbell, along with several Crawfordsville friends, joined a new artillery battery just being organized at Greencastle. Campbell, only 16, was a prep student at Wabash College where his father, John Paxton Campbell was a trustee. As was the fashion of the time, young Campbell decided to keep a journal of his wartime experiences. Unlike so many others, he stayed with it. His record of his three years' service is one of Indiana's great archival treasures. It is now an online project called "Three Years in the Saddle."
The very first entry captures Campbell's youthful enthusiasm for the war.
—Beth Swift, Wabash Archivist

July 12 to August 8, 1862
Enrolled my name in the U.S. Volunteer Service, on the 12 day of July 1862. Aged 16...Enlisted as a private in the 18th Indiana Battery, Eli Lilly Captain. Headquarters at Greencastle Indiana. Left Crawfordsville...for Greencastle in company with the following boys from town James Binford, Fred Sperry, Martin J. Miller, Albert Crawford, Gus Newell, Chas Butcher, James Johnson, Perry Sheppard and Wm. Scott...Received at Greencastle by Captain Lilly, a young looking person with a "summer" mustache...Went to Indianapolis next day drew tents and encamped at Camp Morton. Joined in the evening by detachments from all parts of the country. Battery filling up rapidly more tents and more recruits daily...Crawfordsville boys all furloughed for one week. Gay time at home, left Home forever, never expecting to live through the hardship I shall have to endure bid everybody farewell with a stout heart.

Back at camp Battery organized and drilling. Appointed 2d Bugler a fellow named Anderson 1st. Crawfordsville boys all tent together 18 in one tent, weather hot, Medical examination Aug 6 all passed but myself refused on account of my age, too young thought I was gone sure but Captain Lilly told the Dr. that I was intended for his bugler and that it was "essential to the interests of the service" &c that

235

I should be retained which was finally done. All of mess Number 1 (ours) drowned out last night. Haven't learned the art of ditching our tents yet."

August 21, 1863 I was sitting down just in front of Number 5's gun watching the effects of the shot with the captain's glass. Number 6 had just fired their gun, and at the same instant exactly that the report of our gun rang out through the air and while everyone's attention was engrossed in watching the shot strike, the Rebels fired a shot from a 32 lb James Rifle that they had been mounting during the time they were silent in the large fort direct in our front. The shell whizzed over my head under the axle of Number 5 striking the ground near the trail just at the spot where Corporal McCorkle was lying asleep, cutting his leg entirely off below the knee, ricocheting, struck the right lead horse of the limber, square in the breast passed entirely through him endways, striking the next horse just above the chest, passing clear through hitting the next horse in the throat, splitting his backbone from one end to the other making its exit just above the tail, the wheel horse in the rear of this horse escaped by having his head down close to the ground eating grass. But unfortunately for his mate, the near wheel horse, he had his head around in rear of the off swing horse and the shell struck him in the side of the head, just below his ears carrying his brains entirely out, then passed over the caisson, struck a tree and fell to the ground. The horses were killed so suddenly that their mate never moved. The harness of the lead horse was driven clear through his body.

McCorkle was carried in a blanket to an ambulance and sent back to Poe's Tavern where after lingering a few days, he died and was buried in the valley of Chickamauga the first victim of the 18th Battery. Just as the shot came over, we received orders to limber up and move down in the valley to find a camping place for the night. Had this order come 5 minutes sooner, it would have saved us 1 man and 4 horses. We moved down the valley about 5 miles and camped on the left side of the road near the foot of Waldon's Ridge.

From Archivist Beth Swift...

The frequent diary entries allow the reader to follow this boy as he learns about life in the army and death on the battlefield. As a part of an artillery unit serving in the hills and mountains of east Tennessee, Campbell and his fellow soldiers struggle to haul the cannons through the mountains. The deprivations of an army on the march leave Campbell and his fellow soldiers

> *oftentimes hungry and frequently cold. We learn a lot about these men in the 18th Indiana Artillery, inluding Captain Eli Lilly who returned from the Civil War and started a pharmaceutical company now one of the largest in the world. We learn that Lilly was a man of clear vision and high principles who took young Campbell under his wing and taught him about soldiering.*
>
> *Wabash has a valuable and interesting collection of time-sequenced maps of the Chatanooga area battlefields, centering on Chicamauga. Obtained by George Davis of the Wabash faculty, these maps are in Baxter Hall.*

MACE, EDWARD H. (1841–1877)

Edward Mace was born on 20 November 1841 in Lafayette, Indiana, one of two sons of Mary and Daniel Mace. His father had enrolled briefly at Wabash College in December 1834 but withdrew in January 1835 to study law privately in Crawfordsville. He served in both the Indiana House of Representatives and the U.S. House of Representatives.

The young man was most likely in the Preparatory Department in the late 1850s, but he may have left the college precipitously as his father had and therefore was not credited with being a student. Other sources indicate that he was enrolled at some point and then served in the Civil War. The 1860 census for Lafayette indicates that he was studying law.

In 1860 he enlisted in Company E of the Tenth Indiana Regiment for three months on 18 April 1861. However, on 14 June, before his regiment headed east, he was listed as absent without leave and owed the state of Indiana for his military kit.

On 24 October 1861 Mace was allowed to join the regular army as a second lieutenant of the First Infantry. He was promoted to a first lieutenant on 25 April 1862 and to captain sometime later. He was discharged on 28 May 1864.

Returning to Lafayette, he may have practiced law. On 13 April 1867, he married Henrietta Cumpsten in Warren County. Their only son, William D., was born the following year.

According to the 1870 census, Mace was living in a hotel, with no wife listed, and in the 1872 and 1874 city directories for Lafayette, an E. H. Mace is a lodger on North Fourth Street.

On 5 June 1877 Mace remarried Henrietta Mace in Tippecanoe County. He died two weeks later on 19 June, leaving a complicated will that was contested by the family. He was buried in Greenbush Cemetery.

References: R.P. Dehart, *Past and Present of Tippecanoe County, Indiana* (1909), p. 169; *Biographical Directory of the Indiana General Assembly*, I (1980), p. 257; *Williamsport Republican*, 1 August 1867; Ms. Van Cleef of the Tippecanoe County Historical Association.

MANN, GUSTAVUS A. (1837–1882)

Gustavus Mann was born in Indiana on 21 September 1837, one of two sons of Catherine and Samuel Mann, a prosperous butcher. His brother's name was Horace.

By 1850 the family lived in Terre Haute, and Mann was enrolled in the Preparatory Department at Wabash for the 1851–52 school year.

On 1 November 1861 Mann enrolled for three years as a sergeant in Company H of the Second Cavalry, attached to the Forty-First Regiment. In April 1861 he was demoted to private for some reason, but he completed his commitment and was mustered out at Indianapolis on 4 October 1864.

Mann's career is shrouded in mystery. On his grave marker he is referred to as Dr. Gus, which suggests that he was a physician, although there is no corroborating evidence to this effect. However, it is clear that he had a serious drinking problem and died of alcohol abuse on 10 May 1882. He is buried near his father in Woodlawn Cemetery, Terre Haute.

References: David N. Lewis of the Vigo County Public Library; *Terre Haute Evening Gazette*, 12 May 1882 and 26 January 1892; *Terre Haute Express*, 12 May 1882.

MARSHALL, CHARLES HENRY (1823–1872)

Charles Marshall was born on 11 March 1823 in Dunbarton, New Hampshire, the youngest of nine children of Betsey Goodhue and Benjamin Marshall. His older sister, Sarah, married Caleb Mills, the first faculty member at Wabash College, who also came from Dunbarton.

Marshall graduated with a bachelor of arts degree in June 1844 after spending six years at Wabash. During that time he decided to dedicate his life to the Christian ministry and sought professional training at Yale Divinity School, Andover Seminary, and Lane Theological Seminary. He was ordained in 1849. During these years he apparently married, had two children, and lost his wife. His second marriage to Almira C. Twining of Crawfordsville took place in 1851.

In the following decade, Marshall had parishes in Salem and Lafayette, Indiana; Hudson, Wisconsin; and Jacksonville, Illinois. In 1862 he was called to the prestigious Fourth Presbyterian Church of Indianapolis.

He wished to join the Civil War when others left to go to the front. In the summer of 1864 he became chaplain to the 132nd Indiana Volunteers during their one hundred days of service in Tennessee and Alabama.

Toward the end of the 1860s, Marshall began to show the unmistakable signs of consumption, and on a Sunday in June 1870 he preached his last sermon at Fourth Church. Soon thereafter, he sought a better climate for his health in California, but the travel wearied him, and he eventually returned to Indianapolis, where he died on 27 January 1872. He was buried in Crown Hill Cemetery.

At his funeral the eulogist spoke of how much the minister had been influenced by his years at Wabash College under President White: "I am told that the cast and direction of his life, as far as human influence goes, were largely due to the instruction and inspiration and formation of President White. The pupil admired and fairly adored this great teacher and preacher."

References: *History of the Town of Dumbarton, Merrimack County, New Hampshire* (1860), p. 253; *Wabash Magazine*, XI (March 1872), p. 136; *Wabash Magazine*, XII (June 1872), p. 218; *Indianapolis Sentinel*, 30 and 31 January 1872; *Indianapolis Journal*, 29 January 1872.

MARTIN, THOMAS A. (1842–1926)

Thomas Martin was born on 9 November 1842 in Belmont County, Ohio, the son of Sarah McBride and Robert Martin. His parents settled on farmland in Boone County, Indiana, in about 1844, and young Martin took an active part in the family enterprise until joining the Normal School of Wabash College in 1860–61.

In 1862 he enlisted at Lafayette in Company G of the Seventy-Second Indiana Regiment. By June 1863 his unit was converted to mounted infantry that became a part of John T. Wilder's Lightning Brigade, which fought in Tennessee at Hoover's Gap, Chickamauga, and Murfreesboro. In the summer of 1864, they were among the many forces that laid siege to Atlanta, and after it fell the regiment obtained new horses at Louisville and rode to Nashville, then Selma and Montgomery, Alabama, and finally to Columbus, Georgia. Martin was mustered out at Indianapolis on 6 July 1865.

For a while Martin returned to the family farm and worked at a sawmill. He also taught school, presumably in Boone County. In 1868 he moved to Liberty Township of Daviess County, Missouri, and acquired some farmland, but within a year he returned to Boone County and married Nancy J. Rude on 5 October 1869. They eventually had nine children: Bertha, Eva, Addie, Thomas, Thaddeus, Hugh, Ora, Chauncey, and Charles.

Soon after their marriage, the Martins departed for Missouri and acquired 120 additional acres in Liberty Township, where they cultivated a large orchard of fruit trees. Martin also specialized in breeding shorthorn cattle. For the next forty years they lived on their successful farm until they moved into the town of Gallatin, where Martin died on 29 September 1926. He was buried in Brown Cemetery.

References: John and Buell Leonard, *History of Daviess and Gentry Counties, Missouri* (1922), pp. 412–14; *History of Daviess County, Missouri* (1888), p. 777; *Gallatin North Missourian*, 30 September 1926, p. 1; *Gallatin Democrat*, 5 October 1926.

MASTERSON, WILLIAM S. (1845–1876)

William Masterson was born in Indiana, probably in Crawfordsville, in about 1845, the son of Calvin Masterson, a carpenter. He had a much younger brother, Charles, born in 1857. The family ran a boarding house in Crawfordsville during the 1860s and early 1870s.

Masterson spent two years, 1859–61, in the Normal School of Wabash College. On 28 April 1864 he enrolled for one hundred days in Company D of the 135th Indiana Regiment, whose main duty was to guard railroad lines in Tennessee and Alabama. He was mustered out at Indianapolis on 29 September 1864 and returned to Wabash for a year to study in the English Department.

In 1870 he was still in Crawfordsville, living with his parents and younger brother. However, soon thereafter he went to Washington, DC, as a printer at the *Congressional Record*.

In July 1876 he took seriously ill and decided to move back to Crawfordsville. He died at home on Walnut Street on 31 August 1876, survived by his wife and two children. He is buried in the Masonic Cemetery.

References: Census records; *Saturday Evening Journal* (Crawfordsville), 2 September 1876.

MATTINGLY, CHARLES THOMAS (1845–1919)

Charles Mattingly was born in Corydon, Indiana, on 6 October 1845, the third of seven children of Rachel T. Barnes and Ignatius Mattingly. In 1856 the family moved to Plymouth, where his father was publisher of the *Marshall County Republican*.

On 26 April 1864 Mattingly enlisted in a newly formed regiment, the 138th Indiana Volunteers, for one hundred days. He was back home by September in time to enter Wabash College for the academic year 1864–65 to study in the English Department. The following year he transferred to Oberlin College, where he pursued a commercial curriculum.

In 1866 Mattingly married Evalin L. Paine, and their only child, Ralph, was born in 1880.

He became a partner in the lumber business of Oglesbee, Mattingly and Black in Plymouth in 1867 and later went on to acquire timber companies in Tennessee and Alabama and to speculate in properties in Chicago and other cities. He also invested in 680 acres of farmland near his father in Bourbon, Indiana, where he made a specialty of raising purebred shorthorn cattle. In 1892 he helped found the Plymouth State Bank and served as a director as well as president from 1914 to 1918. His son Ralph assumed responsibility for the Indiana Lumber Company of Nashville, Tennessee, where Mattingly was visiting when he died on 27 January 1919.

References: *Plymouth Democrat*, 30 January 1919; *Plymouth Weekly Republican*, 30 January 1919; 1860, 1870, 1880, and 1900 U.S. census for Plymouth.

MAXWELL, SAMUEL CAMPBELL (1840–1900)

Samuel Maxwell was born on 2 October 1840 in Crawfordsville, the son of Isaphena McCullough and Harvey Henderson Maxwell, who were also the parents of Mary, born four years later. His mother was an older sister of James H. McCullough, also a Wabash College Civil War soldier.

From 1858 to 1860 Maxwell was enrolled in the Normal School of Wabash College. He then spent two more years (1860–62) at the Ladoga Academy, studying science and classics.

In the summer of 1862, he enrolled in Company C of the Seventy-Second Indiana Regiment as a corporal, but while stationed at Lebanon, Kentucky, he was discharged on account of an unspecified medical disability. A year later he joined the Montgomery Light Guards Company, a unit of the Indiana Legion, and was its captain for about a year.

During 1863–64 Maxwell studied medicine with Dr. J. B. Wilson of Ladoga, Montgomery County, and received his medical degree from Rush Medical College in Chicago in 1866.

On 20 June 1865 Maxwell married Jennie Parker, and eventually their family included three girls and two boys, some of whom were Grace, Blanche, Mate, and James. The Maxwells moved to Fowler, where Maxwell practiced medicine and also edited the *Benton County Herald*. Then in 1874 they relocated to Remington in Jasper County, where Maxwell treated patients throughout the neighboring counties of Newton, White, and Benton for fourteen years.

In 1888 the family moved to Duluth, Minnesota, where Maxwell contracted Bright's disease in 1900. He went to California in hopes that the climate would help, but when it was clear that he was failing, he returned to Minnesota and died in Duluth on 13 May 1900.

References: L. C. Blaine et al., *Maxwell History and Genealogy* (1916), pp. 134–37; *Biographical History of Eminent and Self-Made Men of the State of Indiana* (1880), II, p. 28; *Duluth Herald*, 14 May 1900; *History of the Town of Remington, Jasper County, Indiana* (1894), pp. 31, 69, 102–09; Remington-Carpenter Township Public Library.

McCLUNG, JAMES H. JR. (1834–1899)

James McClung Jr. was born on 7 February 1834 in New Albany, Indiana, the younger of two sons of Mary Collins and James H. McClung Sr. His older brother was Samuel A. McClung.

In about 1850 young James took a job as a journeyman printer until he enrolled in the Preparatory Department of Wabash College for one academic year,

1853–54. He then bought a half share with his stepfather, W. H. Green, in the *Connersville Times*. He married Clarissa Goodland on 27 August 1856, and they eventually had three children: William, Mary, and Charles.

The family moved to nearby Liberty, where McClung acquired and became editor of the *Liberty Herald* until the war intervened.

On 17 September 1861 McClung was appointed an orderly sergeant in the Thirty-Sixth Indiana Regiment. He was five feet nine inches tall, with brown hair, grey eyes, and a fair complexion. At the age of twenty-seven, he was older than many of the new inductees and was promoted rapidly to second lieutenant of Company G in February 1862, first lieutenant in April 1862, and captain in March 1863. The Thirty-Sixth saw action at Shiloh, Stones River or Murfreesboro, Chickamauga, Lookout Mountain, and Missionary Ridge. On 26 January 1864 McClung resigned at Tyners Station, Tennessee, because of unstipulated family reasons.

In 1867 he sold his interest in the *Liberty Herald* and purchased a new paper, the *Connersville News*, which later merged with the *Connersville Times*. The 1870 census also listed his occupation as lumberman.

The McClungs resided in Liberty until about 1880, when they moved to the town of Wabash where McClung published the *Plain Dealer*. He and his son Charles purchased the *Muncie Daily and Weekly Times* in October 1887, and soon another son, William, was also working for the paper. Charles died suddenly in 1897, followed by his father on 4 February 1899. McClung was buried in Beech Grove Cemetery in Muncie.

References: Muncie Public Library; *Portrait and Biographical Record of Delaware County, Indiana* (1894), pp. 353–54; *Muncie Daily Herald*, 4 and 6 February 1899; *Muncie Daily Times*, 4 February 1899; *Muncie Daily News*, 5 February 1899; *Muncie Star*, 16 March 1916; military pension file, National Archives, Washington, DC.

McCONNELL, IRA (1842–1919)

In 1905 Wabash College sent a questionnaire to its former students who had graduated with a bachelor of arts degree. Among this select group was Ira McConnell, who indicated on his questionnaire that he had spent recent years in a hospital and was currently living in Michigan City, Indiana. He neglected to mention that he was an inmate of the state penitentiary.

Ira McConnell was born in Cedarville, Ohio, on 28 October 1842, the oldest of eight children of Eliza Beemer (1818–1884) and Robert McConnell (1810–1879), a farmer and carriage maker. His siblings were Sarah, James, Robert, Fernando, Louisa, Joseph, and Joda. In 1848 the family moved to Jay County, Indiana, but when Ira was sixteen years old, he went back to Ohio and worked on a farm near Xenia for a year. Then he joined his uncle William in Thorntown, Indiana, to help with the farming there.

When McConnell joined the army on 28 November 1863, he indicated that his home was in Fairview. At Winchester he signed up for three years as a sergeant in of Company G of the 124th Indiana Regiment. He later reckoned that he had participated in thirteen battles, including Buzzard's Roost, Georgia (7–8 May 1864), Resaca, Sherman's march on Atlanta, and Nashville under General George H. Thomas in late December 1864. He served until well after the war was over and was mustered out on 31 August 1865.

Following the war McConnell spent three years (1866–69) in the Preparatory Department of Wabash College, followed by four more (1869–73) in the Classical Course, indicating that his home during these years was in Muncie. Following graduation he returned to Muncie to begin studying law. He was admitted to the Indiana bar in 1875 and was ready to start practicing in Crawfordsville where he married Hettie D. Powers. They eventually had one son, Frederick.

In the late 1870s he suspended his law practice in order to take up civil engineering. For a few years he was Montgomery County surveyor and then went into business for himself, becoming an expert in the construction of gravel roads. He was also named manager of the Crawfordsville Water Works.

On the surface, McConnell was an upstanding member of the Crawfordsville community, but his family and neighbors observed that he was becoming progressively more violent. As one newspaper wrote, "He slept with a knife under his pillow and ate with a revolver beside his plate. As a result, the members of his household have lived in constant terror." On the evening of 30 November 1900, McConnell returned home in a foul mood. While his wife and their son, Fred, put his horse in the barn, Ira came out of the house brandishing his revolver. He threatened to kill them, and when they ran to escape, he shot twice in their direction. Hettie blew out the lamp she was carrying and hid. Ira ran back into the house and began beating a woman he thought was his wife, but she turned out to be a neighbor. When the sheriff arrived and arrested him, McConnell asked in bewilderment why he was being hauled off to jail.

On 18 March 1901 the case came before the circuit court, and the prosecutor made much of McConnell's pattern of abuse and anger. Fred testified that he and his mother "were compelled at times to stay all night at neighbors as he [McConnell] would lock them out of the house; once they stayed in the college campus until after midnight." It is not known just how long McConnell was at the penitentiary in Michigan City, but eventually he returned to Crawfordsville.

In late February 1919 he fell ill and secured admission to the hospital attached to the soldiers home at Danville, Illinois, where he died on 1 April.

References: *Wabash Magazine*, XII (July 1873), p. 168; alumni directories of Phi Delta Theta; *Wabash Record*, July 1919, p. 56; *Danville Morning Press*, 3 April 1919; *Danville Commercial News*, 2 April 1919; *Crawfordsville Journal and Review*, 18 and 22 December 1943; *Crawfordsville Daily News Review*, 4 February 1901; *Crawfordsville Weekly News Review*, 1 December 1900, 23 and 30 March 1901.

McCORD, WILLIAM A. (1840–1922)

The father of our subject, William M. McCord, was born in Virginia in 1796, and in 1827 in Crawfordsville he married Rebecca Jones, a native of Ohio who was eight years his junior. Later that year the couple moved to a farm two miles south of Delphi. At that time there were only seventeen families in this area of Carroll County and a mere one hundred acres were under cultivation.

Between the years 1828 and 1846, the couple became the parents of eight children: Agnes, Mary, Louise, James, Elizabeth, William, Rebecca, and Eunice. William McCord was born on the family farm on 8 May 1840. His mother died in 1856, and two years later young William made his way to Crawfordsville and to the Normal School of Wabash College.

McCord remained for two years at the college and then, in the summer of 1860, returned to work on the family farm. He pursued these efforts for years to come, with only a brief interruption for military service. On 10 May 1864 he mustered into Company C of the 135th Indiana Regiment. At that time he was described as being five feet eleven inches tall, with a dark complexion, hazel eyes, and black hair. He soon found himself along with other recruits guarding railway lines in Kentucky and Tennessee. The regiment ended up in the latter state when their one hundred days of service were up, and they were formally discharged in Indianapolis on 29 September 1864. Then it was back to the family farm for McCord.

On 10 June 1874 in Carroll County he married Margaretta Galleway, but she died on 7 May 1875 giving birth to their son, George. Since McCord's father had died the previous February, he was left very much alone with his infant son. Fortunately, one of his sisters came to keep house for them.

McCord was still farming when the census taker came around in 1880. Thereafter, for twenty years, his whereabouts are uncertain. The 1900 census shows that George, now age twenty-five, was a telephone inspector in Fremont City, Dodge County, Nebraska. William was also residing in Kearney, Buffalo County, Nebraska, a lodger with his sister, Rebecca, and his brother-in-law, Francis Hamer.

Ten years later McCord was still in Buffalo County but no longer living with his relatives. Soon thereafter he moved to Redondo Beach, Los Angeles County, California, where he died on 12 March 1922.

References: Carroll County Historical Society Museum; Buffalo County (Nebraska) Historical Society Archives; James H. Stewart, *Recollections of the Early Settlement of Carroll County, Indiana* (1872), pp. 20, 27, 57; *Delphi Journal*, 17 February 1875.

McCORKLE, THOMAS HALL (1845–1910)

Thomas McCorkle was born in Thorntown, Indiana, on 4 November 1845, one of seven children of Jane Higgins and Samuel E. McCorkle, a blacksmith. His uncle, William McCorkle, attended Wabash in the early 1840s.

Before the war McCorkle worked as a saddler and was described as being five feet six inches tall, with grey eyes, brown hair. and a fair complexion. In July 1863 he joined Company H of the 102nd Indiana Regiment during Morgan's Raid. Having initially served only eight days, he committed himself to three years' military service in Company D of the Seventy-Second Regiment on 4 January 1864 at Indianapolis. Within a couple of months he was made bugler for the Third Brigade of the Second Cavalry, and in July 1865 he was transferred into Company D of the Forty-Fourth Indiana Regiment. He was mustered out at Nashville on 14 September 1865.

After the war McCorkle spent two years, 1866–68, in the Preparatory Department of Wabash College. He then set about becoming a doctor, studying medicine at the Ohio Medical College in Cincinnati, before settling in Cloverland and establishing a practice there. On 22 December 1877 he married Sarah Gertrude Hawkins of Putnam County.

During 1878–79 he returned to the Ohio Medical College for further training and then returned to Clay County. In 1882 he and his wife moved to Ellsworth, Otter Creek Township, Vigo County, where they remained for the next several decades. In about 1903 the McCorkles moved to Alabama for the sake of McCorkle's health, but they eventually returned to Terre Haute, where he died on 22 March 1910. He is buried in Forest Hill Cemetery, Greencastle.

References: *Journal of the Indiana State Medical Association*, III (April 1910), p. 181; *History of Vigo County, Indiana* (1891), p. 632; *Terre Haute Tribune*, 23 March 1910; *Wabash Magazine*, XII (January 1872), p. 76; alumni catalogues of the Beta Theta Pi fraternity; David N. Lewis of the Vigo County Public Library.

McCOY, THEODORE WILBURFORCE (1839–1896)

Theodore McCoy was born in Decatur County on 31 January 1839, the son of Margaret and James McCoy, a Presbyterian minister. He had one brother, W. N. McCoy, and perhaps two sisters, Mahala and M. E. McCoy.

McCoy came to Wabash as a freshman in the fall of 1856 and stayed for his sophomore year, 1857–1858. He then seems to have studied law in Indianapolis and been admitted to the bar on the eve of the Civil War.

On 23 April 1861 he joined Company I of the Sixth Indiana Regiment for three months, and as soon as this duty was over, he signed up for three years in Company I of the Thirty-Ninth Indiana Volunteer Infantry. Whereas previously he had been a corporal, he was now a second lieutenant. He received promotions to first lieutenant on 3 November 1861 and to captain on 23 May 1862, resigning, presumably for medical reasons, on 1 September 1862 at Stevenson, Alabama.

During the war McCoy apparently maintained a law office in Jeffersonville in partnership with Dr. Flower, and afterwards the Republicans elected him the official reporter for the Indiana Supreme Court. From 1868 to 1872 he served as the court's clerk.

In about 1870 McCoy married Eliza Taggart, and they had three children: Theodora or Dora (1871–1952); Margaret or Maggie (1877–1951); and William T. (1874–1956).

Eventually, he became a Presbyterian minister and moved to Hanover, having done missionary work on the west coast at Puget Sound. His last pastorate was at Salem, beginning in 1894. McCoy died at Hanover on 1 August 1896.

References: *The Hoosier Genealogist*, XXXVI (September 1996), p. 174; L. J. Monks, *Courts and Lawyers of Indiana*, I (1916), p. 306; *Madison Daily Courier*, 3 and 4 August 1896; Register of the Hanover Presbyterian Church; *Bulletin of Hanover College* (December 1938), Duggan Library, Hanover College.

McCULLOUGH, IRVIN A. (1832–1911)

Irvin McCullough was born on 4 August 1832 on a three-hundred-acre farm in Montgomery County, Indiana. He was one of twelve children of Margaret Maxwell and James Brown McCullough. An older brother, James, also attended Wabash and served in the Civil War.

McCullough studied in the Normal School for one year, 1855–56, and on 28 May 1857 he married Angelina Catt in Crawfordsville. The young couple then farmed in Benton County for several years before he enrolled as a sergeant for three years in the Indiana Fifth Cavalry, a unit attached to the Ninetieth Regiment, on 16 August 1862. He was described as five feet ten inches tall, with blue eyes, light hair, and fair complexion. He reported for duty at Indianapolis on 8 October of that year. He was promoted to the rank of first lieutenant in March 1864 at Mount Sterling, Kentucky, and was mustered out at Pulaski, Tennessee, on 15 June 1865.

By 1888 the family was living in Pratt, Kansas, and Angelina had given birth to at least eleven children before she died on 19 July 1890.

On 1 March 1900 McCullough married Mrs. Rachael Hamilton, a widow. They subsequently moved to San Antonio, Texas, where he died on 30 December 1911 and was buried in San Antonio National Cemetery.

References: In addition to information relating to his older brother, James, material for Irvin may be found in: H. W. Beckwith, *History of Montgomery County* (1881), p. 40 and a military pension file at the National Archives in Washington, DC.

McCULLOUGH, JAMES HUGHES (1829–1920)

James McCullough was born on the family farm about two and a half miles from Crawfordsville on 20 November 1829. His parents were Margaret Maxwell (1795–1862) and James Brown McCullough (1788–1868), a farmer and saloon owner. James was the eighth of their twelve children. His younger brother, Irvin, as was seen in the previous biography, also attended Wabash and served in the Civil War.

From 1852 to 1854 McCullough was enrolled in the Scientific Course of Wabash, and he continued for another year as a freshman. In the autumn of 1855, his younger brother, Irvin, followed in his footsteps to the college.

On 19 April 1861 at Ladoga, McCullough enrolled in Company G of the Eleventh Indiana Regiment for three months. These were spent mostly in western Virginia, and he was mustered out at Indianapolis on 4 August.

In the fall of 1861, he registered as a freshman at Northwestern Christian University of Indianapolis, later known as Butler University. He graduated in June 1865.

McCullough married twice. His first wife, Clarissa Shortridge, died in 1860 while giving birth to their son, Clarence. His second marriage to Kittie Latham took place in Springfield, Illinois, and they had two sons, Maxwell and James H. Jr.

McCullough became a pastor in the Disciples of Christ church. Beginning in 1866, he served the Christian church in Terre Haute for ten years, often as an evangelist in neighboring counties. Then he ministered successively to parishes in Rushville; Dayton, Ohio; and Quincy and Bloomington, Illinois.

From 1877 to 1882 he had a church in San Francisco, and he was president of Washington College in Irvington, California, an institution affiliated with the Disciples of Christ, from 1882 to 1887. At some point he was also a pastor of a church in Santa Clara.

In the 1890s McCullough retired from the ministry and settled first on a fruit farm near Irvington and in 1907 in San Jose, where he died on 15 September 1920.

References: H. W. Beckwith, *History of Montgomery County* (1881); F. W. Houston, *Maxwell History and Genealogy* (1916); *Butler University Alumni Quarterly* (1891–1892); *San Jose Mercury*, 16 and 20 September 1920; *History of the Disciples of Christ in California* (1916), p. 302.

McCUNE, WALLACE W. (1839–1907)

Wallace McCune was born in Mecca, Indiana, on 17 March 1839, one of six children of Rosilla and Alexander McCune. His father arrived in Parke County in 1832 and built a sawmill on the site that became the town of Mecca.

Wallace's siblings were Henry, Mary, Benjamin, Samuel, and Horace.

McCune attended the Waveland Academy prior to enrolling in the Preparatory Department of Wabash in 1858. He then spent two years at the college.

In July 1862 he helped organize Company G of the Seventy-First Indiana Volunteer Infantry and on 8 August was commissioned captain of his company. The regiment went immediately to Kentucky, and the raw recruits were thrown into the Battle of Richmond a scant twelve days later. Company G suffered heavy casualties, with six killed and fifteen wounded. Most of the regiment was taken captive, but within a short time they were paroled and allowed to proceed to Terre Haute, where a reorganization of the regiment took place. McCune thought that he should be promoted to lieutenant colonel, and when this did not happen, he resigned on 20 December 1862.

On 19 June 1863 McCune married Sophronia I. Steele, the daughter of General George K. Steele, a partner with his father in the Parke County Bank of Rockville. Their children included Mary, Sallie, Katie, Ross, George, Charles, and Isabel.

After the war McCune returned to Parke County and acquired a farm where he raised livestock and traded in grain, since his father had given up his mill and land in 1860.

Sophronia died in 1880, but McCune remained in Rockville for another decade before moving to the Marion branch of the National Home for Disabled Volunteer Soldiers, where he died on 29 August 1907. He was buried in Dayton, Ohio, where his daughter, Mrs. Kate Newstock, resided.

References: *Parke Place*, II (April 1982), p. 19; I. Strouse, *Centennial Memorial* (1916), p. 80; *History of Parke and Vermillion Counties, Indiana* (1913), pp. 79-85; H. W. Beckwith, *History of Parke and Vigo Counties, Indiana* (1880), pp. 81, 123, 486; *Rockville Republican*, 4 September 1907, p. 1; *Rockville Tribune*, 4 September 1907, p. 8.

McDONALD, AARON ALEXANDER (1835–1907)

Aaron McDonald was born in Vermilion County, Illinois, on 24 January 1835, the older son of Catherine and Alexander McDonald. His younger brother by two years was Milton; their father was a successful farmer. When McDonald entered the Preparatory Department of Wabash College in the fall of 1854, he indicated that his home was Georgetown, Illinois. The following year he became a freshman in the Classical Course of study and completed one more year (1856–57) as a sophomore.

In 1860 he was a schoolteacher in Georgetown, and by 1862 he lived and worked in Pontiac before enrolling in Company D of the 125th Illinois Volunteers on 10 August for three years. At the time he was five feet six inches tall, with light hair, fair complexion, and blue eyes. In early May 1863 his regimental surgeon noted that he had "never been fit for field service, and done very little duty of any kind. He is predisposed to consumption, and now very much affected with it. Disease hereditary in the family." Consequently, McDonald received a formal honorable discharge at Nashville, Tennessee, on 4 May 1863.

On 29 September 1864 he married Sarah Alexander at Cincinnati, and they settled in Danville, Illinois, where they became well established in the community. McDonald and his brother, Milton, went into business together as McDonald and Brothers.

In 1888, while trying to hang a gate, a piece of metal struck him in the right eye and deprived him of sight in that eye. He was much affected by the accident, according to his doctor: "The nervous system was badly shattered at the time of his injury from shock and subsequent physical and mental suffering and has never recovered its 'tone' as manifest in a certain weakness of voice, wavering of step, indecision of action, and uncertainty in method not at all characteristic of the man known to us previous to 1888...."

After thirty-two years the McDonalds left Danville for California and settled in San Diego, where McDonald proposed growing fruit as he had in Illinois. He died there on 31 July 1907.

References: *History of Livingston County, Illinois* (1878), p. 388; *Danville Commercial*, 25 April 1878; Danville (Illinois) Public Library; military pension file, National Archives, Washington, DC.

McDONALD, ARCHIBALD H. (1836–1900)

Archibald McDonald was born in Schenectady, New York, in 1836. His father's name is unknown. His mother, Charlotte, was a widow in 1860 and was both deaf and blind. Archibald and his siblings, Charlotte and Orange, looked after her.

In the fall of 1853, the young man entered the Preparatory Department of Wabash College, staying one academic year. According to the college catalogue, his home was in Danville, Illinois, but this may be an error, since there was another student from Illinois with similar initials, Aaron A. McDonald. More likely, he was from Logansport, Indiana.

When the McDonald family moved from Logansport to Rochester in 1859, Archibald was a printer and founded the *Rochester Sentinel*.

On 2 July 1861 he enrolled in Company A of the Twenty-Sixth Indiana Regiment as a sergeant for three years, although eventually he served for nearly five. Promotions came at regular intervals: second lieutenant on 11 February 1862; first lieutenant, 4 August 1863; and captain, 30 August 1864. On 7 December 1862 he was wounded at the Battle of Prairie Grove, Arkansas. The battle was confusing and indecisive, with Confederates and Federals having about ten thousand troops on each side; both sustained more than one thousand dead and wounded. While a first lieutenant, he was detached from his unit in February

1864 and sent to Brownsville, Texas, to recruit fresh troops, and on 31 August 1865 he went to Louisiana for similar duty. On 7 March 1866 he mustered out while stationed at New Orleans.

McDonald settled in Logansport after the war and went into the grocery business in partnership with B. O. Spencer. Eventually he bought out his partner and ran the store on his own. For three years he was bookkeeper and manager of Dolan's Opera House. In 1890 he was elected county assessor, a post he held for four years before going into the cement contracting business.

McDonald was married twice. His first wife was Louise, who gave birth to two daughters, Mary and Janet. Then, on 24 November 1884 he married Lillie B. Koonz in Jeffersonville, Indiana. Their children were Charlotte, Archibald H. Jr., Richard, and Frederick.

The veteran died at home in Logansport on 20 May 1900 and was buried in Mount Hope Cemetery.

References: Fulton County Public Library; Logansport-Cass County Public Library; W. Peattie, *The Pictorial Story of America* (1896), p. 6; *Combination Atlas and Map of Fulton County Indiana* (1883), p. 20; *Logansport Daily Reporter*, 21 May 1900; military pension file, National Archives, Washington, DC.

McFADDEN, JAMES B. (1827–1888)

James McFadden was born in 1827 in Brown County, Ohio, the oldest of four children of Jane and Charles McFadden. His younger siblings were Cornelius, Louisa, and Nora.

McFadden married Emily Howell in Brown County on 26 December 1849. Their first child, Caroline, arrived the following year, and they moved to Franklin in 1852.

James McFadden entered the Preparatory Department of Wabash College soon thereafter and remained through 1854. In 1856 he purchased 120 acres of land in Johnson County and supplemented his farm income with teaching. By 1860 the McFaddens had three more children: William Henry, James B. Jr., and Frances.

On 9 January 1864 McFadden enrolled in the Ninth Cavalry attached to the 121st Indiana Regiment. He was commissioned a corporal, and at that time he was noted as being five feet nine inches tall, with dark hair, fair complexion, and hazel eyes. Promotion to quartermaster sergeant came at Pulaski, Tennessee, on 4 August 1864. In February 1865, while at Vicksburg, he came down with chronic diarrhea and spent much of the following month in a hospital at New Orleans before being allowed to go home for further medical treatment. He was finally and honorably discharged at Indianapolis on 1 September 1865.

After the war, the veteran resumed farming in Hensley Township until April 1875, when he acquired a farm in Jasper County, Illinois. After only one year, he moved to Cumberland County, where he bought another farm. McFadden died there on 14 March 1888.

References: Johnson County Public Library; military pension file, National Archives, Washington, DC.

McKAMEY, PEACHEA H. (1828–1891)

Peachea McKamey was born in Virginia in about 1828, one of three children of Jane and John McKamey. His siblings were Margaret and Alexander. His first and last names took various forms: McCammy and McCamie, and Preachea and Peach.

McKamey attended the Normal School of Wabash College for one school year, 1855–56. Two years later, on 8 August 1858, he married Georgiana Bladen in Greencastle. They went on to have three daughters and three sons.

In August 1861 McKamey was elected city engineer for Greencastle but probably served only briefly because of the outbreak of the Civil War. In his obituary, he is mentioned as having served in the war, and he later was active in a GAR veterans post. However, it has not been possible to identify his army unit and time served.

Soon after the war the McKamey family moved to New Albany, where they remained for the rest of their lives. McKamey was a carpenter and an active member of the Carpenters and Joiners Union. He died of consumption on 22 November 1891, survived by his wife, who died on 27 August 1897.

References: Betty Menges of the New Albany-Floyd County Public Library; *New Albany Public Press*, 25 November 1891; *New Albany Daily Ledger*, 23 November 1891; *New Albany Public Press*, 1 September 1897; *New Albany Daily Ledger*, 28 August 1897; J. W. Weik, *History of Putnam County, Indiana* (1910), pp. 235–36.

McKINNEY, ARTHUR LAYTON (1819–1901)

McKinney often as not referred to himself by his middle name, Layton, but then on other occasions used his first name, Arthur. He was born on either 13 or 16 September 1819 in either Greene County, or more likely, Mad Township of Clark County, Ohio. His father, James, was born somewhere in Pennsylvania in 1789, while his mother, Mary Flynn (1790–1848), came from Ohio. They married there in 1808. About 1829 they moved to Montgomery County, Indiana, and bought a farm about thirteen miles from Crawfordsville, paying $7 per acre. James McKinney was both a farmer and a preacher, and he and Mary raised a large family, including Jane, Rachael, Margaret, Nancy, Martha, Olive, Watson, Susan, Mary, Ellen, Isaiah, Joseph, and Moses. The last of these attended Wabash

College in 1849–50, but drowned in 1866.

During the 1840s, Arthur McKinney followed his father's example and took a keen interest in the ministry, being ordained in 1848 by the Western Indiana Conference of the Christian Church. He then spent the next six years off and on attending Wabash College: two of those in the Preparatory Department and the rest in the Classical Course of study. To earn money for his education, he both preached and taught. Much of his time was spent living in Crawfordsville, but in 1851 he lived in nearby Covington, Fountain County. He dropped out a year, so it would seem, and for his senior year of 1853–54 he gave his home as Yellow Springs, Ohio. That was because in September 1852 he had also accepted the job of heading the preparatory department of the newly founded Antioch College. Despite all these preoccupations and distractions, he formally graduated from Wabash in June 1854.

McKinney seems to have taken a leave of absence in 1855–1856 to help raise money for Antioch. Ultimately he resigned from the college sometime in 1857. Rumors spread that he, like other faculty members, had been dismissed by the new Antioch president, Horace Mann, because the latter opposed their particular religious beliefs. Mann was a Unitarian who frowned on many of the strict, negative religious practices from the earlier Puritan tradition.

During the course of 1857, Mann insisted that McKinney make some kind of public statement that would exonerate the president. At a church convention in the town of Franklin, on 29 October 1857, McKinney proclaimed that he had resigned for purely personal reasons that had nothing to do with doctrinal controversy. Yet, President Mann seemed dissatisfied with such a pronouncement, and soon wrote McKinney insisting that a fuller explanation be published in the press. McKinney was perplexed and offended. As he wrote Mann on 21 November 1857, "Permit me to say, respectfully, that I take decided exception to the preemptory manner in which you call on me to make a statement through the press, that I was not driven away from the college, etc." Not withstanding his annoyance, McKinney penned a statement and sent it off to a local paper, but when it did not appear in print, President Mann wrote again. He accused McKinney of "colluding" with the editor and others to "keep back the truth."

Finally, on 7 January 1858, the exculpatory words from McKinney appeared in the *Gospel Herald* of Dayton: "I am informed that there are those who state that I was forced to leave my Chair in Antioch College, in consequence of religious opposition. This is incorrect; not one word of truth in it. Nor was I driven away. It was the regret of all, I believe, that I left when I did. Up to the time of my retiring, there had been, so far as I know, harmony of feeling in matters of religion, between members of the faculty and myself. ... For my leaving the College, I alone am responsible."

In the surviving records, there is no clear indication of why McKinney did choose to resign. We do get one clue, however, as to a policy difference between him and President Mann. In an exchange of letters back in July 1857, he denied that "I throw my influence against the administration of the College, and, in some instances, at least, endeavor to prevent students from attending it." "I cannot now call to mind a single instance in which I have given counsel for insubordination in any student to the regulations of the College," he wrote. He admitted that, on several occasions, he might have expressed his opposition to rule 37, however. This referred to a section of the college's *Law and Regulations* governing boardinghouses in town: "Without permission of the Faculty, students will not be allowed to board with families in the village, who take boarders of the other sex." In addition, landlords had to sign a paper promising to report any student lodgers who did not abide by the overall regulations of the college.

On 22 March 1862 McKinney enlisted as a captain and chaplain of the Seventy-First Ohio regiment. He served three full years and was mustered out at New Market, east Tennessee, on 2 March 1865.

His experiences away from his parish may have motivated him to seek political office in Troy, Ohio. In 1866 he was elected county treasurer, and he resigned from his church the following year. In 1868 he was elected to a second term as treasurer. During 1871 he moved to Dayton to help raise money for the Christian Publishing Company. Then, he became a county probation court judge and served two terms, 1872–78. By then he had abandoned all thought of returning to the ministry, and practiced law instead. Between 1894 and 1900 he served three terms as mayor of Troy. Finally, over the years he wrote several books, various pamphlets, and numerous articles.

On 6 April 1841, when McKinney was twenty-one years old, he had married sixteen-year-old Maria McFall in Montgomery County. They may have had three children in all, but we know of only two: Lovina and John. Both of them and their mother survived McKinney's death at Troy on 20 February 1901. Maria died in 1907, and they are both buried in Riverside Cemetery.

References: R. S. Dills, *History of Greene County, Ohio* (1881), pp. 640, 679–85; M. A. Broadstone, *History of Greene County, Ohio*, I (1918), pp. 460–61, 539: *History of Miami County, Ohio* (1900), p. 571; G. Buchanan, *Forward Through the Century, 1857–1957: The Story of the First Congregational Christian Church, Troy, Ohio*, pp. 1–7. See also *Miami Union*, 21 and 28 February and 27 June 1901. Special thanks for all the help provided by the Greene County (Ohio) Library, the Troy (Ohio) Historical Society and the Antioch College Library. Quotations from letters and other materials come from the latter's archival collection.

McKINNEY, THOMAS N. (1835–1910)

Thomas McKinney was born in Washington County on 27 March 1835, the only son of Mary and Alexander McKinney. He had two sisters, Mary and Martha.

When he entered the Preparatory Department of Wabash in the fall of 1854, he lived in Cerro Gordo, Illinois. He remained at the college for only one academic year. On 11 August 1862 McKinney enrolled as a corporal for three years in Company K of the 107th Illinois Regiment. Details of his army experience are lacking except for the fact that he was mustered out on 25 June 1865 at Salisbury, North Carolina.

After the war he returned to Cerro Gordo and farmed his 120 acres in Piatt County until he died on 11 January 1910. He was survived by his wife, Minerva, and two children, Claude, and Pearl.

References: Allerton Public Library, Monticello, Illinois; military service record, Office of the Secretary of State, Springfield, Illinois.

McKINNEY, WILLIAM McCLURE (1835–1864)

For over one hundred years, Wabash College has played an important role in the lives of McKinney men. William McClure McKinney was born on 11 August 1835 on a farm near Newtown that has remained in the possession of the McKinney family in Indiana to the present day. His parents were Sarah and Presley Thompson, whose other children were Susan, Esther, Elizabeth, Mary, and Samuel.

Young William enrolled in the Normal School at Wabash for the 1852–53 academic year, and after two more years in the Preparatory Department, he embarked on the Classical Course and graduated on 13 July 1859, marking the start of a family tradition. Glenn E. McKinney, a half-nephew, was in the class of 1876, but did not graduate. Another Glenn McKinney, great-nephew of William, graduated in the class of 1909, and his son, Lawrence, graduated in 1934.

When McKinney entered Wabash in the early 1850s, he intended to be a minister. However, after his many years at the college, he turned his attention to the law. During 1859–61 he taught school in Covington while studying for the Indiana bar and was ready to be admitted to the legal profession when the war intervened.

McKinney helped to organize Company I of the Fifteenth Indiana Regiment at Lafayette, and on 24 April 1861 he received his commission as a second lieutenant. Once activated on 1 July, the regiment was steadily engaged in western Virginia at the Battles of Rich Mountain and Cheat Mountain, the first campaign of the Civil War in which Robert E. Lee led troops into combat. About this time McKinney was promoted to first lieutenant.

In December 1861 the Fifteenth Regiment transferred to the Army of the Ohio at Louisville, and it engaged in the Battle of Shiloh in April 1862. However, McKinney had been hospitalized for illness and only caught up with his unit toward the end of this major engagement. During the rest of April and May, he took part in the Federal siege of Corinth, and he spent the summer and fall marching and counter-marching throughout northern Mississippi, Alabama, and Tennessee.

On 9 November 1862 he became captain of Company I and led his men into the bloody Battle of Murfreesboro in late December. During 1863 they were in Tennessee, especially in and about Chattanooga.

McKinney kept a diary covering July 1861 to March 1863 that he sent home for safekeeping and which is now in the college archives. We learn from its pages that his life as a soldier was overwhelmingly tedious and uncomfortable, with few heroic moments. What took its toll on him and others was not the risk of battle but the exposure to rain and cold, disease, and fatigue. It was not uncommon for him to spend the night outdoors in bad weather, with no tent for protection.

It is not surprising, then, that he contracted tuberculosis and had to resign from the army on 12 October 1863. On his way home, he was taken captive by Confederate troops in Tennessee and force-marched, and when he fell, he was left to die. Somehow he managed to hire an old mule to carry him to Nashville, and from there to commandeer a train back to Indiana and Newtown, where his family tried to nurse him. However, when it became apparent that his condition was desperate, he was sent to a hospital at Dayton, Ohio. He died three months later on 30 January 1864. His body was brought home and buried in the family cemetery on the McKinney farm.

References: Lawrence McKinney of Covington, Indiana; Gregory M. Britton, *Excerpts of the William McKinney Diary* and *Obituaries of Some Alumni,* Ramsay Archives, Wabash College; *Wabash Magazine*, V (May 1864), p. 239; *History of Fountain County, Indiana* (1883), p. 456.

McMECHAN, THEODORE F. (1841–1895)

Theodore McMechan was born on 19 December 1841 in Dayton, Indiana, the eldest child of Eliza and James G. McMechan, a physician. His siblings were Eva, Ann, and Charles.

McMechan attended the Preparatory Department of Wabash for one school year, 1854–55, then undertook a variety of jobs, including working in a drugstore (which might have been owned by his father), house painting, and clerking in a dry goods store.

On 17 April 1861 he answered the call to the colors and enrolled for three months in Company I of the Eleventh Indiana Regiment. He served mainly in western Virginia and was back in Indianapolis and out of the army by early August. During Morgan's Raid McMechan again enlisted, rushed off, and, like the others who rallied to the call, had to turn around and come right home: he was out of the service after only ten days. Soon thereafter, he moved to Leavenworth, Kansas, where he was employed in a dry goods store for two years. He then became interested in dentistry and in 1865 went to Muncie for instruction and practice. Once qualified, he returned to Crawfordsville, where he married Helen

C. Eaton on 2 June 1870. Two years later she gave birth to a daughter, Maud.

McMechan served several terms as Crawfordsville city clerk (1875–80) and was also active in the local GAR post and the Republican Party. He died just shy of his fifty-fourth birthday, on 17 December 1895, and is buried in Oak Hill Cemetery. He was survived by his wife and daughter.

References: H.W. Beckwith, *History of Montgomery County* (1881), p. 48; records of McPherson Post No. 7, GAR, Crawfordsville, Indiana; *Crawfordsville Journal*, 17 December 1895.

McPHERON, JOHN ERASTUS (1838–1873)

John McPheron was born in Greene County, Tennessee, on 16 March 1838. He had one sister and six brothers. Eventually his family moved to Rogersville Junction, Tennessee, where he did a bit of teaching in the late 1850s. In the fall of 1860 he entered Tusculum College, affiliated with the Presbyterian Church, and remained there two years until the college was forced to shut down because of the war.

McPheron then headed north to Indianapolis and took up the trade of carpentry. Wabash College is in no doubt that McPheron served in the Civil War, as his name is on the memorial tablet affixed to Center Hall. Where and when he served in the army, however, is not known.

In the autumn of 1865 he entered the Preparatory Department of Wabash, and a year later he embarked on the freshman year. During a portion of his sophomore year, 1867–68, he went back to Tusculum, only to return to Wabash in the fall of 1868 for his junior year. While in college he distinguished himself as an orator and held the offices of treasurer and purveyor in the Lyceum literary society. He was also one of the editors of the *Wabash Magazine*.

Poor health forced McPheron to return to Tennessee in April 1869. Gradually he regained his stamina and taught for a while before returning to Wabash in the autumn of 1870 for his senior year. He graduated in July 1871, fervently expecting that he would study theology at Tusculum College, yet illness continued to plague him, and he died at home in Rogersville Junction on 27 August 1873.

References: *Obituaries of Some Alumni*, Ramsay Archives, Wabash College; *Wabash Magazine*, VII (June 1867), p. 91; *Wabash Magazine*, IX (December 1868), p. 56; *Wabash Magazine*, XI (June 1871), pp. 152–53.

MERRILL, SAMUEL JR. (1831–1924)

Samuel Merrill Jr. was born in Indianapolis on 30 May 1831, the son of Lydia Jane Anderson and Samuel Merrill, founder of the well-known firm of

Bobbs-Merrill. The junior Merrill had a significant family heritage and to this day is regarded as one of the town's most illustrious nineteenth-century citizens. Both his maternal and paternal grandfathers fought in the American Revolution, and his father was prominent in Indiana state politics as a legislator and state treasurer. When the state capital moved from Corydon to Indianapolis, Samuel Merrill Sr. was entrusted with seeing that the financial files were safely conveyed to their new location.

At the age of sixteen young Samuel became a freshman at Wabash College, and four years later he graduated with the class of 1851. He then joined his father working in the bookstore in Indianapolis. On 19 July 1859 he married Emily Frances White, the daughter of Wabash College President Charles White. They eventually had five children: Charles, Anna, Mary, Samuel, and Emily.

When the Seventieth Regiment of Indiana Volunteers was formed in 1862 under the command of the future United States President Benjamin Harrison, Merrill joined as a second lieutenant and rose quickly to first lieutenant, captain, major, and finally lieutenant colonel. Once Harrison was transferred to other duties, Merrill commanded the regiment in 1864–65 as Union forces lay siege to Atlanta.

At the end of the war, Merrill returned to the family business, which began to publish books as well as sell them. The firm specialized in books about the Civil War, and in 1900 Merrill wrote his version of the conflict in the form of a history of the Seventieth Regiment.

In 1890 President Benjamin Harrison appointed his friend and fellow officer as the American Consul-General at Calcutta, India, a post he filled for four years.

Upon returning to the United States from India in 1894, Merrill severed his connection with the Indianapolis publishing firm, which was in the capable hands of his son, Charles, and began a new life in the Far West. He and Emily bought an orange and lemon grove near the Sierra Madre mountains and for the next six years described themselves as "ranchers." In about 1900 they moved to Long Beach, California, where Merrill was soon elected to the city's board of trustees, or town council (1904–06). His companion and wife died in 1920, followed the next year by Charles. Confined to bed his last year or so, Merrill died on 2 September 1924.

References: 1905 Wabash College alumni questionnaire; *Indiana Medical Journal*, XXIV May 1906), p. 447; *Indianapolis Star*, 4 September 1924; *Who Was Who in America*; *Wabash Record Bulletin*, September 1924, p. 14; *Long Beach Press-Telegram*, 3 September 1924; A. T. Volwiler, "Letters from a Civil War Officer: Samuel Merrill," *Mississippi Valley Historical Review*, XIV (1928), pp. 508–29.

METCALF, ARTHUR T. (1847–1885)

Arthur Metcalf was born on 11 July 1847 in Plymouth, Indiana, where his father and mother, Uriah and Rebecca, were among the earliest settlers. Five years later his father died, and his mother married George Spalding. Perhaps young Arthur did not get on well with his stepfather, for he left home when only thirteen and went to Jones County, Iowa, where he was living when the Civil War broke out.

Like many youths, Metcalf lied about his age, passing himself off as eighteen, and the captain of Company B, Ninth Iowa Volunteers, apparently believed him because he was inducted on 12 August 1861. Two and a half years later, in January 1864, he re-enlisted in the same regiment and sustained a severe wound at the Battle of Kennesaw Mountain in Georgia. Although he remained nominally attached to his unit, he was given a medical discharge in December 1864.

In the middle of the academic year 1864, Metcalf registered for the English Course at Wabash College, although he did not return the following year. Instead, he became a teacher for a while before choosing to be a printer. In the late 1860s, he married Asvada Nichols, and they had one daughter, Loretta. His wife died after a few years, and he married a young woman from Michigan named Flora. They had a daughter, Minnie.

Metcalf continually battled the effects of his war-related injury and later contracted tuberculosis. In 1884, when his doctor urged him to seek a more congenial climate, he moved to Archer, Florida, where he died on 6 February 1885.

References: 1850, 1870, and 1880 U.S. censuses for Plymouth; Iowa military record, Iowa State Historical Society; *Plymouth Republican*, 19 February 1885.

METEER, JAMES HARRISON (1833–1915)

James Meteer was born in Sharpsburgh, Kentucky, on 16 November 1833. Nothing for certain is known about his family, although his parents may have been John and Mary, while a younger brother could have been Calvin. By the time he entered the Preparatory Department at Wabash College in the fall of 1858, he gave Chicago as his hometown. After two years he embarked on the Classical Course, and completed his freshman and sophomore years (1860–62) before joining the army. While at Wabash he earned a reputation for effective writing and speaking. As his editorial colleagues wrote in the college magazine, "We acknowledged him as our superior, we respected him for his consistent life."

On 1 August 1862 at Franklin, Indiana, Meeter enrolled as a corporal in Company J of the Seventieth Regiment. He was mustered into service the same day at Indianapolis, with the prospect of three years in the army. However, his failing health was alluded to in the pages of the *Wabash Magazine* in December 1863: "At the beginning of the term we were saddened by the announcement that our friend and fellow-student, J. H. Meteer, was lying dangerously ill in hospital at Nashville. We are glad, however, to learn that he is recovering, and has obtained a furlough to spend his convalescent days North." Later the magazine informed its readers that Meteer had spent four months in the Nashville hospital with typhoid fever, and though thin and weak, was sufficiently recovered to pay the college a visit in December 1863. Two months later he was appointed a captain of one of the United States Colored Regiments and served until shortly after the end of the war.

In the autumn of 1865, Meteer returned to Wabash for his junior year and graduated with the class of 1867. He clearly impressed his fellow students, who commented in the *Wabash Magazine*, "From St. Charles, Minnesota, is a man with a frame of a 'physical Ajax,' and a face expressive of strong personal force, a real Ben Butler face, stripped of its harsh, domineering features. . . . His mind scorns all rhetorical blandishments, thrusts such weak things out of the way, and advancing, forces down all opposition by ridicule, sarcasm, and strong, self-evident sense."

For the three years following graduation (1867–70), Meeter attended Union Theological Seminary in New York City and then did two years of missionary work there. As the *Wabash Magazine* noted, he was "Superintendant of one of Dr. Hall's Mission Schools. We learn from his classmate, Mr. Putnam, that the place is a difficult one. But if anyone will master the situation, Meteer will, for he has great energy of mind, moved by a heart full of love for his work."

From 1872 to 1874 he was involved in home missions at Parsons, Kansas, followed by three years as a pastor in Brazil, Indiana. From 1877 to 1889 he was in charge of a Presbyterian church in Sullivan. The year 1889–90 found him back in Crawfordsville as a supply minister, after which he began a series of superintendencies of United States Government Indian Schools. These included the Sisseton reservation in South Dakota (1890–91); Pine Ridge, South Dakota (1891–93); and the Quapaw reservation in the Indian Territory (1893–94). From 1894 to 1908 he oversaw a mission at Richfield, Utah, then moved to Long Beach, California, where he died on 15 February 1915.

A black preacher, the Reverend W. C. Porter, came to Crawfordsville in about 1884 and provided an unusual tribute to Meteer. He admitted that when he joined Meteer's regiment during the war, he had been an ignorant field hand. However, "Under his captain's religious and moral influence he was induced to seek education, religion, improvement of himself and the condition of his people, and that he owed it all to Captain Meteer."

References: *Wabash Magazine*, IV (December 1862), p. 77; *Wabash Magazine*, V (December 1863), p. 75; *Wabash Magazine*, V (February 1864), p. 152; *Wabash Magazine*, (May 1864), p. 179; *Wabash Magazine*, VII (June 1867), p. 23; *Wabash Magazine*, VIII (June 1868), p. 69; *Wabash Record*, October 1904, p. 33; *Wabash Record* supplement, July 1912, p. 15; *Alumni Catalogue of Union Theological Seminary 1836–1926*, p. 177; alumni questionnaire of 1905 and *Tuttle Scrapbook, 1882–1890*, p. 42, Ramsay Archives.

MILFORD, MONROE MORTON (1842–1884)

Monroe Milford was born in Fountain County in 1842, the son of Maria Bantee and Milton Milford. He enrolled in the Preparatory Department at Wabash in 1855 and stayed in college through his junior year in the Classical Course. On 4 April he married a local Crawfordsville girl, Jennie Ramey, and two weeks afterwards enrolled for three months in Company I of the Eleventh Indiana Volunteer Infantry, the regiment in which Isaac Elston was a captain and Lew Wallace a colonel. They fought at Romney, Virginia, one of the early battles of the war, in which the rebels were defeated.

Milford was mustered out at Indianapolis on 4 August and returned to Wabash for his senior year, graduating in 1862. He then began studying law in Attica with his uncle, Marshall M. Milford, who had been a student at Wabash in 1837–38, and was admitted to the Indiana bar.

On 6 August 1870 his wife, Jennie, died. In that same year he ran unsuccessfully for the office of county clerk, but was elected for two terms as mayor of Attica from 1871 to 1876.

On 28 February 1873 Milford married Ellie Poole of Philadelphia, and in 1877 he was elected city attorney in Attica. He died on 16 April 1884 following a series of strokes and was survived by his wife and son Charles from his first marriage.

References: *Wabash Magazine*, III (June 1862), p. 379; H. W. Beckwith, *History of Fountain County, Indiana* (1881), pp. 38, 178; O. S. Clark, *Attica: Fountain County, Indiana* (1932); *Crawfordsville Review*, 19 April 1884; [Crawfordsville] *Evening Argus*, 16 April 1884; *Portrait and Biographical Record of Montgomery, Parke and Fountain Counties, Indiana* (1893), p. 211.

MILLER, ALFRED B. (1836–?)

Alfred Miller is typical of those former Wabash students about whom much less is known than is recalled about their fathers. The elder Miller, Joseph, was born in Oswego, New York, in 1796. He reached Terre Haute, Vigo County, Indiana, in 1817 and for a time took up the milling business. In 1824 he acquired a pork-packing house and eventually became a very large dealer. He sent shipments regularly to New Orleans, sometimes accompanying them either on horseback or by boat.

Miller's mother, Margaret, was born in Virginia in 1805 and gave birth to a large family, including Mary, Elisha, Catherine, Phoebe, William, and Frances. Alfred was born in Terre Haute some time in 1836, the next to the oldest of his siblings. He attended the Preparatory Department of Wabash College for two years, 1851–53. He then presumably went back home to Terre Haute and worked in his father's meatpacking business.

Wabash College records clearly indicate that Miller served in the Civil War, but the regiment is hard to pinpoint. The most likely military service record has to do with an Alfred Miller who was residing in Scotland, Greene County, about forty miles from Terre Haute. This Alfred enrolled in Company A of the Ninety-Seventh Regiment on 20 August 1862. He showed up for duty at Indianapolis on 20 September 1862. He was six feet one inch tall, with dark complexion, black hair, and grey eyes. Entering as a corporal, he received promotions to sergeant and lieutenant and was finally mustered out at Washington, DC, on 9 June 1865.

The only other allusion we have to an Alfred Miller in Terre Haute comes from a city directory of 1876. An Alfred was living on Ohio Street and was a carpenter by trade. Whether this was our student or not is unclear, and there is no other trace of his whereabouts thereafter.

References: David N. Lewis of the Vigo County Public Library; *History of Greene and Sullivan Counties, Indiana* (1884), pp. 158–59; B. Condit, *A History of Early Terre Haute* (1900), pp. 82, 95.

MILLER, CHARLES HENRY (1845–1924)

Charles H. Miller was born in Romney, Indiana, on 7 May 1845, one of five children born to Grizella M. Hutton and George Davidson Miller, an 1840 graduate of Wabash and a Presbyterian minister. His siblings were Mary L., Elisha Baldwin, William P., and Samuel Baxter Miller. His brother Samuel graduated from Wabash in 1871 but did not serve in the Civil War.

On 11 May 1864 Miller enrolled in Company G of the 135th Illinois Regiment for one hundred days. At this time he was he was living in Tuscola, Illinois, and was five feet nine inches tall, with fair complexion, light hair, and blue eyes. Once he was mustered out at Mattoon, Illinois, on 24 September 1864, he entered the Preparatory Department of Wabash College and continued in the English Course for a second year.

On 20 August 1869 Miller married Caroline Page Danford of Normal, Illinois. She presumably died in about 1880, and he married Florence Eliza Phelps of Middleton, Massachusetts, on 7 February 1882. They settled in the small town of Millis, Massachusetts, where he died of pneumonia on 6 January 1924, survived by his wife, who lived until 3 January 1946. They are both buried in the Prospect Hill Cemetery.

References: John Sheehan of Millis, Massachusetts; Ramsay Archives, Wabash College; Millis (Massachusetts) Public Library; and references cited in the biography of Charles's older brother, Elisha Baldwin Miller.

MILLER, ELISHA BALDWIN (1840–1862)

Elisha Miller, often called Baldwin, was born in Crawfordsville on 29 August 1840, the eldest son of Grizella M. Hutton and George Davidson Miller. His father graduated from Wabash a few months before his birth and then went to Lane Theological Seminary in Cincinnati to become ordained as a Presbyterian minister. Miller's siblings were Mary L., William P., Samuel Baxter, and Charles Henry, who also went to Wabash and served in the Civil War and whose biography is given above.

Miller entered the Preparatory Department of Wabash in the fall of 1857 and remained for three years. On 15 July 1862 at Chalmers, near Monticello, he enrolled in Company D of the Twelfth Indiana Volunteers. The regiment left for Lexington, Kentucky, on 23 August, and a week later the raw recruits were thrown into the Battle of Richmond. Among the many casualties was Miller, with a severe wound to his thigh. He lingered in hospital for nearly three weeks and died on 20 September 1862.

References: Lane Theological Seminary, *General Catalogue: 1829–1899*, p. 37; *History of Douglas County, Illinois* (1884), p. 164; *Wabash Magazine*, IV (December 1862), pp. 77, 80; *Wabash Magazine*, IV (July 1863), p. 259; B. H. Miller, *A History of the Millers and Related Families* (1959).

MILLER, LEVIN T. (1838–1908)

Levin Miller was born in Preble County, Ohio, in 1838. His parents were Frances Buell and Lazarus Miller. His father died in 1847 in Williamsport, where Frances and her children were living in 1854 when the young Levin entered the Normal School at Wabash College. He remained for two years.

On 23 April 1861 at Williamsport, Miller enrolled in Company B of the Tenth Indiana Regiment for three months as a first lieutenant. He was mustered out at Indianapolis on 6 August. Later that month he helped to organize a new unit, which became Company K of the Thirty-Third Regiment, and Miller was commissioned its captain. In March of '63 he was one of the four hundred forced to surrender at Thompson's Station, along with their commander John Coburn. Coburn and the other prisoners, Miller included, marched to Libby Prison, but somehow Miller and a few others managed to tunnel their way to freedom. Restored to his regiment, Miller was promoted to major in Coburn's "Redemption Regiment" and took command of the Thirty-Third in May 1864, at the beginning of the Atlanta campaign. Presumably he was released in the spring of 1865.

Returning to Williamsport, he married Sarah C. Kitchens on 20 June 1865. They had two children, Fred and Mary. Prior to the war Miller had been admitted to the Indiana bar, and now he was able to pursue his legal career full time. In the same year he was offered the appointment of territorial governor of Montana but declined because it represented too risky a career move.

In 1881 the Millers moved to Dallas, Texas, and Miller became a partner in the law firm of Crawford and Crawford. They stayed only a year and then settled in Wichita Falls, where Miller resumed his practice of law, supplemented by making real estate loans. He was very popular with the Texans in the county, one of whom said that although he was a "damn Yankee," he was "a fine fellow."

In 1903 the Millers' daughter died, followed in 1904 by her mother. Two years later Miller moved to Pasadena, California, where he died on 1 March 1908. All three are buried in Riverside Cemetery in Wichita Falls.

References: *Wabash Magazine*, IV (July 1863), p. 327; *Biographical History of Tippecanoe, White, ... Counties, Indiana* (1899), pp. 120–21; T. T. Scribner, *Indiana's Role of Honor* (1866), p. 599; *History of Warren County, Indiana* (1883); Kemp Public Library, Wichita Falls, Texas; Louise Kelly, *Wichita County Beginnings* (1982), p. 248.

MILLER, MARTIN J. (1839/40–1865)

Martin Miller was born in 1839–40 in Cologne, Germany. When he entered the Preparatory Department of Wabash College in the fall of 1858, he gave Crawfordsville as his home. He returned for two more years, indicating possibly that he traveled occasionally between Indiana and Cologne. On 18 April 1861 he, along with other Wabash students, interrupted his freshman year to join Company J of the Eleventh Indiana Regiment. They committed to three months' service, much of which took place in western Virginia, and on 4 August they were mustered out in Indianapolis.

Shortly after his sophomore year, on 12 July 1862, Miller re-enlisted for three years in the Eighteenth Light Artillery as a sergeant. On 15 November 1863 he was promoted to second lieutenant, and then to first lieutenant in May 1864.

Miller gained notoriety among his comrades when he drew up a petition on 2 October 1862 against the commander of the battery, Colonel Eli Lilly. Forty-six men signed it, and it was forwarded to Governor Oliver P. Morton. They requested that Lilly be removed from his command because of his overall incompetence, that he was too young, encouraged stealing by his troops, hurled insults at his subordinates, had no knowledge of how to care for horses, and deprived them of their rights as Americans. "We cannot and shall not suffer any longer," the petition read. Governor Morton did nothing about the complaint, and Lilly demoted many of those who had signed it.

Eventually, Miller rose in the esteem of Brigadier General Edward Moody McCook, who made him an aide-de-camp and an assistant adjutant general, entrusted to execute scouting raids. While camped for the night on 2 April 1865, they were surrounded by one hundred Confederates, taken prisoner, and soon afterward shot. Scouts could often be considered as spies, for which execution was permissible. Miller was brought back home and buried at Greencastle.

References: J. W. Rowell, *The Yankee Artilleryman* (1975), pp. 36, 140, 189, 255, 278; *Wabash Magazine*, V (May 1864), pp. 175, 178.

MILLER, ROBERT G. (1837–1869)

Robert Miller was born in Preble County, Ohio, in about 1837, one of six children of Elizabeth and James Miller, a successful farmer. His siblings were William, James, Martha, Mary, and Joseph. In 1860 Miller, a farmer, entered Wabash College as a sophomore in the Classical Course. However, on 18 April 1861 he joined with other Wabash students and committed to three months' service in Company I of the Eleventh Indiana Regiment commanded by Colonel Isaac Elston. Their duty took them to Maryland and Virginia, where Miller contracted measles and, returning to Indianapolis, was confined in a hospital. There, he was mustered out on 6 August 1861.

According to the *Wabash Magazine*, Miller was too ill to return to college that September, but a year later he was better, and on 12 August 1862, he re-entered military service at his county town of Huntington, joining Company A of the Fifth Cavalry attached to the Ninetieth Regiment. He had already endured three bouts with typhoid, and poor health soon forced his medical discharge on 14 November 1862. During these years he was five feet eleven inches tall, with hazel eyes, red hair, and a fair complexion.

By 27 May 1864 Miller must have felt fit enough to be commissioned for three months as a second lieutenant in Company I of the 138th Indiana Regiment, which spent most of its time in Kentucky and Tennessee guarding rail lines.

Meanwhile his parents and siblings had moved to Andrew County, Missouri, where Miller eventually joined them and studied law, ultimately being admitted to the Missouri bar. On 17 March 1867 he married Ruth Webster of Savannah, Georgia. Their daughter, Kate, was born on 18 April 1868, but died eighteen months later. Miller died on 17 January 1869 and was buried in the Savannah Cemetery.

References: Huntington City-Township Public Library; *Wabash Magazine*, IV (July 1863), p. 254; Norman Peters of Washington, DC; military pension file, National Archives, Washington, DC.

MILLER, THOMAS J. (1843–1865)

Thomas Miller was born in Tennessee in 1843, one of three children of Henrietta Davidson and James N. Miller. His siblings were Hattie and Ella. In 1848 the family moved to Troy, Iowa, where his father acquired 125 acres of rich farmland and established a reputation as a stockbreeder and wagon maker.

In the autumn of 1859 Miller enrolled in the Preparatory Department of Wabash College, returning the following year as a freshman. He probably would have continued had not the Civil War intervened. As did many other Wabash students, on 22 April 1861 he joined the recently organized Company I of the Eleventh Indiana Volunteers for three months and was mustered out in August.

Returning home to Iowa, he re-enlisted in Company D of the Third Iowa Cavalry on 26 September 1861 and was soon promoted to the rank of sergeant in March 1862. On 1 February 1864 he volunteered for yet a third assignment, and in April he was promoted to second lieutenant. That June he was among the eight thousand Union troops under the command of General Samuel D. Sturgis that left Memphis and quick-marched to Brice's Crossroads, south of Corinth, Mississippi. Awaiting them were Confederate forces under Nathan Bedford Forrest, whose reputation of attacking northerners and forcing a retreat was displayed: by the end of the day 223 Yankees had lost their lives, 394 were wounded, and 1,500 were taken prisoner. Among the captured wounded was Thomas Miller. Nonetheless, within a month or two he rejoined his regiment and was promoted to first lieutenant in August 1864. Promotion to the rank of captain came in January 1865. The following April his regiment saw action near Columbus, Georgia, under the command of James Harrison Wilson. Federal cavalry captured both Columbus and West Point, but Miller was killed in action on 16 April. He was buried in the nearby national cemetery, while a grave marker in the Troy Cemetery also commemorates his passing.

References: Bloomfield Public Library, Davis County, Iowa; *History of Davis County, Iowa* (1882), pp. 722–23; *The Roster and Record of Iowa Soldiers* (1886), IV, p. 556.

MILLS, BENJAMIN MARSHALL (1846–1869)

Benjamin Mills, usually called Marsh, was born in Crawfordsville on 18 November 1846, the only son of Sarah Marshall and Professor Caleb Mills. He had two sisters, Sarah L. and Julia B. He was registered in the Normal School at Wabash in 1858, progressing to the Preparatory School in 1860. He then entered the college itself in 1861 as a member of the freshman class with an emphasis in the sciences and was known for his "stirring appeals and fierce denunciations of those who were trying to destroy the Nation." Thus, in the summer following his sophomore year, on 11 July 1863, he enrolled in Company C of the 108th Indiana Volunteer Infantry. However, six days later, when Morgan's Raiders were no longer a threat to southern Indiana, he was mustered out in Indianapolis.

Undeterred, he tried to join another regiment, according to a letter from A. P. Andrew of the Twenty-First Indiana Light Artillery, a former student of Caleb Mills. Andrew replied that his regiment was already oversubscribed and regrettably there was no opening for young Marsh. This was on 13 March 1864, but the very next month a place was found for him in the Forty-Ninth U.S. Colored

Infantry with a commission as a first lieutenant, and he enlisted for three years.

Until March 1864 the Forty-Ninth was known as the Eleventh Louisiana Volunteers and was made up almost entirely of "contraband," or liberated, southern slaves, commanded exclusively by white officers. The newly designated Forty-Ninth was ordered to Vicksburg, Mississippi, which had been captured the previous year by Lieutenant General U. S. Grant. When they arrived there on 14 April, Lieutenant Mills joined them, but in June 1865 he took ill and was discharged.

He returned to his home in Crawfordsville and re-entered Wabash in the fall of 1865 as a member of the sophomore class. Over the next few years he regained his health and graduated in the spring of 1868. While in college Mills was known as an excellent scholar "who was bettered for having seen something of reality." He was a member of the Lyceum Literary Society and showed special skill in classical languages. At his graduation on 24 June, he delivered an address titled "Eminence," based on his admiration of Elihu Baldwin, the first president of Wabash College. He then began studying medicine with Dr. McClelland, but his health again failed him, and one day while ice skating he suffered a heart attack. This happened several more times, and on 7 January 1869 he was "compelled to yield to the disease" at the age of twenty-two. He was buried in Oak Hill Cemetery.

References: *Crawfordsville Weekly Journal*, 14 January 1887; *Obituaries of Some Alumni* (1875), Ramsay Archives, Wabash College; *Lyceum Records 1864–1869*; *Wabash Magazine*, V (May 1864), p. 236; *Wabash Magazine*, IX (June 1868), p. 80; *Wabash Magazine* (March 1869), pp. 77–78.

MILLS, EUGENE RUSSELL (1841–1899)

Eugene Mills was born in Chaumont, New York, on 19 June 1841. When he was ten years old his family moved to a farm near Detroit.

On 12 August 1862 he enrolled for three years in Company K of the Twenty-Fourth Michigan Volunteers, and he saw action at the major battles of Fredericksburg, Chancellorsville, and Gettysburg. At Gettysburg he was badly wounded and spent months in army hospitals. While he was recovering he began to keep a diary, which is in the Ramsay Archives of Wabash College, and became a court clerk until he was released from military duties on 1 July 1864.

Back in Detroit, Reverend William A. McCorkle, the Presbyterian minister, urged Mills to consider Wabash College, and Professor Hovey assured him that the college would see to it that his tuition costs were covered by grants from the Presbyterian Church because he had expressed interest in being a clergyman. Consequently Mills spent 1865–66 in the Preparatory Department and then went through the freshman, sophomore, junior, and senior years, graduating in June 1870. At the time he was described as five feet nine inches tall, weighing 146 pounds, and having "dark hair, heavy eyebrows, a high forehead, a sharp nose, and a full face with magnificent whiskers and blue eyes." While still an undergraduate he wrote an article for the *Wabash Magazine* describing his first major battle at Fredericksburg.

From 1870 to 1871 Mills attended Lane Theological Seminary in Cincinnati, and then transferred to Union Theological Seminary in New York City for his final two years, becoming an ordained Presbyterian minister in 1873. His first church was at Cedar Rapids, Iowa, followed by service as a home missionary in Nevada from 1879 to 1883. Thereafter he was a pastor or a Sunday school superintendant in several churches in California before becoming the minister in Glendale. Poor health forced him to resign after four years, but the parish recalled him fondly: "For we realize that that in Reverend Mills we have had not only a beloved pastor but a powerful preacher of the Gospel." He died at Glendale on 24 April 1899.

References: Glendale (California) Public Library; *Glendale Presbyterian Church Diamond Jubilee* (1959), pp. 11–12; *Wabash Magazine* X (December 1869), pp. 57–62; E. R. Mills, *Diary*, Ramsay Archives, Wabash College; *Wabash Magazine*, X (March 1869), p. 79; *Wabash Magazine*, XII (March 1872), p. 148.

MILLS, ISAAC (1843–1923)

Isaac Mills was born in Randolph County on 13 February 1843, one of six children of Elizabeth Thornburgh and Jesse Mills, a prosperous farmer. His siblings were Mary, Joseph, Rachael, Solomon, and Elisha. He was enrolled in the Preparatory Department of Wabash College in 1853–54 and boarded at the house of Professor Caleb Mills in Crawfordsville. Whether he was a relative of the professor is unknown.

On 1 November 1861 he enrolled for three years in Company E of the Fifth Indiana Regiment and was described as five feet seven inches tall, with grey eyes, light hair, and fair complexion. The regiment went first to Louisville, Kentucky, where Mills became ill and spent three weeks in a field hospital. He rejoined his regiment on the eve of the Battle of Pittsburg Landing (Shiloh) in Mississippi, but in May 1862 he almost lost his hand in an accident while unloading a boat, which rendered him unfit for active duty. Nevertheless, he remained for some months as a cook and nurse in a hospital and was given a formal medical discharge on 6 November 1862.

He married Catherine L. Thornburg. Their son, Daniel, was born in 1866. When Catherine died in 1868, Isaac married Jennie Pemberton, who gave birth to three children: Ollie (1873), Henry (1875), and George (1879). Isaac Mills farmed fifty-seven acres in Washington Township until he died in 1923 and was buried in the New Liberty Cemetery, as were his parents.

References: Winchester Community Library; Randolph County Historical Society; E. Tucker, *History of Randolph County, Indiana* (1882), p. 388.

MILLS, NOAH WEBSTER (1834–1862)

Noah Mills, often called Webb, was named after the famous early American lexicographer Noah Webster. He was born near Ladoga, Indiana, on 21 June 1834. His parents were Janet Westfall and Daniel Mills. The memorial tablet on Center Hall lists him as Webster T. Mills, but no such person appears in any college records. He studied in the Preparatory Department of Wabash College from 1850 to 1852 and earned money during those years working in a print shop in Crawfordsville. One of his brothers, Frank M. Mills, later wrote a book about the town. For a year or so after Wabash, Mills worked as a messenger for the Adams Express Company and also studied law when time permitted. He was admitted to the Indiana bar in 1856 and married Sarah Adelia Hackleman. They had a daughter, Kate, in 1858, who died in infancy. They then moved to Des Moines, Iowa, where Mills joined his brother Frank's printing firm.

In 1860 Mills joined the local guards organization, the Wide Awakes, and when war broke out the following spring, he quickly enlisted. On 4 May 1861 he was commissioned second lieutenant of Company D of the Second Iowa Volunteers, and his fellow soldiers elected him captain on 1 June. He distinguished himself at the Battle of Fort Donelson in February of 1862 and was cited for gallantry and coolness under fire. He was also promoted to the rank of major.

At the Battle of Shiloh in April he was slightly wounded in the face, and a further promotion followed, to lieutenant colonel on 22 June 1862. The regiment's colonel was killed on 3 October at Corinth, Mississippi, and Mills became acting colonel. The next day Mills's horse was shot from under him and he sustained a serious wound in the foot while leading a charge. While recovering in a hospital he was promoted to colonel, but infection set in, and he died of lockjaw on 12 October 1862. Shortly before his death he wrote to his family, "In the army I have tried conscientiously and prayerfully to do my duty, and if I am to die in my youth, I prefer to die as a soldier of my country; to do so as a member of the Second Iowa Infantry is glorious enough for me." He was buried at Woodlawn Cemetery in Des Moines, and later his brother Frank compiled a book that memorialized him and others.

References: A. A. Stuart, *Iowa Colonels and Regiments* (1865), pp. 65–70; F. M. Mills, *Early Days in a College Town* (1924), p. 157; D. Stevenson, *Indiana's Role of Honor, II* (1864), pp. 577–78; Iowa State Historical Society, Iowa City.

MITCHELL, JOSHUA ROBINSON (1843–1923)

Joshua Mitchell was born in 1843 in Logansport, the son of Leydia Robinson and William Mitchell. He was a determined student and went straight through the freshman to the senior years (1861–65) at Wabash, culminating in a bachelor of arts degree.

While still at college Mitchell enrolled at Crawfordsville in Company H of the 135th Indiana Regiment on 10 May 1864. He guarded rail lines in Tennessee and Alabama until 29 September, when he was mustered out at Indianapolis with the rank of corporal.

Intent on a career in the ministry, he attended Lane Theological Seminary in Cincinnati from 1865 to 1868, and shortly after graduating he was ordained as a Presbyterian minister. From 1868 to 1872 he was pastor of a church in Lawrenceburg, Indiana, which had previously been served by Henry Ward Beecher.

On 27 June 1870 he married Frances Thornton, and they eventually had four children: Mary, Eleanor, Paul, and Frances. Mitchell served the Fifth Presbyterian Church of Indianapolis from 1872 to 1885, followed by thirteen years at a church in Findley, Ohio. Then, in October 1900 he was called to Pontiac, Michigan, and three years later to Marshall, Michigan. Their final move was to Manistique in 1909. Mitchell was forced to retire in 1919 because of a stroke that left him without speech and little movement. He died on 25 August 1923.

References: 1905 Alumni Questionnaire, Ramsay Archives, Wabash College; *The Wabash*, XXIII (October 1898), p. 23; *The Wabash*, XXV (October 1925), p. 21; *Wabash Magazine*, IX (June 1869), p. 158; *Wabash College Record* (January 1916), p. 176; *Wabash College Record* (January 1904), p. 17; *Wabash College Record* (15 October 1923), p. 12; Phi Delta Theta alumni directories; Lane Theological Seminary, *General Catalogue, 1829–1899*, p. 74; and letter from Mary E. Hagemann.

MITCHELL, MILTON (1835–1866)

Milton Mitchell was born in Indiana, perhaps in Crawfordsville, on 6 April 1835, son of Laura and Joseph T. Mitchell. His parents were both from New York State and moved to Montgomery County in the 1830s. His father died in 1845, leaving his mother as the guardian of six other children beside himself: Alsina, Caroline, Lavinia, Lafayette, Julia, and Mary.

Young Mitchell attended the Preparatory Department of Wabash College for only one school year, 1853-1854, but stayed in Crawfordsville. On 11 July 1863 he responded to the call for troops to meet the sudden threat of Morgan's raiders into southern Indiana by joining Company C of the 108th Indiana Regiment, and when the crisis passed, he was discharged on 17 July.

Milton Mitchell died prematurely on 7 February 1866, survived by his mother, and was buried in Oak Hill Cemetery alongside his father.

References: Crawfordsville Public Library; H.W. Beckwith, *History of Montgomery County* (1881), p. 260; and A.W. Bowen, *History of Montgomery County* (1913), p. 149.

MITCHELL, ROBERT C. (1832–1907)

Robert Mitchell was born at Bloomingburg, Ohio, on 16 September 1832. His family moved to Logansport when he was quite young, and it was from there that he made his way to Wabash College in the fall of 1857. He remained through his senior year and graduated in June 1861. The following year he edited a newspaper in Rensselaer called the *Gazette*.

On 19 July 1862 Mitchell joined Company B of the Seventy-Sixth Indiana Regiment for thirty days, and that December he married Francis Hulburt. During the immediate years after their marriage, the young couple led a peripatetic life centered around journalism. Robert became the editor of the *Daily Union* of St. Joseph, Missouri, in 1867; then in 1868 he undertook the editorial reins of the *Times* of Superior, Wisconsin. In either 1869 or 1870 he was a founder of the Duluth (Minnesota) *Tribune*, and he maintained control of it until 1889. Two years later he started the Duluth *News Tribunal*, and he wrote articles for it until the day he died.

The Mitchells had four sons: Horace, Harold, Robert, and Max. During his many years in Duluth, Mitchell held a number of public offices, including terms as postmaster, county attorney, and registrar of the U.S. Land Office. He died on 26 July 1907, survived by his wife, who lived until February 1929.

References: Duluth (Minnesota) Public Library; *Duluth News Tribunal*, 27 July 1907; *Duluth and St. Louis County, Minnesota*, I (1921), p. 230; *Duluth News Tribunal*, 28 February 1929; alumni directory, Phi Delta Theta fraternity (1888), Wabash College.

MOORE, LEWIS (1844–1916)

Lewis Moore was born on a large farm in Delaware County in August 1844, one of six children of Mary Truitt and Aaron Moore. His siblings were Florence, George, Naomi, Sarah, and Julia.

Moore had two tours of duty during the Civil War. Initially he joined Company A of the 134th Indiana Regiment at Muncie on 30 April 1864 to serve for one hundred days. He spent most of his time guarding railroad lines in Tennessee and northern Alabama and was mustered out at Indianapolis in September. Then, on 22 March 1865, Moore enrolled in Company I of the reorganized Thirteenth Indiana Volunteers at Richmond, Indiana, committing for another year. However, since the war ended soon afterward, he was mustered out at Indianapolis on 18 September 1865.

In the autumn of 1866, he journeyed from Muncie to Crawfordsville to become a member of the Preparatory Department of Wabash College for two years. Then he continued in the freshman and sophomore class until 1870, when he was called home to help run the family farm due to his father's serious illness, an illness that resulted in his death in 1873.

The following year Moore married Ophelia Cones of Delaware County. The family farm now had about 190 acres, and Moore started breeding Jersey cattle.

At some point the Moores moved into the town of Muncie, where Lewis died on 11 May 1916, survived by his wife.

References: Ball State University Library, Muncie, Indiana; F. B. Haimbaugh, *History of Delaware County, Indiana* (1924), II, pp. 584–85; *Portrait and Biographical Record of Delaware and Randolph Counties, Indiana* (1894), p. 580; *Muncie Evening Press*, 11 May 1916.

MOORE, ROBERT S. (1833/4–1911)

Robert Moore was born in Warren, Ohio, in 1833 or 1834, one of three sons of Anna and John Moore, a moderately well-off farmer. His brothers were Cornelius and John. Sometime in the 1840s the family moved to LaPorte County, Indiana, and from there young Moore came to Wabash College in the fall of 1852. He was enrolled for one year in the Preparatory Department and then returned to the farm.

On 8 June 1854 he married Eliza A. Van Tassel, and together they raised a large family that included Mary, Henry, Edith, Milroy, Sadie, Samuel, and Aaron.

Moore enrolled in Company G of the Eighty-Sixth Indiana Regiment for a term of three years on 7 August 1862. He was described at that time as being six feet tall, with dark hair and complexion and blue eyes. He served his full commitment and was mustered out near Washington, DC, on 10 June 1865.

Moore pursued a variety of jobs, including farming, work in a sawmill, and employment as a gas fitter. He took ill and died at Longcliff State Hospital in Logansport on 28 July 1911, survived by Eliza, who lived until 1923. Both are buried in Lamb's Chapel Cemetery at Rolling Prairie, about eight miles northeast of LaPorte.

References: Fern Eddy Schultz of LaPorte, Indiana; Packard, Jasper, *History of LaPorte County, Indiana* (1876) p. 359; LaPorte *Daily Argus Bulletin*, 28 July 1911; LaPorte Public Library.

MOORE, SAMUEL H. (1843–1914)

According to the memorial tablet on the east side of Center Hall, there were two Samuel Moores: one rose to the rank of captain, and the other was a non-commissioned officer. The contemporary evidence is unclear, and it may well be that the two were in fact only one.

Samuel Moore was born near Southport in Marion County on 8 April

1843. He came to Wabash College in the fall of 1860 and was placed in the Preparatory Department. On campus he lived in room number 3 of Forest Hall, as he did again the following year, in what was called "the second prep." He then secured an appointment to the United States Military Academy at West Point and was formally admitted on 1 July 1862. Unfortunately, his freshman year there proved disappointing, and he was discharged in June 1863 because he was "deficient in mathematics."

Nevertheless, Moore's ambition to be a soldier was not quenched, and he joined Company G of the Seventieth Indiana Infantry in November 1863. After three months he was brought back to Indianapolis as a second lieutenant to help recruit a company of the Thirteenth Cavalry of the 131st Regiment. In March 1864 he was promoted, with the title of Adjutant of Field and Staff, and in November he became a first lieutenant while his regiment was at Lookout Valley in Tennessee. A year later, shortly before being honorably discharged in November 1865, he was appointed a captain of Company F. He was only twenty-two at war's end and had indeed distinguished himself in the infantry and cavalry.

After the war Moore enrolled in the Indiana Medical College and fulfilled his dream of becoming a doctor. He practiced in Indianapolis, maintaining an office for forty-two years at the corner of Virginia Avenue and Louisiana Street.

He gained an equally sound reputation as a hunter and woodsman. Nicknamed "Jack Snipe," he won trophies for his trap and wing shooting. Somewhat incongruously, Moore's outdoors image was complemented by the writing and reciting of poetry. He knew most of James Whitcomb Riley's verses by heart and could recite "Little Orphant Annie" at the drop of a hat.

Five years before his death, he had a stroke that forced him into retirement. A few years later another stroke deprived him of speech. He died at home, 732 Fletcher Avenue, on 15 June 1914, survived by his wife and three sons, Harvey, Horace, and Herbert.

References: *Indianapolis News*, 15 June 1914; *Record of the U.S. Military Academy at West Point*; *Journal of the Indiana State Medical Association*, VII (July 1914), p. 340; *Wabash Magazine*, IV (December 1862), p. 78.

MOORES, CHARLES WASHINGTON (1828–1864)

Charles Moores was born in Vermilion County, Illinois on 2 November 1828, son of Jane and Isaac R. Moores, a successful merchant. He had one sister, Matilda. He entered the Preparatory Department of Wabash College in the fall of 1847 and was graduated in June 1852. For the next three years he taught at the Illinois State School for the Deaf.

In 1855 Moores joined former Wabash student Samuel Merrill in the bookselling business that eventually became Bobbs Merrill and Company. This job put him in a good position to meet and eventually marry Samuel's sister, Julia, with whom he had two children: Charles Jr. and Merrill. Charles Jr. graduated from Wabash in 1882.

In July 1863 Moores joined a contingent of the Indiana Legion in response to Morgan's Raid into the southern part of the state, but since this duty only lasted about a week, on 17 May 1864 he formally enrolled in the 132nd Indiana Regiment, Company A, at Indianapolis.

However, one month later he died from a disease that he contracted while stationed at Stevenson, Alabama. A fellow Wabash student, John Cleland, memorialized him years later: "Where is Moores of '52, the man of books, the gentle scholar, the man of honor, the gentleman? Ask that lonely hospital in Alabama, that death place in the dreariest spot on earth, with lack of nursing and lack of tears, and lack of all that makes life worth while."

References: American Biographical Society, *Indiana Men of Affairs* (1923), p. 457; *The Soldier of Indiana in the War of the Union* II (1866), p. 804, published by Moores' brother-in-law, Samuel Merrill; *Wabash Record Bulletin* (15 November 1923), p. 15; J. E. Cleland, "In Memoriam," *The Wabash*, XXVII (March 1903), p. 25.

MORGAN, DAVID N. (1836–1909)

David Morgan was born 2 February 1836 in Piqua, Ohio, one of six children of Margaret and Samuel B. Morgan. His siblings were William, John, Sarah, Margaret, and Martha. All three brothers came to Wabash.

Morgan entered the Preparatory Department in the spring of 1849 and returned the following year. Then he dropped out for several years, returning in the fall of 1852 and re-entering the Preparatory Department before embarking on the four-year Classical Course. He graduated with a bachelor of arts degree in June 1859. For the next couple of years he studied law in Crawfordsville.

Because he was believed to be too short to enter the army, Morgan became a sutler, or civilian merchant who set up stores where soldiers could purchase food, tobacco, shoes and socks, stamps and writing paper, cakes and pies, and novels. Morgan was attached to the Indiana Tenth Regiment. When he returned to Crawfordsville in 1863, he married Elizabeth L. Powers on 10 November.

Toward the end of the war, the Morgans moved to Nashville, Tennessee, where Morgan practiced law and where their first daughter, Mary, was born in 1865. The family moved to Chicago in about 1868, where Morgan continued practicing law for two years.

Toward the end of 1870, they followed David's brother, William, to Kansas City, Missouri, where Morgan became a traveling salesman in his brother's wholesale drug business. About 1876 the Morgans went to Loda, Illinois, so that David could operate his own drugstore, but they came back to Crawfordsville in 1886. In addition to being a druggist, this Morgan served eight years on the Crawfordsville city council. He also ran unsuccessfully for mayor in 1905.

Elizabeth died at the age of sixty-one on 29 December 1900. Her husband followed on 2 November 1909. Both are buried in Oak Hill Cemetery with other members of their extended family.

References: See references for David's older brother, William; *Wabash Magazine*, XI (March 1871), p. 138; 1905 Alumni Questionnaire, Ramsay Archives, Wabash College; *Crawfordsville Journal*, 3 November 1909.

MORGAN, ELISHA P. Jr. (1843–1882)

Elisha Morgan was born in Lawrenceburg on 3 November 1843. His parents were Catherine and Elisha Morgan Sr., a doctor. Elisha Jr. had an older brother whose name is not known. Sometime in the 1850s the family moved to Cincinnati, and young Morgan attended Williston Seminary at Hampton, Massachusetts, before coming to Wabash in 1858. He was initiated into the Beta Theta Pi fraternity, but knowing that his family would be moving to a farm near Beloit, Wisconsin, he secured a copy of the national Beta constitution and organized a chapter at Beloit College.

Morgan stayed at Beloit through his sophomore year (1860–61) but then withdrew, perhaps anticipating his recruitment into the army on 8 August 1862 at Chicago, when he joined Company B of the Seventy-Second Illinois Volunteers for three years. The records show him standing five feet ten inches tall, with fair complexion, light hair, and blue eyes. He received a steady series of promotions during his service: corporal in October 1862, sergeant major in June 1863, second lieutenant of Company E in January 1864, and captain of Company K in September 1864. For the last couple of years he was stationed at Vicksburg, Mississippi, and was mustered out at Montgomery, Alabama, on 7 August 1865.

After the war Morgan remained in the South and tried to grow cotton, but that effort failed. He then moved to Chicago and helped found the firm of Potwin and Morgan, a varnish company. Later he became the vice president of the manufacturing firm Frank Sturgis and Company, which eventually became the Chicago Stamping Company.

In 1880 Morgan moved to Colorado Springs, hoping to find a climate more congenial to his consumptive condition. He died there on 21 February 1882.

References: Pike's Peak Library, Colorado Springs; Newberry Library, Chicago; Illinois State Archives, Springfield; Beloit (Wisconsin) College Library; *Records of the Chi Chapter of Beta Theta Pi at Beloit*; *Beta Catalogue* (1899), p. 189.

MORGAN, JOHN F. (1837–1866)

John Morgan was born in Piqua, Ohio, in December 1837, one of the three sons of Margaret and Samuel B. Morgan that came to Wabash. He had three sisters: Sarah, Margaret, and Martha. His father eventually became a prominent physician in Crawfordsville

In the fall of 1852, Morgan entered the Preparatory Department, where he spent three years and then advanced to the freshman year (1855–57). He then suspended his formal education until 1861, when he returned for his sophomore year.

As in the case of his older brother, David, John was not technically in the army during the war but was a sutler, or provider of food and other supplies to a regiment. He spent months with a regiment, perhaps the Tenth Indiana, camping in the field and foraging for added provisions.

He died in Arkansas on 3 November 1866, and his body was returned to Crawfordsville for burial in Oak Hill Cemetery.

References: H. W. Beckwith, *History of Montgomery County* (1881), p. 236; *Crawfordsville Journal*, 8 November 1866; *Crawfordsville Weekly Review*, 10 November 1866; *Wabash Magazine*, V (May 1864), pp. 175, 179; and those cited for John's older brother, William.

MORGAN, WILLIAM H. (1834–1878)

William Morgan was born in Piqua, Ohio, on 13 March 1834, one of the three sons of Margaret and Samuel B. Morgan attending Wabash, as was shown above. He had three sisters: Sarah, Margaret, and Martha. His father was a prominent physician for many years in Crawfordsville.

In the autumn of 1848, Morgan entered the Preparatory Department of Wabash College, remaining for two years before receiving an appointment to the United States Naval Academy at Annapolis in 1852. He graduated from there with honors in 1856 and spent another year in naval service, but he resigned his commission and returned to Crawfordsville.

For the next few years he followed in his father's footsteps and studied medicine, which included taking a series of lectures at the medical college in Cincinnati.

In April 1861 Morgan was commissioned captain of Company B of the Tenth Indiana Volunteers, and he spent most of his three months' service in Virginia. Mustered out at Indianapolis on 6 August, he immediately sought another commission. On 19 August he was appointed lieutenant colonel in the Twenty-Fifth Indiana Regiment and saw action in Missouri at the battle of Fort Donelson and at Shiloh, where he was acting colonel of the regiment. He was wounded and allowed leave before returning to active duty in May 1862. At that time his status of acting colonel was converted to full-time rank. Later that year he commanded at the Battle of Stones River.

Morgan and his relatively small force were under attack at Davis's Mill, Mississippi (21 December, 1862), from the larger contingent of Confederates commanded by General Earl Van Dorn. Up until then Van Dorn had swept away federal opposition, but this time Morgan stood his ground and inflicted a decisive defeat on his attackers.

On 20 May 1864 Morgan resigned from the army, but at the end of the year he accepted a commission of colonel in the Third Veteran Infantry, First Army Corps (otherwise known as Hancock's Corps). Among other things, this involved training African-Americans. On 13 March 1865 he was brevetted Brigadier General of U.S. Volunteers for his wartime experiences.

Morgan left military service on 6 March 1866, and after a year or two back in Indiana, he headed for Kansas City to take a financial stake in a wholesale drug company. His previous medical training suited him well for this work, but in 1874 he sold his share of this business and began to farm and raise sheep near Westmore, Kansas, where he died on 3 March 1878. His body was brought back to Crawfordsville for burial in Oak Hill Cemetery.

References: "Crawfordsville's Five Civil War Generals," *Indiana Historical Bulletin*, LII (September 1975), p. 111; T. G. Gronert, "Gen. W. H. Morgan: Youngest of Five Civil War Generals," newspaper clipping of about 13 April 1959, presumably from a Crawfordsville newspaper, Ramsay Archives, Wabash College; *Crawfordsville Weekly Review*, 9 March 1878.

NAYLOR, ISAAC ETON GANO (1819–1909)

Isaac Naylor was born in Charleston, Indiana, on 8 October 1819, the son of Lydia Gano and Charles B. Naylor. In 1836 the family moved to Crawfordsville, and Naylor promptly enrolled in the Preparatory Department of Wabash College. He also took a job with the printer and publisher of the *Crawfordsville Record*, I. F. Wade. After two years of studying liberal arts, he applied himself to medicine, working with various doctors in town.

In 1841 Naylor became a teacher in Darlington for two years before returning to Charleston, where he practiced medicine and published the Clark County *Mirror*. Sometime in 1844 or 1845, he went back to Darlington, where he met and married Calista Huffman, a young woman recently arrived from New York State. They eventually had nine children: Charles, George, Kossuth, Ida, Ellen, Fanny, Ransom, Hattie, and John, the eldest of whom served in the Eighty-Sixth Indiana Volunteers and died at Bowling Green, Kentucky.

Naylor practiced medicine and owned a large drugstore in Darlington. On 11 July 1863 he signed on for Morgan's Raid and served briefly as an assistant surgeon. Naylor lived to be nearly ninety years old, dying at home on 21 January 1909. He is buried in the Odd Fellows Cemetery in Darlington.

References: *History of Montgomery County, Indiana* (Bowen & Co., 1913), pp. 321–22; H. W. Beckwith, *History of Montgomery County* (1881), pp. 548–49.

NEAL (NEIL), FRANCIS M. (1838–1912)

About thirty thousand of those severely wounded in the war served in the Invalid Corps as they were recuperating. Although the corps had different duties and different names throughout the course of the war for the North, in general these soldiers and officers were unable to perform direct battlefield duties and served as hospital aides, cooks, wagoneers, and in other jobs demanding less active physical service. Francis Neal was one of them.

Neal was born in Butler County, Ohio, on 16 January 1838. He entered Wabash in the fall of 1854 and remained one academic year. Six years later he was a bookbinder in Cincinnati. On 20 June 1861 he enrolled in Company G of the Fifth Ohio Regiment, committing himself to three years of service. At the time he was five feet six inches tall, with a dark complexion, hazel eyes, and dark brown hair.

Neal's time in the army was fraught with hardship. On 9 June 1862 he was taken prisoner at the Battle of Port Republic in Rockingham County, Virginia, and languished in prison until December. On 12 January 1863 he rejoined his regiment at Dumfries, Virginia, and on 3 July 1863 he was badly wounded at the Battle of Gettysburg. Months of convalescence followed, and almost a year later, on 1 June 1864, he was transferred to the Invalid Corps. With the corps, the command was attempting to solve the problems of soldiers returning home after injuries and not rejoining their units and, just as importantly, declining manpower in the army.

On 10 May 1870 Neal married Joanna Watson at Cincinnati. He became a farmer in Washington Township, Clermont County, Ohio. They eventually had five children: Cleveland, Cora, Lucretia (Ella), Francis (Frank), and Lou (Lulu).

Neal became the mayor of Neville before his death on 15 March 1912.

References: Batavia branch of the Clermont County (Ohio) Library; military service file National Archives, Washington, DC.

NELSON, WILLIAM P. (1827–1879)

Nothing is known of William Nelson's family and his origins other than that he was born somewhere in Indiana about 1827. When he was in the Preparatory Department of Wabash College in 1834–35, he indicated that his home was in Montgomery County.

On 11 April 1855 he married Julia Ann Russell in Linden, and five years later they lived on a farm whose value was a modest $400. Their children were Melinda (1854), who died a year later; Thomas (1857); David (1859); Sarah (1861); and Henry (1875).

At the mature age of thirty-six, on 19 December 1863 Nelson enrolled in Company C of the 120th Indiana Regiment. Early in 1864, while at Nashville, he was involved in an accident when his horse fell on him, injuring his spine and breaking three ribs. Somehow he contrived to remain with his regiment and was eventually mustered out with them at Raleigh, North Carolina, on 8 January 1866.

In the fall of 1868, the family moved to Sadorus, Illinois, known to have some of the finest agricultural land in the country. On 17 April 1876, his wife apparently having died, William Nelson married Nancy J. Phipps in Grundy, Missouri.

Records indicate the Nelsons had five children. Nelson died at Sadonus on 9 April 1879, and Julia followed on 2 December 1887. They were survived by the children of both marriages, one of whom, Henry, was only twelve years old and thus placed under guardianship.

References: H. W. Beckwith, *History of Montgomery County* (1881), p. 88; *History of Montgomery County, Indiana* (Bowen & Co., 1913), p. 155; military record, Archives Division of the Indiana State Library; and his wife's pension file, National Archives, Washington DC.

NETHERTON, ROBERT T. (1830–1865?)

Robert Netherton was among that handful of Wabash students who served in the Confederate Army. He was born about 1830 in Jefferson County, Kentucky. His father, Henry (1807–1842), died when Robert was only about twelve years old. Also left fatherless were two younger brothers, Marcus and John. Their mother was Rebecca Ann Harrison (1809–1884), whose parents had settled in Montgomery County in Indiana, so it was natural for young Robert to enter the Preparatory Department of Wabash in the fall of 1847. He lived at home that first year, but as a freshman (1848–49) he moved onto the campus for what became his last year.

While in Montgomery County, his mother met Bladen Ashby, whom she married in 1850. They settled on a farm near her parents in Clark Township, but Netherton returned to Kentucky to begin studying medicine.

On 3 November 1850 he married Rebecca E. Parris, who had been orphaned at an early age and brought up by her great-uncle, Robert Teator. The Nethertons had three slaves left to Rebecca by her great-uncle. They had three children: Abner, James, and William. By 1860 the Nethertons lived in Simpsonville, Kentucky, where Netherton was a physician.

He entered Company C of the Second Regiment, Tenth Kentucky Cavalry, Confederate States of America, and eventually held the rank of major. Later he was transferred to the Thirteenth Kentucky Cavalry and participated in battles at Owensboro (August 1865) and Geiger's Pike.

On 2 May 1865 Netherton voluntarily surrendered to Union troops at Paris, Tennessee. Ten days later he was allowed to take an oath of allegiance to the United States Government and return home. However, his fine horse was taken away from him, and he was never able to recover it from the Federal army. What happened next is uncertain. He seems to have returned to Jefferson County, where presumably his family had relocated, and probably died later that year.

References: Mary Ann Stokes of Louisville, Kentucky; and two descendants of the Netherton family: Richard F. Johnson of Big Bear Lake, California, and Barbara Wisnewski of Robstown, Texas.

NEWELL, AUGUSTUS E. (1841–1876)

Except for the years that he served with the Eighteenth Indiana Light Artillery, Gus Newell stayed close to home. Born in Crawfordsville on 9 February 1841, he was the son of Rebecca and Hugh Newell. He had twin siblings, two years younger than he: Kate and William. In the autumn of 1853, he entered the Normal School of Wabash College and studied there for two years. Then in mid-June 1856 he began work as a shoemaker.

Although he was active with the Montgomery Guards prior to undertaking formal military service, he had had little preparation for the rigors of three years of continuous duty from July 1862 to June 1865. Quiet and unassuming, he was eventually promoted to the rank of corporal, and as described in his obituary, he was considered "the best gunner in the battery."

Gus never married. In the 1870s he plied his trade of shoemaking with the Crawfordsville firm of T. S. Kelley and Company. About six weeks before he died, he was forced to stop work because he was suffering from severe consumption. He died on 3 August 1876 and is buried in the Masonic Cemetery.

References: 1860 and 1870 U.S. censuses for Montgomery County; *Saturday Evening Journal*, 5 August 1876; J. W. Rowell, *The Yankee Artilleryman* (Knoxville, 1975), pp. 20, 155, 235, 281.

NEWELL, PHOCION P. (1838–1894)

Phocion Newell was born in Attica, Indiana, on 1 January 1838, the oldest of four children born to Caroline Marie Phillips and Davis Newell, an attorney. Young Phocion entered Wabash in the fall of 1849. He spent two years in the Preparatory Department and then began to study law, presumably with his father.

In the mid-1850s the Newell family moved to Minnesota, where Phocion's father married Martha Newell, in 1857. They had two children.

The war intervened in the lives of both father and son, each of whom volunteered for military service. On 13 August 1862, at the age of forty-seven, Davis enrolled in Company H of the Seventh Minnesota Regiment; he died on board the hospital ship *Baltic* on 5 May 1865. Phocion Newell joined Company C of the First Minnesota Regiment on 29 April 1861. Promoted to the rank of corporal, he was transferred to Battery I of the United States Army under the command of William M. Kirby in July 1862 and was stationed near Bolivar, Virginia. On 15 October he was reported absent without leave, and in the coming months the army concluded that he had deserted. It should be noted that not all desertion imputations may have been accurate. Like many soldiers taken ill, he may have been sent to more than one hospital and failed to keep the army adequately informed. According to records, he died on 10 October 1894.

References: Dakota County (Minnesota) Historical Society; military service file, National Archives, Washington, DC.

NOFSINGER, FRANCIS B. (1837–1920)

Francis Nofsinger was born on 6 November 1837 in Ladoga, Indiana, purportedly the first white child born there. His parents were Mary Myers and William Rowland Nofsinger. A younger brother, William Wallace, died when he was five years old.

In the autumn of 1854, Nofsinger came from Indianapolis to Crawfordsville to enter the Preparatory Department of Wabash College. He remained only one school year and then began to study medicine with local doctors, culminating in admission to the Ohio Medical College of Cincinnati in 1861. Later he attended classes at Tennessee Medical College of Nashville, graduating in 1864 and paving his way to become a surgeon in the army.

Nofsinger's military service involved treating patients at the Cumberland General Hospital in Nashville (nine hundred beds) from the spring of 1864 to the spring of 1865. As part of his contract, he not only had to swear not to give aid and comfort to the enemy but also to furnish his own medical instruments. If he did this, the hospital would deduct their cost from his monthly salary of $100.

On 25 October 1865, at Paris, Illinois, he married Julia Baldwin. Their three children were William, Francis B. Jr., and Gertrude.

In 1869 the Nofsingers settled in Kansas City, Missouri, where Nofsinger established one of the city's first meatpacking businesses. Its first year in business, the firm slaughtered and shipped to the East 10,000 hogs and 4,200 cattle, and within a decade they were shipping 100,000 pounds of meat each day. Nofsinger was very active in local politics and community affairs. During 1873–74 he sat on the city council, and from 1874 to 1878 he was president of the Board of Trade. Later, from 1889 to 1893, he was postmaster, and from 1901 to 1905 city assessor. He not only made a good deal of money in his own right, but inherited from his father a grand estate of $150,000.

Nofsinger died on 6 January 1920, survived by his wife and children, and is buried in Mount Washington Cemetery in Fairmont, Missouri.

References: Crawfordsville Public Library; Kansas City Public Library; C. P. R. Walters, *History of Clark Township, Ladoga and part of Scott Township, Montgomery County, Indiana*, p. 137; *United States Biographical Dictionary and Portrait Gallery* III (1878), p. 460; *Kansas City Journal*, 10 May 1901; *Kansas City Times*, 7 and 8 January 1920; military service file, National Archives, Washington, DC.

OAKLEY, CHAUNCEY B. (1833–1903)

Chauncey Oakley was born in Delaware County, New York, on 14 August 1833, one of three children of Harriet Andrews and Benjamin W. Oakley. His other two siblings were Martha and Harriet. Both parents were New Yorkers by birth, and in 1844 they undertook the long trek west to Fort Wayne, Indiana.

Chauncey Oakley spent four years (1847–51) in the Preparatory Department of Wabash College and then was called home to help with the family business in view of his father's poor health. The Oakley family owned a hardware store and was involved in tin and copper smithing as well.

On 9 September 1856 he married Emily A. Evans; she died in 1863. On 11 August 1862 Oakley enrolled at Fort Wayne in Company E of the Eighty-Eighth Indiana Regiment as a captain and was sent to Louisville, Kentucky. At the Battle of Perryville in early October, he was exposed to the elements and harsh conditions for long periods, and by mid-November he came down with liver disease, fever, and facial neuralgia. His health continued to decline, and on 15 December he secured a medical discharge at Nashville and returned to Fort Wayne to work in the family hardware store.

After Oakley's wife died, he re-enlisted in the army in June 1864 as adjutant of the 139th Regiment, one of the one-hundred-day units. He spent most of this time in Kentucky and was released by the end of September. He then signed up again on 3 November as a lieutenant colonel in the 142nd Regiment and was released for the last time at Nashville in July 1865.

After the war he carried on his family's business in Fort Wayne, and on 5 September 1870 he married Mary L. Henry. After living and working for a time in Pennsylvania, the family returned to Fort Wayne and Oakley eventually became secretary of the Fort Wayne Land and Improvement Company. In the late 1880s and early 1890s, he served two terms on the city council, and in 1894 he ran successfully as a Republican for mayor.

On 1 January 1903 he was appointed by the governor to the post of oil inspector for Allen County, but he died four months later on 19 April. When Mary died on 3 November, both were buried in Lindenwood Cemetery near Chauncey's first wife, Emily.

References: Allen County Public Library; *Fort Wayne Journal*, 20 April 1903; *Memorial Record of Northeastern Indiana* (1896), pp. 370–73.

O'NEALL, EDGAR HOWARD (1845–1909)

Edgar O'Neall's name appears in some records as Howard O'Neall. He was born on a farm near Yountsville in 1845, one of four sons and six daughters of Helen (Ellen) and Abijah O'Neall.

In the fall of 1861, he entered the Preparatory Department of Wabash College, and the following year he was in the freshman class. He remained a freshman for two additional years (1863–65).

While still a student he managed to serve one hundred days of military service, between 23 May and 29 September 1964. He was in Company H of the 135th Indiana Regiment and rose to the rank of corporal while serving in Tennessee and Alabama. After the war O'Neall returned to work on the family farm and eventually acquired a homestead of his own.

On 4 December 1877 he married Ida Troutman, and eventually they had four children: Ruth, Russell, a daughter who became Mrs. W. H. Sigmond, and William. In 1900 they left their farm near Yountsville and moved into Crawfordsville in order to make it easier to provide schooling for their children. O'Neall became active in civic affairs, serving as director of the YMCA and as a member of the Culver Union Hospital Board.

In later years O'Neall acquired an interest in two factories in North Dakota that manufactured corrugated culverts and divided his time between the locations of the two plants while still maintaining ties to Indiana, where he was appointed to the state Board of Pardons for a four-year term in 1905.

He died of a heart attack in Fargo on 27 May 1909, and his body was brought back to Crawfordsville for interment in Oak Hill Cemetery.

References: *Moore's Hoosier Cyclopedia* (1905), p. 66; R. G. McCormick, *Yountsville History* (1968), pp. 84–85; *Crawfordsville Journal*, 28 May 1909.

ORCHARD, SAMUEL ADOLPHUS (1835–1914)

Samuel Orchard was born 20 September 1835 in Livonia, the third of eleven children of Amanda M. and Andrew R. Orchard. His brothers and sisters were William Mitchell (also a Wabash student), Margery, Matilda, Isaac Newton, Emily Victoria, John, George, Franklin, Amanda Z., and Elizabeth E.

He attended Wabash College in the Preparatory Department from 1852 to 1854. In 1855 the family moved to Omaha, where his father took up farming. Orchard joined the army, and at some point during the war, he was appointed assistant provost marshal under Captain O. F. Davis.

Between 1865 and 1870 he formed the partnership of Orchard and Preston, a produce and grocery trade business in Omaha. On 3 January 1866 he married Eliza A. Crawford, and they eventually had two children, Charles Colfax and Mabel Gray.

In 1870 Orchard became the first surveyor of customs for the newly opened port on the Missouri River, and between 1872 and 1877 he was Omaha's assistant postmaster. He then went into the furniture business with a new partner, Samuel Bean, and when Bean died in 1881, Orchard continued this very large and successful enterprise in partnership with his son, Charles. Disaster struck in 1892 when the store nearly burned to the ground. It was insured to the impressive amount of $85,000, but the losses ranged upwards of $120,000. Nevertheless, the building was rebuilt and the business carried on.

Orchard died in Omaha on 11 September 1914, survived by his widow and two children.

References: *Omaha Sunday Bee*, 13 September 1914; J. W. Savage and J. S. Bell, *History of the City of Omaha Nebraska* (1894), pp. 567–68; *Historical and Descriptive Review of Omaha* (1892), pp. 91–92.

ORNBAUN, HENRY NEWTON (1837–1863)

Henry Ornbaun was born in Crawfordsville in 1837, one of eight children of Mary Shipley and Andrew Ornbaun. His siblings were Elizabeth, Delilah, John, Mary, Andrew, William, and Alice. Henry spent three years, 1856–59, in the Preparatory Department of Wabash College. He may then have withdrawn because of the death of his father, a wagoner by trade, since Mary was listed in the census as a widow in 1860.

In 1861–62 Ornbaun was licensed to be a minister in the Methodist church. However, on 18 August 1862 he enrolled for two years in Company K of the Seventy-Ninth Indiana Regiment and took part in the Battle of Murfreesboro. He was badly wounded on 25 November 1863 while storming Missionary Ridge, and in spite of being cared for in a hospital at Chattanooga, his injuries proved fatal, and he died on 1 December. His body was returned to Crawfordsville and interred in the Masonic Cemetery.

References: *Wabash Magazine*, V (February 1864), pp. 159–60; William Graham, *Memoirs* (1862–1863), pp. 103–07; *Portrait and Biographical Record of Montgomery, Parke and Fountain Counties, Indiana* (1893), p. 560.

OSBORN(E), MILTON A. (1836–1875)

Milton Osborn was born at Greencastle on 16 March 1836, but when he entered the Preparatory Department of Wabash College in the fall of 1852, he indicated that his home was Bowling Green, Indiana. He remained at Wabash for two years, and then studied law and was admitted to the bar in 1855 or 1856. As prosecuting attorney for the Sixth District (Greencastle), he was in a position to marry Mira I. Hensley on 21 October 1856. They had three children. On 3 June 1862 he received a commission as a first lieutenant of Company D of the Fifty-Fifth Indiana Regiment, and later that year, on 27 October, he became a first lieutenant in the Twenty-Fourth Light Artillery, which position he held until 19 February 1863. On 22 March 1863 Osborn was promoted to captain and transferred to the Twentieth Light Artillery. Details of his service could not be ascertained, except for his resignation on 18 February 1865.

After the war he resumed his law practice, and in 1869 he was elected to one term in the Indiana House of Representatives for Putnam and Hendricks Counties. He died on 24 January 1875 and may be buried in Greencastle.

References: Census and marriage records; *Biographical Directory of the Indiana General Assembly*, I (1980), p. 301.

OTT, JOHN HENRY (1839-1919)

John Ott was among the many local boys who attended Wabash. He was born in Crawfordsville on 4 June 1839, one of seven children of Amanda and Henry Ott, a druggist. He attended the Preparatory Department for one school year, 1854–55.

Ott's military service was brief. On 20 April 1861 he enrolled at Crawfordsville in Company G of the Tenth Indiana Regiment for three months and spent most of this time in Virginia. He was mustered out at Indianapolis on 6 August 1861. Both before and after his stint in the army, he presumably worked for his father in the drugstore.

In the late 1860s Ott moved to Illinois and married Elizabeth. They seem not to have had any children, and in 1883 they relocated to St. Louis, Missouri, where Elizabeth died on 15 September 1889.

Two years later, on 14 May 1891, Ott married Elizabeth A. Fisher in New Richmond, Indiana. They initially lived in St. Louis, but in 1895 settled in Sorento, Illinois, where Elizabeth died, childless, on 15 December 1912. John then moved to Lebanon, Missouri, where he died on 10 May 1919.

References: J. B. Shaw, *History of the Tenth Regiment Indiana Volunteer Infantry* (1912), p. 39; K. Zach, "Family Roots," *Montgomery County Magazine*, XVI (March 1991), p. 10; and military pension file, National Archives, Washington, DC.

PADDOCK, BENJAMIN FRANKLIN (1843–1921)

While at Wabash between January 1860 and July 1861, sixteen-year-old Frank Paddock kept a diary, the original of which is in the Ramsay Archives. Young Paddock was born near Terre Haute on 2 September 1843, the oldest of seven children of Eliza Jane Gunn and William Paddock. His father was a farmer and partner in a flour milling concern.

Paddock's diary records the daily routine of a somewhat lonely student whose big event of the day was to walk downtown and see if any letters had arrived for him at the post office. He tells of going to and from recitations as well as attending church service in town on Sunday and chapel on campus. On one Sabbath he "concluded to go to the Methodists and hear them howl in their accustomed manner," while the college service was not much better in his view: "Went over to chapel as usual on Sunday morning, and got gloriously bored by Prof. Mills. He kept us anxiously sitting for an hour or two . . without interesting us with one remark."

There were times during his first semester when Paddock thought of transferring, but a few weeks of summer vacation at home in Terre Haute convinced him that he longed to be back in Crawfordsville. The fall semester of 1860 went well enough, as he began to study Greek and enjoyed debating in the Calliopean Society. However, when he returned home at Christmas he found his mother ill, and a month later she died. His diary is painfully quiet about this momentous event and only mentions his father's injunction to take his studies seriously when back at school. In the summer of 1861, Paddock enrolled in the University of Michigan for the following fall, but at the end of that academic year, he joined Company I of the Seventy-Sixth Indiana Volunteers for thirty days. He then returned to Terre Haute to help his father in the milling business.

On 5 September 1867 he married Harriet Claxton Rea, and they had five children.

Paddock died in Terre Haute at the home of his son, William, on 2 June 1921.

References: Biographical sketch by Harriet L. Paddock, granddaughter of B. F. Paddock, in the Ramsay Archives, Wabash College; R. Condit, *A History of Early Terre Haute* (1900), p. 145.

PARK, JAMES (1824–1895)

James Park was born in 1824 in Jefferson County, one of the five children of Jannett and James Park, who both came from Scotland. His siblings were Grace, Mary, John, and Alexander.

Park first came to Wabash College in the autumn of 1845 and studied in the Preparatory Department. He then continued into the freshman, sophomore, and junior classes, but for some reason didn't return for his senior year. Once he left college he became a merchant in Williamsport and studied law, passed the bar exam, and started a practice there.

In 1855 he married Eliza, and they had three children: Laura, Ella, and James.

Park was appointed provost marshal for the Eighth Congressional District of Indiana, and during the war he was especially active in recruiting volunteers for the Seventy-Second and Eighty-Sixth Regiments, both organized in Lafayette. For some years afterwards he was a judge of the Court of Common Pleas for Warren and Fountain Counties. His loyal and active service to the Republican Party was rewarded by his being appointed United States Consul to the French town of Aix-la-Chapelle where he lived from 1869 to 1878.

When he returned to the United States, he practiced law in Lafayette. He died there of pneumonia on 18 June 1895.

References: Walter Salts of West Lebanon, Indiana; *Warren Republican*, 20 June 1895; the Madison-Jefferson Public Library.

PARKER, JAMES FREDERICK (1819–1884)

James Parker was born in Hampshire County, Virginia, on 29 October 1819, one of two sons of Elizabeth Sheets and Thornton Parker. Five years later his father died, and in 1826 his widowed mother moved to Tippecanoe County in Indiana.

Parker entered the Preparatory Department of Wabash College in 1837 for one school year, then moved to Oxford, Indiana, and became the county auditor and clerk from 1840 to 1847. In addition he served on the county council in 1846.

On 2 August 1842 he married Rachael N. Justice of Oxford, and they eventually had eleven children. He also became an hotelier and organized the first public dance in 1850 at his Foreign Exchange Hotel. In that year he also began to study law. He was admitted to the bar in 1851 and began practicing, only the second attorney to locate in Oxford. In 1855 and again in 1857 he was elected to the Indiana Senate from Benton County.

On 14 June 1861 Parker was mustered into Company D of the Fifteenth Indiana Regiment as a sergeant for three years. About 1,046 soldiers reported for duty at Indianapolis, where another Wabash man, General Joseph J. Reynolds, took command. In early July they went by rail and boat to Camp Clay in Ohio and then to western Virginia, where they arrived just in time to take part in the Battle of Rich Mountain in July of 1861. On 3 October the Fifteenth fought at Greenbrier, Virginia, and by December they were attached to the Army of the Ohio at Louisville under General D. C. Buell. In February the regiment was at Nashville, and then participated in the Battle of Shiloh and the siege of Corinth. Parker received steady promotions from second to first lieutenant, and on 16 November 1861, to captain of Company D. For reasons of ill health he resigned on 3 June 1862.

After his military duty he went back to Oxford, resumed his legal career, and became county treasurer in 1868. In the later 1870s he moved to Knox County and could have taken up farming. He died there of cancer on 24 December 1884. He is buried in Oxford, Benton County.

References: *Biographical Directory of the Indiana General Assembly*, I (1980), p. 305; J. Birch, *Benton County and Historic Oxford*, I (1928), p. 68; S. Barce, *Benton County, Indiana* (1930), p. 157; manuscript letter from Parker's daughter, Maggie, to W. H. English, 13 November 1888, in the possession of the Indiana Historical Society; T. Scribner, *Indiana's Roll of Honor*, II (1866), pp. 389–94.

PATTERSON, JAMES E. (1835–1864)

James Patterson was born on 27 July 1835 in Covington, Indiana. His parents were Mary Gabriel (1814–1894) and William S. Patterson (1807–1847). He had three siblings: Alva, John, and Horton.

Patterson spent only one year, 1850–51, in the Preparatory Department of Wabash and then became a carpenter. On 30 December 1857 he married Mary E. Spinning from Ohio. There is no record of their having had any children.

Patterson had a distinguished career in the Civil War, rising to the rank of major in the Sixty-Third Indiana Regiment. He was commissioned first lieutenant and adjutant on 21 February 1862 and major on 24 April 1864. However, his life was cut short in May of 1864 at the Battle of Resaca, Georgia. He is buried in the Oak Grove Cemetery in Covington alongside his wife, who died in 1876.

References: Miriam L. Luke of Covington, Indiana.

PATTERSON, THOMAS MCDONALD (1839–1916)

Thomas Patterson was born in County Carlow, Ireland, on 4 November 1839, one of two sons of Margaret Mountjoy and James Patterson. Both of their sons attended Wabash and served in the Civil War.

Once the family settled in Crawfordsville in 1853, Patterson spent three years in the composing room of the *Crawfordsville Review*, and from 1857 until 1861 he assisted his father in the jewelry business.

On 22 April 1861 he enrolled as a sergeant in Company I of the Eleventh Regiment. He was mustered out at Indianapolis on 6 August. In 1862 he entered Asbury College, and in 1863 he married Katherine Grafton of Watertown, New York. They had five children, but only one, Margaret, grew to maturity.

In the fall of 1864, Patterson became a freshman at Wabash. While a sophomore and junior (1865–67), he apparently studied law on the side, because in 1867 he was admitted to the Indiana bar. Consequently, he did not return for his senior year, but rather practiced law in Crawfordsville.

While at Wabash he was one of seventeen who disbanded the Delta Psi

Theta fraternity in December 1865 and then became members of the newly chartered Phi Gamma Delta fraternity in September 1866. The initiation ceremony took place in the Patterson Bookshop on Main Street.

In 1872 Patterson moved to Denver, and in the following year became city attorney. In 1874 he was elected as a Democrat to represent Colorado Territory in the United States House of Representatives. He served from 4 March 1875 to 1 August 1876. Once Colorado was admitted to statehood, he ran again for Congress, serving from 13 December 1877 to 3 March 1879. From 1874 to 1880 he was also a member of the Democratic National Committee.

During the 1890s he purchased two newspapers: the *Rocky Mountain News* and the *Denver Times*. However, politics was still in his blood, and he served as a United States Senator from 4 March 1901 to 3 March 1907. His wife died in 1902, casting a pall over Patterson and his only surviving daughter, Mrs. Richard C. Campbell.

Thomas died on 23 July 1916 and was buried in Fairmount Cemetery in Denver.

References: *Biographical Directory of the American Congress*; *Dictionary of American Biography*; E. H. Ziegler, *Phi Gamma Delta at Wabash* (1941), pp. 16, 24, 38.

PEIRCE, ROBERT BRUCE FRAZIER (1843–1898)

Robert Peirce was born at Laurel on 17 February 1843. His father was Henry, who married twice. Henry's first wife was Harriet B., and she gave birth to at least two sons, Seymour and Harvey. Henry's second wife, Mary, was the mother of John, Mary, Albert, Charles, and Frank. Three of Robert's brothers (Seymour, Harvey, and John) served in the Civil War, though they did not attend Wabash College. Young Robert entered the Preparatory Department in the fall of 1860 and remained there for two years. Then he entered the freshman class in the Classical Course, ultimately receiving his bachelor of arts degree in June 1866.

While at Wabash he enrolled at Crawfordsville in Company H of the 135th Indiana Regiment on 25 April 1864 and received a commission as first lieutenant on 14 May. The regiment spent most of its time in Tennessee and Alabama guarding railroad lines. Peirce was mustered out on 29 September, ready to begin his junior year at Wabash.

On 28 November 1866 he married Hattie Blair of Crawfordsville, whose brother, John, had also attended Wabash. Robert and Hattie eventually had three children: Lois, Frank, and Edwin. At the time of his marriage, Peirce was studying law with B. F. Love of Shelbyville, and after being admitted to the Indiana bar, opened an office in Crawfordsville in 1867. From 1868 to 1874 he served as prosecuting attorney for the counties of Montgomery, Clinton, Boone, Fountain, and Warren.

In 1874 Peirce became general solicitor for the Logansport, Crawfordsville and South-Western Railroad, a post he retained until 1880, when he ran for the United States House of Representatives as a Republican. He defeated Bayliss W. Hanna by a margin of 2,200 votes. He served just one term (4 March 1881 to 3 March 1883) and then was defeated in his bid for re-election. Resuming his law practice in Crawfordsville, he found his corporate and railroad clients expanding to such an extent that eventually, in 1888, he moved to Indianapolis. By then he was also general manager of the Indiana, Decatur and Western Railroad.

Peirce lost his wife, Hattie, on 28 October 1878, and sometime thereafter married Mrs. Alice W. Van Valkenburg. He died at Indianapolis on 5 December 1898 and was buried next to his wife in Oak Hill Cemetery, Crawfordsville.

References: *Biographical Directory of the American Congress*; W. Cumback and J. B. Maynard, *Men of Progress of Indiana* (1899), pp. 394–96; *Wabash Magazine*, V (December 1866), p. 46; *Wabash Magazine*, XI (March 1871), p. 138; *Wabash Magazine*, XII (June 1872), p. 213; *Wabash College Record*, July 1903, p. 28.

PELTON, CHARLES (1843–1900)

Charles Pelton was born in Sparta, Illinois, on 11 March 1843, the son of Martha McClure and Charles B. Pelton. He had one brother. On 4 March 1864 he enrolled at Springfield in Company F of the Second Illinois Cavalry for three years but was mustered out at San Antonio, Texas, on 22 November 1865.

In the autumn of 1866, Pelton came to Wabash College from Carbondale as a freshman in the Classical Course, returning the following year as a sophomore. However, on 7 September 1868, about the time that he was due at Wabash for his junior year, he wrote a letter to Professor E. O. Hovey from Makanda, explaining that he would not be returning because his brother was too ill to work on the family farm and had to go east to act as a bookkeeper for their uncle: "This leaves my parents to my charge while their age and my father's feebleness requires me to be with or near them. It was the Lord's good pleasure and wisdom to withhold from us the peach and apple crop this year . . . It makes us dependent on the sale of some property for the accomplishment of our desire, which is a removal to Crawfordsville."

Eventually the Peltons moved to Montgomery County, and Charles was able to take his senior year at Wabash in 1870–71. He spent the next three years at Lane Theological Seminary in Cincinnati, and a year later he was ordained by the Presbyterian Church at Columbus, Ohio.

He married Georgina Woollard, and they eventually had six children. His pastorates took the family throughout Illinois and the Midwest. They included Worthington, Ohio (1874–78); Cobden, Illinois (1879–81); Cairo, Dongola, Grand Tower, Carterville, Alto Pass, Richview, Dubois and Sumner (all in Illinois, 1881–93); and Milford, Ohio (1893–94).

He was agent for the Municipal Reform League of Cincinnati from 1894 to

1900, and he died there in 1900.

References: Lane Theological Seminary, *General Catalogue*, 1829–1899, p. 86; *Wabash Magazine*, VIII (December 1867), p. 78; *Wabash Magazine*, XI (June 1871), pp. 153–54; *Wabash Magazine*, XII (March 1872), p. 148; *Wabash Record*, July 1903, p. 29; Ramsay Archives, Wabash College.

PERRY, HENRY MITCHELL (1848–1906)

Henry Perry was born on 30 June 1848 in Xenia, Ohio, one of two sons of Nancy McNeice and Richard Perry. He and his older brother, John, attended Wabash and served in the Civil War. They had a sister, Margaret. Both parents died in about 1852, and the two brothers were taken in by relatives, Jane and Richard Harris of Crawfordsville.

At the age of fifteen, the young man persuaded the recruiting officer of the 120th Indiana Volunteers that he was eighteen and thus eligible to enroll into Company B, the same company as his brother. This was in December 1863, and the two Perrys served their full three years, securing discharges at Raleigh, North Carolina, on 8 January 1866. They experienced the battles of Resaca, Kennesaw Mountain, Atlanta, Franklin, Nashville, and Raleigh (March 1865), and it was thought later that excess exposure to combat had impaired the mental stability of the young Henry.

Yet, there were no signs of this instability in the fall of 1868 when he entered the Preparatory Department of Wabash College. The following year he advanced as a freshman, and four years later he graduated in June 1873. He then studied law in Crawfordsville with P. S. Kennedy and W. T. Brush and combined his legal practice with being a notary republic and real estate agent. He lived at 1206 W. Wabash Avenue and maintained his office at 105 N. Washington Street.

Perry's wife was Lillian Britton, daughter of Edward and Mary Britton of Montgomery County. They had three children: Pauline, Lois, and Pierce.

Whatever the cause of his mental instability, whether war battle stress or some inherent condition the war exacerbated, in May 1906 Perry showed signs of such mental distress that he was taken to a sanitarium in Indianapolis, where he died on 23 May. He was survived by his wife. His body was returned to Crawfordsville for burial.

References: Robert M. Perry of Ventura, California; Greene County (Ohio) District Library; 1860 and 1870 U.S. censuses for Montgomery County; Crawfordsville city directories; *Wabash Record*, July 1906, p. 107; *Crawfordsville Journal*, 24 May 1906; *Crawfordsville Journal*, 20 July 1923.

PERRY, JOHN W. (1846?–1923)

As we have seen in the previous sketch, the Perry brothers, John and Henry, were orphaned in 1852 and came to live with relatives in Crawfordsville. Both served in Company B of the 120th Indiana Regiment, and both entered Wabash College in the autumn of 1868. However, John remained at Wabash only one year, then tried running a restaurant in Crawfordsville before buying farmland about two miles east of Mace and four miles northwest of New Ross.

On 23 July 1874 Perry married Esabella Hutching, and they had three children: Earl, Hortense, and Fern. This marriage was dissolved eventually, and Perry married Franklin Brent, daughter of George and Mariam Brent of Brownsburg, on 8 May 1889. They eventually had six children: Hugh M. (1891), Clay L. (1894), Lane (1896), Carl B. (1897), Anna Lucille (1899), and Floyd (1901).

By 1908 Perry had given up farming and joined some of his children on the west coast, settling in Los Angeles and starting a candy-making business. Some years later he returned to the Midwest, then traveled up to Windsor, Canada. Between 1920 and 1922 he lived in a veterans retirement home in Dayton, Ohio, but then went back to California to be near his family. Three of his sons (Clay, Lane, and Floyd) were partners in the Perry Realty Company of Santa Barbara.

On 8 September 1923 Perry was struck down and killed by an automobile. His deafness may have been a contributing factor to his accident. He is buried in Santa Barbara, along with his second wife.

References: See references cited for Henry Perry.

POGUE, WILLIAM CRAWFORD (1834–1910)

Both Union and Confederate armies set up signal corps to telegraph information, give signals by wig-wag, and in the case of the southerners, to spy on the enemy. William Pogue became interested in the skills these soldiers represented and requested transfer to a signal corps unit from his infantry posting. Perhaps he also wished to avoid further action on the battlefield after Chickamauga.

Pogue was born in Crawfordsville on 1 December 1834, the eldest child of Elizabeth Crawford and Silas Pogue, who had a farm east of Mace. His younger siblings were John, Margaret, and Rebecca.

In the autumn of 1853, young Pogue joined the Preparatory Department of Wabash College, remaining for one school year. On 18 September 1861 at Crawfordsville, Pogue enrolled in Company B of the Tenth Indiana Infantry for three years. In height he was five feet eleven inches, with dark complexion, black eyes, and black hair. At the Battle of Chickamauga in September 1863, he tried to slake his thirst from what turned out to be highly polluted water and ended up in hospital for several months. While he was convalescing, his request to be transferred to the United States army signal corps was granted, and as soon as he regained his health, he reported to Chattanooga. He was honorably discharged at Atlanta on 17 September 1864.

In Benton County, Iowa, he met Mary Ann Crawford, and they married on 14 June 1865. Their only child, Edna, was born there in 1868. In 1871 the family returned to Montgomery County and settled on the family farm until 1876, when they left for Florida for six years. Finally, in about 1882 they settled at Northville, Tennessee, where Pogue's wife died in August 1896. Sometime thereafter Pogue moved within the same county to Crossville, where he died on 3 December 1910.

References: C. P. Walters, *Fredericksburg (Mace) and Mace Station* (1970), pp. 16, 19, 93; R. Nees, *Centennial History of the New Ross Community* I, p. 97, and II, p. 3; H. W. Beckwith, *History of Montgomery County* (1881), p. 51; military pension file, National Archives, Washington, DC.

Chickamauga

From Henry Campbell's Diary "Three Years in the Saddle"
September 18, 1863
About 9 o'clock we moved back across the Chattanooga Road and went into position in the edge of the woods on the west side of the road. Picket and skirmish line, remaining as they were. Troops are constantly passing to the left, Thomas' Corps with Crittenden's after it, occupied the entire night in passing. They are hurrying to the left, to prevent the Rebels from getting between us and Chattanooga. The night was dreadfully cold. No fires allowed. No supper. No feed for our horses. The monotonous tramp, tramp, of the passing troops, the rumbling of artillery carriages, and the ominous thoughts of the morrow. All combined rendered it a miserable night. I gathered a few corn stalks for my horse, and lay down on the caisson chests & tried to sleep. With no blankets, this was a chilly proceeding. Our Headquarter wagon got lost in the retiring movement, and did not get up until midnight. Our blankets being with that wagon we shivered it out until they arrived.

September 19, 1863
All of Crittenden's and Thomas' Corps marched past us last night. This morning instead of being the extreme left of the army, we occupy a position on the right center, the extreme right of Thomas' Corps. McCook's Corps arrived after daylight and joined on our right...

It was 8 o'clock before the awful, deathlike stillness that preceded this terrible battle was broken. Then it began far away to the left a low distinct rumbling, gradually approaching, like a distant hail storm, as division after division became hotly engaged repulsing terrible charges from three times their number without faltering or flinching in the least, as the case with Thomas' Corps, actually drove three times their number for more than one mile. We did not get engaged until 10 o'clock when the enemy charged us furiously several times, but they were rolled back with heavy losses each time. The roar is perfectly awful, nothing can be compared with it. If ten million pieces of sheet iron were all shaken at once it wouldn't be a drop in the bucket. The artillery shots were few, compared to the musketry, because the woods were so thick very few positions could be found for the Batteries. About 3 o'clock the Rebels made a furious charge on us, drove the skirmishers back from the ditch in our front, and occupied it.

Captain Lilly moved forward two guns on the left, to a position . . which compelled the Rebels to retreat in confusion. The ditch was literally full of killed and wounded and proved to be a self made grave for hundreds of them.

Brigade made one charge, driving the Rebels back in disorder for at least ½ mile. The tremendous and unceasing roar began to check up as the shades of evening appeared, and ceased entirely about 7 o'clock. All through the forepart of the night, it would occasionally break out, up and down the line in an angry roar as if the troops were afraid of one another advancing. Our loss in the battery was very light considering the terrible fire we had to endure. Andy Johnson was killed while the Battery was moving through a cornfield, he was shot through the lungs and died instantly. Dave Lane wounded in the knee. James Somerville stunned by a spent ball hit on the head. Longstreet's Corps charged us just before dark, but we repulsed them with heavy loss. Fired our guns with thribble charges of canister each discharge would open out great gaps in their ranks. Boys would carry up canister from the caisson by the arm load. . . Rebel sharpshooters tried their best to pick off Captain Lilly who rode his horse all day, and carried canister up from the caisson on horseback when the Rebels charged us. Sergeant Crouse received a shot through the rear of his saddle, passing through his blanket, overcoat & portable writing desk, and lodged in his coat tail.

PORTER, WILLIAM CLAY (1834–1911)

William Porter was born on the Isle of Jersey (England) on 11 May 1834. His parents were Sarah Knight and Jonathan Goodenough Porter, a conservative Methodist preacher. In 1835 the family emigrated to the United States, where his father undertook missionary work in Illinois at Chicago, Naperville, Lockport, and Wilmington.

At the age of fifteen Porter began to train as a blacksmith, a skill that proved very useful in college and seminary. From 1852 to 1856 he attended Knox College in Galesburg, Illinois. Then a friend from Naperville, John V. Cunningham, persuaded him to take his senior year at Wabash, Cunningham's alma mater. Porter spent 1856–57 completing the Classical Course and received his bachelor of arts degree in June.

Intent on entering the Presbyterian ministry, Porter spent two years at Lane Theological Seminary in Cincinnati and was ordained at Plymouth, Indiana, in 1860. In April 1861 he resigned in order to become chaplain of the Twentieth Indiana Volunteers.

He remained with his regiment for four years, primarily attending to the ill and wounded. On one occasion, when his regiment was ordered to retreat, he went forward to warn the pickets and help them withdraw before they could be taken prisoner. He was present at many of the battles involving the Army of the Potomac, including Malvern Hill (1 July 1862), Gettysburg, and Petersburg (15–18 June 1864). As a part of the Twentieth Indiana, he witnessed the naval battle between the *Monitor* and the *Merrimac*. He was also at Appomattox when Robert E. Lee surrendered.

On 25 July 1865 Porter returned home to Naperville, Illinois, and later that year accepted a call to be the minister of a church in Coldwater, Michigan. However, he returned to Naperville on 27 November 1866 to marry John V. Cunningham's sister, Lucinda (Lucy) Isabella. Over the years they had five children: Katherine, Alice, Carolyn, John, and Lucy.

The Porters remained in Coldwater, Michigan, until the end of 1871, then moved to Fort Scott, Kansas, where William began an assignment of thirty-four years as pastor of the First Presbyterian Church. He was especially active as a missionary in that region of the country and traveled to churches and schools on behalf of the American Home Missionary Society.

In 1906 Porter retired, as his health was failing. His wife Lucinda died on 7 February 1909, and he passed away on 21 March 1911. They were both buried at Fort Scott.

References: The public library at Fort Scott; L. A. Ware et al., *Dr. Porter's Life with this Church* (Fort Scott, 1909); *First Presbyterian Church: a History* (1959); Lane Theological Seminary, *General Catalogue*, 1829–1899, p. 65; *The Soldier of Indiana in the War for the Union*, I (1866), p. 488; 1905 Wabash College alumni questionnaire, Ramsay Archives, Wabash College.

POST, JAMES W. (1843–1910)

James Post was born in 1843 in Patterson County, New Jersey. His mother was A. Post, married to J. G. Post, a wagon maker, and he had four brothers and sisters, all born in New Jersey. During the 1850s the family moved to Illinois and settled in Mount Sterling. It was from there, on 14 February 1865, that Post enrolled in Company B of the Fourteenth Illinois Volunteers, noting that he was a farmer. He was five feet four inches tall, with dark complexion, hair, and eyes. While in the army he served as a musician and was mustered out at Fort Leavenworth, Kansas, on 16 September 1865.

In the fall of 1866 Post entered the Preparatory Department of Wabash College and remained for three years, then returned to Mount Sterling, where he continued farming until 1874. After that time he moved to Nebraska for a short while before coming back to Mount Sterling and marrying Gertrude Melany on 12 October 1882. Their children were Francis (1883), Lulu (1885), Elsie (1889), and Mable (1895).

From 1880 onwards Post farmed in Knox County, Missouri, until moving in 1898 to Kirksville, where he died on 24 December 1910. He is buried in the Llewellyn Cemetery there.

References: *Wabash Magazine*, XII (June 1872), pp. 153, 216; military pension file, National Archives, Washington, DC.

POTTS, JOHN (1827–1870)

John Potts was born in Paoli, Indiana, in 1827, son of Ann Smith and Joseph Potts. In 1828 his parents moved to Parke County, where his younger sister, Agatha, was born. Their mother died sometime in the early 1840s, and in 1844 Joseph married Susan Turner.

In the fall of 1846, Potts entered the Preparatory Department of Wabash College, remaining for two years. Then he began to study medicine, most likely with someone in Parke County, and on 15 September 1852 he married Elizabeth McEwen. She died five years later.

In 1858 Potts was admitted to the Parke County Medical Society, and while practicing took a course at Jefferson Medical College in Philadelphia. When the census of 1860 was taken, his practice was in Van Buren Township of Clay County.

On 23 April 1861 Potts enrolled at Rockville in Company A of the Fourteenth Indiana Regiment for three years. He was described as having grey eyes, chestnut hair, and a fair complexion, and he was five feet eleven inches tall. He went with the rest of the Fourteenth to the Battle of Rich Mountain and a lonely and cold posting (without overcoats) on Virginia's Cheat Mountain. On 17 October, Richard Bond, a surgeon in the regiment, wrote Indiana Governor Oli-

A Soldiers' Album

Witter Johnston

John Ketcham

Michael Lawson

Leo Lemmon

Ira McConnell

James Meteer

Eugene Mills

Henry Perry

ver P. Morton recommending Potts for the position of assistant surgeon, should an opening occur. Such a commission in the Fortieth Indiana Regiment came through on 15 April 1862, and he spent the following months at the Cumberland Post Hospital in Maryland. It is not clear why Potts left the army at the end of that year. In any case, he then resumed his medical practice in Clay County.

On 11 January 1869 he married Alsey Heilhart in Parke County. It would seem that he soon died, since only Alsey appears in the Clay County census for 1870.

References: Rockville (Parke County) Public Library; Clay County Genealogical Society; military service file, National Archives, Washington, DC.

POWELL, GEORGE WILLIAM (1842–1915)

When the draft laws went into effect in the North in 1863, new policies also allowed men who paid a not-insignificant sum to be exempted from the draft calls. Substitutes began to be hired. George Powell served on his own early in the war, but later in the conflict, he received a substantial sum for the times (from $300 up) to take the place of another Hoosier. In the latter days some newspaper commentators and others called the results of the draft effort "a rich man's war, a poor man's fight."

George Powell was born on a farm near Parkersburg on 1 April 1842, one of thirteen children of Elizabeth and John W. Powell. Shortly after George's birth the family acquired a larger farm two miles north of New Ross in Montgomery County, where he eventually inherited the more than four hundred acres.

In 1860 Powell enrolled in the Preparatory Department of Wabash College, but before the academic year was over, on 20 April 1861, he joined Company G of the Tenth Indiana Regiment at Crawfordsville for three months. The next year, on 15 October 1862, he enlisted as a corporal in the First Indiana Cavalry attached to the Twenty-Eighth Regiment for nine months. His unit went to Arkansas, and he engaged in the Battle of Helena shortly before being mustered out as a sergeant on 22 July 1863. In his third tour of duty he was paid to substitute for someone else in the Seventy-Ninth Regiment from 24 October 1864 to 11 May 1865. At the time he was described as five feet eleven inches tall, with blue eyes, brown hair, and light complexion.

Returning to Montgomery County, he married sixteen-year-old Henrietta C. Beck on 30 August 1866. Their only child, Eunice, was born in 1880. Powell served as a Walnut Township trustee in 1868. The family moved into the town of New Ross in about 1890. Powell died on 9 May 1915 and is buried in the Pisgah Cemetery in Montgomery County.

References: *Crawfordsville Journal*, 10 May 1915; census, marriage, and death records.

POWELL, JOHN W. (1846–1912)

John Powell was born in Lafayette on 6 October 1846, the son of Eliza J. Baer and Henry Powell. His mother died a few months later, on 6 January 1847. It is not known what became of his father.

The young man was admitted to the Preparatory Department of Wabash College in the autumn of 1861 after serving in the army in Company E of the Tenth Indiana Regiment for three months. However, he had barely begun his studies when he decided to enlist in the Indiana Tenth Light Artillery at Lafayette and was called up for duty at Indianapolis on 17 December 1861. Powell signed up for three years, giving his age as eighteen, although he was only fifteen. He stood five feet nine inches tall, with dark eyes, hair, and complexion. Because of his previous military experience, he entered the Tenth Battery as a corporal, yet his youth and inexperience caught up with him, and he was demoted to private in July 1862. Nonetheless, he served his full term and was honorably discharged on 24 January 1865.

Powell then went to live with his grandfather, Joseph Baer, who had become his court-appointed guardian. When Joseph died, another farmer named Nelson Lutz became Powell's guardian. By implication, he apparently required looking after, a fact that was confirmed in 1906 by legal documents that described him as a "person of unsound mind." When Lutz died, Powell's next guardian was Charles McDill, owner of a farm near Romney. Shortly before he died of heart failure on 3 October 1912, Powell lodged with Philip McCauley at Lafayette. He was buried in Baer Cemetery, Tippecanoe County.

References: Dorothy Van Cleef and the Tippecanoe County Historical Association of Lafayette; *Lafayette Morning Journal*, 4 October 1912; and *History of the Indiana Tenth Volunteer Infantry* (1912), p. 34.

POWERS, IRA C. (1843–1900)

Ira Powers was born on 3 August 1843, one of six sons that Lovia Fields and Jonathan Powers sent to Wabash: David, John, Samuel, George, William, and Ira. Lovia and Jonathan also two daughters, Eliza and Elizabeth. When Jonathan Powers first came to Crawfordsville, before taking up farming full time, he was a partner with Isaac C. Elston in a grocery store near Ristine's tavern. He died in 1855.

Powers attended the Preparatory Department at the college for two years, 1852–54, and then presumably returned to the family farm. Not long afterwards he married Mary E., and they had three children: George, Ella, and William.

In the late 1850s the Powers family moved first to Iowa and then to Illinois, where Ira volunteered for military service. At the age of twenty-nine, he was relatively old to enlist in Company I of the 118th Illinois Regiment, and although his date of entry is uncertain, it was probably sometime in 1862. At the time he was five feet five inches tall, with light hair, fair complexion, and green eyes. He was mustered out at Baton Rouge, Louisiana, on 4 October 1865.

By 1870 the Powers family were back in Crawfordsville, where Powers was a day laborer and then became an agent for a local business. In 1883 he served as the city's assessor. On 7 February 1900 he died of tuberculosis and was buried in Oak Hill Cemetery.

References: *Crawfordsville New Review*, 10 February 1900; *Crawfordsville Weekly Argus News*, 10 February 1900; *Saturday Evening Journal of Crawfordsville*, 6 April 1883; *Crawfordsville Daily Journal*, 5 October 1894; H. W. Beckwith, *History of Montgomery County* (1881), pp. 117, 124, 126; *History of Montgomery County, Indiana* (Bowen & Co., 1913), p. 74.

POWERS, WILLIAM J. (1830–1868)

William Powers was one of six brothers to attend Wabash College, two of whom (see Ira) served in the Civil War. His parents, Lovia Fields and Jonathan Powers, were from Pennsylvania, but William was born in Crawfordsville on 1 August 1830.

Powers spent two years, 1849–51, in the Preparatory Department of Wabash College, and then presumably returned home to help out on the family farm in Montgomery County.

On 30 January 1864 at Crawfordsville, Powers joined Company C of the 120th Indiana Regiment under General Alvin P. Hovey. They joined the Twenty-Third Army Corps in Tennessee, and in April the men marched two hundred miles across the state in order to establish their position at Charleston in East Tennessee. On 2 May the corps became part of Sherman's larger march on Atlanta. They were engaged in a major battle on 15 May at Resaca, and then fought at Kennesaw Mountain. From July to late August they were involved in the siege of Atlanta. For much of October they pursued Confederate forces in Georgia, then went back to Tennessee, fighting in the dreadful Battle of Franklin on 30 November.

During the early months of 1865, Powers was in North Carolina participating in the occupation and guarding of Raleigh. In the summer he did similar work at Charlotte, then returned to Raleigh and was released from service on 8 January 1866 as a corporal.

Returning home to Montgomery County, Powers married Melinda Bastion on 2 March 1866. In addition to farming, he was active in the Christian church and in the International Order of Odd Fellows. He died on 10 October 1868, one of the many victims of tuberculosis, probably contracted during his military service. He is buried in Oak Hill Cemetery.

References: *History of Montgomery County, Indiana* (Bowen & Co., 1913), p. 155; *Crawfordsville Weekly Journal*, 15 October 1868; and the foregoing references for his brother, Ira.

PRATHER, OSCAR (1842–1938)

Oscar Prather was born in Butler County, Ohio, on 29 September 1842, the oldest of six children of Martha and C. W. Prather, a physician. In about 1855 the family moved to Montgomery County, and Dr. Prather opened a practice in Crawfordsville. In 1857 he enrolled his son in the Normal School at Wabash. Oscar lived at home and did not return to the college the following year.

On 30 August 1862 Prather was mustered into Company E of the Sixty-Third Indiana Infantry and eventually marched through Kentucky and Tennessee on the way to taking part in the siege of Atlanta. His regiment pursued Confederate General Hood and participated in the attack on Wilmington, North Carolina, in February 1865 before he was mustered out on 15 May 1865 as a corporal.

He had married Caroline Bowen in Marion County on 24 November 1863, and in 1880 they lived in Kansas City, where he was a house painter. By 1910 he was still in Kansas City, living alone and working as a caretaker. Ten years later he described himself as a custodian. Prather was among the longest-living Civil War veterans among former Wabash students, dying at age ninety-six on 1 December 1938. He is buried in the Mount Moriah Cemetery of Kansas City.

References: H. W. Beckwith, *History of Fountain County, Indiana* (1881), p. 111; Kansas City Public Library; State Historical Society of Missouri; State of Missouri Board of Health.

PRATT, JAMES PEPPER (1841–1864)

James Pratt was born in Logansport on 9 October 1841, the son of Sophia and Daniel Pratt, a very successful lawyer. His siblings were Julia and Charles.

The young Pratt spent two years at Wabash, 1857–59, as a freshman and a sophomore. He then transferred to Yale University for his junior and senior years, 1859–61, and following graduation, returned to Logansport and began studying law with his father.

While at Wabash Pratt kept a diary that is now in the manuscript department of the Indiana State Library. He recorded the incentives that his father offered to turn him into a cultured man of character, encouraging him to earn money by sawing and piling wood and reading books such as William H. Prescott's *Conquest of Mexico* and *Conquest of Peru* and Washington Irving's biography of Columbus. He told of his pride and pleasure in being elected to one of the two literary organizations, the Calliopean Society:

That evening the Society met and we were initiated. We waited in the chapel till the society had met and then filed in. There were five chairs placed in the middle of the room facing the president. Into these we squatted. Then the Constitution and Bylaws were read to us and we were sworn and pronounced Calliopeans. Thus ended the great tragedy.... At the next meeting I was in the debate. The question was resolved that Learning diminishes the power of Eloquence. I was on the affirmative, and one of the last speakers. Before I had come, I felt very grandiloquent in my room, but when I got on the floor I didn't feel half so brave. Still, I managed to get through pretty well without breaking down.

In October 1861 Pratt joined the Nineteenth Regiment of the regular United States Army. He spent the first four months of his service in Indianapolis and then was sent to New York City as a recruiting sergeant from March to November 1862. He then spent four months (November 1862 to February 1863) at Fort Independence, Boston, before beginning his duties as a first lieutenant of Company C, Second Battalion, Eleventh Infantry, of the Army of the Potomac in March 1863.

He saw action at Chancellorsville, and in a letter to his father he recorded the dismal statistics for his battalion at Gettysburg on 2 July: "Nine hundred and fifty strong charged the enemy, and came back three hundred and nineteen strong. My company, four officers and fifty-seven men came back from the charge with twenty-two men and one officer, myself."

On 13 July 1863 he wrote from an encampment near the Antietam River: I fear that the letters on the march were not very edifying, if they were received. There was a touch of whining about them, not manly nor soldier-like. But the truth was, we suffered a great deal, marching 25 and 30 miles a day, lying down in roads, and sleeping a few hours, and before daybreak on our way again, sore feet and stiff joints, empty stomachs, horrible mud, driving rain and roaring streams, never checking our tremendous pace.

Late in the afternoon of 29 May 1864, in the thick of battle near Bethesda Church, Virginia, Pratt was killed by a bullet to his heart and was buried in his blanket nearby. Two weeks before he died, he had written to his father, "It looks dark. We have been fighting seven days now. God grant we may win. If I am killed, do get my body and bury it decently."

After the war his father was able to fulfill this request. His son's body was brought to Logansport for burial in Mount Hope Cemetery, and placed next to his mother who had died two years before.

References: A selection of Pratt's wartime letters to his father are reprinted in *The Soldier of Indiana in the War for the Union*, II (1869), pp. 83, 87, 90, 95–96, 103, 114–15, 629, and 645–48. See also: *Logansport Journal*, 11 June 1864; and Yale University Library.

Pratt probably visited the batttlefield at Antietam when he was stationed there later in the war. Often bullets, military gear, and even bones were visible at the former carnage sites.

PUTNAM, DOUGLAS PERKINS (1844–1905)

Douglas Putnam was born 8 February 1844 in the town of Jersey in Licking County, Ohio, the son of Abby (Abbie) Slocomb Edgerton (1805–1878) and the Reverend Charles Marsh Putnam (1802–1870). His siblings were Henry, Luther, Lydia, David, Howard, and Julia.

On 4 October 1862 Putnam enlisted in Company G of the Ninety-Second Ohio Volunteer Infantry for a term of three years. His health deteriorated during the winter of 1862–63, and he was granted a medical discharge at Carthage, Tennessee, on 21 March 1863. He entered Marietta College in the fall of that year and remained there for his freshman and sophomore years.

In the autumn of 1865, he joined the junior class of Wabash College, indicating that his home was still Jersey, Ohio. He completed his senior year and graduated in June 1867. The college magazine said about him, "His intellect, like his affections, is neither aggressive nor positive, but works as a wooer and persuader. His social capacity is largely developed. He is an intense admirer of the female persuasion, and, with his pale, handsome face, is always acceptable company. His heart is set upon the medical profession." Putnam evidently changed his mind about becoming a physician.

In late 1870 or early 1871, he married Jennie Williamson of Lafayette and then, for ten years, from 1871 to 1881, he served as the minister of the Presbyterian church in Monroe, Michigan, followed by a pastorate in Springfield, Missouri, from 1881 to 1886. In 1887 he embarked on an eleven-year tenure at the Presbyterian church in Logansport, Indiana. In 1899 he moved on to a church in Princeton that had been consumed by flames and presided over its rebuilding.

From 1891 to 1905 he was a member of the board of trustees of Lane Seminary, and in 1904 he was appointed professor of homiletics and pastoral theology. Putnam died at home in Walnut Hills, Ohio, on 25 March 1905 and was buried in Green Lawn Cemetery in Columbus, survived by his wife and children.

References: *Wabash Magazine*, VII (June 1867), p. 24; *Wabash Magazine*, VIII (June 1868), p. 69; *Wabash Magazine*, XI (March 1871), p. 138; *Wabash Magazine*, XII (June 1872), p. 77; *Wabash Record*, May 1892, p. 127; *Wabash Record*, 14 November 1898, p. 23; *Wabash Record*, March 1902, p. 22; *Wabash Record*, July 1903, p. 10; *Wabash Record*, July 1904, pp. 26–27; Lane Theological Seminary, *General Catalogue, 1829–1899*, p. 78; Licking County (Ohio) Genealogical Society; *Granville Times*, 30 March 1905; *Jersey Reform Presbyterian Report*, p. 2; N. N. Hill, *History of Licking County, Ohio* (1881), pp. 476, 508.

RABB, JAMES DAVID (1840–1863)

James Rabb was born in Indiana about 1840, the only child of Fanny S. and James Rabb, a prosperous merchant. When he entered the freshman class at Wabash in the fall of 1856, he gave his hometown as Carrollton, Kentucky He remained two years at the college, completing his sophomore year in the spring of 1858, and then returned home.

Rabb secured an appointment to the United States Military Academy at West Point. He began there on 1 July 1859 and graduated third in his class on 11 June 1863. He was assigned to the Corps of Engineers as a first lieutenant. His first posting was with the Nineteenth Army Corps at Port Hudson, Louisiana. The port had been under federal siege for six weeks during June and July 1863 and was the last on the Mississippi to capitulate. Once Vicksburg surrendered, the Confederates deemed it futile to hold on, so on 8 July thirty thousand of them put down their arms. It was the task of the corps of engineers and officers like Rabb to restore the harbor and facilities. He moved on to New Orleans later that summer and apparently contracted fever and died on 26 August 1863.

References: U.S. Military Academy, West Point, NY.

RABB, JOHN WILSON (1838–1868)

John Rabb was born at Rising Sun on 6 August 1838, son of Margaret J. and David G. Rabb. He came to Wabash College in the autumn of 1855 as a freshman and persevered for the next four years, graduating in July 1859.

Following Wabash, Rabb returned to Rising Sun and studied law with his uncle, James Kelly, and was admitted to the Indiana bar. He launched his legal career there and at the same time edited a newspaper, the *Indiana Weekly Visitor*, from 1860 to 1861.

At the outbreak of war in the spring of 1861, Rabb was one of the first to enlist. On 20 April he was commissioned captain of Company I of the Seventh Indiana Regiment and spent the next three months in western Virginia. He was mustered out in early August and returned to Indiana to marry Julia Fry of Crawfordsville on 16 August 1861, having already committed to further military service.

He received his commission as a first lieutenant in the Second Indiana Light Artillery, a battery commanded by his father. In May 1862 he was taken prisoner at Weston, Missouri, but by June negotiations were underway to exchange him for a Confederate prisoner. In October he was promoted to captain of the Second Battery, which saw action at Boston Mountain and Prairie Grove, Arkansas, during November and December. Rabb seems to have remained in the western theater of war during 1863, mostly in Missouri or Kansas.

On 21 January 1864 Rabb was again promoted, this time to major, and assigned to a different unit, the Second Missouri Battery. In March he accompanied four hundred of his men to Columbus, Kentucky, to reinforce troops against a Confederate attack. Commanders in Missouri and elsewhere sought Rabb's services, which meant his battery was often on the move, going as far south as Mexico in October 1864 to guard a munitions train. In April 1865 he was in middle Tennessee, where he was mustered out on 26 August 1865.

After the war Rabb settled in Leavenworth, Kansas, and practiced law for about six months before relocating to Lafayette, Indiana, in the autumn of 1866. Soon he began to show the familiar and dreadful signs of tuberculosis. He clung to life for about fifteen months, and a week before he died, he returned to his father's home in Rising Sun. He passed away on 19 January 1868, survived by his wife and two children.

References: United States War Department, *The War of the Rebellion: A Compilation of the Official Records of the Union and Confederate Armies*; *Wabash Magazine*, IV (July 1863), p. 328; *Wabash Magazine*, VIII (March 1868), p. 71; alumni directories of the Phi Delta Theta fraternity; *Obituaries of Some Alumni*, Ramsay Archives, Wabash College.

RAGAN, GILLUM TAYLOR (1840–1914)

Gillum Ragan was born on the family farm in Hendricks County, Indiana, in about 1840, one of eight children of Nancy Smith and Robert Ragan. He and his two brothers, William Addison and Reuben Samuel, attended Wabash and also served in the Civil War.

In the fall of 1854, Gillum came from New Winchester to enter the Preparatory Department at Wabash, and two years later he became a freshman. He progressed through his senior year and graduated in 1860.

From 1860 to 1862 Ragan was a teacher and principal at Bainbridge Male and Female Seminary in Putnam County, Indiana, and then joined the army as a clerk in Washington, DC, probably as an employee of the Office of Quartermaster General, where his younger brother worked.

After the war he stayed in Washington and studied medicine at Georgetown University. On 17 May 1866 Ragan married Sallie Osbourne at Louisville, Kentucky, and they eventually had four sons and four daughters. Two of their boys, Robert and Carroll, attended Wabash, and the latter composed several college songs, including the alma mater. Among their other children were Cynthia, Samuel, Belle, Sarah, and Lucia.

Ragan practiced medicine in Indiana from 1866 to 1868 and then moved to Neoga, Illinois, where his brother, Robert, was also a physician. He was active in both local and national medical societies and for thirty years served the Illinois Central Railroad as the company surgeon. He died at Neoga sometime in 1914.

References: Carroll Ragan Black; 1905 alumni questionnaire, Ramsay Archives, Wabash College; *Wabash Magazine*, I (July 1860), p. 319; and the sources cited for his brothers, Reuben and William.

RAGAN, REUBEN SAMUEL (1819–1895)

Reuben Ragan was born in Mercer County, Kentucky, on 10 March 1819, one of three sons of Nancy Smith and Robert Ragan who not only attended Wabash but also served in the Civil War. The others were Gillum and William, whose biographies are given here also. Reuben Ragan grew up on a farm near New Winchester and in the fall of 1845 entered the Preparatory Department of the college, remaining for two years.

Following his years at Wabash, Ragan was a teacher in Perrysville, Kentucky, until the early 1850s, when he married Sally Clifton Burton and began to study law at Indiana University, Bloomington. They eventually had four children: Ella, Jennie, Homer, and Francis.

In 1852 Ragan opened his practice in Greencastle, Indiana. In 1859–60 he served as mayor until elected to a term in the Indiana House of Representatives.

During the war Ragan was a colonel and aide-de-camp of Governor Oliver P. Morton, and afterwards his family continued to live in Greencastle. However, his law practice was somewhat overshadowed by his wholesale fruit-growing and marketing business. He sold produce as far afield as Indianapolis, Lafayette, Evansville, and Louisville, and became an authority on horticulture. He died in Spencer, Indiana, sometime in 1895.

References: Carroll Ragan Black; *Biographical Sketches of Members of the 41st General Assembly* (1861); T. A. Wylie, *Indiana University*: ... (1890); J. S. Ragan, *Historic Sketches of Robert Ragan Sr.; and Descendants* (1928), pp. 11–12; *Biographical Directory of the Indiana General Assembly*, I (1980), p. 321; alumni directories of Beta Theta Pi, Wabash College.

RAGAN, WILLIAM ADDISON (1822–1893)

This Ragan brother was born in Mercer County, Kentucky, on 7 July 1822, one of the three to attend Wabash and also serve in the war. His parents were Nancy Smith and Robert Ragan.

By the time Ragan entered the Preparatory Department of Wabash in 1843, he was living on a farm near New Winchester. After two years he became a freshman in the Classical Course for another two years, then returned home to help his father in the nursery and fruit-growing business in Clayton, Indiana.

On 20 May 1851 Ragan married Mary C. Hopwood, who gave birth to six children: William, Clara, Nannie, Jennie, Charles, and Lillie. The oldest of these attended Wabash. On 15 October 1861 at Richmond, Ragan enrolled in Company K of the Thirty-Fifth Indiana Regiment for three years. In January 1863 at Murfreesboro, Tennessee, he became ill, yet remained in the army until he was mustered out at Nashville on 16 June 1865. He died on 11 March 1893.

References: See citations for his two brothers, Gillum and Reuben.

RAILSBACK, LYCURGUS (1834–1897)

Lycurgus Railsback was born at Richmond, Indiana, on 14 December 1834. His mother's name is unknown. She presumably died in the 1850s, as his father Enoch married Nancy Fouts. According to the census of 1860, Lycurgus had a nine-year-old stepbrother, John.

In 1855 Railsback went to Indianapolis, intent upon pursuing a career in business. His endeavor went well, but he underwent a religious conversion and decided to seek more formal education in order to enter the Presbyterian ministry, so he enrolled in the Preparatory Department of Wabash College in the autumn of 1856. He studied there for two years before undertaking the Classical Course and graduating in four years.

Railsback attended Lane Theological Seminary in Cincinnati from 1862 to 1864 but was increasingly absent doing missionary work among the troops for the American Tract Society. In October 1864 he was ordained a Presbyterian minister and entered the army as a chaplain for the Forty-Fourth Regiment of United States Colored Infantry. He continued this work until 1866, when he returned to Cincinnati for his final year at Lane Seminary.

On 27 September 1866 at Thorntown, Indiana, Railsback married

Elizabeth J. Binford, and for the next two years he worked as superintendant of the Children's Home of Cincinnati.

During 1869–70 he did missionary work in New York City at the Five Point House of Industry, where he and his wife taught English to Chinese, Italians, Cubans, and Spaniards. Two of his Chinese converts later went back to China as Christian missionaries. Other ministerial assignments followed for the minister.

Railsback struck others as both dynamic and eccentric. His Lane Seminary classmate, W. M. Newton, later wrote of him, "He was a preacher of unusual power. As a speaker he was magnetic, sympathetic, mightily in earnest, and frequently broadly humorous."

Prior to going to Kansas City, Railsback wrote to the American Home Missionary Society, expressing his hopes for a new assignment: "Could work among colored people be made a specialty? Is there any Mission field, building up a Sabbath school and church among the poor?"

Railsback died at Shreveport, Louisiana, on 5 August 1897.

References: Wayne County Historical Society of Richmond, Indiana; *Wabash Magazine*, III (February 1862), p. 191; *Wabash Magazine*, III (June 1862), p. 379; *Wabash Magazine*, X (March 1870), p. 70; Kansas City Public Library; J. B. Hill, *The Presbytery of Kansas City and its Predecessors* (1901), pp. 107–09.

RAMSAY, JOHN WILLIAM (1839–1892)

John Ramsay was born in Parkersburg, Indiana, on 2 June 1839, the older of two sons of Maloma Harris and Robert M. Ramsay. His younger brother, Newton, also went to Wabash College and served in the Civil War.

Ramsay's early schooling took place at Waveland Academy, and in the autumn of 1852 he entered the Preparatory Department of Wabash, where he continued through 1857–58, completing his freshman year. He then left college to study law with Henry S. Lane and Colonel Samuel C. Willson of Crawfordsville.

Following in the tradition of his paternal grandfather, who had served in the American Revolution, Ramsay joined the army: Lew Wallace's Zouaves, the Eleventh Indiana Infantry Regiment, for three months from April to August 1861. He then was transferred to the Fifty-First Regiment, where he served as an adjutant from September 1861 to November 1862 and experienced battles at Romney, Kelley's Island, Fort Donelson, Shiloh, Corinth, and Franklin. He also served at Hall's Gap. The wounds from Shiloh troubled him for the rest of his life.

In July 1863, when Governor Morton called up troops for the Morgan raid, he appointed Ramsay a captain in the 108th Indiana Regiment. After nine days the threat dissipated, and so Ramsay was assigned to train Indiana Legion recruits.

On 7 October 1872 he married Alice Rice at Crawfordsville, and for a decade he continued practicing law. He was a lifelong Republican and active in fraternal lodges such as the Knights of Pythias and the Templars. He served as a justice of the peace, and in 1876 he was elected to the first of three terms (1876–84) as mayor of Crawfordsville. He was known for helping reduce the city's debt.

Ramsay died on 27 April 1892, survived by his wife, who lived until 28 November 1918. Both are buried in Oak Hill Cemetery.

References: H. W. Beckwith, *History of Montgomery County* (1881), p. 134, 221; *Crawfordsville Review*, 16 July 1863; *Crawfordsville Journal*, 27 April 1892; *Crawfordsville Review*, 12 April 1884; McPherson Post No. 7, *Descriptive Book*.

RAMSAY, NEWTON LOWRY (1844–1894)

As the son of Maloma Harris and Robert M. Ramsay and younger brother of John William Ramsay, whose life we have just described, Newton Ramsay was born near Parkersburg, Montgomery County, Indiana, on 17 August 1844. After attending local schools, he entered Wabash when he was fifteen years old. His home was in Carpentersville, Putnam County. He remained at the college from 1859 to 1861, studying in the Preparatory Department and Normal School.

In Crawfordsville, on 11 March 1864, Ramsay enlisted in Company A of the Eleventh Indiana Volunteers, indicating that he was a clerk and committing to serve three years. Since the war ended in about a year, he was discharged at Baltimore, Maryland, on 26 July 1865.

He married Mary Eliza Kelley, and they had one son, Robert T.

In the early 1890s they moved to Indianapolis, where Ramsay died in a hospital on 11 June 1894. His body was returned to Crawfordsville, and funeral services were held at the old Ramsay house on West Main Street, where his wife lived until she died on 12 June 1936. Newton is interred in Oak Hill Cemetery, near his brother as well as his wife.

References: Oak Hill Cemetery; Indiana State Archives; *Crawfordsville Journal*, 15 June 1894; *Crawfordsville Star* and *Crawfordsville Journal Review*, 12 June 1936.

READY, MARTIN (?–1872)

When Martin Ready entered the Normal School of Wabash in 1857, he gave Dayton, Indiana, as his home. He did not return the following year. When the 1860 census was taken for Sheffield Township, Ready was working as a plasterer and living with his mother, Harriet, who had come from Ohio and now, presumably widowed, was trying to run a farm worth about $1,200.

On 23 April 1861 he joined Company E of the Tenth Indiana Volunteer Infantry at Lafayette and saw action in western Virginia before being mustered out on 6 August.

By 1870 Ready lived on his own in Vandalia, Illinois, working as a general laborer. A person with his name died in January 1872 and is buried in the Calvary Cemetery, St. Louis.

References: Martin Ready rarely appeared in any printed sources other than census reports.

REYNOLDS, JOSEPH JONES (1822–1899)

One of the most well known graduates who distinguished himself as an officer was Joseph Reynolds. He was born at Flemingsburg, Kentucky, on 4 January 1822, the seventh child of Sarah Longley and Edward Reynolds, a hatter. In 1837 the family moved to Lafayette, and young Joseph entered the scientific course at Wabash in the autumn of 1838. He remained only one year because in 1839 he received an appointment to the United States Military Academy at West Point. He accepted, graduating tenth in his class in July 1843. One of his classmates was Ulysses S. Grant, with whom he maintained a close friendship throughout life.

Reynolds became a second lieutenant in the Fourth Artillery, stationed first at Fortress Monroe, Virginia, and then at Carlisle, Pennsylvania. In 1845 he was attached to troops in Texas, as a prelude to the forthcoming war with Mexico. Then in the fall of 1846, he returned to West Point to be an assistant professor of natural and experimental philosophy. On 3 December married Mary Elizabeth Bainbridge at Fortress Monroe. They eventually had five children.

Reynolds remained on the teaching staff at West Point until 1855, when he was assigned to frontier duty as a first lieutenant at Fort Washita in the Indian Territory. He resigned from the army in 1857 and spent four years dividing his time between teaching engineering at Washington University in St. Louis and partnering with his brother in a Lafayette, Indiana, grocery business.

Soon after war broke out, on 25 April 1861, Reynolds was commissioned as colonel of the Tenth Indiana Volunteer Regiment and spent time in Virginia, where he was promoted to brigadier general of volunteers in June and placed in charge of the Department of West Virginia. Troops under his command were successful in routing the Confederates at Cheat Mountain in September 1861. He seems to have been a strong-minded leader; in August the cold and dissatisfied troops of the Fourteenth Indiana Regiment on Cheat Mountain threatened what can only be regarded as mutiny. Reynolds came from brigade headquarters and read the riot act to them, throwing several non-commissioned officers and enlisted men into the guardhouse. He also replaced offending officers in short order. The matter was over, and the Fourteenth went on to distinguished service.

In December news reached Reynolds of his brother's death in Lafayette, so he resigned from the army in January 1862. He returned to the army in September 1862 as a brigadier general, and on 29 November he was promoted to major general. He was involved at Tullahoma (June and July 1863), Chickamauga, Chattanooga, and Missionary Ridge. In January 1864 he was sent to New

Orleans to organize its defenses, and in July he helped plan the attack on Mobile. From November 1864 to April 1866, he commanded the Department of Arkansas.

At the end of the war, Reynolds chose to remain in the active military, and his volunteer status was converted to the rank of colonel of the United States Army. For the next four years he was with the infantry, being brevetted brigadier and then major general in the latter 1860s, and he served with the federal occupation forces in the southwest, including Texas. In 1870 he was appointed commander of the Third Cavalry, and in 1871 the carpetbaggers in the Texas legislature chose him to represent them in the United States Senate. However, his election was successfully challenged, and he remained in the army. Between 1872 and 1876 he was stationed with troops in Nebraska and Wyoming.

On 17 March 1876 Reynolds was ordered to attack an Indian village on the Powder River in the Montana Territory. After his apparent success, he withdrew so swiftly that he left behind three dead soldiers and one wounded private who was hacked to death by the Indians. He was court martialed and found guilty, but he was pardoned by President Grant and allowed to retire from the army in 1877.

Reynolds spent his retirement in Washington, DC, where he died on 25 February 1899 and was buried in Arlington National Cemetery.

References: United States Military Academy, West Point, New York; *Dictionary of American Biography*; *American National Biography*; E. J. Warner, *Generals in Blue* (1964), pp. 397–98; *Gallant Fourteenth: The Story of an Indiana Civil War Regiment*, p.60.

REYNOLDS, REDERICK H. (1827–1870)

Rederick Reynolds was born on the family farm in Clay County on 24 August 1827, one of eight children of Nancy and James Reynolds. His siblings were Matilda, Richard, Jane, James, Diza, Dobey, and Rebecca.

In the late 1840s Reynolds married a woman named Lydia, who died in 1849.

He spent one year, 1853–54, at Wabash College and then married Sarah Ann Boothe on 20 June 1855. They settled in the town of Highland (now called Staunton) in Clay County, where he was a teamster. They had six children: Perry, Alice, Ida, Samantha, Mary May, and Rosetta, several of whom died young.

On his thirty-fifth birthday Reynolds enrolled at Terre Haute in Company E of the Eighty-Fifth Indiana Volunteers for three years. He saw action in Kentucky and Tennessee before falling ill and being hospitalized in 1863, first in Nashville and then in New Albany, Indiana. He never regained his health and was mustered out in 1865.

Returning to Staunton, Reynolds continued to be plagued by failing health. He died, probably of tuberculosis, on 18 September 1870, survived by his wife. He was buried in Vest Cemetery.

References: Clay County Genealogical Society, Center Point, Indiana; Gale A. Reynolds, *The Reynolds Connection*, pp. 10–12; military pension file, National Archives, Washington, DC.

RHODES, GEORGE W. (1825–1908)

George Rhodes was born in Champaign County, Ohio, on 25 March 1825, the son of Sarah Brittin and John Rhodes. His sister, Abigail, married a Wabash College student, John Grimes.

When Rhodes entered the Preparatory Department of Wabash College in the fall of 1844, the Rhodes family lived on a farm in Miami County. He stayed at college for three academic years and then presumably returned to help on the family farm.

On 10 October 1855 in Fulton County, he married Hannah Theanna Scott, and they eventually had nine children: Henry, Justin, George, Emma, May, William, Franklin, Ellie, and Anna.

Rhodes enrolled in Company I of the Twelfth Indiana Regiment on 9 December 1864 at LaPorte. At the time he was described as six feet one inch tall, with a fair complexion, hazel eyes, and black hair. On 5 May 1865 he was transferred to the Fifty-Ninth Regiment, and he was mustered out at Louisville on 17 July 1865.

Sometime after the war the family relocated to Winfield, Kansas, where Rhodes died on 18 October 1908. He was buried in Winfield's Union Cemetery.

References: Peru (Miami County) Public Library; D. K. Brundage, *Men of 1861–1865 Miami County Indiana and their Families*, p. 879; *Winfield Daily Courier*, 19 and 21 October 1908.

RIBBLE, HENRY H. (1837–1919)

Henry Ribble was born on 10 April 1837 in Clarinda, Iowa, one of ten children of Sarah Surface and George Ribble.

Young Henry came to Wabash College in the autumn of 1856 and stayed one year before returning to his family's farm in Delaware County, Iowa.

On 15 July 1861 at Omaha, Ribble was commissioned as a first lieutenant in the First Regiment of Nebraska Cavalry, described as five feet ten inches tall, with a fair complexion, grey eyes, and brown hair. In January 1862 he was promoted to captain and oversaw relations with the Indians. In March 1865 he contracted typhoid fever and was hospitalized at Plum Creek. He secured a medical discharge on 17 July 1865.

Returning home to Clarinda, Ribble took a job as a clerk with a group that fostered trade with the Indians in Kansas until leaving for Texas, where he practiced law. Because of failing eyesight brought on as a result of the typhoid fever, he had to give up his law practice and became involved with mining companies in New Mexico and Arizona, prospecting as well. In 1877 he again settled in Clarinda, but eventually moved to live with his niece, Mrs. S. E. Crabtree, in Pasadena, California, where he died on 23 September 1919.

References: Dr. John Ribble, Houston, Texas; Clarinda Public Library; Pasadena (California) Public Library.

RICE, JAMES EDWARD (1845–1867)

James Rice was born at Troy, Ohio, the son of Sarah Jane and Daniel Rice. His father had many associations with Wabash College: not only did he send his two sons, James and Charles, to the college, but from 1860 to 1871 he was on the college's board of trustees. As pastor of the Second Presbyterian Church in Lafayette, the senior Rice's building project was supported by then President White of Wabash.

In the fall of 1863, Rice began his freshman year at Wabash. Then, on 10 May 1864 he joined Company A of the 135th Indiana Regiment, committing to one hundred days. Guarding railroad lines in Kentucky, he developed a serious fever caused by constant rain and cold weather, and his health deteriorated when the regiment moved into Alabama for similar duty. He was mustered out at Indianapolis on 29 September 1864.

Rice returned to Wabash for his sophomore year, 1865–66, but it became increasingly apparent that while he was in the army he had contracted consumption, so he sought a healthier climate in St. Paul, Minnesota. He died there on 21 January 1867, and his body was returned to Lafayette for burial.

Their other son, Charles, died of consumption in June 1869, just after graduating from Wabash.

References: Macalester College library; *Wabash Magazine*, VII (April 1867), p. 45; alumni directories of the Phi Delta Theta fraternity; *Lafayette Daily Courier*, 26 and 29 January 1867; *Semi-Centennial of the Second Presbyterian Church, 1840–1890*; *Tuttle Miscellaneous Scrapbooks, 1882–1890*, p. 140, Ramsay Archives, Wabash College.

RICHARDSON, GEORGE W. (1835–1877)

George Richardson was born in Madison in 1835. The names of his parents and siblings are unknown. In the fall of 1856, he entered the sophomore year of Wabash College, staying only one year.

He then read law in Columbus, Indiana, and was admitted to the bar in 1858, the same year that he was elected prosecuting attorney for Bartholomew

County, his home for several years before he returned to Madison on the eve of the Civil War.

On 28 December 1859 he married Helen M. Sheek of Davenport, Iowa, and eventually had two children, Leslie and Charles.

He enrolled for three years as a corporal in Company C of the Sixty-Seventh Indiana Regiment on 8 August 1862 at Madison, and during the spring and summer of 1863, he took part in the siege at Vicksburg. In that swampy, humid, and hot location, he contracted tuberculosis. His captain urged him to seek a medical discharge, but Richardson was determined to remain with his regiment. Late in 1864 he was promoted to a first lieutenant and transferred to Company I of the Twenty-Fourth Indiana Volunteers. While at Carrolton, Louisiana, he came down with malaria and was discharged at New Orleans on 19 July 1865. Back in Madison he sought the help of a local physician, but his health continued to deteriorate.

In 1866 Richardson moved to Columbus and went into partnership with an old acquaintance and fellow lawyer, Ralph Hill, until December 1873, when a serious relapse necessitated his leaving his law practice. Initially he sought improvement in the climate of Denver, Colorado, but returned to Indianapolis and tried again to set up a law practice.

He died in Madison on 6 December 1877, survived by his widow who lived for nearly thirty years in St. Paul, Minnesota; Milwaukee, Wisconsin; and San Francisco. She died on 29 December 1906.

References: *Madison Daily Courier*, 3 January 1860; widow's pension file, National Archives, Washington, DC.

RILEY, GEORGE W. (1837–1864)

On occasion an error creeps into a Civil War veteran's service record and is repeated in secondary sources. To the present day, George Riley's reputation has been impugned because he was said to have been "dishonorably dismissed" from the army. It is now time to set the record straight.

George Riley was born in Crawfordsville on 26 March 1837, one of the seven children of Margaret and James Riley, a retired blacksmith addressed as "Judge." His siblings were Elizabeth, James, John, Margaret, Ambrose, and William. Three of the boys (George, James, and John) attended Wabash, while Ambrose served in the war but was not a college student.

Riley was at Wabash for three years (1853–56) in the Preparatory Department.

On 24 April 1861, within days of the outbreak of war, he went to Lafayette and enrolled for three years in Company E of the Fifteenth Indiana Regiment. He committed himself to three years of military service. When he reported for duty, he was commissioned as a first lieutenant. He spent much of 1862 in Tennessee.

In the archives of the Indiana State Library, Riley's muster roll card in the regimental records indicates that he was dishonorably dismissed from service on 25 January 1863. This allegation is repeated in Terrell's *Report of the Adjutant General of the State of Indiana*, which came out shortly after the war, and reiterated years later by *History of Montgomery County* (Bowen and Co., 1913).

Unfortunately, no one compared these sources with the letter at the National Archives in Washington, DC, that Riley wrote from Murfreesboro, Tennessee, on 22 January 1863 to the Assistant Adjutant General of the Fourteenth Army Corps: "I hereby tender my resignation of the office of 1st Lieut. Co. E 15th Regiment Indiana Foot Volunteers on account of ill health . . . and ask to be relieved of duty at once." His illness is mentioned in another document that indicates that Riley spent part of November and December 1862 in the hospital. When General Rosecranz signed the order on 25 January 1863 relieving Riley of his command, he said only "dismissed from the service." There is no mention of dishonor.

Riley returned to Crawfordsville hoping to regain his health, but he died, probably of tuberculosis, on 10 August 1864. He is buried in the Masonic Cemetery next to his brother, Ambrose. On his tablet is inscribed: "When we at death must part how keen how deep the pain—but we shall still be joined in heart to meet again."

References: W. H. Terrell, *Report of the Adjutant General of the State of Indiana*, II (1869), p. 127; *History of Montgomery County, Indiana* (Bowen & Co., 1913), p. 96; National Archives, Washington, DC.

RISTINE, ALBERT L. (1840–1868)

Albert Ristine was born in Crawfordsville on 14 July 1840, the son of Florinda Humphreys and Benjamin Taylor Ristine (1807–1896). He had five brothers: Harley G. (1838), Theodore Harmon (1845), Hosea D. H. H. (1847), Warren H. (1850), and Charles W. (1856), and one sister, Florinda C., Flora (1853).

The Ristine family has always been one of the most distinguished families in Crawfordsville. Albert's uncle, Major Henry Ristine (1781–1854), moved from Madison, Indiana, to Crawfordsville in 1823 and was one of the first settlers and founders of the town along with his brother, Benjamin. Albert owned a tavern in town, and Benjamin started a dynasty of lawyers.

In 1838, six years after the founding of Wabash College, the newly constructed South Hall sustained a serious fire, and Ben Ristine made a major gift of $100 toward its rebuilding. In gratitude, the college agreed to educate all of his sons without charge, an offer that the family took full advantage of.

At the age of fourteen, Albert Ristine entered the Preparatory Department and remained for the next four years (1854–58). In the fall of 1858, he advanced to the freshman class in the Classical Course and from 1859 to 1861 he repeated his sophomore year due to continuing poor health. Nonetheless, on 31 August

1861 he enrolled in Company I of the Eleventh Regiment Indiana Volunteers for three years. The colonel of this regiment was fellow Crawfordsvillian Lew Wallace. At the time Ristine was five feet eight inches tall, with grey eyes, brown hair, and a light complexion. Ristine was promoted to sergeant and to first lieutenant while participating in battles at Fort Donelson, Shiloh, Corinth, Vicksburg, and the Yazoo Pass Expedition.

In February 1864 the men of the Eleventh Regiment were allowed to go home, but Ristine decided to re-enlist as a veteran volunteer. His last year was spent mainly in Sherman's March to the Sea and the Shenandoah Valley Campaign. According to the *Crawfordsville Journal*, Ristine had a brilliant military career, but having been captured at Vicksburg, he suffered harsh conditions of imprisonment. He was mustered out in Baltimore, Maryland, on 26 July 1865 and returned to Crawfordsville.

For a brief time Ristine attended a commercial college in Cincinnati, but he contracted typhoid fever in 1866. During 1867 he seemed to revive, sustained by members of the Center Presbyterian Church, but he suffered a relapse the following year and died on 6 July 1868. He is buried in Oak Hill Cemetery in Crawfordsville.

References: *Crawfordsville Journal Weekly*, 9 July 1868; H. W. Beckwith, *History of Montgomery County* (1881), p. 195; *History of Montgomery County, Indiana* (Bowen & Co.,1913), p. 119; *Portrait and Biographical Record of Montgomery, Parke and Fountain Counties, Indiana* (1893), p. 293; diaries and scrapbooks of Theodore H. Ristine, Ramsay Archives, Wabash College; *Wabash Magazine*, III (February 1862), p. 190.

RISTINE, HARLEY GREENWOOD (1838–1917)

Harley Ristine was born in Crawfordsville on 21 May 1838, the oldest of seven children of Rhoda Florinda Humphrey and Benjamin Taylor Ristine. Two of his brothers, Albert (1840) and Theodore (1845), studied at Wabash and also served in the Civil War, as did his Uncle Henry (1818).

In the autumn of 1851, Ristine joined the Preparatory Department of the college. He remained through the 1856–57 school year and then advanced to the Classical Course. He completed four years and graduated in 1861 with a bachelor of arts degree. Following graduation, he studied law for a year, presumably with his father.

On 11 August 1862 at Crawfordsville, he enrolled for three years in Company K of the Eighty-Sixth Indiana Regiment. He was five feet four inches tall, with light complexion, dark hair, and blue eyes. Since he was somewhat older than others in the unit, he was made a sergeant, and in 1863 he was promoted to quartermaster. He participated in many of the major battles of the war, including Murfreesboro, Chickamauga, Chattanooga, the siege of Atlanta, and Sherman's March to the Sea. With a leg wound, he was mustered out on 12 February 1865.

After the war Ristine returned to Crawfordsville, but he changed his interest from law to medicine and moved to Cedar Rapids, Iowa, to study with his uncle, Dr. Henry Ristine. He then went to Rush Medical College in Chicago and graduated in 1869. The following autumn he took additional courses at Bellevue Hospital in New York City before becoming a partner with his uncle Henry and cousin John in Cedar Rapids.

In 1872 Ristine began a practice of his own in Fort Dodge, Iowa. He married Carrie (Kittie) Welleson on 21 May 1877. Their son Albert was born in 1878. Their second son, Woolsey, was born in 1881, but complications from his birth claimed Kittie's life.

Ristine went back to New York City in 1886 to take some postgraduate courses and met Eliza P. Lemon of New Preston, Connecticut, whom he married on 10 May 1887. They then returned to Fort Dodge, where Theodore H. Ristine was born in 1889, followed by Carolyne Sallie in 1893. Both of Harley's sons, Albert and Theodore, attended Wabash College.

As a prominent doctor, Ristine involved himself in innumerable activities, usually related to his medical career. He was a medical examiner for the United States government and district surgeon for several railroads, including the Illinois Central and the Minneapolis & St. Louis. At least five nationwide insurance companies used his services. He participated in a variety of medical associations and conferences, writing articles for medical journals, and he helped Iowans through a diphtheria epidemic and the aftermath of a tornado.

Although he might have used an automobile, he persisted in making his rounds throughout the countryside on horseback and was universally loved and respected. He continued working until the very end of his life on 30 January 1917.

References: *Scrapbook of Theodore Ristine*, Ramsay Archives, Wabash College; *Fort Dodge Messenger*, 31 January 1917; *Fort Dodge Daily Chronicle*, 31 January 1917; *Crawfordsville Journal*, 31 January 1917; *The Wabash*, XXVI (June 1902), p. 22; see also the references cited for Albert Ristine.

RISTINE, HENRY JR. (1818-1893)

Henry Ristine Jr. was born in Madison, Indiana, on 21 September 1818, the younger son of Nancy Gray and Major Henry Ristine (1781-1854) whose elder brother was Benjamin Taylor Ristine (1807-1896). He had four sisters: Eliza, Jemima, Jane and Mary.

Nine years after In October 1823 the family moved to the newly organized city of Crawfordsville in 1823, Wabash College opened its doors, and in its second year (1834-1835), Henry Jr. entered the Preparatory Department, dropped out for two years, and then returned from 1838-1840.

In 1840 he enrolled in the Ohio Medical College in Cincinnati, and in 1842 moved to Marion, Linn County, Iowa, where he began his practice. In 1844

Prison camps: a dismal outcome from the effort to save the Union

Many Wabash soldiers found themselves in cold, damp, and potentially dangerous, even fatal, circumstances in the South. Young men used to the comforts of a good fire in Forest Hall and chicken dinners in their school days found themselves starving on thin cabbage soup, parched corn and scummy water. Cruel officers, bitter cold, horrible sanitation, and scarcity of medical care sent thousands to their deaths or lingering illness. Northern prison camps were only a little better.

But what of the stories in some of these narratives of soldiers getting out, being sent home? "Pick up your gear and go away and live to fight another day?" Early in the war that was often the case.

During 1861 relatively few prisoners of war were taken on either side and were exchanged informally. The year 1862 produced many more captured soldiers following the battles of Fort Henry, Fort Donelson, and Shiloh. On 22 July, 1862, a more formal agreement was put into place, with a formula for exchanging prisoners for both sides. Non-commisioned officers were equivalent to two privates; a first lieutenant to four privates; and a general to sixty privates. This arrangement lasted until the spring of 1863, when it was shown to be increasingly unworkable when soldiers cheated and returned to camp. Further undermining the arrangement was the declared policy of the Confederacy in May 1863 that any Negro taken prisoner might be returned to his slave master if appropriate, or might be made a slave even if said Negro was free according to northern criteria. A black slave or free man serving for the North might be executed along with his white officer. Prisoner exchanges therefore pretty well broke down completely. You were caught; you went to prison.

In the South the two most notorious prisons where Wabash students were incarcerated were Libby Prison in Richmond, Virginia, and Andersonville in southwest Georgia. The latter was designed for 10,000 inmates and then expanded until more than 33,000 were confined outdoors in the elements. Of a total of 45,000 northerners incarcerated there, some 13,000 died of maltreatment and disease. The worst of the northern prisons was at Elmira in New York State, but its maximum population was about 9,600, and prisoners were housed inside barracks.

Dreams of the college must have been far off in prison camp.

married Catharine Kirk McMaster of Rockville, Ohio, and in 1847 he opened a drug store in Marion to complement his medical practice, and doubled as druggist for the next 20 years. From 1849-1853, he also served as town postmaster.

In August 1862 he became surgeon for the 20th Iowa Volunteers and was continuously on the march through the Missouri, Arkansas, and Mississippi. He was kept especially busy treating the many casualties suffered in the early stages of the siege of Vicksburg, and fell victim to some disease that caused him to have to resign on 13 May 1863.

The Ristines remained in Marion, Iowa, until 1873 when they moved to Cedar Rapids, Iowa. By then Henry's son, John M., was a qualified doctor and served as a partner in his practice. In 1877 he was honored by being chosen president of the state medical society.

The Ristines had four children. In addition to John, there were Nellie, Belle Minnie, and Mary. In 1893 Henry sustained a stroke, and went for treatment to Pass Christian, Mississippi, where he died on 25 April. His body was taken to Cedar Rapids for burial next to his wife.

References: *Cedar Rapids Gazette*, 26 April 1893; *History of Linn County Iowa*, II (1878), 676; *History of Linn County* (1911), pp. 88-89; *History of Marion, Iowa, 1838-1866*, pp. 139-42; Iowa State Historical Society; Carnegie Library, Marion, Iowa.

RISTINE, THEODORE HARMON (1845-1931)

Theodore Ristine was born in Crawfordsville on 8 January 1845, one of seven children born to Rhoda Florinda Humphrey and Benjamin Taylor Ristine. Along with his older brothers, Albert and Harley, and his uncle, Henry, he served in the Civil War. Among the graduates of Wabash College, few have contributed more to the successful operation and well being of their alma mater.

Ristine entered the Preparatory Department in the fall of 1859 and after two years became a freshman in 1861. He graduated in June 1865, and the diary that he kept during his college years relates just how active he was on campus: he was a member of the Phi Delta Theta fraternity, an editor of the *Wabash Magazine*, and president of the Calliopean literary society.

On 11 July 1863 he joined Company C of the 108th Indiana Regiment, and because Morgan's threat soon dissipated, he was released from service on 17 July. A year later he enrolled in Company H of the 135th Regiment and was appointed a quartermaster clerk. Most of his one hundred days of service took place in Tennessee and Alabama guarding railroad lines, and he was mustered out at Indianapolis on 29 September.

After the war he began to study law with his father and was admitted to the bar late in 1866. He joined the firm of Ristine and Thomson and soon became a partner.

On 28 December 1869 he married Katherine William (Kate or Kittie) Thomson, the daughter of Wabash College Professor Samuel S. Thomson. Theodore and Kate eventually had three children: Harley T., Frank H., and Elizabeth. Their son Harley would become the father of Richard O. Ristine, Wabash graduate and lieutenant governor of Indiana (1961–1965).

Ristine served two terms in the Indiana Senate. Thereafter, he was Crawfordsville city attorney and was elected to the city council. He helped to found a children's orphanage, the YMCA, and local posts of the veterans' GAR.

His contributions to Wabash College were as a trustee for forty years (1883–1931) and treasurer from 1891 to 1911. He was also a generous donor to the college.

He practiced law with his brother, Hosea, in the firm of Ristine and Ristine. He died at the family home at 602 West Wabash Avenue on 4 December 1931, one of the longest living Wabash Civil War vets. His wife died on 8 February 1934. They are both buried in Oak Hill Cemetery.

References: Richard O. Ristine (1920–2009); Theodore Ristine's diary and scrapbook of newspaper clippings, Ramsay Archives, Wabash College; *Biographical Directory of the Indiana General Assembly*, I (1980), p. 641; *Wabash Magazine*, X (March 1870), p. 69; *Ibid.* XII (March 1872), p. 148; *History of Montgomery County, Indiana* (1913), pp. 460, 493, 589; H. W. Beckwith, *History of Montgomery County* (1881), pp. 82, 92, 135, 195; F. M. Mills, *Early Days in a College Town* (1924), pp. 105, 109, 113, 131–32, 134, 137.

ROBINSON, GEORGE W. (1845–1931)

George Robinson was born in Crawfordsville on 1 September 1845, the oldest of six children of Mary E. and John F. Robinson. His siblings were Samuel (1847), John (1849), Charles (1852), Thomas (1854), and Emma (1856).

Robinson spent one year, 1859–60, in the Normal School at Wabash, and then took a job in Crawfordsville as a clerk until southern Indiana was invaded by Confederate cavalry in July 1863. He responded by enlisting in Company C of the 108th Indiana Regiment but served only nine days.

In March 1864 Robinson joined Company I of the Eleventh Indiana Regiment and was promoted to corporal before being mustered out at Baltimore on 26 July 1865. Returning to Crawfordsville, Robinson became an insurance agent. On 28 March 1867 he married Frances (Fannie) M. Naylor, and they had two children: Mary L. and Charles H. In 1891–92 they lived at 106 S. Green Street, but later went to live with their daughter, Mary (Mrs. W. A. Bodell), in Harrisburg, Illinois, where Fannie died on 24 March 1925. After her death, Robinson continued to live with his daughter in Bloomington, Illinois, where he died on 25 October 1931, having outlived most of the other Wabash Civil War veterans. Both he and his wife are buried in Oak Hill Cemetery.

References: *Crawfordsville Journal Review*, 26 October 1931; 1891–92 Crawfordsville city directory.

ROBINSON, JOSEPH J. (1831–1916)

Joseph Robinson was born on his family's farm in Wabash Township, Tippecanoe County, on 14 March 1831. His mother was Rebecca McCrea, and his father, John Robinson, was a prosperous farmer. His siblings were William, Mary, Emily, Nancy, and Charles.

Robinson came to Wabash in the autumn of 1857 and remained for one academic year before becoming a schoolteacher. On 23 May 1864 he enlisted at Lafayette in Company A of the 135th Indiana Infantry Regiment for one hundred days. At the time he was portrayed as having a fair complexion, blue eyes, and brown hair. His assignment was to guard railroad lines in Kentucky and Tennessee, Department of Cumberland, until his release on 29 September.

After returning to Indiana, Robinson resumed teaching, and on 15 January 1865 he married Eliza Ingraham in Jacksonville, Michigan. They eventually had four children: Caroline, Lora Alice, Kate, and Frances. About 1867 they moved to Lamont, Michigan, where Joseph worked as a druggist until he died on 5 December 1916, survived by his wife.

References: Census records; military pension file, National Archives, Washington, DC.

RODERICK, DANIEL GALILEO (1839–1874)

Daniel Roderick was born in about 1839 in Wheeling, Virginia, and entered the Scientific Course at Wabash College in the autumn of 1861. By the time he was a junior in 1865–66, his family had moved to West Milton, Ohio.

As an undergraduate he distinguished himself by winning first prize in a sophomore essay competition and by being one of the senior editors of the *Wabash Magazine*. He was also a member of Phi Delta Theta fraternity.

Like many other students, he volunteered for short terms of duty during two consecutive summers in order not to interrupt his studies. In July 1863 he responded to Morgan's Raid by joining Company C of the 108th Indiana Regiment, and the next summer he enlisted in Company H of the 135th Indiana Regiment for one hundred days. Unfortunately, while guarding railroad lines in Tennessee and Alabama he contracted consumption.

At the time of his graduation in June 1867, the college magazine affectionately described him as "Tall in form, with a superb flaxen beard . . . and a serious, meditative and philosophic face . . . His heart is warm, trustful, and without guile." After taking his bachelor's degree, he began studying law with J. M. Butler, and then in the autumn of 1869 he became principal of the local public school.

In the summer of 1870, when Wabash needed to hire a new tutor for the Preparatory Department, the trustees turned to Roderick as one of their best of their recent graduates. It was said of him, "In mathematics he probably surpassed any who have graduated from Wabash for a number of years." He married Elizabeth Vance on 30 December of that year.

His tenure at the college lasted only one year, and then he resumed the study of law in an effort to achieve his lifelong ambition of becoming an attorney. However, his battle with tuberculosis proved a losing one in spite of his moving to Parsons, Kansas, where he hoped his health would improve. He died there on 30 March 1874 and is buried in the Masonic Cemetery in Crawfordsville. He was survived by his young wife and one child.

References: *Wabash Magazine*, V (December 1863), p. 76; *Wabash Magazine*, VII (June 1867), p. 24; *Wabash Magazine*, VIII (June 1868), p. 64; *Wabash Magazine*, X (March 1870), p. 169; *Wabash Magazine*, XI (March 1871), p. 138; H. W. Beckwith, *History of Montgomery County* (1881), p. 133; *Crawfordsville Journal*, 2 April 1874; and *Crawfordsville Star*, 2 April 1874; minutes of the Prudential Committee of the Board of Trustees, 1 July 1870, Ramsay Archives, Wabash College; 1888 Alumni Directory, Phi Delta Theta fraternity.

ROSS, ABRAHAM TAYLOR (1845–1872)

Abraham Ross, who often went by his middle name, was born in Madison, Indiana, on 11 April 1845, son of Eliza Hillhouse (1806–1894) and Isom Ross (1810–1896), a tanner. His siblings were John, Elizabeth, Catherine, Mary, and Charles.

Ross entered the Preparatory Department of Wabash in the autumn of 1860, but before the school year was over, the war interrupted his studies. Although he had just turned sixteen years old, he enrolled at Crawfordsville for three months in Company I of the Eleventh Indiana Regiment and served from 18 April to 4 August, mostly in western Virginia. Several years later, on 9 May 1864, he joined Company H, 137th Indiana Volunteers as a second lieutenant and was assigned to guard railroad lines in Tennessee or Alabama. He was mustered out on 21 September 1864.

Both before and after his military service, Ross presumably worked in his father's very successful tannery in Madison. During the summer of 1872, he was not feeling well, and he went to Danville, Illinois, to seek some relaxation and improvement. However, this did not happen, and he died there on 1 August 1872. He was buried in Fairmount Cemetery, Madison.

References: *History of Jefferson County, Indiana* (1932), p. 70; *Madison Courier*, 3 August 1872; *Madison Courier*, 16 October 1896; Madison-Jefferson County Public Library.

ROSS, CLIFFORD WENTWORTH (1839–1894)

Clifford Ross was born at Searsport, Maine, on 3 May 1839, the younger of two sons (the other was Frederick) of Salla Rebecca Kidder and John C. Ross. Frederick also attended Wabash and served in the Civil War. Their younger sister was Charlotte.

In 1847 the Rosses moved to Terre Haute, where the father ran the Boston Store, which sold general merchandise.

Ross attended the Preparatory Department of Wabash College for one year, 1856–57, and spent the next two at Miami University in Oxford, Ohio. He then was admitted to the law school at the University of Michigan at Ann Arbor.

On 18 April 1861 at Terre Haute, he enrolled in Company C of the Eleventh Indiana Regiment. After three months in western Virginia, he was mustered out at Indianapolis. The next month, on 5 September 1861, he was commissioned a first lieutenant in Company K of the Thirty-First Indiana Regiment and became an adjutant under General Charles Cruft, a former Wabash student. At the Battle of Shiloh, he was wounded in the head, an injury that bothered him for the rest of his life. At the time, however, he carried on and was promoted to captain of his company on 19 May, but secured a medical discharge on 5 August.

During Morgan's Raid, Ross served in the Seventh Regiment of the Indiana Legion under the command of his older brother, Frederick. In March 1865 he helped organize the 156th Regiment and became a second lieutenant in Company B. By April he was promoted to captain of Company E, and he served out his term before being released in August 1865 at Stevenson's Station, Virginia.

In 1868 Ross embarked for two years on oceangoing voyages, including rounding Cape Horn twice. Settling down in Terre Haute, he practiced law and became involved in the insurance business. He married Frances Ann Morgan on 3 October 1871, and they had one child, John Clifford Ross.

Ross died at home on 19 March 1894, survived by his wife and fifteen-year-old son. He was buried in Highland Lawn Cemetery.

References: David N. Lewis of the Vigo County Public Library; Mrs. Elizabeth Ross Merrill of Terre Haute, Clifford Ross's granddaughter; F. M. Mills, *Early Days in a College Town* (1924), p. 215; *Terre Haute Express*, 21 March 1894; Miami University of Oxford, Ohio.

ROSS, FREDERICK ATHERTON (1834–1899)

Frederick Ross was born in Searsport, Maine, as his brother Clifford had been, on 5 August 1834, one of two sons of Salla Rebecca Kidder and John C. Ross. His father established a mercantile business in 1847 in Terre Haute, where young Frederick learned the trade. In the fall of 1851, Ross came to Crawfordsville and entered the Preparatory Department of Wabash College, remaining for two years. Returning to work in his father's general store, he became a partner, and the store was renamed John C. Ross and Sons.

In 1859 Ross married Frances F. Bradley of Indianapolis, and they eventually had five children: Frank, Lyman, Fred, John, and Katherine. On 19 July 1862 he became a second lieutenant in Company I of the Seventy-Sixth Indiana Regiment. It was a brief commitment of only thirty days, and then he returned to Terre Haute.

The following July when the Confederates threatened southern Indiana, Ross organized a company of Indiana Legion volunteers, but since the danger soon vanished, he again returned to the family business. In May 1864 he accepted a commission as captain of Company D of the 133rd Indiana Regiment for one hundred days, mostly spent guarding railroad lines in Tennessee, and was mustered out in September.

Rather unexpectedly, he sold his business in Terre Haute and moved to Philadelphia for two years, then returned to Terre Haute and started a hardware store, Burnett and Ross, which lasted until 1873, when he decided to devote himself full time to real estate. In 1892 Ross was elected mayor of Terre Haute, and he served for six years. His public service was recognized in his obituary: "He surpassed any other man who ever occupied that position." He died at home on 23 April 1899, survived by his wife and two sons, Frank and Fred, and a daughter, Katherine. He was buried in Highland Lawn Cemetery.

References: See references cited for his brother, Clifford; *Terre Haute Express*, 24 April 1899; *Indiana Commandery* [the Military Order of the Loyal Legion of the United States] (1899), p. 506.

ROSS, LEVI (1829–1863)

Levi Ross was born in Greenfield on 28 August 1829, one of three sons of Elizabeth Wilson and William Olin Ross to go to Wabash College. His eldest brother, Moses W. (1823), was not a Civil War soldier, but William G. (1825) and Levi both served in the war. When his mother died in 1834, having given birth to ten children, his father moved to Crawfordsville and two years later married Julia Harrison.

Ross attended the Preparatory Department of Wabash College for the academic year 1837–38, and then his family moved to a farm in Noble Township of Wabash County, where Ross presumably worked until he left to join the army during the Mexican War. He was in Company F of the First Indiana Regiment, serving just a year, from June 1847 to June 1848. The major, and subsequently the colonel, of this regiment was Henry S. Lane of Crawfordsville.

In 1 November 1849 he married Susan C. Goodlander, and they had four children: William, Susan, Mary, and Levi. Between 1854 and 1856 he prospected for gold and other minerals in California with his older brother, Moses, but he returned to Indiana to work on the family farm as well as start a business in the town of Wabash.

On 5 October 1861 Ross received a commission as a first lieutenant in Company F of the Forty-First Indiana Regiment. He was promoted to captain on 15 April 1862, but in February 1863 he fell seriously ill, and he died at Louisville, Kentucky, on 7 March 1863. He is buried in Falls Cemetery in Wabash, Indiana.

References: T.H. Helm, *History of Wabash County, Indiana* (1884), p. 258; Wabash Carnegie Public Library.

ROSS, WILLIAM G. (1825–1897)

William Ross was born at Greenfield on 2 July 1825, one of three brothers who went to Wabash. His parents were Elizabeth Wilson and William Olin Ross. As we have seen in the case of his younger brother, Levi, by the mid-1830s the Ross family lived in Crawfordsville, which facilitated both boys' attending the Preparatory Department, William for two years, 1836–38.

When the 1850 census was taken, Ross was farming in Wabash County but owned no land. The following year he married seventeen-year-old Emily Smith, and they eventually had five children: Mary, Robert, Allen, Thomas, and John Edward.

By 1860 Ross was continuing to farm, but when the war broke out, he entered Company F of the Forty-First Indiana Regiment, the same unit as his brother, Levi. However, he was fortunate to escape early death and completed his three years of service relatively unscathed. He was mustered out of the army on 4 October 1864 and continued to farm.

He died at home in Roann, Indiana, on 22 August 1897, survived by Emily, who lived until 18 November 1919. Both are buried in the Odd Fellows Cemetery in Roann.

References: T. H. Helm, *History of Wabash County, Indiana* (1884), p. 172; *Wabash Star*, 26 August 1897; *Wabash Times*, 27 August 1897; Wabash Carnegie Public Library.

RUSSELL, BYRON RANDOLPH (1848–1931)

Byron (Barney) Russell was born at Norway, Indiana, on 11 July 1848, the son of Lydia Waymire and Arthur Russell. Both his parents died before he was ten years old, and he went to live with his grandfather.

When Russell turned fifteen, despite his grandfather's objections, he passed himself off as an eighteen-year-old and joined Company G of the Sixty-Third Indiana Regiment. On board a Mississippi riverboat, he injured his eye, but he continued to serve in the campaign in east Tennessee, then went on to the siege of Atlanta in the summer of 1864. He also saw action at Franklin and Nashville. Toward the end of the war, he contracted typhoid fever in North Carolina and was hospitalized at Greensboro. On 22 June 1865 he was mustered out and returned to Indiana.

Living in nearby Yountsville and still as young as most of the other students, Russell secured a place in the Preparatory Department of Wabash College in the fall of 1866 and remained for two years before beginning to study law with Lew Wallace. Later he entered the law department of the University of Michigan, graduating in 1872. For a year and a half he practiced law with Judge E. C. Snyder of Crawfordsville, then started a practice of his own.

On 1 October 1874 Russell married Sylvia E. O'Neall. She gave birth to a daughter, Elsie, the future Mrs. Edward E. Ames of Crawfordsville.

While continuing to practice law, Russell also was one of the founders of the Crawfordsville Building and Loan Company and served as its secretary for thirty-nine years. He was the mayor of Crawfordsville for three terms, 1886–90 and 1902–04, and from 1904 to 1921 he partnered with Gaylord McClure for the practice of law and the sale of real estate.

Sylvia died on 30 April 1905. Russell lived until 30 October 1931. Both are buried in Oak Hill Cemetery.

References: John A. Bowerman, "Russell's Leadership Role Covered Many Areas," *Montgomery Magazine* XI (March 1986), pp. 9–10; Crawfordsville Public Library; *Wabash Record-Bulletin*, 25 November 1921, p. 13; *Crawfordsville Journal*, 1 March 1905, 31 October and 1 November 1921.

SABIN, RICHARD CHAUNCEY (1836–1868)

When Richard Sabin's father Sidney died in 1886, it was speculated that his estate might be worth between $50,000 and $100,000, a huge sum of money in those times. When the will was read, the estate was estimated at even more—$130,000. Of that, $50,000 was left to Wabash College, a sum that was one of the largest bequests to the college during the nineteenth century. The son did not live long enough to be a major supporter of the college, but he played his part in the Civil War, rising to be a lieutenant colonel.

Richard Sabin, called by his middle name Chauncey, was born on 4 June 1836 in New York State, the only child of Ruth C. and Sidney S. Sabin, both Easterners who migrated to Union Mills, LaPorte County, to experience financial success as a family.

In the autumn of 1852, Sabin entered the Preparatory Department of Wabash College. He remained only one school year, living on campus in Forest Hall. Although he did not return, he clearly enjoyed his time at Wabash and shared his pleasure with his parents, who became generous donors to the college.

He married Margaret Loomis at LaPorte on 14 July 1861. On 24 July 1862 he enrolled as a captain of Company H of the Eighty-Seventh Indiana Regiment. He was commissioned major of the regiment on 21 November 1863 and a brevet lieutenant colonel on 5 March 1865, a few months before being honorably discharged along with other members of his regiment.

Following the war the Sabins settled in Arkansas, where Sabin presumably followed the example of his father and took up farming, but he died prematurely on 22 September 1868.

Sabin's mother, Ruth, gave $5,000 for a library alcove in memory of her son, a memorial that later was converted into a fund for the purchase of new books. When she died in 1894, her philanthropic legacies included the founding of the Ruth C. Sabin Home for Women in LaPorte.

References: Thomas Lee Day of the LaPorte County Public Library; Fern Eddy Schultz of the LaPorte County Historical Society; *LaPorte Daily Herald,* 18 and 28 February 1894; the Ruth C. Sabin Home for Women; *LaPorte Herald-Chronicle*, 30 December 1886; *LaPorte Argus*, 30 December 1886.

SANDFORD, EDWARD BRUCE (1839–1874)

Edward Sandford was born on 15 March 1839 on a large farm near Paris, Illinois, the seventh child of Belinda and Isaac Sandford. His father died in 1856, and Sandford was placed with a legal guardian who sent him to Wabash College. He enrolled in the Normal School in 1857, but stayed only one year before moving to Chicago, then to Kansas, and in 1860 to his mother's farm.

It is generally conceded that young Sandford served in the Union army from Kentucky and rose to the rank of lieutenant, but details are lacking.

Three years after the war, he married Mary Howe of Louisville and farmed in Edgar County. However, the depression of 1873 presumably took its toll; on 11 February 1874 Sandford committed suicide at Freeburg near Belleville, Illinois. One of his brothers reported, "Despondency caused by financial troubles had been the cause of such despair." He is buried, along with many other members of the Sandford family, in the Edgar Cemetery in Paris, Illinois.

References: *Belleville Weekly Advocate*, 20 February 1874; the Filson Club, Louisville, Kentucky; Charles A. Hand, Paris, Illinois; Captain Joseph E. Sanders, Vermilion County, Illinois; Mrs. A. Joyce Brown, Brocton, Illinois.

SARGENT, JOHN M. (1842–1905)

John Sargent was born on 31 December 1841 in Pine Township, Warren County, one of five children of Margaret Rhoads and Jesse Sargent. His siblings were Abigail, William, Sarah, and George. His mother died in the 1850s, and his father then married a woman named Jane from Pennsylvania.

During the school year 1857–58 he enrolled at Wabash College in the Normal School for only one year, presumably returning to work on the family farm. He also married Mary, a native of Ohio.

On 4 August 1862 Sargent was mustered in to Company I of the Seventy-Second Indiana Volunteers for a term of three years, and within a few weeks the regiment went to Kentucky and took part in various skirmishes before moving on to Tennessee, reaching Murfreesboro in January 1863. There the regiment was reorganized into mounted infantry and made part of Colonel John T. Wilder's Lightning Brigade. In June 1863 Sargent was in the Tullahoma Campaign (23 June to 3 July 1863) with its major engagement at Hoover's Gap on 24 June. Afterwards he fought at Chattanooga and Chickamauga. In the spring of 1864, the mounted brigade joined General Sherman in the campaign against Atlanta and remained there until it fell. Sargent then witnessed the surrender of Selma and Montgomery, Alabama, in 1865 and was released from the army on 24 July 1865.

After the war the Sargents moved to Danville, Illinois. Three children had been born to them while they lived in Indiana: Albert in 1862, Perry in 1865, and Jesse in 1867. They were later joined by George in 1870, Ada in 1872, Isaac in 1874, and John in 1876.

The family relocated in the 1870s to Six Mile Township of Logan County, Arkansas. Mary died between 1880 and 1887, and Sargent married a widow, Mrs. Sarah Frances Wells, on 30 March 1888. From the time he moved to Arkansas and for the rest of his life, Sargent was a farmer, first in Oliver Springs and then in Van Buren, where there is a headstone commemorating John M. Sargent in Sarah Grove Cemetery. There are no dates on the tombstone, but the date of death, 28 October 1905, has been confirmed electronically. His wife Sarah was interred there in May 1930.

References: Crawford County (Arkansas) Library; *History in Headstones* (1970), p. 404; *History of Crawford County, Arkansas* (2001), p. 476.

SCOONOVER, JEFFERSON (1833–1911)

Jefferson Scoonover was born in Beverly, Virginia, on 10 June 1833, one of nine children of Charlotta Marstiller (1797–1876) and William Schoonover (1795–1865). For years the family spelled their last name "Schoonover," and even Jefferson's younger brother, Crawford, who also attended Wabash College, retained that spelling. However, Jefferson changed his to "Scoonover," though it caused confusion throughout his life.

His parents moved from Virginia to Tippecanoe County in about 1841, so by the time Jefferson Scoonover entered Wabash College in the fall of 1854, he could rightly claim to be a farmer like his father. He devoted only one year to studying in the Normal School and then presumably returned home and resumed farming. However, by 1860 he had settled in Michigan and become a teacher.

On 17 April 1861 he joined Company K of the First Michigan Regiment for a term of three months. He was shown as standing five feet eleven inches tall, with hazel eyes, dark hair, and fair complexion. When he was released from service, he seems to have remained in Michigan for the next two years.

During the summer of 1863, Scoonover returned to Tippecanoe County, and on 8 August he joined the Battle Ground Guards, a local unit of the Indiana Legion, as a first lieutenant. On 14 November 1863 he enrolled in Company I of the Eleventh Indiana Cavalry, which was attached to the 126th Regiment. He entered as a sergeant and in January 1864 was promoted to first sergeant. Within the year he was promoted to lieutenant, but on 30 August 1864 he resigned from the cavalry in order to accept a promotion to captain of Company I of the Twenty-Eighth U.S. Colored Infantry, a post he held until his discharge from the army in January 1866.

In the autumn of 1866, Scoonover settled at Ann Arbor and began to study medicine at the University of Michigan. He remained there two years, and once he completed his course of study, he married Libby Marshall, a local girl. After the wedding they moved to New York City so that Scoonover could take another year of medical training at Columbia College. Once he received his degree in March 1869, he set up his practice in Greenville, Texas, where he remained for at least thirty years. Among his other activities, he was appointed the United States Postmaster in Greenville from 1892 to 1897.

Jefferson and Libby Scoonover had four children: Alice, Floy, Franklin, and Fred. In about 1905 the family moved to Berkeley, California, where, among other projects, Scoonover helped found the Wesley Methodist Church of North Berkeley. He died at home, 1147 Spruce Street, on 12 August 1912, and is buried in the Sunset View Cemetery. He was survived by his wife, who lived until 1928.

References: Berkeley (California) Public Library; Ann Arbor (Michigan) District Library; Columbia University Archives; Bentley Historical Library of the University of Michigan; Mrs. Dorothy Van Cleef, Lafayette, Indiana; Indiana State Library.

SCOTT, JOHN CHAUNCEY (1838–1883)

Nothing is known of John C. Scott's parents, other than that his father was born in New York State and his mother came from Scotland. Scott was born about 1837–38 somewhere in Indiana. By the time of the 1860 census, he was residing in Warren County, sharing a home with some family other than his own and working as a clerk for a railroad.

On 21 July 1862 Scott enlisted in Company H of the Seventy-Second Indiana Volunteers. He indicated his residence was Attica, and he was described as being five feet eleven inches tall, with a fair complexion, black hair, and brown eyes. He signed up for three years of service, entering as a sergeant. In November of that year he was promoted to second lieutenant, followed by a first lieutenancy in June 1863 and a captaincy in December of that year.

The Seventy-Second Regiment saw much action in Tennessee and Georgia, including the Tullahoma Campaign, Chickamauga, and Chattanooga. On 19 June 1864 Scott was badly wounded in the right foot while fighting near Kennesaw Mountain. Weeks if not months of convalescence followed, and it is not clear when he was able to return to duty. It is doubtful that he was with his regiment as part of Sherman's army laying siege to Atlanta in the late summer of 1864. Scott was finally mustered out at Nashville on 26 June 1865.

Returning to Attica, he quickly courted and married Eliza M. Plowman on 6 December 1865. Born about 1841 in Ohio, Eliza usually went by the nickname of Lida. She gave birth to two daughters: Ivy Rae in 1870 and Ruth in 1872. For years Scott carried on a grocery and mercantile business in Attica. This proved successful, unlike his marriage, which ended in divorce in October 1881. Further complicating his life was poor health on top of his injured foot.

Sometime in 1882 he moved to Indianapolis, presumably to be looked after by his mother. He died there on 23 September 1883.

References: Attica Public Library; *Attica Ledger,* 26 September 1883.

SCOTT, WILLIAM HENRY HARRISON JR. (1842–1861)

William Scott Jr. was born in about 1842 in Danville, one of three children of Elizabeth Macay and W. H. H. Scott, a wealthy physician. His two younger sisters were Kate and May.

He was enrolled in the Scientific Course at Wabash during the college year 1860–61 but left Crawfordsville before the end of term and enlisted in the Twelfth Illinois Regiment at Danville on 6 May. One month later, on 17 June, he was discharged on account of disability at Cairo, Illinois.

Curiously, the Scott family does not mention him, either in the obituary of his father in 1876 or in his father's will. Only when his mother died in 1885 was an allusion made to a son, Harry, who had died in the war. The presumption, therefore, is that, instead of being discharged, young William died of disease at Cairo and was buried nearby.

References: Danville (Illinois) Public Library; *Danville Commercial,* 11 May 1876, p. 1 and 4 August 1885, p. 3; Hiram Beckwith, *History of Vermilion County, Illinois* (1879), pp. 398–400.

SCOUTEN, DWIGHT W. (1832–1889)

Dwight Scouten was born at Pitcher Springs, New York, on 12 February 1833, one of five children of Louisa Blood and Richard Scouten. His siblings were Daniel (1839), Charles (1845), Catherine (1848), and Lyman (1850), all born in Terre Haute.

According to the Wabash College records, D. W. Scouten was in the Preparatory Department for two years, 1851–53, when his residence was in Terre Haute. He was also said to have been a captain in the Civil War. However, the college did not record his first name, only his initials, and his surname is subject to various spellings besides "Scouten," such as "Scouton" and "Skouten."

Shortly after the 1850 census was taken for Terre Haute, Scouten and his father headed west in search of gold. They were also counted in the 1850 census for Placerville, California, but returned to Indiana in time for D. W. to enter Wabash in the fall of 1851. In October 1855 his family moved to Deer Creek, Kansas, where his father took up farming, and the following year Scouten joined his father to work on the farm. His mother died on 19 April 1866, followed by his father on 30 January 1881.

Scouten died on 3 February 1889, leaving it a mystery as to when and where he served during the Civil War. It seems clear that he did not join the army in either Indiana or Kansas, nor did he apply for a military pension after the war.

References: Wabash College catalogues; 1850 census for Vigo County, Indiana; Lawrence (Kansas) Public Library; Kansas State Historical Society; Charles S. Gleed (ed.), *The Kansas Memorial Report of the Old Settlers* (1880), p. 248; *Lawrence Daily Journal*, 10 February 1889, p. 3; Mound View Cemetery records, Kanwaka Township; Kansas state censuses for 1865 and 1875.

SEAGER, JOHN C. (1815–1888)

John Seager was born on 15 June 1815 in Patterson, New Jersey, the son of Sarah and George Seager. His father was a mechanic and in the 1830s built a wool-carding mill in Clinton County. The Seagers' 806-acre farm was distinguished not only by its carding machinery but also by its large sawmill.

During the third year of full time operation in 1835–36, Wabash College admitted a student with the name of John Segur to its Preparatory Department. He did not return the following year, but there is every reason to believe that he was that John C. Seager whose family settled in Jefferson Township, Clinton County, in 1830, since his surname was subject to many variant spellings, such as "Segar," "Segur," and "Seager."

During the summer of 1862, the call went out for additional volunteer soldiers from west central Indiana, and when the Eighty-Sixth Regiment was formed including men from Tippecanoe, Carroll, Clinton, Boone, Montgomery, Fountain, and Warren Counties, Seager was commissioned a captain on 19 August. The forty-seven-year-old was formally mustered in on 4 September, but within several months fell victim to typhoid fever. After languishing in a hospital for seven weeks, he resigned on 28 December 1862.

Seager died at home on 18 July 1888 at the age of seventy-three.

References: 1830–1860 U.S. censuses for Clinton County; *History of Clinton County, Indiana* (1886), pp. 727–28; *Friday-Saturday Crescent*, Frankfort, 25 July 1888; *Frankfort Times*, 21 July 1888; J. A. Barnes et al., *The Eighty-Sixth Indiana Volunteer Infantry* (1895), pp. 17–18.

SEATON, JAMES H. (1836–1904)

James Seaton was born on his family's farm near Grantsburg on 29 November 1836. His parents were Winifred and James Seaton, and his siblings were George, John, Elizabeth, and Minerva.

From 1853 to 1856 Seaton was enrolled at Wabash in the Preparatory or Scientific Department, but didn't pursue the Classical Course that lead to a bachelor of arts degree.

On 18 September 1861 he enlisted in Company K of the Thirty-Eighth Indiana Volunteers and then re-enlisted in December 1863 as a first lieutenant. His family recalled his describing General Sherman's 1864 March to the Sea in Georgia. In July 1865 he was mustered out at Louisville, Kentucky.

On 9 January 1870 Seaton married Mary A. Jones of Crawford County, and a year later they acquired the first of several farms in Fulton County, Illinois. Eventually they had three children: Sherman, Lulu, and Albert. In 1880 they moved to Hennepin, and Seaton also ran a local drugstore, but by 1900 the family was living near St. David. Two years later they acquired yet another farm about a mile south of Bryant, where Seaton died on 26 November 1904. He was interred in the Marysville Cemetery.

References: Canton (Illinois) Public Library; *Canton Daily Register*, 28 November 1904; Henry F. Perry, *History of the Thirty-Eighth Regiment Indiana Volunteers* (1906), p. 289.

SELLERS, JOHN LAYMAN (1836–1924)

John Sellers was born on the family farm in Putnam County three and a half miles south of Greencastle on 25 August 1836. His parents were Fannie Brown and John Crawford Sellers, who had thirteen children. Another son, Joseph, also attended Wabash and served in the Civil War.

When Sellers registered for the Normal School of Wabash College in the fall of 1856, he gave Putnamville as his hometown. He stayed only one year.

On 4 September 1862 at Indianapolis, Sellers enrolled for three years in Company L of the Forty-Fifth Indiana Regiment, known also as the Indiana Third Cavalry. Later he was transferred to Company A of the Thirty-Ninth Regiment, otherwise known as the Indiana Eighth Cavalry. Records at that time show him as six feet tall, with dark complexion, black hair, and blue eyes.

Mustered out of service at Lexington, North Carolina, on 20 July 1865, Sellers returned to Putnam County, and on 11 December 1866 he married Mary J. Matkins. Over the years they had six children: Edward, Katie, Jennie, Nancy, Minnie, and Ida May. When Mary died in 1879 or 1880, Sellers took a second wife, Elizabeth (Lizzie) Wells, on 3 August 1880, and they went on to have four children.

Sellers worked on the family farm until he died on 18 March 1924, followed by Elizabeth on 11 December 1925. They share a gravestone in the Putnamville Cemetery.

References: *Greencastle Herald*, 19 March 1924; DePauw University Archives, Greencastle.

SELLERS, JOSEPH B. (1843–1914)

The Twenty-Seventh Indiana Regiment liked to promote itself as the "Giants" because of the height of many of its soldiers. On 1 September 1861 Joseph Sellers enrolled for three years as a sergeant in Company I of the Twenty-Seventh Indiana Volunteer Infantry at Indianapolis. He was described as six feet three inches tall, with fair complexion, auburn hair, and blue eyes, and his significant height made him an appropriate member of the "Giants."

Joseph Sellers, the younger brother of John Sellers discussed above, was also born on the family farm south of Greencastle in 1843, one of thirteen children of Fannie Brown and John Crawford Sellers. Sellers was a student in the Normal School at Wabash College during the 1860–61 academic year. In 1862, along with the other members of the Twenty-Seventh, he was in the battles of Newtown, Virginia, on 22 May; Winchester, 23 May; and Cedar Mountain, 9 August, when he was shot through the lower right leg. He was in the hospital until November. In May 1863 he was under severe fire at the Battle of Chancellorsville and was shot again through the right leg in the Battle of Resaca in May 1864, necessitating the leg's amputation. On 8 July 1864 his father came and took him home, and Sellers was discharged in August.

In 1866 Sellers returned to the farm east of Greencastle and was elected county sheriff and treasurer of Putnam County as a Republican. From 1867 to 1871 he was county treasurer. On 27 September 1868 he married Viola E. Kiser. They had six children: Cora, Grant, Homer, Frank, Ernest, and Stella Grace. The family settled on a farm two miles from the old homestead and engaged in stock raising until 1891, when they moved to North Salem and bought a flourmill and the Central Hotel.

Sellers was active in civic affairs in Putnamville. He was commander of the GAR post and a member of the Odd Fellows and the Knights of Honor. In 1895 he was still being described as "a large, robust man, weighting 275 pounds, and stand[ing] six feet three and one-half inches high."

He died on 12 April 1914, survived by his wife, and is buried in the Putnamville Cemetery.

References: *Greencastle Herald*, 24 April 1914; *A Journey Through Putnam County History* (1966), p. 366; J. W. Weik, *History of Putnam County, Indiana*, pp. 61 and 472; *Biographical and Historical Record of Putnam County, Indiana* (1887), p. 265, 270; DePauw University Archives, Greencastle.

SESTON, CHARLES H. (1840–1864)

In 1975 the U.S. Army Reserve Center at Camp Atterbury was named after Sergeant Charles Seston. His memory as a proud Civil War soldier from Indiana and color bearer lives on.

Charles Seston was born in New Albany in 1840. His mother died soon after his birth, and his father, John Seston, a saddler, married Catherine S. McClary in 1842. He had a stepsister, Anna.

In the fall of 1860, Seston entered the Normal School of Wabash College but did not finish the school year because he enrolled in the Eleventh Indiana Regiment for three months. After guarding railway lines in western Virginia, he was mustered out at Indianapolis on 4 August.

Less than four weeks later, Seston re-enlisted in Company I of the Eleventh for three years. At this time he gave his residence as Johnson County, not New Albany. In September 1864 the forces under General Philip Sheridan were trying to clear the Confederates out of the Shenandoah Valley. As a sergeant, Seston distinguished himself during the Third Battle of Winchester, Virginia, the largest and bloodiest battle in the Shenandoah Valley. He was killed in action. Posthumously, he was awarded the Medal of Honor for "gallant and meritorious service in carrying the regimental colors." Although buried on the battlefield, his body was returned for burial in New Albany in May 1865.

References: *Wabash Magazine*, III (February 1862), p. 190; *New Albany Daily Ledger*, 12 May 1865; J. R. H. Spears, "Sergeant Charles M. Seston: Citizen Soldier," *Indiana Historical Bulletin*, LII (April 1975), pp. 45–46; *New Albany Ledger*, 6 October 1864.

SEWARD, FREDERICK DWIGHT (1842–1928)

Frederick Seward was born on 11 December 1842 at Laketown, the son of Pleiades B. Barber and Amos Dudley Seward, a civil engineer and teacher. In 1855 the family moved to Mankato, Minnesota, where his father taught school. To that town the Presbyterian minister Reverend James Thomson had come from Crawfordsville to build a new church. The family was to become closely associated with him in years to come.

On 19 August 1862 Seward was mustered into Company E of the Ninth Minnesota Infantry and committed to three years of service. Promotion to corporal came in 1863, and later that year he became a first lieutenant and was transferred to the Seventy-Second Regiment Infantry, United States Colored Troops. During 1864–65 Seward served as a captain in the 117th Regiment Infantry, United States Colored Troops.

After the war he returned briefly to Mankato and then entered the Preparatory Department of Wabash College in the fall of 1865, due, no doubt, to the family's acquaintance with Reverend Thomson, who was one of the founders of Wabash. The following year Seward went to Western Reserve College in Cleveland, graduating in June 1870. Determined to become a minister, he spent the year 1870–71 at Lane Theological Seminary in Cincinnati. Seward married Emma A. Hoyt on 30 June 1871, and eventually they had three children.

After Seward was ordained and served in several pastorates, in 1881 the family moved to California, where Seward became the pastor of the Presbyterian church in Ventura. From 1887 to 1894 he traveled extensively doing home missionary work, and from 1895 to 1897 he was pastor in Fresno, followed by churches in Beaumont and Banning between 1897 and 1900, with other assignments and accomplishments to follow. All told, Seward served, or helped found, about thirty-eight churches throughout California.

In 1909 his wife died, and on 1 November 1910 he married Binne Pinneo of Los Angeles. Seward died on 10 June 1928, survived by a son from his first marriage, E. D. Seward of San Pedro, and his second wife.

References: Minnesota Historical Society; Los Angeles Public Library; *Mankato: Its First Fifty Years, 1852–1902* (1903), pp. 13, 64, 305; *Minnesota in the Civil and Indian Wars*, I, p. 446; *Los Angeles Times*, 23 and 25 June 1928; E. A. Wicher, *The Presbyterian Church in California* (1927), pp. 214, 232, 234, 239; *General Biographical Catalogue of Auburn Theological Seminary, 1919–1940* (1960), p. 30; *The Presbyterian*, 9 August 1928, p. 18; and Lane Theological Seminary, *General Catalogue*, 1829–1899, p. 85.

SHANKLIN, JAMES MAYNARD (1836–1863)

James Shanklin was born in Evansville, the eldest of five children of Philura French and John Shanklin. Prior to coming to Wabash in the fall of 1850, he was tutored privately, and he became a freshman when he was only fourteen years old. Unfortunately, he was restricted by poor health and had to leave the college after his first year. He spent some time in the East and returned to Wabash as a sophomore in 1852–53. He then transferred to the University of Michigan at Ann Arbor but was once more forced to leave because of his health. After working hard in the wilds of Michigan, he spent fifteen months in the Kansas and Nebraska territories.

Shanklin was instrumental in organizing the Forty-Second Indiana Infantry. He was commissioned a major on 12 September 1862 and made lieutenant colonel of the regiment one month later on 21 October. He received a head wound at the Battle of Wartrace, Tennessee (11 April 1862), about which he wrote an account in *The Soldier of Indiana in the War for the Union*, published in 1866. At the Battle of Stones River he was captured and held at Libby Prison in Richmond, Virginia. After his release he was taken ill with acute laryngitis at his home in Evansville and died the next day on 23 May 1863. He was mourned by his unit as a good officer, brave soldier, and decent man. He was only twenty-seven years old.

References: S. F. Horrall, *History of the Forty-Second Indiana Volunteer Infantry* (1892), pp. 93–94.

SHAW, JAMES BIRNEY (1842–1922)

James Shaw was born at Pittsburg, Indiana, on 28 May 1842, the oldest of six children of Cornelia Mudge and William H. Shaw. As a child, he worked on the family farm, and when the Monon Railroad began passenger service, he sold peanuts aboard the train. Later he stoked wood-burning locomotives for the Panhandle Railroad.

When young James entered Wabash College in the fall of 1857, his family lived in Bradford, Indiana. He spent three years in the college's Normal School, and by 1859–60 he had moved back to Pittsburg in Carroll County.

On 6 September 1861 at Lafayette, he enrolled for three years in Company D of the Tenth Indiana Regiment, and in July 1862 he became a hospital steward, a job he performed for the remainder of his military service. He lost much of his hearing during the Tullahoma campaign on the Elk River in Tennessee in July 1863, and the following year he spent 120 days in the Atlanta campaign and took part in the march of Sherman's forces to Savannah and the sea. He was mustered out at Indianapolis on 19 September 1864.

After the war he settled briefly in Remington and then moved to Watseka, Illinois. There, he courted and married Martha Jane Morgan and worked as a railroad dispatcher and telegrapher. By the late 1870s the Shaws relocated to Lafayette, Indiana, where Shaw continued his railroad work. When the Lake Erie and Western line closed its Lafayette office in 1885, Shaw was elected a justice of the peace and supplemented his income by running an agency for the prosecution of pension claims.

In 1912 Shaw's account of his regiment was published in Lafayette: *History of the Tenth Regiment Indiana Volunteer Infantry: Three Months and Three Years Organizations.*

He died of a stroke on 11 July 1922, survived by his wife and children, and was buried in Springvale Cemetery.

References: *Indianapolis News*, 11 July 1922; R. Banta, *Indiana Authors and their Books* (1949), p. 288; R. P. DeHart, *Past and Present of Tippecanoe County, Indiana*, II (1909), pp. 678–70; J. B. Shaw; *History of the Tenth Regiment Indiana Volunteer Infantry* (1912); Tippecanoe County Historical Association, Lafayette.

SHELBY, DAVID (1827–1864)

David Shelby was the oldest of five children born to Rezin (1791–1856) and Jane Thompson Shelby. The date of his birth is not known, but it was probably sometime in 1827. He grew up in Eugene Township, Vermillion County. The family was comfortably well off, with the father pursuing a legal career and serving as a judge.

In 1842 Shelby enrolled in Wabash's Preparatory Department, advanced to the freshman year in 1844, and carried on until the middle of his senior year. In January 1848, Shelby and his roommate held a particularly rowdy party in their dormitory room. The group then headed for town, met up with several recent college graduates, and extended the celebration with much noise and profanity. This brought down the wrath of the faculty upon Shelby's head, and when he seemed unrepentant, he was expelled. Returning to the college in the autumn of 1853, he then successfully completed his requirements for the bachelor of arts degree and graduated with the class of 1854. Immediately upon graduation, he returned home and was elected to the post of county auditor. Five years later he was similarly chosen county surveyor. He farmed a good-sized piece of land.

On 12 August 1862 Shelby helped form Company K of the Ninety-Seventh Indiana Volunteers at his hometown of Eugene and assumed the rank of captain. He had signed up for three years of military service, but in less than two, he died of disease at Altoona Pass, Georgia, on 13 June 1864. His body was returned to Vermillion County, where he was interred in the Shelby family cemetery near where the Vermillion and Wabash Rivers meet.

References: Mrs. William A. Heidbreder of Cayuga, Indiana; Indiana State Archives.

SHIDELER, GABRIEL (1825–1897)

Gabriel Shideler was born in Ohio on 18 February 1825, the youngest of three sons of Anna Swihart and Joseph Shideler. His brothers were Joseph (1821) and Jonathan (1822). From 1844 to 1848 he was in the Preparatory Department at Wabash College. He then worked as a carpenter.

On 16 May 1861 he enrolled at Lafayette in Company H of the Fifteenth Indiana Regiment, but by 14 June he had switched to Company A and committed to three years of service. While at Nashville, he transferred to the Fourth U.S. Cavalry on 18 November 1862, and at the Battle of Chickamauga in September 1863, his horse stumbled and fell, pinning his left leg so that he had to spend the better part of six weeks in hospital. Once back in active service, the leg flared up again, forcing an extended stay in a convalescent camp at Huntsville, Alabama, during May and June of 1864. Back with his comrades at Kennesaw, Georgia, he continued to serve well past three years. He was released at San Antonio, Texas, on 13 December 1865.

For the next ten years he lived in Attica, Indiana, and was limited to doing odd jobs, since his health prevented him from resuming his trade of carpentry. Sometime prior to 1880 he moved to Colorado and worked at first in Conejos County as a canvassing agent. In 1883 he was living in Del Norte, where his health was again deteriorating, and by 1890 he was on crutches, unable to work, and living mainly on local charity. He applied without success for a military pension and returned in 1893 to Lafayette, Indiana, where he secured a modest pension of $12 per month. Sometime later he moved to Paxton, Illinois, and in June 1897 he was declared insane. He died at Paxton on 21 July 1897.

References: H. W. Shideler, *History of the Shideler Family* (1931), p. 46; military pension file, National Archives, Washington, DC.

SHIPP, SANFORD CATTERLIN (1837–1890)

Sanford Shipp was born at Frankfort, Indiana, on 19 April 1837, one of eleven children of Mary Catterlin (1820–1883) and Samuel Copeland Shipp (1810–1884), a successful merchant. His siblings were Milton, Sarah, Caroline, Emma, Fannie, James, Matilda, Maggie, Samuel, and Mary. He attended Wabash for one academic year, 1854–55, and then moved with his family to Thorntown. On 12 June 1861 the young man enlisted in the Seventeenth Indiana Regiment, Company B. His regiment saw action in numerous skirmishes in Kentucky and participated in major battles in Tennessee in 1863: at Hoover's Gap in June and Chickamauga in September. He served his full term of three years and was released on 21 June 1864.

In Indianapolis Shipp worked as a clerk in a dry goods business. On 5 November 1873 he married Mary Walter. By 1880 the Shipps lived in Darlington, where Shipp was a grocer, and they had three children: Mary, six; Della, four; and a one-month-old girl. He died on 5 November 1890 in Indianapolis.

References: Frankfort Public Library; *Frankfort Crescent*, 17 January 1883 and 16 April 1884.

> **Everybody went down and enlisted together...**
> **Fact vs. College Tradition**
>
> Over the years the college has repeated the claim that when the Civil War broke out, thirty students immediately went downtown and enlisted in Company I of the Eleventh Regiment, commanded by Captain Isaac Elston. The lore also maintains that six out of seven seniors signed up.
>
> According to our research, an impressive twenty-three students joined Company I, but none were seniors. Some were juniors, others sophomores, and several were freshmen. Edward Kingsbury, Monroe Milford, and Joseph Webster were juniors; William Black, Henry Groenendyke, James Carnahan, Robert Miller, Oliver Spencer, and Lane Willson were sophomores; and James Gookins, Horace Foote, Martin Miller, and Thomas Miller were freshmen. Six more were in the Preparatory Department: Samuel Lingerman, Thomas Stevens, Arthur Deming, Enos Hornaday, and Abram Ross. And there were five future teachers from the Normal School: John Carter, James Grisard, Isaac Taylor, Charles Seston, and James Patterson.
>
> There were eight seniors at college in the spring of 1861, five of whom subsequently joined the army, but not at the time that the twenty-three students mentioned above went en masse downtown to enlist in Company I of the Eleventh Regiment on 22 April.

SHORTRIDGE, WILLIAM BURKE (1832–1908)

William Shortridge was born on a farm in Fairfield Township, Tippecanoe County, on 15 February 1832, the third of seven children of Clarissa Burks and Morgan Shortridge. Morgan Shortridge was the first sheriff of Tippecanoe County from 1828 to 1832 and served in the Indiana House of Representatives from 1832 to 1833 and again in 1840–41.

Young William attended the Preparatory Department of Wabash College from 1851 to 1852 and then returned to the family farm. His father died on 22 December 1858, leaving him to help his mother until President Lincoln's call for troops in 1861. On 7 September he enrolled in Company A of the Fortieth Indiana Volunteer Infantry for a term of three years and was mustered in on 31 October 1861 at Lafayette. At the time he enlisted he was twenty-nine years old, five feet eleven inches tall, and had a dark complexion with black eyes and black hair.

While Shortridge was in the army, he fought in many of the most significant battles: Chickamauga, Lookout Mountain, Mission Ridge, Shiloh, Stones River,

Perryville, Dallas (26 May to 4 June 1864), Kennesaw Mountain, the crossing of the Chattahoochee River, Peach Tree Creek, and Nashville. He also took part in the siege of Atlanta and the occupation of Chattanooga. His regiment lost five officers and 143 enlisted men in combat, and another five officers and 206 enlisted men succumbed to disease. Shortridge was honorably discharged as an orderly sergeant on 12 October 1863.

Returning home to Tippecanoe County, he married Leah Van Scoy on 10 May 1865. They eventually had six children, including Jessie F., Anna Augusta, William A., Edgar S., May Luella. Their first son, Samuel Morgan, died at the age of four months. Shortridge ran as a Republican and was elected justice of the peace in Wea Township for two terms.

Shortridge died on 5 March 1908. He, his wife, and his mother were all buried in Wild Cat Cemetery, Wea Township, Tippecanoe County.

References: *Biographical Record and Portrait Album of Tippecanoe County, Indiana* (1888), pp. 616–19; *Biographical Directory of the Indiana General Assembly*, I (1880), p. 355.

SIMPSON, EDWIN STANLEY (1845–1904)

Edwin Simpson was born in Crawfordsville on 12 May 1845, one of five sons of Maria and John Simpson. Edwin and his brother, Joseph, both went to Wabash and served in the Civil War. Their other brothers were Philo, James, William, and Samuel.

Simpson was enrolled in the Preparatory Department of Wabash for one academic year, 1859–60 and then presumably returned home to work on the family farm.

On 29 July 1862 he joined Company A of the Fourth Cavalry, attached to the Seventy-Seventh Indiana Regiment, and soon found himself in Kentucky. By January 1863 the regiment had moved on to Tennessee, and during February and March the regiment was engaged near Murfreesboro. It also took part in the Battle of Chickamauga on 19–20 September. In May 1864 the Seventy-Seventh joined Sherman in the campaign against Atlanta, but once the city fell, the cavalry returned to Tennessee and Kentucky. In 1865 it was sent back to Alabama and Georgia, and its last months of active duty were spent in Tennessee, where Simpson was mustered out at Edgefield on 29 June.

Simpson returned to Crawfordsville and pursued various jobs, including assistant county clerk and three terms as county engineer. During his tenure in this job, he supervised the laying of concrete sidewalks and gutters in Crawfordsville.

Simpson never enjoyed robust health, and he died on 30 November 1904.

References: *Crawfordsville Daily Journal*, 2 December 1904; R. J. Reid, *Fourth Indiana Cavalry Regiment: A History* (1994) p. 207.

SIMPSON, JOSEPH B. (1840–1886)

Joseph Simpson was born in Crawfordsville on 15 September 1840, the older brother of Edwin, who also attended Wabash and served in the Civil War, as described in the preceding biography. His parents were Maria and John Simpson, and his other siblings were Philo, James, William, and Samuel.

In the autumn of 1853 Simpson entered the Preparatory Department of Wabash College, remaining for one year before leaving for a couple of years. He then returned in 1855 for a year in the Normal School. Until the outbreak of war, he worked for the dry goods firm of Graham and Brothers.

On 20 April 1861 at Crawfordsville, he enrolled as a corporal for three months in Company G of the Tenth Indiana Volunteers and served briefly in Virginia, before he was mustered out at Indianapolis on 6 August. On 5 May 1863 he received a commission as a first lieutenant in Company I of the Eleventh Indiana Regiment. On 26 November 1864 he was promoted to captain, and in April 1865 he was stationed at Baltimore, Maryland. He was mustered out on 26 July.

Back in Crawfordsville Simpson became one of the founding members of the GAR Post No. 1 on 18 September 1866 and seems to have devoted himself to the dry goods business for the rest of his life. In 1870 he lodged with Lew Wallace and family, but later lived on his own in Spring Street.

After the war Simpson was plagued by poor health. He died on 5 June 1886 and was interred in Oak Hill Cemetery.

References: *Saturday Evening Journal* (Crawfordsville), 12 June 1886; *Crawfordsville Review*, 12 June 1886

SIMPSON, ROBERT GLENN (1845–?)

Robert Simpson was born in Switzerland County on 10 May 1845. In 1860 he lived on his own in Pleasant Township there. On 26 September 1861 he enrolled at Bennington in Company H of the Sixth Indiana Voluntary Infantry for three years, saying that he was seventeen, whereas in fact, he was sixteen. This subterfuge worked for a while, and he was mustered in at Madison on 31 December 1861. However, once his deception was discovered, he was discharged on 16 June 1862.

On 27 February 1864, having moved to Mason, Illinois, Simpson enrolled at Mattoon in Company E of the Sixty-Second Illinois Regiment. This time he gave his correct age as eighteen and claimed that he was a farmer. He was described as being five feet six inches tall, with brown hair, blue eyes, and a light complexion. He remained on active duty for two years, spent partially at Little Rock, Arkansas, and was released on 6 March 1866.

After the war Simpson farmed until the spring of 1867, when he enrolled in the Preparatory Department at Wabash College, studying there for two years. On 1 September 1870 he married Mary E. Marsh of Bennington, and they eventually had seven children: Eva, Perry, Hettie, Howard, Carine, Carrie, and Harvey. In the fall of 1871, he returned to Wabash in the Preparatory Department, and at some point in 1872 he began to study medicine at Bennington with Dr. P. C Holland. He was ultimately accepted at Ohio Medical College in Cincinnati, from which he graduated in 1877.

Returning to Switzerland County, Simpson established his medical practice in Florence, but after eighteen months he moved to East Enterprise, where he remained for four years until finally settling at Bennington.

References: *History of Dearborn, Ohio and Switzerland Counties, Indiana* (1885), pp. 1068–69, 1270; Switzerland County Public Library, Vevay, Indiana.

SIMS, JAMES NOBLE (1817–1899)

James Sims was born on 5 January 1817 at Connersville, one of thirteen children of Elizabeth McCarty and Stephan Sims. In 1834 his mother died, and the family moved to Clinton Township, Boone County, where Sims was living when he entered the Preparatory Department of Wabash. He stayed for two years, but once his family settled in Frankfort in 1836, he began teaching and reading law with a local attorney.

In 1839–40, Sims attended classes at Asbury University. He was admitted to the Indiana bar in 1844. Four years later he set up his own practice in Frankfort, which continued for the next fifty years. He supplemented his legal work by occasional forays into politics. He was a Whig until 1854, when he became a Republican, and he was a proud supporter of Lincoln, whose nomination for president he witnessed at the Republican convention in Chicago in 1860.

At the relatively old age of forty-five, Sims joined the 100th Indiana Volunteer Regiment that was organized at Fort Wayne in August 1862 and secured a commission as captain of Company I on 12 September. The company was known as the Clinton County Excelsiors. In November the regiment went to Memphis, where it was merged with the Second Battalion, First Division, of the Army of the Tennessee, commanded by Ulysses S. Grant. In 1863 they were involved in the critical victory at Vicksburg on 4 July, and a week later they attacked Jackson, Mississippi. Sims was discharged on 11 August 1863 due to poor health.

On 14 November 1865 Sims married Margaret A. Allen of Clinton County. She gave birth to two children: Frederick, in about 1868, and Grace, in about 1869.

Sims died in Frankfort on 20 February 1899, survived by his wife, who lived until 1 November 1912. He was interred in the IOOF Cemetery in Frankfort.

References: *Combination Atlas Map of Clinton County, Indiana* (1878), pp. 35–36;

L. J. Monks, *Courts and Lawyers of Indiana*, II (1916), pp. 611–12; *Frankfort Crescent*, 24 February 1899.

SKINNER, CLARK (1829–1903)

Clark Skinner was born in Cincinnati on 30 August 1829, the son of Lavina Scudder and Corson Clark Skinner. Before coming to Wabash in 1851, he was a teacher in Peru, Indiana. He studied in the Preparatory Department for two years and then apparently began to prepare for life as a minister. He was admitted to the Methodist Northern Indiana Conference in 1856.

On 31 March 1857 Skinner married Nannie C. Sewell of Newtown, Indiana. She had five children before she died on 2 January 1870. Clark then married Martha E. Voliva on 8 February 1871.

In 1861 Skinner worked at the Methodist church in LaPorte, which was struggling and badly in debt. He stayed there about a year and helped to raise money and restore solvency. At some point in 1862 or 1863, he volunteered as a chaplain for a few months before ministering in South Bend.

From 1865 to 1867 Skinner was pastor of the Methodist church in Crawfordsville. He returned to South Bend in about 1887 and died there on 1 June 1903.

References: S. F. Taylor, *History of LaPorte County, Indiana* (1876), p. 405; Methodist Archives, DePauw University, Greencastle, Indiana.

SMITH, HORACE B. (1843–1864)

Most volunteers like Horace Smith could not afford their military clothing and equipment when they enlisted early in the war. The state paid for their items of apparel and then presumably recovered the cost from the soldier's pay. Smith recorded that when he joined the Eleventh Indiana in April of 1861, he was provided with a uniform and shirts for $10; drawers for 80 cents; socks and shoes for $1.15; and cap for $1.

Smith was born in Ohio in about 1843, the son of Mary and Charles Smith. His siblings were America, Ellen, James, and Astus.

The family seems to have settled in Montgomery County sometime after 1850, but when young Horace came to Wabash in the fall of 1858, he had no family in Crawfordsville, and so he "boarded at the Jewett household." He remained in the Normal School for two years, 1858–60, and then signed up for military service a year later in Crawfordsville. Like so many others at Wabash, he joined Company I of the Eleventh Regiment on 18 April 1861. They were all mustered in at Indianapolis on the 22nd, served their three months, and were mustered out at Indianapolis on 4 August.

On 20 February 1862 Smith re-enlisted, this time in Company B of the Eighty-Second Ohio infantry. He signed up for three years and was soon promoted to the rank of corporal within a month's time. Sergeant's stripes were forthcoming in July 1862 and promotion to first sergeant in June 1863.

Smith was wounded and taken prisoner at the Battle of Gettysburg on 1 July 1863. His initial confinement was on Belle Island, but then he was sent to the dreaded confines of Andersonville, Georgia. He died there on 13 March 1864.

References: Crawfordsville Public Library; H. W. Beckwith, *History of Montgomery County* (1881), pp. 49, 110; military service file, National Archives, Washington, DC.

SMITH, JOHN NEWTON (1836–1913)

John Smith was born at Hopewell, New York, on 14 December 1836, the only son of Eunice Newton and China B. Smith. In 1837 the family moved to Indiana, to a farm in or near Middlebury, where Eunice died in 1840. Two years later Newton married Nancy Davis, and they eventually had nine children.

John Smith entered the Preparatory Department of Wabash College in the autumn of 1854 and remained only one year. On 3 July 1861 he enrolled in the Third Virginia Volunteer Cavalry Regiment as a second lieutenant. Why he joined the Confederate Army is puzzling, since his father came from Maine and his mother from Connecticut. The regiment fought in many conflicts from Williamsburg to Fredericksburg, and it participated in General Jubal Early's operations in the Shenandoah Valley and the Appomattox Campaign. Smith remained on active duty until 1865.

After the war he trained in medicine, and in about 1883 he moved to Bartow, Florida, where he married Mela M. and established a medical practice. His wife died on 17 January 1899. Smith died on 13 November 1913 in Jacksonville, where he may have been seeking medical assistance. They are buried in Oak Hill Cemetery in Bartow.

References: Elkhart Public Library; *History of Elkhart County, Indiana* (1881); *A Twentieth Century History and Biographical Record of Elkhart County, Indiana* (1905); Historical and Genealogical Library, Bartow, Florida; (Bartow) *Courier Informant*, 18 January 1899 and 13 November 1913.

SMITH, THOMAS GREENIP (1823–1894)

Thomas Smith was born in Kendall, England, in about 1823. In 1853, when he entered the Scientific Course at Wabash, he indicated that his home was Dumfries, Scotland, although before coming to Crawfordsville, he spent some years in Albion, Illinois, where he apparently became a Presbyterian and resolved to enter the ministry. By the time he was at college, he was married and had two children. His wife, Jane Brown, had been born in Manchester, England. Eventually they had six children: Herbert, James, Thomas Jr., Mary, George, and Otis. Both Thomas Jr. and Otis later graduated from Wabash College.

Smith spent only one year at Wabash. At the age of thirty, he was anxious to begin a career in the Presbyterian ministry. In 1857 he was appointed minister to the church in Albion, was formally ordained in 1869, and served as its pastor off and on for the next twenty years.

Uncertainly surrounds his military service. One source claimed that he served for three years and eight months, while another suggested two years or less. He probably was assigned as a chaplain to a unit of the regular United States Army, since he does not appear in the military records of either Illinois or Indiana.

In April 1866 he resumed his pastorate in Albion, but left there in 1877 for a church in Bridgeport, Illinois. A few years later he went to the Sharon Presbyterian Church in Enfield, Illinois, and stayed until 1883. He died in 1894.

References: *The History of the Albion Presbyterian Church, 1843–1943*; *History of White County* (1883), pp. 867–68; Albion Public Library, Edwards County; Carmi Public Library, White County. Since two of Thomas Smith's sons attended Wabash, there is information in the college archives about their father's career.

SMITH, WILLIAM (1841–1865)

William Smith was born in Fayette County, Kentucky, on 6 November 1841. His parents were Mary J. (1827–1864) and George W. Smith (1810–1869).

In the autumn of 1859, Smith came to Crawfordsville and joined the Preparatory Department of Wabash College. He gave his hometown as Lexington, Kentucky. In the summer of 1860, Smith was lodging in town with the William K. Wallace family, but later moved in with his own family, who had come to Indiana sometime in 1860 and settled in Crawfordsville while Smith completed his third year at Wabash. In 1864 his mother died.

The following year, on 22 March 1865, he went to Lafayette and enrolled in Company K of the 154th Indiana Regiment for one year, induced to serve in part by a bounty of one hundred dollars, which he received in two installments: one-third upon enlistment and the rest to be paid at the end of his tour of duty. He was then twenty-three years old, five feet nine inches tall, with brown hair, hazel eyes, and a fair complexion. At first his regiment trained in Indiana and then went to Kentucky, his home state. A story circulated that Smith crossed the Wabash campus carrying a Confederate flag. A minor riot ensued, and Smith feared for life and limb.

In June of 1865, he fell ill in Maryland and was admitted to an army hospital at Cumberland. He died there on 30 June, and his body was returned to Crawfordsville for burial in the Masonic Cemetery with both of his parents.

References: The story of Smith and the Confederate flag comes from an unidentified newspaper clipping in the James A. Greene scrapbook at the Crawfordsville Public Library. A handwritten date on the cutting is 17 June 1902. See also: *Crawfordsville Weekly Journal*, 14 October 1869; H. W. Beckwith, *History of Montgomery County* (1881), p. 109; military service file, National Archives, Washington, DC.

SPEED, SIDNEY ALLEN (1846–1923)

Sidney Speed was born in Crawfordsville on 25 June 1846, the fourth of five children of Margaret Baxter and John Speed, both natives of Scotland. Sidney's siblings were Margaret, Cecilia, Frank, and Robert Bruce. His father was a stonemason, which took the family to Pennsylvania, Virginia, and Washington DC, where he worked on various public works and monuments. In 1834 he came to Indiana in anticipation of using his talent on the new state capital in Indianapolis. However, this did not happen, and he settled in Crawfordsville, building a substantial log house at the corner of Grant Avenue and North Street.

The Speed cabin later achieved notoriety as a station on the Underground Railroad for escaping slaves, a line that ran through Alamo, Yountsville, Crawfordsville, and Darlington. Occasionally, the Speeds concealed a dozen fugitives in the loft of the house, and members of the family made small additional purchases of food so as not to arouse suspicion as to how many mouths they were feeding. Part of the house remains in Crawfordsville on the grounds of the Lane House.

Speed entered the Normal School of Wabash College sometime during the academic year of 1860–61. He returned for a second year, but several months shy of his sixteenth birthday, he lied about his age and enrolled in the Indiana Eighteenth Light Artillery on 12 April 1862. He served until 12 April 1865. On 21 April 1863 the unit in which Speed served was involved in skirmishes at McMinnville, Tennessee. In a letter to his sister, he described the way in which the Federal troops punished the community: "That night we burned two large cotton factories, the depot, the court house, several houses of leading Rebels, and seven grist mills." Later that year, on 18 September at Chickamauga, Speed demonstrated his coolness under fire when a Confederate shell landed near him and his comrades with its fuse still burning. Speed picked it up and hurled it aside before it had a chance to explode. Not surprisingly, he was promoted to corporal a few months later.

Returning to Crawfordsville he enrolled for one more year of college (1865–66) before leaving for California, only to turn around quite soon and return to Crawfordsville.

In 1867 Speed began his own business in drain tiles, but this lasted only a few years. Then he became a representative for the Howe Sewing Machine Company in Crawfordsville, Terre Haute, Frankfort, and Logansport. On his twenty-sixth birthday, 25 June 1872, he married Margaret Seimantel of Lawrenceburg,

Indiana. They had one daughter, Mable.

In 1875 he introduced a new business in Crawfordsville as a stonecutter and dealer in marble and granite monuments, with business premises at 104 South Water Street. During the 1890s he successfully designed monuments for the Chickamauga and Chattanooga military parks and also submitted plans for the Andersonville Prison memorial site and a monument for Shiloh.

Speed was forced to retire from active business in 1911 because of a partial stroke and paralysis. However, he lived in Crawfordsville until his death on 12 July 1923, survived by his widow, who died on 8 December 1937. Both were cremated and later buried at Oak Hill Cemetery.

References: *The Soldier of Indiana in the War for the Union*, II (1866), p. 203; *History of Montgomery County, Indiana* (Bowen & Co., 1913), pp. 176, 506–08; *Portrait and Biographical Record of Montgomery, Parke and Fountain Counties, Indiana* (1893); T. E. Gronert, *Sugar Creek Saga* (1958), pp. 145–46, 179–82; J. W. Rowell, *Yankee Artillerymen* (1875), pp. 71–72, 168, 235, 276; *Crawfordsville Journal*, 13 July 1923; *Crawfordsville Journal Review*, 9 December 1937; *Wabash Record–Bulletin*, summer 1923, p. 23; P. Cline, *Crawfordsville: A Pictorial History* (1991), pp. 36, 42–44, 47, 55.

SPELMAN, JOHN ADAMS (1834–1885)

John Spelman was born on 22 July 1834 in Edinburg, Ohio, one of nine children of Lavinia and Ohel Spelman. His siblings were Rhoda, Thomas, Stephen, Mable, Ellen, Jane, Martha, and a brother Levi who also attended Wabash. In 1838 the family moved from New York State to a farm near Boonville in the Hoosier state.

Spelman was apparently a natural student, for he not only completed two years in the Preparatory Department of Wabash College, 1851–53, but also four more years in the Classical Course, 1854–58. He graduated with a bachelor of arts degree and began the study of law. After a year or two he went to Sterling, Iowa, and Lexington, Minnesota.

On 4 October 1861 he enrolled in Company I of the Third Minnesota Volunteer Infantry as a musician. From Fort Snelling in St. Paul, his regiment went to Tennessee, and in July 1862 he was taken prisoner and briefly incarcerated in Libby Prison in Richmond, Virginia. He rejoined his regiment at Murfreesboro and went westward to Missouri and Arkansas, where he was mustered out at De Vall's Bluff on 14 November 1863.

At the beginning of 1864, he re-enlisted and rejoined his old comrades in the Minnesota Third and was promoted to corporal and sergeant. However, for reasons unknown he requested that he be demoted to the rank of private, and early in 1865 he secured a medical discharge but stayed in Little Rock working for the army sanitation department.

After the war Spelman settled in Owatonna, Minnesota, and in 1867 became the editor of the *Vendetta*, which merged with the Owatonna *Journal*. Soon he became part-proprietor and also did job-printing. He retained the newspaper until 1873, when he became a partner in a new bookstore.

On 27 November 1873 he married Ellen Grosvenor, and they eventually had four children: George, Mable, Herbert, and John A. II.

While in Owatonna, Spelman was very active in municipal and county affairs, including as a correspondent for the *New York World* and the *St. Paul Pioneer Press*, county superintendant of schools, county treasurer, and county assessor. As his health grew precarious, he decided to leave Minnesota for the drier climate of North Dakota, where he settled in 1882. He died in Ellendale on 2 January 1885 and was buried in the Ellendale Cemetery. The following year the local GAR veterans' post was named after him.

References: Boonville, Owatonna, and Ellendale (Minnesota) Public Libraries; Minnesota Historical Society; Owatonna *Weekly Journal*, 23 December 1904; *History of Dickey County, North Dakota* (1930); Phi Delta Theta alumni directories; Roger Scanlan; military service record, National Archives, Washington, DC.

SPENCER, GEORGE WASHINGTON (1834–1876)

George Spencer was born in Monticello on 7 January 1834, one of seven children of Sarah Reynolds and George Armstrong Spencer. His siblings were Lucinda, Melissa, Mary, Matilda, Calvin, and Isaac. He grew up on a farm. In the autumn of 1856, he enrolled in the Preparatory Department of Wabash, completing only one academic year, and then went back to White County.

He married Eliza Ann Bunnell on 14 April 1858. On 13 October 1861 Spencer traveled to nearby Brunettsville and enrolled for three years in the Forty-Sixth Indiana Regiment. The new recruits were formally mustered in at Logansport on 5 November and soon headed for Kentucky. Spencer was promoted rapidly to the rank of sergeant major that December.

At the time of his enlistment, he was five feet nine inches tall, with black eyes, dark hair, and dark complexion. The following year, on 12 June 1862, he was promoted to lieutenant of Company E. His regiment positioned itself along the Mississippi River, both at New Madrid and Island No. 10, and served with Grant's forces as he laid siege to Vicksburg. Spencer received an honorable discharge on 7 June 1863.

On 5 August 1876 he accidentally ingested poison and lingered for a few hours, but died the following day. He was buried in the Old Monticello Cemetery, pre-deceased by his wife on 24 October 1872.

References: Monticello Public Library; *Monticello Herald*, 10 August 1876; James S. Spencer, *History of the Spencer Family in White County*, pp. 1 and 7.

SPENCER, JAMES S. (1838–1920)

James Spencer was born on 18 March 1838 in Adelphi, Ohio, the son of Nancy Ellen Barnet and Robert Armstrong Spencer, a physician. He was one of three brothers to attend Wabash and to serve in the Civil War. The others were William G. and Robert A. James also had an older brother, Benjamin, and a younger sister, Margaret, who died in infancy.

Young Spencer was enrolled in the Preparatory Department of Wabash for one school year, 1856–1857, and then returned to White County and embarked on his career as a printer. In 1858 he began the *Rensselaer Gazette*, and the following year he inaugurated a Monticello paper, the *Spectator*, later known as the *Herald*.

On Christmas Day 1860 Spencer married Emma L. Skinner from Valparaiso. They went on to have seven children, three of whom died in infancy. Those surviving to adulthood were Schuyler, Defoe, Bessie, and James.

On 21 August 1862 Spencer joined the Seventy-Third Indiana Regiment of Volunteers, the same unit in which his father and older brother served as surgeons. He was described as five feet seven inches tall, with light complexion, auburn hair, and hazel eyes. Although he committed to two years of military service, he fell ill within six months and obtained a "surgeon's certificate of disability" at Nashville, Tennessee, on 12 February 1863, possibly due to family connections. Spencer's ailments did not prove fatal, but those of his father did.

Back in Monticello Spencer went into business as a druggist for the next eight years and bought a farm north of town. Among his other activities, he served as a justice of the peace. His wife died on 22 March 1912, and Spencer moved in with his daughter, Bessie MacOwan, who lived north of Monticello. He died there of cancer on 11 June 1920. Both he and his wife were buried at Riverview Cemetery.

References: Monticello–Union Township Public Library; James S. Spencer, *The Spencer Families of White County Indiana* (1913?), pp. 5–8; W. H. Hammelle, *White County History* (1915), p. 503; Monticello *Evening Journal*, 11 June 1920.

SPENCER, OLIVER HAMMOND (1840–1892)

Oliver Spencer was born in Lafayette on 20 August 1840, the son of Israel Spencer and his second wife, Charlotte Bartholomew. Israel had four children by his first wife, Elizabeth, two of whom, James M. and David, attended Wabash. Oliver was one of Charlotte's three children; the other two were George and Flora. Charlotte died in 1845, and Israel married Helen Virginia, who bore six more children. Israel pursued a variety of careers: in the 1830s he was a carpenter and part owner of the Lafayette Flour Mill, in the 1840s he ran a dry goods and grocery store, and in the 1850s he owned a drugstore. He amassed considerable wealth.

Oliver Spencer was one of those relatively rare students who pursued the Classical Course at Wabash and graduated in June 1863 while at the same time fitting in two tours of military duty. First, on 18 April 1861 he enrolled at Crawfordsville in Company I of the Eleventh Regiment for three months, and after some skirmishes in western Virginia, he was mustered out at Indianapolis on 4 August. Between his junior and senior years he served another thirty days, this time in Company G of the Seventy-Sixth Regiment, and was mustered out on 20 August 1862 in time to return to Wabash for his senior year.

After graduating Spencer presumably returned to Lafayette for a while, and then moved to Leavenworth, Kansas, where he studied law and worked as a teacher for a few years.

In 1869 he traveled to San Francisco, was admitted to the California bar, and practiced law while teaching on the side. He died on 5 March 1892. His body was returned to Lafayette for burial in Greenbush Cemetery.

References: *Wabash Magazine*, IV (July 1863), p. 265; *Indiana Eagle* (Lafayette), 27 November 1839; *Wabash Record* (July 1903), p. 27; California Historical Society; San Francisco (California) Public Library; Tippecanoe County Historical Association; California State Bar Association; as well as the references cited in the account of his brother, James Spencer.

SPENCER, ROBERT ARMSTRONG JR. (1842–1882)

Robert Spencer Jr. was born in Uniontown, Ohio, on 25 June 1842, one of three brothers who attended Wabash College and who also served in the Civil War. The others were James S. and William G. His parents were Nancy Ellen Barnet and Robert Armstrong Spencer. Robert Spencer Sr. was a physician, and during the latter 1850s and early 1860s, he combined a medical practice at home with an academic assignment as a professor of anatomy and physiology at the Cincinnati College of Medicine and Surgery.

Robert Spencer Jr. attended the Normal School of Wabash for one school year, 1856–57, and then returned to Monticello and worked in a drugstore. In the summer of 1862, Spencer Sr. joined the Seventy-Third Indiana Regiment Volunteers as a surgeon, and a few months later Spencer Jr. enlisted in Company G of the Sixty-Third Indiana Regiment. Almost immediately he was appointed a hospital steward, a post he filled for the next three years. He was mustered out at Indianapolis on 23 June 1865.

After the war it is likely that Spencer trained to become a physician like his father. On the other hand, when he moved to Burlington, Iowa, in 1872, he did not pursue medicine but worked as an insurance agent. In about 1875 he married Alice Kendall, the daughter of a local grocer. They had a daughter, Ella, who died in infancy, and a son, Frank, who grew to maturity.

In January 1881 Spencer's tubercular condition, which dated from the time he was in the army, forced him into retirement. He sought warmer temperatures in Atlanta, Georgia, but returned to Burlington in February 1882 and died there on 1 June 1882, survived by his wife, who lived until 14 April 1925. Both are interred in the Burlington Cemetery.

References: White County Public Library; Burlington (Iowa) Public Library; J. S. Spencer, *History of the Spencer Families of White County Indiana,* pp. 6–7; *Daily Hawk Eye* (Burlington), 3 June 1882 and 14 April 1925; *Monticello Herald,* 8 June 1882.

SPENCER, WILLIAM G. (1833–1901)

William Spencer was born in Zanesville, Ohio, on either 5 or 6 November 1833, the oldest of three brothers who attended Wabash and also served in the Civil War, followed elsewhere. His parents were Nancy Eleanor (Ellen) Barnet and Robert Armstrong Spencer, and the brothers who were soldiers were James S. and Robert A. Jr. There was also an older brother, Benjamin, and a younger sister, Margaret, who died in infancy. Almost more remarkable was the fact that Robert Spencer Sr. also joined the army as a surgeon. William, who was also a physician, ended up serving in the same Seventy-Third Regiment as his father.

Spencer spent only his freshman year at Wabash, 1852–53, and then returned to Monticello to study medicine with his father. He spent 1854–55 at the Jefferson Medical College at Philadelphia and then joined his father's practice, a medical partnership that lasted until the Civil War.

On 1 January 1856 he married Harriet V. Kistler, and eventually they had three children: Charles, Gertrude, and May. Charles died in infancy.

During the late summer and fall of 1861, Spencer helped to raise a company of volunteers and was chosen its captain. He formally took charge of Company E of the Forty-Sixth Indiana Regiment that October, but he resigned his commission in order to become a military doctor. On 20 March 1863 he became an assistant surgeon in his father's Seventy-Third Indiana Regiment. A little over a month later, on 30 April, he was taken prisoner while tending the sick in Morgan County, Alabama. He spent seven months in Libby Prison in Richmond as a hostage for Confederate Dr. Green, who was in Union hands. In part through the intervention of Indiana's governor, Oliver P. Morton, an exchange was made, and Spencer was released on 22 November 1863. He rejoined the Seventy-Third until being promoted to full surgeon with the Tenth Tennessee Cavalry on 18 April 1864, and he continued serving with them until he was discharged at Nashville on 1 August 1865.

After the war, Spencer continued practicing medicine in Monticello and acquired two thousand acres in White County. He also became part owner of a bank in Fowler, Indiana. He died on 26 October 1901, predeceased by his wife in 1888. Both are buried in Riverview Cemetery.

References: See references for two brothers, James and Robert; *History of White and Pulaski Counties, Indiana* (1883), p. 243; military pension file, National Archives, Washington, DC; *Monticello Herald*, 31 October 1901, p. 1.

SPERRY, FREDERICK L. (1844–?)

Frederick Sperry was born in Ogdensburg, New York, in 1844, one of four children of Margaret and Henry Sperry, who moved from New York State to Crawfordsville in 1845. He had an older sister, Julia, and two younger brothers, Orman and Eber.

The young student entered the Normal School of Wabash in the fall of 1855 and stayed one academic year. The college catalogue indicates that he was living with his mother in town.

In the summer of 1862, Sperry was one of a number of local young men who responded to Eli Lilly's call for recruits into his new battery, the Eighteenth Indiana Light Artillery. He was brought in as a corporal but was demoted to private during the next year. Otherwise, he was well regarded by his fellow soldiers.

He was released in June 1865 and returned to Crawfordsville to continue working as a miller, his father's occupation. He was one of the first to sign up for membership in the Grand Army of the Republic, Post No. 1, in September 1866. Sometime between 1865 and 1870, Sperry married a woman named Anna, according to the 1870 census, who presumably died about 1873 since he married Nancy Berry on 14 May 1874. They presumably left Montgomery County by 1880, since they are not in the local federal census. Their son, George, died in February 1918, and their other son, Frank, the following June.

Sperry's mother, Margaret, died as early as 1858 and is buried in the Masonic Cemetery of Crawfordsville, where there is a grave marker for F. L. Sperry, a Civil War sergeant in the Eighteenth Infantry. No dates are affixed to the marker, so there is no way of knowing when Sperry was interred. Whoever arranged the burial may have confused the Eighteenth Light Artillery with the Eighteenth Regiment and also been mistaken about Sperry's rank.

References: U.S. census for Montgomery County; Montgomery County marriage records; *The People's Guide... of Montgomery County* (1874), p. 186; J. W. Rowell, *Yankee Artillerymen* (1975), pp. 20, 280; Crawfordsville *Journal Weekly*, 15 February and 21 June 1918.

SPILMAN, JAMES FLETCHER (1829–1868)

James Spilman was born in Allen, Kentucky, on 10 January 1829, one of four brothers who came to Wabash: James Fletcher, Marcus Ireneus (Ira), Robert Bruce, and William Elbridge. Their parents were Dorcas Jane Garrison and William Russell Spilman, and they had an older sister, Mary. The name "Spilman" was sometimes spelled "Spillman" or "Spellman." In about 1835 the family settled on a farm near the town of Rockville, and it was from there that Spilman enrolled in the Preparatory Department of Wabash in the autumn of 1847.

He embarked on the Classical Course but switched to the Scientific Course, which he pursued until 1851. At some point in 1850, the family moved to Crawfordsville so that the brothers could live at home while attending school.

Between 1850 and 1860 Spilman was a farmer as well as a teacher. During Morgan's Raid, he joined the hastily raised 108th Indiana Regiment of Volunteers. He was made the clerk of Company C, and the regiment headed for Indianapolis. It scarcely had time to reach there when the emergency was over, and the regiment was disbanded on 17 July.

Spilman was made an honorary member of the class of 1854 and awarded an honorary MA degree in 1866. He died sometime in 1868 at the age of thirty-nine. He seems not to have been buried with other members of his family in Montgomery County. His father, William, died on 20 March 1876 and is buried in the Odd Fellows Cemetery of Crawfordsville.

References: The Wabash College catalogue for 1880–81 indicates that he died in 1868 at the age of 39. Later alumni directories say that he died in 1878. See also references for his brothers.

SPILMAN, MARCUS IRENEUS (IRA) (1832–1902)

Marcus Spilman was born in Parke County, Indiana, on 25 January 1832, one of four brothers previously mentioned who came to Wabash: James Fletcher, Marcus Ireneus (Ira), Robert Bruce, and William Elbridge. Their parents were Dorcas Jane Garrison and William Russell Spilman, and they had an older sister, Mary.

The young man was enrolled in the Preparatory Department at Wabash College for the school year 1851–52. On 4 February 1865 Spilman enrolled in Company K of the 154th Indiana Regiment of Volunteers at Lafayette for one year of service. Within a few months the war was over, but his regiment nonetheless took up a position at Stevenson Heights, Virginia. From there he was mustered out on 4 August 1865.

Returning to Crawfordsville, Spilman took up his occupation of laborer and carpenter, living with his parents until 1870. Sometime during the next year he married Agnes Rebecca Lyons, and they eventually had three children: Frank, Theodore Bruce, and Mark. Rebecca died on 14 May 1887, and for the next fifteen years Spilman continued with his usual work, admitting that he was employed only about six months out of every year. He lived south of Crawfordsville on an extension of South Grant Avenue, sharing his house with sons Frank and Mark. Troubled by kidney failure and rheumatism, Spilman died of a heart condition on 4 October 1902. He is buried in the Odd Fellows Cemetery, next to his father and his brother, James.

References: *Crawfordsville Journal*, 4 and 10 October 1902. See also sources for Robert.

SPILMAN, ROBERT BRUCE (1840–1898)

Robert Spilman was born on 7 August 1840 on a farm about three miles from Rockville, the youngest of five children of Dorcas Jane Garrison and William Russell Spilman. The other children were Mary Frances, Marcus Ireneus, James Fletcher, and William Elbridge. James and Marcus, covered elsewhere in this account, attended Wabash College and also served in the Civil War.

In 1850 the Spilman family moved to Crawfordsville and Robert followed his older brothers to Wabash College, where he was in the Preparatory and Normal School from 1853 to 1857. He then continued for four more years, graduating with a bachelor of arts degree in 1861. All three brothers received BA degrees, an unusual accomplishment.

On 11 August 1862 Spilman enrolled in Company K of the Eighty-Sixth Indiana Regiment, committing to three years' service. Promotions came rapidly. In December 1862 he was promoted to sergeant, in March 1864 to lieutenant, and by June 1864 to captain. He saw action at Murfreesboro and participated in the protracted Atlanta campaign, then was formally discharged at Nashville on 6 June 1865.

Before entering the army, Spilman had begun to study law with an attorney in Crawfordsville. He continued after the war and was admitted to the Indiana bar in March 1866.

He then moved to Manhattan, Kansas, where on 10 May 1868 he married Hannah A. Russell, a fellow Hoosier. Their children were: William Russell (1870), Catherine (Katrina) (1872), Robert Bruce Jr. (1875), Clara (1880), Elbert (1882), and Harold Addison (1883). One of their sons, Robert Jr., attended Wabash College for several years in the 1890s.

Establishing a practice in Manhattan, Spilman became Riley County attorney in 1870, and in 1873 he was elected to the first of three terms as mayor of Manhattan. He also spent two years, 1879–81, in the Kansas state legislature. He also served as a county superintendent and spent a total of thirteen years, off and on, as county attorney. In 1885 Spilman retired from his law practice in order to run for election to the district court. He served successfully for two terms as judge, elected in 1885 and again in 1889. Over the years he enjoyed remunerative investments in land.

Spilman died at Manhattan on 19 October 1898, survived by his widow, who lived until 1929. Both are buried in the Sunset Cemetery.

References: Riley County (Kansas) Historical Society; *Wabash Magazine*, VIII (June 1868), p. 68; *Wabash Magazine*, X (March 1870), p. 167; *Wabash Magazine*, XXIII (November 1898), p. 77; Riley County (Kansas) Genealogical Society, *Pioneers of the Bluestem Prairie* (1976), p. 459; *Portrait and Biographical Album of Washington, Clay and Riley Counties, Kansas* (1890), pp. 636–38. See also the references for brothers James and Marcus.

SPITLER, MARION LYCURGUS (1836–1899)

Marion Spitler was born on 12 March 1836 in West Lebanon, where his father, George W. Spitler, was a teacher. His mother was Melinda Hershman from Ohio.

About 1841 the family settled on a farm near Rensselaer, and it was from there that Spitler made his way to Crawfordsville to attend Wabash in the autumn of 1848. He completed the final year of the Preparatory Department two years later. He then embarked on four years of college work and graduated with a bachelor of arts degree in June 1855.

For the next few years he combined teaching with clerking in the general store of Isaac D. Stackhouse in Rensselaer. He married Mary E. Burnham of Biddeford, Maine, in 1859. The Spitlers eventually had six children: Mariam E. Learning, Marian E., George T., Charles G., Maud E., and Marion L. Jr., who was a member of the Wabash College class of 1898.

On 9 August 1862 Spitler assumed a commission of second lieutenant in Company A of the Eighty-Seventh Indiana Volunteer Infantry. He was promoted to first lieutenant in June 1863 when his regiment was attached to the Army of the Cumberland. For unknown reasons he resigned from the army in September of that year.

Following the war, Spitler took up the study and practice of law, and between 1868 and 1876 he served as Jasper County clerk. He then joined the Rensselaer law firm of Simon P. and David J. Thompson and remained with them for the rest of his active career. He was for years a member of the Rensselaer town board and of the school board. In 1895 he was a successful candidate for the Indiana General Assembly, representing Jasper and Newton Counties in the House of Representatives.

Spitler retired from his law firm in 1896 and died in Rensselaer on 19 November 1899. He was buried in Weston Cemetery.

References: 1880 U.S. census for Jasper County; Indiana Historical Bureau, *Biographical Directory of the Indiana General Assembly*, I (1980), p. 367; *Biographical History of Tippecanoe, White, Jasper, Newton, Benton, Warren and Pulaski Counties, Indiana* (1899), pp. 647–50; L. H. Hamilton, *Jasper and Newton Counties Indiana* II, (1916), pp. 451–53.

STAFFORD, GEORGE WASHINGTON (1815–1902)

George Stafford was born in Giles County, Virginia, on 24 September 1815, son of Ruth Neel and Thomas Stafford. He was one of their ten children, all of whom lived to maturity. In 1832 his father and mother came to Indiana and settled in Attica. The young George was reared at home and studied under the direction of Reverend James Dixon. He returned to Virginia in 1836 and experienced a conversion to Methodism. In 1840 he was ordained a deacon by Bishop Soule at Indianapolis and an elder by Bishop Morris at Centreville in 1842.

The Wabash College catalogue for 1841–42 lists a Granville Stafford, but this name must have been recorded in error, since George lodged with Circuit Court Judge Honorable James Stitt, whose daughter Rachael R. Stitt he married in March 1842. Rachael and George Stafford eventually had eleven children, but only five lived until the end of the century: James T., William, George W., Edward, and Mary.

In 1861 Stafford permanently located at Crawfordsville, where he purchased a large farm and served as an itinerant minister throughout the state until 1878. During his ministry he was one of the most successful evangelists in the Methodist Church, having received 3,500 persons into membership. He was also an earnest worker on behalf of temperance and signed the first temperance pledge in America.

In 1862 Reverend Stafford enlisted as chaplain in the Fortieth Indiana Infantry, organized at Lafayette. He served in Georgia and accompanied his regiment during the battles of Chickamauga and Mission Ridge. He followed Sherman to Atlanta, where he encouraged his men and performed hundreds of last rites. When he himself became ill and was taken to hospital, he resigned and came home.

He returned to Crawfordsville and became an active Mason and Odd Fellow as well as continuing his circuit ministry. Rachael died in November 1899 at their home, and George Stafford died two years later on 1 February 1902.

References: 1905 Wabash College alumni questionnaire; Methodist Episcopal Church, Minutes of the Northwest Conference, September 1902, p. 271; *Crawfordsville Journal*, 1 February 1902; Crawfordsville *Weekly Journal*, 3 November 1899.

STANLEY, JAMES BARTHOLOMEW (1837–1908)

It's often assumed, even by those who know history fairly well, that divorce was difficult to obtain in the nineteenth century. In the case of Indiana, at least, the opposite is true. Indiana became known as the home of easy divorces, granted for almost any reason. The state was, according to newspapers of the day, a "Divorce Mill." Judges usually granted divorces to anyone applying if the other partner in the marriage did not contest the action. Residency was a requirement, but since the law did not state how long a person had had to live in Indiana, dissatisfied marriage partners from other states flocked to the Hoosier state for a few months' stay.

Indiana did reform its divorce laws in the mid-1870s, but by that time other states had made it considerably easier to get a divorce. Multiple divorces are sometimes seen in this collection of Civil War soldiers. James Stanley, the subject of this piece, was married four times and was divorced three times. What might be the causes of a divorce in these times when marriages were early and considered sacred? One newspaper of the time, the *Chicago Press and Tribune*, said on 13 October 1858 that divorce happened when women struggled to be free of "sots, beasts, and debauchers." Men had their reasons, too. We do not know if these sins or difficulties were the reasons James Stanley and his wives parted.

Stanley was born on 11 December 1837 at Cedar Valley, Ohio, one of five children of John Bratton Stanley (1799–1873) and his first wife. His siblings were William, Jonathan, John, and Mary. In about 1840 James's father, with his wife either dead or divorced, moved to Pleasant Township, Wabash County, Indiana, and married Elsie Ann Lowry. They became the parents of Nathan, Leander, George, and Sarah.

In the autumn of 1854, Stanley made his way to Crawfordsville and enrolled in the first year of the Preparatory Department at Wabash, remaining one school year. He presumably then returned to work on his family farm.

In 1862 Stanley married Anna Caroline Kraner, an Ohio native. They had three children, Clark, Octavia, and John, all born in Indiana. On 18 February 1865 Stanley was mustered into Company E of the Eighty-Ninth Indiana Regiment, which took part in Sherman's March to the Sea. He was described as six feet tall, with grey eyes, dark complexion, and black hair. That June he transferred to the Twenty-Sixth Regiment of Indiana Volunteer Infantry but came down with chronic diarrhea while stationed at Mobile and was mustered out of the service on 15 January 1866. This condition continued to distress him throughout his life.

By 1870 his family lived in Westchester, on a fairly prosperous farm, but not long after the birth of another child, James and Caroline were divorced. Stanley married Susan E. Head in about 1874, and they had four children: Alfred, Joseph, Emily, and Edward. However, their marriage ended in divorce in 1885, although Stanley took custody of their four children.

Stanley then moved from Indiana to Kansas and found another bride, Elizabeth Arnold, but their marriage lasted only a year. He married for a fourth time in Jewell County, on 14 April 1889 to Maggie McMullen. He died in Ellinwood, Kansas, on 25 October 1908 of consumption.

References: Military pension file, National Archives, Washington, DC.

ST(E)ARNS, DANIEL W. (1842–1926)

Daniel Stearns was born on 21 October 1842 at Wallace, the eldest of fourteen children of Katherine and Henry Starns. Daniel's father spelled the name "Starns," while Daniel spelled it "Stearns."

Stearns lived and worked on the family farm until the fall of 1859, when he entered the Preparatory Department of Wabash. On 18 September 1861 he enrolled at Lafayette in Company B of the Tenth Indiana Regiment for a term of three years. He was at that time described as being five feet nine inches tall, with fair complexion, blue eyes, and brown hair. He saw action at many of the key battles of the war: Nashville, Shiloh, the siege of Corinth, Perryville, Chickamauga, the siege of Chattanooga, the storming of Missionary Ridge, and Sherman's Atlanta campaign. He was mustered out at Indianapolis on 19 September 1864.

Stearns's release from the army came just in time to permit him to return to Wabash for the 1864–1865 school year, which he spent studying in the Scientific Course. On 6 March 1866 he married Mary E. Miller, and they eventually had six children: Herbert, Kate, Sue, Harry, Ethel, and Hollie. In 1866 he also ran unsuccessfully as a Republican candidate for the state legislature. At about this time he began to apprentice with the Covington law firm of Stillwell and Wood. Two years later he was admitted to the Indiana bar.

In 1868 the Stearns family moved to Hillsboro, where he taught for several years before coming to Crawfordsville in 1871. Stearns went to work for the grocer A. F. Ramsey, and in 1879 he joined another grocer in town, T. N. Lucas. During these years he was a frequent contributor to various newspapers. Using the pen name Frank Mayfield, he placed poems with the *Cincinnati Gazette*, the *Toledo Blade,* and the *Indianapolis Journal.*

In 1886 the family moved to Lawrenceburg, Tennessee, where he continued to write, adding another nom de plume, James Upton Keene, for his prose articles. He published more than three hundred poems and magazine pieces during his lifetime.

In 1896 Stearns tried his hand again at politics, but with equally dismal results. It was too much to hope that a Republican could be elected in postwar Tennessee to the state senate. By 1904 he was ready to return to the law and formed a partnership with Jonathan Crews. In 1905 he was also appointed United States Postmaster for Lawrenceburg, an appointment he held throughout both the Taft and Wilson administrations. Daniel Stearns died at home on 22 February 1926 and was buried in Mimosa Cemetery.

References: Crawfordsville's McPherson Post No. 7, *Descriptive Book and Roster*; J. B. Shaw, *History of the Tenth Regiment Indiana Volunteer Infantry* (1912); T. E. Gronert, *Sugar Creek Saga* (1958), pp. 171, 230; H. W. Beckwith, *History of Montgomery County* (1881), pp. 236–37; Kathy Niedergeses of Lawrenceburg, Tennessee; *Lawrence Democrat*, 24 February 1926; military pension file, National Archives, Washington, DC.

STEELE, WILLIAM HOVEY (1841–1923)

William Steele was born in Owen County on 17 April 1841, one of twelve children of Margaret Nail and John Sloan Steele. In the autumn of 1859, he entered the Preparatory Department of Wabash College, indicating that his home was Gosport. He remained one academic year.

Once the war broke out, Steele served for three months in the Fifty-Fifth Indiana Infantry as well as a short stint in the Eighty-Fifth Indiana Regiment before joining Company E of the Thirty-Third Regiment on 29 August 1862. The regiment, formed in Owen County, went first to Tennessee, where the Battle of Thompson's Station took place on 5 March 1863. In July the regiment marched to Tullahoma, Georgia, and in September it was called back to Murfreesboro. From May to September 1864 it took an active part in the Atlanta campaign and lost three hundred men in addition to a great many wounded. By November those still standing joined Sherman's March to the Sea. For a time in the spring of 1865, the regiment was in North Carolina, and finally, on 21 June 1865, they were mustered out at Louisville, Kentucky. Steele miraculously managed to survive all of these conflicts. Following the war he returned to Owen County and married Cynthia Anna Melick on 21 December 1865. They eventually had eight children.

At some point the family moved to Nebraska and then to Kansas, but they returned to Owen County where they settled in several places before gravitating to the region where Steele grew up in Gosport.

Cynthia died in 1885, and Steele married Rebecca Bean on 13 March 1890. She also died, and he married Eliza Seay on 29 August 1911. A doctor described Steele shortly before his death as five feet nine inches tall, with fair complexion and blue eyes and weighing 124 pounds. He died in Gosport on 12 October 1923 and was buried in Gosport Cemetery.

References: Owen County Public Library; military pension file, National Archives, Washington, DC.

STEPHENSON, AMOS LESLIE (1845–1932)

Amos Stephenson was born in Lagro on 16 February 1845, the oldest of seven children of Maria Jane Thompson and Hugh McDonald Stephenson. His younger siblings were William Hartwell, Ella, Joseph T., Frank, and Fome. Another sibling died in infancy.

Stephenson came to Crawfordsville at the age of twelve, in the fall of 1857, and enrolled in the Normal School of Wabash College. In 1858 he entered the Preparatory Department, and in 1860 he became a freshman, but he did not return in 1861.

On 11 March 1862 he was mustered into the Fourteenth Indiana Light

Artillery for three years at Wabash, Indiana. He was five feet eight inches tall, with light hair and grey eyes, and was a painter by occupation. While in the service he received several promotions: corporal on 20 March 1864, second lieutenant on 1 May 1864, and first lieutenant on 1 July 1865. He saw action at the battles of Nashville and of Spanish Fort, Alabama. He was mustered out in Indianapolis on 1 September 1865.

Returning to the town of Wabash, Stephenson studied dentistry with Drs. Bechtol and Spaw and later opened his own dental practice, which functioned until his retirement in 1902. He was a charter member of the Wabash GAR post and a member of the Masons and the Elks.

On 24 November 1870 Stephenson had married Alice Eagle, who died on 20 January 1902. Ten years later, on 23 January 1912, he married Lena Blanche Thurston. He died of pneumonia on 30 June 1932 and was buried in Falls Memorial Gardens, Wabash. His death date would seem to indicate that he was the last of the Wabash College veterans to "cross over the river and rest beneath the shade of the trees," as Stonewall Jackson said.

References: Records of Falls Cemetery, Wabash County; C. W. Weesner, *History of Wabash County, Indiana* (1914), pp. 919–20.

STEVENS, AARON LEWIS (1828–1901)

Aaron Stevens usually went by his middle name, and he was born on the family farm in Richland Township, Fountain County, on 21 May 1828. When he came to Wabash in 1848, he either spelled his name as "Stephens" or the college recorded it in that form. Ordinarily, however, the name shows up as "Stevens." His mother was Susannah Lucas, and his father, David, was a farmer. His siblings were Elizabeth, William, John, Maria, Amelia, Ann, Mary Ann, and Andrew.

Stevens attended the Preparatory Department of Wabash College from 1848 to 1849. He married Martha Brady of Crawfordsville on 20 July 1849. Their two sons, George and Owen, died in infancy, and Martha did not live beyond the decade of the 1850s.

In 1860 Stevens married Sarah A. Sigler of Warren County, and they settled on a farm near Rainsville. Ultimately their children included Marvin, Rollins, Thaddeus, and Sylvia. Two others died in infancy.

On 9 August 1862 Stevens took command of Company D of the Eighty-Sixth Indiana Regiment as its captain. He was thirty-four years old and committed himself to three years of service. He was wounded at the Battle of Stones River in 1863 and convalesced for five months. He also took part in the battles of Chickamauga and Chattanooga, the series of battles involved in the Atlanta campaign, and the Battle of Nashville. He was mustered out at Camp Harker near Nashville on 6 June 1865.

After the war he resumed farming in Indiana, but poor health from his war wounds followed him. In 1870 the family moved to Floral, Cowley County, Kansas, where Stevens hoped to regain his health. He acquired and worked six hundred acres of land on which he grew corn and wheat while also raising cattle.

He died on 22 June 1901. Sarah lived until 29 December 1908. They are both buried in Floral.

References: Because the name *Lewis Stevens* was a common one in Indiana, he was confused with another from Howard County. Fortunately, a descendant of our Wabash student, Roger M. Stevens of Burke, Virginia, provided the correct information.

STEVENS, THOMAS J. (1840–1887)

Thomas Stevens was one of ten children fathered by Thomas Sr. from two marriages, the second with Nancy DeWeese. Thomas Jr. was fifth in line and was born in Harrison County in 1840.

The Stevens family settled early in Harrison County, and their family papers, housed in the Corydon Public Library, consist of several hundreds of pages. Complicating the biographical search, there were two men named Thomas J. Stevens who were distantly related. One was the son of Thomas Sr., while the other, born in 1852, was a grandson from his first marriage.

Thomas Jr. came to Wabash College in the fall of 1859 and spent two years in the Preparatory Department before advancing to his freshman year. However, prior to that year, he inserted three months of military service (April–August 1861) with Lew Wallace's Eleventh Indiana Volunteers, and he subsequently re-enlisted for three years in the Eighty-First Indiana Regiment. He was badly wounded at the Battle of Stones River, at Murfreesboro, and on 31 October 1863 he was named first lieutenant of Company C.

After the war Stevens studied medicine and established a practice in Harrison County. On 9 July 1867 he married Elizabeth A. Hisey, and they had two children, Gennie and Annie. Elizabeth died in the early 1880s, and Stevens married Florence Martin on 30 December 1884. The veteran died on 18 September 1887 at the comparatively young at the age of forty-four.

References: Corydon Public Library; 1880 U.S. census for Harrison County census; WPA marriage and death records for Harrison County.

STONE, VALENTINE HUGHES (1840–1867)

Valentine Stone has one of the most interesting military careers of all the Wabash College soldiers. He spent the most significant part of his wartime career at the southernmost tip of America, in the Dry Tortugas, guarding incarcerated, notorious prisoners.

Stone was born in Bath County, Kentucky, in 1840, one of three sons of Sally and Samuel Stone. His siblings were Alfred and James, also born in Kentucky. Young Valentine came to Wabash College in the fall of 1851 to enter the Preparatory Department, but stayed only one school year.

On 18 April 1861 he joined Lew Wallace's Eleventh Indiana Regiment at Crawfordsville, enrolling in Company I for three months as a corporal. One month later he was promoted to second lieutenant and transferred to the Fifth Battery of the regular United States Army, and in June he rose to the rank of first lieutenant. He initially worked at the battery's headquarters in Harrisburg, Pennsylvania, but in March 1862 he was a member of an expeditionary force that landed on the Peninsula as part of General McClellan's forces. Later that summer, because of chronic illness, he was assigned to the Sixth Army Corps.

By the fall of 1864, Stone was fit enough to return to the Fifth Battery with General Philip Sheridan in the Shenandoah Valley. He was made a brevet captain in January 1865 and a brevet major in March 1865 for "gallant and meritorious service," and he marched to Washington in June 1865.

Stone stayed in the regular army after the war, although he was demoted to a lieutenant. By July 1866 he was promoted to captain, and in April 1867 he became a major and commanded Fort Jefferson on the Dry Tortugas near Key West, Florida. Here were confined, under his guardianship and those of the troops, the John Wilkes Booth conspirators who had escaped hanging or deportation but were sentenced to incarceration for life. One died, but Dr. Samuel Mudd and Edman Spangler were first held in close confinement in the debilitating tropical atmosphere of the prison. They were then given more freedom as they performed small carpentering tasks and made themselves amenable to the fort life.

At some point during the war, Major Stone had married. He and his wife Julia had one son, Ralph Lowe Stone, born on 13 September 1864. The family lived in the fort, and Julia was reported to be the life and joy of the fort. According to a *New York Times* article some years after the war, she, Dr. Mudd, and Major Stone tended prisoners when a devastating yellow fever epidemic hit Fort Jefferson in 1867. Both Valentine and Julia contracted yellow fever in August 1867 and died the following month, she on 21 September and he on the 24th. They had sent their son north to relatives, and he grew up to become a physician, but falling into serious depression, took his own life.

References: Indiana State Archives; *New York Times*, "Three Military Prisons," year and author not identified; and the National Archives, Washington, DC.

STROTHER, LYMAN THOMPSON (1840–1922)

Lyman Strother was born at Dayton, Tippecanoe County, on 28 December 1840. In the census of 1860 for Sheffield Township, Tippecanoe County, his parents are not listed, possibly because they had died. His siblings were Belle and Turressa.

Strother entered the Preparatory Department of Wabash College in the autumn of 1860 and interrupted his second year by enrolling at Lafayette in the Tenth Indiana Light Artillery on 3 January 1862. At the time he was described as being five feet eight inches tall, with fair complexion, grey eyes, and dark hair. He served for three years, including at the Battle of Shiloh, and was mustered out at Nashville on 24 January 1865.

Returning to Dayton, Strother apprenticed with a local doctor and then secured admission to Rush Medical College in Chicago, where he received his diploma on 6 February 1867. He added another diploma from Jefferson Medical College in Philadelphia on 12 March 1873. He married Martha (Mattie) A. Bartness on 21 October 1869, and they had two children: William O. (1871) and Harry R. (1877).

In June 1884 the family moved to Mound Valley, Labette County, Kansas, where Dr. Strother continued his medical practice. In March 1895 they settled in Notawa, Cherokee Indian Territory, which became the forty-sixth state of Oklahoma in 1907.

Strother died in Notawa on 10 July 1922 and was buried in the Nowata Memorial Park Cemetery.

References: *Wabash Magazine*, III (February 1862), p. 190; *Wabash Magazine*, VII (June 1866), p. 8; military pension file, National Archives, Washington, DC; Katy Matthews of Topeka, Kansas, and Nita Wesson of Nowata, Kansas; Nowata *Daily Star*, 10 July 1922 and 20 July 1922.

SWAN, MILTON JAMES (1841?–1911)

Milton Swan's family origins are confused. Although he was brought up by Joseph C. H. Swan and his wife, Catherine, it is not clear whether Joseph was Milton's father. It is quite certain, however, that Catherine was not his mother.

Milton was born about 1841–42 in Indiana. His father married Catherine Wilhite of Crawfordsville (born 1823 in Kentucky) in 1845, and she had at least seven children. These included Conia (or Conie) (1846), Julia S. (1847), Laura (1849–1850), Walter (1853–1854), Mary (1856), and May (1860). Milton Swan lived with this family until he married.

In the autumn of 1853, Swan entered the Preparatory Department of Wabash College, where he remained for two years. When the census of 1860 was taken in Crawfordsville, Milton was a nineteen-year-old laborer.

On 21 September 1861 at Lafayette, he joined Company H of the Tenth Indiana Regiment for three years. At the time he was five feet seven inches tall and had light hair, a light complexion, and blue eyes. He was wounded twice during the war: in April 1862, which resulted in a medical furlough for about three weeks; and on 19 September 1863, the first day of the Battle at Chickamauga, when a bullet struck the left side of his body and passed through his groin, leading to a hospital stay of over three months. He was mustered out on or about 22 September 1864.

After the war he returned to Crawfordsville and married Frances M. Galey. They lived for many years next door to her family. Their first son, Charles, was born in 1868 and was followed by another boy, Guy. Still later they adopted a girl, Laurie.

Sometime in the early 1870s the Swan family moved to Frankfort, where Swan had a dry goods business and a grocery store on the east side of the town square that he shared with his son, Guy. Swan was elected to the city council.

The sale of his grocery business in 1908 facilitated the family's leaving Frankfort for Texas, where Charles already lived. Frances died there in 1910, and Swan died on 26 September of that year. He is buried in Houston.

References: Military pension file at the National Archives, Washington, DC. See also: *Frankfort Times*, 30 September 1911; *Frankfort News*, 28 September 1911; Jean Swann, *Roots and Branches*, (1985), p. 1; Kingman Bros. *Combined Atlas and Maps of Clinton County* (1878), p. 14; *History of Clinton County, Indiana*, (1886), p. 514.

SWANK, JOHN W. (1842–1919)

John Swank was born on 8 March 1842 at Croydon, Harrison County, one of ten children of Christiana Edelman and William H. Swank.

In the early 1850s the family moved to Huron Township, Des Moines County, Iowa, and it was from there that the youth came to Crawfordsville in the autumn of 1851 to enroll in the Preparatory Department. He studied for only one school year and returned home to work on the family farm.

On 19 September 1861 Swank and his older brother, William H. H. Swank, enrolled at Burlington, Iowa, in Company C of the First Missouri Engineers. They both were mustered into service on 31 October and were transferred to the Missouri Engineers West, but John Swank was in the east at war's end. On 2 November 1864 his three years of service ended, and he was mustered out at Chattanooga.

Swank presumably resumed farming, although his father died in 1865. By 1868 he and his wife, Martha, lived in Missouri, where their first daughter, Ollie, was born. By 1870 they were in Nebraska, where a son, William S. was born. In 1875 they had another daughter, identified only with the initial L. About 1876–77 they moved to Columbia, in Washington Territory, where another daughter, Della, was born in 1878.

In 1887 the family was living on a farm eight miles from Pomeroy, Garfield County, Washington. That February Martha died, and for a few years Swank remained single, looking after his children. On 21 May 1891 he married Mary E. McNeill. Their son, Clay, arrived in May 1892.

Swank died on 2 November 1919 in Retsil, Washington.

References: Rose Mele of Des Moines, Iowa, and Quest Keatts of Pomeroy, Washington. See also: *An Illustrated History of Southeastern Washington* (1906); E. V. Kuykendall, *History of Garfield County, Washington* (1948); *Washington Independent* of Pomeroy, 14 February 1887, 6 December 1888, 21 May 1891, and 7 July 1892; military service file, National Archives, Washington, DC.

TABER, HUMPHREY (1842–1869)

Humphrey Taber was born in Logansport on 2 December 1842, one of eight children of Deborah Ann Coles and Cyrus Taber. An older brother, Paul, attended Wabash from 1847 to 1853 and graduated from the Classical Course. Their father died in 1855, but Humphrey was able to attend Wabash for several years. From 1858 to 1860 he studied in the Preparatory Department. He then dropped out for two years and returned in 1862–63.

At the end of this latter year Taber joined Company H of the 110th Indiana Infantry for the Morgan episode and was released from service on 15 July.

Taber presumably went back to Logansport but seems never to have married. He did become a member of the Tipton fire company. His early death deprived him of carving out much of a career. He died while residing at Fort Wayne on 24 September 1869 and is buried in Mount Hope Cemetery at Logansport.

References: Logansport *Journal*, 29 September 1869.

TALBOT, JESSE NICHOLAS (1840–1908)

Jesse Talbot was born on 15 August 1840 near Quincy, Illinois, the son of Drucilla Bowles and Coleman Talbott (sic). He returned to the Midwest from Santa Rosa, California, where his family had settled after leaving Illinois.

He was twenty-three when he joined Company H of the 135th Indiana Infantry in May 1864 and served his obligatory one hundred days guarding railroad lines in Tennessee and Alabama.

In September 1864 he took advantage of being able to start the autumn term and entered the Preparatory Department of Wabash College, where he spent the next two years. He then continued as a freshman until his funds were exhausted in 1867 and he decided to take up the study of medicine with local physicians.

Talbot set up his medical practice in Fountain County and married Lucretia Clore on 24 October 1871. They settled in Jacksonville, now Wallace. Their eldest daughter, Lucy, was born in 1872, daughter Grace was born in 1874, and twins Jessica and Marshall were born in 1882.

Sometime in the 1880s or 1890s Talbot and his family moved to Alamo in Montgomery County and then retired and relocated to Crawfordsville. Lucretia Talbot died in 1906 and Jesse in 1908. Both are buried in Oak Hill Cemetery.

References: 1880 U.S. census for Fountain County; 1900 U.S. census for Montgomery County; *Crawfordsville Journal*, 6 January 1908.

TALBOT(T), JOHN TURLEY (1845–1880)

John Talbot was born in Hendricks County sometime in 1845, the third of eleven children of Nancy McCoun (1821–1898) and Willis Talbot (1811–1881). His father and mother were Kentuckian by birth, but they moved in 1841 to Eel River Township, Hendricks County, where Willis farmed for many years.

Talbot worked on his father's farm until the outbreak of war. On 19 July 1862 at Danville, he enrolled in Company K of the Seventieth Indiana Regiment. As a private, he committed to serving for three years. He was badly wounded when attacking Confederate defenses at the Battle of Kennesaw Mountain. A minie ball passed through both of his thighs, and he almost died but recovered sufficiently to rejoin his regiment and participate in Sherman's March to the Sea through Georgia. He was mustered out of service as a corporal near Washington, DC, on 8 June 1865.

That fall he entered the Preparatory Department of Wabash College. The following year, 1866–67, he was promoted to the sophomore class. His junior year was interrupted by family and personal business, and instead of returning for his senior year, he purchased (presumably with his father's assistance) a half share in the local newspaper, the *Crawfordsville Journal*, and became its editor. He continued in this role until he was forced by ill health to sell his share in the paper in 1876 to his partner, T. H. B. McCain.

Talbot moved to California and settled in the Santa Rosa area, where he took up farming. He died of consumption at Hanford, California, on 9 April 1880. He seems never to have married.

References: *Wabash Magazine*, VIII (March 1868), p. 70; *Wabash Magazine*, IX (June 1869), p. 84; J. V. Hadley, *History of Hendricks County, Indiana* (1914), p. 753; *History of Hendricks County, Indiana* (1885), p. 378; *The People's Guide* (1874), p. 187; T. E. Gronert, *Sugar Creek Saga* (1958), p. 340; *Crawfordsville Journal*, Souvenir Edition (1894), p. 12; *Saturday Evening Journal of Crawfordsville*, 17 April 1880.

TAYLOR, ALVAH (1839–1923)

Alvah Taylor was the only child of Anna Tyner and Freeman T. Taylor and was born on 30 June 1839 in Harrisburg, Indiana. His father supplemented his farming by becoming a minister of the Old School Baptist Church and in 1856 moved the family to Lagro.

After attending high school in the town of Wabash, Taylor became a freshman in the Classical Course at Wabash College in the fall of 1861. He graduated with a bachelor of arts degree in June 1865. While at Wabash he was a member of the Phi Delta Theta fraternity. During the summer of 1864, he served as a sergeant for one hundred days in Company G of the 138th Indiana Regiment and was released from the army in September, in time to continue his senior year at college. He had married Anastasia Stratton on 23 May 1864.

Taylor returned to the town of Wabash and secured a position in the law firm of John U. Pettit. He was admitted to the Indiana bar in 1868 and became a partner with Pettit until Pettit became a judge in 1873, after which Taylor continued on his own until about 1920. He was also active in the local school board and the local veterans group. His wife died on 28 April 1883, leaving two children, Horace and Grace. Horace died at the age of nineteen in 1887.

On 8 May 1884 Taylor married Mrs. Mary L. McClure of Wabash.

In about 1920 he retired from his law practice and went to live with his daughter in Marion, where he died on 23 January 1923. He is buried in the Falls Memorial Gardens, Wabash County.

References: *Memorial Record of Northeastern Indiana* (1896), pp. 225–27; W. Cumback and J. B. Maynard, *Men of Progress* (1899), p. 185; *Wabash College Record*, July 1903, p. 287; *Wabash Record-Bulletin*, 26 March 1923, p. 31; and 1905 Wabash College alumni questionnaire, Ramsay Archives.

TAYLOR, ISAAC (1836–1923)

It is difficult to ascertain who among these five hundred veterans lived in the most places in America after the war. Ours was a restless nation, and new opportunities, land holdings, and career advancement called these people. Or perhaps they just couldn't make it in one place. Isaac Taylor may hold the record for relocations, having settled and resettled twelve times.

Taylor was born in Boone County on Christmas Day, 1836. He was one of six children of Elizabeth Cross and William Taylor. Their children besides Isaac were Wesley (1824?), William (1826?), Mary (1829?), Martha, (1835?), and Elizabeth (1839?).

In the autumn of 1860, Taylor came to Crawfordsville from Whitestown and entered the Normal School at Wabash College. The following spring he joined many of his fellow students and enrolled in Company I of the Eleventh Indiana Regiment on 18 April 1861. The regiment proceeded to Virginia, where Taylor completed his obligatory three months' service and was mustered out at Indianapolis on 4 August.

Taylor then acquired some farmland, and on 8 December 1864 he married a native of Boone County, eighteen-year-old Melissa Ann Phillips. They eventually had six children: Albert (1865), Charles (1867), Florence (1870), Melissa (1871), Emma (1873), and Alvah (1878).

In 1877 the family made the first of many moves to a number of farms and locales. From 1877 to 1880 they were in Prairie City, Kansas; then they spent two years in Deming, Indiana, followed by two in Lebanon, Boone County. From 1884 to 1897 they settled in King's Point, Dade County, Missouri, interrupted by two years at Gray Horse, Oklahoma. They returned to King's Point in 1899, where Taylor retired for medical reasons and lived on a veteran's pension. Of their six children, one had died, but the youngest son, Alvah, still lived with his parents.

They continued their wanderings, settling in Homestead, Oklahoma, from 1900 to 1902 before returning again to King's Point in 1902–03. The years 1903 to 1906 found them in Argonia, Kansas, and then back to Gray Horse for 1906–09. In 1910 they moved to Butterfield, Barry County, Missouri, and four years later Taylor entered the National Veterans Hospital at Leavenworth, Kansas, where he died on 24 December 1923. He is buried in the national cemetery there.

References: Tri-City Library of Jamestown, Indiana; and Lavern Wing of Lebanon, Indiana.

TAYLOR, JOHN (1840–1891)

Uncertainty surrounds John Taylor's middle initial, for sometimes it is recorded as T and sometimes as A. However, it can be established that he was born in Mishawaka on 29 April 1840, the son of Janett and Andrew Taylor, whose other children were Christopher, Joanna, and James.

The family settled in Mishawaka in the 1830s and was living there when Taylor entered the Preparatory Department of Wabash College in the fall of 1855. He remained for two years.

On 17 April 1861 Taylor enrolled as a sergeant in Company I of the Ninth Indiana Regiment for a term of three months. He was mustered out on 29 July, and on 17 September he re-enlisted at LaPorte as a sergeant in Company F of the Twenty-Ninth Regiment. He was said to be five feet eight inches tall, with blue eyes, brown hair, and light complexion.

Taylor was promoted rapidly from first lieutenant in January 1862 to captain in March 1862. He participated in battles at Bowling Green, Shiloh, Corinth, and Chickamauga. Although he escaped the heavy casualties sustained in this last battle, he received a dishonorable discharge for "flagrant disobedience of orders in allowing and abetting his men in pillaging while posted as pickets." He appealed this ruling unsuccessfully and was formally dismissed on 23 October 1863.

In about 1870 he moved to Illinois and eventually settled in Chicago, where he worked during the 1880s as a clerk for the Pittsburgh, Fort Wayne and Chicago Railroad. He died of pneumonia on 23 February 1891. His body was returned to Mishawaka for burial.

References: Mrs. Margaret Topps of Chicago. See also: *Mishawaka Enterprise*, 27

February 1891; *History of St. Joseph County, Indiana* (1880), pp. 414, 421, 438; T. E. Howard, *A History of St. Joseph County, Indiana* (1907), pp. 418, 720–21, 728, 735.

TAYLOR, MARSHALL B. (1834–1879)

Marsh Taylor was born in Indiana about 1834, the eldest child of John Taylor and his first wife, whose name has not survived. Other children from this marriage were a son with the initials N. C. T.; a daughter, Ellen; R. J., presumably another son; and perhaps young Charles, who also may have been an offspring from John's second marriage to Emma, mother of Harry, Frederick, and Grace.

The family was living in Lafayette as early as 1847–48 when Taylor enrolled for one academic year in the Preparatory Department of Wabash College. Afterwards he joined a business in Lafayette called Taylor and Company.

In 1860 he was listed as a lawyer in Lafayette. He married Susan (Sudie) Rose, who was not from Tippecanoe County, and there is no indication of any children.

On 26 August 1861 he became captain of Company H of the Tenth Indiana Regiment. He was promoted to major in August 1862, lieutenant colonel in December 1862, and colonel in June 1863. He was mustered out at Indianapolis on 19 September 1864.

When the call came for eleven new regiments on 20 December 1864, Taylor raised one in Lafayette and became colonel of the 150th Indiana Regiment that saw action in Virginia at Harper's Ferry, Charleston, and Winchester, after which he was mustered out of service.

After the war Taylor may have returned to Lafayette and resumed practicing law. He died on 3 August 1879, and in 1886 the local GAR veterans association named their post after him.

References: *Biographical Record and Portrait Album of Tippecanoe County, Indiana* (1888), pp. 231, 237, 239–40; and Dorothy Van Cleef of the Tippecanoe County Historical Association.

THOMAS, CHARLES LAMBERT (1832–1917)

Charles Thomas was born on 24 December 1832 in Bucks County, Pennsylvania. His father, Horatio, and his mother, Rebecca Day, moved to Warren County in Indiana, in 1835. Charles was the second of eight children, six of whom attended Wabash: Joseph, Charles, Horace, Erasmus Darwin, Albert and Benjamin.

Thomas joined the Preparatory Department of Wabash College in the fall of 1850. After two years he became a freshman in the Scientific Course and completed this in June 1855. However, as he explained in his alumni questionnaire, there was no bachelor of arts degree awarded to such students. "When I finished my course in 1855 no one was allowed a diploma except the 'Classics' [students], but Dr. [President] White gave me a certificate showing I had completed the course, and in it stated I would be entitled to a diploma should the college ever recognize the course." In 1868 Thomas was awarded an honorary master of arts degree from Wabash.

He responded to the question concerning athletics, "[there] were none in those times. Time was devoted to getting an education." As for membership in clubs, "[there] were none except those held over the students by the four or five professors."

Thomas spent 1856–59 at the Ohio Medical College of Cincinnati and then returned to Warren County and began to practice medicine. On 9 July 1862 he enrolled as an assistant surgeon in the newly formed Twenty-Fifth Indiana Infantry, and he was promoted to surgeon on 20 October 1862 at LaGrange, Tennessee. He spent most of 1863 in Tennessee and joined General Sherman the following year in his Atlanta campaign and March to the Sea. He was mustered out of service at Louisville on 17 July 1865.

Instead of resuming his medical practice in Warren County, Thomas settled in Crawfordsville, and on 24 May 1866 he married Martha (Mattie) Binford. Their son, Samuel, was born in 1867 and their daughter, Mattie, in 1870. Complications from Mattie's birth may have contributed to Martha's death later that year.

Thomas gave up his medical career in 1867 and began to study law. Once he was admitted to the bar, he went into practice with his brother Albert. During the early 1870s he also served as United States Deputy Collector of Internal Revenue for Montgomery County.

Thomas later married the daughter of the president of Wabash College, Josephine Tuttle. He died at home on 4 March 1917 and is buried in Oak Hill Cemetery. Josephine lived until the age of ninety-two, dying on 11 March 1935. She is also buried in Oak Hill Cemetery.

References: *Crawfordsville Journal*, 5 March 1917; H. W. Beckwith, *History of Montgomery County* (1881), p. 304; and 1905 Wabash College alumni questionnaire, Ramsay Archives.

THOMAS, ERASMUS DARWIN (1837–1929)

Erasmus Thomas was born at Williamsport in March 1837, one of the six sons of Rebecca Day and Horatio Thomas. In addition to his elder brother Charles, four other brothers attended Wabash.

Darwin, as he was often called, entered the Preparatory Department in the fall of 1855 and spent two years there before advancing to his freshman and last year, 1857–58. Thereafter he lived with his older brother Horace and worked as a clerk. Two years later, when he joined the army, he gave farming as his occupation.

On 15 August 1862 Thomas enrolled at Marshfield in Company E of the Eighty-Sixth Indiana Regiment, committing to three years of service. As a private, he was described as being five feet ten inches tall, with a dark complexion and black hair and eyes. The regiment assembled in Indianapolis on 4 September, and on 29 May 1863 he was promoted to regimental adjutant. He was mustered out on 6 June 1865.

After the war Thomas presumably worked for the army, since he went to Santa Fe, California, in 1880 to work in the army's commissary department and later was in Boston and St. Paul, Minnesota (1892), attached to the commissary office at Fort Snelling. Thomas worked here until about 1924. He died in St. Paul on 9 January 1929.

References: In addition to the sources cited for his brother, Charles, see also: *St. Paul Pioneer Dispatch*, 10 January 1929; *Warren Republican*, 24 January 1929; the Minnesota Historical Society, and Walter Salts of West Lebanon, Warren County.

THOMPSON, SAMUEL FINLEY (1840–1903)

Samuel Thompson, who went by his middle name Finley, was born in Carlisle, Maryland, on 12 March 1840, the son of Mary A. Crowe and Charles K. Thompson. His siblings were Mary O. and Charles A.

Thompson entered the Preparatory Department of Wabash College in the fall of 1851 and remained for three years. He then transferred to Hanover College, which he attended from 1855 to 1859, graduating in 1859 with a bachelor of arts degree.

On 18 September he enrolled at Indianapolis in Company I of the Tenth Regiment for three years as a sergeant. At the time he was five feet nine inches tall, with blue eyes, dark hair, and a fair complexion, and gave as his occupation as professor. He was later promoted to sergeant major and was mustered out at Indianapolis on 19 September 1864.

After his release from the army, Thompson settled in Philadelphia, where he was a confidential clerk for an insurance company. He died at home, 2022 North 17th Street, on 21 May 1903.

References: *Hanover Alumni Record* (1913), p. 36. See also: *Philadelphia Public Ledger*, 22 May 1903 and *Philadelphia Evening Bulletin*, 22 May 1903, both furnished by the Free Library of Philadelphia.

THOMSON, CHESTER G. (1833–1911)

The father of our student was James A. Thomson, who had been born in Kentucky about 1799. His wife, Martha M. Blair, was born about 1804 in Tennessee. The couple was married in the early 1820s and came to Boone County in time to appear there in the 1830 census. Thereafter James pursued farming as a career, and by the time the 1850 census was taken, he had amassed real estate worth some $3,000.

Chester Thomson was born at Shannondale on 8 May 1833, the son of James and his wife Martha M. Blair. His siblings were Joseph (1825), Mary (1826), Levi (1828), Wallace (1831), Martin (1835), Susan (1838), Cynthia (1840), and William (1843). At the age of seventeen, Thomson declared himself a farmer for census purposes in 1850, like his older brothers and his father.

When Thomson entered the Preparatory Department of Wabash College in the fall of 1854, he gave Thorntown as his residence. He stayed at college only one school year, followed by a year at Bacon's Commercial School in Cincinnati. In 1856 he moved to Omaha, but the financial panic of 1857 sent him to Brunswick, Missouri, where he taught school until the outbreak of war.

On 2 August 1862 he enrolled in Company F of the Seventy-Second Indiana Volunteers at Lafayette for three years. He began as a first lieutenant and was promoted to captain on 17 February 1863 and to lieutenant colonel on 6 December 1864. He was mustered out at Nashville, Tennessee, on 20 June 1865.

After the war Thomson settled in Lafayette and married Sarah Dougherty on 10 October 1871. They had one son, John D. Thomson. The father established the C. G. Thomson pork and beef packing company, from which he retired in 1892 and established a grocery store at the corner of Sixth and Main Street. When he gave up this business, he farmed in Benton County and elsewhere.

Thomson was active in volunteer work, serving on the board of the Tippecanoe County Children's Orphanage Home and on the board of the Indiana Boys School at Plainfield. He died at home in Lafayette on 11 November 1911 and is buried in Springfield Cemetery.

References: Lafayette Public Library and Mrs. Dorothy Van Cleef of Lafayette.

THOMSON, WILLIAM HALL (1833–1891)

William Thomson was born in Crawfordsville on 8 August 1833, one of six children born to Mariah Hall and James Thomson, the minister at the local Presbyterian church and one of the founders of Wabash College. Two of his siblings died in infancy, but Juliet, Mary Ann, and James grew up alongside William.

James was a Presbyterian minister who had been born in Springfield, Ohio, in 1801. Mariah was similar in age, growing up in Pennsylvania. The couple came to Crawfordsville in 1827, where James helped establish a Presbyterian church.

About 1843 he became pastor of a church in the town of Wabash and remained there off and on until another move took the family to Mankato, Minnesota, in 1854.

William Thomson enrolled for four years (1849–53) in the Preparatory Department of Wabash College and lived at home. His older cousin, William Hanna Thomson, was also at the college during these years, leading to confusion among historians of the Thomson family.

In 1854 Thomson took up farming in Mankato, where his father had been called. However, on 19 August 1862 he joined Company E of the Ninth Minnesota Regiment at Fort Snelling as a private, committing to three years of service.

Guarding Native Americans on the frontier, he contracted pneumonia, and for most of 1863 he was furloughed either in hospital or at home in Mankato, trying to recover his health. He rejoined his regiment in Rolla, Missouri, in November, but by January 1864 he secured a medical discharge from the army and returned to his family, presumably to resume farming.

Thomson's father died in 1873, perhaps prompting his son to leave Minnesota and settle in Logansport, Indiana, where he married Susan Vigus Grinnell [Germell/Mermill] on 12 October 1875. They had no children.

The Thomsons moved to Nashville, Tennessee, in about 1882, where Thomson was a wagonmaker. William died there on 28 January 1891. He is buried in Mount Olivet Cemetery. Susan died on 9 May 1907.

References: *Portrait and Biographical Record of Montgomery, Parke and Fountain Counties, Indiana* (1893), pp. 300–02; the Ramsay Archives, Wabash College, *Seventy-Fifth Anniversary of the Founding of the First Presbyterian Church of Mankato*, 1930; National Archives, Washington, DC; the Minnesota Historical Society of St. Paul; and Richard O. Ristine, a descendant of the Thomson family.

THOMSON, WILLIAM HANNA (1833–1918)

William H. Thomson was born on 1 November 1833 in Beirut, Syria, a part of the Ottoman Empire. His father was William McClure Thomson and his mother was Elizabeth Hanna Thomson, both of whom were Presbyterian missionaries.

When he was about nine years old, he traveled to Crawfordsville, where four of his uncles—James Thomson, John S. Thomson, Samuel S. Thomson, and Alexander Thomson were intimately involved in the establishment and furtherance of Wabash College. He entered the Preparatory Department in the autumn of 1845 and remained through his junior year, but then returned to Syria in the summer of 1850.

Deciding to study medicine, Thomson returned to the United States to complete his degree in 1859 at Albany Medical College. He intended to return to Syria, but the dangerous conditions there deterred him, and he opted instead to work at New York City's Quarantine Hospital.

On 7 May 1861 Thomson married Catherine Sarah Jackson, and they eventually had eight children.

When the war began Thomson became an army medical inspector, examining troops that passed through New York to determine their fitness for military service. He narrowly escaped the violence that occurred when the draft was introduced in 1863.

Following the war he practiced medicine at various hospitals in New York City, but he gradually was attracted to the academic side of medicine. He was an early convert to Louis Pasteur's germ theory of disease, and from 1868 to 1890 he was named professor of materia medica and diseases of the nervous system at New York University. He also lectured on morals and religion during the years 1890–97.

Thomson was a prolific published author. His books included *The Great Argument: or Jesus Christ and the Old Testament* (1884), *The Parables by the Lake* (1885), *Brain and Personality* (1907), *What is Physical Life?* (1909), *Some Wonders of Biology* (1909), *Death and Immortality* (1911), *Life and Times of the Patriarchs* (1912), and *Clinical Medicine* (1914).

Thomson died in New York City on 18 January 1918.

References: *National Cyclopedia of American Biography*, XXIII, pp. 321–22; Theodore Ristine (comp.), *A Digest of the Minutes of the Board of Trustees of Wabash College* (1928), p. 19; and the *New York Times*, 19 January 1918.

TODD, WILLIAM ADDISON (1838–1897)

William Todd was born in Danville on 4 April 1838, one of five children of Serena Henton and Henry G. Todd (1811–1893), a medical doctor and state senator who also served in the Civil War. William's siblings were Minerva, Laura, Marshall, and Henrietta.

Young Todd attended Wabash College in the Preparatory Department from 1852 to 1855 and continued as a freshman until he took seriously ill. He then began studying medicine with his father, and within the year he went to Oskaloosa, Iowa, where he established a drugstore.

On 3 October 1861 Todd married Orpha Tuttle Goodwin of Eddyfield, Iowa. They had two sons, Edward, who died in infancy, and Henry Oliver.

In 1862 he attended medical school at the University of Michigan, Ann Arbor, and afterwards returned to Hendricks County and began to practice medicine. During that year his father had become a surgeon in the Fifty-Third Indiana Regiment, and later, on 19 April 1865, William followed suit, securing a commission as assistant surgeon in the Eleventh Indiana Regiment. He served from 13 May until 26 July.

After the war the Todds settled in Garden Grove, Iowa, where Todd practiced medicine until the spring of 1883, when he set himself up in practice at Chariton, Iowa.

Todd died on 24 March 1897 as the result of an accident involving a runaway horse. He and his wife are both buried in the Chariton Cemetery.

References: *History of Hendricks County, Indiana* (1885), p. 306; T. Throckmorton, *History of Medicine in Lucas County, Iowa*; and the Lucas County (Iowa) Genealogical Society.

TRABUE, WILLIAM DAVID *alias* TRIBETTE, WILLIAM H. (1828–1897)

William D. Trabue led a life of adventure and myth-making. As a result, he is somewhat difficult to portray. He was born on 2 August 1828 in Woodford County, Kentucky, one of two sons of Elizabeth Long and Ephraim Trabue.

In the late 1840s, when Trabue entered the Preparatory Department of Wabash College, his family lived in Howard County. Whether he completed his first year, 1849, is unknown. Legend developed that he ran away from home and family because of a blighted love affair; in any case, he made his way to New Orleans and afterwards to Cuba, where he hoped to join the Lopez expedition, which sought to liberate Cuba from Spain. When this uprising failed, he took passage to France. While in Paris Trabue traced his family's French roots and learned that the name "Trabue" had evolved out of "Tribette."

About 1853 he signed on as a sailor aboard a ship bound for Sidney, Australia. Liking what he found there and deciding to remain, he changed his name to Tribette and eluded his ship's officers long enough for them to leave without him. While in Australia he became involved in the whale oil business and went into a partnership as an import-export merchant. They did well until his partner absconded with the profits and left Trabue (Tribette) penniless. In 1859 he found employment that eventually enabled him to return to America.

In New Orleans he explored Alabama and Mississippi, settling in the town of Terry, Mississippi, where he began his own dry goods company. When the war was nearing the town of Terry, he abandoned his store and joined the Confederate Army. It is said that he was taken prisoner by the Union forces on three separate occasions. He succeeded in escaping the first two times, but the third time he fled he had to spend the rest of the war in a northern prison camp. When he was released in 1865, he went home to Indiana wearing his Confederate uniform and was promptly shunned.

After the war Trabue reclaimed his store in Terry, although it had been thoroughly looted. Slowly he built up his business and within two decades boasted a bank balance of over $60,000, much of which he risked by investing in Mississippi state bonds that yielded $300,000. The war being over for a while and money as usual talking, he returned to Howard County as a prosperous entrepreneur and was greeted as a prodigal son.

In 1897 he went to New York City in search of medical treatment and contemplated going to Germany for the same reason. However, his condition worsened, and he had to enter a sanitarium at Clifton Springs, New York, where he died on 13 November 1897. Trabue's body was sent to Kokomo with the expectation that he would be buried there. However, the inhabitants of Terry, Mississippi, pleaded that the body be interred there, which it was.

References: Paul McKibben of Kokomo, Indiana; the Mississippi Department of Archives and History; *Kokomo Tribune*, 11 November 1897; *Kokomo Tribune Diamond Issue*, October 1925; *Terry Daily Clarion-Ledger*, 15 November 1897; M. C. Landin, *The Old Cemeteries of Hinds County, Mississippi, 1811 to the Present*, p. 23; *Biographical and Historical Memoirs of Mississippi* (1891), p. 177.

TRAFTON, LUCAS WILLIAM (1837–1877)

Lucas Trafton was born in Evansville, Indiana, on 9 April 1837, the only child of America Butler and Dr. William Trafton (1792–1847).

In the autumn of 1852, the youth entered the Preparatory Department of Wabash College. The following fall he joined the freshman class but was injured while hunting. He lost part of his arm and didn't return to college, but rather worked as a clerk in a law office in Henderson County, Kentucky. After further study he was admitted to the Kentucky bar in 1858 and became a county judge in 1859.

On 23 August 1862 he enlisted at Pavis County, Kentucky, in Company H of the Confederate Tenth Kentucky Cavalry (Johnson's Cavalry) as a private commiting to three years of service. At the time he was five feet six inches tall, with a fair complexion, brown hair, and grey eyes. He became captain and assistant quartermaster the following November.

His regiment was under the command of General John Hunt Morgan, who undertook the ill-fated raid on southern Indiana in July 1863. Meeting resistance, the raiders turned eastward and were eventually forced to surrender in Gallia County, along the Ohio River, on 21 July 1863.

Initially Trafton was confined at Cincinnati, but he and his fellow prisoners were transferred successively to Columbus and Sandusky in Ohio, Fort Delaware, and finally Aikens Landing in Virginia. A prisoner exchange took place in October 1864, allowing him to rejoin his cavalry unit. He was badly wounded while fighting in Georgia but was nursed back to health by a local inhabitant, Mrs. Mary Spalding.

He voluntarily surrendered to Union troops at Atlanta on 12 May 1865 and was therefore qualified to take an oath of allegiance to the United States Government, which he did on 25 May. This enabled him to return home to Henderson, where he continued practicing law.

On 23 November 1865 he married Helen Gibbs. Their only son, Spalding, was named after the woman who had cared for him during the war. Trafton died in Henderson on 6 April 1877.

References: *History of Henderson County, Kentucky* (1887), pp. 751–53. Also the Tri-State Genealogical Society and the National Archives, Washington, DC.

TWINEHAM, ARTHUR PERRY (1847–1921)

Arthur Twineham was born at Bennington on 16 August 1847, the only son of Sarah Ann Brant and William Twineham, a bookseller. He had one sister, Frances.

In about 1861 he began as a clerk in a store owned by U. P. Schenck in Vevay, Indiana, and also did some teaching. He entered Company I of the Fifth Ohio Cavalry as a private in August 1864 at Cincinnati by lying about his age and claiming he was eighteen. He served for not quite a year and was mustered out at Raleigh, North Carolina, on 26 June 1865. He saw action at the battles of Rocky Creek Church, Georgia (2 December 1864) and Fayetteville and Averysboro in North Carolina on 16 March 1865.

In the fall of 1866, he enrolled in the Preparatory Department of Wabash College. He advanced as a freshman into the Classical Course in 1867–68 and continued as a sophomore in 1868–69. He then transferred to Indiana University at Bloomington, where he was given senior standing, and graduated with a bachelor of arts degree in June 1870.

That fall Twineham took a job as principal of the high school in Greenfield, followed by the headship of schools in Rockville in January 1871. At the same time he studied law at Indiana University, and in September 1872 he took a job with Judge H. W. Harrington of St. Louis. He remained there until November 1873, when he joined Judge William M. Land of Princeton, Indiana, in a law partnership. A year later he started his own practice in Princeton. He was appointed town attorney in 1874–76, later being named Gibson County attorney.

In 1879 he married Letta R. Behymer, who died in the early 1880s. His second marriage to Agnes Lockhart took place in 1894, and they had three children.

While serving as the chairman of the Gibson County Republican Central Committee, Twineham was elected to the Indiana House of Representatives in 1885, but failed in his bid to be sent to the U.S. House of Representatives in 1892.

He was elected mayor of Princeton in 1907–08, and postmaster from 1908 to 1913. Twineham died on 29 August 1921.

References: C. C. Hough, *Biographical Sketches of Members of the Indiana State Government* (1885), pp. 206–07; *Wabash Magazine*, XI (1871), p. 127; *Biographical Directory of the Indiana General Assembly* I (1980), p. 39

TWINING, EDWARD HENRY (1833–1902)

Edward Twining was born on 3 October 1833 in Lowell, Massachusetts, where his father, William (1805–1884), was a Presbyterian minister. The senior Twining taught philosophy, math, and astronomy at Wabash College from 1843 to 1854. Edward's mother, Margaret Eliza Johnson (1808–1873), was from New York City. Edward had six siblings: Almira, Catharine, William J., Helen, Charles, and Mary.

William Twining held his teaching post until he resigned in 1854. He continued living in Crawfordsville until 1859.

Edward Twining's parents enrolled him in the Preparatory Department of Wabash in the fall of 1844, and he remained through the spring of 1847. He then embarked on the Classical Course in 1847 and received his bachelor of arts degree in 1852. He took a postgraduate year at the Sheffield School of Science in New Haven and then returned to Crawfordsville until he took a job at Knox College in Galesburg, Illinois.

Twining married Harriet Sperry (1835–1876), and they had three children: Almira, Jane, and William. During 1855–56 he undertook theological studies in New Haven and then accepted the post of assistant professor of analytical chemistry at Yale College for two years, 1857–59, followed by two years of teaching in Tennessee. In 1861 he taught in Jacksonville, Morgan County, Illinois.

On 21 August 1861 he enlisted as a private in Company K of the Thirty-Third Illinois Regiment at Springfield for three years. At age twenty-eight, he was recorded as being five feet eight inches tall, with a fair complexion, brown hair, and grey eyes. He reported for duty on 2 September at Camp Butler, Springfield, and on 1 July 1862 he was promoted to captain while at New Orleans. Two years later, on 28 September 1864, he became aide-de-camp to his divisional commander. He was mustered out of service on 21 October 1865.

From 1866 to 1868 Twining taught chemistry at Washington and Jefferson College in Pennsylvania. He then accepted other teaching positions before combining his talents as a civil engineer for the United States Mississippi River Commission in St. Louis, New York City, and Chicago.

He retired in 1904 and lived in Webster Grove, Missouri, until 1906 when he moved to Brooklyn, New York. Twining died in Montreal on 20 March 1920.

References: *Wabash Magazine*, XXV (June 1901); *Wabash Magazine*, IX (June 1869), p. 158; 1905 Wabash College alumni questionnaire, Ramsay Archives; Archives of the University of Minnesota: "An Appreciation of Professor Twining," *Minnesota Alumni Weekly*, XIX (12 April 1920), pp. 9–10; and the Yale University Library.

TWINING, WILLIAM JOHNSON (1839–1882)

William Twining was born on 2 August 1839 at Madison, four years before the family moved to Crawfordsville (see the account of his older brother Edward, above). His parents were Margaret Eliza Johnson and William Twining. William Sr. taught at Wabash College from 1843 to 1854.

Twining enrolled in the Preparatory Department for two years, 1851–53, and then went on as a freshmen, sophomore, and junior. In 1858, when his older brother was teaching at Yale, he went to New Haven with a view to studying there, but poor health prevented him from doing so.

However, an unexpected opening at the United States Military Academy for someone from the Eighth Congressional District of Indiana enabled him to secure an appointment at West Point on 1 July 1859. Four years later he graduated fourth in his class, with his health much improved. On 11 June 1863 he was made a first lieutenant of engineers attached to the Army of the Cumberland and worked on various Tennessee rivers. He also took part in two major battles, Chickamauga in September and Chattanooga in November. He was promoted to captain and aide-de-camp on 30 June 1864 and in September was transferred to the Army of the Ohio. The following December he was named a brevet lieutenant colonel, and he resigned on 30 August 1865. He was decorated on several occasions for gallant and meritorious conduct stemming from his bravery at the siege of Nashville and during the Atlanta campaign.

In December 1865 Twining was appointed a captain in the regular United States Army and returned to West Point as an assistant professor of engineering. Two years later he was sent to the Dakotas, attached to the joint commission for surveying and demarcating the northern boundary between the United States and Canada. This involved mapping the eight hundred miles of the forty-ninth parallel between Lake of the Woods and the Rocky Mountains and resulted in his being promoted to chief astronomer for the commission. When this project ended in 1876, he measured the miles covered by the Union and Central Pacific Railroads.

On 16 August 1877 he was promoted to major and assigned to Washington, DC, where he became one of three engineers responsible for developing the newly organized District of Columbia, including planning for an adequate supply of water, the disposal of sewage, the construction of roads, and the draining of swamps.

Twining died at Washington on 5 May 1882. He was survived by his fiancée, whose name has not been preserved. His funeral and burial were impressive, monumental in scope, as described in the West Point alumni magazine: "Outside the church could be heard the tramping of the troops of the escort taking their places in line, and presently the procession was formed. It was headed by all the troops of the Army, Navy, Marine Corps and Militia present in the city; it was followed by the President and Cabinet, by his colleagues on the Board of Commissioners, by the whole body of his subordinates, by civic bodies, by his friends."

His body was taken to West Point for burial.

References: See those for his older brother, Edward. See also *Annual Reunion of the Association of Graduates, United States Military Academy at West Point* (1882), pp. 94, 101, and the academy's archivist.

VAIL, HOLMAN ABRAHAM (1843–1907)

Holman Vail was born at Aurora, Dearborn County, Indiana, on 27 April 1843, the son of Mary Ann Holman and Peter B. Vail, a druggist. He had one brother, James, born in 1842.

The young man spent two years in the Preparatory Department of Wabash College, 1859–61. He then was admitted to the United States Naval Academy at Annapolis and matriculated on 28 September 1861.

During the war Vail remained a full-time cadet at the academy, graduating in October 1865. He then had a series of tours of duty for the navy that took him to Chattanooga (1866), Pensacola (1867), Saginaw (1868), Jamestown (1869), Severn (1870–71), Hartford (1873–75), Trenton (1877–79), and Whachusett (1881–85). Between these assignments he worked in Aurora with the hydrographic office and the Naval Observatory and inspected lighthouses.

He married Mary Gertrude Haines on 26 April 1888 in Aurora.

Vail formally retired from the navy with the rank of commander on 4 December 1890. He and his family lived for a time in Colorado Springs, Colorado, and in Memphis, Tennessee, settling in Washington, DC, where Vail died on 2 December 1907. He is buried in the Riverview Cemetery at Aurora.

References: *Wabash Magazine*, III (December 1861), p. 93; *The Wabash*, XXX (February 1906), p. 149; Lawrenceburg Public Library; *Lawrenceburg Register*, 12 December 1907; the Nimitz Library of the U.S. Naval Academy at Annapolis.

VANCE, HARVEY B. (ca. 1842–1876)

Harvey Vance was born about 1842 in Indianapolis, one of five children of Mary J. Bates and Lawrence Martin Vance Sr. His siblings were Samuel C., George P., Mary Ann, and Lawrence M. Jr.

On 31 August 1861 he enrolled as a private at Indianapolis in Company F of the Eleventh Voluntary Infantry Regiment (Zouaves) to serve for three years. Colonel Lew Wallace was its commander, and Vance became his orderly. At the time he was five feet five inches tall, and he indicated that he was a bookkeeper.

On 7 July 1862, while camped at Helena, Arkansas, he suffered the first of many asthma attacks that seemed to affect his heart and caused him to be given a medical discharge at Indianapolis on 17 January 1863. Later that year he entered the Preparatory Department of Wabash but had to withdraw in June 1864.

Doubtless hoping that a change of climate would restore his health, Vance settled first in Gilroy, California, and later in Cheyenne, Laramie County, Wyoming Territory, where he became a music teacher and telegraph operator.

Vance died at Cheyenne on 18 February 1876, but his body was brought back to Indiana to be buried alongside other family members in Crown Hill Cemetery, Indianapolis.

References: 1850 U.S. census for Indianapolis; alumni directories of the Beta Theta Pi fraternity at Wabash College; and military pension file, National Archives, Washington, DC.

VANCE, LAWRENCE MARTIN (1847–1935)

Lawrence Vance was born in Indianapolis on 5 December 1847 to Mary J. Bates and Lawrence Martin Vance Sr. His mother's younger brother, Hervey, attended Wabash College, as did her three sons, Lawrence, Harvey and Samuel.

In May 1864 Vance committed to one hundred days in the 132nd Indiana Regiment, whose colonel was his older brother, Samuel. He became an orderly and was mustered out of military service the following September. He entered the freshman class at Wabash in the autumn of 1870. For unknown reasons, he did not return for his senior year (1873–74).

In July 1875 Vance married Rosaline Stewart, formerly from the state of Maine. They had one child, Marie S. Vance. Rosaline died in 1886, and Lawrence married Minnehaha (Minnie) Paine of Indianapolis. They had three children, Daniel Lawrence, Marjean, and David. For some years they lived in Indianapolis, but they eventually moved to Los Angeles, where Vance worked as an electrician.

Vance died at the age of eighty-five on 22 January 1935.

References: California Historical Society; California State Library; *Indianapolis Sentinel*, 19 July 1875; Nowland, *Sketches of Prominent Citizens of 1876* (1877), pp. 187–88.

VANCE, SAMUEL COLVILLE (1839–1913)

Samuel C. Vance was the eldest son of Mary J. Bates and Lawrence Martin Vance Sr., born in Indianapolis on 22 August 1839. His two younger brothers, Harvey and Lawrence M., mentioned elsewhere in this narrative, also attended Wabash and served in the Civil War.

Samuel Vance spent one year (1855–56) in the Preparatory Department at Wabash and the following year (1856–57) as a freshman. Two years later, in the autumn of 1859, he entered Amherst College as a sophomore, but he withdrew on 9 October 1861 to enlist as a captain in the Twenty-Seventh Massachusetts Volunteers.

On 10 March 1862 he accepted a commission as a second lieutenant of Company F of the Tenth Indiana Infantry, and on 20 May he became a first lieutenant.

Vance married Minnie Harrington of West Springfield, Massachusetts, on 14 July 1862. She died on 13 April 1865. His second marriage was to Mary Breckenridge of Lafayette, Indiana, on 22 June 1865. They had three daughters (Jesse, Mary, and a daughter who later became Mrs. L. C. Gifford) and one son, Arthur.

On 9 August 1862 Vance was transferred to the newly organized Seventieth Indiana Infantry and made a major. His regiment spent the autumn marching through Kentucky, and from November to June 1863 it was at Gallatin, Tennessee, guarding the rail link with Nashville.

For unknown reasons, he resigned his commission on 10 April 1863 and organized a regiment of the Indiana Legion called the Indianapolis Guards. Then on 17 May 1864 he accepted a commission as colonel of the 132nd Indiana Regiment, again guarding railroad lines in Tennessee and Alabama. He was mustered out in September 1864.

From 1865 to 1870 Vance was a partner in the Indiana Banking Company of Indianapolis. He stayed in Indianapolis as a bookseller from 1871 to 1875, and then he became an agent for the Connecticut Mutual Life Insurance Company between 1875 and 1877.

In 1877 he moved to Verdiere, Florida, where he took up farming and orange growing. By 1886 he was living in Jacksonville and was affiliated with the National Bank and the Barnett National Bank of Jacksonville. He died at Jacksonville on 3 November 1913 and first was buried in Jacksonville in the Evergreen Cemetery. Later he was brought to Indianapolis and interred in Crown Hill Cemetery alongside his father, Lawrence, and his brothers George and Harvey.

References: John Lancaster of the Amherst College Archives; Jacksonville (Florida) Public Library; alumni directories of the Beta Theta Pi fraternity; *Indianapolis Journal*, 19 July 1862 and 26 June 1865. Crown Hill Cemetery lists Samuel's death as 1910, but this is an error made presumably when his body was reinterred.

VANCLEAVE, BENJAMIN MILTON (1842–1928)

Benjamin VanCleave was born on 19 May 1842 at the family farm located about ten miles south of Crawfordsville near the town of Parkersburg, one of seven children of Sarah Jane and David VanCleave. His siblings were William, James, Elizabeth, Eunice, Aaron, and Sarah.

VanCleave enrolled as a private in Company B of the Tenth Indiana Regiment on 18 September 1861. He committed to three years of service, but he was badly wounded on 19 January 1862 at Mill Spring, Kentucky. After convalescing in a hospital, he rejoined his unit and saw action at Lookout Mountain and Chickamauga, and then participated in Sherman's March to the Sea. He was mustered out at Indianapolis on 19 September 1864.

After the war VanCleave enrolled in the Preparatory Department at Wabash College for one school year, 1865–66. Following that, he returned to the family farm, and on 24 December 1868 he married Mary Elizabeth Chase of Parkersburg. Eventually they had eight children.

In 1881 the VanCleave family moved to Clebourne, Texas, and in 1888 to Topeka, Kansas, where they remained for more than forty years. VanCleave worked in the storehouse of the Santa Fe Railroad until he retired in 1909. Mary Elizabeth died on 18 March 1920, and VanCleave lived with one of his daughters until he died on 21 November 1928.

References: Robert VanCleave, the nephew of Benjamin Milton; Kansas Historical Society of Topeka; *Topeka Capital*, 19 March 1920 and 22 November 1928; J. B. Shaw, *History of the Tenth Regiment Indiana Volunteer Infantry* (1912), p. 70.

VEALE, GEORGE W. (1833–1916)

George Veale was born on the family farm at Comer's Point, five miles south of Washington, Indiana, on 20 May 1833. His mother was Eleanor Aikman and his father, James C. Veale, was the first teacher in Daviess County. Together they had ten children.

Young George followed in his older brother James's footsteps and came to Wabash in 1853, but he stayed only one year in the Preparatory Department. His family relocated to Evansville, and he took a job as a clerk in a dry goods store. He married Nannie Johnson on 20 January 1857. They had four children, one of whom died in infancy. The others were George Jr., Quindaro, and Walter.

A few months after they were married, the Veales took a river steamer, the *White Cloud*, to Quindaro, Kansas, where Veale became a merchant and its first sheriff. In due course he became a farmer, edited a newspaper, and organized a freight shipping company that carried cargo between Topeka and Leavenworth by riverboat and teams of oxen.

On 29 April 1861 Veale organized a company of volunteers at Topeka and became its captain. It was integrated into the Fourth Kansas Cavalry, and his wife, with a group of women, sewed a large battle flag for the company. A year later he was in Tennessee, with his regiment under the command of General U.S. Grant, seeing action at Shiloh and Pea Ridge. In his three years of service, Veale estimated that he took part in twenty-seven engagements.

Once he had mustered out of the cavalry, he almost immediately became colonel of the Second Kansas Militia for Shawnee County on 12 October 1864 as a result of a series of cavalry raids into Missouri by the Confederate Major General Sterling "Pap" Price, who tried to overwhelm Veale's militia by sheer numbers at the Big Blue River. Two days later, at the Battle of Westport, the Confederates were decisively beaten and withdrew from the area.

The family relocated to Topeka, and Veale established a dry goods store called Hamilton and Company while at the same time investing in land that railroads found attractive. He also did tax work for the Union Pacific and helped found the Acheson, Topeka and Santa Fe line. A contribution of $1,000 plus three-quarters of a section of land led to the establishment of Lincoln College, which later became known as Washburn College, where George Jr. attended. Veale was instrumental in starting the Topeka Bank and Savings Institution and oversaw the construction of a large office building that was called the Veale Block.

Although a resident of Topeka for only a couple of years, Veale was elected to the Kansas State Senate in 1867 and 1868, and in 1871 he began fourteen years in the state's lower house. He died on 28 November 1916 and is buried in the Topeka Cemetery.

References: Katy Matthews, Topeka, Kansas; F.W. Blackmar, *Kansas*, I (1912), pp. 352–55; *Topeka Daily Capital*, 29 November 1916 and 26 June 1933; and J. L. King, *History of Shawnee County, Kansas* (1905), pp. 84–86.

VIGUS, JORDAN ROSS JR. (1825–?)

Jordan Ross Vigus Jr. was born in Corydon on 18 September 1825, the only son of Elizabeth W. (1789–1841) and Jordon R. Vigus. He went by various names, such as Ross Vigus, J. Ross, and Jordan R. His older siblings were Elizabeth and Harriet.

The young man spent two years in the Preparatory Department at Wabash, 1844–46. In 1850, according to the federal census for Logansport, he was working as some kind of clerk. He joined Company D of the Ninth Indiana Regiment on 22 April 1861. His term of service was three months, and he was mustered out at Indianapolis on 29 July 1861.

After the war he continued as a laborer in and around Logansport, living with one or another relative. Vigus may be buried at Mount Hope Cemetery in Logansport together with his father and other relatives. However, there is no record of this, so we were unable to ascertain for certain where and when he died.

References: Logansport-Cass County Public Library and the Cass County Historical Society Museum. Also Jordan Ross Vigus Sr.'s will; J. Z. Powell, *History of Cass County, Indiana* (1913), p. 1206; T. B. Helm, *History of Cass County, Indiana* (1886), p. 270; N. A. Armstrong and D. Riker, *The Letters of John Tipton*, I (1942), p. 169.

WALLACE, DIXON HALL (1844–?)

Dixon Wallace was born at Canton, Mississippi, in 1844. His mother's name was Elizabeth, but there is no record of his father. His siblings were Mahala,

James, Thomas, and Susanna.

In the fall of 1851, at age seven or eight, the very young Dixon came to Wabash as a student in the Preparatory Department. He remained through the spring of 1856.

At the beginning of 1862, tempted by a bounty of $50, he became a private in Company D of the First Choctaw and Chickasaw Mounted Rifles, which was part of the so-called Second Indian Brigade. His brigade commander, Colonel Tandy Walker, wrote about his role during the fight on 19 April 1864 at Poison Springs, Arkansas: "I deem it proper here to mention the name of Private Dixon Wallace . . .who in the pursuit was the first man to the [enemy's] artillery, and mounting astride one of the guns gave a whoop, which was followed by such a succession of whoops from his comrades as made the woods reverberate for miles around." The Confederate victory that day netted 198 Federal wagons.

During the war Wallace secured a leave in order to return to Canton to marry his childhood sweetheart, Katharine Mae from Ohio, who was fourteen or fifteen years old at the time. In the spring of 1865 Wallace was an army mail clerk, and in 1870 he and Kate lived in Brandon, Rankin County, Mississippi, where Dixon was a store clerk. They moved to Goodman, Holmes County, Mississippi, for a while before returning to Canton, where the Confederate veteran and Wabash alumnus died, presumably prior to 1930, when his wife applied for a widow's pension from the state of Mississippi.

References: Madison County-Canton (Mississippi) Public Library; Mississippi Department of Archives and History, Jackson, Mississippi; Wallace's military service file at the National Archives, Washington, DC. The quotation is from *War of the Rebellion*, series I, vol. XXXIV, p. 849.

WALLACE, GEORGE (1837–1905)

George Wallace was born in Indiana in 1837 and grew up in Bethlehem, Clark County. His parents were Sarah and Thomas Wallace, a farmer. He had an older brother William who preceded him at Wabash, and two younger siblings, Margaret and John.

He entered the Preparatory Department of Wabash College in the fall of 1854 and in 1856–57 was a member of the freshman class. The family moved to Switzerland County, where Wallace farmed until he enlisted in Company A of the Third Cavalry attached to the Forty-Fifth Regiment of Indiana Volunteers on 22 August 1861. During 1862 he was in Maryland and fought in the battles of South Mountain and Antietam, and he was also involved at the Battle of Gettysburg and the pursuit of General Robert E. Lee's army. He was mustered out in August 1864.

In 1867 Wallace married Maggie Gordon from Ohio Township, Spencer County, Indiana. They eventually had three children: Thomas (1868), Bessie

(1871), and Walter (1875). About 1889 they came to Crawfordsville, but eventually took up residence in Chicago, where Wallace died on 18 June 1905. His body was brought to Spencer County for burial in the Rockport Cemetery.

References: Spencer County Public Library; *Rockport Journal*, 23 June 1905; and *Rockport Democrat*, 23 June 1905.

WALLACE, JOHN MILTON (1820–1866)

John Wallace was born in Brookville on 2 January 1820, the youngest of eight children of Eleanor and Andrew Wallace.

At the age of eighteen, Wallace entered the Preparatory Department of Wabash College, indicating that his home was Indianapolis, perhaps because he was living with his oldest brother, David, who was governor of Indiana. He did not complete the school year, however, because on 21 February 1839 his brother appointed him his private secretary. Wallace didn't return to the college but instead supplemented his secretarial duties by studying law in Indianapolis.

Once admitted to the bar, Wallace was appointed the youngest of the state's prosecuting attorneys by the Indiana General Assembly. As a resident of Anderson, he was responsible for the eleventh judicial circuit. Although his post was renewed in 1843, he moved to Fort Wayne, where he was elected mayor.

In 1845 Wallace moved to Marion, where practiced law for the next twenty years, interrupted by his service in the war with Mexico as a captain of Company A, Fourth Indiana Regiment, along the Rio Grande. Like many others, he was forced to resign due to ill health.

In 1848 he married Miriam C. Weeks (1824–1915), and they eventually had four children: Lewis Andrew (1849), John Milton Jr. (1853), Joseph L. (1856), and Charles (1858). In 1854 Wallace was elected judge of the Eleventh Circuit and presided for six years.

Soon after the Civil War broke out, Wallace replaced his nephew, Lew, who had taken up the command of the Eleventh Regiment, as Indiana's adjutant general. On 7 May he himself was commissioned a colonel of the Twelfth Indiana Regiment, but not long afterwards, on 6 August 1861, he was forced to resign due to poor health. Undeterred, and determined to serve his country, Wallace procured the post of paymaster general for the United States Army. This too proved beyond his physical stamina. He returned to Marion for a few years and died there on 25 August 1866.

References: *History of Grant County, Indiana* (1886), p. 702; G. S. Wallace, *Wallace Genealogical Data* (1927), p. 144.

WALLACE, LEWIS (1827–1905)

Lew Wallace was born in Brookville on 10 April 1827, the second of four sons of Esther Test French and David Wallace. His brothers were William, John, and Edward.

In 1832 the family moved to Covington, where Lew's mother died of consumption in 1834. As a result, the boys boarded in Crawfordsville, where Lew, at the age of seven, entered the Preparatory Department of Wabash College and stayed for two years.

In 1836 Wallace's father married Zerelda Gray Sanders and ran successfully for governor. The family moved to Indianapolis, where Wallace studied law in his father's office and worked for Robert B. Duncan in the office of the Marion County clerk. When the Mexican War began in 1846, Wallace enlisted as a second lieutenant in the First Indiana Regiment, but he saw little action and was mustered out in 1847. He believed the First Indiana Regiment had been slighted in recognition after the war, and it strengthened his determination to find honor and seek advancement and glory.

He was admitted to the Indiana bar in 1849 and briefly practiced law in Indianapolis. In 1851 he was named a state prosecuting attorney for the eighth judicial circuit, a post he held for two years. On 6 May 1852 he married Susan Arnold Elston of Crawfordsville, and they had one child, Henry Lane Wallace. Four years later the family moved to Crawfordsville, and Lew Wallace was elected to the state senate, where he served for two terms, 1857–61. During these years he organized the Montgomery County Guards for purposes of marching and drill. Militia units were organizing and marching all over the state, but Wallace's was cited as being the most impressive, best drilled, and most determined, no doubt reflecting the character of its leader.

On 15 April 1861 Wallace was appointed by Governor Morton to the post of state adjutant general, but ten days later he accepted a commission as colonel of the newly formed Eleventh Indiana Infantry, much preferring the field to a desk job. His uncle, John Milton Wallace, succeeded him as adjutant general.

Initially, the Eleventh Regiment was recruited for only three months, but later it was reorganized for a term of three years. Wallace rose rapidly in rank from brigadier general to major general following the Union victory at Fort Donelson in February 1862. However, in early April the troops under his command were late reaching the battlefield of Shiloh, and his superiors held this against him, especially Secretary of War Edward M. Stanton. The controversy, which haunted him all of his life, seems to have been caused by a misunderstanding between Grant and Wallace regarding roads to Pittsburg Landing. Contrary to initial expectations, Union troops were being strongly engaged by Confederates, and on the morning of 5 April, Grant believed he ordered Wallace to come to Pittsburg Landing to join the battle by what he thought he was calling "the River Road." Wallace understood the road intended to be the Shunpike, which Wallace's men had improved and which he thought was passable through the swampy terrain.

He did not arrive until late in the day and did not aid his general's troops. The battle, which caused near to thirteen thousand Union casualties and ten thousand for the Confederacy, resulted in the Confederates withdrawing south, but the controversy went on for years. Before he died, Grant, revisiting reports from all sides, finally said he believed he understood why Wallace was confused. In June of that momentous year of Shiloh, however, General Grant dismissed Wallace, and he rather ignominiously spent time hunting and fishing at his hideaway on the Kankakee River, awaiting a further assignment.

In August Governor Morton asked him to take charge of the Sixty-Sixth Indiana Volunteer Regiment in spite of there being no authorization by the War Department. Early in September he successfully fended off Confederate raiders in Cincinnati under General Kirby Smith and then took charge of forces at Camp Chase in Columbus, Ohio. Between November 1862 and May 1863 he was commissioned to look into the conduct of Major General Don Carlos Buell, which, once Buell was exonerated, left Wallace without a specific assignment, so he returned to Crawfordsville.

On 9 July 1864 troops under Wallace's command fended off the Confederate attack on Washington led by General Jubal Early. Commanding one-year troops, most of whom had not seen battle, Wallace stationed troops along the Monocacy River to deceive and delay Early. Although he did not achieve a victory, he held Early back long enough for the nation's capital to be prepared, and in the face of strong opposition, Early retired.

Wallace was mustered out of service on 30 November 1865 as a major general and then served on the commission looking into the conspiracy behind the assassination of President Lincoln. He also was a member of the tribunal examining the conduct of the commandant of Andersonville, the notorious Confederate prison camp.

In 1870 Wallace ran unsuccessfully as a Republican for the United States House of Representatives. He published the first of many books in 1873, *The Fair God*, which told the story of Hernando Cortez's conquest of Mexico.

From 1877 to 1881 he was governor of the New Mexico territory, and during this time there he wrote and published his most famous novel, *Ben-Hur: A Tale of the Christ*, in 1880. From 1881 to 1885 he lived in Constantinople as the American ambassador to the Ottoman Empire.

Returning to Crawfordsville, he continued to write both fiction and nonfiction, including *The Boyhood of Christ* (1888), *The Life and Public Service of Benjamin Harrison* (1892), *The Prince of India* (1893), and his *Autobiography* (1906), published posthumously.

Lew Wallace died at Crawfordsville on 15 February 1905. He and Susan are both buried in Oak Hill Cemetery.

References: A recent Indiana Historical Society Press book by Wallace scholar Gail Stephens, *Shadow at Shiloh* (2010), examines in fairly clear detail the Shunpike/River Road misunderstanding that stood at the core of Grant's displeasure after the battle. Stephens also evaluates Monocacy with fresh insights. Earlier studies of value are E. J. Warner, *Generals in Blue* (1964), pp. 535–36; I. McKee, "The Early Life of Lew Wallace," *Indiana Magazine of History*, XXXVII (September 1941), pp. 205–16; L. Wallace, *An Autobiography* (1906); E. and K. M. Morsberger, *Lew Wallace: Militant Romantic* (1980); *American National Biography* XXII (1999), pp. 537–39; *Dictionary of American Biography* XIX (1936), pp. 375–76; *Biographical Directory of the Indiana General Assembly*, I (1980), p. 406.

WALTER, ALPHA (ca. 1837–1862)

Alpha Walter was born about 1837, one of four children of Margaret and Alpha Walter. His siblings were Isabel, Frank, and Margaret. His father served during 1846–47 in the war with Mexico and died prior to 1850, when his family lived in Charlestown, Indiana.

Walter entered the Preparatory Department of Wabash in the autumn of 1856 and for unknown reasons was dismissed during the academic year.

On 1 October 1859 he married Elizabeth Ann.

Soon after the Civil War broke out, Walter enrolled in Company I of the Twenty-Third Indiana Regiment on 8 July 1861 for a term of three years. He joined as a corporal, being older than many recruits. He died of typhoid fever on 3 March 1862, and his only child, also named Alpha, was born on 12 June 1862. Elizabeth secured a military pension for herself and her son and lived until 1925 in Louisville, Kentucky.

References: 1850 U.S. census and the application for a widow's pension, National Archives, Washington, DC.

WARNER, NATHANIEL (ca. 1831–1895)

Nathaniel Warner was born in New York State about 1831 and grew up in Jamesport, Long Island. His parents were Betsey Terry and Nathaniel Warner, whose other children were Mary, Abigail, John, Rosalin and Austin.

Following his brother, Austin, who attended Wabash College from 1847 to 1849, Nathaniel Warner entered the Preparatory Department in the fall of 1849 and continued in the Scientific Program in 1850–51.

In the late 1850s Warner made his way to Saline County, Missouri, where he met Elizabeth J. Steele Medcalf, a recent widow. They married on 31 May 1860. She had a three-year-old son, John, from her first marriage, and subsequently gave birth to Leila Minerva (Minnie) (1861), Terry (1863), Nathaniel Arthur (1864), and William, who died in infancy.

In 1862 or early 1863, the Warners moved from Missouri to Mound City Township in Kansas, where Warner took up farming and taught school. He also served in the Kansas Home Guard, his Civil War experience. In 1869 the family moved to Fort Scott in Bourbon County, and Warner continued to farm.

In the 1880s or early 1890s, their son, Terry, moved to Parker, Kansas, to practice medicine, and his parents joined him. Warner died there in 1895, while Elizabeth lived until 1912.

References: Katy Matthews of Topeka, Kansas; Ola May Earnest of the Linn County (Kansas) Historical Society; Suffolk County (New York) Historical Society. See also: W. E. Connelley (ed.), *History of Kansas State and People*, IV (1928), pp. 1791–92; *Parker Message*, 5 January 1912, 2 February 1912, and 30 December 1937.

WASSON, JAMES HENRY (1839–1919)

James Henry Wasson, often called Henry, was born in Crawfordsville in 1839 to Elizabeth and James Wasson, a farmer and blacksmith.

In the autumn of 1857, Wasson entered the Normal School of Wabash College. On 27 May 1858 married Elizabeth P. Bennett. He ceased his formal education in 1860 and took employment initially as a clerk and later as part owner of a dry goods store. Wasson was county auditor between 1879 and 1883 while also serving as a bookkeeper and cashier of the Indiana Natural Gas Company.

In late April 1861 he enrolled in the Tenth Indiana Regiment at Crawfordsville, served his agreed-upon three months in Virginia, and was mustered out on 6 August.

Henry and Elizabeth Wasson had no children of their own, but they adopted a young girl, Ethel, who took the Wasson surname and became a teacher in Crawfordsville.

After his wife died, Wasson married Elizabeth Albright Voris on 12 December 1900, and they remained in Crawfordsville for several years. Wasson then accepted a job with the Rural Free Delivery branch of the post office, which took him first to Chicago, then to Cincinnati, and finally to Indianapolis, where he retired in about 1909. He died of heart failure on 3 December 1919 and was buried in Oak Hill Cemetery at Crawfordsville.

References: *Wabash College Record*, January 1920, p. 127; H. W. Beckwith, *History of Montgomery County* (1881), p. 115; Crawfordsville *Journal*, 3 December 1919; *Indianapolis Star*, 4 December 1919; and archives of the GAR McPherson Post No. 7.

WATERS, ROBERT S. (ca. 1830–1895)

Robert Waters was born in Eel River Township in Hendricks County, the son of Samuel D. Waters. His mother's name is not recorded, but she bore another son, Nathan, before she died in about 1840. Robert's father married Elizabeth in 1844, and they had six children: Julie Ann, Sarah, Eliza, Harvey, Samuel, and George.

The young man was enrolled in the Preparatory Department of Wabash College from 1843 to 1846. He then went to Kentucky in the early 1850s, and on 18 January 1854 he married Arrinda Payton of Gallatin County. The couple must have moved back to Indiana for a few years, since their eldest son, Silas, was born there. However, their next two sons, Lee and James, and a daughter were born in Kentucky. Their last child, Edward, was born in Indiana about 1874.

Waters's muster roll card at the Indiana State Archives gives his last name as Walters, not Waters. On 8 October 1864 at Columbus, he enrolled in Company E of the 140th Indiana Regiment for a term of one year. He was described as being five feet six inches tall, with blue eyes, sandy hair, and a fair complexion.

On 20 January 1865, as his regiment was marching from Murfreesboro to Clifton, Tennessee, Waters contracted malaria, or what the doctors (mistakenly) called "breakebone fever." He was briefly hospitalized and put on a boat for Louisville, where he was treated at two different hospitals and finally given a medical discharge on 7 June 1865.

After the war the Waters family settled in the town of Patriot, Indiana. Waters pursued farming and worked as a boatman. Between 1884 and 1892 they moved back to Gallatin County where Waters died on 26 February 1895.

References: Dr. Carl Cowen of Indianapolis; Switzerland County Public Library; military pension file at the National Archives, Washington, DC.

WAY, WILLIAM H. (ca. 1839–1862)

William Way was born in Indiana in about 1839. His mother's name was Hannah, but his father's first name is unknown. Prior to 1849, Way's father died, and his mother married Thomas White of Columbus, Bartholomew County, Indiana. Way came to Wabash College in 1856–57 from Louisville, Kentucky, so was presumably living with relatives at the time.

At the outbreak of war, he was in Columbus and enrolled as a private in Company C of the Sixth Indiana Regiment on 20 August 1861. A month elapsed before he was mustered into service at Madison and proceeded to Kentucky, where he spent the winter at a camp in Bowling Green and contracted measles.

He died in a hospital at Woodsonville, Kentucky, on 14 April 1862.

References: Bartholomew County Public Library.

WEBSTER, JOSEPH RAWSON (1839–1917)

Joseph Webster was born in Bombay in India on 5 May 1839, where his parents, Maryette Rawson and Elijah Ashley Webster, were missionaries. The family returned to America in 1842, going first to New York State but settling in LaGrange County, Indiana, in 1847, where his father was elected to the Indiana House of Representatives. Joseph had two siblings, Eunice and Charles.

Webster enrolled in the Classical Course at Wabash in the fall of 1858 and received his bachelor of arts degree on 25 June 1862. He was chosen as one of the class speakers at the graduation ceremony. His topic was "The Creative and the Executive."

With the outbreak of war, Webster was one of the first to enlist, cutting short his junior year at Wabash. With many other students, he joined Company I of the Eleventh Indiana Regiment and was mustered in on 22 April 1861, spent a short time in western Virginia, and was mustered out at Indianapolis on 4 August.

On 6 August 1862 he was commissioned captain of Company G of his former Eleventh Regiment, but later transferred to the Eighty-Eighth Regiment and was promoted to the rank of major on 31 October 1864. On 18 May 1864 he became lieutenant colonel of the United States Forty-Fourth Regiment of colored infantry and remained with them until honorably discharged in January 1866.

After the war Webster bought land in Bolivar County, Mississippi, with the idea of growing cotton, but he soon gave up this enterprise and headed north to Council Bluffs, Iowa, where he remained only briefly before finally settling in Lincoln, Nebraska. Practicing as a lawyer, he was elected to the Nebraska state legislature in 1868 and attorney general in 1873.

On 12 June 1873 he married Sarah Cooper Thompson. Their only child, Joy Louise, was born in 1874. From 1878 to 1879 Webster was a judge in Lancaster County, the county seat of Lincoln, the capital of Nebraska.

In 1893 Webster became a professor in the law school of the University of Nebraska, resigning in 1900 after he was named first assistant attorney general of the United States at Washington, DC. His wife, Sarah, died there in March 1904.

On 29 November 1906 he married Dr. Lenore Perky, a medical doctor who was instrumental in urging the Nebraska state legislature to found a hospital for birth-deformed adults and children. Webster died on 9 January 1917 in Washington, DC.

References: *Wabash Magazine*, III (June 1862), p. 379; *Wabash Magazine*, IV (December 1863), p. 74; *Wabash Magazine*, IX (June 1869), p. 156; Nebraska State Historical Society; *Nebraska State Journal*, 10 January 1917, p. 7; unpublished letter from Webster to the dean of the University of Nebraska law school, 12 February 1900, in the possession of the State Historical Society; *Sunday State Journal*, 6 May 1917. For background on Elijah Webster, see: *Biographical Directory of the Indiana General Assembly*, I (1980), p. 410.

WHITE, CHARLES BREMAN (1826–1882)

Charles B. White was born in Thetford, Vermont, on 14 February 1826, one of ten children of Martha Carter and Charles White. Three of his siblings were William, Edmond, and Emily. The family moved to Crawfordsville when Charles White Sr. was appointed the second president of Wabash College (1841–1861).

In the autumn of 1842, at the age of sixteen, son Charles became a student at Wabash. He graduated four years later in June 1846, returning to the East to begin his theological training at Andover Seminary.

In the winter of 1848–49 White suffered an acute infection of the lungs, diagnosed as incurable tuberculosis, and was given six weeks to live. His only hope seemed to be to leave New England for the warmth of the Deep South. Accordingly, he went to Alabama and began to study medicine informally, and in 1850 he entered the medical department of the University of Louisiana, graduating in 1852. That same year he married Evelyn Starr and established a thriving medical practice in New Orleans.

The outbreak of the Civil War presented him with a dilemma: he had been graciously accepted in his new southern surroundings, but his Yankee upbringing made him loyal to the North. The death of his wife in 1863 prompted his decision to join the Union army, and he plunged into the routine of a U.S. Army assistant surgeon. In 1864 he was promoted to a full surgeon, and he eventually became medical director of the Thirteenth Army Corps.

In spite of his service in the Union army, White was welcomed back into New Orleans society after the war and forged a national reputation in the area of public sanitation. He held a number of prestigious offices within the medical community, including president of the Louisiana State Board of Health (1868–76) and president of the American Public Health Association.

White maintained his ties to Wabash through a gift of botanical and zoological specimens to the college, and his brother, William Carter White, was a member of the faculty for more than twenty years. White died on 16 April 1882. His remains were conveyed to Crawfordsville and buried in Oak Hill Cemetery.

References: *New Orleans Medical and Surgical Journal*, IX (1882), pp. 873–74; S. V. Butler (ed.), *The Medical Register and Directory of the United States* (Philadelphia, 1878), p. 295; Rudolph Matas Medical Library of Tulane University, New Orleans.

WHITE, JOHN M. (1841–1863)

John White was born in 1841 in Marion County. Because the name White was so common, it was impossible to pinpoint the members of his family.

When he entered the Preparatory Department of Wabash College in the fall of 1856, he lived in Southport. He remained at Wabash for two years and then began studying medicine, probably with a local Crawfordsville doctor.

On 1 September 1859 White married Irena B. Wert of Crawfordsville.

White enrolled in Company G of the Seventieth Indiana Regiment at Indianapolis on 19 July 1862, stating that he was a physician. He was commissioned a first lieutenant on 7 August and served at Gallatin, Tennessee. He became an assistant surgeon on 6 December 1862.

He died at a hospital in Gallatin on 31 August 1863.

References: Samuel Merrill, *The Seventieth Indiana Volunteer Infantry* (1900), p. 292.

WHITEFORD, MATTHEW MACKIE (1840–1931)

Matthew Whiteford was born at Kilbernie, Ayrshire, Scotland, on 11 March 1840, the son of Esther and Robert Mackie. In 1859 he came to the United States and settled in Pomeroy, Ohio, and joined the Presbyterian church there in 1860.

In the autumn of 1861, he entered the Preparatory Department of Wabash College for two years, then became a freshman in the Classical Course in the fall of 1863, graduating in June 1867. While at Wabash Whiteford was an editor of the *Wabash Magazine* for several years and a member of the Phi Delta Theta fraternity, and he was recognized as a gifted public speaker. During his junior year he won first prize in declamation.

When leaving Wabash in 1867, Whiteford intended to be a lawyer, and for a year or two he studied law and may have practiced briefly in Crawfordsville. He married Julia Dumont Naylor of Crawfordsville on 16 January 1868. They had two children: Robert Naylor (1870) and William (1878).

During the summer of 1864, while still at Wabash, Whiteford joined Company D of the 135th Indiana Regiment on 23 May for one hundred days, spent mostly in Tennessee and Alabama guarding railroad lines. He was mustered out on 29 September and continued at Wabash as a sophomore.

Beginning in September 1869 Whiteford became a tutor in the Preparatory Department of Wabash, serving as associate principal in the fall of 1872. In the spring of 1875, he determined on a career in the Presbyterian ministry and spent the next two years at Princeton Theological Seminary, graduating with a bachelor of divinity degree. He accepted a call to be pastor at the First Presbyterian Church of Peru, Indiana, in May 1877, a post he filled until 1883.

His wife, Julia, died in 1879, making it easier for him to return to Scotland from 1883 to 1885 and become involved in churches in Glasgow and Edinburgh. Once back in America, he married Julia's sister, Mary D. Naylor, on 8 June 1886 and served a succession of churches in Ohio, Wisconsin, Illinois, Iowa, and South Dakota until he retired in 1910.

For some years thereafter Whiteford lived in Missouri, and he eventually settled near his son, Robert (who graduated from Wabash in 1890) in Toledo, Ohio, where he died on 27 June 1931.

References: Princeton Theological Seminary; *Wabash Magazine*, VII (June 1867), p. 113; *Wabash Magazine*, IX (June 1869), p. 158; *Wabash Magazine*, X ((December 1869), p. 83; J. H. Stephens, *History of Miami County, Indiana* (1896), p. 148; *Wabash Record*, July 1904, p. 23; *Wabash Bulletin*, February 1932, p. 32.

WHITEHEAD, COLUMBUS DELANO (1848–1919)

Columbus Delano Whitehead, or Del as he liked to be called, was born in Licking County, Ohio, on 21 March 1848, one of five children of Mary Green and Abram Whitehead. His siblings were Richard, Eliza, Asa, and Wickliffe.

He was one of the youngest Wabash students to serve in the Civil War, and since his service took place before he entered Wabash, the particulars have been impossible to discover. Presumably he entered an Ohio regiment or militia unit, although his name is not listed on the usual roster of such recruits.

By the time Whitehead entered Wabash in the fall of 1869, he gave his home address as Columbia Center, Ohio. He began with the freshman class and stayed until he graduated in June 1873. While in college Whitehead earned money by sawing or chopping wood, providing janitorial services for a local church, and selling books to anyone who would buy them. As a representative for the National Publishing Company, he sold twenty copies of John Bunyan's complete works and thirty copies of Mark Twain's *Innocents Abroad*. He was a member of the Phi Delta Theta fraternity and was especially active in public speaking, winning the coveted Baldwin oratorical contest.

Upon graduation, Whitehead went to Indianapolis to study law with the firm of Barbour, Jackson and Williams, following in the steps of his older brother, Wick, Wabash class of 1871, who was also a lawyer. Whitehead was admitted to the Indiana bar in 1874, practiced law for the next few years, and was elected judge of the Marion County criminal circuit court in 1878.

On 22 September 1875 he married Mary Maxwell Wilson, and eventually they had four children: Emma, Mary, Howard, and Joseph.

In 1879 the family moved to Maryville, Missouri, where Whitehead left the law for the grain shipping business. Five years later they moved again, this time to Kansas City, where he became involved in the insurance business and ran for United States Congress. As he later mused, "Made the race for Congress on the Populist ticket in 5th Missouri district. Was on the wrong side of the river to win."

Between 1898 and 1904 he was a salesman in Kansas City. Then, in 1905 he joined his son Joseph to work at the Kansas City branch of the Philip Carey Manufacturing Company. He worked there until 1909, when he and Mary moved to Wichita, Kansas, where she died on 3 May 1910. Del died nine years later from injuries suffered from a fall from the roof of his house on 29 May 1919. Both are buried in Elmwood Cemetery, Kansas City.

References: 1905 Wabash College alumni questionnaire, Ramsay Archives; C. A. Kannouse's circular letter to the class of 1873, sent out in 1879, Ramsay Archives; *Wabash Record*, July 1903, p. 30; *Wabash Magazine*, XI (June 1871), pp. 207–08; *Freshman Clipper*, 13 December 1873; Mary E. Burt of Kansas City; *Kansas City Star*, 5 May 1910; the Stein-McClure funeral home, Kansas City; and the records of Elmwood Cemetery.

WHITENACK, DAVID S. (1837–1931)

David Whitenack was born in Johnson County on 30 January 1837. His parents were Elvira Harris and Peter Whitenack, whose other son, George, served with his brother in the same company and regiment during the war.

When Whitenack entered the Preparatory Department of Wabash in the fall of 1857, he came from Greenwood in Johnson County. He remained at the college through the spring term of 1860.

On 1 January 1861 he married Sylvia R. Unthank, and they eventually had ten children, though four died in infancy.

Whitenack enrolled in Company F of the Fifth Cavalry on 28 December 1863 at Greenwood and was mustered in at Indianapolis on 5 January 1864, noting that he was a farmer. At the time he was six feet tall, with blue eyes, auburn hair, and a fair complexion.

On 31 July 1864 both brothers were captured and sent to Andersonville. David wrote of those harrowing days,

> Everything of value was taken from us, money, watches, jewelry, many articles of clothing, and even the photographs of our friends, while we were threatened with being shot or hung, and were abused as thieves and robbers. After we had been deprived of what few comforts we possessed, we were driven, like so many hogs, into the stockade, where already thirty-two thousand souls were confined. There were four hundred and forty of us, the rest of General Stoneman's command having escaped. What a sight met our eyes! At least fifty dead were lying near the gate, waiting for the return of the "dead wagon." Starvation was apparent in almost every living man. Some were almost entirely destitute of clothing. Many were unable to walk by reason of scurvy, while hundreds were in a dying condition.

The brothers were lucky. On 16 September 1864 they were transferred to a prison at Florence, South Carolina, where the chances of survival were slightly better. In fact, after three days they made a successful escape. They were at large for nine days and covered one hundred miles, but their pursuers, including bloodhounds, were too much, and they were again taken captive. They spent six weeks in a jail at Columbia, South Carolina, followed by a return to Florence and a stint at Richmond. In February 1865 both brothers were paroled and went initially to

Annapolis, Maryland, where George sought medical treatment. David remained with his brother until he could arrange to take him home.

In early April 1865 David rejoined his regiment at Pulaski, Tennessee, and was formally discharged on 27 June 1865, only to rejoin the Sixth Indiana Cavalry attached to the Seventy-First Regiment on 1 July as a second lieutenant, mustering out at Murfreesboro on 15 September.

When he returned to Johnson County, Whitenack taught school in the winter and farmed in the summer. In 1883 he moved from the country into the town of Greenwood and managed a hotel, also becoming an undertaker and acquiring a furniture store.

For seventy-one years he was an elder in the Presbyterian church. He died on 16 April 1931 and is buried in the Old Greenwood Cemetery.

References: The quotation about Andersonville is from Merrill & Co., *The Soldier of Indiana in the War of the Union*, II (1866), pp. 751–53; *History of Johnson County, Indiana* (1888), p. 555; E. L. Branigin, *History of Johnson County, Indiana* (1913), p. 321; *Indianapolis News*, 16 April 1931; and the Greenwood Public Library.

WHITESIDE, MORRIS LATHAN (1841–1916)

Morris L. Whiteside's name posed multiple problems when it came to identifying him. A Lt. R. Whiteside served in the war, but there is no record of his attending Wabash. On the other hand, a Morris L. Whiteside was in the Normal School from 1855 to 1857, and he served in the war. It is possible there were two Whitesides at Wabash.

Lathan (Morris) Whiteside was born in Ohio in 1841, the son of Susan Dungon and Abram Whiteside, a successful merchant. His siblings were Charles, Sarah, and Susan.

On 22 April 1861 Whiteside enrolled for three months in Company B of the Sixth Indiana Regiment. He married Carie Kindside, and they had three children who died in infancy.

During the 1870s he was a dentist in Paris, Edgar County, Illinois, and in 1876 he served on the Paris city council. He died on 27 May 1916 and is buried in Edgar County.

References: Charles A. Hand of Paris, Illinois, plus census and military service records.

WILLSON, LANE (ca. 1842–ca. 1878)

Lane Willson was born in Crawfordsville about 1842, the oldest of seven children of Laura Virginia Mattox and Samuel Campbell Willson. His siblings were Ann, Julia, Levi, Lucy, Robert, and James. His father was for sixteen years a law partner of Henry S. Lane, longtime Indiana statesman and United States senator, after whom he was presumably named.

In the fall of 1853, Willson entered the Normal School of Wabash College, where he spent three years and was then promoted to the Preparatory Department, in which he spent three more years. In 1860 he was living with his family in Crawfordsville and claimed to be a druggist.

On 18 April 1861 he was among the first to enlist in Company I of the Eleventh Indiana Regiment under Colonel Lew Wallace for three months. His tour of duty took him briefly to western Virginia, and he was mustered out at Indianapolis on 4 August. When Morgan raided southern Indiana in July 1863, Willson again volunteered and served for only nine days.

In 1870 he was living in Crawfordsville with his parents, but later he moved to Indianapolis, where he died in about 1878. He was initially buried in Mills Cemetery of Crawfordsville, but on 18 May 1880 his remains were interred in Oak Hill Cemetery, where his father was laid to rest in 1881 and his mother in 1888.

References: *Wabash Record*, October 1904, p. 1; *Crawfordsville Weekly Review*, 25 June 1881; records of Oak Hill Cemetery; C. W. Taylor, *The Bench and Bar of Indiana* (1899), p. 2297; *A Biographical History of Eminent and Self-Made Men of the State of Indiana*, II (1880), pp. 53–54.

WILLSON, SAMUEL J. (1839-1897)

Samuel Willson was born on 24 February 1839 at Roseboom, Otsego County, New York, one of three sons of Maria Campbell and James S. Willson. All three served in the Civil War, but Robert C and Albert W. did not attend Wabash.

In 1859–60 Willson attended Westfield Academy in Chautauqua County and then came to Indiana in the autumn of 1860 and enrolled in the Preparatory Department of Wabash College. The following spring he volunteered for military service on 21 April 1861 and joined Company H of the Eleventh Indiana Regiment at Indianapolis for three months. For a brief time he went to western Virginia, but he was mustered out on 4 August. Later that month, on 24 August, he received a commission as a second lieutenant in the same company and regiment and committed to serving three years. He was described as six feet tall, with blue eyes, brown hair, and a light complexion. Before being forced to resign on 1 August 1862 because of poor health, he took part in battles at Fort Donelson and Shiloh and was transferred to the signal corps at Paducah, Kentucky.

The following September Willson was offered a commission as captain of Company K of the Fifty-Fourth Indiana Regiment, and at the Battle of Chickasaw Bluffs in December 1862, he was wounded in the head by a shell fragment.

Back with his regiment in the spring of 1863, he took part in the battles of Magnolia Hill, Jackson, and Vicksburg. In August he was assigned to New Orleans and contracted malaria, causing him to spend some months in hospital. He was released from duty in December 1863.

Returning home to New York State, he married Sarah E. Shove of Ripley, Chautauqua County, on 3 February 1864. They eventually had seven children: Charles, John, Mary, Sarah, Albert, Robert, and Anna. Willson always wanted to farm, so shortly after marrying he moved to Attica in Fountain County, Indiana, but then returned to New York State. In the fall of 1867, the Willsons relocated to Iowa, where they stayed until 1874, but finally they settled in Royal Oak, Michigan, where they rented 160 acres and later bought 40 acres of their own. Willson supplemented farming by serving on the school board, acting as a school inspector, and being a justice of the peace.

He died at Royal Oak on 16 October 1897, survived by his wife, who died on 14 December 1912.

References: Military pension file for Willson at the National Archives, Washington, DC; Royal Oak (Michigan) Public Library; *Portrait and Biographical Album of Oakland County, Michigan* (1891), pp. 289–90; C. Fey, *City of Royal Oak Michigan, 1817–1954* (1954), pp. 79–80.

WILSON, JAMES (1825–1867)

James Wilson was born on 9 April 1825 and is thought to have been the first white male child born in Crawfordsville. His father, John, attended Wabash in 1834–35, as did his brothers (William, Samuel, John Wardsworth, and George), three of whom served in the Civil War. His mother was Margaret McKee, a Virginian.

James Wilson joined the Preparatory Department at the age of nine and stayed through graduation in 1842. He then studied law with Tilghman A. Howard of Rockville and opened his own law office in Crawfordsville in 1845. According to one local historian, he "at once jumped meteor-like to the head of his chosen profession. He became a leader, and his superiority to all was conceded. He swayed juries at his will, and held vast audiences entranced by the power of his eloquence."

When the war with Mexico broke out, Wilson enlisted in the United States Army and served from June 1846 to June 1847. In November 1856 he ran as a Republican and abolitionist for the United States House of Representatives from the Ninth District, and he was active in the many debates over slavery. After another term in Congress, he married Emma Ingersoll of Crawfordsville on 4 March 1849, and they eventually had four children. One died in infancy, but the other three distinguished themselves. John Lockwood Wilson became United States representative from the new state of Washington; Tilghman Howard Wilson honored the memory of his father James's legal mentor; and Henry Lane Wilson was appointed United States ambassador to Mexico.

On 26 November 1862 Wilson was commissioned captain and assistant quartermaster of the Twenty-Sixth United States Army Regiment. In 1865 he was promoted to major and made a brevet lieutenant colonel on the eve of his honorable discharge in December.

Wilson's return to Crawfordsville was short lived, as President Andrew Johnson named him minister resident to Venezuela. After successfully settling many disputed claims between the two countries, he declared his wish to resume practicing law and sent his family home while he awaited the arrival of his successor. Unfortunately he contracted malaria and died on 8 August 1867. He is buried in Oak Hill Cemetery.

References: *Biographical Directory of the American Congress*; Francis B. Heitman, *Historical Register and Dictionary of the United States Army* (1903); 1860 U.S. census for Montgomery County; *Wabash Magazine*, X (December 1869); *Indianapolis Journal*, 11 December 1889.

WILSON, JOHN WARDSWORTH (1836–1866)

John Wardsworth Wilson was born in Crawfordsville in 1836, one of the brothers (see Samuel, William, and James) who attended Wabash and served in the Civil War. His parents were Margaret and John Wilson. He often went by a variant of his middle name, calling himself Ward.

In 1847 he enrolled in the Preparatory Department of Wabash College, remaining through the academic year 1851–52. He joined the Indiana Volunteer Infantry in December 1861, citing his residence as Romney. He was named a first lieutenant in Company C of the Fortieth Indiana Regiment and served for one year before resigning.

For the next two years he lived in Lafayette, and in October 1864 he accepted a commission as a first lieutenant in the Eleventh Cavalry of the 126th Regiment, serving with them until the end of the war. He returned to Crawfordsville in poor health and died on 23 November 1866. He is buried in Oak Hill Cemetery.

References: *Crawfordsville Weekly Review*, 24 November 1866; *History of Montgomery County* (Bowen & CO., 1913), p. 588.

WILSON, SAMUEL MCKEE (1831–1864)

Samuel Wilson was born on 21 June 1831 in Crawfordsville, one of the four sons of Margaret and John Wilson (see James, John, and William) who attended Wabash College and also served in the Civil War.

At the age of twelve, Samuel enrolled in the Preparatory Department of Wabash for four years. He then turned his attention to farming in Tippecanoe County.

In April 1861 he responded to the call and joined Company D of the Tenth Indiana Regiment, and one month later was promoted from second lieutenant to captain. After three months of service spent mostly in Virginia, he again enlisted the following March in the Indiana Sixteenth Light Artillery for three years and resumed his rank of second lieutenant.

At the Battle of Antietam he sustained an injury from which he never fully recovered, although he remained with his regiment for many months more. In May 1864 he was forced into retirement by medical necessity and returned to Crawfordsville, where he died on 24 July 1864. He is buried in Oak Hill Cemetery.

References: *History of Montgomery County* (Bowen & Co., 1913), pp. 586–97; *Crawfordsville Daily Review*, 30 July 1864.

WILSON, OLIVER MORRIS (1836–1907)

Oliver Wilson was born in Logansport on 16 August 1836, the son of Mary Todd Barbee and Lazarus Brown Wilson, a surveyor who worked on the extension of the National Road. He had two siblings, Henry and Alma.

He was a student at Marion County Seminary before coming to Wabash from New Albany in the fall of 1852 to enroll in the Scientific Course. He stayed for the academic year 1853–54 and then transferred to Hamilton College in New York State, where he was graduated in 1858.

Wilson returned to Indianapolis and studied law, securing admission to the bar in 1859 and marrying Mary Adelia Allen in 1860. His marriage would eventually result in the birth of six children. However, the newlyweds soon found their lives disrupted by the coming of war

Wilson's appointment as clerk to the Indiana Sinking Fund Commission and the Swamps Land Commission in 1862 was short lived, as once the war started, he responded to the call for additional troops and became a lieutenant in Company B of the Fifty-Fourth Indiana Regiment on 22 September. One month later, on 16 October 1862, he was promoted to captain of his company, and at the beginning of January 1863 he became major.

After Wilson was honorably discharged at New Orleans on 8 December 1863, he returned to Indianapolis, where he and Mary built a house next to his parents at the corner of Capitol and Maryland Streets. Between 1865 and 1869 he supplemented his law practice by being secretary to the Indiana State Senate, and he was named assistant U.S. district attorney for Indiana by Ulysses S. Grant. In 1871 he successfully contested a seat in the Indiana House of Representatives as a Republican from Marion County. Using his varied experience with state government, he authored and published in 1880 *Primitive Governments and their Parliaments*.

In 1887 Wilson and his family moved to Arkansas City, Kansas, then took up residence in Independence, Missouri, and later in Kansas City, where he died on 19 July 1907.

References: *Biographical Directory of the Indiana General Assembly*, I, (1980), p. 422; *Indiana State Bar Association, Papers and Addresses* (1922), pp. 73–74; *National Cyclopedia of American Biography*.

WILSON, WILLIAM COCHRAN (1827–1891)

William C. Wilson was born in Crawfordsville on 22 November 1827, one of four sons of Margaret McKee and John Wilson who attended Wabash (see James, John, and Samuel).

He and his older brother James were two of the earliest students to enroll in the recently founded Wabash College in 1834. In fact, William may hold the record for the number of years attending the college: thirteen, from the time he entered the Preparatory Department until he graduated in 1847. The following two years he studied for a law degree at Indiana University, and in 1849 he became prosecuting attorney for Montgomery County. In 1850 he established a law practice in Lafayette with a former Wabash student, Daniel Mace, as his partner, and when Mace was elected to the United States House of Representatives, Wilson acquired a new partner, George Gardner.

In 1853 Wilson married Sarah Bonnell. Apparently they had no surviving children.

During the war Wilson compiled a distinguished military career. On 19 April 1861 he became the captain of Company D of the Tenth Indiana Regiment and in a matter of weeks was promoted to major. The regiment made its way to western Virginia and merged with the troops under the command of General Rosecrans, and on 11 July they routed the Confederates at Rich Mountain, but Wilson was one of those wounded. Once he recuperated he raised another regiment, the Fortieth Infantry, and became its colonel in September 1861. Joining the Army of the Cumberland under General Thomas, he commanded his regiment until May 1862, when illness forced him to resign. He raised and led the 108th Regiment in the Morgan furor. Many of the summer soldiers who served under him were past or current students at Wabash. The spring of 1864 found him appointed colonel of the newly constituted 135th Regiment, whose assignment was to guard railroad lines in Tennessee and Alabama.

Following the war Wilson resumed his law practice in Lafayette and also became a city council member. When his former partner, Daniel Mace, died in 1867, leaving vacant the job of postmaster, Wilson served in his stead. Eventually he took on a new law partner, Jay H. Adams.

On two occasions Wilson ran for public office, but his bid for state senator in 1878 and for state attorney general in 1884 were both unsuccessful. He died in Lafayette on 25 September 1891, survived by his wife.

References: *History of Montgomery County* (Bowen & Co., 1913), pp. 484–89; C. W. Taylor, *Biographical Sketches and Record of the Bench and Bar of Indiana* (1895), pp. 726–28.

WISHARD, JOSEPH MILTON (1828–1905)

Joseph Wishard was born on 1 January 1828 on a large farm near Greenwood. He was one of six children of Nancy Henderson Oliver and John Wishard, and his siblings were William, Samuel, Margaret, Martha, and John. His mother died in 1849, the year he entered the Normal School of Wabash College for two years. Afterwards he taught for a few years in Johnson County.

On 14 April 1852 Wishard married Rachael A. Lyons, and eventually they had eight children. In 1854 he enrolled at the Ohio Medical College of Cincinnati. After completing his courses he began practicing in Greenwood in 1857.

When the war broke out, he realized that his skills as a doctor were badly needed, so on 21 October 1862 he joined the Fifth Cavalry attached to the Ninetieth Indiana Regiment as an assistant surgeon. On 6 October 1863 he was promoted to surgeon and served until 27 June 1865, when he was mustered out at Pulaski, Tennessee.

In 1903 he fell and dislocated both hips, leaving him much infirmed. His ninety-year-old brother, Dr. William Niles Wishard, for whom Wishard Memorial Hospital in Indianapolis is named, visited him daily in Greenwood until he died on 31 May 1905.

References: H. H. Hardesty, *Presidents, Soldiers and Statesmen* (1895), pp. 1238–39; *Indianapolis and Vicinity: Commemorative Biographical Record* (1908), pp. 471–72; *Franklin Republican*, 2 June 1905; *Franklin Democrat*, 2 June 1905.

WOLFE, EDWARD T. (1847–?)

Edward Wolfe was born in 1847 at Romney, the younger of two sons of Sarah and Matthew Wolfe who attended Wabash and served in the war. His siblings were Caroline, William, and Matthew.

In the 1850s the Wolfe family moved to Montgomery County, where Matthew Wolfe farmed on a small scale. During the school year 1862–63 Edward was enrolled in the Normal School at Wabash.

Responding to Morgan's raid, Wolfe joined Company C of the 108th Indiana Infantry Regiment from 11 to 17 July. In 1880 Wolfe and his wife Charlotte lived in York, Illinois, where he claimed to be a painter, whether of canvasses or houses is unknown.

A Clark County newspaper of January 1896 states that Wolfe resigned his position with the pension office in Washington and moved with his wife to a farm in Arkansas.

References: 1850 and 1860 U.S. censuses; H. W. Beckwith, *History of Montgomery County Indiana* (1881); *Clark County Democrat*, 8 January 1896, p. 10; and Clark County Genealogical Library.

WOLFE, WILLIAM J. M. (1844–1902)

William Wolfe was born in 1844 at Romney, the elder of two sons of Sarah and Matthew Wolfe who went to Wabash as well as served in the Civil War. He had two brothers, Edward and Matthew, and a sister, Caroline.

In the fall of 1857, he entered the Preparatory Department and remained there for three years before entering the freshman class, where he spent the next two years. On 12 July 1862, at Crawfordsville, he enrolled in Eli Lilly's Eighteenth Indiana Light Artillery Battery for three years' service.

On 17 July 1864 at the Battle of Atlanta, he was stunned by exploding shells but not actually wounded. According to a letter he wrote to his brother, he and his fellow soldiers of the Eighteenth were particularly restive under Captain Lilly and wondered if there was some way he could wangle a transfer, saying he would do "anything to get me from under command of the tyrannical captain who I am under now." However, he remained with the regiment until his discharge on 30 June 1865. Years later, in 1892, he presided at a reunion of artillery veterans gathered under a tent at the colonel's home.

On 13 February 1868 Wolfe married Arabella Porte of Clay County, and they eventually had four children: Claude, Lotte, Maude, and Mady.

Wolfe established himself as a dentist in Bowling Green, Clay County, in the 1870s, and later located his practice in Brazil, where he died on 4 October 1902. He is buried in the Cottage Hill Cemetery.

References: See the citations for his younger brother, Edward; also J. W. Rowell, *The Yankee Artillerymen* (1975), pp. 36, 200, 211, 270, 273; Joyce Oehler of Brazil, Indiana; *Terre Haute Weekly Gazette*, 9 October 1902.

WOLVERTON, WILLIAM B. (1835–1865)

William Wolverton was born on 8 May 1835 in Butler County, Ohio, one of five children of Rebecca Alston and John H. Wolverton. His siblings were Susan, Emma, Laura, and Edwin.

In 1836 the Wolvertons moved to Crawfordsville. At the time John Wolverton was a tailor, but over the years he also worked as a mechanic, a coroner, and a farmer. They lived in town for about twenty years and then acquired a farm in Montgomery County.

William Wolverton entered the Preparatory Department of Wabash in the autumn of 1848. He spent two years there and then helped his father on the farm, made saddles, and did other odd jobs.

On 5 December 1861 he enrolled at Alamo in the Ninth Indiana Light Artillery for a term of three years. During April 1862 he took part in the battles of Shiloh and Corinth, and the following year he spent time south of Vicksburg on the Mississippi River and the Tennessee River. In January 1865 he and others were passengers on a riverboat, the *Eclipse*, docked at Johnsonville, awaiting departure for the north and honorable discharges. On the 27th the ship's boiler exploded, badly wounding thirty-seven of the seventy soldiers aboard. Wolverton died of his burns two days later on 29 January. His body was returned to Crawfordsville for burial in the Masonic Cemetery.

References: Biographical sketch of John Wolverton by Ryan Fegan (1991) in the Crawfordsville Public Library; *Atlas of Montgomery County* (1878), pp. 55–56; H. W. Beckwith, *History of Montgomery County* (1881), pp. 101, 103, 298; *History of Montgomery County* (Bowen & Co., 1913), p. 173.

WOOD, CHARLES OGDEN (1836–1891)

Ogden Wood, as he was most often called, was born in Terre Haute in 1836, the eldest of three children of Cornelia Hitchcock and Charles Wood. He had a younger sister and brother, Sarah and Maxwell. His name and that of his brother, Maxwell, both appear on the memorial tablet on the east wall of Center Hall honoring Civil War veterans. In the annual catalogue for 1851–52, and in the handwritten student index volume, Ogden Wood's name appears as Charles R. Woodward.

On 3 December 1860 Wood married Marie Cook Roome, a widow with two children, in Cleveland, Ohio. Together they had one child, Charles, born in 1865.

After being active in the Vigo County Marching Club called the Wabash Guards, he was chosen to serve as a major of field and staff in the Eleventh Indiana Volunteers in April 1861. Colonel Lew Wallace drew heavily from the Wabash Guards of Terre Haute, the Montgomery Guards of Crawfordsville, and the City Guards of Indianapolis to form his own unit.

On 25 May 1861 Wood entered the Ninth Indiana Regiment and worked his way through the ranks of second lieutenant, first lieutenant, and captain by 30 May 1863. He played a key role in subduing the mobs during the draft riots in New York City in July 1863, and later that year he was transferred to the staff of former Wabash student Major General Edward R. S. Canby, commander of Union troops in New York harbor.

Sometime in 1864 or early 1865, he was sent to the Presidio in San Francisco to help organize an Eighth Regiment of California volunteers, and for a brief time he commanded the troops on the island of Alcatraz as a lieutenant colonel and then as brevet colonel. On 24 October 1865 Wood returned to the Presidio, only to be sent to Nevada to command troops at Fort Churchill.

Following the United States's acquisition of Alaska from Russia in 1867, Wood was put in charge of some soldiers stationed at Sitka. He was now a brevet major but was charged with the unprovoked assault of a fellow officer in a barroom brawl. He was subsequently court-martialed and found guilty. Instead of being dismissed from the service, he appealed successfully and was suspended in rank and pay for six months. Later that year he was transferred to the department of the Platte River, and in August 1870 he requested and was granted an honorable discharge from the army.

Returning to Terre Haute, he pursued his father's career of pharmacist and periodically sought reinstatement in the army. He lamented that his resignation had been "the mistake of my life." In about 1880 he went to Cincinnati and secured employment with the Louisville and Nashville Railroad Company. However, the election of Benjamin Harrison in 1888 prompted him to move to Washington in search of a political appointment. This eluded him, and he died of "the grippe" on 17 April 1891. He was buried in Arlington National Cemetery.

References: Vigo County Public Library; the descendants of Charles Ogden Wood: Thomas E. Wood and James Olstad; also: C. C. Oakey, *Greater Terre Haute and Vigo County* (1908), p. 185; Terre Haute city directories, 1858–80; *Evening Star* (Washington, DC), 20 April 1891; R. Condit, *A History of Early Terre Haute* (1900), p. 171; *Terre Haute Express*, 21 April 1891; and *Terre Haute Weekly Gazette*, 24 September 1891.

WOOD, GUSTAVUS ADOLPHUS (1825–1891)

Gus Wood, as he was later called, was born at Galena, Delaware County, Ohio, on 12 January 1825. There are no records of his parents or possible siblings.

He entered the Preparatory Department of Wabash in the fall of 1843, giving his home as Lafayette, Indiana. He stayed for one year then returned in the fall of 1845 as a sophomore in the Classical Department. The war in Mexico drew him away from his studies, and he secured an appointment as a first lieutenant in Company K of the First Indiana Infantry in 1846. He was stationed at the mouth of the Rio Grande, near Monterey. He was honorably discharged on 14 June 1847. For the third time, he entered Wabash as a junior in 1847–48, but that November the college banned all secret organizations. He expressed his displeasure in intemperate language that resulted in censure by the faculty and a refusal to sanction an honorable dismissal, so Wood left.

Returning to Lafayette, he studied law and was admitted to the Indiana bar, becoming Tippecanoe County prosecuting attorney in 1850. In 1854 he was appointed a common pleas judge, the youngest in the state.

In the late 1840s he married an Irish girl, Honor, who died in 1850. On 26 May 1851 at Columbus, Indiana, he wedded Lydia Caroline Carpenter. Their first child died, but they later had three sons, William, Gus, and Hewitt, and two daughters, Elizabeth and Mary (Minnie).

On 15 May 1861 he was appointed captain of Company K of the Fifteenth Indiana Infantry, and one week later became a major. A year later, on 9 March 1862, he was made a lieutenant colonel, and he achieved the rank of colonel in June 1863. He was cited for bravery at the Battle of Stones River at Murfreesboro, where his troops captured troops of the Twentieth Louisiana Regiment. Other battles that Wood participated in were Rich Mountain, Shiloh, and Perryville.

He was later captured and imprisoned at the dreaded Libby Prison in Richmond. Rejoining his regiment, he took part in the Battle of Missionary Ridge, where his horse was shot out from under him. He emerged unscathed and was mustered out on 24 June 1864.

In August 1865 Wood and his family settled at Chattanooga, where he resumed his law practice. His firm, Wood and Burt, was well known. He also devoted two years to being Chattanooga city attorney and six years as a Hamilton County judge.

Wood died on 11 August 1891 at Highland Park Station near Chattanooga, within sight of Missionary Ridge, where he had fought.

References: The Chattanooga-Hamilton County (Tennessee) Public Library; *Chattanooga Times*, 12 August 1891; Tippecanoe County Historical Association; R. P. DeHart, *Past and Present of Tippecanoe County, Indiana* (1909), p. 165; *History of Montgomery County* (Bowen & Co., 1913), p. 88; military pension file, National Archives, Washington, DC.

WOOD, MAXWELL COHEN (1843–1891)

Max Wood was born in 1843 at Terre Haute. His parents were Cornelia Hitchcock and Charles Ogden Wood, and his siblings were Ogden and Sarah. As we have seen, Ogden studied at Wabash and also served in the war.

In the fall of 1859, Wood entered the grammar school connected to Kenyon College, Gambier, Ohio. The next year he transferred to Wabash for the 1860–61 school year.

On 29 July 1862 at Evansville, he enrolled in Company I of the Seventy-Sixth Indiana Regiment for thirty days. During the summer of 1863, he became a second lieutenant in the Union Rifles, a unit of the Indiana Legion in Vigo County. His third military experience began on 7 May 1864, when he was commissioned first lieutenant in Company D of the 133th Indiana Regiment and served for one hundred days in Tennessee and Alabama guarding railroad lines.

After the war Wood returned to Terre Haute and joined his father to work for the Vandalia Railroad for the next twenty-five years as a clerk in the auditor's office of the railroad.

In the late 1860s Wood married Elizabeth L. Floyd of Keokuk, Iowa. Together they had three children: Charles, Grace, and Maxwell.

Wood died at Terre Haute on 19 September 1891, survived by his wife and children, and was buried in Woodlawn Cemetery.

References: David N. Lewis of the Vigo County Public Library; *Terre Haute Weekly Gazette*, 24 September 1891; and the Kenyon College archives.

WOODROW, EDWARD R. (ca. 1845–1909)

Edward Woodrow was born about 1845 at Chillicothe, Ohio, one of three sons of Harriet and David Woodrow. His brothers were Charles and Henry. When he entered Wabash in the fall of 1863, he lived on a farm in Franklin County, Ohio, about two and a half miles from Columbus. Before completing his freshman year (1863–64), he enrolled for three years in Company I of the Eleventh Indiana Regiment at Crawfordsville on 28 March 1864. At the time he was described as standing five feet nine inches tall, with blue eyes, light hair, and a fair complexion. His regiment took part in Philip Sheridan's campaign through the Shenandoah Valley. In September 1864 at the Battle of Fisher's Hill in Virginia, Union forces had the Rebels on the run, but as Woodrow later recounted, he "accidentally fell over a precipice and down a distance of some 6 or 7 feet, falling with the small of his back striking a large stone as he reached the bottom, causing a severe injury to his spine but which did not immediately disable him from continuing on duty although producing much pain and distress in that region."

Woodrow's spinal injury grew worse in the coming weeks, and he was moved from a field hospital to Jarvis Hospital in Baltimore in October. The following month his brother Henry and his mother traveled to Baltimore, hoping to bring him back home. Although the attending doctor thought the trip might be fatal, he agreed to let Woodrow make the journey by train. His brother Charles met him at Columbus and conveyed him to the family farm in a horse-drawn carriage. Initially he was virtually bedridden and received regular medical attention from the Seminary Hospital in Columbus.

On 27 February 1865 his formal medical discharge came through from the army. It took another year before he could resume a normal routine, but for the rest of his life he had to avoid manual labor. He remained in Franklin County until 1870, when he moved to Pickaway County to take a job as a bookkeeper for three years. Returning to Columbus, he and two partners established a furniture dealership partnership, Woodrow, Scott and McAllister.

He moved to Larned, Kansas, in late 1885, and on 16 June 1886 he married Lydia Jane Curlette. Their two children were Helen (1887) and William (1889).

Woodrow died on 9 September 1909, either in Larned, Kansas, or in Columbus, Ohio.

References: Military pension file at the National Archives, Washington, DC.

WOODWARD, CHARLES R. JR.(1830–1903)

Charles Woodward/Woodard was born at Madison in September 1830, the son of Deborah Wood and Charles Woodward Sr. His siblings were Henry C., Maria, and Albert.

According to the Wabash College catalogue for 1851–52, Charles was in the Preparatory Department. After one year at Wabash, he returned home and became a sugar-maker or confectioner.

On 9 August 1862 Woodward enrolled for three years in Company C of the Sixty-Seventh Indiana Volunteers. That December his regiment was encamped at Milliken's Island, Louisiana, and moved to the swamps and bayous nearer Vicksburg. Fatigue and exposure to wet and cold brought on rheumatism, diarrhea, liver problems, lung disease, and an inflamed throat, and by February 1863 he was on sick leave. When he did not improve, he was given a medical discharge on 24 July.

Back in Madison, Woodward set up shop as a tobacconist and cigar maker. About 1871 he moved to Indianapolis, then later to Galesburg, Illinois, and to Jeffersonville, Indiana. By 1884 he was again in Madison, still making cigars.

Over the years Woodward's health declined, and in February 1903 he was so afflicted with mental disability that a guardian was appointed for him. He died on 12 December 1903 and is buried in Springdale Cemetery.

References: Madison-Jefferson County Public Library; military pension file, in which his surname is spelled "Woodard," National Archives, Washington, DC.

WOOLFOLK, AUSTIN (1837–1871)

Austin Woolfolk was born in 1837 in Louisiana. His father was also named Austin, and his mother died after giving birth to his sister Margaret in 1839. An older brother, Joseph, had been born in 1833. Austin Sr. married Emily Sparks on 7 October 1839, and the newly married couple moved to Iberville Parish.

Several other boys came to Wabash College from Iberville Parish in the early 1850s. Although his father died in 1847, young Austin was able to study at the college for one year, returning home to help with the plantation.

On 1 September 1862 Woolfolk enrolled at New Roads in Company I of the Second Louisiana Cavalry, commanded by Captain Allen Jumel. Woolfolk was then five feet six inches tall, with a fair complexion, dark eyes, and black hair. At first he thrived in the military, but a childhood injury flared up, and he was given a month's furlough in January 1863, never to return to active duty. He secured a medical discharge on 26 March 1863.

He never married and died in 1871. He was buried in the Woolfolk Cemetery at Rosedale, Iberville Parish.

References: Iberville Parish (Louisiana) Library; Judy Riffel, *A Bayou House*; *Maringouin Library and Museum*, a pamphlet published in 1985; and military service file, National Archives, Washington, DC.

WORT, ERASMUS DARWIN (1827–1890)

Erasmus Wort was born in Brownstown, Indiana, in 1827, possibly coincident with the death of his mother, Maria G. Wort. His father was Samuel A. Wort, and he had one older brother, Samuel.

Wort spent one year, 1843–44, at Wabash College, and then returned home to be an apprentice in his father's medical practice, eventually becoming a member of the medical society soon after its organization.

On 10 May 1849 he married a local Jackson County girl, Mary Indiana Noble, who gave birth to three boys: Velpeau, Aramus, and Elmer. In 1855 the Worts moved to Marengo, Iowa, where Wort established a medical practice, but on 21 August 1862 he volunteered for military service as a physician, enrolling in Company E of the Twenty-Fourth Iowa Volunteers. He may have had medical, or perhaps psychological, problems before entering the army, because he was given a medical discharge on 19 February 1863 at Helena, Arkansas.

At some point the Wort family returned to Jackson County, where Erasmus practiced medicine in Seymour in spite of serious disability. When his wife died in 1872, he came to rely on the charity of friends, and from time to time he resided in the local poorhouse in Brownstone, where he died on 10 December 1890.

References: Jackson County Public Library; Pension Office, National Archives, Washington, DC.

WRIGHT, IRVIN B. (1842–1905)

Irvin Wright grew up in a wealthy family. His father, John W. Wright, was an attorney in Logansport with real property valued at $28,500. By the time the 1860 census was taken, that figure had risen to $70,000. John was born in Ohio about 1813, while his wife, Mary Jane, was born in Pennsylvania four years later. Irvin Wright was presumably born in Eel Township of Cass County on 2 February 1842. His siblings included John, Edward, Williamson, David, and Philip.

Wright attended Wabash College's Preparatory Department for two years, 1855–57. The 1860 census indicated that he was still a student, but where he was studying is unknown.

On 18 April 1861 Wright joined the Twentieth Regiment of Ohio volunteers and was duly mustered out on 1 June. On 19 February 1862 he received a commission as a second lieutenant in the Eleventh Regiment of United States Volunteer Infantry. On 15 December 1862 he was promoted to first lieutenant of the same regiment. From July 1862 to January 1863, he was assigned to recruiting service.

During the course of 1863, Wright's regiment was attached to the Army of the Potomac and at the beginning of July was at Gettysburg. Wright emerged from that conflict unscathed and was recommended for promotion to brevet captain due to his "gallant and meritorious" conduct during the battle. During August and September of that year, his regiment saw duty in New York City providing stability and order following the draft riots of earlier that summer. Wright's unit then rejoined the Army of the Potomac and in the early months of 1864 was assigned to duty in Washington, DC. For a time Wright was with the provost marshal's office on Maryland Avenue as well as the Sixth Street wharf.

Between May and July 1865 Wright was attached to the provost marshal's office in the Department of Virginia, with headquarters in Richmond. He continued there until late 1865 and then secured a furlough for several months. Early in 1866 he was back in Richmond, and it looks as if he might have contemplated a career in the army. He was offered the rank of captain in the Twentieth Regiment of the regular United States army in September 1866, but by then he had decided to resign from his military career, which took place on 1 November 1866.

Once discharged from the army, Wright set about finding a wife. Ninna was born in Ohio and was two years older than Irvin. Her maiden name is not known. They presumably married in 1866, and their first child, Mary Jane, was born the following year. By then they were living in Washington, DC. About 1869 their son, John, was born in Indiana, and soon thereafter they relocated to Cincinnati.

Wright must have inherited some of his father's wealth, since the 1870 census for Ohio shows him with real property of $25,000 and cash of $10,000. By then he was a lawyer, and he continued practice in Cincinnati for at least ten years, as recorded by the 1880 census. Then the details of his life become murky.

By the time Wright died, his wife and daughter were living somewhere in Maryland, suggesting that the parents were either estranged or divorced. The source of such an estrangement may have stemmed from his growing medical problems. Later he attributed his nervous prostration and melancholy to the death of some twenty-six family members in the years 1884 to 1889. He also came to suffer heart problems, rheumatism, and rectal dysfunction. By 1897 Wright was residing in a soldiers home in Sandusky, Ohio, where he lived out the rest of his life. He died there on 7 August 1905. His body was returned to his earlier home of Logansport and was buried in Mount Hope Cemetery.

References: Logansport Cass County Public Library; *Logansport Journal* 12 August 1905; *Logansport Daily Pharos*, 12 August 1905; burial record extract from Mount Hope Cemetery; military pension file, National Archives, Washington, DC; Cincinnati Historical Society Library.

WRIGHT, JOHN B. (1843–1924)

John Wright was born on a farm a few miles from Marshall on 7 March 1843. His father Prior had been born in Richmond, Virginia, and his mother, Julia Beard, was a Hoosier. Their other children were Mary, William, Daniel, Salmon, George, and Prior.

In 1830 Prior opened a general store at the "Narrows" of Sugar Creek and also served as postmaster in the new town of Lusk Springs. Later he built a gristmill on the creek, which thrived until the floods of 1847 washed it away. Prior rebuilt a mill during the next year, and the 1850 census testified to his prosperity by valuing his real property at $12,000.

Sometime, presumably in the 1850s, the family secured a farm near Montezuma, and young John joined his father in this pursuit. In the autumn of 1861, however, he was sent to Wabash to pursue a course of study in the Normal School. This lasted one academic year.

On 2 August 1862 at Annapolis, Indiana, Wright signed up for three years' service in Company A of the Eighty-Fifth Regiment. At this time Wright was a youth of five feet seven inches tall, with a fair complexion, blue eyes, and dark hair. He served his full term, not being mustered out at Washington, DC, until 12 June 1865.

After the war Wright returned to Parke County and took up farming again. He remained there until about 1870 and then settled in nearby Vermillion County. It was there that he met and married Augusta Johnson on 24 December 1872. Their children were Lydia (1873), Lizzie (1875), Prier (spelled a different way than his grandfather) (1878), Annie (1880), Kate (1883), and John (1885). For many years the Wrights lived at Cayuga, and it was there that Augusta died in 1896.

A year or two later, Wright and his children moved to Douglas County, Illinois. Wright returned to his familiar surroundings of Parke County long enough to marry Lucinda Rubottom at Bloomingdale on 4 January 1899. The family moved several more times, but ties with old Wabash were maintained because Wright's son, Prier, went to college there and graduated in 1901.

Wright died at Tuscola, Illinois, on 24 August 1924. He is buried in the Johnson cemetery near Newport, a reminder presumably of his first wife's family name. Lucinda survived John, but her later whereabouts are unknown.

References: Military pension file, National Archives, Washington, DC.

WRIGHT, JOHN MARSHALL (1845–1890)

John Marshall Wright was born in 1845 in Madison, Indiana, the son of Mary A. and Williamson Wright, an extraordinarily successful lawyer. He had an older sister, Eliza. His mother died sometime in the 1850s and his father married again, providing young John with two half sisters, Kate and Elizabeth, and a half brother, William.

Wright entered Wabash as a freshman in the autumn of 1862 and managed to fit three short-term tours of duty in the army while still remaining in college, graduating in June 1866. Just before coming to Wabash, he enrolled in Company A of the Eighty-Sixth Ohio Regiment on 28 May 1862. Between 12 and 15 July 1863 he became a member of the 110th Indiana Regiment during Morgan's Raid. Beginning on 25 April 1864 he served one hundred days in Company H of the 135th Indiana Volunteers, mainly guarding railroad lines in Tennessee and Alabama. He was mustered out on 29 September 1864 in time to return to classes.

After the war Wright studied law, and by 1875 he practiced in Chicago. In 1877–78 he had a law office in Washington, DC, where he met his wife, Catharine (Caddie) Lois Coburn. They married in Philadelphia on 23 December 1882, and some years later they moved to Lincoln, Indiana, where their only child, Mary, was born in 1887.

Wright died on 14 April 1890 from consumption, from which he had suffered for many years.

One of the minor peculiarities of Wright's life was that he slightly changed his name when entering the army. Instead of John M. he was John W. This may have simply been a clerical error that haunted him later when seeking a pension, or it may have been a deliberate way to avoid using his middle name. Later, when Caddie applied for a pension for herself and her daughter, she pointed out this discrepancy.

References: Logansport-Cass County Public Library; *Logansport Daily Journal*, 15 April 1890; and his military pension file, National Archives, Washington, DC.

YOUNG, CLAIBORN ADDISON (1843–1912)

Claiborn Young was born in Boone County, near Thorntown, on 29 May 1843, the son of Mary Russell and the Reverend Claiborn Young, a Presbyterian minister. His siblings were William, Margaret, Harriet, Robert, Eliza Jane, Susan, and Lorilla.

Young Claiborn entered the Preparatory Department of Wabash in the autumn of 1860. He completed one year before joining Company G of the Eleventh Indiana Regiment for three years. On 2 January 1864 at New Orleans, he was given a commission as second lieutenant in the Eighty-Fifth United States

Colored Infantry, sometimes referred to as the Corps d'Afrique, and was honorably discharged in the spring of 1865 before the end of term at Wabash. That fall he became a freshman and continued to his senior year and graduation in June 1869.

Young had always intended to follow his father and train for the Presbyterian ministry, so he went to Union Theological Seminary in New York for the 1869–70 academic year. However, he found Trinitarian doctrines less and less to his liking and decided to study Unitarianism. With this in mind he spent 1870–71 at Harvard Divinity School. Still feeling some kind of religious calling, but hesitating to commit to organized religion, he worked among Native Americans in Maine and also went south for a while to be a missionary among black freedmen.

On 8 May 1890 he married Lucy Conant Farnham, and the following September he was formally ordained in the Unitarian Society and assigned to Lancaster, New Hampshire. The Youngs had a son whose name has not survived. In 1893 Young accepted a call from the Unitarian Society in Norton, Massachusetts, where he remained for three years, then moved to Canton, Massachusetts.

He published a book of poetry in 1897, *Way Songs and Wanderings*, and soon thereafter his wife and son both died. With nothing to hold him to Canton, he returned to Crawfordsville, but he found it increasingly difficult to get around due to partial paralysis. In July 1902 he was admitted to the Soldiers and Sailors Home near Lafayette, and he died there on 3 November 1912. A few years later, three fellow Wabash alumni published another of Young's volumes of poetry, *In the Red Man's Land*, whose title came from his experiences as a missionary.

References: *Boone: Your County Magazine*, II (January 1975), p. 6; *Wabash Magazine*, III (December 1861), p. 94; *Wabash Magazine*, VI (June 1866), p. 6; *Wabash Magazine*, IX (June 1869), p. 85; *Wabash Magazine*, X (December 1869), p. 85; *Wabash Magazine*, XI (March 1871), p. 138; Indiana Veterans Home of Lafayette; Canton (Massachusetts) Public Library; Mrs. Margaret Howells of Crawfordsville; and the Unitarian Universalist Association of Boston.

YOUNG, GEORGE THOMAS (1841–1918)

George Young was a first cousin of Claiborn Addison Young. George was born at Shannondale on 12 April 1841. His father was William Young, a farmer, and his mother was Mary Vannice Young, William's second wife. John V. Young was his half-brother.

George attended Thorntown Academy before entering the Normal School of Wabash College in the fall of 1859, where he remained for only one school year.

On 11 September 1862 at Lebanon, Young married Margaret Catherine (Kitty) Burroughs. Over the years they had ten children, four of whom died in infancy. Those who grew to maturity were Malinda, Nora, Myrtle, a daughter who became Mrs. Wishard Beasley, and Otis.

Many George Youngs served during the Civil War from the state of Indiana. However, the most likely one with a Wabash connection enrolled in Company D of the 107th Indiana Regiment on 9 July 1863 at Indianapolis, when the Confederates threatened southern Indiana, and after six days he was released.

Young spent most of the rest of his life on a large farm seven miles southeast of Lebanon in Boone County. He served two terms as Jefferson Township trustee and one term as county assessor. He and Kitty settled briefly in the town of Dover, where she died on 5 October 1910. Young was residing with his daughter Malinda in the town of Economy when he died on 16 January 1918. Both he and his wife are buried in the Shannondale Cemetery.

References: Margaret Howell of Crawfordsville, a granddaughter of George Young; *Lebanon Pioneer*, 17 January 1918; *Early Life and Times in Boone County, Indiana* (1887), pp. 24, 391; *The People's Guide to Boone County* (1874), p. 306; *History of Boone County, Indiana* (1915), p. 389; *Lebanon Reporter*, 17 January 1918.

A Soldiers' Album

James Pratt

Daniel Roderick

Richard Sabin

James Shanklin

Thomas Smith

Edward Woodrow

AFTERWORD

Some note should be taken of conclusions we reached after completing this project of Civil War soldiers from Wabash College. What did we find as we looked over all five hundred plus of these biographies? There are several answers to that question.

First of all, although it cannot be proven definitively, it is likely that Wabash College sent more students to the war, proportional to its size, than did any other college in America. This possibility is reinforced by the record number of enlistments from the state of Indiana, either as volunteers or draftees. Estimates suggest that 74 percent of eligible military-age Hoosiers participated in the war for shorter or longer terms, and of these, 57 percent signed up for three years. This meant that Indiana produced the second-highest number of soldiers in the nation proportional to its population. Nearly 200,000 young men enlisted in Indiana, of whom about 7,243 died of battlefield wounds and another 17,785 of disease, indicating that about 12 percent never returned home. The loss of life among the former Wabash students is consistent with this percentage.

Many of these young men came from the area in and around Crawfordsville. Of the 436 young men who came to Wabash from Indiana, 112 resided in Crawfordsville at the time of their admission. Many others moved to Crawfordsville intending to go to the college. There were many Hoosiers; 435 veterans hailed from Indiana between 1833 and 1876, with Illinois a distant second at 31. Alphabetically, our veterans came from California (1), Iowa (7), Kentucky (8), Louisiana (1), Michigan (5), Minnesota (3), Mississippi (1), New Hampshire (1), New Jersey (1), New York (5), Ohio (9), Tennessee (1), and Wisconsin (1). In addition, a handful came from abroad: Scotland (2) and Syria (1).

It might have been thought that most of the Wabash students who entered military service were in their late teens or early twenties, having been born in late 1830 or 1840, yet sixteen of the veterans were born between 1811 and 1819, making them in their forties when they served. Several of these older soldiers joined in July 1863 when John Hunt Morgan and his Confederate cavalry threatened southern Indiana. As forty-year-olds, they ran little risk, since they often served for only about one week. Most of the soldiers as a whole enlisted as privates or sergeants, and a few rose to become captains or colonels; two of them became either a brigadier or a major general.

The huge totals leaving for camp and field did affect the college. As the war started, a fairly large number of students went downtown and enrolled in Crawfordsville, causing the college to worry whether there would be enough students to hold classes if the call for soldiers grew louder and more insistent. From the autumn of 1860 to the late spring of 1865, 101 students joined the army, and many started college during the war, stayed for a while, and then enlisted, while parents often urged their sons to postpone serving until they were older or were needed less on the family farm. Our total was swelled by students who were formerly at the college or who came after the war.

Since the college was founded to encourage young men to be ministers or teachers in Indiana and the Midwest, is not surprising to find 35 clergymen and 13 educators among about 400 whose jobs we could identify. At least 82 went into some form of business, 74 into law, 78 into farming, and 50 into medicine. The number of medical doctors is notable, because at that time the college emphasized classical languages and literature and offered a minimum of science courses. Other occupations included 14 artisans and craftsmen, 11 clerical staff, 7 professional soldiers, 23 government employees, 2 painters, 12 printers and journalists, 5 United States congressmen, and 14 state legislators.

Looking at deaths by decade, 84 died during the 1860s and 62 directly from military service. As is the case for all military casualties, many succumbed from disease or accidents rather than from battle casualties. During the four war years, 1861 to 1865, they lost their lives in Alabama (5), Georgia (8), Kentucky (5), Illinois (5), Indiana (12), Ohio (1), Maryland (1), Mississippi (6), Pennsylvania (1), South Carolina (1), Tennessee (1), Texas (2), and Virginia (10), and in unknown places, 4. Those who died in Indiana succumbed from their wounds or disease after returning home, hoping to recover. A surprising amount of deaths in years after the conflict can be attributed to debilitation during the war.

Those who erected the memorial tablets on Center Hall probably assumed, as we did, that all of the Wabash men were Union sympathizers. However, nine students volunteered for Confederate military service, and of these, the Lowry brothers, Samuel and William, were sons of an early Wabash trustee and fought on opposite sides of the conflict. Most of the nine were born in the South and enlisted after they left the college, so during the war itself no student left the campus to join the Confederate military service.

Finally, the soldiers' own views and general dedication came out of a culture that was both widespread in the United States of the 1860s, close enough to the time of the Revolutionary War to still inspire the generation seventy years later, and refined by Wabash College itself.

Officially, the college did its best to encourage patriotism among its students and alumni: "According to an arrangement of the Faculty, a military company has been formed; and all (unless excused by Faculty), are compelled to drill twice a week." Individual faculty members also encouraged students to become soldiers. Writing to a recent recruit, Professor Caleb Mills, however, expressed ambivalent feelings:

> Since you left, the condition of our beloved country has assumed such an aspect as to make it the duty of many of her sons to respond to the call of arms. I honor the young man who is willing to drop his books and answer her demand. If one leaves the plow, another his tools and another the counter, counting house or office and goes to the camp and battlefield, I see no reason why the student of sufficient years and

strength should not say to his books, lie there until I have served my country and then I will resume my communion with you. I am glad to learn that you have volunteered though I would take as much pleasure in teaching you as anyone ever under my instruction.

It is true that as the war dragged on into July 1863, the mood of the students became more subdued, as *Wabash Magazine* noted:

Wabash has suffered deeply in this war. The sad list is increasing of her departed heroes. As they leave the world, and us and as we think of those still in the field, the touching refrain comes to us again and again—brave boys are they—gone at their country's call; and yet, and yet, we cannot forget, that many brave boys must fall.

Wabash did not forget its own. A formal dedication of a large plaque June 17, 1902, called the Roll of Honor, saw many Civil War vets returning to their college. The spirit of the dedication can be found in these lines from an editorial on "The Sons of Wabash" written for the *Indianapolis News* by Dr. Louis Howland:

It is well that this roll of honor should be spread before the world. A college is great not in what it has in wealth and endowment and equipment, but in its memories, and in those unobtrusive influences which guide and mold lives. So Wabash College may become rich and powerful, but it can have nothing that it will prize more highly than the record of the deeds of its sons that was dedicated today. It is good to know . . . that men who have had special advantages are eager to use them for the general good, and ready to recognize the binding force of the Scriptural injunction, Unto whomsoever much is given, of him much shall be required.

The Roll of Honor on the outside wall of Center Hall is still on the tour of families considering the college. Another plaque, the frontispiece of this book, was dedicated in 1913. So through the years the college has paid tribute.

This volume is also a tribute to the students whose work contributed to our belated history of those Wabash men who took part in the Civil War. There may have been more of these soldiers than all of us were able to discover, but these individual biographies are intended to provide as full a picture as was possible of those who attended Wabash from 1833 to 1870 and left it to serve. They richly testify to the dedication and pride shown by our forebears, who boldly declared, "Other Colleges! Can you show such a record?"

The honor of your presence is requested at

the Dedication of the

Wabash College Memorial Tablet

The Roll of Honor of her sons who served

in the Civil War

Wabash College Campus

Crawfordsville

Tuesday the Seventeenth day of June

One Thousand Nine Hundred and Two